# America in Italian Culture

# America in Italian Culture

*The Rise of a New Model of Modernity, 1861–1943*

GUIDO BONSAVER

Great Clarendon Street, Oxford, OX2 6DP,
United Kingdom

Oxford University Press is a department of the University of Oxford.
It furthers the University's objective of excellence in research, scholarship,
and education by publishing worldwide. Oxford is a registered trade mark of
Oxford University Press in the UK and in certain other countries

© Guido Bonsaver 2023

The moral rights of the author have been asserted

All rights reserved. No part of this publication may be reproduced, stored in
a retrieval system, or transmitted, in any form or by any means, without the
prior permission in writing of Oxford University Press, or as expressly permitted
by law, by licence or under terms agreed with the appropriate reprographics
rights organization. Enquiries concerning reproduction outside the scope of the
above should be sent to the Rights Department, Oxford University Press, at the
address above

You must not circulate this work in any other form
and you must impose this same condition on any acquirer

Published in the United States of America by Oxford University Press
198 Madison Avenue, New York, NY 10016, United States of America

British Library Cataloguing in Publication Data
Data available

Library of Congress Control Number: 2023934668

ISBN 978-0-19-884946-9

DOI: 10.1093/oso/9780198849469.001.0001

Printed and bound in the UK by
Clays Ltd, Elcograf S.p.A.

Links to third party websites are provided by Oxford in good faith and
for information only. Oxford disclaims any responsibility for the materials
contained in any third party website referenced in this work.

*To Laura, Matthew, Renato and Alessio.
My new world.*

# Preface

This book is the result of a long journey, forged by collaborative projects and countless exchanges. At the same time, like all monographs, it is driven by a desire to shed light on a specific topic. In this case, the topic is multifaceted: the perception and influence of American culture in Italy throughout the decades between the country's unification and the fall of Fascism. It is more than a study aimed at filling a scholarly gap in the field, however. As my interest grew, I took stock of the relevance of studying a period during which Italian culture—in its myriad of local and individual variations—experienced an epochal move from one hegemonic, foreign model of modernity to another: from France to America. The educated elite in nineteenth-century Italy were steeped in French culture: they spoke French and viewed Paris as a beacon of intellectual and lifestyle fashions. Paris was—to paraphrase Walter Benjamin—the cultural capital of nineteenth-century Europe.[1]

Of course, other metropolises—Berlin, Vienna, London—vied for cultural dominance, but few doubted that, in literary and artistic terms, Paris was the 'place-to-be'. When America emerged, it was at a key juncture in Western history. The technological advances brought about by the diffusion of electricity and the combustion engine towards the end of the nineteenth century ushered in a new industrial revolution. It vastly sped up the capacity of news, ideas, and artefacts to travel internationally. Material and intellectual goods—cars, books, vinyl records, and so on—could be replicated in previously unthinkable numbers. Furthermore, much-improved levels of literacy together with large-scale social reforms produced a working class with increased time and money to be spent on leisure, all of which facilitated a cultural market of unprecedented size. The United States of America showed its skills in mastering and blending these two aspects: mass industrial production at the service of mass culture.

The odd use of the term 'transnational' throughout this book highlights the importance of understanding the interaction with American culture as an epoch-making phenomenon that Italy shared with other countries around the world. As transnational history is informed by a study of the circulation of goods, people, and ideas across national borders, the period under consideration here, 1861–1943, marks a fertile study case. Italy in those decades witnessed radical developments in its social and economic structure, and much of it was related to its interaction

---

[1] Walter Benjamin, 'Paris, Capital of the 19th Century' [originally titled 'Paris, die Hauptstadt des XIX. Jahrhunderts', 1935], *Perspecta*, 12 (1969), 163–72.

with the rest of the world. From the start, the 'making' of Italians—the citizens of a young nation state in the 1860s—was a complicated business. Among the many tensions, there was the gulf between a Francophile educated elite and a mass of poorly-literate individuals, many of whom turned their back on their country of birth in search of a better life. The former eagerly read the latest news from Paris; the latter dreamt of America.

Meanwhile, the world was shrinking. By the end of the nineteenth century, a peasant family from the Veneto or Sicily could hoard enough money to cross the Atlantic Ocean. By the 1920s, millions of Italians were encountering America through Hollywood films. In the 1930s, short-wave transmissions instantly brought the sound of jazz bands in Chicago and New York to every owner of a radio set. Technological advancement and social transformations allowed America to enter the lives of entire communities in previously unimaginable ways. America offered a model of modernity that flouted national borders and spoke to all. It could be rejected, adored, or transformed for one's personal use, but it could not be ignored.

Richard Kuisel has recently argued that 'Americanization' should be considered as an early stage of the process of globalization that engulfed a large part of the world, Europe first of all.[2] One could argue that French culture had played a similar role in earlier periods, but only for a limited sphere of people. The culture and lifestyle radiating from Paris during the nineteenth century—and well before—was an influential model, but only for those who could access it by reading, travelling, and purchasing material goods. An elite transnational model was slowly replaced by one that could reach all levels of society. The mass appeal of New York was greatly helped by the other great culture capital of America: Hollywood. During the interwar years, each and every Italian, regardless of his or her geographical or social origin, ineluctably felt the influence of America. Perversely, Italy was by then in the hands of the most nationalistic of all political regimes, Mussolini's Fascism. This is another aspect that makes the Italian case particularly interesting. What were the effects of protectionist policies, censorship, and autarkic campaigns aimed at protecting Italians from this supposedly pernicious foreign influence? The transnational and the totalitarian, in those years, came head-to-head.

This book aims at a cultural history—what Italians read, listened to, and watched—during Italy's protracted entry into the modern world. It seeks to shed light on the cultural make-up of Italians, both as individuals and as a national community in contact and in dialogue with the rest of the world. When the Eiffel Tower was built in 1889, it was the tallest building on earth, at 312 meters high. It immediately became an international icon of France's modernity. Just a few years earlier Gustave Eiffel had contributed to the construction of the Statue of Liberty, which the French people had donated to the Americans. It was just under 100 metres

---

[2] Richard F. Kuisel, 'The End of Americanization? or Reinventing a Research Field for Historians of Europe', *Journal of Modern History*, 92 (September 2020), 602–34.

in height, but this was appropriate for a young nation that was beginning to stretch its limbs. The height matter was put to rest in 1931 when the Empire State building was erected, soaring to 443 metres. One could, of course, see this as a phallic articulation of nationalistic pride—and in a Freudian sense it was—but it is equally symbolic of where the economic and cultural centre of gravity of the Western world was moving. This book is about the cultural fallout of this shift across the Italian peninsula and its isles.

# Acknowledgements

Many colleagues and friends have helped me in researching and writing this book. My warmest thanks go to those who kindly found the time to read and comment on different parts of the typescript. The mistakes and misjudgements left in the book are entirely mine, but their number has certainly been limited thanks to: Giorgio Bertellini, Richard Bosworth, Victoria De Grazia, Robert Gordon, Peter Hainsworth, Stephen Gundle, Axel Körner, Charles Leavitt, Martin McLaughlin, David Robey, Cinzia Scarpino, Sara Sullam, and Simona Storchi. I am particularly thankful to David Ellwood and Donald Sassoon for reading and commenting on the entire manuscript.

Others have helped on specific queries along the way. Again, their respective expertise has been most helpful. A big thank you to Walter Adamson, Silvio Alovisio, Gioacchino Balistreri, Raffaele Bedarida, Paola Bonsaver, Lucia Borghese Bruschi, Stefano Bragato, Alessandro Carlucci, Pietro Corsi, Luca Cottini, John Dickie, Massimo Fanfani, Giorgio Farabegoli, Valerio Ferme, Lidio Ferrando, David Forgacs, Emilio Franzina, Donna Gabaccia, Patricia Gaborik, Nicholas Gaskill, Margherita Ghilardi, Marie Kokubo, Stéphanie Lanfranchi-Guilloux, Paolo Leoncini, Thomas Leslie, Martino Marazzi, Mauro Maspero, Adriano Mazzoletti, Amoreno Martellini, Graham Nelson, Fabio Pezzetti Tonion, Paolo Prato, Matteo Sanfilippo, Matthew Seelinger, Anthony Julian Tamburri, and Roberto Vezzani.

An affectionate thank you goes to three younger colleagues whose suggestions, *ad hoc* research, and prose-style tips allowed me to enrich and polish my typescript: Alice Gussoni, Lachlan Hughes, and Joseph Kelly. Their assistance was guaranteed by financial support from the Oxford Faculty of Medieval and Modern Languages and Pembroke College, both of which also funded a number of research trips abroad. Back home, a collective, warm thank you goes to both the kind, efficient staff of the many libraries at Oxford—a bookworm's earthly paradise—and to the editorial team who turned my manuscript into a professional publication: Saraswathi Ethiraju, Cathryn Steele and Hilary Walford.

Finally, Caterina's love, care, and tolerance allowed this book to interfere with our daily life for too many years. Un abbraccio e un bacio.

# Contents

*List of Illustrations*     xv

    Introduction     1

### PART 1. THE DISCOVERY OF AMERICA, 1861–1919

1. Cross-National Influence in Post-Unification Italy     23
2. The Idea of America in Italy's Two Nations     47
3. American Mass Production and the Dawn of Italian Mass Culture     107
4. American Literature, Opera Librettos, and Pragmatism     132
5. The First World War and the Arrival of Jazz     151

### PART 2. AMERICAN CULTURE IN FASCIST ITALY, 1922–1943

6. America as a Mirror of Modernity     175
7. The Craze for American Literature and Comics, and the Plight of the English Language     247
8. Dancing to Jazz on Fascist Airwaves     296
9. The Lure of Hollywood     334
10. American Culture in Fascism's Final Years, 1938–1943     418

    Conclusion     490

*Bibliography*     503
*Index*     539

# List of Illustrations

0.1. Publicity poster of Walt Disney's *Mickey Mouse: The Jazz Fool* (1929). (courtesy of Rodney Rogers, New Orleans) — 4

0.2. Charlie Chaplin comically facing Primo Carnera in a signed photo. (courtesy of Adriano Mazzoletti, Rome) — 16

1.1. Print advertising the 1889 Exposition Universelle. (courtesy of Universitats Darmstadts) — 33

1.2. Front page of the 1910 annual guide of *Il café chantant*. (courtesy of Biblioteca Luigi Chiarini, CSC, Rome) — 40

1.3. Milan's Galleria Vittorio Emanuele II (1877). (author's personal collection) — 41

2.1. US military uniforms and the slave market in South Carolina. (courtesy of Biblioteca Nazionale Centrale, Rome) — 53

2.2. The Women's Pavilion at Philadelphia Centennial Exhibition. (courtesy of Centro Studi per L'arte del libro, Novara) — 58

2.3. A slightly tarnished photo of Adolfo Rossi in 1883. (courtesy of Archivio di Stato di Rovigo) — 61

2.4. Front page of *L'Italia. Giornale del Popolo*, of 29–30 April 1884. (courtesy of Biblioteca Nazionale Centrale, Rome) — 64

2.5. Front page of *L'Italia. Giornale del Popolo*, 1–2 May 1884. (courtesy of Biblioteca Nazionale Centrale, Rome) — 65

2.6. Cover of *La Domenica del Corriere*, 23 June 1901. (courtesy of Biblioteca di Storia Moderna e Contemporanea, Rome) — 70

2.7. Chicago's and New York's early skyscapers at the end of the nineteenth century. (respectively, courtesy of Thomas Leslie and author's personal collection) — 71

2.8. The Library of Congress Building. (author's personal collection) — 72

2.9. Bill Cody with four Native American chiefs in a Venetian gondola. (courtesy of the Buffalo Bill Centre of the West, Cody WY) — 86

2.10. A 'Pellerossa' attack on a Wells Fargo stagecoach as re-enacted in Bill Cody's Wild West. (courtesy of BSMC, Rome) — 87

2.11. Italian copy of the Wild West programme, 1906. (courtesy of the Buffalo Bill Centre of the West, Cody WY) — 89

2.12. Copy of commemorative postcard of Annie Oakley, c.1885. (author's personal collection) — 90

2.13. Front page of the first instalment of *Buffalo Bill*. (courtesy of Princeton University Library, Princeton, NJ) — 92

xvi   LIST OF ILLUSTRATIONS

2.14. Front-cover of *La Domenica del Corriere* of 8 December 1901. (courtesy of BMSC, Rome)   95

3.1. Dante approves of Olivetti's US-inspired typewriter in a publicity poster of 1912. (courtesy of Fondazione Adriano Olivetti, Ivrea)   110

3.2. Still from Luigi Maggi's western *Il bersaglio vivente*, Ambrosio, 1913. (courtesy of Museo Nazionale del Cinema, Turin)   116

3.3. The headed paper of Photo Drama. (courtesy of Manuscript Division, Library of Congress, Washington, DC)   119

3.4. The newly built FIAT factory in Poughkeepsie, NY, 1909. (courtesy of Centro Storico FIAT, Turin)   126

3.5. From the official catalogue of the Esposizione internazionale di automobili, Turin, 18 January–2 February 1908. (courtesy of Centro Documentazione—Museo Nazionale dell'Automobile, Turin)   129

4.1. Front cover of the first edition of the libretto of Puccini's *La fanciulla del West* (1910). (courtesy of the Weston Library, Oxford)   141

5.1. Ernest Hemingway in the American Red Cross uniform with Nurse Agnes Von Kurowski. (courtesy of the John F. Kennedy Presidential Library and Museum, Boston MA)   157

5.2. Map of all the centres run by the American Red Cross in Italy in January 1919. (courtesy of the National Library of Medicine, Bethesda, MD)   159

5.3. Front-page illustration of *La Domenica del Corriere*, 28 (14-21 July 1918), dedicated to the celebrations of The Fourth of July in Milan's Piazza del Duomo. (courtesy of BSMC, Rome)   161

5.4. Fiorello La Guardia surrounded by Italian and US officers. (courtesy of La Guardia and Wagner Archives, New York City)   166

5.5. The American Jazz Band, wearing Italian army helmets, presumably in Milan, 1918. (courtesy of C. B. Barlow, USAAS Section 563)   171

6.1. Josephine Baker's iconic banana skirt, *La Folie du jour*, Folies-Bergère, 1926. (courtesy of Everett Collection/Alamy Stock)   181

6.2. Depero's advertising image for Campari inspired by New York's skyline (1931). (courtesy of Museo Campari, Milan)   184

6.3. New York skyscrapers, 1932. (courtesy of Prints and Photographs Division, Library of Congress, Washington, DC)   185

6.4. Artist's illustration of Palanti's plan for a giant skyscraper to be built in Rome's city centre. (courtesy of Bodleian Library, Oxford)   188

6.5. Carlo Levi's front cover image for Mario Soldati's *America primo amore*, Florence: Bemporad, 1935. (courtesy of the Bodleian Library, Oxford)   190

6.6. Commemorative postcard celebrating the record-breaking crossing of the Atlantic by the Italian liner *Rex*. (author's personal collection)   192

6.7. Detail from two articles published in *La Domenica del Corriere*, February and March 1930. (courtesy of BSMC, Rome)   202

LIST OF ILLUSTRATIONS    xvii

6.8. Three photos dedicated to America's economic and architectural might in *La Rivista illustrata del Popolo d'Italia*, 15/10 (October 1930). (courtesy of BSMC, Rome)    203

6.9. A set of traffic lights featuring fasces decoration, next to New York's Empire State Building, published in *La Rivista illustrata del Popolo d'Italia*, 13/1 (January 1935). (courtesy of BSMC, Rome)    205

6.10. Detail of the front page of *Il Popolo d'Italia*, 10 October 1918. (courtesy of BSMC, Rome)    207

6.11. Mussolini's signature appearing on the frontispiece of Margherita Sarfatti's biography of 1925. (courtesy of the Bodleian Library, Oxford)    217

6.12. De Pinedo's and Lindbergh's aviation feats in the *Corriere della Sera*, 24 May 1927. (courtesy of BNC, Rome)    225

6.13. Mussolini being instructed by Balbo at the commands of a Savoia Marchetti S.62, c.1932. (courtesy of BNC, Rome)    228

6.14. Vittorio De Sica in a still from Mario Camerini's *Il signor Max* (1937). (DVD screenshot)    232

6.15. Advert for American beauty products appearing in *La Rivista cinematografica*, 1 (1921). (courtesy of Museo Nazionale del Cinema, Turin)    238

7.1. Front page of the second issue of Giovanni Papini's *La Vraie Italie* (March 1919). (courtesy of CIRCE, University of Trento)    254

7.2. Translations from French, English, and German, 1896–1953. (data from Viallet, 'Statistiques et histoire des relations culturelles franco-italiannes')    259

7.3. Cover of the first issue of Ugo Ojetti's *Pegaso* (January 1929). (courtesy of Fondazione Alfred Lewin—Biblioteca Gino Bianco, Forlì)    270

7.4. Front cover of the first novel published in Mondadori's 'I Romanzi della Palma' series, 1932. (author's personal collection)    272

7.5. Front page of a 1928 issue of *Corriere dei Piccoli*, featuring a story of Signor Bonaventura. (courtesy of Bernd Zillich, Munich)    284

7.6. The head title of Lucio l'Avanguardista (Rob the Rover). (courtesy of giornalepop.com)    285

7.7. Front page of *Topolino*'s first issue, 31 December 1932. (courtesy of Leonardo Gori, private collection)    287

7.8. Front page of *L'Avventuroso*'s first issue of 14 October 1934. (courtesy of Donald at annitrenta.blogspot.com)    289

7.9. Copy of the twentieth instalment of the comics story 'Ulceda', by Guido Moroni Celsi. (courtesy of giornalepop.it)    293

7.10. The 'Mickey-Mouse-inspired' character of Formichino in the *Corriere dei Piccoli* of 9 June 1940. (author's personal collection)    294

8.1. Front cover of Anton Giulio Bragaglia, *Jazz Band* (1929). (courtesy of Museo Nazionale del Cinema, Turin)    302

xviii  LIST OF ILLUSTRATIONS

8.2. Ugo Filippini's Black & White Jazz Band in October 1922. (courtesy of Adriano Mazzoletti, Rome) 307

8.3. 'Fox-trott, ballo sovrano!', article in Rome's *La Tribuna illustrata*, 22–9 February 1920. (courtesy of Digiteca, BSMC, Rome) 309

8.4. Front cover of the music sheet of 'Villico Black Bottom'. (author's personal collection) 311

8.5. Carlo Benzi and Milietto Nervetti on their arrival in New York, in 1928. (courtesy of Adriano Mazzoletti, Rome) 313

8.6. Front cover illustration of *Radiocorriere*, 9/30 (23–30 July 1933). (courtesy of Biblioteca Nazionale Centrale, Florence) 322

8.7. Front cover illustration of *Radiocorriere*, 9/32 (6–13 August 1933). (courtesy of Biblioteca Nazionale Centrale, Florence) 323

8.8. 'Pippo' Barzizza as conductor of EIAR's Orchestra Cetra in the late 1930s. (courtesy of Adriano Mazzoletti, Rome) 326

9.1. First page of an article signed 'Metro Goldwin' (*sic*) devoted to MGM's film *The Midshipman* (1925), in *Comoedia*, 5/8 (August 1926). (courtesy of BNC, Rome) 339

9.2. *Exhibitors Herald*'s article of 21 January 1922 celebrating the eighteen-year anniversary of Fox Film. (courtesy of MHDL, Wisconsin Center for Film and Theater Research) 341

9.3. American and Italian theatrical release posters of Archie Mayo's *The Adventures of Marco Polo* (1938). (courtesy of Mauro Maspero, Cantù) 348

9.4. Illustrations accompanying Vittorio Mussolini's article 'Emancipazione del cinema italiano', *Cinema*, 1/6 (25 September 1936). (courtesy of Cineteca, Bologna) 361

9.5. Benito Mussolini standing next to his son Vittorio during a visit to the construction site of Cinecittà, in 1936. (courtesy of Mitchell Wolfson Jr Collection, Genoa) 363

9.6. The advertisement page used by the Anti-Nazi League for the Defence of American Democracy to protest against Vittorio Mussolini's visit. (author's personal collection) 368

9.7. Signed photograph by Shirley Temple after her meeting with Vittorio Mussolini at Fox Studios, Hollywood, October 1937 (from Vittorio Mussolini's memoir, *Vita con mio padre*; courtesy of BNC, Rome) 369

9.8. Goebbels and Alfieri during the former's visit to the Venice Film Festival, 1936. (anonymous photo; courtesy of Wikimedia Commons) 374

9.9. Two-page advertisement of Meehan's *Naughty Nanette* (1927). (courtesy of Biblioteca Luigi Chiarini, CSC, Rome) 378

9.10. Vittorio Mussolini and Mario Camerini accompany Angelo Rizzoli during his visit to the Cinecittà studios. (courtesy of Cineteca, Bologna) 380

LIST OF ILLUSTRATIONS xix

9.11. A selection of 1930s covers. (courtesy of Media History Digital Library, Wisconsin Center for Film and Theatre Research; and Cineteca, Bologna) 382

9.12. The impoverished Professor Bensi (Vittorio De Sica) and his butler (Camillo Pilotto) in a still from Mattoli's *Tempo massimo* (1934). (DVD screenshot) 401

9.13. Poster advertising the film *I quattro moschettieri* (1936). (courtesy of Cineteca, Bologna) 403

9.14. A stage photo taken during the production of *I quattro moschettieri* (1936). (courtesy of Cineteca, Bologna) 403

9.15. Work at CAIR's studio for the production of *Le avventure di Pinocchio* (1935). (courtesy of Archivio Romolo Bacchini at Wikipedia Common) 405

9.16. Still from the animation film *Le avventure di Pinocchio* (1935). (courtesy of Archivio Romolo Bacchini at Wikipedia Common) 407

9.17. Front cover of *Lo Schermo* of July 1938 dedicated to Walt Disney's *Snow White and the Seven Dwarfs*. (courtesy of Cineteca, Bologna) 408

9.18. FIAT's Lingotto factory in Turin, designed by Giacomo Matté-Trucco and completed in 1923. (courtesy of Archivio Storico FIAT, Turin) 411

9.19. A 1938 photo from FIAT's archive celebrating the arrival in New York of a Fiat 500 to be sold in the USA. (courtesy of Archivio Storico FIAT, Turin) 412

9.20. Front cover of *Cinema illustrazione* dedicated to the main cast of Matarazzo's *Joe il rosso* (1936). (courtesy of CSC, Rome) 415

10.1. The November 1938 issue of *Rivista illustrata del Popolo d'Italia*. (courtesy of BSMC, Rome) 426

10.2. Airmen of SAAF 7 Squadron toy with a part-dismantled Breda Ba.88 left behind by the Italian Air Force. (photo by Capt. Robert Abbot Fenner; courtesy of his sons Bill and Bob, and of Tinus le Roux) 429

10.3. Marcello Piacentini's Torrione INA in Brescia (1932), and his Torre dell'orologio in Genoa (1940). (courtesy, respectively, of Wolfang Moroder and of Lidio Ferrando) 432

10.4. The Italian pavilion of Marcello Piacentini, Giuseppe Pagano, and Cesare Valle at the 1937 International Exposition in Paris. (courtesy of La Photolith, Wikipedia Commons) 434

10.5. Bird's-eye view of the initial project for EUR42 presented to Mussolini by Marcello Piacentini and his collaborators on 28 April 1937. (courtesy of BNC, Rome) 435

10.6. The model of the initial version of EUR42 showing the four central skyscrapers along the main axis of the complex. (courtesy of BNC, Rome) 435

10.7. The Palazzo della Civiltà Italiana of Giovanni Guerrini, Ernesto La Padula, and Mario Romano in Rome's EUR district, 1940. (author's personal collection) 437

## xx  LIST OF ILLUSTRATIONS

| | | |
|---|---|---|
| 10.8. | Detail of the top section of the Palazzo della Civiltà Italiana in Rome's EUR district, 1940. (author's personal collection) | 438 |
| 10.9. | The official poster promoting EUR42, featuring Adalberto Libera's arch; and Eero Saarinen's Gateway arch designed for the Jefferson Memorial. (courtesy, respectively, of BNC, Rome, and of Hendrickson Photography/Shutterstock) | 439 |
| 10.10. | Cover of a 1940 album dedicated to Fulmine, published by Vittoria. (courtesy of giornalepop.it) | 456 |
| 10.11. | Mondadori's Tuffolino replacing Topolino's characters, from May 1942. (courtesy of Donald at annitrenta.blogspot.com) | 456 |
| 10.12. | Detail from *Radiocorriere* containing the publicity of Rabagliati's solo programme, *Radiocorriere*, 17/48 (29 November 1941), 12. (courtesy of BNC, Florence) | 461 |
| 10.13. | Osvaldo Campassi, 'Coppie', *Cinema illustrazione*, 13/38 (21 September 1938), 5. (courtesy of Cineteca, Bologna) | 466 |
| 10.14. | 'Falsa vita di Hollywood', *Cinema illustrazione*, 13/47 (23 November 1938), 6. (courtesy of Cineteca, Bologna) | 468 |
| 10.15. | Detail of the contents page of *Bianco e nero*, 3/2 (February 1939), 181. (courtesy of Cineteca, Bologna) | 469 |
| 10.16. | A cameo appearance of Gorni Kramer in Riccardo Freda's *Tutta la città canta* (1946). (courtesy of Cineteca di Milano) | 487 |
| 11.1. | The Mussolini family: left, the cover of *Time*, 26/18 (8 October 1935), featuring Mussolini with his sons Bruno (left) and Vittorio (right) (courtesy of BNC, Rome); right, Edda Mussolini with a group of blackshirts during a cruise to India of the Naval League, on 21 February 1929. (courtesy of Archivio Luce, Rome) | 495 |
| 11.2. | Film still from Fellini's *La dolce vita* (1960), with Adriano Celentano, in the middle, singing 'Ready Teddy' in his makeshift English. (courtesy of Legenda, Cambridge) | 501 |

# Introduction

In the minds of many Italian intellectuals at the end of the nineteenth century, the word 'americanismo' conjured up disquieting images of modernity. It spoke of mass-produced goods, feverish consumerism, dumb conformism, and a relentless pursuit of materialistic pleasure. A parallel between American culture and modernity was also promulgated by the Vatican through its interpretation of 'Americanism' as a sinister, materialistic degeneration that risked engulfing the entire Catholic community in the USA.

These voices, however, represented only one side of the debate. Positive interest was growing. The political and military role of the USA on the international stage had started to attract attention, first in the Spanish–American war of 1898 and then, more prominently, during the First World War. America's economic strength was praised not just for its capacity for mass production and technological innovation but also for the enviable lifestyle that, among the lower and middle classes, was by then far more affluent than that of their European counterparts. Americanism for many meant social mobility and emancipation from tradition, it meant new forms of entertainment and a cult of modernity in all its expressions, from skyscrapers to jazz music, cinema, and the radio. Among the most enthusiastic philo-Americans were the Futurists, who were the first in Italy to rave about jazz and to identify New York as the new Paris of the twentieth century.

America began to loom more and more largely over the cultural horizon of many Europeans. In Britain, both newspaper editor W. T. Stead and literary author H. G. Wells saw America as envisioning Europe's future, and as rising to the status of being the place where—in Wells's words—'the leadership of progress must ultimately rest'. American philosopher William James added a prophetic tone in one of his foundational lectures: 'Our children, one may say, are almost born scientific.' American entrepreneurs proved the most successful in grabbing hold of the new opportunities offered by technological advances and in leaving their mark on the modern world that was taking shape on both sides of the Atlantic.[1]

The progressive influence of American culture produced a shift from the expression 'Americanism' to 'Americanization', which implied a threatening,

---

[1] W. T. Stead, *The Americanization of the World or The Trend of the Twentieth Century* (New York and London: H. Markey, 1901). H. G. Wells, *The Future in America* (New York and London: Harper and Brothers Publishers, 1906), 257. William James, *Pragmatism: A New Name for Some Old Ways of Thinking* (Cambridge, MA: Harvard University Press, 1907), 14.

foreign presence. Paris, the most cosmopolitan of all European capitals, which had welcomed American culture and American intellectuals, was also the centre of a counter-discourse that presented America as a perverse excrescence of European culture. The values and traditions of the old continent had to be defended.[2]

In Italy, more than 'americanismo' or 'americanizzazione', the neologism that best characterized the response of much of the Italian intelligentsia to American culture was 'americanata'. The term was coined in the late nineteenth century to describe a spectacular act born out of a ridiculous and childish desire to impress. This neologism became so trendy that it was even used as a headline for a series of articles on American *faits divers* published by Italy's most popular illustrated magazine, *La Domenica del Corriere*, between 1908 and 1913. The term has also survived the test of time and is still present in the Italian language today. In its early usage it was part of the condescending, self-defensive attitude with which much of the Italian media described America.

At the turn of the century, Camillo Olivetti and Giovanni Agnelli—each the father of a manufacturing empire—travelled to the USA in search of lessons to be learnt. But these were isolated cases. In general, Liberal Italy's educated elite preferred to stay at home and read about 'americanate' in the pages of *La Domenica del Corriere*. The view of America as a violent land of extremes, populated by poorly educated men and morally dubious women, even in its north-eastern, industrialized version, remained dominant. It was a sort of motorized, skyscrapered version of Buffalo Bill's world: a 'Wild East'.

At the same time, unexpectedly, masses of semi-illiterate Italians began to leave Italy, fleeing the newly unified nation state, which, according to *Risorgimento* narratives, had made the dream of the Italian people finally come true. Economic historians can illuminate us on what went wrong, but a cultural look at the response to this demographic revolution yields surprising results. How was early migration discussed in the media? How was it represented through literary works? Outright condemnation and a sense of embarrassment were the recurrent tones in the press. At the turn of the century, if daily papers dealt with migration, it was mainly to report on some disaster, the sinking of a ship, overcrowded with third-class passengers, or the deadly collapse of a mine in some distant corner of the world. The implicit message was that migration had been a tragic mistake, which nationalists mixed with cries about the humiliation and degradation suffered by the noble Italian race. Literary works did not even do that. They mainly ignored the matter, to the point that Italy's major expert on migration literature,

---

[2] On this, see Philippe Roger, *The American Enemy: The History of French Anti-Americanism* (Chicago: Chicago University Press, 2005); and Seth Armus, *French Anti-Americanism (1930–1948)* (Lanham, MD: Lexington Books, 2008).

Sebastiano Martelli, has concluded that the great novel of Italian migration is yet to be written.[3]

It took the Italian government until 1901 before a raft of legislation attempted fully to regulate migration and tackle the exploitation and misery attached to it. By then about half a million men and women were leaving Italy, every year. The political class, the media, and literary authors had woken up late to a phenomenon that did not square with their nationalistic values. This generated the co-habitation of two images of America: the imagined promised land of popular belief, and the caricaturized depiction of the printed press.

After the First World War, it became impossible to dismiss America as a sum of its 'americanate'. A condescending attitude was still at work, but the voice of those seeing something else became stronger and stronger. The multidisciplinary approach of this book will allow us to see how different cultural fields reacted in different ways and at different times to the rising presence of the USA as an economic and cultural superpower. By the 1920s, Hollywood had become the ultimate locus of all there was to love and hate about America. It had also become the capital of world cinema. And it established itself as a beacon from which the flickering image of America entered the eyes and minds of people in every corner of the world. The 'Americanization' of the planet, if nothing else, was partly a visual invasion, and America became an imagined country.

Cinema was a powerful new art, born out of French technology—the Lumière brothers won the first round with their *cinématographe*, beating Thomas Edison's kinetoscope as the key hardware in the film industry—but quickly fallen into American hands. This happened thanks to US protectionist policies, followed by the collapse of European markets during the First World War. Film was a new narrative form that slowly began to fight for recognition as an art. It was also the most transmedial of all arts: photographic mainly, but based on literary scripts and performed by actors with the complement of sound that, by the late 1920s, no longer meant the occasional presence of a group of musicians performing live.

By a wise twist of fate, the first ever sound film was entitled *The Jazz Singer* (1927). If the 1920s are today remembered as the jazz age, it is because its syncopated rhythms, the pounding presence of the drum kit (jazz's gift to world music), the popularity of its dance movements, became the music score of those very years. Even linguistically, the move from the pre-war 'Belle Époque' to the 'Jazz Age' is indicative of a major shift in Europe's cultural balance. The eminent historian Eric Hobsbawn, also a jazz connoisseur under the pen name of Francis Newton, humorously wrote that 'the social history of the twentieth-century arts

---

[3] Sebastiano Martelli, 'Dal vecchio mondo al sogno americano: Realtà e immaginario dell'emigrazione nella letteratura italiana', in Piero Bevilacqua, Andreina De Clementi, and Emilio Franzina, *Storia della migrazione italiana. Partenze*, i (Rome: Donzelli, 2001), 433–55.

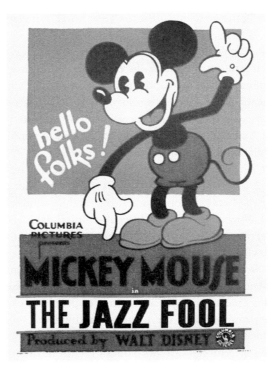

**Fig. 0.1.** Publicity poster of Walt Disney's *Mickey Mouse: The Jazz Fool* (1929). (courtesy of Rodney Rogers, New Orleans)

will contain only a footnote or two about Scottish Highland music or gypsy lore, but it will have to deal at some length with the vogue for jazz'.[4]

And a vogue it was. Jazz travelled far thanks to the technology of vinyl records and the radio, but it also travelled thanks to cinema, often smuggled as accompanying music for the comic shorts by Buster Keaton and Charlie Chaplin, or through Walt Disney's early cartoons featuring Mickey Mouse. One of the early sound animations by Disney was *Mickey Mouse: The Jazz Fool* (1929), which the following year reached the first-run cinema theatres of most Italian cities with the title *Topolino ama il jazz*.

Mention of Walt Disney takes us to another cultural field where his products fought valiantly and became part of America's imaginary invasion of Italy: comics. By the mid-1930s, Mickey Mouse had become the main character of Italy's most popular comics magazine, aptly named *Topolino*. But by then the 'American craze' for comics was already in full swing, led by a colourful collection of superheroes mainly licensed by the powerful King Features Syndicate. Italian teenagers found themselves catapulted from the starched and tame

[4] Francis Newton, *The Jazz Scene* (Goring by Sea: McGibbon & Key, 1959), 14.

stories narrated in rhymed couplets by the *Corriere dei Piccoli* to the wild, science- and sensual-driven adventures featuring Flash Gordon or Mandrake. As Umberto Eco has suggested, those narratives were part of an increasing presence of American culture in Italy, often in direct contrast with the nationalistic vision promoted by Fascism's pedagogues.[5]

This brief, historical overview touching upon a number of different fields is an indirect argument for the need of a multidisciplinary approach in order to give an adequate sense of how American culture entered Italy. It is also an argument towards the need to pay attention to the economic and social context that generated those cultural artefacts and the one that received, replicated, and elaborated them.

When the USA emerged as an economic superpower at the start of the twentieth century, William Cody, better known as Buffalo Bill, was still touring Europe with his spectacular Wild West show. The popularity of Buffalo Bill serves as a reminder that there was another America that populated the minds of Europeans up until the late nineteenth century, and it was an America in many ways opposed to the image of the USA as an urbanized, technologically minded, and pleasure-seeking nation. It was a primitive land, violent and unforgiving, the vast theatre of romantic stories of individuals fighting for their survival. The popularity of the Western genre—in film as much as in literature and comics—allowed this image to continue into the twentieth century and coexist with the new vision of America as a modern civilization defined by the futuristic skyline of Manhattan's skyscrapers. What did Italians make of these opposing images?

Mention of Italians brings us to another introductory caveat: there was no such thing as a homogeneous entity of 'Italians'. Beyond the regional differences that still characterize Italy today, the cultural make-up of Italy's educated elite—the less than 5 per cent of the population that entered the classroom of a Ginnasio-Liceo—was very distant from the semi-illiterate rest of the country. It was so distant that one of the most respected historians on Italian migration, Donna Gabaccia, has written of it as 'two peoples who often seemed as different as two races'. This is particularly important in a study of Italy–USA relations, since one 'race' formed the vast majority of those millions who criss-crossed the Atlantic in search of a better life. And the other 'race' was the educated minority who wrote about America in periodicals and travel books.[6]

A literary narrative of a failed encounter between these two peoples can be found in Mario Soldati's early masterpiece, his travel memoir *America primo amore* (1935). In the chapter entitled 'Italo-americani', the young Turinese intellectual forces himself to spend some time with a family of proudly Italian American immigrants from the South. Soldati boasts about having learnt English

---

[5] Umberto Eco, 'Il modello americano', in Umberto Eco, Remo Ceserani, and Beniamino Placido (eds), *La riscoperta dell'America* (Rome and Bari: Laterza, 1984), 3–32.
[6] Donna Gabaccia, *Italy's Many Diasporas* (London: UCL Press, 2000), 19.

from scratch in his first six months there. His interlocutors, instead, only communicated using 'a curious Sicilian–American jargon'. When invited into their home, Soldati barely tolerates the poor quality of their food, wine, and conversation, so much so that he finds escape in the reminiscence of superior parties back in Turin, which he glorifies with the quotation of a verse from Baudelaire's poem in praise of wine, obviously in the French original. America meant different things to different people. Where a family of migrants were eagerly displaying their version of the 'American dream', a young Italian intellectual could only disapprove of America's—and these new Americans'—lack of *finesse*.[7]

But, even among *literati* such as Mario Soldati, what was their knowledge of America? Looking at Italian correspondents and travel writers in the USA, Michel Beynet has argued that Italian commentators lacked expertise. Even during the interwar years, the near-totality of books on America were written by non-specialists—often simple collections of articles written during a journey through the USA—free from references to other works on the subject. More than a coherent debate, there was a cacophony of many voices, each concentrating on his or her own impressions. There were no 'americanisti' in the universities either, to the point that the entry on 'Stati Uniti d'America' for Italy's most prestigious state-sponsored encyclopaedia, the Treccani, was oddly given to a classicist.[8]

One of the first scholars to buck the trend was Mario Praz, who taught English Literature at Rome University but developed an interest in American literature. When he wrote about American travellers in nineteenth-century Italy, Praz warned his readers that the history of cultural relations between Italy and America was a troubled one, 'often involving disguise and misunderstandings'.[9] This was also due to the fact that the number of Italian intellectuals who had first-hand knowledge of America—not necessarily because they had been there but simply because they were familiar with the English language—was very limited. As we will see, the publishing industry relied on French translations as a source for their Italian versions of American fiction well into the interwar years. One gets a similar impression of a 'French connection' in debates concerning cinema. When Florence's most sophisticated literary journal, *Solaria*, devoted an entire issue to cinema in 1927, the discussion was an Italian supplement to what had happened in Paris the year before. *Les Cahiers du mois* had published its own

---

[7] Mario Soldati's *America primo amore* (Florence: Bemporad, 1935); then in *America e altri amori: Diari e scritti di viaggio* (Milan: Mondadori, 2011), 40–9. The line of Baudelaire's poem comes from 'L'Âme du vin' in his *Les Fleurs du mal*.

[8] Michel Beynet, *L'Image de L'Amerique dans la culture italiennes de l'entre-deux guerres*, 3 vols (Aix-Marseille: Publications de l'Université de Provence, 1990), i. 6–8. The ninety-page-long encyclopedic entry, published in 1932, was coordinated by Angelo Taccone, then professor of Ancient Greek literature at Turin University. This is mentioned by Giorgio Spini in his 'Prefazione' to Giorgio Spini, Gian Giacomo Migone, and Massimo Teodori (eds), *Italia e America dalla Grande Guerra a oggi* (Venice: Marsilio, 1976), 9–22 (13).

[9] Mario Praz, 'Impressioni italiane di americani nell'ottocento', *Studi americani*, 4 (1958), 85–107 (88).

dedicated issue on cinema, and most of the critical references used by the *solariani* referred to the French debate, even when discussing American cinema. Equally telling was the adoption of the French nickname for Charlie Chaplin's iconic tramp character, Charlot. Italian film critics used it indiscriminately, often as an awkward synonym for Charlie Chaplin the filmmaker himself.

The question of knowledge of the English language takes us to the field of school education, which needed to be explored in order to understand the extent to which French prolonged its influential role in the cosmopolitan make-up of Italy's educated elite. This also raised questions of gender, following the creation of the Liceo Femminile, in 1923. But, rather than tackle this topic here, I will use it as a sign of the need to present the context and content of this book more systematically. The next section will dwell on the field of studies on American culture in Italy, after which I will outline the specific contribution of this book.

## The Academic Context

Today, no historian of twentieth-century Italy would question the major role played by American culture, sometimes welcomed with open arms, other times appropriated and reshaped in creative ways, or fought against and demonized as a sign of spiritual decadence. The study of the presence of American culture in Italy goes back a few decades. It found a literary forum in *Studi americani*, Agostino Lombardo's journal founded in 1955. It is easy to imagine how in those years the geopolitical context must have turned any discussion centring on the USA into a potential field for ideological entrenching. Stephen Gundle's study of the cultural policies of the Italian Communist Party during that period reveals this in some depth.[10] Furthermore, the development of cultural studies in the late 1960s created an interest in mass media and mass culture that inevitably put the spotlight on America. In Italy, however, this new discipline was slow to be established, and so debates around Italy's 'Americanization' remained within the fields of sociology and intellectual history.

A much-needed milestone contribution arrived only in 1991 in the form of the hefty, collective volume *Nemici per la pelle: Sogno americano e mito sovietico nell'Italia contemporanea*, with a scholarly introduction by Pier Paolo D'Attorre, who sadly passed away prematurely only a few years afterwards. Its twenty-three essays provided a wide range of studies to which a number of international scholars contributed. Then, following the end of the 'American century', a score of in-depth monographs concentrated on American culture in Europe and so, partly, on Italy too. In 2005, two of the most prominent figures in the study of

---

[10] Stephen Gundle, *Between Hollywood and Moscow. The Italian Communists and the Challenge of Mass Culture, 1943–1991* (Durham, NC: Duke University Press, 2000).

American mass culture abroad, Robert W. Rydell and Rob Kroes, published a volume—*Buffalo Bill in Bologna: The Americanization of the World. 1869-1922*—which examined the early phase of the expansion of American culture. Rydell and Kroes's mention of Bill Cody's Wild West performance in Bologna, however, was provocative rather than illustrative of a specific interest in Italy. It could have been London, Paris, Vienna, or any other historic European town visited by the Wild West show.[11]

In the same year, another monograph dedicated to the subject was published by a historian well rooted in Italian studies who had contributed to D'Attorre's book: Victoria De Grazia. Her *Irresistible Empire: America's Advance through 20th-Century Europe* came in the wake of her stimulating work of the 1980s and 1990s. It showed how America provided a model of economic strategies and social emancipation—from Hollywood's marketing ploys to the Rotary Club—which spread throughout Europe with the intensity of a religious fever. After that came two other volumes published in 2012. They were the more traditional study of diplomatic and intellectual history by Mary Nolan—*The Transatlantic Century: Europe and America, 1890-2010*—which developed the notion of a two-way relation between Europe and the USA, and David W. Ellwood's scholarly *tour de force*: *The Shock of America: Europe and the Challenge of the Century*. Ellwood, like De Grazia, is a historian whose research has often concentrated on Italy. In this book, beyond presenting a political history of the phenomenon, Ellwood provided countless examples of the deep impact of American culture abroad, with many examples focusing specifically on the Italian peninsula.[12]

Mention of four volumes by American and British historians raises the question of where Italian scholarship stood during those early years of the twenty-first century. Indeed, Italy's leading Americanist of his generation, Maurizio Vaudagna, co-edited not one but two volumes in English. His own research interests, however, concentrated on economic policies, and so the cultural dimension was a secondary concern. Another 'americanista', Massimo Teodori, produced a book entitled *Maledetti americani*, which was more of a long discussion-essay than a scholarly work. The following year he coupled it with its anti-thesis, *Benedetti americani*, both books revealing how the polemics related to the political role of the USA in the post-WWII years were still fuelling attempts at historical analysis.[13]

---

[11] Pier Paolo D'Attorre (ed.), *Sogno americano e mito sovietico nell'Italia contemporanea* (Milan: Franco Angeli, 1991). D'Attorre became director of the Fondazione Gramsci Emilia-Romagna in 1992, was then mayor of Ravenna until he died of tumor in April 1997, at the age of forty-six. Robert W. Rydell and Rob Kroes, *Buffalo Bill in Bologna: The Americanization of the World, 1869-1922* (Chicago: Chicago University Press, 2005).

[12] Victoria De Grazia, *Irresistible Empire: America's Advance through 20th-Century Europe* (Cambridge, MA: Harvard University Press, 2005). Mary Nolan, *The Transatlantic Century: Europe and America, 1890-2010* (Cambridge: Cambridge University Press, 2012); David W. Ellwood, *The Shock of America: Europe and the Challenge of the Century* (Oxford: Oxford University Press, 2012).

[13] David K. Adams and Maurizio Vaudagna (eds), *Transatlantic Encounters: Essays on the Use and Misuse of History in Europe and America* (Amsterdam: VU University Press, 2000). R. Lawrence Moore and Maurizio Vaudagna (eds), *The American Century in Europe* (Ithaca, NY: Cornell University

Again, the cultural dimension remained somehow in the background, and D'Attorre's book of 1991 remained unequalled. An Italian scholar who might have written an insightful book about the influence of American culture was Umberto Eco. Starting from his foundational work in semiotics and Italian cultural studies in the 1960s and 1970s, Eco paid particular attention to American culture as a paradigm of popular, mass-produced artefacts. Inspiring and entertaining were also his journalistic pieces written from 'the province of the American empire', to paraphrase the title of one of the books that collected them, *Dalla periferia dell'impero* (1977). These many thoughts and small contributions, however, were never condensed into a monograph. Instead, at the start of the twenty-first century, Eco produced a novel, the most autobiographical of his fictional *oeuvre*—*La misteriosa fiamma della regina Loana* (2004). Recalling his own childhood during the interwar years, Eco dwelt at length on the importance of American comics in shaping his vision of the world during the Fascist regime. But, however stimulating this novel is, it was hardly a substitute for a scholarly study on American culture in twentieth-century Italy.[14]

The books just mentioned, and many other, shorter contributions, allowed me to form a detailed picture of the research field and of the portions that remained uncultivated. I had decided that my approach was going to be multidisciplinary but, in itself, such a line of investigation required a number of key methodological decisions. Help came from a hefty volume, once again by a historian of Europe with a particular interest in Italy. This is Donald Sassoon's *The Culture of the Europeans: From 1800 to the Present*. Its sixteen-hundred pages are the inevitable consequence of an ambitious chronological span and disciplinary breadth. At the same time, the book provides an erudite and thought-provoking reading that taught me two lessons. First, the importance of the connection between cultural artefacts and the social and economic context within which they find their place. Pierre Bourdieu's notion of 'cultural capital'—acknowledged in Sassoon's introduction—was a telltale sign of his intention to question high-culture canons and sedimented national narratives by simply looking at how artefacts fared within their specific fields and how they moved from one part of Europe to another. The second lesson concerned cultural models. Chapter 46 of his book is entitled 'Mass Culture: The American Challenge'. At the same time, the preceding 934 pages dwell often on the importance of France, and of Paris as a constant paradigm of the latest fashion. For a specialist in Italian culture, this chimed with something that, for years, I had wanted to get to the bottom of, ever since I had encountered an epigrammatic note by Antonio Gramsci that reads: 'We will

---

Press, 2003). Massimo Teodori, *Maledetti americani: Destra, sinistra e cattolici: Storia del pregiudizio antiamericano* (Milan: Mondadori, 2002); and *Benedetti americani: Dall'alleanza atlantica alla guerra al terrorismo* (Milan: Mondadori, 2003).

[14] Umberto Eco, *La misteriosa fiamma della regina Loana* (Milan: Bompiani, 2004); trans. in English as *The Mysterious Flame of Queen Loana* (London: Secker & Warburg, 2005).

understand very little of Italian culture until 1900 unless we study it as a phenomenon of French provincialism.'[15]

To my knowledge, nobody has written extensively on the 'Frenchization' of Italian culture, and the inelegance of this expression has perhaps defied any temptation. At the same time, when studying the cultural upbringing of the Italian educated elite throughout the nineteenth century—even before the Unification, whether in Francophile Piedmont, Austrian-ruled Lombardy, the Vatican's Rome, or Spanish-sub-ruled Sicily—if there was one unifying thread, it was that of the presence of the French language and of Parisian culture in particular as models of a coveted cosmopolitan status and of a 'modern' lifestyle. The library of every self-respecting noble or upper-bourgeois family would have included a collection of French books, often accompanied by a subscription to one or two Parisian journals. Learning English or German was an exception, left predominantly to scientists and philosophy scholars. Reading and speaking French was the expectation. As Sassoon showed, this was taking place in Italy as much as in other parts of Europe. Throughout the nineteenth century, when it came to marketing its lifestyle, France remained—as recently defined by a British economic historian—'a Velvet Empire'.[16]

No academic study, has fully traced this tension between French and American culture as it developed throughout the first decades following Italy's unification, all the way until the First World War. The same can be said for the interwar years. In 1993, David Forgacs had insisted on the need to move back to the Fascist period in order to understand how American influence in Italy had taken shape. In the same year, Italian historian Emilio Gentile produced an essay on American culture and the Fascist regime, which provided a stimulating first answer although the role of French culture was still left in the margins.[17]

In more recent years, much has been written on the cultural history of the interwar period, and, although no single volume has been dedicated to foreign influence, the specific role of American culture has been touched upon by various scholars, from Ruth Ben-Ghiat to Forgacs himself together with Stephen Gundle. Most welcome was Daniela Rossini's book on the 'mito americano' in the First World War. Mention of the 'mito americano' will remind many that, in the literary field, this had been a recurrent topic of study, based on the controversial thesis that interest in American

---

[15] Donald Sassoon, *The Culture of the Europeans: From 1800 to the Present* (London: Harper Press, 2006). Antonio Gramsci, Quaderno 14 (1932–35); §37. All references to Gramsci's *Quaderni del carcere* are based on the four-volume edition by Valentino Gerratana (Turin, Einaudi, 1975). The entire text is now freely available online at https://quadernidelcarcere.wordpress.com (accessed 14 April 2023). Unless stated otherwise, all translations are mine.

[16] David Todd, *A Velvet Empire: French Informal Imperialism in the Nineteenth Century* (Princeton: Princeton University Press, 2021).

[17] David Forgacs, 'Americanisation: The Italian Case, 1938–1956', *Borderlines. Studies in American Culture*, 1/2 (1993), 157–69 (161). Emilio Gentile, 'Impending Modernity: Fascism and the Ambivalent Image of the United States', *Journal of Contemporary History*, 28/1 (1993), 7–29 (later repr. as part of his volume *The Struggle for Modernity: Nationalism, Futurism, and Fascism* (Westport, CT: Praeger, 2003), 161–80).

literature equated to anti-Fascism. On this, the recent, sadly posthumous, volume by Jane Dunnett—*The 'Mito Americano' and Italian Literary Culture under Fascism*—has shed much light. Overall, however, many questions remained unanswered, and the post-unification years stayed as an unexplored land if one excludes the work of diplomatic and political historians such as Giorgio Spini and, more recently, Daniele Fiorentino. Hence my resolution to concentrate this study on the period between Italy's unification and the implosion of the Fascist regime in July 1943, by which time America had started to come to Italy in the shape of GI soldiers.[18]

At its boundaries, the pre-unification period was aptly covered by a recent volume by Axel Körner, whereas the impact of the arrival of Allied troops during the last phase of the Nazi-led Repubblica Sociale Italiana has already been examined in detail by the seminal study of David Ellwood, *Italy 1943–1945*.[19]

As to my personal interest and contribution to this field of study, I should start by saying that until a dozen years ago my research interests focused exclusively on the fields of literature and film. At the same time, my interest in cultural history was slowly taking over. It took its first shape in a conference and an edited book on censorship in modern Italy, in collaboration with Robert Gordon, back in 2005. After that came an attempt to make sense of the demographic and cultural revolution that contemporary Italy was going through in those years. The former poor country that had seen millions of its citizens migrate to different parts of the world, America included, was now a wealthy country receiving waves of immigrants, in an epochal process that had started spectacularly across the Adriatic with the implosion of the Albanian regime in 1991. Again, this took the shape of a conference and book.[20]

Pondering on the past, present, and future impact of migration on Italian culture brought forth a notion that is as generic as it is fundamental for understanding who we are: cultural change. If Italy had been a crossroad of different civilizations throughout the centuries, to what extent could change be understood

---

[18] Ruth Ben-Ghiat, *Fascist Modernities: Italy, 1922–1945* (Berkeley and Los Angeles: University of California Press, 2001). David Forgacs and Stephen Gundle, *Mass Culture and Italian Society: From Fascism to the Cold War* (Bloomington, IN: Indiana University Press, 2007). Daniela Rossini, *Il mito americano nell'Italia della Grande Guerra* (Rome and Bari: Laterza, 2000); pub. in English as *Woodrow Wilson and the American Myth in Italy* (Cambridge, MA: Harvard University Press, 2008). Jane Dunnett, *The 'Mito Americano' and Italian Literary Culture under Fascism* (Rome: Aracne, 2015). A notable contribution by Giorgio Spini is the co-editorship and preface to *Italia e America dal settecento al'età dell'imperialismo* (Venice: Marsilio, 1976), which was paired to a second, complementary volume: *Italia e America dalla Grande Guerra a oggi* (Venice: Marsilio, 1976). By Daniele Fiorentino, see *Gli Stati Uniti e il Risorgimento d'Italia, 1848–1901* (Rome: Gangemi, 2013).

[19] Axel Körner, *America in Italy: The United States in the Political Thought and Imagination of the Italian Risorgimento, 1763–1865* (Princeton and Oxford: Princeton University Press, 2017). David W. Ellwood, *Italy 1943–1945* (Leicester: Leicester University Press, 1985).

[20] Guido Bonsaver and Robert Gordon (eds), *Culture, Censorship and the State in 20th Century Italy* (Oxford: Legenda: 2005). Emma Bond, Guido Bonsaver, and Federico Faloppa (eds), *Destination Italy: Representing Migration in Contemporary Media and Narrative* (Oxford: Peter Lang, 2015).

through a study of the cultural history of the Italian peninsula? This was an ambitious research question, which introduced me to the challenge of discussing cultural change across different disciplines. More importantly, as a modernist, I was brought to focus on the study of the key phase of the arrival of American culture in competition with—and often mediated by—the historic foreign model of intellectual exercise and lifestyle fashion: France, or, better, Paris. This took me to another collaborative project, this time with Alessandro Carlucci and Matthew Reza, which produced a conference in 2016, a theoretical essay, and an edited volume entitled *Italy and the USA: Understanding Cultural Change in Language and Narrative*. My contribution to that volume is an early version of the third chapter of this book.[21]

By then I was sure about the need to study the arrival of American culture as strictly linked to Italy's entry into the modern world of mass production and mass culture. The solitary journey leading to this book had started.

## Questions of Methodology

Mention so far of two familiar names—Gramsci and Bourdieu—is an indication of my interest in connecting the social and cultural relevance of the objects of this study. Attached to it is the more recent field of world literature. Whether through Franco Moretti's *Atlas of the European Novel* or Pascale Casanova's *La République mondiale des lettres*, the perception of the wider horizon and of the many different journeys of literary works has made me familiar with a transnational mind frame. The wider, global context will be privileged as an agent in the cultural make-up of individuals and communities. The decades under scrutiny here witness a major shift in the strength and importance of transnational flows.[22]

At the same time, this approach has been enriched by other fields of research. The ambitious attempts at system theory by semioticians of the calibre of Umberto Eco and Yuri Lotman have allowed me to perceive the complexity and endless variations of the dynamics of cultural encounters and exchanges. I have also learnt much from the field of contact linguistics for their analytical and

---

[21] Guido Bonsaver, Alessandro Carlucci, and Matthew Reza, *Italy and the USA: Understanding Cultural Change in Language and Narrative* (Cambridge: Legenda, 2019). Guido Bonsaver, Alessandro Carlucci, and Matthew Reza, 'The Dynamics of Cultural Change: A Theoretical Frame with Reference to Italy–USA Relations', *900 Transnazionale/Transnational 900*, 3/1 (2019), 107–30.

[22] Franco Moretti, *Atlas of the European Novel, 1800–1900* (London: Verso 1998); Pascale Casanova, *La République mondiale des lettres* (Paris: Éditions du Seuil, 1999); trans. into English as *The World Republic of Letters* (Cambridge, MA: Harvard University Press, 2004). Overall, I agree with Sven Beckert's definition of transnational history as 'a way of seeing' rather than a methodology, paying attention to networks and processes transcending politically defined spaces. See C. A. Bayly, Sven Beckert, et al., 'AHR Conversation: On Transnational History', *American Historical Review*, 111/5 (2006), 1441–64 (1454, 1459).

data-driven study of the organic variations of languages exposed to foreign borrowings. From these two areas of study I have derived the concept of the three phases through which foreign artefacts (material and immaterial such as an idea, a technique, or a word) are perceived, assimilated, and elaborated by the receiving cultural system: transfer, replica, and invention. The first, transfer, refers to the process of recognition and ostentation (as defined by Eco) in which a cultural artefact is identified and imported; replica takes place when the receiving culture starts to produce its own version of that artefact; and invention concerns the phase in which the process of elaboration comes to a stage whereby what is produced is only vaguely related to the originally imported artefact. The reality of cultural exchange is obviously more complicated and multidirectional. It is a simplification, however, which has helped me to conceptualize cultural change across different fields and different kinds of artefacts.[23]

It should also be mentioned that reception theory has added clear awareness of the subjective paths through which a cultural object 'makes sense' while interacting with the notions, attitudes, and intentions of its individual consumers. Individuals and groups are also capable of re-elaborating and producing an artefact entirely emancipated from—and indeed sometimes in opposition to—the original. This is one of the basic premises that allowed studies of American cultural influence to move away from its analysis as a one-way process of cultural imperialism or, as famously worded, 'Coca-colonization'.[24] Jazz music, and a few decades later, rock'n'roll music, travelled across the Atlantic and provoked a myriad of different reactions that radiated in different directions, both socially and geographically, some recrossing the ocean and hitting America with equal force. As when four singing moptops reached New York City in February 1964 and spread Beatlemania across the USA. Or when, in the same year, the most autochthonous of all American literary and film genres, the western, was given a sharp twist by Italian director Sergio Leone, who began to play with its codes in *Per un pugno di dollari*.

Cultural history is a field of research that sits awkwardly between the stools of more established disciplines. This book is first and foremost a historical narrative,

---

[23] This classification derives mainly from Eco's typology of the modes of sign production in his *Theory of Semiotics* (London: Macmillan, 1977; 1975 in Italian edn). The development of Eco's model is detailed in the already mentioned theoretical article, Bonsaver, Carlucci, and Reza, 'The Dynamics of Cultural Change'. The term 'transfer' comes from contact linguistics; see, e.g., Sarah Grey Thomason, 'Contact as a Source of Language Change', in Brian D. Joseph and Richard D. Janda (eds), *The Handbook of Historical Linguistics* (Oxford: Blackwell, 2004), 687–712. As for Lotman, the concept of semiosphere as developed in his *Universe of the Mind: A Semiotic Theory of Culture* (London: Tauris, 1990), although not used here specifically, has been stimulating to an understanding of the endless metamorphoses through which individuals and communities form a sense of being in relation to the environment in which they are immersed.

[24] The reference here is naturally to Reinhold Wagnleitner, *Coca-Colonization and the Cold War: The Cultural Mission of the United States in Austria after the Second World War* (Chapel Hill, NC: The University of North Carolina Press, 1994).

and the monographs on European cultural history mentioned above have been instructive models. They also taught me not to lose sight of the particular. If I were to think of an inspiring forefather, then Carlo Ginzburg's classic, *Il formaggio e i vermi* (*The Cheese and the Worms*, 1976) deserves first mention. His microhistorical approach has always encouraged me to search for stories of individuals that allow us to sense the spirit of a period, or of the connections between places. The notion of 'national identity' is a delicate one and has often proved to be a theoretical construction rather than the actual experience of individuals: for this reason, no simplistic categorization of 'Italians' and 'Americans' will be applied. At the same time, during the years under consideration here, American culture began to acquire a defining presence in the lives and minds of people living in Italy, and as such it interfered with their sense of identity. It is a cultural historian's work to study this in all its many variations.

Most importantly, I should explain the selection of cultural fields explored by this book. Those examined in depth are six. The first concerns the discussion and representation of America in periodicals—from newspapers to illustrated and literary magazines. This provides much of the material towards an understanding of the many discourses that circulated in Italy. Then come the creative elaborations and theoretical discussions pertaining to the narrative arts: the traditional one, literature (from fiction to travel books), and the newly born one, film. The fourth field is that of music, made compulsory by the already mentioned importance of jazz, but also useful in order to see how the world of opera—historic territory for Italian composers—reacted to the emergence of American culture. The last two concern the interwar years, which brought new forms of cultural production beyond film in the form of the mass medium of radio and of comics. The latter were a first symptom before the post-Second World War explosion of what we now call 'youth culture'.

These six fields are complemented by other, secondary ones that simply presented themselves and needed to be discussed for better understanding of how America reached Italy. The first is the already mentioned field of foreign-language learning in the Italian school system. The perception of American culture throughout the entire period under scrutiny here was in many ways prejudiced by the fact that knowledge of the English language was limited to a small minority of the educated elite. Then came architecture, made compelling by the iconic presence of American skyscrapers, particularly so when asking what the Fascists made of their implicit challenge to Fascism's own ambition as a 'modernist' regime that intended to give a distinctive shape to every walk of life, buildings included. The same can be said about aviation, the technology which embodied modernity in the 20th century. Philosophy too knocked at the door, given the interest in American pragmatism shown at the start of the century by the Florentine *enfant terrible* Giovanni Papini, and passed on to the young Benito Mussolini himself. Finally came economic history, made necessary by the fact that America's Taylor-styled industries played a substantial part in America's image.

Overall, it goes without saying that for some of these fields of study I had to sit on the shoulders of their respective giants. At the same time, I thoroughly enjoyed the learning process of delving into each field's primary works. Studying the use of steel frame and concrete in high-rise buildings, or following the diaspora of New Orleans jazz musicians—some of Sicilian origin like Dominic James 'Nick' La Rocca—and the role of transatlantic ocean liners in providing a vehicle for Italian jazz musicians eager to reach America: these have been formative experiences whose excitement, I hope, is still detectable in the pages of this book. On top of this, those individual strands often coexisted and came entwined with one another. Sometimes this created narrative and visual 'knots'. One such experience is condensed in the second illustration of this Introduction. It shows two icons of the interwar years: Charlie Chaplin, one of America's greatest filmmakers, comically challenging Primo Carnera. The latter was then Italy's most famous heavyweight boxer. A few months after this picture was taken, Carnera became world champion but then, on the eve of Italy's invasion of Ethiopia—ironically, and embarrassingly for Fascist propagandists—he was defeated by African American boxer, Joe Louis. And, if the worlds of cinema, sport, and politics are conflated in the image, it is equally symbolic that this copy of the photograph should be a signed gift made by Carnera to Carlo Benzi, one of Italy's most prominent jazz musicians at the time. The two had befriended each other during an Atlantic crossing on the liner *Conte Grande*, in whose orchestra Benzi had played the saxophone. So, music is indirectly part of this photograph too, and the role of ocean liners—themselves much exalted as a symbol of Fascist Italy's technological achievements. Cinema, sport, politics, naval technology and jazz music: all converged and asked for 'their' story to be told, individual and collective.

Among the absent fields, one should say a word about the two most conspicuous omissions. First, there is no specific exploration of the fine arts. This is mainly due to the fact that, while the visual dimension is extremely important in the shape of film and photographs in illustrated magazines—and those are treated in depth—there was little transfer, indeed, perception, of American artistic production before the Second World War. Edward Hopper's suspended images of an American dream in crisis can rightly be put in parallel with Giorgio De Chirico's metaphysical art. However, it is a painting by De Chirico that was exhibited in New York in 1921. The impact of Hopper's work did not fully reach Italy—physically or artistically—until the post-war years. Indeed, Marla Stone's groundbreaking book on Italian fine arts during the Fascist years has very little to say about America, while, of course, this is a field that would compel extended treatment when dealing with the post-Second World War years.[25]

---

[25] Marla Stone, *The Patron State: Culture and Politics in Fascist Italy* (Princeton: Princeton University Press, 1998). On the late reception of American art in Italy, see Catherine Dossin, *The Rise and Fall of American Art, 1940s–1980s: A Geopolitics of the Western Art World* (Farnham: Ashgate, 2015), 21–7.

16 AMERICA IN ITALIAN CULTURE

**Fig. 0.2.** Charlie Chaplin comically facing Primo Carnera in a signed photo, which Carnera donated in 1930 to jazz musician Carlo Benzi during their crossing of the Atlantic on the liner *Conte Grande*. (courtesy of Adriano Mazzoletti, Rome)

The second absent field concerns the wider area of material culture—that is, how Italians changed their daily habits as a consequence of their contact—real or imaginary—with American culture. There is no doubt that things began to change during the chronological span of this book—and indeed some reference to these changes will be found in sections that address the experience of return migrants, for example. However, as in the case of fine arts, I would argue that this is a phenomenon that—for example, with regard to food culture—mainly concerns the post-WWII years. Fast-food restaurants were certainly mentioned by astounded Italian travellers to America during the interwar years, but there is no trace of that having any effect whatsoever on how Italians continued to eat their meals. Even the most Americanophile Futurists, when accompanying their performances in the Milanese and Roman nightclubs with alcoholic drinks, would sternly stick to champagne. Nobody was taken by the American predilection for bourbon whiskey (whereas the champagne versus whiskey topos is subtly displayed by Federico Fellini in his 1950s nightclub sequence of *La dolce vita*).[26]

---

[26] I expand on this in an essay entitled '"Senti'n po', a Gregori Pècche...": Shavelson's *It Started in Naples* and Fellini's *La dolce vita* between Italian and US Culture', in Guido Bonsaver, Brian

Clothing is another branch of material culture that has not found space here apart from a few notes about fashion in films that explicitly addressed the topic. Again, I would argue that it is not a field in which American culture had much influence before 1945. Sport and leisure time were more difficult fields to leave aside. No doubt Italian travellers to the USA commented on the dedication of Americans to leisure activities, and particularly shocking was the sight of young women playing sport with the vigour and competitiveness of their male counterparts. Mussolini's Fascism paid equal attention to sport and *dopo-lavoro*, and therefore parallels were offered. A study of the organization of sport and leisure time in Fascist Italy will probably show how America provided the example of a country already well developed in that direction. Indeed, Victoria De Grazia's monograph on women under Fascism already signals this.[27]

Perhaps it is fairer to admit that material culture is simply not at the centre of this book. I dwell on aspects of it when they emerge as relevant. At the same time, the core of this study is an understanding of 'culture' as the production of artefacts that are intended for intellectual pleasure: a newspaper article or a comic, a book, a film, a piece of music. Surely, food, clothing, and sport carry significant cultural connotations, but they principally serve non-intellectual functions. This is not an attempt at a hierarchy of cultural artefacts and social habits but simply a clarification of the main sphere of interests pertaining to this book.

As for the internal hierarchy and canons in each cultural field, following the cultural studies turn of yesteryear, I treat definitions of high and low culture with due caution. At the same time, it will be interesting to see the role this differentiation played in the judgement of Italians looking at American artefacts. The identification of America with mass production had enormous influence. Hollywood became a controversial paradigm of this process, constantly accused of allowing the commercial drive for mass appreciation to spoil the development of film aesthetics. American novels too, as we will see, were first seen as coming from 'below'. Before respectable bookshops began to display the best of contemporary American novelists—the stuff that fuelled the 'mito americano' in the 1930s—the stalls of street vendors and news kiosks were already crowded with scores of crime and adventure novels, and the craze for Jack London was already in full swing. What some of those works had in common was their middlebrow status. Americans were good at that. Even in the field of comics, when the Fascists eventually imposed anti-American measures in 1938, one expected response was that Italian magazines should give up those speech balloons and return to the dignified

---

Richardson, and Giuseppe Stellardi (eds), *Cultural Reception, Translation and Transformation from Medieval to Modern Italy: Essays in Honour of Martin McLaughlin* (Cambridge: Legenda, 2017), 331–51.

[27] Victoria De Grazia, *How Fascism Ruled Women: Italy, 1922-1945* (Berkeley and Los Angeles: University of California Press, 1993).

literary tradition of rhymed couplets. A 'higher-brow' idea of children's entertainment was re-established.[28]

Beyond the disciplines that have been mentioned so far, there is one that has always been implicit and now merits a comment: political history. The change from Liberal to Fascist Italy was so radical that we will need to consider its impact on cultural production and on the perception of America. The totalitarian and leader-centred make-up of the Fascist regime—at least in its intentions—turned Benito Mussolini into the ultimate judge of what constituted good or bad culture. His ideas on American politics, society, and culture are of great importance, whether or not Italians followed them in their multifarious practices. Mussolini might not have read comics, and he considered jazz to be only a type of dance music, but he was an avid reader of newspapers and books, and his weekly screenings of documentary and fiction films at Villa Torlonia are part of the history of Italian cinema, if nothing else because one of his sons, Vittorio, turned himself into an authoritative film critic and film producer.

The political dimension has been a recurring thread in my research interests even during the years in which literature and cinema were my main field of work. I constantly ended up focusing on authors and filmmakers whose political interests were worn on their sleeves. Working on censorship was also an exploration of the meeting point between cultural production and political power. If I look back, there is a work that is worth mentioning here, since it relates to politics and also provides a good bridge to another methodological question: the narrative style adopted in this book. In 2010, I wrote the biography of an extraordinary man called Gaetano Pilati, whose papers I had discovered in a Florentine archive. His life offered an ideal micro-story through which to narrate the radical changes that the Italian working class had gone through during its social and political emancipation in the early years of the twentieth century. The son of a semi-illiterate Bolognese farmer, Pilati moved to Florence in 1907 to become a modernizing builder (constructing affordable housing with reinforced concrete) and a militant socialist, finally elected to parliament in 1919. Under Fascism, he became a likely target and was eventually killed in cold blood, in the middle of the night, during the last anti-socialist pogrom of 24 October 1925.[29]

---

[28] The notion of 'middlebrow' will be used in this study to refer to those literary works that mediated between the intellectual sophistication and ambitions of 'high-brow' literature and the commercially driven and coded characteristics of cheap paperback fiction. On this notion, in relation to the Italian publishing industry during the period under consideration, see Sara Sullam, '(Middle)browsing Mondadori's Archive: British Novels in the *Medusa* Series, 1933–1945', *Textus: English Studies in Italy*, 28/3 (2015), 179–201; Elke D'hoker and Sarah Bonciarelli, 'Extending the Middlebrow: Italian Fiction in the Early Twentieth Century', *Belphégor*, 15/2 (2017), 1–16; and Fabio Guidali, 'Developing Middlebrow Culture in Fascist Italy: The Case of Rizzoli's Illustrated Magazines', *Journal of European Periodical Studies*, 4/2 (2019), 106–21.

[29] Guido Bonsaver, *Vita e omicidio di Gaetano Pilati: 1881–1925* (Florence: Cesati, 2010). The works on censorship I refer to are *Censorship and Literature in Fascist Italy* (Toronto: Toronto

When I wrote his story, I decided that the narrative should be a fabric weaving together written text and the visual clues from the images I had collected—old photos, documents, the odd memorabilia. It was a dialogue between text and image that was partially spurred on by the example of personal favourites such as W. G. Sebald's *Austerlitz* (2001), Benedetta Tobagi's *Come mi batte forte il cuore* (2009), and Edmund De Waal's *The Hare with Amber Eyes* (2010). Equally, though, it went back to a fond memory of my childhood: spending hours browsing through my father's four shelves of books, in particular through his illustrated history of the Second World War. I remember poring over those black and white photographs, some overexposed, some out of focus, trying to make sense of the three-dimensional reality they represented. This is the reason why this book comes with over a hundred images, all connected to the text. The visual journey contained within this book is not an appendix, but part and parcel of the narrative.

I should also add that my considerations will often be enriched by direct quotations. Similar to the decision to include illustrations, the purpose of this is to try and transmit the flavour and voice of those years. As cultural anthropologist Tim Ingold suggests, 'people grow in knowledge not only through direct encounters with others, but also through hearing their stories told'. He refers to stories of migration in distant lands, but I would argue that it is a similar question in relation to stories coming from a distant past, told by the people who experienced them and not just paraphrased by a historian.[30]

A note is also due concerning the use of America and American as synonyms for the United States of America and the US citizen. This is still the practised norm today, despite the terms' implicit ambiguity as a potential reference to the continent and the people living in both Americas. This book will not attempt to raise a linguistic crusade (although I applaud how the replacement of 'Indian' with 'native American' has eventually put right the centuries-old linguistic coda of one of the biggest blunders in human geography). At the same time, for the sake of clarity, the abbreviation USA and its adjective US will be used when abstracting from the historical setting and referring to the country and its citizens in a political sense. As for the use of Italian American with or without hyphen, I have come to the conclusion that 'Italian American' is the most respectful approximation, and I thank American friends and colleagues for helping me reach this conclusion.

The organization of the ten chapters of this book is, I hope, easily deductible from the table of contents. The First World War presented itself as a natural

---

University Press, 2007); and *Mussolini censore: Storie di letteratura, dissenso e ipocrisia* (Rome and Bari: Laterza, 2013).

[30] Tim Ingold, *Being Alive: Essays on Movement, Knowledge and Description* (London: Routledge, 2011), 161. I should also apologise for the lack of the original text in the many quotations from sources in Italian. It was present at first but had to be cut in order to contain the length of the book.

watershed, hence the division into two parts. Within each section, five chapters deal with the perception and presence of American culture, starting from the public debate and progressively concentrating on different cultural fields. The subdivision of the Fascist years comes from the need to underline the profound changes that Mussolini imposed in 1938 to the regime's cultural policies and how they impacted on the perception and representation of America.

Overall, these ten chapters should provide a stimulating angle through which to follow the development of Italian culture at a time of radical changes. By the 1920s, images of America were familiar to all Italians. Some remained suspicious, such as the country's leading playwright, Luigi Pirandello. Asked about it in 1929 during one of his long stays abroad, Pirandello had no doubts: 'Americanism is engulfing us. I think that a new beacon of civilization has turned on over there.' In Pirandello's mind, Americanism meant the end of Europe as he knew it, and the last bastion against this invasion was to be found in Paris. From his prison cell, Antonio Gramsci read the article and left a note about it in his notebook. He did not share Pirandello's apocalyptic tones. Better, he did not think that what was coming from across the Atlantic was such an alien, annihilating force. To him, 'it is an organic extension and an intensification of European civilization'.[31]

What the two agreed on, however, was that America offered a new paradigm, a new model of what the future might have in store for Italy, for Europe, and for the rest of the world.

---

[31] Corrado Alvaro, 'Pirandello della Germania del cinema sonoro e di altre cose', interview in *La Fiera letteraria*, 14 April 1929, pp. 17–19; now in Ivan Pupo (ed.), *Interviste a Pirandello: 'Parole da dire, uomo, agli altri uomini'* (Soveria Mannelli: Rubbettino, 2002), 427–31 (429). Antonio Gramsci's note appears in his Quaderno 22 (1934), §15.

PART 1

# THE DISCOVERY OF AMERICA, 1861–1919

# 1
# Cross-National Influence in Post-Unification Italy

When the Italian nation state was born, in March 1861, and Rome was eventually taken from the Vatican and proclaimed capital, in February 1871, the peninsula's political unity had been a long time coming. In Giuseppe Mazzini's prophetic language, the 'third Rome' of the Italian people—a successor to imperial and papal Rome—had eventually come into being. Despite its great economic and cultural prosperity, the Italian Renaissance had brought no political unification, and for centuries the aspirations of patriots had lived solely in the realm of literature. With increasing parts of the peninsula falling under foreign domination following the descent of Charles VIII's French army in 1494, by the start of the nineteenth century Italy was predominantly under foreign rule. When the dust settled, after the earthquake of the French Revolution and the Napoleonic wars, Austria returned to dominate. It controlled most of the north, while the Papal State in the centre and the Spanish Bourbons in the south lay in the shadow of Austria's military power. However, the foreign nation that had indubitably fascinated, shaken, and bewitched Italian intellectuals was, before and after defeat, France.

During the age of the Enlightenment, Paris had established itself as the cultural capital of Europe. French had replaced Latin as the language of diplomacy and of high culture. In 1784, one of the most renowned French polemicists at the time, Antoine Rivaroli (or le Comte de Rivarol, as he preferred to call himself in an attempt to conceal his father's Italian origin) wrote an essay in praise of French as a universal language. It won a prestigious competition on the subject held by the Prussian Academy of Sciences, in line with Frederick II's Francophile views in cultural matters.[1]

The educated elite of Europe, from the British Isles, to western Russia, down to the Mediterranean coasts of Italy and Spain, not only learnt and spoke French as their mark of distinction: they all looked to the fashions and lifestyle of the Parisian upper classes—*le goût parisien*—as a model of modernity, however much occasionally tinged with envious scorn. Whether *gallomani* or *gallofobi* ('Gallophiles' or' Gallophobes'), to use the expressions in vogue at the time, most Italian intellectuals shaped their tastes and lifestyles either in conformity with or in contrast

---

[1] Antoine de Rivarol, *De l'universalité de la langue française* (Paris: Bailly-Dessenne, 1784).

to the French model. The young aristocrat of the renowned satirical poem by Giuseppe Parini, *Il giorno* (1763–5), embodied in mock-epic style a sample of this 'Frenchization' of the Italian elite. Among the servants present at his late morning bed-rise, the French tutor is described in the most detail. Here is his arrival:

> The Tutor of the gentle language
> Who from the Seine, Graces' mother,
> Has just arrived, bringing divine ambrosia
> To drip on the sickened Italian lips.[2]

The poem then makes reference to the French nationality of Italian poetry's most revered female figure, Petrarch's Laura, adding even more weight to this mock self-vilification of Italian culture.

Closer to the topic of this book, interest in the independence war of the thirteen British colonies and their creation of the United States of America, in 1776, came to Italy mainly via France. Periodicals such as the *Journal des savants* and the *Journal encyclopédique* were the principal sources of information, whether consumed directly through a subscription or through the selective mediation of Italian journals. A very influential volume was Guillaume Thomas Raynal's *Historique philosophique et politique des établissement et du commerce des Européens dans les deux Indes* (1770) to which Diderot contributed. As for non-French writings, it was rare for a foreign work on America to be translated directly into Italian before a French translation had already led the way.[3]

Then, all of a sudden, the revolution of 1789 imposed France as a groundbreaking political experiment, welcomed by some, though mostly feared by the European elites. Its repercussions shook continental Europe to its very foundations. The ideals of Liberty, Equality, and Fraternity, however interpreted, glorified or betrayed throughout the last decade of the eighteenth century and the first of the nineteenth century, spread themselves all over Europe. In Italy they arrived in 1796 sewn into the flags of the French republican army, providing Italian patriots with inspiration and much-needed military help in their struggle towards unification. As boasted by the narrator of Nievo's *Confessioni di un italiano*—a key novel about the Italian *Risorgimento*—'the number of souls who consecrated themselves to the cult of liberty and other human rights proclaimed in France, was in Italy far bigger than anywhere else'; or, as Francesco de Sanctis vividly put it in his seminal history of Italian literature of 1873, it was 'propaganda helped by

---

[2] Giuseppe Parini, *Il giorno* [1763–5], ed. Dante Isella (Parma: Guanda, 1996), 9 (ll. 184–203).
[3] On this, see Piero del Negro, *Il mito americano nella Venezia del Settecento* (Rome: Atti della Accademia Nazionale dei Lincei [18], 1975), 445–657; Stefania Buccini, *The Americas in Italian Literature and Culture, 1700–1825* (University Park, PA: Pennsylvania State University Press, 1996); and Körner, *America in Italy*, 9–13, 27.

cannons which in a few short years achieved what properly should have taken a century'.[4]

The Congress of Vienna—whose proceedings were written in French—was an attempt to turn back the political clock, but France's influence did not decline with military defeat. It retained its position as a dominant source of 'soft power', exporting culture as much as luxury goods. In his long introduction to his erudite, literary, 2,000-page-long guide to Paris published in 1867, Victor Hugo expressed no doubt in his belief in the universal mission of the French capital: 'In the 20th century, there will be an extraordinary nation. [...] That nation will have Paris as capital, and it will not be named France; it will be named Europe.'[5] Even politically and militarily, France had returned to a central position in the Italian mind. When unification eventually arrived, in 1861, it was thanks to an alliance between the Piedmontese and the France of Napoleon III.

However, beyond political, diplomatic, and economic history, to what extent was France still a cultural model during the second half of the nineteenth century? After all, the diffusion of Romanticism in the early decades of the century, though opposed in numerous Italian circles, had sparked an enthusiastic interest in the culture of northern European countries. The literature of the British–Irish and Germanic traditions had become an object of study and admiration, from the epic poetry of the mythical Ossian to the works of Shakespeare and the fever caused by Goethe's *Die Leiden des jungen Werthers* (*The Sorrows of Young Werther*, 1774), which swept through Europe and materialized in Italy in the pages of Ugo Foscolo's *Le ultime lettere di Jacopo Ortis* (1802). Moreover, before the Romantic excesses of Byronism, British culture had already been cultivated by Italian intellectuals in the eighteenth century, identified for its wit and sense of humour. The neologism *umorista* became so popular that it was included in Niccolò Tommaseo's historic *Dizionario della lingua italiana* (1861–79). The entry deserves full quotation for the sharp, personal comment at its end:

HUMORIST

Of gay, fantastic writer, and originally lively.

Humour is a fundamental trait of the English people, and an original one that is poorly copied by Italians, who are unable to combine fair, good, and dark humour. Our humorist writers, and our humourism, are pitiful forgeries. Humour, which has replaced Esprit, demonstrates our recurrent slavery.[6]

---

[4] Ippolito Nievo, *Confessioni di un italiano* [pub. posthumously in 1867], 2 vols (Milan: Garzanti, 1973), i. 305. Francesco de Sanctis, *Storia della letteratura Italiana* (1873; Turin: Einaudi, 1965), 861.

[5] On France's soft power, see Todd, A *Velvet Empire*, 123–74. Victor Hugo, 'Introduction', in Louis Ulbach (ed.) *Paris Guide par le principaux ècrivains et artistes de la France*, 2 vols (Paris: Librairie Internationale, 1867), i, pp. i–xlvi (pp. i, iv).

[6] A digital edition of Nicolò Tommaseo and Bernardo Bellini, *Dizionario della lingua italiana* (Turin: Società L'Unione Tipografico-editrice, 1861–79), is available on the website of the Accademia della Crusca. The entry 'Umorista' can be found in vol. IV, tome II, p. 1664.

If, in the specific area of humorist writing, the English were taking over from the French—and note Tommaseo's blunt condemnation of Italy's xenophilia—evidence suggests that French culture continued to play a crucial role in the perception of the outside world by Italian intellectuals. This is indirectly proven if one follows the route taken by English writings—the most influential school of literature in the nineteenth century, after France, according to Franco Moretti.[7] Appreciation of English literature commonly arrived via France. If *The Spectator* was the most influential among early periodicals produced in Britain, when Milan's most entrepreneurial editor, Antonio Fortunato Stella, created *Lo Spettatore Italiano*, in 1814, his model was not Addison's and Steel's journal but rather the French *Le Spectateur* by Conrad Malthe-Brun. In its initial version, *Lo Spettatore italiano* carried only translations from the French magazine, save for an appendix about Italian matters, to which the young poet Giacomo Leopardi was to contribute. Moreover, and more importantly, the battle between Romantics and Neoclassicists, which held central stage in Italian literary circles, was initiated by an essay written in 1816 by the most prominent and provocative cultural figure in Paris at the time, Madame Germaine De Staël. Her invitation to translate contemporary foreign literature was received by many Italian intellectuals as an insult to their cherished cultivation of classical culture. And, indicatively, those who followed De Staël's advice began to translate in the wake of the French publishing industry.

Just about every influential work published in English or German during the nineteenth century acquired an Italian translation after a French version had already appeared years in advance. More often than not, these Italian translations were heavily influenced by their French predecessors, to the point that in many cases the translator relied entirely on the French text. The late-eighteenth-century translation of Shakespeare's plays by Jean-François Ducis, however crude in their treatment of the original, formed the basis of several Italian editions in the following decades. Likewise, a fundamental work of Romantic culture, the historical novels by Walter Scott, found its way into Italy through French translations. Four novels—including *Waverley* (1814) and *Ivanhoe* (1819)—were first published in 1822, and all were based on French editions.[8] The role of mediator played by the French publishing industry with regard to British culture continued during the

---

[7] Moretti, *Atlas of the European Novel*, 174–85.

[8] Throughout the nineteenth century, the practice of producing a translation based on translations in other foreign languages was entirely accepted in Italy, even in the more sacred territory of classical literature. The most prestigious translation of Homer's *Iliad* in those decades was that of Vincenzo Monti (1825), who did not know Ancient Greek and who, for this reason, was sarcastically called by Ugo Foscolo 'traduttor de' traduttori' ('translator of translators'). Tolerance in making use of translations in other languages was widespread in Western culture. On Shakespeare's translations in Italy, see Irina Zvereva, 'Per una storia della riflessione teorica sulla traduzione in Italia: La sfortuna di Shakespeare', *Entymema*, 11 (2013), 257–68. On the history of the term *romantico* and on Walter Scott's novels, see David Robey, '*Romantic, romantico, romanzesco*: An Aspect of Walter Scott's Reception in Italy', in Bonsaver, Richardson, and Stellardi (eds), *Cultural Reception, Translation and Transformation from Medieval to Modern Italy*, 199–214.

second half of the nineteenth century. For example, the much-discussed writings on social Darwinism by Herbert Spencer came to Italy via France, and the fictional production of Edgar Allan Poe circulated through Italian translations based on Charles Baudelaire's versions, clearly marked by the French author's poetic licences.[9]

Indeed, in his book about literary 'Anglomania' in eighteenth-century Italy, Arturo Graf, the erudite scholar and co-founder of the *Giornale storico della letteratura italiana* (1883), had no doubt about the dominant role played by French culture: 'this craze too came, like many others, from France'.[10] Graf's chapter devoted to the British capital is entitled 'Parigi e Londra', and, before dealing with the latter, he spends sixteen pages on Paris as the obligatory stop of any Italian intellectuals on their way to London. According to him, Italians saw in Paris 'the seat of pleasure, the temple of fame, the model city, from which all others take norm and example'.[11] When he eventually concentrates on London, Graf devotes only ten pages to it, dwelling on the odd Anglophile who spent time there. And when it comes to suggesting further reading, he laments the lack of books on London in Italian and recommends two volumes in French.

On the German front, A. W. Schlegel's lectures on drama and literature (*Über dramatische Kunst und Literatur*, 1809), which offered the definition of Romanticism much adopted and discussed in Italy, were popularized by De Staël in her *De l'Allemagne* (1810) and were translated into Italian only in 1817. This might seem surprising, given that the first Italian writings in support of Romanticism were circulated in 1816. But not if one considers that the first use of the term *romantico* with a Schlegelian understanding appeared in 1814, thanks to the Italian translation of a favourable review of De Staël's *De l'Allemagne* published in the already mentioned *Le Spectateur*. Finally, another fundamental work of Romantic culture, the Grimm Brothers' collection of fairy tales (1812–22) was translated into French in 1824, while the first Italian translations of a selection of the fairy tales appeared only forty years later.[12]

These preliminary notes should not detract from the notion of a cross-national exchange and dialogue that went beyond the influential role played by French culture. Interest in other cultures went in phases. If Anglomania had swept through eighteenth-century Italy, the latter part of the nineteenth century saw an increasing interest in German culture, despite the political and military conflicts

---

[9] On Spencer, see Giovanni Busino, 'Il nazionalismo italiano e il nazionalismo europeo', in anon. (ed.), *La cultura italiana tra '800 e '900 e le origini del nazionalismo* (Florence: Olschki, 1981), 47–68. We will return to Poe's translations in Chapter 4.
[10] Arturo Graf, *L'anglomania e l'influsso inglese in Italia nel secolo XVIII* (Turin: Loescher, 1911), 32.
[11] Graf, *L'anglomania e l'influsso inglese*, 160.
[12] On the Grimm Brothers' translations, see Lucia Borghese, 'Storia della ricezione delle fiabe grimmiane in Toscana e della loro prima traduzione italiana', in Pietro Clemente and Mariano Fresta (eds), *Interni e dintorni del Pinocchio: Folkoristi italiani del tempo del Collo*di (Pescia: Editori del Grifo, 1986), 49–58; and Bernhard Lauer, 'Les contes des Grimm dans les langues du monde : aller et retour', in Dominique Peyrache-Leborgne (ed.), Vies et métamorphoses des contes de Grimm. Traductions, réceptions, adaptations (Rennes: Presses universitaires de Rennes, 2017), pp. 17–23.

of only a few years before. The next section of this chapter will be devoted to this phenomenon, so that we can have a better sense of the overall context within which American culture found its place.

## 1.1 The New Germany

Like Italy, the German Reich was born on the nationalistic wave that swept through the European continent during the nineteenth century. However, it was not so much the similarity in the timing of the two countries' unification (1871 for Germany) that brought them together. By then the military might of Bismarck's Prussia had already provided the Piedmontese with another ally through which to continue paving their road to national unity at the expense of the Austro-Hungarian Empire. The third and final war of independence in 1866 saw Italy and Prussia fight Austria from different fronts, thanks to an alliance brokered by Napoleon III. This meant that, despite the dismal performance of Italy's national army (it was the first war fought by the newly created Kingdom of Italy), the Austrian defeat by the Prussian army resulted in the northern regions of Lombardy and Veneto eventually joining the rest of the kingdom.

By then, Rome and its surrounding territories had remained the most symbolic piece of Italy waiting to be annexed to the Italian nation state. The Pope had ruled over Rome and substantial parts of central Italy since the eighth century. What was left of the Papal State was under the protection of France, and so the Italian government had to wait until the humiliating defeat of Napoleon III's army in the Franco-Prussian war of 1870 before being able to make a move. Politically at least, the occupation of Rome, which quickly became the capital of the nation, opened up a period of closer ties between Italy and the German-speaking nations. Bismark's secular policies—his 'cultural battle' against German Catholicism—chimed with Italy's *questione romana*. Moreover, after the so-called Historic Left came into power, in 1875, Germanophilia was widespread in government circles. The friction with France resulting from Italy's first moves towards a colonial presence in North Africa added momentum to the shift. This finally peaked in the defensive military treaty—the Triple Alliance—signed by Austria, Germany, and Italy in 1882. In later years, to many nationalist leaders such as Alfredo Rocco, the future Minister of Justice in Mussolini's early governments, Germany's autocratic system became a model to be followed as against the weaknesses of French and British parliamentary democracy.[13]

---

[13] On the influence of German culture in the late nineteenth century, see Luisa Mangoni, *Civiltà della crisi: Cultura e politica in Italia tra otto e novecento* (Rome: Viella, 2013). For the later years, see Emilio Gentile, *Il mito dello stato nuovo dall'antigiolittismo al fascismo* (Rome and Bari: Laterza, 1982).

Politics, moreover, was not the only area in which the new Germany exercised its influence. Its economic strength—both industrial and financial—was much respected. The latter played a pivotal role when the Italian banking system spiralled into crisis in the early 1890s, ending with the scandal of the Banca Generale's management, which involved politicians at the highest level and provoked the fall of one of Giolitti's liberal governments, in December 1893. Order and financial stability returned thanks to the involvement of the German banking system, which created a healthier new institution in the form of the Banca Commerciale Italiana, based in Milan, and directed by the Prussian-born Otto Joel.[14]

Beyond the political and economic sphere, Germany's scholarly production was much revered, particularly in the fields of philosophy, archaeology, economics, jurisprudence, and the natural sciences. In the late nineteenth century, German culture was particularly associated with positivistic values: logical and scientific premises, clear methodology, and efficient practice. The most scientific of all literary disciplines, philology, saw Germany as its main exponent. Some young Italian intellectuals even went to Germany to complete their studies, as did Luigi Pirandello, who completed his degree in Romance Philology—of all subjects—at the University of Bonn, in 1891. Likewise, the future educationalist and politician Luigi Credaro went to Leipzig in 1889 to study philosophy and psychology. Scientific disciplines were also thought to be taught at the highest level in German universities. Italy's most prominent physiologist at the time, Angelo Mosso, had studied in Turin under Jacob Moleschott before continuing his studies in Leipzig. The association between his expertise and German culture was so close that, when he was invited by the Massachusetts State Normal School (now Worcester State University) in 1899 to address an audience of science teachers, he did so in German.[15]

Beyond scholarly production stood the great achievements of German culture in the literary and musical fields. And, if the former mainly came through the intermediary of France, the latter crossed the Alps more directly. From Beethoven to Mendelssohn, Wagner, and Brahms, the richness of Germany's nineteenth-century musical tradition was astounding and played a major role in changing the status of music as an art form. Wagner's concept of the *Gesamtkunstwerk* ('Total art work') was influential beyond the musical sphere

---

[14] On this, see chapter 3 of Peter Hertner, *Il capitale tedesco in Italia dall'Unità alla prima guerra mondiale* (Bologna: Il Mulino, 1984).

[15] It is indicative to note that, despite his Germanophile education, when Mosso founded a biology journal in 1882, in Turin, in order to give it an international profile, the choice was for the French language: *Archives italiennes de biologie*. Similarly, when Turinese enthusiasts created a journal of art photography, *Fotografia artistica*, in 1904, they decided that the articles should appear in both Italian and French. On this see Cottini, *The Art of Objects*, 63. On Mosso's lecture at Worcester's Normal School, see an article in Turin's *La Stampa*: anon., 'Angelo Mosso in America', *La Stampa*, 10 June 1899, p. 2. On Mosso as a central figure of Italian positivism, see Luisa Mangoni, *Una crisi fine secolo: La cultura italiana e la Francia tra otto e novecento* (Turin: Einaudi, 1985), 70, 202.

with its proto-modernist idea of multimedia artistic productions, which the Futurists were to embrace despite their dismissal of Wagner as a composer.[16]

However, despite all this, even Germany's most fervent admirers would not argue that the divide and reciprocal misunderstandings between the Germanic and Latin civilizations had been overcome. The tone in the early post-unification years was set, to some extent, by Pasquale Villari, then a prominent historian and political figure. In his book-length comparison between the Latin and the German spirit, entitled *L'Italia, la civiltà latina e la civiltà germanica* (1861), Villari identified the fundamental contribution of German culture to the development of modern Europe in a particular attitude: its pragmatism and its cult of individual entrepreneurship coupled with a solid concept of the state. At the same time, the book offered an equal celebration of the Latin spirit, which, having absorbed those Germanic qualities, would bring 'a new triumph of the Latin people'.[17] This nationalistic stance was understandably prevalent in the immediate years following Italy's unification. The already mentioned, paradigm-setting history of Italian literature by Francesco de Sanctis aimed at strengthening the self-identity of Italian intellectuals, adopting a teleology that presented the progress of both Italian letters and the country's unification as inevitable. Attached to this was a tendency to undervalue foreign influences, as in the following comment on Romantic literature: 'Romanticism, in its German and French exaggeration, did not take root in Italy and was only able to scratch its surface. The few attempts only had the effect of better accentuating the repugnance of the Italian genius.'[18] It was a genius that ultimately found its identity in the opposition between Latin and Germanic culture.

Moreover, in the minds of many Italians, Austria and Germany were combined as one single culture, and many nationalists found it impossible to forget the fact that, post-1870, the last Italian-speaking territories still under foreign domination—the provinces of Trento and Trieste in the north-east—were both part of the Austro-Hungarian Empire. In other words, the attraction of Germany—its cultural richness and the political alliance of those years—was counterbalanced by the notion of historical and cultural conflicts that could easily intensify and turn into Germanophobia.

Such a turn began in the early years of the twentieth century, when a generation of nationalist intellectuals began to drum up the need for Italy to flex its

---

[16] On the Italian craze for Wagner, particularly among intellectual circles in the city of Bologna, see Axel Körner, *Politics and Culture in Liberal Italy: From Unification to Fascism* (London: Routledge, 1999), 234–66. On the cultural influence of Germany, see Gustavo Corni, 'Il modello tedesco visto dall'Italia', in Agostino Giovagnoli and Giorgio Del Zanna (eds), *Il mondo visto dall'Italia* (Milan: Guerini, 2004), 34–54.
[17] Pasquale Villari, *L'Italia, la civiltà latina e la civiltà germanica* (Florence: Le Monnier, 1861), 72.
[18] De Sanctis, *Storia della letteratura Italiana*, 891.

muscles on the international stage and reclaim its *terre irredente* rather than feed on the leftovers from the colonial carving-up of Africa. From the Florentine circle led by Giovanni Papini and Giuseppe Prezzolini, and their periodicals—*Leonardo* (1903-7) and then *La Voce* (1908-16)—came the bellicose call for a new Italy, which should claim back its Italian-speaking territories under Austria. When it came to Trentino, the Alpine province next to South Tyrol, Prezzolini asked a young contributor to the journal, then working in Trento, to write a long report about the condition of Italians there. The young contributor was at that time a fairly unknown revolutionary socialist who worked as assistant editor at a local Italian daily, *Il Popolo*. Founder and director of the newspaper was the fervent Italophile socialist and future national hero Cesare Battisti, who was to be hanged as a traitor in 1916 after he had fled to Italy, joined the Italian army, and was eventually made prisoner by the Austrians. The assistant editor's name was Benito Mussolini, and his report was published by *La Voce* in 1911.[19]

At the loftier level of cultural policies, Giuseppe Prezzolini devoted an entire chapter of his *La coltura italiana* to lamenting the crisis of classical studies in Italian schools and universities, which, as he saw it, had come as a result of the adoption of the German philological approach. 'Science entered from the door, and poetry fled from the window.'[20] German culture and positivism began to be presented as unnatural to the Italian spirit. Not by chance, it is in these years that two philosophers who were due to play a major role in the following decades, Benedetto Croce and Giovanni Gentile, began to move Italian philosophy away from positivism into the territory of neo-idealism.[21]

Unsurprisingly, when the First World War broke out, Italian nationalists from all walks of life united in demanding Italy's intervention on the side of the Triple Entente. Standing out among a number of small books published in the months before Italy's entry into the war—the near equivalent of today's instant books—is *L'Italia e la civiltà tedesca* by Ugo Ojetti, one of Italy's most respected literary and art critics at the time. From the Romantic to the positivist age, German culture is presented by Ojetti as a toxic presence in Europe, bringing him to the conclusion that the German civilization is 'fatally anti-Latin and incompatible with our civilization'.[22]

The Italian government eventually joined in. Despite the political and military ties with the German-speaking nations, Prime Minister Antonio Salandra and the

---

[19] On Mussolini's writings for *La Voce*, see Emilio Gentile, 'A Revolution for the Third Italy', in Spencer M. Di Scala and Emilio Gentile (eds), *Mussolini 1883-1915: Triumph and Transformation of a Revolutionary Socialist* (New York: Palgrave Macmillan, 2016), 257-95.
[20] Giuseppe Prezzolini, *La coltura italiana* (Florence: Lumachi, 1906; Florence: La Voce, 1923), 30.
[21] On the coexistence of neo-idealist and nationalistic trends within the critique of positivism at the turn of the century, in both France and Italy, see Mangoni, *Una crisi fine secolo*, 216-28.
[22] Ugo Ojetti, *L'Italia e la civiltà tedesca* (Milan: Rava, 1915), 30.

anglophile foreign minister Sidney Sonnino secretly negotiated a more generous offer from the Triple Entente and brought Italy into the war in May 1915. War propaganda did the rest in bringing Germanophobia to the masses.

Finally, on a different note, but relevant for the scope of this book, it is important to mention that, like Italy, Germany was beginning to fall under the spell of America's influence by the early twentieth century. Particular attention is paid to this by Victoria De Grazia in her *Irresistible Empire*, but, from a strictly Italian viewpoint, the issue was raised by the Germanophile novelist and critic Giuseppe Antonio Borgese, who spent two years in Berlin, and in 1909 published his impressions in the hefty volume *La nuova Germania*. When it came to describing its capital, Borgese presented it as a most 'American' city:

> With a look of indulgent disdain, flying past Paris, the decadent metropolis, past a sooty and foggy London, past the great provincial Vienna, he [the Berliner] stops with proud emulation over Chicago and New York. The Berliner is already the most American man that Europe can give birth to, and his city looks like him as the footprint resembles the foot which pressed it into shape. [...] whoever wants to see America, and a bigger America, must come to Berlin [...][23]

A similar, later view of Berlin as the ultimate 'American' city was held by the German author and film theorist Siegfried Kracauer. At the start of the new century, Berlin embraced modernity and was competing with London and Paris for the crown of Europe's most forward-looking city. It was a move that Kracauer, like Borgese, saw as intoxicated with a sense of admiration for America as a model of entrepreneurial spirit, cutting-edge technology, consumerism, and a *joie de vivre* extended to the masses, all coming together in a new explosive combination. In Germany, wrote Kracauer about a circus show, 'the animal world, too, has fallen for jazz'.[24] Other European capitals (Paris in particular) had a more nuanced relationship with American culture, absorbing rather than reflecting it. Indeed, as Miriam Bratu Hansen concludes, in her study of Kracaurer's cultural horizon: 'Like Benjamin, Kracauer found a counter-image to contemporary Berlin in the city of Paris.'[25]

---

[23] Giuseppe Antonio Borgese, *La nuova Germania* (Milan: Fratelli Bocca, 1909), 277. For De Grazia's discussion of American influence in Weimar Germany, see in particular *Irresistible Empire*, 15–16, 22–5, 38–49, 164–70, 239–40.

[24] Miriam Bratu Hansen, 'America, Paris, the Alps: Kracauer (and Benjamin) on Cinema and Modernity', in Leo Charney and Vanessa Schwartz (eds), *Cinema and the Invention of Modern Life* (Berkeley and Los Angeles: University of California Press, 1995), 362–402 (372). The quotation, translated by Bratu Hansen, comes from an article entitled 'Zirkus Hagenbeck', *FZ* 19 June 1926.

[25] Bratu Hansen, 'America, Paris, the Alps', 385.

## 1.2 The French Model

Metaphorically, if Austria and Germany were next-door neighbours whom Italians respected but never understood or fully trusted, France was a rich relative from a big city whose appearance produced a combination of awe, envy, and concealed annoyance. Culturally, as we have already started to see, France played a central role. In iconic terms, the most conspicuous attempt to reaffirm Paris as the cultural capital of Europe in the second half of the nineteenth century was the construction of the Eiffel Tower, the gate and giant beacon of the Universal Exhibition of 1889. While glorifying the centennial of the French Revolution, the Eiffel Tower proved even more successful as a symbol of the cutting-edge modernity of contemporary Parisian culture. Beyond its much-debated engineering and architectural majesty, the tower struck a chord with its curved lines, which turned it into a symbol of the new artistic taste of the *fin de siècle*. Its structure, like all world fair constructions, had been planned to be easily dismantled, and the Tour Eiffel was supposed to be taken down after twenty years. Instead, it became integral to the identity of Paris as a metropolis that was preparing to face the new century with a renewed sense of its *grandeur*.

Echoes of the fascination of Parisian culture travelled to the other side of the Atlantic and could be heard even beyond the urban centres of the east coast. When Adolfo Rossi, an Italian journalist who spent almost five years in the USA,

**Fig. 1.1.** Print advertising the 1889 Exposition Universelle stretching from the Seine along the Champ de Mars. (courtesy of Universitats Darmstadts)

between 1887 and 1892, wrote about the life of the 'cowboys' in the vast plains of the south-west, he reported a new phenomenon, the arrival of eccentric young men of a cultured kind, attracted by the outdoor lifestyle. Some of them, Rossi wrote, were fluent in French, rode for miles in order to collect their issue of the *Vie parisienne* and dreamt of getting drunk 'in the arms of a forty-year-old Jennie or a Minnie who will make him believe she sang in Paris'.[26]

As for Italy's relationship with the Parisian model, beyond questions of lifestyle—as there is little doubt that the *goût parisien* dictated fashion throughout Europe—its influence was enormous in all the arts, literary and otherwise. No other foreign city could attract Italian intellectuals more than Paris. Some moved there for good, as the greatest Italian playwright of his generation, Carlo Goldoni, had done a few decades before, or two of the country's greatest opera composers of the early nineteenth century, Gioachino Rossini and Vincenzo Bellini, both buried at Paris's Père-Lachaise cemetery. The third one, Gaetano Donizetti, gravitated around Paris much more than he did around Vienna, despite his Austrian citizenship. Finally, the dominant Italian literary figure of his generation, Alessandro Manzoni, joined his mother in Paris, in the summer of 1805, and took up semi-permanent residence for five years. After that, during his monastic years in his family home in Milan, Manzoni's main contact with the intellectual world, beyond the small circle of Milanese friends, was through his correspondence with Claude Fauriel, an influential figure in the Romantic movement, close friend of both Manzoni and Madame de Staël. Fauriel would sometimes visit the Manzonis, and a second Parisian period followed in 1819–20. Throughout all this toing and froing, French remained a language much in use by Manzoni and his family, and French translations remained a major intermediary in his explorations of German and English literature, starting with Pierre Le Tourneur's French version of Shakespeare's plays.

Before and in addition to any long stays or visits by the Italian intelligentsia to the French capital, Parisian periodicals provided them with the necessary flow of news and cultural stimuli. This had already been the case in the late eighteenth century, given that, in conservative circles of the post-revolutionary years, journals were created with the specific aim of providing Italian readers with alternative, non-French viewpoints. One of them was the *Giornale della letteratura straniera*, founded by a group of reactionary intellectuals in the Duchy of Mantua, in 1793 (then under Austrian rule), in order 'to stop, as much as possible, the dissemination and reading among us of journals from France'.[27] In this case the cause of such defensive action was mainly political, but in others it was purely cultural, as when Sidney Sonnino—the most cosmopolitan Italian politician at the time (whose mother was English)—founded the *Rassegna settimanale di politica, scienze, lettere ed arti* (1878–82), together with Leopoldo Franchetti.

---

[26] Adolfo Rossi, *Il paese dei dollari* (Milan: Tipografia degli Operai, 1892), 62–3.
[27] [Anon.], 'Introduzione', *Giornale della letteratura straniera*, 1 (1793), pp. i–iv (p. iii).

Their intention was to create a periodical that provided, in addition to a forum on Italian matters, first-hand news about cultural and political debates in different parts of Europe. Plainly based on the London *Saturday Review of Politics, Literature, Science and Art* (1855–1938), the *Rassegna* contained a section with a selection of articles from British, French, and German periodicals in the original language.[28]

Those were exceptions, however, which indirectly confirmed the strength of Italy's connections with the French press and publishing industry. As the literary historian Luisa Mangoni has shown in detail, French journals such as the *Revue des deux mondes* were a constant source of comment and debate, echoed in Italian periodicals such as Florence's prestigious *Nuova antologia di lettere, scienze ed arti*, founded in 1866. Indeed, when introducing her monograph on Italian culture in the late nineteenth century, Mangoni admitted an unexpected turn in her studies. The further she explored the primary bibliography related to those years, the more she realized how important French culture had been as a source of knowledge about the outside world:

> This research, which was born as a study on the shift in Italy from the nineteenth century to the twentieth, was subjected to radical modification caused by the object of study. For example, the reference to French culture acquired a centrality that I had not entirely expected. The French model, often criticized, implicitly or explicitly, appeared constantly, even in authors who were traditionally or academically linked to Germany. Implicit comments were particularly significant: within disparate contexts, the same sentences and references appeared in almost identical form, as if drawn from the same source; moreover, it seemed obvious that such references would be immediately recognized by the average, cultured reader at the time.[29]

In literature, as Sassoon concisely put it, 'Italy's literary scene remained essentially imitative and dependent on France'.[30]

During the second half of the nineteenth century, French Naturalism provided the most influential literary expression of the positivistic turn in Western culture. The manifesto-like prefaces of the novels by the Goncourt Brothers, Émile Zola, and others became guidelines that in Italy were absorbed and turned into the foundations of the *verismo* school led by Giovanni Verga and Luigi Capuana. Equally, French symbolist poetry and the 'decadent' phase of the French letters as epitomized by Joris-Karl Huysman's novel *À rebours* (1884) had a clear influence

---

[28] On the *Rassegna settimanale*, see Chiara Beria, 'La "Rassegna Settimanale" e la cultura europea', in Romano Luperini (ed.), *Il verismo italiano fra naturalismo francese e cultura europea* (Lecce: Manni, 2007), 119–49.
[29] Mangoni, *Una crisi fine secolo*, p. viii.
[30] Sassoon, *The Culture of the Europeans*, 166.

on contemporary Italian authors such as Italy's turn-of-the-century writer *par excellence*, Gabriele D'Annunzio. Pursued by his creditors, D'Annunzio was to move to France in the spring of 1910, where he lived for about four years, contributing to Paris's cosmopolitan intellectual life. A memorable case was his four-thousand-lines-long French play *Le Martyre de Saint Sebastien* (1911). This work, despite the collaboration by the Russian ballet designer Léon Bakst, music by Claude Debussy, and a striking performance by the legendary Ida Rubinstein in the transvestite part of the saint, was coldly received. By 1911, D'Annunzio's late-Romantic, erudite sensuality was considered *passé* by the novelty-seeking Parisian audience.[31]

Italian literati also had their Parisian outpost in the figure of Ricciotto Canudo, the poet, cinema theorist, and literary critic who had settled there in 1902 and two years later had started to contribute a column called 'Lettres italiennes' to the prestigious *Mercure de France*. Through his familiarity with the avant-garde circles frequented by literati, artists, and musicians, Canudo provided a point of contact from which D'Annunzio too was to benefit. More generally, as suggested by Amotz Giladi, still in the early twentieth century, 'in Italy, the prestige of Paris is such that being successful there opens doors, to writers, within their own country'. Likewise, being mentioned in or, even better, contributing to French literary journals, such as the *Mercure* or *La Nouvelle Revue Française*, was considered the pinnacle of an Italian author's career. It happened to D'Annunzio, to Marinetti, to Pirandello, and to Giovanni Papini, who, in 1913, took over the column on Italian literature from Canudo.[32]

In the art world, a more indirect but equally paradigm-shifting impact was produced by French impressionism, and, more importantly, Paris became a magnet for aspiring artists. A 'Paris period' was a recurrent feature in the biographies

---

[31] Marcel Proust was impressed by D'Annunzio's mastery of the French verse, but he too dismissed the play with the following words: 'I found the play quite boring, apart from a few moments', cruelly adding, 'the publicity and orchestra quite huge for those few farts'. On D'Annunzio's work and his years in France, see John Woodhouse, *Gabriele D'Annunzio: Defiant Archangel* (Oxford: Oxford University Press, 1998), 250–82; and Andrea Mirabile, *Multimedia Archeologies: Gabriele D'Annunzio, Belle Époque Paris, and the Total Artwork* (Amsterdam: Rodopi, 2014). Proust's quotation comes from a letter to Reynaldo Hahn, of 23 May 1911, quoted by Rubens Tedeschi in his essay 'Mal di melodramma', in Luca Ronconi (ed.), *D'Annunzio. La scena del vate* (Milan: Electa, 1988), 19–26 (25). On the influence of French naturalism on Italian *verismo*, see, e.g., Judith Davies, *The Realism of Luigi Capuana: A Study in the Evolution of Late Nineteenth-Century Narrative in Italy* (London: Modern Humanities Research Association, 1979); and Romano Luperini (ed.), *Il verismo italiano fra naturalismo francese e cultura europea* (Lecce: Manni, 2007).

[32] On Italian writers and French culture, see François Livi, 'Le "Saut vital": Le Monde littéraire italien à Paris (1900–1914)', in André Kaspi and Antoine Marès (eds), *Le Paris des étrangers: Depuis un siècle* (Paris: Imprimerie nationale, 1989), 313–27; and Amotz Giladi, 'Les Écrivains florentins d'avant-garde et la France: Échanges, rivalités et conflits, 1900–1920', *Australian Journal of French Studies*, 54/2–3 (2017), 218–34. See also Shirley Vinall, 'In the Footsteps of D'Annunzio: *Anthologie-Revue de France et d'Italie* and the Promotion of Italian Culture in France', *The Italianist*, 26 (2006), 274–310. The *Anthologie-Revue* was a journal founded in Milan in 1897 but written in French, in order to promote Italian literature abroad. The then young Filippo Tommaso Marinetti was one of its sub-editors.

of most Italian artists at the time, and many settled there for good: from Giovanni Baldini, the most famous Italian portrait painter of his generation, who moved there in 1872, followed two years later by Federico Zandomeneghi, to others who made Paris their home, such as the renowned sculptor Medardo Rosso, Italy's greatest publicity artist of his generation Leonetto Cappiello, and Amedeo Modigliani, whose move in 1906 metamorphosed him into a world-famous artist. Italy's most prominent avant-garde movement, Futurism, was also born in Paris. Its founder, Filippo Tommaso Marinetti, had studied there, and from the pages of *Le Figaro* launched the movement's manifesto, on 20 February 1909 (just as Jean Moréas had done with the publication of his Symbolist manifesto in 1886).

As late as 1914, Futurism's most talented artist, Umberto Boccioni (who was tragically to die as a volunteer in the First World War), would write: 'There are no trends today, in Europe and in the world, in painting and in sculpture, genuinely preoccupied with what forms the plastic dimension, which are not derived from French impressionism: from Manet to Cézanne.'[33]

More broadly, scholars see a clear influence of French culture on the general intellectual debate at the turn of the century, from which Italian modernism was to emerge. A leading scholar on modern Italy's cultural history, Walter L. Adamson, writes of the city of Florence: 'All the key figures in the Italian modernist avant-gardes, including Marinetti, Papini, Soffici, and Prezzolini, had crucial formative experiences in Paris, imbibing its art and philosophy as well as the culture of its soirées and revues.' This was all part of the 'Myth of Paris', as he calls it.[34]

Ardengo Soffici's stay in the French capital was to last seven years, during which time he became part of the cosmopolitan circles of the artistic and literary avant-garde. And, when France entered the First World War, in August 1914, Soffici and Papini co-authored a long editorial published on the front page of their periodical, *Lacerba*, entitled 'Ciò che dobbiamo alla Francia' ('What we owe to France'). The nationalistic passion that dominated the journal was reflected in the fact that the first two paragraphs of the article were dedicated to a list of Italians who had played key parts in French history—from Cardinal Mazarin to Émile Zola, 'the son of a citizen from the Veneto'. After that, however, Papini and Soffici dwelled on the huge cultural debt of post-1870 Italy towards their French

---

[33] Umberto Boccioni, 'Perché non siamo impressionisti', in Boccioni, *Pittura scultura futuriste (dinamismo plastico)* (Milan: Edizioni futuriste di 'Poesia', 1914), 81–99 (81).
[34] Walter L. Adamson, 'Modernism in Florence: The Politics of Avant-Garde Culture in the Early Twentieth Century', in Luca Somigli and Mario Moroni (eds), *Italian Modernism: Italian Culture between Decadentism and Avant-Garde* (Toronto: University of Toronto Press, 2004), 221–42 (225–6). The expression 'Myth of Paris' comes from his earlier monograph *Avant-Garde Florence: From Modernism to Fascism* (Cambridge, MA: Harvard University Press, 1993); see, in particular, pp. 52–63. On the cultural influence of nineteenth-century Paris, see Christopher Prendergast, *Paris and the Nineteenth Century* (Oxford: Blackwell, 1992).

cousins and boasted that solely on this basis, Italians should waste no time in entering the war on their side.[35]

Even in the field of opera, which the Italian tradition had dominated since its birth, as reflected in the pre-eminence of Italian as the language of librettos, by the nineteenth century the French capital was perceived as the genre's most prestigious venue. As Sassoon put it:

> The advent of Rossini put an end to the great debate of the mid-eighteenth century between the champions of French music and those of Italian opera. The Italians had won. However, the nineteenth-century capital of opera was Paris, whose pull was so remarkable that no Italian city, not even Naples with its San Carlo or Milan with La Scala, could rival it. The major Italian composers, from Rossini and Verdi, once they had achieved fame in Italy sought the ultimate consecration: a Parisian triumph. Paris functioned as a kind of global legitimation of one's success.[36]

If, in the world of opera, the Italian tradition was the most prestigious, when it came to 'lower' forms of musical entertainment—for example, the so-called *caffè concerto* or *café chantant*—French culture was once again leading Europe. The *café chantant* became popular in Paris during the nineteenth century, and it consisted of an evening entertainment—usually mixed with dance and other variety shows—based around the performance of songs, the most famous of which could be found in print for the pleasure of *habitués*. It reached its climax with venues such as the Folies Bergère, which opened in 1869, and the Théatre-Concert du Moulin Rouge (1889), and it helped mark Paris as the embodiment of the *Belle époque* and the European capital of light entertainment of the more sensual kind.[37]

In Italy, the *café chantant* spread to most regional capitals within the space of a few years, sometimes in the form of barely tolerated venues, sometimes fully supported by the local elite as an example of the emancipation of their lifestyle. The latter was the case in Naples, where the Salone Margherita was opened in 1890 as part of the monumental Galleria Umberto I in the heart of the city, seating about five hundred people. Its opening night was attended by the city's *crème de la crème*, and all publicity had been written in French for the occasion, as were the artists' contracts, the programme, and the menu. The catering staff, too, were asked to speak only in French.[38]

---

[35] Giovanni Papini and Ardengo Soffici, 'Ciò che dobbiamo alla Francia', *Lacerba*, 2/17 (September 1914), 1–2.

[36] Sassoon, *The Culture of the Europeans*, 269.

[37] On Paris as 'the pleasure capital of Europe', see Rosemary Wakeman, *A Modern History of European Cities: 1815 to the Present* (London: Bloomsbury Academic, 2020).

[38] On Naples's Salone Margherita, see Vittorio Paliotti, *Il salone Margherita e la belle époque* (Rome: Benincasa, 1975); and Paolo Sommaiolo, *Il café-chantant: Artisti e ribalte nella Napoli Belle Époque* (Naples: Tempo Lungo, 1998), 67–101.

A privileged lens through which to study the *café chantant* as it spread throughout Italy at the turn of the century is provided by an illustrated weekly created in 1897, printed in Naples, and later attached to the association of variety artists, founded in 1909. Its name was *Il Café chantant*, and the title of its hefty annual guide made its French model even more explicit: *Il Café chantant: Guida del varieté italiano*. The journal and its guide aimed to provide both a useful guide to those in the variety business, with detailed information about the most important venues in the Italian circuit, and a publicity forum in which Italian and foreign artists could advertise their talents.[39]

The size of some venues helps us understand the success of these variety shows during this period. In Rome, two theatres had a capacity of around a thousand customers—the Salone Margherita (naming venues and products after the king and queen of Italy was a popular and officially tolerated initiative at the time), opened in 1889; and the Olympia, opened in 1896, which two years later hosted the Roman première of the Lumière brothers' cinematography. Even bigger was the Jovinelli, opened in 1909, which could host up to two thousand people.[40] Another striking feature emerging from the journal's pages is the regular use of French *noms de plume* adopted by Italian female singers and dancers: from Gina De Chamery, to Gina Lillière, Nina De Charny, Antonietta Dubry, Lina De Ferny, and many others. Equally, in the small adverts that peppered *Il Café chantant*, the French expressions *divette* and *étoile* were commonly used for female artists. The dominance of the French language is also suggested by a short story that accompanies the 1910 annual guide, written by Antonio Morosi and entitled 'La cena di Natale'. Set at a Christmas dinner organized by the managers of a variety theatre for their artists, the short story pokes gentle fun at the social aspirations of this small community, their dialogues predominantly in French.[41]

Mention of the opening of Naples's Galleria Umberto I, in 1890, is a reminder of another field in which Paris proved a cultural beacon to the rest of Europe: urban architecture. The Galleria was a giant arcade, a clear attempt to bring the Parisian *belle époque* to Naples. By the second half of the nineteenth century, the fashion of the construction of monumental arcades was in full swing all over Europe. Their antecedents were the covered passages of Paris, which became a characteristic feature of the city, with more than a hundred scattered around the city.

---

[39] On the history of the *café chantant* in Italy and on the periodical *Il Café chantant*, see Doriana Legge, 'Il café chantant: Quella sarabanda attorno al magro albero della cuccagna, 1900–1928', *Teatro e storia*, 38 (2017), 179–208.

[40] On the architectural evolution of Rome's theatrical venues, see Maria Grazia Turco (ed.), *Dal teatro all'italiana alle sale cinematografiche: Questioni di storia e prospettive di valorizzazione* (Rome: Quasar, 2017).

[41] Antonio Morosi, 'La cena di Natale', *Il café chantant: Guida del varieté italiano*, 1 (1910), 11–12. Morosi had previously published a book devoted entirely to variety shows: *Il teatro di varietà in Italia* (Florence: Calvetti, 1901).

40   AMERICA IN ITALIAN CULTURE

**Fig. 1.2.** Front page of the 1910 annual guide of *Il café chantant*. (courtesy of Biblioteca Luigi Chiarini, CSC, Rome)

One of the earliest and most iconic of these is the Passage des Panoramas, in Montmartre, which opened in 1800 and boasted a metal and glass roof and, by 1817, gas lighting. Its name came from two rotundas (no longer existing) that displayed another electric novelty of urban entertainment: 360-degree, back-lit painted cloth panels, which gave the impression of a quasi-three-dimensional view of the city's landscapes painted on them. Walter Benjamin considered these spacious, covered precincts such a defining feature of Parisian scenery that he devoted much of his later years to a study of them, resulting in his unfinished and posthumously published *Passagen-Werk* (*Arcades Project*). A monumental proto-arcade was already in Paris by the mid-1780s, in the form of Louis Philippe II's restructuring of the Palais-Royal. The colonnades around the palace garden became the first shopping arcade, complemented on one side by the Galeries de Bois, whose wooden structure provided a first, safe shopping haven—it hosted more than a hundred *boutiques*—for Paris's aristocracy and aspiring bourgeoisie.

As for Italy, although one could lay claim to a historical connection with the *portici* of Italian medieval towns, the modern arcade came late. The first, large *galerie* was built in Milan soon after the country's unification. The spectacular

**Fig. 1.3.** Milan's Galleria Vittorio Emanuele II (1877) in a postcard dated 1890. (author's personal collection)

Galleria Vittorio Emanuele II, opened in 1877, connected the city's cathedral to its opera house, La Scala, and quickly became known as 'Milan's salon'.[42]

Gramsci's comment on the Francophile provincialism of nineteenth-century Italian culture, as we saw in the Introduction, bordered on the unkind, but it was

---

[42] On the history of arcades—which, symbolically, American architects were later to develop into shopping malls in the twentieth century—see Johann Friedrich Geist, *Arcades: The History of a Building Type* (Cambridge, MA: MIT Press, 1985); on Milan, see pp. 366–402. See also Walter Benjamin, *The Arcades Project* (1982; Cambridge, MA: Belknap Press, 1999).

an intuition that facts tend to corroborate. Paris was the place—and French was the language—through which, not just French culture, but also other foreign cultures and fashions were absorbed by Italian intellectuals. The *Tout-Paris* of literary, artistic, and musical circles were the first port of call for Italians who aspired to be *à la page* regarding the most recent developments in the arts. It was not just a question of taste and fashion: it was also dictated by the dependence of Italy's culture industry on French resources.[43]

A further example is provided by the field of journalism. With the exponential growth in the number of newspapers throughout nineteenth-century Europe and their development from polemical and opinion-making vehicles into sources of up-to-date, factual information about world events (facilitated by the arrival of the telegraph), the role of press agencies became vital. Italy's Agenzia Stefani, founded in Turin in 1853, established itself as the sole press agency in the newly formed Kingdom of Italy thanks to the patronage of one of its founders, the statesman Camillo Benso di Cavour. However, the Agenzia Stefani had by then developed a close relationship with Havas, its vastly more powerful French counterpart, as detailed in their agreement of June 1867. Havas imposed its control over Stefani, acting as a gatekeeper for the transmission both of world news going to Stefani and of Italian news from Stefani to other, non-French press agencies. This was a consequence of the earlier agreement of 1859 between the three dominant press agencies in Europe: the French Havas, the British Reuters, and the German Wolff. Havas's gatekeeping of news from and into Italy was questioned only when Italy's foreign policy became increasingly philo-German, particularly following the Franco-Italian tensions over Tunisia in 1881, culminating in the Triple Alliance of 1882. However, strengthened by the massive debt that the Stefani family—which still controlled the agency—had accumulated towards Havas, the latter was able to maintain its grip on the Italian agency even during those years.

It is with the premiership of Francesco Crispi, in 1887, that the Italian government begins its attempts to free Italy's main press agency from its French counterpart. This was only partially achieved, since, although Stefani was cleared of its financial relationship with Havas, in practice the latter continued to remain the source of information for most world news that Stefani distributed. As for the relationship with the press agencies of Germany and the Austro-Hungarian Empire, it is indicative that as late as April 1914, when responding to complaints by the German agency Wolff about Stefani's reluctance to make use of the newly installed telephonic service from Berlin, Stefani's director replied that he had only five stenographers in his offices in Rome and Turin, and they all worked in French. He then made a comment about the difficulty of finding German-speaking

---

[43] Gramsci too, after all, frequently benefited from the French publishing industry. When he was working on his notes on Americanism and Fordism, for example, he relied on three books by Henry Ford, two of which he owned in their French translation. On this see Bruno Settis, 'Rethinking Fordism', in Francesca Antonini et al. (eds), *Revisiting Gramsci's* Notebooks (Leiden: Brill, 2020), 376–87.

stenographers, an obstacle he had already encountered when trying to find one for an Austrian agency. In any case, the political events of that year were to bring any pro-German developments to a sudden halt. All contacts with the German and Austrian agencies stopped on 29 September 1914. As for the new allies, the director of the Agenzia Stefani complained to the Italian Foreign Office during the same month that most of Reuters telegraph dispatches from London were still travelling first through the Paris offices of Havas.[44]

In the following chapter, a few pages will be devoted to the coverage of America by the Italian press and Italian travel writers. Although the first resident correspondent in New York was established by the *Corriere della Sera* as late as 1909, Italian journalists were sent to the USA from time to time, to report on dramatic events such as the New Orleans lynching of eleven Italians in 1891 and the American–Hispanic war of 1898. Travel books on the USA also began to be published. Beyond that, however, minor news and *faits divers* concerning the USA arrived in Italy either through the filter of Havas or picked up from newspapers and periodicals in other languages. The French press, as we have seen with the early case of *Lo Spettatore italiano*, was again and again the main source.

The gatekeeping role played by Havas, together with mention of Stefani's difficulty in finding German-speaking stenographers, brings up the question of the knowledge of foreign languages in late-nineteenth- and early twentieth-century Italy. This takes us to a field often left to the margins of Italy's cultural history: the impact of the teaching of modern languages in the school system of post-unification Italy.

In line with a tradition shared by Europe's ruling classes, the study of foreign languages up until the end of the nineteenth century—in both secondary schools and universities—was focused chiefly on learning Latin and Ancient Greek. Modern languages were to be learnt elsewhere, in the family through the employment of foreign private tutors and governesses, and thanks to the occasional long stay abroad. The model of secondary school that dominated Italy's school system was the Ginnasio–Liceo, a combination of the Prussian model of the Gymnasium, which had led school reform in Europe since the late eighteenth century, and the French Licée, created in the Napoleonic years as a secular state school that supplanted the old system of colleges and seminaries run by religious orders. In Piedmont, after various attempts, the Ginnasio–Liceo system—five years of Ginnasio followed by three years of Liceo—was eventually enshrined in law by the Legge Casati of 1859, before being adopted by the newly unified Kingdom of

---

[44] On the history of Agenzia Stefani, see Sergio Lepri, Francesco Arbitrio, and Giuseppe Cultrera, *L'agenzia Stefani da Cavour a Mussolini: Informazione e potere in un secolo di storia italiana* (Florence: Le Monnier, 2001). Havas's control of 50% of the Agenzia Stefani's profits ceased only in 1900, after Teodoro Mayer—an influential banker and politician—convinced the Stefani family to allow him to enter in co-ownership. Mayer was later influential in allowing Manlio Morgagni, a close collaborator of Mussolini, to take control of the entire company in 1924. It is only in the post-First World War years that the Agenzia Stefani created its own international network of correspondents in open competition with Havas and Reuters.

Italy. Religious schools continued to exercise a central role in most parts of Italy, but they had to adapt to the format of the Ginnasio–Liceo, which was the only course of study allowing access to university degrees in the humanities and law. It was, therefore, the educational pillar for the formation of the country's politicians, judiciary, and intellectuals.

As for modern foreign languages, the first programmes that followed the Casati law did not include any. This does not mean that French was not taught at all, but it was an optional subject and taken up only if the parents who requested it were prepared to pay. It appeared as a compulsory subject in all *Licei* only as late as in 1892. Other than French, the less-prestigious technical schools, which provided access to science degree courses, were invited to offer German or English. These languages were understood as useful only for the formation of future scientists and engineers.[45]

Once introduced, the teaching of French in the Ginnasio–Liceo system was limited to the final three years of the Ginnasio, and it was taught to a minimal level: two hours a week, compared to twice as many in Latin and a similar number of hours in ancient Greek, which continued to be studied in the Liceo years. Educated Italians were, therefore, steeped in classical literature and, when forced to use a modern language, would rely on French. This does not mean that a small number of Italian intellectuals, diplomats, and businessmen did not learn other modern languages. They were, however, a tiny minority, fully overshadowed by the dominance of French teaching in schools and by the fact that French remained the language of culture and diplomacy throughout the nineteenth century. The latter is in itself a remarkable fact at a global level: considering that the nineteenth century saw the British Empire as the economic and military superpower across the continents, it is extraordinary that French culture and the language should have managed to retain international predominance.[46]

It was only in 1911 that a forward-looking, liberal Minister of Education, Luigi Credaro, followed the recommendations of a Royal Commission and proposed a challenge to the dominance of the Liceo in the education of Italy's elites. His plan foresaw the introduction of a tripartite system, which, after the Ginnasio, offered a Liceo Classico flanked by a Liceo Scientifico and a Liceo Moderno. The latter

---

[45] On the history of language teaching in Italy, see Paolo Balboni, *Storia dell'educazione linguistica in Italia: Dalla Legge Casati alla Riforma Gelmini* (Turin: UTET, 2009). For a detailed overview of Italian secondary schools in the 1870s, see Luisa Montevecchi and Marino Raicich (eds), *L'inchiesta Scialoja sulla istruzione secondaria maschile e femminile (1872–1875)* (Rome: Ministero per i beni culturali e ambientali, 1995); and Gaetano Bonetta and Gigliola Fioravanti (eds), *L'istruzione classica (1860–1910)* (Rome: Ministero per i beni culturali e ambientali, 1995).

[46] The focus here is on secondary schools, since, as one can imagine, for the newly unified Italian nation, the main priority at the level of compulsory education (i.e. primary schools) was to introduce pupils to the Italian language, which, for the vast majority of them, was a foreign romance language, given their own almost exclusive use of dialect outside the classroom. On France's capacity to outplay the British Empire in matters of 'soft power', see Todd, *The Velvet Empire*, 7–9, 123–74.

offered two modern languages in the shape of French with either English or German, to the detriment of Ancient Greek. Credaro, a philosopher converted to Herbart's pedagogical theories, had spent a year in Germany and was a vocal promoter of the study of modern languages. The Liceo Moderno model, however, proved unpopular among local administrations. It was introduced only in a few provinces of the Kingdom and was eventually abolished in 1923 as part of the school reform by Fascism's first Minister of Education, the philosopher Giovanni Gentile.[47]

In the cultural sphere, French remained the dominant language. In matters of lifestyle, entertainment, and what is generally referred to as 'high culture', the French language was not just necessary: it was a distinguishing trait of membership of the educated upper classes of Europe. One has only to sample a few novels set in the nineteenth century. The presence of a French tutor was a common feature of an educated household, and the peppering of urbane conversation with French expressions was equally a familiar trait. Without the extremes of Tolstoy's *War and Peace* (1868–9), famously opening with a dialogue between two Russian aristocrats taking place entirely in French, one can find examples of the pervasiveness of French culture among the Italian elite in just about all late-nineteenth-century Italian novels set among the Italian educated classes. In *Giacomo l'idealista* (1897), by the Milanese Emilio de Marchi, the Lombard gentry pepper their conversation with Latin and French expressions. When Count Lorenzo Magnenzio, whose family is at the centre of the narrative, bursts into a tirade against the influence of foreign culture, France is his sole target:

> The count, who cultivated an old grudge against France as a result of his readings about the time of the Terror, could not forgive the damaging influence that French books continue to exert on the style of our journalists and authors [...]
> —Frenchified language, frenchified bonnets, frenchified Madonnas and Sacred Hearts: if this frenchified obsession continues at this rate, we'll wake up one fine morning with a bomb under our bed.[48]

When it comes to the aristocracy of the Roman capital, Gabriele D'Annunzio's fiction provides a peculiar but revealing viewpoint. In his first 'decadent' novel, *Il piacere* (1889)—much inspired by Huysman's *À rebours*—the narrative is enriched by learned references to English literature and German classical music, suggestive of the nobility's cosmopolitan high culture. In line with the novel's political undercurrent—an elitist denunciation of the vulgarity of democracy—the Roman

---

[47] On Credaro's educational policies, see Carlo Graziani, 'Luigi Credaro e la politica scolastica nell'età giolittiana', *Problemi della pedagogia*, 1–2 (1961), 76–106, 276–90; and Luigi Ambrosoli, 'Luigi Credaro e la scuola italiana nell'età giolittiana', *Scuola e città*, 5 (1980), 199–206.

[48] Emilio De Marchi, *Giacomo l'idealista* (Milan: Hoepli, 1897), 35.

nobles are presented as superior individuals, even with respect to the rest of Italy's educated elite. However, despite those references to other European cultures, it is once again the French language that makes its appearance in their dialogues.

As for southern Italy, if *verismo* authors concentrated on the life of the lower classes, and Verga's project to move up the social ladder through a series of novels was interrupted before it reached the upper steps, a notable exception is Federico De Roberto's work, in particular his novel *I viceré* (1894). Its plot traces the life of a noble Sicilian family during the troubled years of the *Risorgimento*. De Roberto's linguistic flattening of his prose style and dialogues to a Tuscan Italian, free from dialect and foreign languages, does not allow for any direct presence of the French language, but whenever the narrative dwells on the trips abroad of a family member, their knowledge of French and the obsessive mention of Paris are sufficient evidence. Hence, it should not be surprising to note that, as late as 1914, Naples was the place of publication of *La Jeune Fille*, a magazine for the refinement of young women that was written entirely in French. A later, convincing reconstruction of nineteenth-century southern Italian aristocratic life is provided by Giuseppe Tomasi di Lampedusa's masterpiece *Il gattopardo*, published posthumously in 1958. Once again, the fascination with French culture is ubiquitous. Already in the first chapter we are given a sense of the ease with which the protagonist—Principe Salina—lingers on memories of visits to Paris, and of lines of French poetry, while in his daily life at the time of Garibaldi's expedition to Sicily, in May 1860, he first derides the Italian flag as an 'aping of the French' and then finds consolation in reading the latest issue of the *Journal des savants*. At the same time—and this offers a fitting anticipation of our next chapter—American culture makes a single appearance in the novel. Prince Salina remembers reading about a new medicine recently discovered in America and immediately dismisses it as a 'crude substitute for the stoicism of the ancients and for Christian fortitude'. The association of American culture with eccentric scientific discoveries that deserve derision more than respect is, as we will see, one way in which the European elite—including the Italian—tended to belittle the first signs of America's status as a rising economic and cultural powerhouse.[49]

---

[49] Giuseppe Tomasi di Lampedusa, *Il gattopardo* (1958; Milan: Feltrinelli, 1967), 43, 45; English trans. by Archibald Colquhoun, *The Leopard* (New York: Pantheon, 1960). On *La Jeune Fille*, published from 1914 until 1919, see Daniela Rossini, 'La donna nuova Americana nell'illustrazione: Reazioni italiane tra Belle Époque e fascismo', in Rossini (ed.), *Le americane: Donne e immagini di donne fra belle époque e fascismo* (Rome: Biblink, 2008), 95–114 (99).

# 2
# The Idea of America in Italy's Two Nations

If Benjamin Disraeli's expression 'two nations' aptly described the huge divide between rich and poor in Victorian England, it can easily be adopted for the present study, since the situation was very similar, in fact worse, in the new Kingdom of Italy. The economic divide was accompanied by a cultural divide, greater in Italy owing to a poorer record of school attendance and literacy. In 1861 only about 27 per cent of Italians could read, a figure far below that of Britain, which was closer to 70 per cent. As already mentioned, in her influential book on Italian migration around the world, Donna Gabaccia addressed the question of Italy's social make-up by saying that rich and poor were almost 'different races'. It is a provocative statement but one that is close to an uncomfortable truth.[1]

Statistical figures relating to the USA help us to add substance to it. In a survey done in 1882, Italian data on levels of literacy were compared to those of other nations. The figures concerning the United States of America were oddly broken down into white and black populations. Their 1870 census showed an impressive figure for the white community: 89 per cent of the population aged 10 and above were literate. This was clear evidence of the huge success of public education in the USA, with levels that outstripped even those of northern European countries. African Americans were nowhere near as fortunate: their literacy level peaked at 19 per cent. Considering that these were the levels of a community that, until five years before, had largely been kept chained to the condition of slavery, it is of no little importance to point out that, if Italy's average for the same year had risen to 33 per cent (25 per cent among women), several provinces in central and southern Italy had similar if not inferior percentages to those among African Americans.[2]

For this vast majority of the population, printed matter—whether books or periodicals—held little importance. This is a key issue with regard to the perception of America in the early decades of Italy's unification. Journalist and historian

---

[1] Disraeli's expression refers to his political novel *Sibyl or the Two Nations* (1845). Regional variations in Italy were substantial, moving between above 50% of literacy in Piedmont down to 10% in a number of provinces formerly belonging to the Vatican (such as Romagna) and the Kingdom of the Two Sicilies. Data on education in nineteenth-century Italy and Britain can be found in Giovanni Vecchi, *Measuring Wellbeing: A History of Italian Living Standards* (Oxford: Oxford University Press, 2017), 178–80. Gabaccia, *Italy's Many Diasporas*, 19.

[2] Data from Ministero di agricoltura, industria e commercio, *Risultati parziali del censimento della popolazione al 31 dicembre 1881 riguardo al numero degli analfabeti e confronti internazionali* (Rome: Tipografia Elzeviriana, 1882), 14–15. On individual regions, see M. Girolama Caruso and Frank Heim, 'Il livello di istruzione in Italia negli ultimi 150 anni: I dati', in Sveva Avveduto (ed.), *Italia 150 anni: Popolazione, welfare, scienza e società* (Rome: Gangemi, 2015), 121–34 (125).

---

*America in Italian Culture: The Rise of a New Model of Modernity, 1861–1943.* Guido Bonsaver, Oxford University Press.
© Guido Bonsaver 2023. DOI: 10.1093/oso/9780198849469.003.0003

Sergio Romano suggested that 'America was paradoxically more familiar to southern peasants than to the lower and middle bourgeoisie'.[3] This is a statement that, as we will see, needs some fine-tuning, but that, overall, points to a real issue. Educated Italians formed an idea of America that was very different from the part-mythical, part-real notion that brought millions of near-illiterate Italians to embark on a long journey of migration.

For this reason, this chapter will focus first on the views of Italy's educated elite, before exploring the ways and forms in which the vast mass of Italians built a vision of the United States of America. In between the two, a section will be devoted to an event that, at the turn of the century, added a popular, first-hand experience to the Italian perception of America: the impressive spectacle of the Wild West, brought to the Italian peninsula twice, in 1890 and in 1906, by the grand itinerant show led by William Cody, better known as Buffalo Bill.

## 2.1 Describing America in Print

The USA was a remote country: geographically, linguistically, and culturally. The American War of Independence (1775–83) had been the most debated issue both then and in the early decades of the nineteenth century. Some had perceived it as a contagious case of revolutionary republicanism, as exemplified by Vittorio Alfieri's fervorous five odes of *America libera* (1783). Others praised it as the rise of a young nation that, unlike the French two decades later, was able to preserve the democratic principles of its foundation. The latter was the view of an influential historian in early nineteenth-century Italy, Carlo Botta. His *Storia della guerra d'indipendenza degli Stati Uniti d'America* was published in 1809, in Paris, where he had settled following the vicissitudes of his early life as a militant republican and later as a pro-Napoleonic administrator. Botta saw the formation of the USA as a lesson of what should have happened in the old continent in the wake of the French Revolution. For this reason, his portrait of George Washington as a selfless leader is easily understood as a moral comparison with power-consumed Napoleon Bonaparte.

Beyond founding fathers such as Washington and Benjamin Franklin, the first American president who achieved popularity in post-unification Italy was Abraham Lincoln. His stance on slavery and his leadership during the Civil War earned him a level of fame that was somehow sanctified by his assassination on 15 April 1865. The funeral train that transported his body from Washington to Springfield in a tortuous journey allowing tens of thousands of Americans to mourn him at his passing provided the inspiration for the similarly symbolic

---

[3] Sergio Romano, 'Prefazione', in Teodori, *Maledetti americani*, pp. vii–xi (p. viii).

journey from Pisa to Genoa of the embalmed body of *Risorgimento* hero Giuseppe Mazzini, in 1872.[4]

At the same time, beyond the political realm, the Italian elite shared a certain disinterest and detachment towards the USA. Neither the pre-unification regional states nor the newly unified kingdom had stakes invested in the American continent. Economic relations were minimal and so, before the late 1880s, was the demographic connection created by migration. If Italian explorers had played a pivotal role in the discovery of the Americas, no substantial colony of Italians was ever formed in North America before the second half of the nineteenth century. Moreover, Giorgio Spini points to the religious dimension that made the mainly Protestant north of less interest than the southern and central part of the Americas (Mexico included), whose population was uniformly Roman Catholic.[5] This scant interest was often mixed with condescension, particularly in cultural matters. It was a viewpoint shared by other European elites, even the French, despite the political ties fostered by shared republican ideals.

In terms of book publications, there was no shortage of available works on the USA, though the quantity of such works was limited compared to British and French counterparts. It was nonetheless sufficient for providing an informed opinion, with a mixture of travelogues and monographs based on statistical, second-hand information.[6]

When we look at the entire span of the five decades between Italy's unification and the First World War, it seems appropriate to speak of two different phases in the representation and discussion of the USA. The first shows a genuine exploration of the geographical, social, and economic fabric of the country, often by travellers with a scientific background. It peaks at the time of Philadelphia's Centennial Exhibition of 1876—which is seen as an extolment of America's economic strength and entrepreneurial skills. This phase roughly ends in the 1880s, coinciding with the presence of two Italians—Adolfo Rossi and Dario Papa—whose American experience was to leave a significant mark in their work as journalists. Towards the turn of the century, what emerges is an added interest that is brought about by two main factors. First, the striking originality of America's big

---

[4] On the historical and literary debate on America in pre-unification Italy and, in particular, on Botta's American history, see chapter 1 of Körner, *America in Italy*, 2–37. Körner also dispels the myth of the American War of Independence as constituting a model for Italian revolutionaries during the Risorgimento years. For a historical study of the European perception of America in the eighteenth and nineteenth centuries, see also Antonello Gerbi, *The Dispute of the New World: The History of a Polemic, 1750–1900* (Pittsburgh, PA: University of Pittsburgh Press, 1973).

[5] Giorgio Spini, 'I Puritani della Nuova Inghilterra e la cultura italiana', in Raimondo Luraghi (ed.), *Atti del I Congresso Internazionale di Storia Americana. Italia e Stati Uniti dall'indipendenza americana ad oggi (1776–1976)* (Genoa: Tilgher, 1978), 23–31.

[6] For an extensive survey of Italian travel books on the USA during this period, see Andrew J. Torrielli, *Italian Opinion on America: As Revealed by Italian Travellers, 1850–1900* (Cambridge, MA: Harvard University Press, 1941).

cities, New York in particular. Secondly, the presence of millions of Italian migrants, which somehow complicates the idea of America.

At the same time, if there is a thread running through the entire period, it is an ambivalent attitude combining praise and ridicule, sometimes within the same breath of discourse. The admiration for the independent spirit and the enlightened principles of the Constitution around which the USA had been founded was a recurring topic. Their repercussions on society at large were perceived in various walks of life, from the exemplary development of compulsory education, to dynamism in commerce, and less rigid class barriers. At the same time, the romantic idea of America as a virginal country allowed ample space to a degree of paternalism, which tended to produce a counter-image of American society as naïve, unsophisticated, violent, and always prone to extravagant if not childlike extremes. In this respect, America's thin layer of cultural history (from the perspective of Western civilization, obviously) in comparison with the centuries-old stratification of culture in the Old World, and in Italy in particular, provided a continuous source of reminders of the still precarious cultural roots of this young country. This is an attitude that, remarkably, became even stronger in the second of these two phases.

To concentrate now on the post-unification years, a first book on the USA was written by a young geologist from Bologna university, Giovanni Capellini. He had travelled through the country when it was still engulfed in the Civil War, in 1863, and, following his scientific interests, a large part of the journey was devoted to the mountainous areas of the north-east.[7] A defining stylistic trait is Cappellini's factual tone, even in the most extreme situations. For example, when witnessing a brutal example of racism—a group of children throwing stones from a shore of the Ohio river at the floating corpse of an African American, in plain view of the adults—Capellini limits himself to a line recording the contradiction of a Unionist country that, while at war to abolish slavery, is at the same time treating its own African American population with utter disdain.[8] Or, when he devotes twenty pages to an accurate description of the appearance and customs of two native tribes—Omahas and Ponkas—it is the cynical policies of the US administration in depriving the tribes of their freedom of movement that are described with an objective tone, leaving any judgement to the reader, as he explicitly says at the end of this section.[9]

A second publication is *Gli Stati Uniti d'America nel 1876*, written by an economist, Salvatore Cognetti de Martiis, to coincide with the centennial of American independence. The economic policies under President Lincoln's administration

---

[7] Giovanni Capellini, *Ricordi di un viaggio scientifico nell'America settentrionale nel 1863* (Bologna: Tipografia Vitali, 1867).
[8] Capellini, *Ricordi di un viaggio scientifico*, 234–5.
[9] Capellini, *Ricordi di un viaggio scientifico*, 186.

had been the subject of Cognetti de Martiis's studies in previous years, to which he had added a small biographical volume in 1873. *Gli Stati Uniti d'America* consists of a number of informative essays on the country's society and economy. It appeared first in instalments in the Milanese conservative newspaper *La Perseveranza* in 1876, and it was then published as a monograph the following year.[10] Cognetti de Martiis too provided a very factual description, praising in particular the organization and secularism of US public education. This was a theme that emerged repeatedly in travelogues that described the country's cultural policies. Using the lexis derived from the Darwinist ethnography current at the time, the author did not restrain himself from defining the white population as the 'razza dominante' ('dominant race'), and when describing the native population—alternatively called 'Pelle Rossa' ('Red Skins') or 'nativi colorati' ('coloured natives')—he offered a simple demonstration of their superiority over the African American population by stating that, before the Civil War, the Cherokee tribes were also owners of black slaves.[11]

Cognetti de Martiis's study was paralleled by the work of an agronomist, Francesco Carega di Muricce, a Tuscan patriot who had been involved in the region's 'soft' revolution of 1860, which had seen the moderate Duke of Lorena peacefully flee from Florence. After his political career had ended, and before he returned to his profession as an agronomist and to his interests as a landowner, Carega had travelled extensively through the Americas in 1871-2, and his views had been published by Florence's *Gazzetta d'Italia*. From those writings he derived the two volumes of *In America*, which were published in 1875. Like Cognetti de Martiis, Carega showed particular interest in investigating the USA's social and economic fabric; but, in his case, the anecdotal aspect stemming from his first-hand experience added a warmer, narrative tone to his chapters.[12]

In the 1880s another two volumes were published by economists. The first was Egisto Rossi's *Gli Stati Uniti e la concorrenza americana*, printed in Florence in 1884. This book was closely connected to the parliamentary debate related to the introduction of protectionist policies, the subject of a heated debate by the so-called Historic Left. Indeed, Egisto Rossi was the secretary and close collaborator of leading textile industrialist and MP Alessandro Rossi, who for years had fought for the introduction of protectionist measures against imports from across the Atlantic. Egisto Rossi's aim was to produce a book that clearly showed the size and strength of the US economy, and he did so with a detailed study that, running to almost 800 pages and enriched with statistical tables, illustrations, and maps, provided convincing evidence of the giant steps that were quickly bringing the US

---

[10] Salvatore Cognetti de Martiis, *Gli Stati Uniti d'America nel 1876* (Milan: Stab. Tip. della Perseveranza, 1877).
[11] Cognetti de Martiis, *Gli Stati Uniti d'America*, 62-3.
[12] Francesco Carega di Muricce, *In America (1871-1872)*, 2 vols (Florence and Rome: Banco Annunzi, 1875).

economy to a commanding global position. Rossi's introduction to the book left no doubt about his views: he lamented the lack of interest towards the USA from the Italian press compared with those in Britain, France, and Germany, and stated his belief in the future world dominance of the American nation: 'Americanism, which is the most virile and robust achievement of the Anglo-Saxon people, will soon achieve economic primacy over the entire globe and it will force all nations to bear its consequences in the political and social field [...]'.[13] Rossi's book was influential in the debate concerning the increase of Italy's protectionist policies in 1887, particularly in relation to wheat and sugar imports, for which the USA was a major exporter.

In 1887 it was the turn of Giuseppe Sormani, then chief editor of the Milanese business paper *Il Commercio*, to tour the USA. His correspondence was published in the following year and provided yet another narrative of the economic might being developed in both industry and agriculture, thanks to intense mechanization and constant technological development. In the case of Sormani, however, his enthusiastic support of 'the American way' in business, of its money-making drive, and of its main streets plastered with advertising placards is counterbalanced by a strong degree of criticism of America's social mores. When it comes to culture and the arts, Sormani is constantly dismissive of American society, often in association with a reminder of the vast superiority of Latin/Italian civilization:

> The American man, whose inclination turns him towards business, cannot have a sophisticated artistic judgement; however, in these last few years he has been so busy copying beauty that it is possible to imagine the beginning of such appreciation: that spark, which all the world envies, and which has been a constant presence, between the Adriatic and Mediterranean seas.[14]

This is an attitude that was present in Italy's illustrated magazines too. An early example of this can be found in the 16 March 1861 issue of *Il Mondo illustrato: Giornale universale*, Italy's first illustrated magazine, founded in Turin in 1847 (in the wake of the Parisian *L'Illustration: Journal universel*). The magazine scarcely devoted any attention to the USA other than to touch upon the odd exotic and curious item of news. In this case, an article was devoted to two topics, both accompanied by a large image. The attitude of the journalist was patronizing and dismissive: the first concerned the uniforms adopted by the US Army, which the

---

[13] Egisto Rossi, *Gli Stati Uniti e la concorrenza americana: Studi di agricultura, industria e commercio da un recente viaggio* (Florence: Tipografia Barbera, 1884), p. xix. On the reverberations of Egisto Rossi's work in the Italian parliamentary debate, see Raffaele Romanelli, *L'Italia liberale* (Bologna: Il Mulino, 1979), 244–5. On Alessandro Rossi's economic thought, see Silvio Lanaro, 'Mercantilismo agrario e formazione del capitale nel pensiero di Alessandro Rossi', *Quaderni storici*, 6/16 (1971), 48–156.

[14] Giuseppe Sormani, *Eco d'America* (Milan: Tipografia degli Operai, 1888), 260.

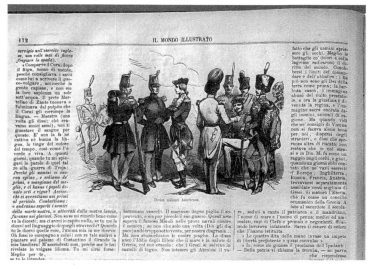

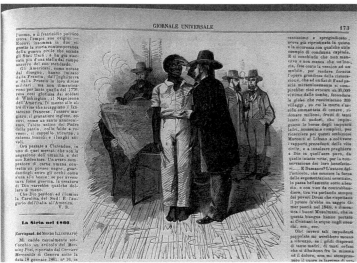

Fig. 2.1. US military uniforms and the slave market in South Carolina; illustrations from the Turin magazine *Il Mondo illustrato*, 16 March 1861. (courtesy of Biblioteca Nazionale Centrale, Rome)

article presented as a laughable plagiarism from different European nations. The second touched upon slavery as an offensive contradiction of American democracy and ended with the following line: 'May God forgive and enlighten South Carolina. This is Italy's wish for America.'[15]

---

[15] VS, 'Le divise militari americane e il mercato degli schiavi nella Carolina del Sud', *Il Mondo illustrato*, 4/11 (16 March 1861), 172–3. In its early years, the magazine's section devoted to foreign news

The comparison with Italian culture, charged with patronizing overtones, continued to be present in other contemporary travelogues by authors who concentrated on questions of culture and lifestyle. For example, it is a defining trait in *Una corsa nel nuovo mondo* (1878), by Francesco Varvaro Pojero, a young Sicilian travel writer who, after visiting Philadelphia's Centennial Exposition of 1876, decided to cross the country from coast to coast. It is also present in *Ricordi d'America* (1878), by Gustavo Winderling, a Milanese dental surgeon who was at Philadelphia's world fair as a contributor to the Italian pavilion.[16]

Patriotic pride takes a violent, racist turn in the travelogue of Ferdinando Fontana, journalist, poet, playwright, and librettist (he wrote the libretto of Puccini's first two operas). Fontana visited New York in 1882 and devotes almost ten pages of his book to the description of a single event. While walking through the streets of Manhattan, he happened to notice a shoeshiner kneeling down at the feet of a well-dressed, imposing African American with a cigar in his mouth. When Fontana realized that the shoeshiner was of Italian origin, the event triggered a stream of jingoistic rhetoric:

> There were two men, one kneeling in front of the other, at the corner of a street. The man standing belonged to one of the races which are least prone to noble and grand thought, which are more resistant to any civil progress; he belonged to that race which, for a long time, was considered unworthy of the adjective 'human'. [...]
> You will have already understood that the man standing there was a negro.
> The man kneeling down in front of him belonged to the most superior race in humanity; better, he belonged to the youth of this superior race. His fathers had dominated the world three times and this made him three times feared and commendable amongst men. [...]
> And it seemed that that negro shouted from every pore at the 'genteel Latin blood' curved in front of him: 'Grandson of Julius Caesar and Marco Polo; cousin of Beato Angelico; seed of Dante Alighieri; relative of Raphael, Domenichino and Michelangelo; son of Giordano Bruno; brother of Garibaldi and Cavour; polish,

---

would always open with a long report on French affairs, and no other country was covered in each issue. The first article concerning the USA is similarly symbolic of the above-mentioned attitude: on the one hand, it praised the introduction of telegraph lines as a technological achievement; on the other hand, it dwelt on the detail of the line between New York and Philadelphia being interrupted by an owl, which was electrocuted on the live wire (anon., 'Stati Uniti d'America', *Il Mondo illustrato*, 5 (30 January 1847), 68). On the early history of Italian illustrated magazines, see Michele Giordano, *La stampa illustrata in Italia: Dalle origini alla Grande Guerra 1834–1915* (Milan: Guanda, 1983).

[16] Francesco Varvaro Pojero, *Una corsa nel nuovo mondo*, 2 vols (Milan: Treves, 1878). Before this volume, Varvaro Pojero had published a travelogue of his journey through Eastern Europe and Russia (1875). He came from a rich family of textile traders and was Honorary Consul for the Austro-Hungarian Empire in Palermo. Gustavo Winderling, *Ricordi d'America* (Milan: Treves, 1878). In the book's preface, Winderling tells us that he had been asked by the Italian ministry of education to use his journey to the USA to examine and report on the teaching of medical sciences in American universities. Giuseppe Massara dwells on both books in his *Viaggiatori italiani in America (1860–1970)* (Rome: Edizioni di storia e letteratura, 1976), 33–42.

polish well the leather of my shoes!—Of my shoes, of me, John, the negro, who loves so much what the white civilization produces...alcoholic drinks!...Me, who amongst my ancestors (and not that far back!) can boast great cannibals![17]

Fontana's reaction is indicative of the blurred distinction between patriotism and racism, which could turn into rage when emancipation challenged the status of one's own people. Opposition to slavery did not mean a belief in equality among different communities.[18]

At the same time, this passage introduces us to the sense of shame and patriotic dismay that occurred when wealthy Italian travellers came into contact with the first traces of economic migration by Italy's near-illiterate masses. This is a factor that was to become more and more prominent as Italian migration escalated towards the turn of the century.

However, it is important first to dwell on the Philadelphia exhibition, in 1876, which marked the centenary of US independence and played a catalyst role. It was America's big chance to show the world its entrepreneurial and industrial potential.[19] Thirty-seven countries, Italy included, took part. The fair's main pavilion covered the largest area of any building in the world: 21.5 acres, supported by 672 columns. Unsurprisingly, one finds that a clutch of books devoted to the USA were published in Italy at the time, not all written by Italians. In 1876, the prestigious Milanese publishing house Treves produced two travelogues on the USA, and a third came out in 1879, all translated from French. Illustrated magazines played their part too. The Sonzogno publishing house in Milan created an illustrated, periodical publication for the purpose called *L'Esposizione universale di Filadelfia del 1876*, whose instalments, once collected in two volumes, formed a comprehensive guide to the world fair.[20]

Illustrated magazines provide an insightful viewpoint, as they bridged the gap between, on the one hand, the mainly political interests of newspapers and the limited circulation of travel books, and, on the other, the need to cater for a new,

---

[17] Ferdinando Fontana and Dario Papa, *New York* (Milan: Galli Editore, 1884), 173–9. Fontana authored the first half of the book, Papa, on whom we will concentrate later, the second.

[18] A similar tendency is shown by French authors, which Philippe Roger defines as 'a time of backsliding' in *The American Enemy*, 207–10 (207).

[19] Before the Philadelphia exhibition, a first attempt had been New York's Exhibition of the Industries of All Nations of 1853, a smaller-scale affair that had drawn criticism for its attempt to imitate London's Crystal Palace exhibition of 1851 (whose official name was The Great Exhibition of the Works of Industry of all Nations). The Philadelphia exhibition was the first one approved and backed by the US government and Congress. On the role of world fairs in defining the cultural identity of post-Civil War USA, see Rydell and Kroes, *Buffalo Bill in Bologna*, 47–72.

[20] The eighty instalments were sold in bookshops and news kiosks, but subscribers to the entire series would receive as a gift a copy of an illustrated *Storia dell'indipendenza degli Stati Uniti d'America*. The publicity did not specify its author, but it was probably an early edition of Carlo Romussi, *Storia degli Stati Uniti d'America* (Milan: Sonzogno, 1877). Romussi specialized in illustrated, non-academic national histories for Sonzogno: in 1875 he had published *Storia d'Italia narrata al popolo*, and in 1876 *Storia di Francia narrata al popolo*.

wider reservoir of readers, comprising upper-class, educated women and people from the lower-middle classes—shop owners and white-collar workers—and the urban working classes. The progress of Italy's industrialization and its battle against illiteracy were slowly bringing a greater stratification of the reading public, which illustrated magazines tried to intercept. Turin's *Il Mondo illustrato* had stopped publication in September 1861. It was in Milan that its most important successor was born, published twice a week by Treves, from November 1869. Its name was *L'Illustrazione popolare*, and in its first issue the chief editor, Carlo d'Ormeville—an established librettist and theatre impresario—clearly stated his intention of reaching out to a less-educated readership. This was reflected in the content of the periodical; most of the first issue, for example, was taken up by a long biographical piece on George Stephenson, the father of railway transport, presented as a working-class man who, thanks to his genius, had become rich and famous, and the first instalment of a French novel, *Le confessioni di un operajo* (*Confessions d'un ouvrier* (1851)), a minor work by Émile Souvestre. In the fourth issue, d'Ormeville wrote of a circulation of 40,000 copies nationwide, and boasted that it had raised to 70,000, the following year. These were figures that outstripped those of most Italian newspapers, which typically had regional circulations.[21]

When it came to Philadelphia's centennial fair, its coverage in *L'Illustrazione popolare* began soon after its inauguration, with a full-page image of the fair's main building in the issue of 28 May 1876 (which was also the first time that the USA appeared in any form in the journal pages for that year). It then continued with articles and large illustrations of different buildings in almost all of its weekly issues, peaking on 2 July with a five-page coverage of the Declaration of Independence, replete with pictures of all American presidents. The following week the anonymous chronicler of the fair stated—armed with patriotic pride more than with factual evidence—that the Italian pavilion had been unanimously declared the best of them all.[22]

America was unusually present in almost every issue of *L'Illustrazione popolare* during the second half of 1876. With regard to Philadelphia's fair, it is interesting to note that, despite the many descriptions and illustrations, no attention was paid to a controversial and groundbreaking aspect of the fair—that is, the presence of a building dedicated entirely to women. The Women's Pavilion had been built thanks to funding raised by a women's committee led by Elizabeth Duane Gillespie, great-granddaughter of Benjamin Franklin, despite the reluctance of the fair's organizers. It would be unduly forceful to read a specific intention in this

---

[21] *Corriere della Sera* reached 50,000 copies only eleven years later, in 1887. Milan's then major daily, *Il Secolo*, had the highest circulation at the time; it reached 100,000 in 1895. The latter's success was also due to its attempt to cater for a wider readership, embracing the *faits divers* that characterized illustrated magazines. See Valerio Castronovo, Luciana Giacheri Fossati, and Nicola Tranfaglia, *La stampa italiana nell'età liberale* (Rome and Bari: Laterza, 1979), 107–13.

[22] Anon., 'Le nostre incisioni', *L'Illustrazione popolare*, 36 (9 July 1876), 562.

omission, particularly so if one considers that the Sonzogno ad hoc publication gave it pride of place, with a front-page illustration (see Fig. 2.2). In the accompanying long, approbatory text, a comment addressed the Italian readership in no uncertain terms:

> But it seems to us that what feminine culture should really be about in order to benefit the woman who procures it and the children whom she will educate, is not known by many in Italy. Today the rich woman is not educated, and the woman of modest means is not given a useful occupation. The real emancipation of women will happen through labour only; thanks to its fruits she will make herself independent from seduction, from material needs, from man: that is real freedom![23]

The author of this anonymous article must have been close to feminist or socialist circles. It is an open denunciation that was uncommon in the popular press at the time. The Women's Pavilion was also mentioned in two long articles dedicated to the exhibition by *L'Illustrazione italiana*, another illustrated magazine by Treves, and in Turin's *La Stampa*. While the former was simply factual in presenting the women's pavilion, the latter ended its description with the following comment: 'I saw so much stuff of that sort of thing there; it's enough to make you think that these *ladies* will actually become independent. Who knows, one day they might even sit in parliament!'[24]

The journalist's prediction would become reality in 1916 (exactly thirty years before Italy followed suit), but what is particularly interesting is the tone of the sentence. It is slightly ambivalent in the fact that its sensationalizing exclamation mark could be interpreted either as an enthusiastic wish or as an ironic emphasis. Indeed, when discussing the role of women in American society as seen by Italian commentators, this ambivalent tone is more prevalent than any feminist enthusiasm.

This takes us to some consideration on the prevailing themes in the perception of American society by Italian commentators during this earlier period. The status of women, particularly in an urban environment, is a recurring topic. Their degree of emancipation was startling to the Italian traveller. American women often revealed a level of culture and sophistication that was superior to that of their male peers, and more than anything else they showed an outspoken independence of mind and body. According to one of the founding mothers of Italian

---

[23] Anon., 'Il padiglione della donne', *L'Esposizione universale di Filadelfia del 1876*, instalment no. 10 [no date specified; presumably May or June 1876], 73–4.

[24] Created in 1875, *L'Illustrazione italiana* was aimed at a slightly more educated readership than *L'Illustrazione popolare*. This is reflected in its price, 50 cents against only 10 for the latter. The two journals' layout and illustrations, however, were very similar and would sometimes share the same material. The articles mentioned are A. Favaro, 'A proposito della prossima Esposizione universale di Filadelfia', *L'Illustrazione italiana*, 23 (2 April 1876), 359–62; MV, 'Una gita di corsa all'Esposizione', *La Stampa*, 18 July 1876, p. 2.

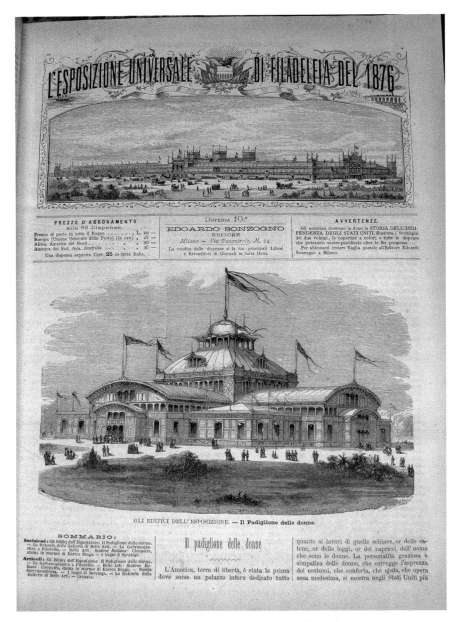

**Fig. 2.2.** The Women's Pavilion at Philadelphia Centennial Exhibition as it appeared in an instalment of Sonzogno's *L'Esposizione universale di Filadelfia dl 1876*. (courtesy of Centro Studi per L'arte del libro, Novara)

feminism, Anna Maria Mozzoni, this was the result of better access to education. In one of her early works, *Un passo avanti nella cultura femminile*, published in 1866, the Milanese intellectual had proposed a plan for the reform of Italy's education system to the advantage of women. Before concentrating on her ideas, the book presented an extended overview of almost one hundred pages on the state of women in various European and American countries. The USA was apportioned the longest and most passionate section, containing what Mozzoni considered an exemplary model of further education for women—the academic programme of a liberal college, Vassar, which was reproduced in full.[25]

Some male travellers such as Carega di Muricce were in awe of this, and in 1871 he described in detail the life both inside and outside the house of 'an Anglo-American woman' (as he defined her, clarifying that her status was not shared by African American and Latin American women). Equally impressed was a young engineer called Camillo Olivetti, future founder of the prestigious family industry in Ivrea (on which we will dwell in Chapter 3), as he wrote in his letters home during his journey through the USA in search of industrial innovation.[26] The majority, however, were of a more conservative opinion. Among them was Cognetti de Martiis, who regretted the excesses reached by women's independence and, as an economist, considered the presence of a strong female labour force deleterious to overall conditions of employment. Likewise, in journalist Dario Papa's 1884 book on New York, the description of women's independence is coloured by a constant reminder of the arrogance and frivolousness that it generates.[27]

A second topic that recurs in travelogues at the time is related to the country's booming economy. Just about every description of a major city begins with a comment on the bustling activity along its streets, the noise, the odours, and most symbolically the ever-present advertising placards for which American businessmen seemed to have an obsession. From New York, Fontana addressed the subject with an elaborate metaphor:

> If the Dollar is the king of America, and its slave is the machine, publicity is the sovereign empress, the arrogant, squashing, incredibly dominant queen. [...] Genius and Stupidity met one day, by chance, they slept together—and publicity

---

[25] Anna Maria Mozzoni, *Un passo avanti nella cultura femminile: Tesi e progetto* (Milan: Tipografia internazionale, 1866), 63–77. On the perception of the emancipation of women as a defining trait of American culture in nineteenth-century Europe, see Nicola Miller, 'Liberty, Lipstick, and Lobsters', in Körner Axel, Nicola Miller, and Adam I. P. Smith (eds), *America Imagined: Explaining the United States in Nineteenth-Century Europe and Latin America* (New York: Palgrave Macmillan, 2012), 81–117.

[26] Olivetti travelled from coast to coast in 1893-4. His letters were posthumously published as Camillo Olivetti, *Lettere americane* (Milan: Edizioni di Comunità, 1968) (see pp. 16, 53–4, 71).

[27] Carega di Muricce, *In America (1871–1872)*, i. 72–103. Cognetti de Martiis, *Gli Stati Uniti d'America*, 69. Fontana and Papa, *New York*, 257–71. As already mentioned, Fontana authored the first half of the book, Papa the second.

was born; a daughter who inherited for the most part the qualities of her mother, but who did honour, every now and then, her paternal blood.[28]

Once again, praise and denigration stood side by side (and one should also note the implicit misogyny in imagining Genius as a man and Stupidity as a woman).

Likewise, after describing in detailed and admiring terms the hectic efficiency of a barrel factory in Brooklyn, Fontana ends his chapter with a mock toast referring to the famous circus impresario, P. T. Barnum: 'Homeland of Barnum, cheers!'[29] In a sense, it seems that the aggressive and uncouth forms of American capitalism—whose achievements were praised by economists—triggered a feeling of amused admiration, rarely free from a patronizing sense of cultural superiority whenever commentators looked at its manifestations in America's urban life.

If the American man was portrayed as the ultimate businessman with no time for the aesthetic pleasures of life, Italians were brought in and praised as the exemplary opposite end of the spectrum—that is, men gifted with genuine talent and a love of the arts. It is a stereotype that is challenged only by an author who wrote from the perspective of an Italian who had settled down in the country. This is Adolfo Rossi, a journalist, whose biography deserves a full paragraph.

Adolfo Rossi—no relation to Alessandro and Egisto Rossi—migrated from his native village near Rovigo, in the Veneto, to New York in the summer of 1879. He was then a young white-collar employee in the local post office, bored by his occupation—he had to stop his Ginnasio–Liceo studies and find a job after the death of his father—and raring for a new start and opportunities to cultivate his literary ambitions. As he explained, the choice of New York came as a result of reading those very books that had been published around 1876: he mentions Carega di Muricce, Varvaro Pojero, and Louis Simonin, the French travel writer whose two works on America had been translated by Treves. Rossi was to live in the USA for five years, first from hand to mouth—following the theft of his savings during the journey—and moving from job to job, learning to speak and write in English, working first in a New York factory, then as a pastry maker, as an accountant, and as a waiter in the prestigious Brunswick hotel.[30]

After about a year, by chance, his literary aspirations found an opening in the offer to write for *Il Progresso Italo-Americano*, New York's daily in Italian. As Rossi explains, by 1880 New York hosted an Italian community of about 25,000 immigrants, mostly from southern Italy. It was a reality that was totally ignored in Italy;

---

[28] Fontana and Papa, *New York*, 10–11.   [29] Fontana and Papa, *New York*, 130.

[30] Rossi's American memoirs were published in two different volumes. First, *Nacociù, la Venere americana: Avventure degli emigranti al Nuovo Mondo* (Rome: Edoardo Perino, 1889); this book saw two further editions with different titles: *Vita d'America* (Rome: Edoardo Perino, 1891) and *Un italiano in America* (Milan: Treves, 1892)—the third edition is slightly expanded but does not contain the final chapter referring to the native American princess Nacociù. Second, *Il paese dei dollari* (Milan: Tip. degli Operai, 1892), which had a later edition, *Nel paese dei dollari (Tre anni a New York)* (Milan: Max Kantorowicz Editore, 1893). The reference to his readings before he left for America are in *Nacociù, la venere americana*, 8.

none of the books he had read mentioned it.[31] The *Progresso* was the second periodical born in New York (following the weekly *L'Eco d'Italia*), and Rossi became its main editor in December 1880. However, after a few months he left the job and decided to see more of the country. He worked as an accountant for a railway company employing Italian immigrants in Colorado, and he eventually settled down in Denver, where he befriended an Italian with whom he decided to put in verse the legend of a Native American princess (hence the title of the first edition of the book, which contains long extracts of the poem). Rossi eventually returned to New York and to his preferred occupation as editor in chief of the *Progresso*, and he met and befriended the already mentioned Ferdinando Fontana and Dario Papa. Rossi convinced Papa to contribute to his paper during his months in America, after which both returned to Italy, in early 1884. It is likely that Rossi's budding career as a journalist in Italy was helped by Papa's established status at the *Corriere della Sera*, though neither ever mentioned this explicitly.[32]

Characteristic of Rossi's travel books is the lack of prejudice shown towards American society, as well as his first-hand experience of life as a poor immigrant, which prevented him from espousing the facile patriotism of other Italian

**Fig. 2.3.** A slightly tarnished photo of Adolfo Rossi (far left) in 1883, during a visit to the house in Staten Island in which Antonio Meucci hosted Garibaldi during his American exile. (courtesy of Archivio di Stato di Rovigo)

---

[31] Rossi, *Nacociù, la venere americana*, 38.
[32] Dario Papa was an esteemed journalist, writing for *Corriere della Sera* in its early years, and then acting as chief editor of various papers in Milan and Verona. He was in the USA in 1881–3.

authors. We will return to his books later on in this chapter, but, generally speaking, I would argue that his two books contain the best mixture of objective observation and entertaining narrative of the travel literature of these first thirty years following the country's unification.

Rossi's extended experience as a journalist in New York was also instrumental in his familiarity with the American press. He became a great fan of it, and his enthusiasm was shared by Dario Papa, who dedicated an entire chapter of his book to praise of the press. This is an aspect of American society that, unsurprisingly, was commented upon only by authors who had a good command of the English language. In his book, Papa concentrated on the *New York Herald* as an example of journalism capable of properly informing its readers, as opposed to the convoluted and subjective literary sophistications of the Italian press. Papa also praised America's major news agency, the Associated Press, for the variety of its news items contrasted with the scant political offerings of its Italian equivalent, the Agenzia Stefani. Papa's views took no prisoners in judging the Italian dailies, which he knew well:

> The offices of American papers are not, like ours, infested by men of letters, who think themselves too good to serve the public, and who always cough up great ideas, but flee from the job of actually making the paper a vehicle of news, rather than an academy. [...]
>
> The fact is that a newspaper there is created not, as it is in Italy, by journalists working in their rooms, basing their material on minimal information passed on by the police, and adorning it with rhetorical embellishments [...] The newspaper is made in the street, in the open air, based on one's notebook, on reality, collecting the news where it happens to be, informing the public speedily first of all, and then in detail.[33]

Adolfo Rossi also praised the American press in both his books on the USA and did not refrain from addressing the limitations of Italian papers, which he too saw as stylistically over-literary and semantically uninformative.[34]

In both cases, the American experience had a direct effect on their professional practices. Inspired by the *New York Herald*, when back in Italy Papa attempted the creation of a similar product in Milan. In April 1884, the paper he directed, *L'Italia: Giornale del popolo*, began to adopt an 'American' approach in both writing style and pagination. Papa's aim was to move towards a less convoluted prose style and more fact-based content. The latter is particularly detectable in the organization of the newspaper's front page. This can be seen through comparison between the old-style front page of the 29–30 April 1884 issue and the

---

[33] Fontana and Papa, *New York*, 471, 474.
[34] Rossi, *Nacociù, la venere americana*, 63–7; *Nel paese dei dollari*, 131–41.

1–2 May 1884 issue (the paper was published every second day). As the two illustrations show, the traditional version presents three of the five columns taken over by one single article of local importance. In contrast, the new version is dominated by news items coming from different cities of Italy and Europe, as evidenced by their headlines in bold. The paper's use of two different telegraphic networks—a sign of technological advancement at the time (Italy's first telegraphic service began in 1875)—is also highlighted on the front page, distinguishing between its use of Agenzia Stefani news and its in-house telegraphic system (see Figs 2.4 and 2.5).

It is a layout that seems to echo Rossi's words when writing about American newspapers:

> What, amongst us [in Italy], are called editorials but are often little more than tedious rigmaroles and soliloquies by editors who insist on judging everybody and talking about everything, including matters they know very little about, in north-American newspapers are reduced to short and rich notes, to brief comments, which express the opinions of competent men on what happened. In the United States one thinks that a paper should mainly be a bulletin with news coming from all over the world: judgements have to be left to the wide readership.[35]

It was not a revolution, but those changes were enough to put Papa at loggerheads with the paper's management board (part of which, it must be said, was also opposed to his open republicanism).

His experiments were also spurned by other papers which preferred to stick to the tradition of long editorials. Papa eventually resigned as chief editor of *L'Italia* in June 1890, and the 'American' experiment was abandoned. What remained dominant in the Italian newspapers at the time was the persona of the 'giornalista stanziale' ('resident journalist'), to use Nello Ajello's expression—that is, journalists whose status derived from their sophisticated prose-style rather than from their capacity to investigate news items. At the same time, other dailies began to develop a more dynamic approach towards news reporting, such as Rome's *Il Messaggero* and the *Corriere della Sera*.[36]

As for Adolfo Rossi, he returned to Italy to become one of the most popular correspondents of his generation and eventually chief editor of the *Corriere della Sera* in 1889. Continuing with the factual reporting style he had learnt in the USA,

---

[35] Rossi, *Nel paese dei dollari*, 138.
[36] Nello Ajello, 'I maestri del colore (appunti per una storia del giornalismo letterario in Italia)', *Problemi dell'informazione*, 1/4 (1976), 556–7; quoted in Castronovo, Giacheri Fossati, and Tranfaglia, *La stampa italiana nell'età liberale*, 102 (Papa's experiment is discussed in this volume at pp. 101–5). Before Papa's *L'Italia*, a newspaper that had innovated its front page was Milan's *Il Secolo*, which, in 1869, had introduced an illustration, very much in the wake of French *feuilletons*. On both Papa's *L'Italia* and the other dailies, see Mauro Forno, *Informazione e potere: Storia del giornalismo italiano* (Rome and Bari: Laterza, 2012), 37–40.

Fig. 2.4. Front page of *L'Italia. Giornale del Popolo*, of 29–30 April 1884. (courtesy of Biblioteca Nazionale Centrale, Rome)

Fig. 2.5. Front page of *L'Italia. Giornale del Popolo*, 1–2 May 1884. (courtesy of Biblioteca Nazionale Centrale, Rome)

Rossi's defiant articles contributed to the growing sales of Rome's newspaper *La Tribuna* at the turn of the century. Even in Rossi's case, though, his approach was not always welcome. For example, when in November 1895 he joined the Italian army in north-east Africa to report for the *Corriere della Sera* on Italy's stumbling efforts to expand its colonial possessions, he was forced to return to Italy after a few weeks. His frank and detailed reporting on logistical inefficiencies and the inadequacies of commanding officers had turned him into a *persona non grata*.[37]

Rossi's journalistic persona, at the antipodes of the *giornalista stanziale*, is condensed in his humorous—almost 'proto-Hemingwayesque'—reply to his chief editor's request, in November 1894, to change plans and, rather than travelling to St Petersburg to report on the Tzar's funeral, to go instead to a remote place in Sardinia, to cover a bloody battle between brigands and policemen: 'my suitcase is ready; all I need is to replace my black suit with a pair of boots and the Baedeker guide with a revolver.'[38]

It was in those years that Rossi returned to his American experience and wrote the two books of memoirs published respectively in 1889 and 1893. The second one—*Il paese dei dollari (tre anni a New York)*—is devoted to his years as chief editor of *Il Progresso Italo-Americano*. His 'American' journalistic mindset is palpable in every chapter. The book begins with a specific case of an Italian immigrant, Angelo Cornetta, a semi-illiterate barrel-organ player, who was first arrested on suspicion of mistreating his Irish partner. Rossi met him when he was on death row for killing a fellow during a row while they were peeling potatoes. It is a chapter that introduces us to Italian migration and to the violent face of American society, institutionalized in the death penalty. The narrative, however, is entirely focused on the humanity of Cornetta, whom Rossi visited in jail a number of times. It is a psychological study that does not attempt to generalize about migration and violence. Rather, it stays close to the facts, to the details of a human being who cannot understand why he is condemned to die and eventually takes refuge in an insane daydream that he is going to be let free on the day of his execution.

The rest of the book continues in this vein. When Rossi tackles the much-debated topic of the American woman, he first warns us against the prejudices of Italian travellers and then concentrates on another case: Mary, a young woman, born in New York and well educated (she is the daughter of an Italian architect). Mary enters a long dialogue with Rossi that carries on for multiple chapters. Indeed, she becomes a Ciceronian guide not just to the life of an educated American woman but to American society at large. One day, the two travel

---

[37] On Papa and Rossi, see also Castronovo, Giacheri Fossati, and Tranfaglia, *La stampa italiana nell'età liberale*, 101–3. An anthology of Rossi's correspondence has been published recently: Adolfo Rossi, *L'Italia della vergogna nelle cronache di Adolfo Rossi (1875–1921)* (Ravenna: Longo, 2010).

[38] These lines come from Rossi's first article from Sardinia: 'Viaggiando in Sardegna', *Corriere della Sera*, 22–3 November 1894, p. 1.

through the entire length of Manhattan using the elevated railroad so that Mary can answer all the questions that come to Rossi's mind when looking inside and outside their compartment. The final chapter is dedicated to his return to Italy and to his disappointment in seeing the many failings of Italian society. The concluding comment has an almost prophetic ring to it. Rossi predicts that the limitations of Italy's educational system and democratic life will produce violent struggles and violent statesmen. It is difficult not to think forward to the eventual implosion of liberal Italy at the hands of Mussolini and his Fascist squads.

The second phase of the coverage of the USA by Italian authors begins roughly in the 1890s and has its own climax at the time of the Hispanic–American war of 1898. This is the ten-week war that saw the defeat of Spain in defending its last colonial holds in Cuba, Puerto Rico, and the Philippines. It also marked the first time that the US military flexed its muscles on the international stage. It was now impossible for Italy's intellectual elites to ignore the size and strength of America's economic and military power. The press coverage of the war by the *Corriere della Sera* is exemplary of this development. When the war broke out, in April 1898, there were no Italian correspondents in either Cuba or the USA. The *Corriere della Sera* had to rely on telegraphic news coming in from different news agencies and foreign papers, mainly French and British. Only a week later, though, an Italian correspondent started to send his reports from Madrid. It was Adolfo Rossi, of all people. His first article of 29–30 April recalled his train journey through France—where he recorded the strong anti-American feelings held by all French passengers—and Catalonia—where he noticed the poor state of the Spanish conscript army. Rossi's articles, however, were given limited space, and he did not author any of the front-page editorials on the war.[39]

It was only in late June that the *Corriere della Sera* eventually sent its 'special envoy' to the USA. And it was a very different type of journalist from Adolfo Rossi. The choice fell on the rising star of Roman journalism, Ugo Ojetti, who was then a well-known, young author of erudite literary interests with a sophisticated prose style. His book of interviews with twenty-six leading figures of Italian literature, from Carducci to D'Annunzio—*Alla scoperta dei letterati* (1895)—had revealed his rare talent in sketching vivid human profiles and condensing erudite conversations into a few lines. They were gifts that lent themselves to journalism of a literary kind, and, indeed, Ojetti became a model of 'giornalista-letterato', as Isabella Nardi defines him.[40]

---

[39] The editorials were written by Arturo Colautti (under the pseudonym 'Fram.'), then *Corriere della Sera*'s expert on military conflict. A fervent nationalist, Colautti wrote articles that maintained a critical distance from the two factions. On the other hand, Catholic papers such as the Jesuits' *Civiltà cattolica* and the Vatican's *Osservatore romano* were vocal supporters of Spain.

[40] Isabella Nardi, *Il primo passo: Note sulla formazione di un giornalista-letterato: Ugo Ojetti* (Naples: Edizioni Scientifiche Italiane, 1990).

Before being sent to the USA, Ojetti had cut his teeth on correspondence work with an Egyptian trip to Luxor, for which he reported for the Roman daily *La Tribuna*. By the time Ojetti arrived in New York, the Hispanic–American war was at its end. His first article, published on 6–7 July 1898, missed the final naval battle of Santiago de Cuba, of 3 July, which saw the Spanish squadron entirely destroyed by the US fleet. For Rossi, this would have been an embarrassment. For Ojetti, it was an opportunity to tour the north-east, interview a few leading figures, and comment on American literature and the arts.

Ojetti spent three months between New York and Washington, and his articles regularly featured on the *Corriere della Sera*'s front page. We will dwell later on his writings, but, at a more general level, his arrival as an American correspondent marked an approach and style totally different from Rossi's. He was the first of a long line of 'giornalisti-letterati' who were to travel to America, for whom the literary quality of their prose was of equal importance to the topic under consideration.

Another trait of this new phase is the fact that commentators displayed interest not so much in America's industrial fabric or open spaces, but rather in the social and cultural matter of its main cities, particularly when displaying some eccentricity. This takes us to a key expression already mentioned in the Introduction, a neologism that came to define this approach: 'americanata'. Still present in contemporary Italian usage, etymological dictionaries tell us that the term refers to an odd, spectacular event resulting from the childish ambition and graceless enthusiasm of its organizers. In the late nineteenth century, it specifically referred to something happening in the USA, although its very first appearance, to my knowledge, dates back to 25 September 1877. It appears in a short, anonymous article in the *Corriere della Sera* about the bizarre success of an Italian composer in Peru.[41] The first article directly referring to the USA, entitled 'Americanate', is instead dated 17 November 1878 and tells the curious story of the theft of the corpse of an American millionaire in New York. By the late 1880s the neologism must have entered common usage if Sormani, in his book of 1887, could lament the scarce coverage of the USA by Italian journalists, coming to the conclusion that second-hand reporting on 'americanate' was the easy solution adopted by the Italian press.[42]

The increasing use and familiarity of the expression came to its height a few years later, in 1908, when 'Americanate' became the headline of a series of short articles in the illustrated magazine *La Domenica del Corriere*. Its readers were served with odd news confirming the cliché of American society as a cabinet of

---

[41] Anon., 'Corriere teatrale', *Corriere della Sera*, 25 September 1877, p. 3. At the end of the short article the author concludes: 'What *Americanate!* will say our readers. Yes…, but *nice ones* we add' (emphasis in the original). From this one can infer that the expression must already have been in colloquial use at the time.

[42] Anon., 'Americanate', *Corriere della Sera*, 17 November 1878, p. 3. Sormani, *Eco d'America*, 16. When looking at articles on America in both *Corriere della Sera* and *La Stampa* during the very early years of 1900, Giuseppe Gadda Conti comes to the same conclusion that 'americanate' seemed to be the most characteristic category of news. Giuseppe Gadda Conti, 'L'America nel *Corriere della Sera* e nella *Stampa*: Mark Twain', *Studi americani*, 19–20 (1973), 133–54.

bizarre curiosities. The first article came out in the 16–23 February issue of 1908 (about house servants forming trade unions and going on strike), signed by Carlo de Flaviis, who was presumably their main author, considering that the twenty-three articles I found—published between then and June 1913—were either signed by him or anonymous. The little biographical information we have about de Flaviis tells us that he was a Neapolitan playwright, song lyricist, and occasional contributor to Naples's *Il Giorno* and Milan's *Corriere della Sera*. His day job was as a manager at Naples's provincial post office, and there is no trace of an American background; hence one is led to imagine that his source of information must have been either items from news agencies or articles from the foreign press.[43]

An overview of the most popular illustrated magazines—*L'Illustrazione popolare*, *L'Illustrazione italiana*, and *La Domenica del Corriere*—allows us to gain better knowledge of the coverage of the USA at the time.[44] It confirms an increasing interest that by 1910 rivals the interest in France: that is, by 1910 there is at least one article on both countries each week. However, whereas serious political news is foremost in articles on France, articles on the USA concentrate on *faits divers* and are often dedicated to minor 'americanate'. In other words, American culture is progressively discussed more frequently: it is associated with modernity, technology, and adventure, but more often than not the events that are described are extremes that are more ludicrous than informative. It is equally indicative that, while events in France regularly gain the prestigious front-cover illustration of those magazines, those in America rarely do. In the *Domenica del Corriere*, for example, it is only after more than a hundred issues that a first cover illustration is devoted to the USA, on 23 June 1901: it is about an adventurous event but, indicatively, one with a peculiar twist. It depicts the attempted single crossing of the Atlantic in a sailing boat. This category of crossing had already been completed twice in the recent past, but what made businessman Howard Blackburn's attempt noteworthy was the fact that the man was disabled. He was maneuvering the boat despite missing all his fingers from both hands.[45]

Two Italian travel books, published at roughly the same time, bear testimony of this new trend, though at a higher cultural level. The first, *Impressioni d'America*, was published in 1898 by Giuseppe Giacosa, one of Italy's most famous librettists

---

[43] Salvatore Battaglia's *Grande dizionario della lingua italiana* does not give a reference to the first use of 'americanata', and the Sabatini Coletti indicates 1890 as the year of the first usage, which is contradicted by its presence in the pages of the *Corriere della Sera* since 1877. A discussion of the representation of America in *La Domenica del Corriere* can be found in Angela dall'Osso, *Voglia d'America: Il mito americano in Italia tra otto e novecento* (Rome: Donzelli, 2007). I am thankful to the linguist Alessandro Carlucci for helping me get to the bottom of the genesis of this intriguing neologism, which does not appear to have an equivalent in any major European language.
[44] I am very grateful to my young colleague Alice Gussoni, who, with the support of university funding, composed a first, annotated catalogue of the content of those papers for the years 1899 and 1910.
[45] On *La Domenica del Corriere*'s illustrations, see Giovanna Ginex, 'L'arte dell'illustrazione nelle pagine de "La Domenica del Corriere" (1899–1989)', in Giovana Ginex (ed.), *La Domenica del Corriere: Il novecento illustrato* (Milan: Skira, 2007), 17–27. Blackburn's fingers had been amputated after he had almost frozen to death in a previous boating accident.

**Fig. 2.6.** Cover of *La Domenica del Corriere*, 23 June 1901; the illustration is dedicated to Howard Blackburn's single crossing of the Atlantic. (courtesy of Biblioteca di Storia Moderna e Contemporanea, Rome)

and playwrights at the time. The second, *America vittoriosa*, the collection of Ugo Ojetti's correspondence, came out in 1899.[46]

Giacosa had travelled to the USA to discuss the staging of one of his plays, and his movements were confined to the cities of New York and Chicago. His descriptions of the two metropolises move constantly between two extremes: on the one

---

[46] Giuseppe Giacosa, *Impressioni d'America* (Milan: Cogliati, 1898); the book collects essays previously published in *Nuova antologia* in 1892 and 1893. Ugo Ojetti, *America vittoriosa* (Milan: Treves, 1899).

hand, a sense of patronizing superiority towards America's lack of a historical past, as evidenced by its urban architecture and its citizens' habits; on the other, a sense of admiration for the entrepreneurial and optimistic spirit that seemed to pervade America's urban life. The modernity of the skyline inspired a similarly ambivalent response, which could be defined as a sort of 'admiring rejection'. These are the years in which Chicago and New York began to rival each other in constructing high-rise buildings, the forefathers of the fully-fledged skyscrapers of the early twentieth century. Chicago was then slightly ahead, although the year after Giacosa's visit New York staked its claim to the world's tallest building with the construction of the Park Row Building, the first high rise in the two cities that was more than 100 metres high (391 feet). Giacosa defined them as 'Babel-like masses that attack the Chicago sky with a boldness bordering on madness'.[47] Later on in the book, however, his criticism is literally juxtaposed to a show of appreciation:

> At first sight the city looked abominable; reflecting on it I recognized it as admirable beyond words. I would not want to live there for all the money in the world; I believe that those who ignore it will not be able fully to understand our century, of which it is the ultimate expression.[48]

Fig. 2.7. Chicago's and New York's early skyscapers at the end of the nineteenth century. On the left, a postcard image of Chicago's Luminous Reliance Building, completed in 1895; on the right, New York's Park Row Building, completed in 1899. (respectively, courtesy of Thomas Leslie and author's personal collection)

---

[47] Giacosa, *Impressioni d'America*, 50.    [48] Giacosa, *Impressioni d'America*, 199.

As we know, Ugo Ojetti also limited his American stay to the north-east. During his visit to the federal capital, Ojetti was particularly struck by the ambitious attempts of the US government to assert the country's status by challenging Europe in architectural construction. The building that attracted him most was the Library of Congress (today known as the Thomas Jefferson Building). After it had opened, in November 1897, Ojetti was one of the first Italian intellectuals to visit it:

> When, on Capitol Hill, one walks past the flower beds and the sycamore trees that take you from the Congress building (the US Capitol) to the Library of Congress, one has the clearest proof not only of the strength and ambition of this new people, but also of their intellectual potential, which is only known to us thanks to a few amazing industrial discoveries from Fulton to Edison, thanks to two or three poets who show a virile and wild originality such as Whitman, Emerson, or Poe, thanks to two or three acute and balanced philosophers such as W. James or Baldwin, or thanks to two or three intensely modern and descriptive painters such as Sargent or Vedder, to name only the extreme poles.[49]

Ojetti here pays homage to the buildings as much as to the humanistic culture of the USA. At the same time, the description is somehow counterbalanced by

**Fig. 2.8.** The Library of Congress Building (renamed Thomas Jefferson Building in 1980), which was built in 1890–7. (author's personal collection)

---

[49] Ojetti, *America vittoriosa*, 117.

the repetition of 'two or three', which adds the sense of a fledgling culture, still green in its offshoots. America cannot yet boast a great tradition of artists: at most they have 'two or three' good writers, 'two or three' good philosophers, 'two or three' good painters. Even when it comes to praising American scientific discoveries, the adverb *mirabolante* ('amazing') adds a fairground 'americanata' flavour to the description. A few lines further, Ojetti's line of thought comes to the fore:

> This immense and luxurious building, which was finished yesterday (1888–1897) at a cost of thirty millions, with a Treasure of almost one million volumes and almost three hundred thousand prints, possesses something miraculous in the vertiginous speed of its construction, a speed that frightens our Latin minds, more used to the slow and centuries-long stratifications of science and art. All their anxious thirst to know, to know a lot, of knowledge, to know everything that has been thought and dreamt of in the world, completely, dominating the past and the future since the present is already well within their grasp, all this is clearly manifested here, in all its frenetic and almost childish exaggeration and at the same time in all the beauty of its noble, superior or, untamable desire.[50]

On the one hand, Ojetti clearly comprehended America's towering economic power; on the other, his condescending attitude is epitomized by the adjective *puerile* ('childish'). Add to this that Italy is later presented as the ultimate repository of Classical and Christian culture, and it is no surprise that Ojetti's eventually commented: 'In truth, Rome lies further from America than geography suggests.'[51]

A later and more extreme example comes from a work by Alberto Pecorini, an Italian journalist who settled in New York at the turn of the century. In 1909 Pecorini published a hefty volume dedicated to the USA, which was part of a series devoted to foreign cultures by Treves. It was entitled *Gli americani nella vita moderna osservati da un italiano* ('Americans in Modern Life as Seen by an Italian'). When dealing with the arts, Pecorini not only shared the argument of the superiority of Italians' *senso del bello* ('perception of beauty'); his protests reached a peak in demanding that even the teaching of art history should be left entirely in Latin hands—that is, lecturing on Italian literature and fine arts in American universities should be the preserve of scholars from Italy.[52]

Pecorini's and Ojetti's views were also infused by the centuries-old notion of a clear division between Germanic and Latin civilizations. The latter saw this as part of a necessary Renaissance of Italian culture, which could be reached only through a rejection of the positivistic, 'Germanic' mindset that had dominated in preceding decades. American society was seen as reproducing in the extreme the

---

[50] Ojetti, *America vittoriosa*, 118.   [51] Ojetti, *America vittoriosa*, 131.
[52] Alberto Pecorini, *Gli americani nella vita moderna osservati da un italiano* (Milan: Treves, 1909), 404.

virtues and vices of Germanic culture. And, when it came to questions of morality, Protestant was synonymous with Germanic.

Economist and sociologist Vilfredo Pareto had no doubts in drawing a clear distinction between Germanic and Latin culture. According to Pareto's essay of 1911, American culture was a clear example of the internal contradictions of Protestant morality: it legislated according to strict Protestant principles and at the same time allowed its younger generation—particularly women—to run wild as a consequence of their liberty of movement and thought generated by America's economic wealth. It was a view that, as we will see in later chapters, was to resonate well into the interwar years.[53]

But what about the presence of the Italian immigrant community? Until then, Adolfo Rossi's books were the only ones that had tackled this reality armed with facts and a non-nationalistic attitude. In this respect, it is important to note that, in the few pages that Rossi added to the new edition of *Nacociù, la Venere americana*, in its 1892 edition for Treves re-entitled *Un italiano in America*, he had written at length on New York's Five Points area and strongly denounced the brutal exploitation of poor immigrants on the part of fellow countrymen who acted as agents of labour.[54] Consistent with his interest in the social impact of migration, once he had left his journalistic career, Rossi was to take up the job of inspector for Italy's eventually created government Directorate for Migration (the Commissariato generale dell'emigrazione), in 1902.

At the turn of the century, mass migration to the USA had reached a size that could hardly be ignored, particularly in the big industrial cities in the north-east. In his writings, however, Pareto ignored the topic; and, despite his three-month-long American experience, Ojetti too avoided the topic. He confirmed this attitude in a shorter book on the USA that he published in 1905, entitled *L'America e l'avvenire*. His treatment of American culture makes it clear that he considered the USA to be a country characterized entirely by Protestant, Anglo-Saxon culture, to the exclusion of all other influences.[55]

Giuseppe Giacosa, on the other hand, devoted the final three chapters of his book to Italian migrants. We must remember that he was writing during the months following one of the most traumatic events in the early history of the Italian community: the lynching of eleven Italian immigrants in New Orleans during the night of 14 March 1891. The reason behind the lynching was the presumption that they had somehow been involved in the murder of David Hennessy, the city's head of police, five months earlier. Hennessy had been investigating the feud between two Sicilian families, the Provenzano and Matranga, suspected of fighting

---

[53] Vilfredo Pareto, 'Il mito virtuista e la letteratura immorale', first pub. in French as *Le Mythe vertuiste et la literature immorale* (Paris: Rivière, 1911); rev., trans., and pub. in Italian in 1914; now in Pareto, *Scritti sociologici* (Turin: UTET, 1966), 481–652.

[54] Rossi, *Un italiano in America*, 67–9.

[55] Ugo Ojetti, *L'America e l'avvenire* (Milan: Treves, 1905).

for control over the docks in relation to the imported fruit trade. The mass lynching of suspects who had only just been found not guilty in court caused open tension between the Italian and US government. It also revealed the strength of anti-Italian sentiment at the time. Indeed, the American press was largely sympathetic to the lynching.[56] Without mentioning any specific event, Giacosa took a strongly defensive stance on behalf of the Italian immigrant community:

> The bad reputation of Italians in the big cities derives mainly from the sobriety of their behaviour and from their frugality. [...] The main accusation that Americans throw at Italian migrants concerns both their sordid, degrading and incurable abstinence, and their willingness to accept the most humble and vulgar and lowly-paid jobs.[57]

Giacosa did not refrain from describing the squalor in which many Italians lived, both in New York and in Chicago, but, even in those circumstances, his aim was to defend the honour of the Italian migrant:

> Such miserable spectacles can be found only in those few streets in which the scum of Italian migration accumulates, which is in any way a hundred times more preferable to the Irish scum, whose degradation derives from vice and not, as it happens with ours, from virtues gone desperate, from economic prejudices, and from lack of education.[58]

Giacosa's patriotism is detectable throughout the three chapters, to the point that the last one—which is also the concluding chapter of the book—is entirely devoted to a biographical sketch of two Italian migrants who brought fame and honour to their mother country. The first is Florentine Antonio Meucci, unrecognized inventor of the telephone and briefly employer in his candle factory of the then fugitive Giuseppe Garibaldi. The second is the less known Piedmontese Count Luigi Palma di Cesnola, who, after a brilliant military career during the Civil War, later became a diplomat and an archeologist, before finally being appointed the first director of New York's Metropolitan Museum of Art in 1879.

A few years earlier than Giacosa, another Italian traveller with a literary reputation as a librettist, had tackled the subject in a very similar way. This is the already mentioned Ferdinando Fontana. The last chapter of his *New York* is dedicated to

---

[56] The New Orleans lynching of Italian migrants was not the only, nor was it destined to be the last, of these episodes. Thirty-nine Italians were murdered in similar circumstances between 1879 and 1910. On the lynching of Italians in nineteenth-century USA, see Patrizia Salvetti, *Corda e sapone: Storie di linciaggi di italiani negli Stati Uniti* (Milan: Donzelli, 2003); and Jessica Barbata Jackson, *Dixie's Italians: Sicilians, Race and Citizens in the Jim Crow Gulf South* (Baton Rouge, LA: Louisiana State University Press, 2020).
[57] Giacosa, *Impressioni d'America*, 166.    [58] Giacosa, *Impressioni d'America*, 186.

the Italian community. After having described the miserable state of the Italian immigrants in the Five Points neighbourhood, Fontana first praised the Italians in comparison with another community at the margins of society, the Irish, and later defended them from the accusation of resorting too easily to the use of knives, with the contention that their violence is simply a justified act of self-defence.[59] As Giacosa did, Fontana too ended the chapter with a narrative of successful Italians who were able to prove the virtues and values of the Italian people.

Once we move beyond the turn of the century, the patriotic attitude towards Italian migration continues. A detailed account of the USA in the very early twentieth century comes from Vico Mantegazza, a travel writer and journalist, then chief editor of Florence's daily, *La Nazione*. His *Agli Stati Uniti: Il pericolo americano* ('On the United States: The American Danger') was published in 1910 by Treves.[60] Mantegazza travelled much more extensively than Ojetti and Giacosa, spending in particular a few weeks in Texas. This relatively unexploited and unpopulated territory allowed Mantegazza to dwell on the possibility of Italian migrants settling there and achieving a similar social status to the earlier waves of migrants from the British Isles and from Germany, who had formed the land-owning backbone of other US states. He also saw it as a way of combating the risk of Italian migrants being swallowed up by the exploitative world of New York and Chicago, where they had little opportunity for social and economic progress.

These hopes were shared by others; indeed, the establishment of a small community of Italian migrants in the village on which Mantegazza concentrates, Dickinson, came as a result of the initiative of the local Consular Agent of the Italian government. What is more revealing, however, is the way in which the author almost totally ignores the fact that Italian immigration in the Southern states had already been going on for decades, and episodes like the New Orleans lynching had shown the very low regard in which Italian migrants were held. The parallel between the treatment of African Americans and Italian migrants in the Southern states is also carefully avoided in Mantegazza's chapter on the state of the black population in post-Civil War USA. This is particularly revealing when he discusses the life of the renowned black activist Booker T. Washington, to whom a whole five pages are devoted. Since by then Washington had already published his autobiography, (*Up from Slavery*, 1901), Mantegazza was able to include a number of biographical details, particularly in relation to Washington's childhood as a slave in south-west Virginia. However, while he mentions the fact that Washington was a mulatto, he adds that 'he does not know anything about his family'.[61] In fact, Washington never made a mystery of the fact that his natural

---

[59] Fontana and Papa, *New York*, 188–93.
[60] Vico Mantegazza, *Agli Stati Uniti: Il pericolo americano* (Milan: Treves, 1910). The title of the book is strongly reminiscent of one of the most vocal anti-American books published in France in the wake of the Hispanic-American war: Octave de Noël, *Le Péril américaine* (Paris: De Soye et Fils, 1899).
[61] Mantegazza, *Agli Stati Uniti*, 98.

father was an Italian named Taliaferro, who lived in a neighbouring plantation. He never met him, but when he found out about him from his mother, as he explains in his autobiography, he decided to pay testimony to his origin by adding the T. of Taliaferro to the surname of his stepfather, Washington. Mantegazza simply ignores this significant detail and eliminates any potential association with Italy by removing the 'T.' altogether.[62]

Even more intriguing are Mantegazza's considerations on the crime of lynching. Despite the fact that in the preceding pages he had presented a factual description of the past and present segregation of the black community, when it comes to lynching Mantegazza adopts a surprisingly accommodating stance. In short, after presenting Booker Washington as an example of a virtuous black man, Mantegazza proceeds to judge him as an exception to the perceived intellectual and moral inferiority of African Americans:

> This is too little to prove the capacity for regeneration of the black race in America.
>
> Black people here, like everywhere, are depraved drunkards, with no feeling at all for their families. They swap their women like animals, and if it were not for the fact that they live in the countryside and that they are very prolific, the question of the negroes would cease to exist because, little by little, their numbers would dwindle and eventually disappear. A negro man is unable to save. He spends all he has, in liquor and overindulgence, and, when he is drunk, he is prey to the lowest instincts, so much so that no threat or certainty of punishment—nearly always in the form of hanging and lynching—can stop him. It must be said that almost every day newspapers contain the news of some negro being lynched by the crowd because he raped—and often raped and killed—a white woman.[63]

It is possible that the censorship of Booker Washington's 'T.' was part of Mantegazza's careful avoidance of the fact that the status of Italian migrants in the Southern states was not far from that of the community that only a few years before had been freed from slavery. A similar attempt to defend the identity and dignity of Italian migrants, this time by asserting their alleged superiority over other subaltern communities such as the Chinese, African, and Native American, can be found in another traveller to the Southern states, the diplomat Edmondo Mayor des Planches.[64]

---

[62] The surname Taliaferro originates from Tagliaferro or Tagliaferri, an Italian surname typical of the north Italian regions. The history of the Taliaferro in the USA is peculiar. They became a prominent family in Maryland and Virginia, originating from a Taliaferro who migrated in the seventeenth century from London, where the family name appears as early as 1562. By the nineteenth century, various Taliaferro households had become established and wealthy landowners in the USA. It is likely, therefore, that Booker T. Washington's natural father was not so much a poor Italian migrant but, rather, a wealthy landowner.

[63] Mantegazza, *Agli Stati Uniti*, 99–100.

[64] Edmondo Mayor des Planches, *Attraverso gli Stati Uniti: Per l'emigrazione italiana* (Turin: Unione Tipografica Torinese, 1913; see in particular pp. 48–59). See also Matteo Sanfilippo, 'La grande

As for the explicit racism directed towards African Americans, Mantegazza's views were uncomfortably widespread. Alberto Pecorini, mentioned above, devoted an entire chapter to America's black population entitled 'Black Blood'. In no uncertain terms, Pecorini presented their emancipation at the end of the Civil War as a disastrous reform that had not only wrecked the economy of the Southern states but had backfired against the black population, since 'in practice it did not abolish their economic slavery and brought on them a feeling of hatred that did not exist before'.[65] It follows that Pecorini too seems to ignore the lynching episodes involving Italians of a few years before and comes instead to a lenient view of this practice, commenting that it was triggered by the increase in crimes against white women perpetrated by black males.

Another chapter of Pecorini's book is dedicated to Italian migrants. Here, like that of Mantegazza and others, his representation of the degrading conditions in which many migrants live in the slums of the big metropolises, is counterbalanced by the argument that it should be the responsibility of local American administrations to tackle what is—as he calls it—an 'Italo-Americano' issue.[66] Something similar is done by the *Corriere della Sera*'s most prestigious non-resident correspondent at the time, Luigi Barzini. During the months he spent in the USA, in 1908, Barzini wrote two articles that are interesting in this respect. On 22 April 1908, he wrote about violence against Italian immigrants in Virginia, and on 8 September he discussed the lynching of African Americans. In the first case, Barzini was careful to specify that the gunshot attack at the lodgings of Italian workers on the part of an illegal militia had nothing to do with racism. It was the result of tensions following the economic crisis. At the same time, in a long article about lynching, Barzini treated it as the consequence of the uncivilized nature of the African American population. The second part of Barzini's article presented an apology of lynching. First he deplored the emancipation of black slaves and considered it the root of the hatred they were subjected to because of their newly acquired powers as voters; then he denied that better education could lift them socially; finally he came to the conclusion that lynching was a necessary evil:

> Like ferocious mastiffs around a vast herd of wild animals, lynchers keep a close watch on the negroes. The terror they maintain creates a boundary between the two races. Their task is hateful but necessary. Woe betide us the day in which negroes have no more fear![67]

emigrazione nelle pagine dei viaggiatori', in Sebastiano Martelli (ed.), *Il sogno italo-americano: Realtà e immaginario dell'emigrazione negli Stati Uniti* (Naples: CUEN, 1998), 351–76.

[65] Pecorini, *Gli americani nella vita moderna*, 300.
[66] Pecorini, *Gli americani nella vita moderna*, 398.
[67] Luigi Barzini, 'I "cavalieri della notte" alla caccia degli italiani', and 'Bianchi e neri', *Corriere della Sera*, 5 April 1908, p. 5, and 5 September 1908, p. 3.

Barzini too, in order to adopt a position that was sympathetic to lynching, had to omit the fact that Italian immigrants had been subject to it.

At this point it would be appropriate to wonder whether the anti-African American sentiment present in these authors was somehow connected to Italy's colonial efforts in Africa, which had started in the mid-1880s and had been marked by humiliating defeats against Abyssinian troops first at Dogali (1887) and then at Adwa (1896). It was, after all, the first time in which the Italian nation had been directly involved in a confrontation with a community originating from Africa. Among the works considered here whose publication post-dates the battles of Dogali and Adwa, none of them makes a connection between the African American community and Italy's colonial struggles, which are never mentioned. Only Ojetti, in his 1905 essay, dares to allude to Italy's tragic embarrassments in Africa, but does so with a revealing rhetorical style. Before a long defence of Latin culture, he briefly lists the arguments of philo-American authors—unnamed—who decry the decadence of Latin culture by referring to recent historical events such as: France being defeated by Germany, Greece by Turkey, Spain by the USA, and Italy by Abyssinia. Only, this opinion is qualified as 'the stupidity of chance and prophesies!', and therefore dismissed. Beyond this brief reference, Ojetti makes no other mention of Italy's colonial efforts, nor does he ever refer to the African American community. This is consistent with his view of American society: populated by Anglo-Saxons, with the existence of millions of African Americans and Italian Americans discreetly left out of the picture.[68]

To return now to the subtitle of Mantegazza's book, 'The American Danger', this forms the subject matter of his final chapter, in which the author warns his readers against the rising economic and military power of the USA. It is a recognition of America's rising strength, which, paradoxically, is constantly accompanied by a sense of superiority. America is a nation of *parvenus*, naïve, savage, childlike citizens, a nation of former peasants. Mantegazza's attitude reaches a sarcastic peak when he dwells on America's potential for an autonomous cultural identity:

> Little by little they are also forging an English language of their own, and, who knows, there are those who seriously think that, given all that can be done and achieved with dollars, there is the possibility that they will manufacture a Shakespeare or a local Byron so that they shall no longer be indebted to Europe even from the point of view of literature and culture![69]

---

[68] Ojetti, *L'America e l'avvenire*, 17.
[69] Mantegazza, Vico, *Agli Stati Uniti*, 325–6.

Mantegazza's final comment is exemplary of this overview of the perception of the USA in the Italian press and travel literature of the early twentieth century. By then, no Italian intellectual could deny the great economic power of the USA. However, when it came to the cultural sphere, they asserted the vast superiority of the old continent.

Ojetti too accused Americans of simply emulating European culture, and disparaged their original contributions, such as skyscrapers, as sterile, since they lacked 'the notion of eternity that we, Mediterranean people, possess'. Indeed, Ojetti comes to the conclusion that Europeans should not worry about the USA, since their people's character will soon develop Latin traits. Such metamorphosis is seen by Ojetti not as a consequence of the increasing presence of southern European migrants but, rather, as part of the process of refinement of every civilization.[70]

A more militant interest towards Italian migration was to be found in Italian Catholic circles. The main thrust came from the bishop of the northern city of Piacenza, Monsignor Giovanni Battista Scalabrini. Born in 1839 near Lake Como, in a family of eight children, two of whom were to migrate to the Americas, Scalabrini became deeply involved in the provision of aid to the masses of Italian migrants around the world. Papal support allowed Scalabrini to create first a male (1888) and then a female (1895) missionary order for the purpose. Named after San Carlo Borromeo, but commonly known as 'Scalabriniani', the orders quickly set up a network reaching the main destination cities around the world. New York was among the first. Scalabrini's writings were influential in bringing the Italian elite to a more open and humane attitude towards migration. It is no coincidence that the first legislation by the Italian government fully to address the question of migration, in 1901 (tackling the flaws of the 1888 law on migration), came in the wake of Scalabrini's constant denunciation of the need to protect migrants abroad.[71]

At the same time, the Catholic church had developed its own vision of the USA. Right up until the beginning of the twentieth century, the Vatican defined America as missionary territory. Indeed, the defence of the welfare and religious faith of Italian migrants was Bishop Scalabrini's main aim, rather than their integration into American society. This created tensions with Catholic hierarchies in the USA, which were mainly of Irish origin. Moreover, in the same years, the US Catholic church had come under scrutiny from the Vatican for its unorthodox tendencies, which were deemed to be the result of the influence of a Protestant-dominated, pluralist, materialistic society. The critique came to a head in 1899 with the encyclical *Testem benevolentiae nostrae* ('Witness to

---

[70] Ojetti, *L'America e l'avvenire*, 25.
[71] On Scalabrini, see Mark I. Choate, *Emigrant Nation: The Making of Italy Abroad* (Cambridge, MA: Harvard University Press, 2008), 129–37; Silvano Tomasi (ed.), *For the Love of Immigrants: Migration Writings and Letters of Bishop John Baptist Scalabrini* (New York: Center for Migration Studies, 2000).

our Good Will') by Pope Leo XIII to Cardinal James Gibbons, Archbishop of Baltimore. In his letter, the Pope warned US bishops about the dangers of 'Americanism'—that is, a move away from the spiritual rulings of the Roman Catholic Church in order to seek a smoother assimilation in American society. In conclusion, if, on the one hand, the Vatican was denouncing the way in which the Italian elite ignored the phenomenon of migration, on the other, through the concept of 'Americanism', it contributed to the perception of the USA as the country that embodied the virtues and vices of Protestant modernity—that is, materialistic values that were essentially non-Catholic, and by extension non-Italian.[72]

Finally, we should return to a factor that played a major role in the perception of the USA: the lack of coverage by resident correspondents. In 1886, when involved in the set-up of New York's Italian newspaper, *Il Progresso Italo-Americano*, Adolfo Rossi mentioned the lack of journalists who could write in Italian. Two years later, Giuseppe Sormani echoed these views by lamenting that no Italian newspaper had a correspondent in the USA.[73] Indeed, journalists were sent over to cover prominent events such as the Civil War in the 1860s or the Spanish–American war of 1898, but, until 1909, no Italian newspaper seemed to think that the USA deserved constant journalistic coverage. Even on the occasion of a historic and much publicized event such as the inauguration of the State of Liberty, on 28 October 1886, which saw hundreds of thousands of New Yorkers cheer the parade led by President Cleveland, the *Corriere della Sera* published an article the following day that began with the complaint that Italy's main news agency, the Agenzia Stefani, had not bothered to circulate even a single news dispatch concerning the event.[74]

The creation of the first position of resident correspondent in New York is part of the history of the *Corriere della Sera* during its reshaping at the hands of volcanic Luigi Albertini, who, at only 29 years old, succeeded Torelli Viollier as director, in July 1900. These are the years in which the *Corriere della Sera* surpassed *Il Secolo* as Italy's most popular newspaper and established itself as the most authoritative voice on foreign news. Before taking his post at the helm, Albertini had worked for a few months in 1894 as an apprentice at London's *The Times*, and four years later, by then a *Corriere della Sera* employee, he had

---

[72] On this, see Ornella Confessore, *L'americanismo cattolico in Italia* (Rome: Edizioni Studium, 1984).
[73] Sormani, *Eco d'America*, 15–16. Rossi's reference to the lack of journalists writing in Italian comes from *Nacociù, la venere americana*, 98.
[74] The anonymous, front-page article in *Corriere della Sera*, 29–30 October 1886, was entitled 'La statua della Libertà a New York' and contained statistical data about the history and construction of the statue. It should be noted that, oddly, in France too the event was not treated by the press as significant; hence it is possible that Havas did not pass on any news items related to the event to the Agenzia Stefani. On the French press, see Roger, *The American Enemy*, 101–4.

travelled through France, Germany, and England in order to assess the best printing set-up. He came to the conclusion that *The Times* represented a leading example and, indeed, its headquarters provided the model for the *Corriere della Sera*'s historic site in Milan's Via Solferino, built in 1903. However, when it came to printing technology, Albertini decided that it had to be American, and Hoe's printed presses were imported from New York (as *The Times* itself had done). This technological innovation allowed the *Corriere della Sera* to add more pages, moving from the traditional four of nineteenth-century dailies, to eight and eventually ten in 1910. It also allowed Albertini to create a more informative and diverse paper. Foreign news was gathered though collaborative deals with leading European papers—the first ones being Paris's *Le Matin* and London's *The Times*—and, equally, Albertini invested in the creation of a network of correspondents.[75]

We have already met Luigi Barzini, who, in 1908, was an 'inviato speciale' in the USA. His fame had peaked with his coverage of the legendary automobile race Bejing–Paris, launched in 1907 by *Le Matin* and won by the Italian car in which Barzini travelled as a journalist–passenger (all five cars in the race had one, so that they could telegraph news of their progress). Few remember, however, that, when Barzini joined the Itala crew in Bejing, he was coming from San Francisco. Barzini's previous assignment had been an American one. He had reached New York in April 1907 to report on the trial of the year: millionaire Harry Thaw had murdered renowned architect Stanford White in the rooftop restaurant of Madison Square Garden (which White himself had designed) to defend the honour of his wife, fashion model and future Hollywood star Evelyn Nesbit. Crossing the country to catch a ship that would carry him to China for his following assignment must have wet Barzini's appetite for a more extensive coverage of the USA. After the Bejing–Paris race and a few weeks' rest, Barzini returned to New York in December 1908. Among the items to report there was the first 'American scandal' within Italy's royal family. This relates to the adventurous and carefree life of Luigi Amedeo di Savoia, better known as the Duca degli Abruzzi (a first cousin of King Victor Emmanuel III). The Duca degli Abruzzi was a navy officer who was renowned for his adventurous feats as an alpinist and explorer. In 1908 he had become engaged to Katherine Elkins, daughter of a rich American senator, Stephen Benton Elkins. The two had met in 1907 in Washington, at a private event organized by President Theodore Roosevelt. The papers' gossip was rife with innuendos about opposition from within the royal family and accusations against the duke, presented as a 'dowry-grabber'. Barzini defended the Italian aristocrat from any accusation and announced that, according to his insiders' confidential information, Miss Elkins and the duke were due to be happily married in

---

[75] On Albertini, see Lorenzo Benadusi, *Il Corriere della Sera di Luigi Albertini: Nascita e sviluppo della prima industria culturale di massa* (Rome: Aracne, 2012).

the autumn. History was to prove him wrong, since the two never tied the knot and eventually parted ways in 1912.[76] Barzini was to remain in the USA until November 1908, travelling through the country to report on FIAT cars competing in American motor races, aviation events, the winning presidential campaign by William Howard Taft, and the Italianate premiere of *Aida* with Toscanini and Caruso at the Metropolitan opera house (more on this in Chapter 4).

After his second stint in the USA, Barzini moved back to Europe. Luigi Albertini, however, must have thought that the time had come to have a resident correspondent in New York. His choice fell on Felice Ferrero, who in the previous months had been the *Corriere della Sera*'s correspondent in Berlin. Ferrero's first article appeared on 24 February 1909, praising the military might of the US fleet coming back home after its tour of the world. After that, Ferrero almost metronomically sent one or two articles per month. When he paid a visit to President Taft, the latter openly praised the *Corriere della Sera*'s decision, saying that a resident correspondent would allow Italians to be better informed about America and would 'give a less legendary and fantastic colour to news about Americans; to know better what Italian migrants do here, since, for their mother country, they are like a part of their population which disappeared into the unknown'.

Whether Ferrero managed to fulfil this augur is doubtful. If one reads his articles published between 1909 and the First World War, what emerges is a certain scornful and ironic detachment from both American society and the Italian migrant community. When he dwells on the latter in one of his early articles, it is difficult not to perceive a touch of class-related snobbery: the masses of semi-illiterate migrants are dismissed as brutes, because they are either ignorant, or incompetent (the best ones have moved on in search for work and opportunities), or criminals; and, he adds: 'if one could make a statistic out of how many of them have learnt to use soap before leaving certain savage and unfortunate parts of Italy, there would not be much to count'. At the same time, Ferrero showers the Italian consul and his wife with praise for their organization of refined charity events. His treatment of organized crime in New York's Little Italy also deserves particular attention.

The question of the existence and activities of the *Mano Nera* (Black Hand)— the extortion racket linked to the Italian American communities—had been mainly ignored by Italian authors, in both book and press articles. What brought it to the fore was the murder of NYPD Lieutenant Giuseppe Petrosino on the evening of 12 April 1909. Petrosino was in Palermo, investigating past convictions of Italian American criminals, hoping to find sufficient evidence to deport them back to Italy. The murder of Petrosino took place during Ferrero's watch as correspondent at the *Corriere della Sera*, but the two long articles published on 14 April

---

[76] Luigi Barzini, 'La fantasia dei giornalisti americani', *Corriere della Sera*, 22 April 1908, p. 3.

did not see his involvement. The first, as one would expect, was written from Palermo, but the second, which gave a very informative picture of Petrosino's work in his battle against New York's Black Hand, was signed 'l.b.'. Its content confirms that the initials stand for Luigi Barzini. The article begins with Barzini recalling a casual conversation with Petrosino in which the latter had asked him to write about organized crime in the Italian community and invited him to visit him at NYPD's central office. Barzini never took up the proposal, but he claims that he had started to research the matter and had accumulated potentially explosive evidence about criminal acts in the Mulberry Street area during the early months of 1908. The article spells out a number of examples, and Barzini admits that, at the time, 'I recoiled from it with a mixture of horror and shame'. His article of 1909 was somehow a reparation for his past reluctance.[77]

Felice Ferrero took a different view. When Petrosino's body was taken back to New York and given a state funeral on 12 April that saw two thousand NYPD officers join the procession and more than a hundred thousand people behind it, the *Corriere della Sera* devoted only a brief, anonymous piece on it, which was actually an excerpt from an article run by London's *Daily Telegraph*. Ferrero did not touch upon Black Hand crime until more than a year later. This took the unusual shape of two articles published on 11 and 23 August 1910. In the first article Ferrero begins by casting doubt on the actual size of the phenomenon. He suggests that many cases of arson or explosions attributed to the Black Hand are in fact insurance-money frauds organized by the alleged victims themselves. He then concentrates on the phenomenon of *omertà* ('code of silence') on the part of the immigrant population, who, being mainly southerners, are well used, he tells us, to similar exploitations by the Camorra and the Mafia. Two weeks later, Ferrero met a Sicilian doctor whose son had been kidnapped by the Black Hand. The doctor had given up on the police and was waiting for the right time to come to an understanding with the criminals. Here Ferrero returns to a drastic class-based distinction, whereby the doctor and his wife are described as dignified representatives of Italy's educated middle-class, surrounded by the squalid rabble, which knocks at his door to be seen by him, some of whom are probably the gang's informers and know very well who the culprits are and where the boy is kept in hiding.

Ferrero did not return to the subject after these two articles, but a similar class-based distinction is at the root of a piece he wrote a few months later about the cost of living in New York. The prompt to his piece was a public inquiry that concentrated on the population struggling around the poverty line. According to Ferrero, however, 'the real victims of New York, the abused and maltreated slaves',

---

[77] l.b. [Luigi Barzini], 'Petrosino e la mano nera', *Corriere della Sera*, 14 March 1909, p. 3.

are the middle classes, as they cannot afford the space and comforts that their status deserves.[78]

On the whole, Ferrero concentrated on the Anglo-Saxon elite, with profiles of famous politicians and businessmen, with a penchant for their gala evenings at the Metropolitan opera, which gave him a chance to write about the opera season and praise the work of Arturo Toscanini. When he was dealing with successful Americans, Ferrero's tone was never free from condescending irony. President Taft is described as a 'fanciullo ben nutrito' ('a well-fed child') and the Oval Office as a place more typical of the studio of a commercial firm. And when he meets an ageing J. P. Morgan (caricatured into 'signor Geppi'), who by then works from the monumental library in his New York mansion, Ferrero describes his collection of rare books and manuscripts as pristine, since in that house 'nobody reads, and in all probability nobody knows how to read'. Ferrero's articles are also peppered with slightly misogynistic undertones, as, for example, when he describes in ironic tones a strike by women workers in the clothing industry or when, at the end of the account of his visit to J.P. Morgan, he devotes the final paragraph to Morgan's dog, who, Ferrero tells us, hates women. The animal is described as being friendly to all the men in the house while snubbing the female red-haired librarian who looks after the manuscripts. This, he tells us in the final line of the article, is proof that the dog is 'a beast gifted with reason'.[79] For a more open-minded resident correspondent, readers had to wait until *La Stampa* decided to add its own man in New York, Amerigo Ruggiero, twenty years later.

## 2.2 America Comes to Italy: William Cody's Wild West

The combination of admiration for the American entrepreneurial sway and a patronizing attitude towards its culture found a perfect embodiment in the most famous American show that toured Europe at the turn of the century: the Wild West. Buffalo Bill is today synonymous with the open spaces, rough living, and violent conflict of the western frontier. In the late nineteenth century, his persona was the result of William Cody's success in building a legendary narrative around his own life. He did so in a grandiose manner, bringing to Europe a complex, itinerant machine for mass entertainment.

---

[78] Felice Ferrero, 'La mano nera', Corriere della Sera, 11 and 23 August 1910, p. 3, and 'Gli accampamenti cittadini', 3 February 1911, p. 3. The theme of kidnapping by Italian *mafiosi* provided the narrative thread to a major American film production of 1916: *Poor Little Peppina*, directed by Sidney Olcott and featuring Mary Pickford and America's best Italian actors at the time—Antonio Maiori and Cesare Gravina. On this, see Giuliana Muscio, *Naples/New York/Hollywood: Film between Italy and the United States* (New York: Fordham University Press, 2019), 29–31.

[79] Felice Ferrero, 'Battaglia di donne', 'Geppi', Corriere della Sera, 28 January 1910, p. 3, and 3 February 1910, p. 3.

Four trains were used in order to transport his hundreds of staff and horses and all the props and structures from one city to the next. The show's arrival in each new town was a master class in logistics on a massive, almost military scale. Bill Cody's 'American' flair for publicity would also take over the printed press with a welter of initiatives, from adverts in local papers, to interviews and publicity stunts—including having a group of his Native Americans climb the Eiffel Tour at the 1889 World Exhibition. In this respect, Bill Cody himself was the perfect embodiment of the American businessman in the minds of the European intelligentsia: a man of limited education, who nevertheless showed exceptional skills in managing a daring, ambitious business.

The first Italian leg of Bill Cody's European tours was relatively brief. Between January and April 1890, Bill Cody's trains visited six major cities: Naples, Rome, Florence, Bologna, Verona, and Milan. He was to return sixteen years later, this time reaching no less than thirty-five Italian cities between March and May 1906. According to the local press, on both occasions the show was sold out almost everywhere.[80] The most memorable of Bill Cody's Italian stunts was in Rome in

Fig. 2.9. Bill Cody with four Native American chiefs in a Venetian gondola, during a pause in his first Italian tour in 1890. (courtesy of the Buffalo Bill Centre of the West, Cody WY)

---

[80] On Bill Cody's Italian shows, see the informative Mario Busoni, *Buffalo Bill in Italia: L'epopea del Wild West Show* (Fidenza: Mattioli 1885, 2011); and the more scholarly Alessandra Magrin, 'Rough

1890, with his visit to the Vatican accompanied by some of his Native Americans, where they received the papal blessing and were challenged to tame wild horses against local *butteri* (the closest Italian equivalent to cowboys), an event that took place south of the city, at Cisterna di Latina. According to the Italian press, the challenge was won by the locals, though, when interviewed, Bill Cody stated the opposite. Every photo opportunity was taken, and the Italian press eagerly played along. This was hardly surprising, given that articles on the Far West and on the wild and exotic practices of America's 'redskins' appeared constantly in Italy's illustrated magazines. On the eve of the Wild West's first visit to Milan in April 1890, *L'Illustrazione popolare* dedicated a long article and two pages of illustrations to the event, presenting it as a great occasion to see a 'coloured race that was on the verge of extinction'.[81]

In some cities it is estimated that about ten thousand people watched the show. This brings us to a relevant question: how wide a cross-section of the local population actually got to watch Cody's show? We know that the price of the 1906 tour

Fig. 2.10. Full-page illustration of a 'Pellerossa' attack on a Wells Fargo stagecoach as re-enacted in Bill Cody's Wild West, from *L'Illustrazione popolare*, 9 March 1890. (courtesy of BSMC, Rome)

Riders in the Cradle of Civilization: Buffalo Bill's Wild West Show in Italy and the Challenge of American Cultural Scarcity at the fin-de-siècle', *European Journal of American Culture*, 36/1 (2017), 23–38; and Luca Cottini, 'Buffalo Bill and the Italian Myth of the American West', in Bonsaver, Carlucci and Reza (eds), *Italy and the USA*, 89–102.
[81] Anon., 'Buffalo-Bill', *L'Illustrazione popolare*, 10 (9 March 1890), 147–9.

ranged from about 1 lira and 20 cents to 8 lire for a reserved seat in the main stand. According to archival data, the minimum gross pay for a qualified worker in a big factory in Turin was, in the same year, 40 cents an hour. This would suggest that the cheapest tickets were affordable to the urban working classes. Indeed, a description of the crowd in a *New York Times* article written after the performances held in Verona on 15–16 April 1890 mentions seeing humbly dressed women attending with babies in their arms.[82] In any case, considering that the street publicity regarding the show is unlikely to have reached beyond the confines of the towns, the vast majority of the audiences were urban dwellers. Newspaper adverts and reviews obviously travelled further, but would have reached only the few educated readers who could easily afford the trip to town to watch the show. Buffalo Bill's Wild West show would, therefore, have had little impact on the image of America in the minds of the millions of Italians who resided in the countryside, many of whom were about to migrate to the Americas. Nonetheless, it was an epoch-making event: for the first time America had come to visit Italy. It was there for everybody to watch, and affordably so. A successful culinary sideshow was provided by the American popcorn and caramel sold by dealers who travelled with the show.

The content of the Wild West should not be written off as pure entertainment. If the birth of American cinema in later years was to be marked by the ambitious epic narratives of D. W. Griffith—I am thinking in particular of *Intolerance* (1916)—Bill Cody's Wild West had a similar penchant for storytelling of biblical proportions. 'The Drama of Civilization' was the ambitious title of the entire narrative of the show, which, divided into five acts, went from 'The Primaeval Forest' in which Native Americans freely roamed the plains, to various stages of occupation by white pioneers, who constantly fought for their survival against repeated attacks by 'Indians'. Towards the end, a dramatic climax was provided by a re-enactment of the historic Battle of the Little Bighorn of June 1876, during which an alliance of Native American tribes led by chief Sitting Bull overcame the troops of General Custer. Symbolically, this marked only a temporary setback in the steamrolling advance of civilization through the plains of America, and, to underscore this, Buffalo Bill would appear once the battle was over with a huge banner saying 'Too Late!'. It was a reminder of Buffalo Bill's role in the history of the conquest of the West: his presence during the war as a scout but also his killing and scalping of the young Cheyenne chief Yellow Hair, the first act of reprisal on the

---

[82] Ticket prices varied slightly in different cities. The cheapest ticket ranged between 1.2 and 2 lire (and 50 cents was the price to visit the Show Annex, which presented a range of Wild West items on display). The figure for workers' pay is specified in the official agreement signed in 1906 by the car manufacturer Itala of Turin and FIOM, the Italian trade union for workers in the metal industry. See 'Contratto Itala-Fiom, 1906', in *Archivio Fiom*, http://archivio.fiom.cgil.it/itala.htm (accessed 2 July 2023). The description of the crowd attending the Verona show can be found in: anon., 'Cowboys in Old Verona', *New York Times*, 18 May 1890, p. 17.

part of the US Army. This gruesome episode was not acted out, but it was narrated and illustrated in the show's programme. Bill Cody preferred instead a narrative of reconciliation, with all riders parading together at the end of the show, Native Americans included, amicably led by Cody himself.[83]

In the 1906 version of the show there was an added part called 'The Congress of Rough Riders of the World'. Cody had opened up to an international outlook, featuring riders from different corners of the world. This part had been introduced in 1893, and by the time it reached Italy the expression 'rough riders' had acquired a political connotation linked to the US Army. 'Rough riders' were what future President Theodore Roosevelt had famously called his cavalry unit during the Hispanic–American war.

Cultural historians have assessed other ways through which the Wild West came to embody contemporary America. First, the ample use of electric lighting in the evening performances added dramatic effect, to say nothing of its function as a technological showcase. Thomas Edison was behind the creation of what was at the time the biggest mobile power unit in the world. Secondly, the presence of

Fig. 2.11. Italian copy of the Wild West programme, 1906: right: internal front page of the programme; left: one of the show's sponsors, the American car and bicycle tyre manufacturer Dunlop. (courtesy of the Buffalo Bill Centre of the West, Cody WY)

---

[83] The archive of the Buffalo Bill Center of the West in Wyoming holds a copy of the eighty-page-long programme printed in Milan for the show. The illustrated pages dedicated to Buffalo Bill's killing and scalping of the young chief are at pp. 39–40. The next section of the programme was dedicated to the weapons used in the Wild West, under the chilling title: 'The rifle is an agent of civilization' (p. 40).

Fig. 2.12. Copy of commemorative postcard of Annie Oakley, c.1885. (author's personal collection)

female characters in the shape of artists and infallible sharpshooters—among them the legendary Annie Oakley—was an example of the much-discussed emancipation of American women. Thirdly, the emergence of the international role of the USA was suggested by the world-encompassing reach of the 'rough riders'. In this respect, as Rydell and Kroes have rightly suggested, Bill Cody was in tune with the rising popularity of world fairs, through which the USA was beginning to show its industrial muscle.[84]

At the same time, we should not underestimate the dominant tone and style of the Wild West: it was an equestrian show with a historical narrative. This played straight into the romanticized view of the USA as a land of vast open spaces and primeval forces. In this sense, the Wild West presented an America that was closer to the colonization of Africa. It was a 'new world', a continent where European pioneers had met a state of nature—and primitive communities—that had disappeared centuries before in the old continent.[85]

---

[84] Rydell and Kroes, *Buffalo Bill in Bologna*, 105–11.

[85] It is also the conclusion reached by historian Daniele Fiorentino in his analysis of the press coverage of Buffalo Bill's first tour. See Daniele Fiorentino, '"Those Red-Brick Faces": European Press Reactions to the Indians of Buffalo Bill's Wild West Show', in Christian Feest (ed.), *Indians and Europe: An Interdisciplinary Collection of Essays* (Aachen: Rader, 1987), 403–14.

The arrival of the railroad in these narratives was symbolic of the civilizing mission that was bringing America into the realm of modernity. But the memory of Custer's humiliating defeat went back only as far as 1876; it was recent history. From this viewpoint, Cottini is right to point to the connection with Italy's own history as a colonizing nation, late on the international stage, and fresh from the humiliating defeats of Dogali and Adwa. The struggles of Far West pioneers and Buffalo Bill's revenge and pacification following the Battle of the Little Bighorn played as a metaphorical, assuaging narrative of Italy's own efforts in the horn of Africa. It also presented a narrative that entirely justified the subjugation of 'barbarous' locals on the part of white-men settlers.[86]

Among Bill Cody's publicity tricks was his routine of asking local journalists to take part as passengers in the scene of the Wells Fargo coach being attacked by 'Indians'. In April 1890, when the Wild West stopped in Verona for the first time, journalist and author Emilio Salgari volunteered to sit inside the coach. In the strangest encounter of Ancient Classical culture with American entertainment, the show was being performed inside the city's well-preserved Roman amphitheatre (it had been Bill Cody's compensation for the disappointment of not being able to use Rome's Colosseum). Salgari was then a young Veronese journalist whose fame as Italy's Jules Verne was only beginning to take shape. At the time, his exotic adventure stories were set in the Far East, but he nonetheless showed good knowledge of the Far West and of the life of Buffalo Bill (or 'Guglielmo il bufalo' as he called him). His review of the Verona show was enthusiastic, though he lamented that the limitations imposed by the size of the Roman arena much reduced the capacity of staging some major acts.[87] A few years later, Salgari was to produce seven novels set in the Far West. The first was *Il re della prateria* (1896), but it is *La sovrana del campo d'oro* (1905) that is considered Salgari's first fully-fledged western novel. The book was published only a few months before the Wild West's second passage through Italy. It is not by chance that the female protagonist's name, Annie Clayfert, is strongly reminiscent of the Wild West's famous sharpshooter Annie Oakley. Moreover, halfway through the novel, the protagonists meet Buffalo Bill, who then features throughout the rest of narrative. *La sovrana del campo d'oro* is part of a crop of western novels that were connected to Bill Cody's passage through Italy.

---

[86] Cottini, 'Buffalo Bill and the Italian Myth', 93, 97. This narrative is seen by Irene Lottini as working as successfully in the larger European context; see 'When Buffalo Bill Crossed the Ocean: Native American Scenes in Early Twentieth Century European Culture', *European Journal of American Culture*, 31/3 (2012), 187–203.

[87] Salgari's three articles on the Wild West show have been reprinted in a small volume: Emilio Salgari, *Arriva Buffalo Bill!* (Verona: Perosini, 1993). On the importance of the Wild West show as part of Salgari's interest in America, see Luca Di Gregorio, 'Per un pugno di romanzi: L'immaginario del West di Emilio Salgari, tra "selvaggismo nero" e western americano (1896–1910)', in Matteo Pollone (ed.), *Il western in Italia: Cinema, musica, letteratura e fumetto* (Turin: Graphot, 2020), 23–36.

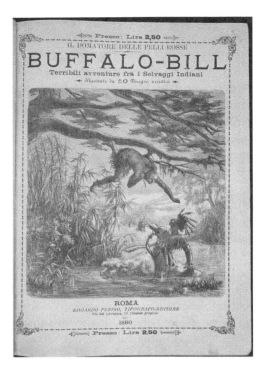

Fig. 2.13. Front page of the first instalment of *Buffalo Bill*, published by Perino in 1890. (courtesy of Princeton University Library, Princeton, NJ)

One such book, the equivalent of an American dime novel, was produced in time to profit directly from the popularity of the very first arrival of the Wild West show in 1890: the anonymous *Buffalo Bill: Il domatore delle pelli rosse*. The publisher was Edoardo Perino, which we have already met in relation to Adolfo Rossi's American travel books.[88] The-320 page-long novel could be purchased either in instalments for 5 cents each or as a single volume costing 2.5 lire. The author is unknown, but, judging from the illustrations—some signed by British artist Richard Ansdell, and others, including the front cover, by French painter Paul Philippoteaux—it seems almost certain that the book was a translation from a similar publication either in English or in French.[89] Another one, of Italian origin, was Roberto Tanfani's *I figli del deserto: Romanzo d'avventure fra le pelli-rosse* (1891), again published by Perino.

[88] Edoardo Perino was a Turinese printer who had settled in Rome soon after it became capital of the Kingdom. There, his publishing house aimed mainly at the middlebrow market, producing affordable, often illustrated, editions of books together with magazines for both adults and children. Its activity was similar to that of Milan's Sonzogno, only it quickly went out of business after its founder's death in 1895.

[89] Paul Dominique Philippoteaux spent several weeks in the USA in 1882 when he was commissioned to paint the cyclorama of the Battle of Gettysburg, which, almost 100 metres long, was at the time the world's largest painting. It is therefore possible that the publication originated first in America, and it cannot be excluded that Bill Cody might have been involved in its Italian edition as part of his publicity campaign.

Bill Cody's show added fuel to Italians' interest in the USA, catering to middle-brow publishers in both illustrated magazines and other publications. However, while Philadelphia's Centennial Exhibition of 1876 had spurred interest in the real country—hence an increase in publications looking at America's social and economic fabric—the Wild West shows of 1890 and 1906 were connected to narratives of a particular kind, related to a romantic and adventurous phase of American history that had recently come to an end. By the time of Bill Cody's second European tour, a new narrative art was making its first steps: cinema. Destined to become a major vehicle of mass culture, cinema was going to continue the tradition of Wild West narratives and, through the western, forge the most iconic and most 'American' film genre of the twentieth century. Bill Cody's Wild West was the subject of documentary film shorts, some produced as early as 1894 as part of Thomas Edison's first steps in filmmaking. We know that at least two of them reached Italy in 1896 and 1897, thus contributing to the fame of Buffalo Bill. But, more importantly, the second Wild West tour of 1906 contributed to the interest in western narratives on the part of the newly born Italian film industry. Documentaries on the Wild West show were produced in Brescia and Rome and distributed in the same year. As we will see in the Chapter 3, western films began to be produced in Italy as well.[90]

Finally, Italy's most renowned opera composer of the early twentieth century, Giacomo Puccini, was among the spectators on the occasion of Bill Cody's second passage through Milan, in April 1906. He wrote briefly but positively about it, and, although it would be excessive to draw a direct line between this event and Puccini's American opera of 1910, *La fanciulla del West*, there is little doubt that Cody's Wild West was part of Puccini's increasing interest in American culture. As we will see in Chapter 4, it was an interest dictated also by the rise of New York's Metropolitan Opera as one of the leading opera houses in the world.

## 2.3 What America did Most Italians Dream of?

In Emanuele Crialese's award-winning film on the migration to America of a family of peasants from early twentieth-century Sicily—*Nuovomondo (Golden Door* (2006))—what finally convinces the head of the family to embark on such a perilous journey are two postcard images, the first showing coins growing on a tree, the second showing two American peasants next to a giant hen. Throughout the film, this image of America as a marvelous land of plenty is developed through a number of surreal, poetic moments showing the family members handling enormous, imagined carrots or bathing in a river of milk. Such images did exist,

---

[90] On the Wild West show and early cinema, see Silvio Alovisio, 'Immaginare un nuovo mondo: Sulle tracce del western nel cinema muto italiano', in Pollone (ed.), *Il western in Italia*, 49–66.

concocted on photographic paper or more simply talked about by people interested in promoting migration. So, how did it all start, and on what knowledge did semi-illiterate citizens base their decision to move their lives to America, across an ocean they had never seen? This question is particularly relevant for the first waves of Italian migrants in the last decades of the nineteenth century, who did not benefit from either the views of returned migrants or the pull of chain migration. Strangely enough, despite the growth of the by now well-established discipline of migration studies, this is an issue on which historical research still has some way to go.[91]

Pre-unification states had already had to deal with the issue of migration, and their policies, like those of the new Italian governments, seemed to focus on the single issue of containment in defence of social order. During the early years of the Kingdom of Italy, various surveys—most famously the one on Sicily by Leopoldo Franchetti and Sidney Sonnino (1877) and the parliamentary inquiry led by Senator Stefano Jacini on rural Italy (1877-86)—revealed the widespread poverty and squalid living condition of millions of Italian peasants. At the same time, migration was not seen favourably by Italy's ruling elite. Politically, it was an embarrassing phenomenon: it could be interpreted as signalling both a lack of devotion to the mother country as well as a weak national economy unable to feed its citizens. It also raised reactionary fears—that allowing vast numbers of lower-class citizens freely to decide their destiny might fuel demands for radical reforms from those left behind.

Emilio Franzina's studies on the public debate on migration in the late nineteenth century, particularly in north-east Italy, give several examples of politicians and landowners using their influence on the press to try and stem migration through articles and reports discouraging it.[92] A similar survey limited to Sicily's leading newspaper, *Il Giornale di Sicilia*—a survey that I personally made for the years 1890-5—confirmed this trend, with the regular publication of articles concentrating on disastrous and tragic news relating to migration. Illustrated magazines too were indicatively more interested in the exotic dimension of America—hence the many articles and images of Native Americans or eccentric *faits divers*—and ignored the increasing presence of Italian communities in the major cities of the north-east and in southern towns such as New Orleans. *Corriere della Sera*'s offshoot, *La Domenica del Corriere*,

---

[91] For a general discussion on the relative lack of historical research on early Italian migration, see Emilio Franzina, *La storia è altrove: Casi nazionali e casi regionali nelle moderne migrazioni di massa* (Verona: Cierre, 1998), 7-19. Recent works on early migration to the Americas confirming this scholarly gap are Matteo Sanfilippo, 'L'emigrazione siciliana', *Archivio storico dell'emigrazione Italiana*, 3/1 (2007), 79-95; Giuseppe Moricola, *L'albero della cuccagna: L'affare emigrazione nel grande esodo tra '800 e '900* (Rome: Aracne, 2016); and Amoreno Martellini, *Abasso di un firmamento sconosciuto: Un secolo di emigrazione italiana nelle fonti autonarrative* (Bologna: Il Mulino, 2018). I am particularly grateful to senior figures in the history of Italian migration—Emilio Franzina, Donna Gabaccia, and Matteo Sanfilippo—for the constant dialogue on these issues.

[92] See two works by Emilio Franzina: *La grande emigrazione: L'esodo dei rurali dal Veneto durante il secolo XIX* (Venice: Marsilio, 1976); and *L'immaginario degli emigranti: Miti e raffigurazioni dell'esperienza italiana all'estero fra i due secoli* (Treviso: Pagus, 1992).

created in 1899 and quickly established as the most popular weekly magazine with its iconic front-cover illustrations, when it came to migration produced only images that underlined its tragic features. The first three covers dedicated to it were produced only in 1901, in the wake of the parliamentary debate on the matter. The dominant tone was of despair and doom, with no attempt to depict the economic reality that was bringing millions of Italians to such desperate measures in order to find work.

**Fig. 2.14.** Front-cover of *La Domenica del Corriere* of 8 December 1901; the caption reads 'The Sad Departure from Genoa of Northern Italian Peasants Migrating to America'. (courtesy of BMSC, Rome)

In his study of early migration, Fernando Mazzotti comes to a similar conclusion when assessing the position of the press during the late nineteenth century. This points to an embarrassing parallel in relation to Italy's colonial ambitions, which, on the contrary, were ever present:

> A paradoxical situation was therefore emerging. Where the powers of the state had failed, the poor and ragged had succeeded. The state had committed to colonial enterprises and had tried to stem migration, to no avail. The anonymous masses, instead, had left the country and formed free colonies, which were beginning to become a source of wealth and also a source of pride.[93]

Politicians and economists in those years used to distinguish between temporary and permanent migration. The first, also called *migrazione impropria* ('improper migration'), was deemed beneficial to the country. Its temporary nature meant that labour moved seasonally according to opportunities without disrupting family units and also ensuring that earnings would contribute to the national economy. At the other end of the spectrum, permanent migration, also called *migrazione propria* ('proper migration'), was deemed detrimental, since it was perceived as a net loss of both labour and earnings to the country of origin. As one can imagine, migration over the Atlantic mainly fell into this second category.

The liberal economic policies of the first Italian governments, despite the findings of the above-mentioned inquiries, avoided a heavy-handed approach. A *laissez-faire* attitude and the absence of migration quotas resulted in a massive expansion of migration with very little overall control. Table 2.1 shows the flow of migrants from two of the regions that contributed most to the first waves: the Veneto in the north-east and Sicily in the south. Recorded data go back only to 1876, and the figures in each column show the peak year in each decade. Early migration involved *Veneti* first, whereas Sicilians migrated later but eventually in higher numbers.

For better or worse, it took politicians more than twenty years to produce legislation on migration that went beyond matters of law and order.[94]

The law of January 1901 attempted to regulate and institutionalize the practices of the so-called *agenti di emigrazione* ('agents of migration'), who had been promoting and organizing the migration of hundreds of thousands of peasants all over the country. It also required careful monitoring of the navigation industry in order to ensure fair prices and to prevent fraud by rogue companies often based

---

[93] Fernando Manzotti, *La polemica sull'emigrazione nell'Italia Unita* (Milan: Dante Alighieri Editrice, 1962; rev. edn, 1969), 99–100.

[94] On the political and economic debate on migration in this period, see Choate, *Emigrant Nation*, 77–100; and Francesca Fauri, *Storia economica delle migrazioni italiane* (Bologna: Il Mulino, 2015), 13–106.

Table 2.1. Number of Italians officially migrating abroad from the regions of the Veneto and Sicily

| Years | Migration from Veneto (total in peak year) | Migration from Sicily (total in peak year) |
| --- | --- | --- |
| 1876–1880 | 17,127 (1877) | 1,228 (1876) |
| 1881–1890 | 93,405 (1888) | 11,308 (1889) |
| 1891–1900 | 97,314 (1891) | 28,838 (1900) |
| 1901–1910 | 70,701 (1907) | 127,603 (1906) |

*Source*: Enzo Caffarelli, 'Appendice 2: Statistiche' in Tiziana Grassi et al. (eds), *Dizionario enciclopedico delle migrazioni italiane nel mondo* (Rome: SER, 2014), 841–6.

abroad. Lastly, following pressure from Catholic circles led by Bishop Scalabrini, the government took on responsibility for its migrating citizens at both ends of the journey through the creation of government agencies and facilities for accommodation. Article 17 of the law began with a strict warning to navigation companies: 'Navigation companies and their representatives are forbidden from public incitement to migration.' Equally interesting are Articles 2, 3, and 4, devoted entirely to the protection of minors. They were meant to tackle an issue that had been troubling Italian embassies and consulates abroad: the use of children as mendicant music players—mainly of barrel organs—which had been mushrooming in the big cities of Europe and even across the Atlantic. Many of these children had been 'rented' from poor peasant families and were left for years entirely in the hands of often unscrupulous masters.[95]

In traditional push-and-pull terms, it is not difficult to identify the factors that attracted Italians along with many other Europeans to the Americas during the second half of the nineteenth century. The Latin American nations (Brazil and Argentina in particular), facing their first decades of independence, were in dire need of a demographic injection, ideally of farmers able to assist in cultivating the vast lands that lay untouched and unpopulated. The USA, further north, had started its economic recovery following the end of the Civil War in 1865, and was developing a process of rapid industrialization on a scale unseen in the Western world. This created a great need for labour, particularly in the metropolises of the north-east, in the neighbouring mining and stone-cutting industries, and further west along the railway lines that were bringing the country together. Farming hands were still needed—particularly in the southern states and on the west coast—but the conditions were mostly different from Latin America: landownership by then was a more difficult dream to fulfil.

[95] On mendicant music players, see John E. Zucchi, *The Little Slaves of the Harp: Italian Child Street Musicians in Nineteenth Century Paris, London and New York* (Montreal and Kingston: McGill-Queen's University Press, 1992).

But what pushed Italian peasants to choose between different migration destinations? Poverty and unemployment led most people away from their homes. The traditional destinations—the big cities, for northern Italians the richer economies over the Alps—continued to absorb their share of migration, but steam-powered sea travel—its relatively low cost and high speed—had opened the new floodgate of transatlantic migration. Crossing the Atlantic was now an option: but to which nation? How could a near-illiterate peasant living in the remote countryside make an informed decision on where to go?

Historical evidence shows that the major trends were engineered by a combination of factors, mainly beyond the reach of the migrant's personal choice. South American countries such as Argentina and Brazil were the first to set up government-sponsored schemes in order to attract European migration. In this they found a natural ally in the navigation companies, whose profits greatly benefited from the creation of steady flows of poor migrants along their routes (third-class passengers commonly accounted for about 90 per cent of the total number of passengers on transatlantic liners). Throughout the second half of the nineteenth century, the port of Genoa, in the north-east, was the dominant hub. Newspaper articles and police reports tell of a constant flow of peasants, mainly arriving by train: groups of men, or entire families carrying what was left from the sale of all their belongings. By then, many had already purchased their tickets or had signed a contract that involved free transportation, but often delays of a bureaucratic or other nature forced them to camp out for days and nights in the streets of the port area. Figures show that the regions adjacent to Genoa—Liguria, Piedmont, Lombardy, and Tuscany—provided much of the very first waves of Italian migrants.

However, the big reservoir of poorly employed labour in northern Italy was further east, in the Veneto. Local government and police officers in the province of Venice reported on the level of desperation and anger that was driving peasants, hundreds at a time, away from their villages. Anger was aimed equally at the *signori*, exploitative landowners, and at local bureaucrats, who were slow in providing passports. South American countries were initially the main destination, because those were the countries promoted by agents of migration, who visited rural fairs or could be found on certain days in the local inn. Some of these intermediaries were locals whom people trusted, including parish priests. The resentment towards the *signori* is well encapsulated in a passage in ungrammatical Italian from a letter dated 23 April 1878 which deserves to be quoted in the original:

> vi fasio sapere che io mi trovo con tento di essere venuto inamerica per che qua si e sicuri di non morire di fame, che qua valle più 2 giorni di lavoro che in in

italia 2 mesi [...] I Signori di talia diceva che in america si trova delle bestie feroce, in italia sono le bestie che son i signori.[96]

I'm letting you know that I am happy I have come to America because one cannot starve here, since here 2 days of work are worth more than 2 months in Italy. [...] The Signori in Italy used to say that there are ferocious beasts in America, but the beasts are in Italy and they are the Signori.

As for southern Italians, we know that early migration flows were created on the back of former export routes for citrus fruit. The gulf of Palermo had for centuries been a highly fertile land for the cultivation of oranges and lemons, and much of the produce was shipped to the rest of Europe and, from the eighteenth century onwards, to the Americas. The ports of New York and of New Orleans had been the gates through which Sicilian citrus fruit was then distributed throughout the USA. However, by the second half of the nineteenth century, the internal production of southern states such as Florida, Arizona, and later California greatly diminished the need for foreign imports. In order to maintain their quota of business, navigation companies had to find a new niche in the market, and migration provided the solution. This happened particularly in relation to New Orleans, where there was another party with a vested interest: the state of Louisiana. In 1866, under pressure from plantation landowners suffering from lack of labour as a result of freed African Americans moving to more tolerant areas of the USA, the government of Louisiana created the Louisiana Bureau of Immigration, an agency responsible for promoting migration to the state. Sicilian peasants were identified as fit for the purpose: they were good labourers, used to harsh working conditions. American social and labour historians have documented how the combined interests of Louisiana landowners and navigation companies created a steady flow of Sicilian migrants, most of whom were recruited in various villages around the Palermo area, from Cefalù in the east to Trapani in the west. They estimate that over 90 per cent of Italians migrating to Louisiana in the later part of the

---

[96] The letter was sent from a village in the Cordoba province of Argentina; quoted in Emilio Franzina, *Merica! Merica! Emigrazione e colonizzazione nelle lettere dei contadini veneti e friulani in America Latina; 1876-1902* (Verona: Cierre, 1994), 87. At the same time, it is interesting to note how, in the migrants' letters, the native Americans are described in the margins as little more than a nuisance in the way of their colonizing effort (pp. 117, 125). On the figure of the *agenti di migrazione*, see Piero Brunello, 'Agenti di emigrazione, contadini e immagini dell'America nella provincia di Venezia', *Rivista di storia contemporanea*, 11/1 (1982), 95-122; then in Emilio Franzina (ed.), *Un altro Veneto: Saggi e studi di storia dell'emigrazione nei secoli XIX e XX* (Abano Terme: Francisci, 1983), 138-67; Amoreno Morellini, 'Il commercio dell'emigrazione: Intermediari e agenti', in Bevilacqua, De Clementi, and Franzina (eds), *Storia dell'emigrazione italiana*, i. 293-308; and Antonio Cortese and Maria Carmela Miccoli, 'Il ruolo degli agenti di emigrazione e delle compagnie di navigazione nei flussi in uscita dall'Italia sino alla Prima Guerra Mondiale', *Polis*, V/I (2017), 261-73.

nineteenth century were Sicilians. Most came via New Orleans and some via New York, where the Louisiana Bureau of Immigration had an office.[97]

All this would suggest that the predilection of northern Italians for South America as much as that of southern Italians, and Sicilians in particular, for the USA, was the result of material pull factors, rather than individual choice or informed opinion. Importantly, the fact that the first big wave of migrants came from northern Italy is the main reason why they were the ones who were mainly directed towards South America. By the end of the nineteenth century, when migration flows began to show a steady increase in the number of southern migrants, South America was less and less of a 'pulling' area. This happened as a result of the growing instability of the Argentinian and Brazilian economies, of the end of government-sponsored promotional schemes, and also as a consequence of diplomatic issues between Italy and these two nations. The USA, in contrast, progressively emerged as the bigger player. Figures began to turn around in 1900, the year in which for the first time the USA attracted more migrants than Argentina and Brazil combined. By then, migration to the USA had become firmly dominated by Italian southerners. As early as 1877, Campania—the region of Naples—had become the biggest exporter of migrants to the USA and Canada, and since then a southern region has always been at the top of the annual statistics, with peaks of 55,169 migrants from Campania in 1902, then outnumbered by Sicily, which presented the highest ever regional peak of 111,159 migrants in 1913.[98] By then migration chains and return migrants had made people wiser about what lay ahead of them. They became less dependent on exploitative agents, and the increasing preference for the metropolises of the north-east was justified by the much higher salaries on offer there. However, for the early waves of peasant migrants, before chain migration allowed them to benefit from the knowledge of their peers, it was more probable that choice was based on what was offered to them at a particular time and place, rather than being the result of informed opinion. Even for those who could read, there was little public information they

---

[97] Jean Ann Scarpaci, *Italian Immigrants in Louisiana's Sugar Parishes: Recuitment, Labor Conditions, and Community Relations, 1880-1910* (New York: Arno Press, 1980); Anthony V. Margravio and Jerome J. Salomone, *Bread and Respect: The Italians of Louisiana* (Gretna, LA: Pelican, 2002). With Alice Gussoni, I have recently expanded on this issue in a co-written essay entitled 'From Sicily to Louisiana: Early Migration and Historiographical Issues', in Lauren Braun-Strumfels, Daniele Fiorentino, and Maddalena Marinari (eds), *Managing Migration in Italy and the United States* (Berlin: De Gruyter, forthcoming 2023).

[98] A different story concerns the smaller number of migrants who were attached to a specific profession. This seems particularly the case of northern communities living in the valleys of the Alps, which had a centuries-old history of seasonal migration. In their case, the switch to a transatlantic form of migration was linked to the demands of a specific market in the Americas, such as, for example, that of *scalpellini* ('stonemasons'), who were in high demand in the north-east of the USA. On this, see Patrizia Audenino, *Un mestiere per partire: Tradizione migratoria, lavoro e comunità in una vallata alpina* (Milan: Franco Angeli, 1990); and her 'The Paths of the Trade: Italian Stonemasons in the United States', in George E. Pozzetta (ed.), *Emigration & Immigration: The Old World Confronts the New* (New York: Garland Publishing, 1991), 31-47.

could access. The vast majority of 'guides' for migrants directed to the USA was published in the years following the 1901 legislation.[99]

Images of America as a land of plenty certainly circulated. They were part of a centuries-old literary and folkloric tradition of utopian places sometimes called 'Paese di Bengodi' ('The Land of Goodpleasure'), sometimes 'Paese della Cuccagna' ('The Land of Plenty'). We know of prints and calendars sold at fairs, representing these new worlds across the oceans and printed in the thousands for a market of non-educated readers. However, the notion of 'La Merica' (as America was sometimes misspelled) that these images spread was of a generic kind, which might have provided a general impulse towards migration, but which was unlikely to direct the choice of one particular place against another. We have instances of migrants referring to America in their correspondence, even when they had eventually reached a different continent such as Australia.[100]

The same conclusion is suggested by socio-linguistic studies of the notion of 'America' in dialects across Italy as well as other European countries. 'America' was a distant place, remote but at the same time alluring, often with little or no connection to the actual land across the Atlantic. In its different variations, 'to discover America' in several dialects simply meant 'to strike it rich'. This vague notion of America was shared even by early western films produced in Italy before the First World War. Some of these, despite the presence of the iconic cowboys and 'Red Skins', were set in other distant places such as Australia and South Africa. Early westerns in Italy did not really connect with America as a historical and geographical notion. America was a country of the imagination, such as in a 1911 film version of *Pinocchio*, in which it turns out that, after Pinocchio and Geppetto have been swallowed by a whale, they are transported to an unknown shore across the ocean, where they are kidnapped by a tribe of *pellerossa*.[101]

Once we move beyond the first wave of migrants, we need to consider the important issue of the influence of return migration. Unlike those of other nationalities, Italian migrants showed a high tendency to return to their place of

---

[99] Only seven out of sixty-six guides for migrants identified by Luigi Monga were published before 1901. Luigi Monga, 'Handbooks for Italian Emigrants to the United States: A Bibliographical Survey', *Resources for American Literary Study*, 6/2 (1976), 209–21.

[100] The state of research on nineteeth-century illlustrated prints for the non-educated public, some of which addressed the new world of the Americas, is not advanced enough to allow a clear understanding of their actual influence on the population that migrated. On this, the most comprehensive study remains Franzina, *L'immaginario degli emigranti*, in particular pp. 61–112. See also Marcello Zane, 'Strisce senza stelle: Per uno studio sull'iconografia italiana dell'emigrazione negli Stati Uniti', in Martelli (ed.), *Il sogno italo-americano*, 322–49; and Martellini, *Abasso di un firmamento sconosciuto*, 19–23.

[101] On the notion of America, see, e.g., Max Paul Friedman, 'Beyond "Voting with their Feet": Toward a Conceptual History of "America" in European Migrant Sending Communities, 1860s to 1914', *Journal of Social History*, 40/3 (2007), 557–75. On the notion of 'Paese di Bengodi' in European popular culture, see Dieter Richter, *Il paese di Cuccagna: Storia di un'utopia popolare* (Florence: Nuova Italia, 1998). On the western entitled *Pinocchio*, see Alovisio, 'Immaginare un nuovo mondo', 61–2. For more on early Italian western films, see Chapter 3. Ignazio Silone's most famous novel, *Fontamara* (1933), presents the recurrent turn of phrase—'to discover America'—amongst Abruzzesi peasants, meaning 'to strike it rich'.

origin. For example, in 1905 (we have no precise data for returns before that year), if 316,797 Italians migrated to the USA, 68,515 crossed the Atlantic in the opposite direction. A broader figure was produced by a US study that estimated that, between 1900 and 1914, more than 1.3 million Italians left the USA to return home.[102] Return migrants certainly influenced the image of the USA that poorly educated Italians were beginning to form in those years. No doubt the importance of chain migration is a consequence of this uncut umbilical cord, which fed news and mobilized people back home. Even those who did not return were able to influence relatives and friends at home through their correspondence, which often was read and discussed well outside family circles.

However, for the purposes of our study, the key question is whether return migrants became 'vehicles of America' in the way they had absorbed customs and usages that locals saw as foreign. A journalist and militant scholar who addressed this question with regard to the first waves of return migrants is Amy Allemande Bernardy. Born in Florence in 1880, daughter of a mother of Piedmontese origin and of the US consul in the city, Bernardy became a prestigious journalist and historian particularly interested in Italian migration. Having studied under Pasquale Villari, with whom she corresponded throughout her life, she shared his nationalistic sentiment and felt constantly compelled to denounce how the virtues of the Italian people were under threat when migrating to foreign lands. A restless traveller through both Italy and the USA, in one of her volumes, published in 1913, Bernardy dwelt on the impact of return migrants in the Marsica area, in the Appennine mountains west of Rome. In a chapter aptly entitled 'Come l'America ritorna da noi' ('How America comes back to us'), she criticized a deterioration in the moral character of return migrants as a consequence of their exposure to the American lifestyle: 'here we can witness the material and moral languishing of the rural Italianness of the race, replaced by foreign traits such as mechanization and the arrogance of shapeless and uncultivated industrialism.'[103] Bernardy's lyrical prose is sometimes a hindrance to her sociological aims, but she is very clear in condemning just about every aspect of American influence on people's lives: from alcoholism to free-time activities such as non-traditional dancing; even worse, to people becoming arrogant and spendthrift, to ill health (tuberculosis, syphilis, and rheumatism as American-absorbed diseases). Even women's emancipation is surprisingly described by Bernardy as toxic to the 'the ancient and sturdy virtues of the race'.[104] Beneath the intended condemnation,

---

[102] Betty Boyd Caroli, *Italian Repatriation from the United States, 1900–1914* (New York: Center for Migration Studies, 1973), 11. The 1905 statistics are extracted from 'Appendice statistica' in Gianfausto Rosoli (ed.), *Un secolo di emigrazione italiana 1876–1976* (Rome: Centro Studi Emigrazione, 1978), 343–83.

[103] Amy Allemande Bernardy, *Italia randagia attraverso gli Stati Uniti* (Turin: Bocca, 1913), 300.

[104] Bernardy, *Italia randagia*, 336.

what emerges is the first picture of how return migrants' newly acquired lifestyles continue and become a visible example of 'La Merica' in the eyes of locals. On the positive side, Bernardy mentions only their economic impact, since many of them have managed to save enough money to repair their old houses or build new ones on newly acquired land. Local churches and religious festivals also benefited from the donations of return migrants.

Bernardy's impressions, stripped of moralistic tones, are confirmed by a parliamentary inquiry on the state of peasants in southern Italy published in 1911. In the section of the final report devoted to migrants, the author, Senator Eugenio Faina, touched upon similar issues—alcoholism, the spread of diseases, more liberal customs, the use of remittances to buy properties and fund religious events—as typical effects of return migration. Faina, though, avoided Bernardy's nationalistic praise of Italians and acknowledged less laudable traits. He suggested that among the migrant population there were a number who were simply criminals fleeing from the law and who were unlikely to become models of good citizenship once abroad, even less so when back home. The phenomenon of *delitti d'onore* ('honour killing') perpetrated by return migrants on discovering that their wives had allegedly been unfaithful to them was also mentioned as a pernicious result of return migration. As Faina emphatically concluded: 'Honour! honour! how many crimes are committed in your name!'[105]

To return to Amy Bernardy, another revealing aspect she tackles concerns language. Once again, the general tone is one of condemnation: in her view, when return migrants speak to her in English, they are more abrupt and disrespectful. Dialect makes them return to their gentle manners. As for the Italian language, she observes that in these mountain villages it is less known than English:

'Yes', they answer with no hesitation, fifty if not seventy-five percent of the people between Avezzano and Alfedena you happen to speak to, as if they totally ignored the existence of a 'sì'. And only a few do not understand you if you speak to them in English; how many exactly? I do not know; certainly less than those who do not understand you if you speak pure Italian to them.[106]

Once again, Bernardy's views need to be taken with caution. However, they point to the beginning of a process that linguists have found particularly interesting:

---

[105] Eugenio Faina, *Inchiesta parlamentare sulle condizioni dei contadini nelle province meridionali e nella Sicilia*, viii. *Relazione finale* (Rome: Tipografia Nazionale, 1911), 48–58. For a revealing study on the lives of the wives of Sicilian migrants—in particular from the village of Sutera—see Linda Reeder, *Widows in White: Migration and the Transformation of Rural Women, Sicily 1880-1928* (Toronto: University of Toronto Press, 2003).
[106] Bernardy, *Italia randagia*, 310–45 (pp. 327–8). On Bernardy, see Maddalena Tirabassi, *Ripensare la patria grande: Gli scritti di Amy Allemande Bernardy sulle migrazioni italiane (1900-1930)* (Isernia: Cosmo Iannone, 2005).

that is, the way in which the language learned abroad—American English in our case—tended to interfere only with the migrants' main language, their local dialect. Standard Italian, on the other hand, remained somehow unaffected by this process; it was a form of communication that semi-illiterate Italians had never really made their own.

Remittances were by far the main influence of return migrants on the local communities in which they resettled. Their investments were welcome, since, when successful, they had a positive impact at both the personal and the public level. First, they allowed family units to emerge out of poverty, and, secondly, the new wealth (inflated by a currency exchange rate massively in favour of the US dollar) impacted on the community through donations, most often in the form of contributions either to the restoration and embellishment of local churches or to the yearly *festa padronale* ('feast of the Patron Saint'), which, particularly in southern Italy, carried with it colourful processions and celebrations.

During his journey through southern Italy, in 1905, Angelo Mosso condensed this issue in one observation: 'To form a good idea of mobility towards America, and of the degree of wellbeing among migrants, it suffices to visit the local parish. If the church displays some luxury, one can be certain that migration is well on its course.'[107] Apart from the question of money, though, and beyond Bernardy's preoccupations, it is likely that return migrants, rather than being a model of a foreign culture, were living examples of the possibility of moving to a distant country in order to find better living conditions. Equal if not more value was given to the fact that they had not lost contact with traditional values and habits. After all, chain migration represented an attractive prospect specifically because it promised a journey to a faraway country that was geographically but not culturally distant. Particularly in the first years of the twentieth century, when the USA saw a huge increase in the migration of southerners to the big cities of the northeast, the prospect of arriving and, at least temporarily, settling in districts entirely dominated by a migrant community that spoke their language, often their local dialect, was a strong element of attraction.

Chain migration was based on the belief that the journey was worth it because it allowed better economic prospects without the total loss of one's homeland: the human landscape in America was going to be a familiar one. This is also suggested by the title of some of the few, early guides for migrants: *L'Italia in America: Notizie per gli emigranti* (*Italy in America: News for Migrants* (1883)) or *Guida Metelli della colonia italiana negli Stati Uniti* (*The Metelli Guide to the Italian Colony in the United States* (1885)). For this reason, return migrants, paradoxically,

---

[107] Angelo Mosso, *Vita moderna degli italiani* (Milan: Treves, 1906), 121. On return migration, see also Francesco Paolo Cerase, 'L'onda di ritorno: I rimpatri', in Bevilacqua, De Clementi, and Franzina (eds), *Storia dell'emigrazione italiana*, i. 113–25; Russell King, *Il ritorno in Patria: Return Migration to Italy in Historical Perspective* (Durham: Geography Department, University of Durham, 1988); and Matteo Pretelli, *L'emigrazione italiana negli Stati Uniti* (Bologna: Il Mulino, 2011).

were expected to show that, beyond their new wealth—however real—little had changed: their ways—beliefs, daily practices, cultural and religious references—had stayed the same.[108]

As a consequence, on the one hand, the USA was seen as a different, exotic place, full of social and economic opportunities; on the other, it was perceived as a safe destination where migrants could immediately be reassured by the presence of familiar habits, sounds, and more or less disinterested help.

To return to the question in the title of this section, there is a sense that the America dreamt of by the first waves of semi-illiterate Italians in the late nineteenth century was more a vague idea of good working conditions than a specific geographical place. Argentina, Brazil, the USA, Canada: it is difficult to imagine that Italian peasants with no more than two or three years of primary school (often none), who in most cases had never left their native villages, could access the necessary information in order to be able to distinguish between one country and the other. In the early stages, external circumstances often dictated the choice. In the case of the vast reservoir of the rural north-east, in Veneto, we know how agents of migration operated, and the extent to which they were linked to labour demand from the Americas. We are less informed about southern Italy. Donna Gabaccia, in what is still today the most insightful analysis of early migration from Sicily, concentrated on the small, rural town of Sambuca, about fifty miles south of Palermo. She showed how tensions caused by the economic crisis and by philo-socialist militancy were some of the 'pushing' reasons encouraging the dream of a better life abroad. It might well be that this dovetailed with a 'pulling' factor that had already been at work. The first ships carrying Sicilian peasants to New Orleans arrived as early as March 1865, before the Civil War had even ended. The connection provided by the import of citrus fruit meant that shipping lines were already in operation. It was merely a question of switching from fruit to people. Moreover, in those years it was legal to offer contracts stipulating that transport costs were free but would be detracted from the migrants' salaries once they had reached the plantations. Socially and geographically (even within New Orleans' neighbourhoods), those Sicilian migrants found themselves shoulder to shoulder with the African American community. It is no wonder that Sicilian Americans played a central role in the development of ragtime and jazz music in Louisiana, as will be discussed in Chapter 4.[109]

---

[108] A similar conclusion is reached by Linda Reeder: migrants' remittances opened up new opportunities for rapid social elevation—typically through the construction of a new house—and access for women to consumer culture, but gender relations and social norms often remained unchanged. Reeder, *Widows in White*, 142–67.

[109] Donna Gabaccia, *Militants and Migrants: Rural Sicilians Become American Workers* (New Brunswick, NJ: Rutgers University Press, 1988). On early migration from Veneto, see, e.g., Franzina, *La storia è altrove*, 224–81. The arrival of ships carrying Sicilian peasants is recorded by New Orleans's Italian consul on 30 March 1865 (Archive of Ministry of Foreign Affairs, Rome, in MDAE 1861–1887, b.895 'Rapporti dei Consolati', f.257; quoted in Bonsaver and Gussoni, 'From Sicily to Louisiana', forthcoming 2023).

Whatever the image of America that migrants brought with them during their long transatlantic journey, it was no doubt very different from the one familiar to the educated elite. Nationalistic feelings and a pan-European sense of superiority were absent from their views. America was a place to live a better life. It was a hope more than an opinion.

# 3
# American Mass Production and the Dawn of Italian Mass Culture

The image of America in the minds of educated Italians was constantly coloured by a factor that had much to do with the economic sphere—that is, the capacity of the American industry to deliver production on a mass scale. As we saw in the previous chapter, the prevailing view was that Americans were entrepreneurial people, naïve and rough around the edges, but excellent at putting together an ambitious business plan, and at delivering it. This is amply shown in the early part of Victoria De Grazia's *Irresistible Empire*, where she concentrates on the arrival of American business practices in Europe. The widespread dissemination of the Rotary Club's network throughout Europe is a sign of how Europe's middle and upper bourgeoisie looked up to America as an ideal society where their peers were not only its powerful engine but also an exemplary social force in all other fields, political and cultural. At the time, the reason for this success, from a cultural viewpoint, was well understood by Antonio Gramsci when he was writing on Fordism from his Fascist prison cell, in 1927: the American middle classes had been benefiting from having developed in a country free from the ties of past European history, in particular from the presence of a noble class that in many ways acted as a hindrance to progress and to the attempted hegemony by Europe's middle classes.[1]

At the turn of the century, one of Italy's 'America-enlightened' bourgeois entrepreneurs was Camillo Olivetti. After receiving his degree in industrial engineering at Turin's prestigious polytechnic, in December 1891, Olivetti spent more than a year in Britain, working in a London factory of electrical instruments while perfecting his English. This made him a rare example of a late-nineteenth-century educated Italian who could travel to the USA and properly immerse himself in its culture. He first went to Chicago as an assistant to his former university supervisor, and on that occasion he decided to extend his stay—a stay that included a semester of teaching at Stanford University. His correspondence dating between August 1893 and July 1894—and similarly the one relating to his third US trip, in 1908–9 (no correspondence survives of Olivetti's second trip to the USA in 1896)—presents him as an attentive observer of the American

---

[1] De Grazia, *Irresistible Empire*, ch. 1, 'The Service Ethic', 15–74. Antonio Gramsci, *Americanismo e Fordismo: Quaderno 22* (Turin: Einaudi, 1978), 13–32; also in Quaderno 22 (1934), §2.

economy as much as of its society. He was no uncritical enthusiast of America—he describes Americans as childlike and he disliked New York's high-rise buildings—but at the same time Olivetti was eager to acquire detailed knowledge of the innovative potential of US industry. This started with a meeting between Thomas Edison and his university supervisor, Professor Galileo Ferraris (a renowned inventor himself in the newly expanding electrical engineering field), whom Olivetti had been helping as an assistant and an interpreter. Edison took Ferraris and Olivetti for a tour of his engineering workshops in Llewellyn Park, proudly showing them his first attempts at a phonograph and the already developed models of kinetograph and kinetoscope, America's first machines for shooting and watching movies.[2]

In his first long, solitary journey from coast to coast, Olivetti paid a visit to several cutting-edge industrial firms specializing in electrical devices. At the same time he had a clear interest in one other product of cutting-edge technology in which the American excelled: typewriters. Olivetti had no romantic interest in the old America which Buffalo Bill Cody was bringing to Europe. In fact, in his long train journeys he brought with him a bicycle—another new product of the modern industrial world—which allowed him to move around in the areas where he stopped and avoid hiring a horse. He was not blind to the human and natural landscapes, but there is little doubt that his main goal was to absorb as much as possible of the spirit and practices of US industry.[3]

Once back in Italy from his first trip, he created his first factory in Ivrea—north-east of Turin—constructing electrical instrumentation. The breakthrough came with the creation of the first Italian factory for the production of typewriters, in 1908, which quickly became a model of industrial entrepreneurship. The second and third trips to the USA had been aimed at ordering machinery and observing production lines in preparation for his own factory. In Hartford, CT, Olivetti was taken for a visit of Underwood, the then world-leading company in typewriters, producing seventy thousand machines per year—as Olivetti wrote to his wife on 19 December 1908, underlining the figure. About fifty years later, Camillo's son, Adriano Olivetti, was to inherit such a successful business that in 1959 he was able to buy out their American competitor. Even the main building of the typewriter factory in Ivrea became an example of industrial innovation: its apparently traditional red-brick facades hid a cutting-edge structure in reinforced concrete, which again had been modelled on American factories. Olivetti was groundbreaking also in his approach to human resources: as a harsh critic of Italy's education system at both ends—the education of the masses was too scarce,

---

[2] Olivetti, *Lettere americane*, 5–13, 165. On Olivetti's early years as an industrialist, see Bruno Caizzi, *Camillo e Adriano Olivetti* (Turin: Unione Tipografico–editrice Torinese, 1962), 1–68.

[3] On the symbolic status of the bicycle as an icon of modernity in turn-of-the-century Italian culture, see Luca Cottini, *The Art of Objects: The Birth of Italian Industrial Culture, 1878–1928* (Toronto: University of Toronto Press, 2018), 73–102.

the technical teaching of the specialists too theoretical—he decided to create in-house courses, initially taught by him, designed to prepare his staff for the specific challenges of his industrial endeavour.

No little part in this was played by his Socialist ideals and militancy, which were to complicate his life at a later stage, during the Fascist years. Olivetti was also very aware of the need to be innovative and hard-nosed in the marketing of his products—another field in which Americans excelled. Inserting the father of Italian culture, Dante Alighieri, in an image advertising his typewriters was a daring short circuit between Italy's cultural roots and the new technologies being developed at the turn of the century (see Fig. 3.1).

Camillo Olivetti is a good example of the few Italian entrepreneurs who, in those years, saw the American industry as a model to be studied in detail. Cultural historian Alberto Saibene associates Olivetti's experience with that of Giovanni Agnelli and Alberto Pirelli and talks of an 'American Grand Tour' taken by future leading industrialists in the early twentieth century. This is true, although it should be emphasized that it concerned a very limited number of individuals.[4]

Around the same time, in 1902, the economist Giuseppe Maria Fiamingo wrote an essay for the *Nuova antologia* menacingly entitled 'L'invasione economica dell'America' ('The Economic Invasion by America'). It is notable how his analysis very much reflects the first-hand impressions of Olivetti during his American trips. The advantage of US industry, beyond the size of its internal market, lay, according to Fiamingo, in the different disposition of its people: the constant drive for innovation of its industrialists and the high level of competence of its working class. He then added a list of the industrial fields in which American knowhow had become dominant: culture-related fields were not exempt, from typewriters to linotype printing in the publishing industry. His concluding comment was unwavering: 'This has turned the United States into the richest ever country with an export figure of seven billions and with plans to achieve nothing less than absolute economic domination of the world.'[5]

A few years later, in their influential history of the American civilization, Charles and Mary Beard described the beginning of America's 'Machine Age' as marked by the arrival of electricity and the combustion engine. Mass production made mass culture a possibility, and the three areas that the authors chose as most representative of this shift at the very start of the twentieth century were the car industry, cinema, and the radio.[6]

---

[4] Alberto Saibene, 'Il secolo americano di Adriano Olivetti', in Adriano Olivetti, *Dall'America: Lettere ai familiari (1925–26)* (Rome and Ivrea: Edizioni di Comunità, 2016), pp. 118–39 (121).
[5] Giuseppe Maria Fiamingo, 'L'invasione economica dell'America', *Nuova antologia di lettere, scienze e arti*, 98 (March–April 1902), 484–92 (492). Despite his perception of the 'American peril', Fiamingo had previously published a volume vehemently in favour of liberalism in Europe: *Il protezionismo sociale contemporaneo* (Turin: Roux Frassati & Co., 1896).
[6] Charles A. and Mary R. Beard, *The Rise of American Civilization* (New York: Macmillan, 1927), 745–7.

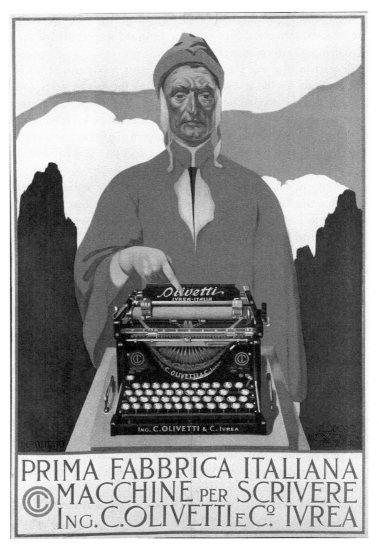

**Fig. 3.1.** Dante approves of Olivetti's US-inspired typewriter in a publicity poster of 1912. (courtesy of Fondazione Adriano Olivetti, Ivrea)

The role of wireless broadcasting in Italy will be considered in Chapter 8. However, with regard to cars and film, a case will be made here for a parallel treatment, with specific reference to one of the capitals of Italy's industry, Turin. A first question to be answered is of a geographical nature: why Turin? A reason behind this choice is linked to the city's role in the history of silent cinema. As is well known, during the first decade of the twentieth century, when cinema took its first steps, Turin could lay claim to being the most important centre of this new culture industry. Film historian Gianni Rondolino went so far as to call it Italy's

'Hollywood' of that decade.[7] At the same time, Turin can also easily be considered as the most Francophile of Italy's main cities. This is for obvious historical and geographical reasons. The combination of these two factors makes it an interesting case for the study of the way in which American culture entered Italian society in a field like cinema, which was dominated by France in its very first stages. Thirdly, the decision to extend this study to the car industry is also linked to Turin's dominant status in this other, newly born industry. But these are not the only reasons. Other, interesting parallels between the film and car industries can be drawn.

The new technology of the automobile, as we will see, also came to Italy mainly through France and at the same time had to face the growing importance of its equivalent development across the Atlantic. Moreover, both industries—cars and film—were an expression of new technologies, which brought a fundamental and soul-defining contribution to twentieth-century culture. I would argue that even from an aesthetic viewpoint the two can easily be connected. One of the earliest Italian films, shot in 1904 by the pioneers of Turin's film industry, Roberto Omegna and Arturo Ambrosio, documented a car race, the *Prima corsa automobilistica Susa Moncenisio*. Here it was, a newly born form of representation, cinema, used in order to immortalize another newly born phenomenon, the automobile. This is coincidental, but at the same time it signals the impact of the car as a cultural object and, as such, also an object of beauty and art. In Futurism's 1909 Manifesto by Filippo Tommaso Marinetti, it is a car that provides the rebirth of the artist in the narrative preface. Point four of the manifesto then famously continues with a glorification of the car, which peaks in the provocative statement that a roaring car is 'more beautiful than the Victory of Samothrace'.[8] Marinetti in those years tried to give the neologism 'automobile' a masculine gender—*un automobile*—since he saw it as a virile expression of power. He failed in this, but he was not alone in his glorifying tones. The car played a central role, not just as a revolutionary mode of transport, but also as the ultimate symbol of modernity, and of a new idea of beauty, made out of scientific precision and industrial labour.

As Charles and Mary Beard suggested, the automobile, with cinema and the radio, had come to represent the irrepressible entry of technology into modern society. America led the way: by the early twentieth century this epoch-making move had cascaded down to the lower steps of the social ladder, in a way still unknown in most of Europe:

---

[7] Gianni Rondolino, *Torino Come Hollywood* (Bologna: Capelli, 1980).
[8] Filippo Tommaso Marinetti, *Fondazione e Manifesto del futurismo*, first pub. in French in *Le Figaro*, 20 February 1909; then in Marinetti, *I manifesti del futurismo* (Florence: Edizioni di 'Lacerba', 1914). On Futurism and cars, see Samuele Pardini, 'The Automobile', in Sascha Bru, Luca Somigli, and Bart Van den Bossche (eds), *Futurism: A Microhistory* (Oxford: Legenda, 2017), 48–58. On the philosophical context of Marinetti's praise of speed, see Jeffrey Schnapp, 'Why Speed is a Religion-Morality', in Schnapp, *Modernitalia* (Bern: Peter Lang, 2012), 1–21.

By the millions, cheap automobiles, new and second-hand, telephones, radios, labor-saving implements and other commodities, classed in more sparing societies as luxuries, found their way into the possession of those who labored with their hands at plow or forge. Whereas the proletariat of older cultures, Rome for instance, had to be amused with circuses and supplied with free bread, the industrial multitudes of the United States, like the middle class, paid for their own diversions and bought their own loaves.[9]

## 3.1 Turin between French and American Culture: The Film Industry in 1904–1914

A few considerations are needed about the first steps of the film industry in Turin.[10] In particular, it is important to grasp how the fledgling Turinese film industry positioned itself among the two emerging giants that the French and American film industries had quickly become. One of the most authoritative historians of early Italian cinema, Paolo Cherchi Usai, warns us of the complexity of a study of the influential forces of these early years. New ideas, inventions, and practices were mushrooming in different parts of Europe and America, and it is difficult, often impossible, to determine when transfers took place or whether a particular development in a particular place should be considered a replica or a genuine invention. The challenge for the historian is to find out the extent to which any filmmaker or producer was aware of what was being done by his or her peers.[11] With this in mind, these pages will try to unravel the history of how the Turinese film industry faced, with a few years' delay, the challenges of developing this new and most transnational technology.

France had a great start owing to the fact that the hardware developed by the Lumière Brothers—the *cinématographe*, first used in public in 1895—quickly proved more popular than its American equivalent—Thomas Edison's kinetoscope—which was cumbersome and did not allow for collective screening. Film production too saw the French lead the way. In the first decade of the new century, Paris-based Pathé-Frères became the dominant company in the newly born film industry, and one with clear global ambitions, exporting its artefacts across the oceans. Furthermore, it was not just in terms of production and distribution that France dominated. Pathé was also pioneering in the development of where films

---

[9] Beard and Beard, *The Rise of the American Civilization*, 751.
[10] Sections 3.1 and 3.2 are an expanded version of an essay of mine published in Bonsaver, Carlucci, Reza (eds), *Italy and the USA*, entitled 'Turin between French and US Culture: The Car and Film Industries, 1904–14', 156–83. The paragraphs on Cines and on early Italian westerns are new.
[11] Paolo Cherchi Usai, 'On the Concept of "Influence" in Early Cinema', in Roland Cosandey and François Albera (eds), *Cinéma sans frontières 1896–1918: Images across Borders* (Payot, Québec: Nuit Blanche Editeur, 1995), 275–86.

could be screened, leading the move away from fairground entertainment to venues that could compete with theatre and opera. By 1908, Paris had more than one hundred permanent cinemas, twenty of which were managed directly by Pathé. This also meant elevating the artistic status of cinema in order to attract the interest of the cultured elites: the *Société du Film d'Art*, founded by Paul Lafitte (with Pathé's financial help) in 1908, began the trend, making ample use of literary adaptations. Two years later Pathé followed suit with its own *Séries d'art*, and at the same time one other emerging French giant, Gaumont, launched its *Le Film esthétique*.[12]

The American film industry, in these early years, found itself on the defensive. Pathé not only dominated the European market: in 1906 it was distributing about six films a week in the USA, each printed in seventy-five copies. By 1908, the figure had risen to ten films a week, distributed in about two hundred copies. This made Pathé not just the largest single source of films in the American market: its distribution was twice the size of all the American productions put together. Only protectionist policies could shield the US industry from French competition, and this was achieved thanks to the relentless efforts of Thomas Edison. In 1908 he led the creation of a trust, the Motion Pictures Patents Company (also known as the Edison Trust), in order to streamline film distribution in the USA, but more than anything else to establish a system of near-monopoly that could keep foreign competitors at bay.[13]

In those same years, the Italian film industry was taking its first steps. In Turin, the two leading companies, Ambrosio and Itala Film, were founded respectively in 1906 and 1907. Although the very first film screening took place in Turin on 21 April 1895 using an Edison kinetoscope, once Italians had begun to manufacture and screen their own films, their hardware, modes of production, and distribution were undoubtedly imported from France. Itala Film, in particular, in its first year, when still called Carlo Rossi & C., was staffed with personnel directly poached from Pathé. Their artistic director, Charles Lucien Lépine, had been general director of Pathé's factory outside Paris, Indeed, he was successfully sued by his old company for breach of confidential industrial knowledge. When the young Giovanni Pastrone became the driving force of the company, the following year, France was still the model: suffice it to say that, consistent with his decision to compete in the niche market of comical films, he went across the Alps and hired

---

[12] Richard Abel, *The Ciné Goes to Town: French Cinema, 1896–1914* (Berkeley and Los Angeles: University of California Press, 1994), 9–58. See also, by the same author: 'The Perils of Pathé, or the Americanization of American Cinema', in Charney and Schwartz (eds), *Cinema and the Invention of Modern Life*, 183–223.

[13] Kristin Thompson, *Exporting Entertainment: America in the World Film Market 1907–34* (London: BFI Publishing, 1985), 4–19. See also Gerben Bakker's studies, 'The Decline and Fall of the European Film Industry: Sunk Costs, Market Size, and Market Structure, 1890–1927', *Economic History Review*, 58/2 (2005), 310–51; and *Entertainment Industrialised: The Emergence of the International Film Industry, 1890–1940* (Cambridge: Cambridge University Press, 2009).

one of the then most popular French actors at the time, André Deed, who had been working with Georges Méliès and Pathé. With Itala Film, Deed started the popular series based around the comical character of 'Cretinetti', which ensured international fame for the Italian film company. Others followed suit, with Ambrosio in 1910 hiring another comedian active in France, Marcel Fabre, to appear in its popular comic series as Robinet.[14]

These few details can already give us a sense of the entrepreneurial boldness of this first generation of Italian filmmakers. There were no reservations in taking the fight to the most powerful of Europe's film industries. At the same time, everything in the world of early cinema was changing very rapidly. The already mentioned protectionist near-embargo on French imports in the USA—fought on the grounds of morality as much as of financial interest—allowed the US industry to develop quickly, and, by the time its internal market had been adequately stretched to the size of thousands of cinemas, it had become a clear leader in terms of both production and international competitiveness. This development was somewhat mirrored by the presence of American films in Italy. In the early years, up until 1915, the distribution of about the total amount was in the hands of Pathé and Gaumont. It was only after the First World War that American production companies were able to free themselves entirely from the dominance of their French competitors.[15]

So, how could the fledgling Italian film industry stand up to such ever-growing giants? Initially, it very much followed the example of its French neighbour and developed production in the four main markets, which were already being coded in four *genres*: (i) documentary footage on contemporary life (so-called *actualités*); (ii) the description of extraordinary places or events; (iii) narratives based on historical or literary/biblical material; and (iv) comedies. Of these four, it was the production of films set in ancient times, whether historically or literary based, that began to give Italian companies a leading edge. Italy's association with Ancient Rome and classical culture was a factor but only to some extent: after all, when Pastrone began to work on the production of *Cabiria*, in 1912, he went to the Louvre in Paris in order to study examples of classical antiquity. Equally important was Italy's established excellence in the staging of operas, a practice that was not so distant from building monumental, static sets designed to accomodate dozens of extras.

---

[14] Aldo Bernardini, *Cinema muto italiano*, i. *Ambiente, spettacoli e spettatori 1896–1904* (Rome and Bari: Laterza, 1980), 9–64; Silvio Alovisio, '"The Pastrone System": Itala Film from its Origins to World War I', *Film History*, 12/3 (2000), 250–61; Maria Adriana Prolo, 'Francesi nel cinema italiano muto', *Bianco e nero*, 14/8–9 (1953), 69–74. On André Deed, see Jean A. Gili, *André Deed: Boireau, cretinetti, gribouille* (Bologna: Cineteca Bologna, 2005).

[15] On this, see Federico Di Chio, *Il cinema americano in Italia: Industria, società, immaginari: Dalle origini alla seconda guerra mondiale* (Milano: Vita e Pensiero, 2021), 1–48.

Italians were also quick to grab the opportunities for longer and more complex narratives offered by the growing length of available reels. The first international success was Ambrosio's *Gli ultimi giorni di Pompei*, co-directed by Arturo Ambrosio and Luigi Maggi, the first of a series of films based on the eponymous 1834 historical novel by Edward Bulwer-Lytton. Produced in 1908 with a length of approximately 360 metres (lasting about sixteen minutes), the film was received enthusiastically, much praised for its attention to the reconstruction of an ancient Roman city and for its dramatic effects in the eruption sequence.[16] The distribution of Italian films in American cinemas began to grow. If only 8 Italian films were screened in the USA in 1906, figures increased massively: two years later there were 105 (83 of which were Turinese); and that rose to 255 films in 1910 (194 Turinese). In that year, Itala had established two releases a week in New York, while Ambrosio and Cines contented themselves with one each.[17]

Italian production companies were also quick to try their hand at the autochthonous genre of the western. In the wake of the French film industry, by 1910 Italian companies had begun to produce home-made westerns, some of which were distributed in the USA. Precise data are missing, but, according to Silvio Alovisio, it is likely that Itala Film's *La voce del sangue* of 1910—a five-minute story of a white young man, captured and raised among 'Indians'—was the first Italian western. Sadly, none of these early westerns has survived apart from a few stills. Fig. 3.2 is an example from a 1913 film produced by Ambrosio whose plot seems somehow inspired by Bill Cody's Wild West. The protagonist is a cowboy who, like Annie Oakley and her husband Frank Butler, the Wild West's most famous sharpshooters, decides to earn a living by performing in front of crowds. Ironically, judging from the critical comment of a reviewer in 1914, if there was a defining trait of those films, it was the fact that the ever-present cowboy hero tended to appear with a perfect hairstyle and in pristine clothes, untouched by the furious action.[18]

By 1910, technological advances and screening practices had enabled the full development of the production of long feature films. Set over four or more reels,

---

[16] Davide Turconi, 'I film storici italiani e la critica americana dal 1910 alla fine del muto', *Bianco e nero*, 1/2 (1963), 40–54 (41).

[17] Paolo Cherchi Usai, 'Maciste all'Hell's Kitchen: Il cinema muto torinese negli Stati Uniti', in Paolo Bertetto and Gianni Rondolino (eds), *Cabiria e il suo tempo* (Milan: Il Castoro, 1998), 132–48. See also Aldo Bernardini, *Cinema muto italiano*, iii. *Arte, divismo e mercato 1910–1914* (Bari and Rome: Laterza, 1982), 145; and Giorgio Bertellini, 'Epica spettacolare e splendori del vero. L'influenza del cinema storico italiano in America (1908–1915)', in Gian Paolo Brunetta, *Storia del cinema mondiale* (Turin: Einaudi, 1999), ii. 227–65. On other regional realities, such as that of Neapolitan early cinema, see, e.g.,., Muscio, *Napoli/New York/Hollywood*.

[18] Among the directors of Italian early westerns was Roberto Roberti, father of the future king of Spaghetti western, Sergio Leone. His *La vampira indiana*, of 1913, starred Bice Waleran, future wife of Roberti and mother of Sergio. See Alovisio, 'Immaginare un nuovo mondo'; and Vittorio Martinelli, 'Laggiù nell'Arizona', *Bianco e nero*, 58/3 (July–September 1997), 107–13. The 1914 review comes from *La cinematografia italiana ed estera* (October 1914); quoted in Martinelli, 'Laggiù nell'Arizona', 108.

**Fig. 3.2.** Still from Luigi Maggi's western *Il bersaglio vivente*, Ambrosio, 1913. (courtesy of Museo Nazionale del Cinema, Turin)

narratives could last more than an hour. Now individual films could compete with theatre and opera productions, and Italy contributed substantially to the elevation and prestige of cinema as an art. The first Italian long feature film that achieved international success was a four-reel adaptation of Dante Alighieri's work *L'Inferno*, directed by Francesco Bartolini and Adolfo Padoan, and distributed in 1911 by Milano Film. In the same year, Itala Film successfully produced *La caduta di Troia*, directed by Pastrone and Luigi Romano Borgnetto. Of a shorter length—two reels for a duration of about thirty minutes—the film was lauded abroad for its *mise en scène* deploying a realistic set, moving beyond the traditional use of canvas backdrops. In the same period, the leading film company in Rome, Cines, achieved fame on the international scene with historical epics such as the three-reeler *La Gerusalemme liberata* (1911), inspired by Torquato Tasso's eponymous literary masterpiece. These were the films that sparked interest in the Italian industry and particularly so on the part of one of the most entrepreneurial distributors in the USA, George Kleine.[19]

Chicago-based, Kleine had started to import and distribute foreign films in 1903 and had tried to resist Thomas Edison's protectionist drive towards a total

---

[19] These years also saw the birth of dozens of film magazines, some addressing distributors and cinema managers, others aimed directly at filmgoers. On Italian film criticism in the pre-sound years, see Silvio Alovisio, 'Le riviste del cinema muto: Una fonte per la ricerca tecnologica?', *Bianco e nero*, 549 (2004), 31–44; and Francesco Casetti with Silvio Alovisio and Luca Mazzei (eds), *Early Film Theories in Italy: 1896–1920* (Amsterdam: Amsterdam University Press, 2017).

regimentation of the American film market. He eventually became a member of the Edison Trust but still continued to pursue his own interest in the foreign market as an independent distributor, concentrating in particular on Italian productions. In 1913, he masterminded the arrival of Italian historical epics, not just in American cinemas around the country, but even in the heart of New York's theatre land: Broadway. This particular project was aimed at raising interest in the screening of a film so that it would achieve the prestige normally enjoyed by theatre and opera premieres. A full orchestra was hired to accompany the screening. Ticket prices were high, in an attempt to lure the wealthy, educated crowds who would normally spurn cinema as an inferior form of art. The film at the centre of this operation was Cines's *Quo Vadis?* (1912), directed by Enrico Guazzoni and based on Henryk Sienkiewicz's eponymous historical–religious novel of 1896. The gamble paid off, and the film was hailed as an example of the artistic heights reached by Italian cinema.[20]

On the Turinese front, other blockbusters followed in the wake of this success, with Ambrosio's *Spartaco* (based on an eponymous Italian novel published in 1874) and a much longer remake of *Gli ultimi giorni di Pompei*. On his part, Giovanni Pastrone at Itala Film had been working on his own blockbuster since the previous year: once it was finished in 1914, its premiere around the world was to turn it into an icon of the historical epic. I am referring to the almost two-hour-long *Cabiria*. Set during Rome's Carthaginian wars and vaguely inspired by the novel *Cartagine in fiamme* (1908) by popular novelist Emilio Salgari, *Cabiria* tells the story of the rescue of a Roman noble girl by her servant and a duo of Roman spies—all while, around them, the historical figures of Scipio, Hannibal, Massinissa, and Queen Sophonisba open up the film to a grand reconstruction of luxurious interiors and epic battles. Pastrone was relentless in his eye for detail as much as in his intention to create 'art'. Italy's most famous literary figure at the time, Gabriele D'Annunzio, was hired to add his prestigious touch to the film's intertitles. And for the music score Pastrone gave another prestigious figure, Ildebrando Pizzetti, the task of composing an *ad hoc* piece for the most spectacular scene of the sacrifice of children at the monumental temple of Moloch. In the USA, *Cabiria* was distributed by the *ad hoc* created Itala Film Company of America, which took advantage of the opportunity, making a considerable profit, despite the enormous expenses relating to the advertising campaign and the cost of a live orchestra.[21]

By then, George Kleine had already decided that his links with the Italian film industry had to be nurtured and taken to new heights. His correspondence with Italian producers shows the extent of his eagerness to exploit Italy's newly

---

[20] See Turconi, 'I film storici italiani e la critica americana', 40–54.
[21] On the making of *Cabiria*, see Paolo Cherchi Usai (ed.), *Giovanni Pastrone: Gli anni d'oro del cinema a Torino* (Turin: UTET, 1985).

achieved fame, as he suggested topics and themes around which films should be made. In other words, the US distributor of Italian films was keen to become a producer himself, and he proceeded to do so.

The correspondence relating to Kleine's relationship with Cines suggests that his attempt to exploit the sensational success of *Quo Vadis?* had been hampered by Cines's limitations in producing films both at the agreed rate (600 metres per week) and of sufficient quality. The latter was the object of a number of complaints by Kleine: the film used by Cines (which produced its own film material) was not chemically stable, plus the perforation adopted was of insufficient precision, such that reels were often damaged during projection. The Turinese companies were more reliable on that front—hence Kleine's decision to invest there and at the same time aim to retain as much control as possible.[22]

The first move was to sign an exclusive contract with Ambrosio, in April 1913, in which the latter was to produce the already mentioned remake of *Gli ultimi giorni di Pompei*. The contract specified that the film was to be of similar length and spectacular value as *Quo Vadis?* and that Kleine's company would retain full ownership. Another four films were to follow under similar conditions.[23] A few months later, Ambrosio offered Kleine the opportunity to enter into co-production with his firm, but Kleine declined: he wanted executive control. After a long negotiation and a number of meetings (Ambrosio and Kleine had first met in New York, in 1911, after which the latter visited Italy twice during his European tours, in 1911 and 1913), a deal was struck between Kleine, Alfredo Gandolfi (Ambrosio's then financial director), and Mario Alberto Stevani. The latter had been a partner of Kleine, since 1912, exporting European films to the USA, and he was a chief administrator at Cines.[24]

The result was the creation of Photo Drama, a film production company based in Turin. The three immediately went ahead with the acquisition of the land necessary to build a fully functional studio on the outskirts of the city, in Brugliasco. The Photo Drama company was legally founded only in March 1914, and by then the construction of the new studios was already in full swing. Indeed, by the summer of the same year they were fully functional. In the long telegram in which, from Italy, Kleine announced to his Chicago associates that Photo Drama was now a reality, on 12 December 1913, he described it as follows:

[22] Documents in The George Kleine Papers, Washington: Library of Congress [GKP], Box 7 'Cines'. Paolo Cherchi-Usai came to the same conclusion in his groundbreaking essay on George Kleine: 'Un americain à Turin à la conquête de l'Italie. George Kleine à Grugliasco 1913–1914', *Archives*, 22–3 (1989), 1–20 (5). A later issue of *Archives*, 26–7 (1989), contained a selection of documents from the Kleine Papers. On George Kleine, see Joel Frykholm, *George Kleine and American Cinema: The Movie Business and Film Culture in the Silent Era* (London: Palgrave Macmillan, 2015).

[23] They were *Othello*, *The Lion of Venice*, *Madame du Barry*, and *Delenda Carthago!*. Only the first three were completed.

[24] On Stevani at Cines, see Riccardo Redi, *La Cines: Storia di una casa di produzione italiana* (Bologna: Persiani, 2011), 45.

You are now at liberty to announce formation of Photodrama production company of Italy by myself and two associates stop have bought beautiful estate permitting staging of fifty scene [sic] simultaneously in varied natural and artificial setting stop policy is to combine artistic perfection of italian with virility of american method taking the best out of both schools stop big features only stop [...] Important features being made for me by other plants are nearly ready.[25]

In the telegraphic words of Kleine, feminine Italian art was about to marry American masculine entrepreneurship. The following January, Kleine was in Turin to follow the construction of the studios. Given the reciprocal lack of knowledge of the other's language, all communications between Kleine and Gandolfi took place in French. Together they planned the first round of productions to which the Photo Drama studios were supposed to give birth. Spanish director Segundo de Chomòn, a famous name in French silent cinema who, for Pathé, had rivalled Georges Méliès as a master in special effects, had been hired by Ambrosio since 1912: he was contracted to be the director of Photo Drama's early films. The first to go into production, in the summer of 1915, was a film adaptation of Arrigo Boito's opera *Mefistofele* (1868). Other films equally based on opera works were supposed to follow.

By then, however, on 24 May 1915, Italy had entered the First World War, and the financial prospects of the new company quickly lost their appeal. In a series of telegrams, Gandolfi tried to convince Kleine to stay faithful to the project, but by then the American entrepreneur had decided that the drastic setback suffered by the European film industry demanded a cautious approach. As a consequence, Gandolfi stopped production and instead rented the studios out to Ambrosio's

Fig. 3.3. The headed paper of Photo Drama in a letter sent by Gandolfi to Kleine on 25 June 1914. (courtesy of Manuscript Division, Library of Congress, Washington, DC)

---

[25] Telegram by George Kleine to Led Sterokinet, 12 December 1913; in GKP, Box 30 'Kleine European Trips', file 'European Trip 1913–14'.

main competitor, Itala Film. Personal tragedy was soon to follow: one of the three partners, Stevani, turned out to have accumulated so much debt that he eventually committed suicide, in July 1915. Stevani's widow asked for the company to go into liquidation so that she could rescue some money, and, unable to convince Kleine to intervene, Gandolfi was forced to follow that path. Photo Drama ceased to exist in 1919 (company liquidations were frozen during the war years), and its Brugliasco studios were taken over by the city council and converted for other purposes.

As already evidenced in the footnotes, this important episode in Turin's early cinema history has been studied by more than one film historian. However, one aspect that, in my view, still remains unclear, relates to the role of Arturo Ambrosio.

Judging from Kleine's correspondence, Ambrosio was initially keen to collaborate with him. However, since the latter had decided to create his own company, there must have been inevitable competition between Ambrosio Film and Photo Drama. Moreover, Gandolfi's resignation from Ambrosio Film in order to become an associate of Kleine should not necessarily be considered as an act of collaboration. Indeed, in his own correspondence, once he had moved to Photo Drama, Gandolfi never mentioned Ambrosio, either as a collaborator or as a possible source of help during the company's final crisis. The fact that the studios were eventually rented out to Ambrosio's main rival, Itala Film, is another sign that the creation of Photo Drama had perhaps taken place at the expense of the relationship of Ambrosio with both Kleine and his former financial director, Gandolfi.

Two other details emerging from the correspondence seem to point in that direction. First, when Stevani, on 27 May 1914, wrote to Kleine from Paris to report on the disappointing results of the first films produced by Ambrosio on Photo Drama's account (*The Lion of Venice*, *Othello*, and *Madame du Barry*), he made mention of the fact that at the same time Ambrosio had launched on the market his own historical epic—*The Destruction of Carthage*—and was selling it at a much lower price. Stefani also found it to be of a better quality than the Photo Drama ones; hence, in order to try to stem its competition, he was forced to buy the distribution world rights to Ambrosio's film at a very high price. The implicit comment of Stevani's long report was that the films produced by Ambrosio for Photo Drama were clearly of an inferior quality to that of the film the firm had produced under its own aegis. When replying to Stevani from Chicago, Kleine also dropped two comments relating to Ambrosio that appear slightly derogatory. First he warned Stevani, who at the time was Ambrosio's agent for the distribution of its films in the USA, that he knew for certain that Ambrosio was trying to replace him. Secondly, he mentioned having read in the *Moving Picture World* that Ambrosio had employed an American as its new Commercial Director General and that the firm 'had begun to install American push into the business by engaging numerous high salaried people in all departments'. He accompanied this piece of information with a dry comment: 'It is to laugh.'[26]

The First World War provided a watershed in the history of early cinema, since it created enormous difficulties for the European film industries. The Italian industry began to spiral into a crisis from which it did not recover until the Fascist government came to its rescue in the mid-1930s. The demise of Photo Drama was part of this process, as much as the demise of the Turinese film industry. Rome was to impose itself in the interwar years as the new capital of the Italian film industry. However, these few pages should have provided a sense of the way in which Turinese filmmakers developed their business while negotiating their relations with the leading industries of France and the USA. What emerges is the picture of a generation of filmmakers who had few fears in facing international competition and the world markets. The success of Italian historical/literary films certainly emboldened this attitude. At the same time, there is a clear sense that, if France was, in the early years, the model from which to import ideas, hardware, and human knowhow, by the 1910s the pendulum was swinging towards the USA. No doubt this was the result of the enormous prospects for export, given the size of the US cinema market. Equally important, however, is the perception that the Italian film industry had to a good extent emancipated itself from its dependence on France. Despite Kleine's sarcasm, it is true that Ambrosio in 1914 was attempting to 'Americanize' its staff, starting with the appointment of Frank Joseph Goldsoll as its new Commercial Director General.[27] As for Photo Drama, apart from Kleine's explicit intention to hire US actors to make its productions more attractive to the American market, it is interesting to note that, when the company hired its staff, the traditional French brain drain and head-hunting that had characterized the early years of Italian cinema had disappeared: in the list of all staff employed by Photo Drama on 28 February 1915, there is not a single surname of French origin among the technical personnel.[28]

Finally, the popularity in the USA of Italy's 'kolossals' such as *L'Inferno* and *Cabiria* marked a short but intense period—1911 to 1914—during which the relationship between the Italian and American film industries spoke of reciprocal influence in different areas. As Kleine had envisaged, the capacity of American entrepreneurs to organize and deliver entertainment on a large, industrial scale was able to merge with the Italian tradition of artistic refinement and artisanal skills. Film historians constantly remind us that the father figure of US cinema, D. W. Griffith, was deeply influenced by the spectacular settings of Italian epic

[26] Letter from G. Kleine to A. Gandolfi, dated 21 July 1914; in GKP, Box 54, File 'Mario Stevani 1913–1914'.
[27] The appointment was also announced in an anonymous short article entitled 'F. J. Goldsoll's New Post', which appeared in the *New York Times*, 1 July 1914 (p. 3).
[28] The document containing the full list of personnel working at the Brugliasco studios of Photo Drama is in GKP, Box 44, File 'Photo Drama Producing Co. General 1913–1917'.

films. Equally telling, though, is the fact that Griffith admired other, although similar, Italian skills when he visited Italy's pavilion at San Francisco's Panama–Atlantic International Exposition of 1915. He was impressed by the reconstruction of historical buildings (the Doge's Palace was the main one), and that was the quality he had in mind when he planned to build a film set for the Babylonian episode of *Intolerance* (1916) inspired by Pastrone's *Cabiria*. As his young assistant director at the time, Joseph Henabery, remembers, Griffith sent him all the way to San Francisco to try and find the artisans who had been working at the Italian pavilion, so that they could be hired for his film production. Henabery found that the art and building restoration business in San Francisco was in the hands of Italians, and he managed to track down and employ some of the artisans and artists who had been working on the Italian pavilion. Irony dictates that one of them turned out to be French.[29]

Griffith's passion for expensive, spectacular historical reconstructions was to be his Achilles heel, which eventually made him an outdated figure in the commercially savvy world of post-First World War Hollywood. The Italian film industry too was showing strength as much as weakness. Its attention to epic historical landscapes and its obsession with *mise en scène* and scenography, at the expense of the development of coherent, well-paced narratives, might have brought it to a crisis even if the First World War had not taken place. This weakness was noted with regard to Cines as early as 1910. An eighty-page-long report following an inspection of Cines's financial state by its main creditor, the Banco di Roma, in August 1910, concluded that there was an unhealthy imbalance between production funds invested in *mise en scène* and costumes as against those spent on the development of treatment (*soggetto*) and script, whose quality was often inferior to that of the competition. Its author was Alberto Fassini, a Banco di Roma manager who, in 1909, had joined Cines's governing board. In December 1910, in the wake of his report, he was appointed as one of the three members of Cines's Comitato Direttivo together with the already mentioned Alberto Stevani.[30]

The arrival of the first multi-reel films brought Cines great commercial success in the shape of the already mentioned *La Gerusalemme liberata* (1911) and *Quo Vadis?* (1912). Whether this was the result of Fassini's constructive criticism or of the artistic skills of Enrico Guazzoni as director remains to be seen. Indeed, the fact that Guazzoni's *Quo Vadis?* was mainly complimented by film critics for

---

[29] See the long interview with Joseph Henabery by silent film historian Kevin Brownlow in his *The Parade's Gone By...* (New York: Alfred Kopf, 1968), 43–52. The story of Italian migrants helping to build the sets of D. W. Griffith films was liberally used by the Brothers Taviani in their 1987 film *Good Morning Babylon*.

[30] Long extracts of the report, by Banco di Roma's Alberto Fassini, are quoted in Redi, *La Cines*, 30–7. The full report is held at the Archivio Storico del Banco di Roma at the Archivio Storico UniCredit Banca di Roma, Rome.

its *mise en scène* and use of outdoor sets makes one think that the latter was more likely.

This chapter has concentrated thus far on the development of film companies based in Turin, but the story of Roman Cines confirms a similar pattern of steadfast and ambitious commitment in the competition with the American and French giants of the day. Sadly, Cines too was to face eventual bankruptcy during the crisis years following the First World War. Before then, however, Cines ambitiously attempted to achieve vertical control of distribution and screening abroad through the acquisition of a number of movie theatres in Germany, in the 1910s, supported by American financial backing. One of them was the Lichtspielhaus in Nollendorf Square, in Berlin, which accommodated about one thousand spectators and was later taken over by UFA. It was an ambitious attempt to enter foreign territory, which, as one can easily imagine, was entirely thwarted by the fact that Italy and Germany found themselves on opposite fronts in the war.[31]

Another area in which Cines had ambitiously planned to take on the big American and French competitors—in this case Kodak and Lumière—was related to the production of celluloid film. In 1907, Cines decided to invest in its own production by spending the then huge amount of one and a half million lire in order to buy the knowhow, patents, and technical assistance from the two leading French companies—Lumière and Planchion—and it proceeded to convert a factory outside Padua, with the grand plan of displacing foreign competition in Italy and ideally exporting its own produce. The proposal, approved by Cines's governing body on 13 May 1907 and requiring a huge injection of new capital, gave little space to modesty. In the words of its management board, this development would make Cines 'the only firm in the world that combines cinematography and film, thus achieving a formidable position'.[32]

By December 1907, the Padua factory had started production, employing about 600 workers. However, as we have already seen in Kleine's disappointment with Cines's reels, the quality of the film was never consistently at the level of Kodak's and Lumière's, and by December 1910, the decision had been made to concentrate on the production of celluloid for other purposes, mainly fabric for clothing ('artificial silk', as it was called). Fassini was made director general of Cines Seta, and he was to become one of the leading managers in Italy's celluloid production during the interwar years.[33]

---

[31] On Cines, in addition to Redi, *La Cines*, see Kimberly Tomadjoglou, 'Rome's Premiere Film Studio: Società Italiana Cines', *Film History*, 12/3 (2000), 262–75.

[32] Minutes of Cines' Consiglio d'amministrazione, 13 May 1907; in Archivo Storico Banco di Roma; quoted in Redi, *La Cines*, 54.

[33] Alfred Kallmann, *Die Konzernierung in der Filmindustrie, erläutert an den Filmindustrien Deutschlands und Amerikas* (Würzburg, 1932 (doctoral thesis available online); Kallmann's study concentrates, as the title suggests, on the German and American film industries; his comments on Cines appear on p. 3. On Germany's film market and its progressive 'Americanization' in Weimar Germany,

Back in Turin, by 1916 even Arturo Ambrosio himself seemed to be aware of the dead end that Italian cinema was approaching with its insistence on historical narratives dominated by spectacular *mise en scène*. In an interview with *La Vita cinematografica*, after his return from a trip to the USA, he admitted that the *stile italiano* in cinema was becoming less and less popular in the USA.[34] The first meeting between American and Italian cinema had taken place during the few but intense years before the great storm of the First World War. Italy came slightly late to the international stage, but it had quickly shown its intention to establish itself as a major player. Through Kleine, Italian artistry and American entrepreneurship seemed for a moment to find a powerful synergy. But it was not to be.

Finally, and at a more general level, it should be noted that there was one more reason behind the meeting of Italian and American culture in relation to historical settings. For both countries, ancient history was raw material on which to build a sense of national identity; it was a heritage providing the reassurance of a prestigious past. Since its separation from the colonial motherland, the USA had been developing a separate identity through a cultural shift that privileged the classical roots of Western culture as against the north European gothic tradition celebrated in nineteenth-century Britain. The choice of neoclassical architecture in Washington's main government buildings made Italy's ancient past a shared heritage. The arrival of cinema nurtured this through the monumental reconstructions of cities such as Pompey and Rome. It is not surprising that in the post-war years, once the fever for Italian historical films was over, George Kleine's activity should open up to the distribution of Italian vintage films in American schools and universities. There, they were presented as illustrative historical reconstructions rather than as entertaining narratives.[35]

## 3.2 Turin between French and American Culture: The Car Industry in 1904–1914

As with film, France's contribution to the birth of the automobile is indisputable. Once again, however, it would be problematic and ultimately of little use to try to put together a timeline of 'who-invented-what' at a time when internal combustion engines and their application to vehicles were being developed in many corners of Europe and across the Atlantic. Nevertheless, all car historians would

---

see Thomas J. Saunders, *Hollywood in Berlin: American Cinema and Weimar Germany* (Berkeley and Los Angeles: California University Press, 1994).

[34] Veritas [pseudonym], 'Il cavaliere Ambrosio di ritorno dall'America', *La Vita cinematografica*, 7/15 (February 1916), 74.

[35] On the role of classical culture in shaping American national identity, and on the combined role of American and Italian cinema, see the work of Maria Wyke, in particular her *Projecting the Past: Ancient Rome, Cinema and History* (London: Routledge, 1997).

agree on two facts: first, the forefather of the automobile is Nicholas-Joseph Cugnot, a French military engineer who in 1770 tested a steam-propelled cart. Secondly, if Germany managed to produce the most reliable and paradigm-setting engines in the second half of the nineteenth century, it was France that dominated car production in its early years. In 1891 Panhard et Levassor produced its four-wheeled vehicle, which was to set the standard for the years to come (front engine, sliding gearbox, rear-wheel drive). The historic names of Peugeot and Renault added their capacity to blend technological innovation and industrial production, and by the end of the century the French car industry dominated the world market. By 1903, France was still producing nearly half of all the cars in the entire world, almost three times more than the USA.[36]

France's leading edge left its mark on the industry's lexis too. The French neologism 'automobile' temporarily defeated the competition of 'horseless carriage' (USA), 'motor car' (Britain), and *Selbstfahrer* (Germany) and became the model for many European languages, Italian included. The same for other key expressions such as *carburateur, chassis, volant,* and *garage*. Similarly, in the newly born world of motor racing, the expression *grand prix* was to dominate, despite the resistance from the US motoring press, which, until 1908, tried to replace it with the anglicized version 'grand prize'.[37]

As far as Italy is concerned, beyond various prototypes that were developed in different parts of the country, the fledgling Italian car industry rose to a new level with the 1899 foundation of a company led by a group of Turinese motor enthusiasts: the Fabbrica Italiana Automobili Torino. Among them was Giovanni Agnelli, who became FIAT's managing director in 1901, brought in his family to control the company, and led it personally until the end of the Second World War. Agnelli and his other associates involved in the creation of FIAT were a group of Turinese aristocrats and rich bourgeois (Giovanni's father had been a successful entrepreneur in the silk industry), whose interest in car manufacturing derived from neighbouring France. The announcement of the first pioneering Paris–Rouen motor race, in 1894 (won by two cars, a Panhard et Levassor and a Peugeot Frères), fired the imagination of many, all eager to enter the competition with an Italian-made vehicle. We also know that Giovanni Agnelli's first contacts with the motoring world came partly via Luigi Storero, a Turinese mechanic who imported French tricycle cars. One of the first decisions taken by the newly formed

---

[36] Serge Bellu, *Histoire mondiale de l'automobile* (Paris: Flammarion, 1998), 18. See also James Laux, *In First Gear: The French Automobile Industry to 1914* (Liverpool: Liverpool University Press, 1976); and Gijs Mon, *Atlantic Automobilism: The Emergence and Persistence of the Car: 1890–1940* (New York: Berghahn, 2014).

[37] Charles Bishop, *La France et l'automobile* (Paris: Génin, 1971), 7.

company was to acquire the latest Panhard et Levassor model in order to study it in detail.[38]

The first years saw the company move from one financial crisis to another. Giovanni Agnelli was the most vocal about the need to step away from an expensive artisanal approach, producing individually tailored models, and move instead towards a well-structured and financially viable industrial production. This became a reality only in 1908, with the production of the Fiat Tipo1, which, particularly in its taxi version (aptly named 'Fiacre'), became FIAT's first commercial success, with a total of about 1,600 vehicles being produced, many of which were exported to the main cities of Europe and the USA. The relatively underdeveloped circulation of cars in Italy made export a necessity: in the year 1908, out of 1,215 cars produced by FIAT, 747 were sold abroad.[39]

By then, Giovanni Agnelli had already set his sights on a new paradigm: the US car industry and its enormous internal market. Agnelli's first visit to the USA dates to the autumn of 1905, when he travelled to New York together with the firm's president, Lodovico Scarfiotti, in order to discuss sales in the USA and to consider the possibility of building a factory over there.[40] Protectionist tariffs hindered car exports to the USA—hence Agnelli's idea of creating a US subsidiary. Four years later, in the autumn of 1909, FIAT built its own factory in Poughkeepsie, north of New York City, and production of luxury and racing cars began the following year. About 700 vehicles were built in the first two years.[41]

Fig. 3.4. The newly built FIAT factory in Poughkeepsie, NY, 1909. (courtesy of Centro Storico FIAT, Turin)

[38] Valerio Castronovo, *Giovanni Agnelli: La FIAT dal 1899 al 1945* (Turin: Einaudi, 1977), 9–10. Valerio Castronovo, *FIAT 1899-1999: Un secolo di storia italiana* (Milan: Rizzoli, 1999), 7, 12. See also Progetto Archivio Storico FIAT, *FIAT 1899-1930. Storia e documenti* (Milan: Fabbri, 1991).

[39] Precise production data can be found in Archivio Storico FIAT (ASF), *FIAT: Le fasi della crescita: Le cifre dello sviluppo aziendale* (Turin: Scriptorium, 1996).

[40] Historians disagree on the exact timing of this first visit. However, the minutes of FIAT's administrative board meetings present incontrovertible evidence: the meeting of 13 November 1905 contains a report on the visit to the USA by FIAT's President and its Director ('Amministratore delegato'), Giovanni Agnelli. No firm dates are mentioned, but the timing and content of the report make it clear that the two visited the USA in the weeks preceding November 1905. See Progetto Archivio Storico FIAT, *I primi quindici anni della FIAT: Verbali dei Consigli di amministrazione 1899-1915* (Milan: Franco Angeli, 1987), 347–8.

[41] On FIAT's activity in the USA, see Giuseppe Capirone, 'Fiat "compra" in America, storia di cent'anni', *Il Registro*, 28/4 (October–December 2014), 12–17; and Antonio Amadelli, 'La Fiat in USA: Le origini', *La Manovella*, 1983 (printout held at ASF). See also Giuseppe Volpato, 'L'internazionalizzazione

How did FIAT's development and its early access to the American market fit with the development of the car industry in the USA at the time? As had happened in Europe, a plethora of small, artisanal companies had been born in the final years of the nineteenth century. From these emerged the future giants of the industry, and among them was Henry Ford, who, after leading a number of pioneering attempts, managed to secure the funding for the creation of the Ford Motor Company, in 1903. Thanks to his efforts and that of other established firms such as Oldsmobile and Rambler, the following year the USA's car industry began to overtake that of France in overall production figures, and their leadership increased exponentially from that date: by 1907, US car production was almost double that of France (c.44,000 units versus c.25,000).[42]

The first to develop car production to an advanced industrial level was Henry Ford, with his Model T, whose production in Detroit started in 1908. It was a car designed to be built quickly, and to be reliable, easily maintained, and, more than anything else, affordable. Its success spoke for itself: in 1909 production rose to 10,666 vehicles; in 1910 it reached 19,050. The much-mentioned assembly-line method was introduced in the new Ford factory only in 1912, but by then Henry Ford had already made a name for himself as a careful practitioner of the approach to the scientific management of industrial production theorized by Frederick W. Taylor. Every stage of assemblage was studied in detail and organized so as to streamline production and reduce costs. The net result was that the sale price of the Ford Model T, at $680 in 1911, was a fraction of the cost of any other vehicle of similar size and class. By making cars affordable to the lower middle classes and later on even to his own workers, Ford led the car industry to much wider markets. In 1913, production of the Model T rose to 170,211 units. The European car industry, by then, was a very distant second. In that year, the USA produced 485,000 out of the 606,124 vehicles produced in the whole world.[43]

During one of his visits to the USA, in 1911, Giovanni Agnelli made sure he was able to meet Henry Ford and to be taken on a tour of his factory. Agnelli came to the firm opinion that it was vital to move towards a similar, standardized, low-cost production structure. He arranged for his engineers to visit Ford's factories in order to study and compare the reciprocal organization of labour and assemblage.[44] FIAT's ultimate aim was to produce a similarly economical car to

---

dell'industria automobilistica italiana', in Archivio Storico Fiat, *L'industria italiana nel mercato mondiale: Dalla fine dell'800 alla metà del 900* (Turin: Fiat, 1993), 157–216. See also various documentation in ASF, file 'La Fiat all'estero', box 10, file VII.

[42] James Flink, *The Automobile Age* (Cambridge, MA: MIT Press, 1988), 25.

[43] Flink, *The Automobile Age*, 25.

[44] The full report of the 1918 visit is held at ASF, box 1, file 'Relazione Tecnica, Ing. Maraini'. In 1918, the differential between Ford's and FIAT's assemblage times was still huge: assembling the doors, for instance, varied from 2 minutes in a Ford factory against 15 at FIAT; painting a vehicle differed from 2 hours 40 minutes in a Ford factory against 17 hours 25 minutes at FIAT (pp. 16, 18,

Ford's Model T. The first attempt was the Fiat Zero, a four-seater of which about 2,000 units were produced between 1912 and 1915 (after which the factory was converted for war production). It was, however, a far cry from its American rival, in terms of both production levels and price. An entirely new factory was needed in order radically to move forward. The path was set in 1914, when Agnelli commissioned architect Giacomo Matté Trucco to plan a cutting-edge factory adopting Ford's moving assembly line. The project, however, saw its completion only after the First World War, and so we will consider this in the second part of this book, in Chapter 9.

In actual fact, Giovanni Agnelli's relationship with the USA was not exactly one of grateful admiration. As he knew well, the extraordinary growth of the US car industry posed a serious threat to European car manufacturers. We have already seen how Giovanni Agnelli had no deferential fears. The creation of a factory on US soil was a clear move into his competitor's territory. Giovanni Agnelli was also particularly active in making use of the prestige that could be derived from the success of FIAT racing cars. Since the early years of car racing in the USA, FIAT cars were present, and successfully so. On the occasion of the first Grand Prix in the USA, the American Grand Prize, which took place in Savannah, Georgia, on Thanksgiving Day, on 26 November 1908, Agnelli sent an official FIAT racing team, which fielded three cars, driven respectively by a French, an Italian, and an American driver. Only eleven of the twenty cars on the starting line finished the race, but all three FIATs completed it and secured two podium places (first and third) as well as the ninth position. French, German, and another Italian car manufacturer (Itala; no relation to Itala Film) occupied the other places, with the first US-built car clocking an embarrassing eleventh position and arriving forty-one minutes behind the leaders. Given that this was happening during the same year in which Henry Ford was beginning to produce his Model T by the tens of thousands, it suggests that Agnelli's initial strategy was to concentrate on the luxury market and sport cars. This, after all, had been the profile of European manufacturers from the very beginning. Indeed, that is what the US factory in Poughkeepsie was set up to do.[45]

Back in Italy, however, it was important to keep the Americans at arm's length, or at least to come to terms with them. Initially this seemed to take the shape of collaboration. Ford arrived in Italy in 1905: this was the first year in which the US company appeared at the Esposizione internazionale di automobile in Turin, Italy's principal motor show. It had a single stand, represented by its European distributor, H. B. White, which was based in Paris. The Ford Motor Company was

in the report). See also Pier Luigi Bassignana, 'Tayloristi loro malgrado', in Bassignana (ed), *Taylorismo e fordismo alla Fiat nelle relazioni di viaggio di tecnici e ingegneri (1919–1955)* (Turin: AMMA, 1998), 7–36.

[45] See Bruno Bottiglieri, 'Strategie di sviluppo, assetti organizzativi e scelte finanziarie nel primo trentennio di vita della Fiat', in Progetto ASF, *FIAT 1899–1930*, 13–40.

absent in the following two years, until in 1908 it came back to the Esposizione internazionale in a big way. This time it shared an imposing set of stands with Italy's leading car factory, FIAT. What had happened is that in that year the official distributor and repairer of FIAT cars—Garages Riuniti (which was part-owned by FIAT)—had acquired the sales and maintenance services of Ford cars too. This surprising 'marriage' lasted for only two years, after which Ford returned to being independently represented. On the part of Agnelli, this seems to have been the result of an attempt to keep Ford under FIAT's roof, which would have had two obvious advantages: on the one hand, the acquisition of a detailed knowledge of Ford's cars and marketing strategies, and, on the other, the ability to influence its distribution in Italy.[46]

Luckily for the Italian car industry, Henry Ford did consider the Italian market to be of sufficient size to deserve particular interest. In the pre-First World War years, the circulation of cars in the peninsula was greatly inferior to that of more

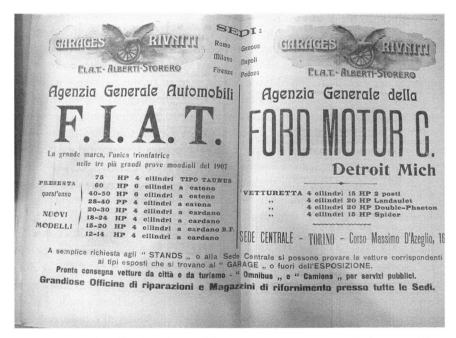

Fig. 3.5. From the official catalogue of the Esposizione internazionale di automobili, Turin, 18 January–2 February 1908. (courtesy of Centro Documentazione—Museo Nazionale dell'Automobile, Turin)

---

[46] Years later, in March 1930, at the peak of FIAT's battle to defend the Italian market from Ford's potential presence, Giovanni Agnelli made a similar move when he offered Ford a manufacturing alliance that would have seen the two companies near-monopolize the Italian market. The offer was turned down by Ford, as recently revealed in an article by economic historian Pier Angelo Toninelli, 'Between Agnelli and Mussolini: Ford's Unsuccessful Attempt and the Italian Automobile Market in the Interwar Period', *Enterprise & Society*, 10/2 (2009), 335–75.

developed European countries. In 1910, for example, there were fewer than eight thousand registered vehicles on the road in Italy, compared to about one hundred thousand in Great Britain.[47] It was only in the post-war years that Ford and the other US giant, General Motors, began a more aggressive campaign towards securing their presence in Europe, Italy included. As we will see, there and then Giovanni Agnelli had to work towards the creation of protectionist policies similar to those that had closed the door to French films in early twentieth-century America. His friendly relationship with Benito Mussolini was to come to good use.

## Concluding Remarks

Looking at Turin in the early years of the twentieth century, while concentrating on the film and car industries, has provided an opportunity to study the development of two products that very much defined twentieth-century culture at a time when the USA was beginning to assert its economic power. In both cases, it is clear that, from the Italian perspective, a shift from France to the USA took place in a matter of a few years, well before the First World War. Another common factor is the degree of self-assuredness demonstrated by Turinese entrepreneurs. The recognition of the dominance of a certain foreign industry did not imply a sense of inferiority, nor did it create adulation towards its model. Arturo Ambrosio as much as Giovanni Agnelli—and the same can be said for Camillo Olivetti—were representatives of an entrepreneurial class who boldly developed their business and simply looked at what the international market had to offer.

A final question relating to the presence and influence of American products in these two industries remains to be tackled: why did the development happen so quickly, in comparison with other areas of Italian culture? There are two probable causes. First of all, both films and automobiles are commodities that are highly dependent on technology. This is an area in which the American economy was capable of competing with its European rivals at the turn of the century and—with regard to mass production and distribution—was already showing its supremacy over the old continent. In both fields, France had been a leading country, but within a few years a number of factors—including the huge potential of the US internal market, the world's largest at the time—allowed the USA to take the upper hand. The First World War certainly gave an enormous advantage to the American film industry (there was no disruption to either its production or its national market), but it is doubtful whether the process would have been very different without it. FIAT and the car industry in general benefited from the war—FIAT's army truck 18BL became, after all, FIAT's first mass-produced

---

[47] See Sara Moscatelli, 'Il veicolo della modernità: L'automobile', in Paride Rugafiori (ed.), *La capitale dell'automobile: Imprenditori, cultura e società a Torino* (Venice: Marsilio, 1999), 65–138 (78–80).

vehicle—but once it was over, they would have suffered the same destiny as Italy's film industry, if it were not for the protectionist policies that kept the USA outside the national borders. If 'Hollywood on the Tiber' was to become a reality in later years, it was political and economic interests that ensured that the USA was never allowed a 'Detroit on the Po river'.

The second point concerns the fact that cinema and automobiles were entirely new products. In both cases, the USA did not have to face a European, sedimented tradition that somehow gave it an initial advantage. In fact, the weight of the past came to function as a hindrance. Intellectual snobbery towards the medium of film persisted in European intellectual circles for decades. One of the consequences of this is the American birth of Film Studies as an academic subject, something that European universities were slower to adopt. The car industry fared better, although a classic example is the persistence of the 'horse-friendly' 1865 Locomotive Act of the British parliament, which stated that self-propelled vehicles on public roads had to be preceded by a man on foot armed with a red flag. By the time the law was repealed, in 1898, the British car industry had lost precious ground.[48] More importantly, beyond the intrinsic conservatism of established cultures, films and cars happened to be born at the time at which the USA was ready to show the strength of its economy. As such, both became icons of modernity and symbols of mass culture.

---

[48] On the early history of Film Studies as an academic subject, see Dana Polan, *Scenes of Instruction: The Beginnings of the US Study of Film* (Berkeley and Los Angeles: University of California Press, 2007). On the 1865 Locomotive Act, see Brian Ladd, *Autophobia: Love and Hate in the Automotive Age* (Chicago: University of Chicago Press, 2008), 14–28.

# 4
# American Literature, Opera Librettos, and Pragmatism

The knowledge and appreciation of American literature in the decades preceding the First World War are closely connected to the dominant image of America among Italy's educated elite. On the whole, American literature was considered a minor offshoot of its British progenitor, coloured by the romanticized traits of a young nation, close to nature, genuine but unrefined, unless Europeanized to its core, such as in the work of Henry James. Its circulation was closely linked to the scarce knowledge of the English language among Italians. This had a direct influence on the discovery of American literature, since French translations regularly acted as a cultural go-between. Even the fact that millions of Italians migrated to the Americas in the decades around the turn of the century did not encourage better knowledge of the English language (or of Spanish too, for that matter).

This cultural resistance is also somehow connected to the near-absence of the theme of migration to the USA in the literary production of Italian authors. Despite the fact that millions of Italians from all over the peninsula and islands were crossing the Atlantic in search of a better present and future, both the interest in the language and literature of those distant places and the interest in representing the experience of migration remained minimal.

In order to pay adequate attention to these factors, the following pages will first trace the features and channels of the initial appreciation of American literature. Some considerations will also be devoted to opera librettos, a genre that showed a similar tension between French and American influence. The second section will dwell on the treatment, however scarce, of the theme of migration to the USA in fictional works, and a final section will discuss the interest in American pragmatist philosophy, which also concerned a young socialist revolutionary called Benito Mussolini.

## 4.1 American Literature and the Middlebrow

Some of the most celebrated nineteenth-century American authors did travel to Italy, and their visits left their mark on their fictional production. Nathaniel Hawthorne was in Italy for almost a year, in 1858–9, although his Protestant outlook was to colour negatively his vision of the *Belpaese,* which he projected into the neo-Gothic landscape of his last novel, *The Marble Faun* (1860). The most Italophile among this group was Henry James, who visited Italy eleven times between 1877 and 1907, sometimes for a few weeks but sometimes for up to six months. Much of his first, successful novel, *Roderick Hudson* (1875), was written during his stay in Florence, the previous year, and Italy's art cities surround its American protagonist.

However, none of these authors played a major role in the discovery of American literature by Italian intellectuals. During the second half of the nineteenth century, the interest in the New World and, more specifically in the USA, had already taken literary shape in the form of hugely popular works of middle-brow literature. The first is James Fenimore Cooper's adventure novel *The Last of the Mohicans* (1826). The best of his so-called Leatherstockings series, the novel became a sensation in Europe and has much to do with the creation of the most American genre, the frontier's novel, which was to become the western once the frontier moved further west.[1]

The second one is Harriet Beecher Stowe's *Uncle Tom's Cabin* (1852). Soon after its publication, Italian translations began to mushroom in different corners of Italy, from Turin, to Genoa, Venice, Florence, and Naples: ten different editions were published in two years (one, oddly, in French). The abolitionist cause became the subject of even a ballet, *Bianchi e neri*, composed in 1853 by Giuseppe Rota and performed at Milan's La Scala and in most of Italy's major theatres, often combined with an opera by Giuseppe Verdi. In the end, twenty-five Italian editions of *Uncle Tom's Cabin* were published between 1852 and the end of the century, for either adult or young readers, and, together with several stage adaptations, they sparked interest in the New World of the United States of America. It was a rural portrait of the USA in which the issue of slavery added an element of backwardness that fitted well with the image of the USA as a young country, proudly independent, but still well behind Europe in terms of social norms and lifestyle.[2]

---

[1] Fenimore Cooper's novel set during the American War of Independence—*The Spy* (1821)—was also very popular: it saw more editions than any other of his novels in nineteenth-century Italy. On Cooper's translations, see James Woodress, 'The Fortunes of Cooper in Italy', *Studi americani*, 10/2 (1965), 53–76. Incidentally, James Fenimore Cooper had spent almost two years in Italy during his long stay in Europe in 1826–33. His—mainly disappointing—experience of Italy was recollected in his travel book *Excursions to Italy* (1838) and in the political novel set in Venice, *The Bravo* (1831).

[2] See Frederick Jackson, 'An Italian Uncle Tom's Cabin', *Italica*, 35/1 (1958), 38–42; and Axel Körner, 'Uncle Tom on the Ballet Stage: Italy's Barbarous America, 1850–1900', *Journal of Modern History*, 83/4 (2011), 721–52; and, by the same author, 'Masked Faces: Verdi, Uncle Tom and the Unification of Italy', *Journal of Modern Italian Studies*, 18/2 (2013), 176–89. The material of both essays is re-elaborated in chapter 5 of Körner's recent monograph, *America in Italy*. See also Enrico Botta, 'Da una guerra civile all'altra: Lo zio Tom, la secessione e l'unità d'Italia', *Ácoma*, 21 (2021), 22–42. Huge interest in Stowe's novel did not engender equal interest in her other works. Together with most of them, her novel set in Renaissance Italy, *Agnes of Sorrento* (1861), was, to my knowledge, never translated into Italian.

A third, very popular middlebrow novel was the work of another woman writer, Louisa May Alcott. Her *Little Women* (1868-9) was also destined to become a classic in adult and then in children's literature, but its circulation in Italy flourished at a later stage. It was first known through its French translation of 1896 and was eventually brought into Italian only in 1908. Another author to receive late recognition was American's most famous humorist, Mark Twain, whose work was translated and critically praised only at the start of the twentieth century, a few years before his death. Mark Twain too had travelled extensively throughout Italy, in 1867, an experience that became part of his travel book *The Innocents Abroad: A New Pilgrims' Progress* (1869).

Beyond the vast popularity of these works, two other authors came to represent American literature, neither of whom had ever set foot on Italian soil. They were Walt Whitman and Edgar Allan Poe. Their appreciation—in some cases their cult—was initiated by Italy's first scholar in American literature, Enrico Nencioni. In a number of essays published in Florence's prestigious cultural journal *Nuova antologia*, Nencioni introduced the Italian elite to the contemporary work of American authors. A poet in his younger years, Nencioni had come into contact with the small community of British and American expats living in Florence. Among them were Robert and Elizabeth Browning, and, indeed, Nencioni's first essay for *Nuova antologia*, in 1867, was dedicated to the former's poetry, and his subsequent literary writings moved between English and American literature. On the whole, Nencioni proved more of a literary journalist than a scholar—despite his career as an academic in Italian literature—and, indeed, his essays reveal today the limitations of views coming from an insightful but rather superficial and over-digressive reader.

At the time, however, his essays established Nencioni as the most authoritative Italian voice on American literature. It was he who developed a vision that was to become dominant in the following decades. Walt Whitman's poetry was presented as the most characteristic of this young, national tradition: a naïve but wilful, anti-intellectual literature able to connect a primitive, romanticized bond to the natural world with a praise of modernity in both its social and technological expression. Edgar Allan Poe's work, at the same time, was seen as embodying the nocturnal, dark side of this vision: a hallucinatory but formally sophisticated exploration of nightmarish landscapes where—to paraphrase Goya's famous etching—the sleep of reason generates literary monsters. Nencioni's work proved influential on leading Italian literary figures at the time. Both Giosuè Carducci and Giovanni Pascoli eagerly read his essays and wrote themselves in praise of Whitman, and so did the younger Gabriele D'Annunzio, who, however, mistook the democratic, ordinary 'I' of Whitman's poetry for a variation on his own Nietzschean and elitist view of the *Übermensch*. At the same time, the neo-Gothic and perturbing traits of Poe's fiction were much appreciated among the avant-garde group of Milanese authors called the *Scapigliatura*. From them was to flourish Italy's peculiar genre of *letteratura fantastica*.

What these literary appreciations had in common was the idea of American literature as the bearer of a sort of antidote to the rhetorical and over-self-conscious Italian tradition. In many respects, the literary *mito americano*, which was to develop in the 1930s, was already present, *in nuce*, in Nencioni's years. The main difference, however, was that the Italian literati of the late nineteenth century interpreted it from a condescending, superior viewpoint: the work of authors such as Whitman and Poe was a stimulus, a call to a return to a less scholarly notion of literature. It was far from being an accolade for the entire body of American literature as an emerging national tradition. Typical, in this respect, was Ugo Ojetti's view, expressed in 1898 and quoted in Chapter 2: the USA could be thought of as being able to produce 'two or three' great artists, 'two or three' great authors at most; no more than that.

Nencioni's role was also typical in the fact that he did not write nor lecture on American literature as an academic. It would be naïve to expect that American literature should have entered the doors of Italian academia in the late nineteenth century; this did not happen in the rest of Europe either. At the same time, this remained the case in Italy for decades, well into the mid-twentieth century. The first generations of 'americanisti' were either scholars who developed their interest as an aside to their actual specialism, or enthusiasts who belonged to the world of journalism and popular literature. Indeed, the first monograph in the field of American literature is a short history entitled *Manuale di letteratura americana* (1884), written by Gustavo Strafforello and published by Hoepli, a Milanese publisher aiming at the new market of lesser-educated readers.

Strafforello was a journalist and a publicist specializing in publications with a similar readership—suffice it to mention other books he authored such as *La scienza per tutti* (*Science for Everybody* (1869)) and *I fenomeni della vita industriale spiegati al popolo* (*The Phenomena of Industrial Life Explained to the People* (1870)). He also wrote an improbable adventure novel set in America, *Il nuovo Monte Cristo: Memorie di un emigrante* (*The New Monte Cristo: Memoirs of a Migrant* (1856)), featuring, not an Italian, but an Irish migrant during the Californian gold rush. In his handbook on American literature, Strafforello took the word 'literature' as a synonym for the more generic term 'publications', as his chapters list the life and works of literary authors just as much as those of philosophers, scholars, and scientists. Indeed, Strafforello's work is informative rather than erudite, and, unsurprisingly, it was mainly ignored by post-Second World War Italian historians of American literature. The fact that the book is derivative from similar publications in English by American and British publishers makes us infer that Strafforello must have had a good command of the language. More importantly, the 'middlebrow dimension' within which this publication arose chimes with the popularity of American literature as it was to develop in the early decades of the twentieth century.[3]

As we will see, before the 'decade of translations', as the 1930s were famously called by Cesare Pavese, American literature continued to be translated and popular in its middlebrow version, with Jack London as its leading champion in the 1920s. This is confirmed by Valerio Ferme's analysis of translations from American publications even for the years preceding the First World War. At that time, too, the list of American books translated into Italian was led by Beecher Stowe, Fenimore Cooper, Poe, and Twain.[4]

To return to literary criticism, the next monograph that followed Strafforello's handbook came from a similarly unorthodox figure. The author of a volume on Walt Whitman (1898) was Pasquale Jannaccone, a young enthusiast of American literature who was actually an economist. At the time Jannaccone was a young academic studying under the direction of Salvatore Cognetti de Martiis, whom we encountered in Chapter 2 as the author of one of the first monographs on the USA. Jannaccone's studies as an economist were then focused on workers' rights in British industry, but, perhaps in connection with his supervisor's focus on the USA, he developed an interest in American literature. It was a passing phase, though. After his book on Whitman's poetry, and an essay on Poe published in *Nuova antologia*, in 1895, Jannaccone concentrated entirely on his profession as an economist. He was eventually to inherit the prestigious chair of Economia politica at Turin university that had been held by Cognetti De Martiis.

When it comes to the early years of the twentieth century, American literature was still the territory of non-specialists. From Florence, Giovanni Papini added his voice in praise of Walt Whitman in a 1908 essay, again published in *Nuova antologia*, in the wake of the first complete Italian translation of *Leaves of Grass* (1907). With a mind frame similar to that of D'Annunzio's, Papini too interpreted Whitman through a Nietzschean perspective, which was more at the service of his nationalistic call for an elitist renewal of Italian letters than a well-contextualized appreciation of Whitman's poetry.[5]

This tendency in Italian criticism was coupled with a trait that has emerged repeatedly in these early chapters: the French connection. The discovery of American literature was firmly guided by the literary debate across the Alps. The case of Edgar Allan Poe is typical: his European fortune started in Paris, and it became utterly dependent on the dedication of Charles Baudelaire. Its impact can easily be found in Italy: every single short story by Poe was translated into French

---

[3] On Strafforello, see Anna De Biasio, 'Appunti sui primi studi americanistici in Italia: Gustavo Strafforello e il suo *Manuale di letteratura italiana* (1884)', *Annali di Ca' Foscari*, 39/1–2 (2000), 113–33.

[4] Valerio Ferme, 'Appendice', in Ferme, *Tradurre è tradire: La traduzione come sovversione culturale sotto il fascismo* (Ravenna: Longo, 2003), 223–8.

[5] See Maria Camboni, 'Giovanni Papini e Walt Whitman tra Pragmatismo, Nietzsche e Futurismo', *900 Transnazionale/Transnational 900*, 2/1 (2018), 26–41.

before somebody thought of producing an Italian version. Many were translated by Baudelaire himself, including Poe's most famous short story, *Murders of the Rue Morgue* (1841), which was the clear model for the first five Italian versions published between 1863 and 1894. This is revealed by the migration of the liberties that Baudelaire took in lexis and syntax from the French into the Italian translation, including the title itself, with Baudelaire's change of 'Murders' into 'Double assassinat' fully reflected in all five Italian translations with 'Doppio assassinio'. As for Poe's only novel, *The Adventures of Gordon Pym* (1838), it is indicative that Baudelaire's French translation of 1858 is held today by forty Italian libraries, whereas the later Italian translation is held by only nine. This adds weight to the suggestion that, at the turn of the century, English-writing authors—Americans among them—were more likely to be read in their French translation. Similar considerations could be made about the critical debate. When a young Emilio Cecchi first wrote about Poe's poetry, as late as 1910, he concentrated on the French translations.[6]

The first appreciation of Whitman's poetry was similarly derived from France. Nencioni had first heard of Walt Whitman through the mediation of an expert of French literature, Girolamo Ragusa Moleti, who was the Italian translator and early exegetist of Baudelaire's work. Ragusa Moleti had also encouraged his friend Luigi Gamberale to translate Whitman's poetry into Italian. Indeed, Gamberale was the translator of all three editions of Whitman's poetry mentioned before.[7]

As for the Italian poets who were influenced by American literature, while Carducci eagerly tried to learn English in order to enjoy the original texts, Pascoli and D'Annunzio never mastered it: so much so that, when Pascoli tried his hand at a translation of Poe's celebrated poem, *The Raven*, he modelled it around Mallarmé's French translation. And, although D'Annunzio's private library holds an original edition of Whitman's *Leaves of Grass*, this sits next to the two volumes of its French translation. Finally, a study on the Milanese *Scapigliati* shows how their reception of Poe's work came entirely through France, Baudelaire *in primis*.[8]

---

[6] Library data are extracted from the Italian national catalogue databank (Catalogo OPAC SBN del Servizio Bibliotecario Nazionale). They are indicative but approximate for two reasons: first, there is the chance that copies of books printed in the late nineteenth century might have been acquired by a library at a later date. Secondly, not all Italian public libraries have uploaded their data on the system. On Poe, see Costanza Melani, *Effetto Poe: Influssi delle scrittore americano sulla letteratura italiana* (Florence: Florence University Press, 2006). Emilio Cecchi wrote on Poe's poetry in *Cronache letterarie* of 12 June 1910; he then returned to the Italian translations of Poe's work on 9 February 1913.

[7] On the fortune on Whitman's poetry abroad, see Gay Wilson Allen (ed.), *Walt Whitman Abroad* (Syracuse, NY: Syracuse University Press, 1955), 187–98, on Italy.

[8] On Pascoli, see Giovanni Getto, 'Pascoli e l'America', in Getto, *Carducci e Pascoli* (Bologna: Zanichelli, 1957), 154–84. D'Annunzio's library is today public at the Vittoriale museum in Gardone, on Lake Garda. On the *Scapigliatura*, see Sergio Rossi, 'E. A. Poe e la scapigliatura lombarda', *Studi americani*, 5 (1959) 119–39. D'Annunzio's knowledge of the English language was, in Praz's words, 'rudimentary', hence he always turned to French translations for assistance (Mario Praz, *Il patto col serpente* (Milan: Mondadori, 1972), 400).

Between Poe and Whitman, it was the former who proved extremely popular in the then growing market of low- to middlebrow fiction. In this sector, as Gramsci had expanded upon in one of his prison notebooks, the Italian book industry was lagging behind its north European counterpart, owing to its elite's incapacity to produce a home-grown 'national-popular' literature.[9] Once again, France was the leading light, with scores of translations of French sentimental novels and short stories finding their way into Italian bookshops and the literary sections of periodicals and newspapers. At the same time, the early nineteenth century had seen a growing interest in new narrative genres: the British neo-Gothic novel was feeding a growing market for stories of mysterious and heinous murders; once this trend met the urban settings of the modern metropolis, it was to develop into the ever-popular genre of crime fiction. Poe is considered a father figure of the genre, largely because of the already mentioned 'Murders in the Rue Morgue' and other stories that used Paris as the backdrop for the investigations of Monsieur Dupin. By then, the genre had already been established in France through the fictional memoirs of Eugene François Vidocq, the first head of the French police. His four volumes of stories—actually ghost-written by two journalists and published between 1828 and 1829—were a huge success: the character of Vidocq acquired a legendary reputation decades before Conan Doyle was to bring Sherlock Holmes to literary fame.

One notable exception concerns an iconic figure of American popular detective fiction: Nick Carter. His stories, initially written by John R. Coryell, were imported into Italy via a German company, Eichler, which represented the American publisher Street & Smith in parts of Europe. This used a sister publisher in Milan, called Casa Americana, which between 1908 and 1911 produced 150 issues of the dime novel series *Nick Carter Weekly*, which in Italian became *Nick Carter, il gran poliziotto americano*. Between 1901 and 1912, Casa Americana had also been distributing the Italian version of Street & Smith's dime novels dedicated to Buffalo Bill, translated as: *Bufalo Bill: L'eroe del Far West*. This underlines the importance of German publishers in the introduction of American dime novels throughout continental Europe. However, when it comes to the circulation of American fiction in a more sophisticated, middlebrow version, such as the publication of James Fenimore Cooper's adventure novels, literary historians have no doubts about placing France as the main channel through which this new genre reached Italy. Years before Salgari produced his first western novel in 1896, Italian publishers had already been translating the popular French followers of Cooper's fiction in the shape of the American adventure novels by Gabriel Ferry and Gustave Aimard.[10]

---

[9] I am referring to Notebook 14 (1932–35), the one from which the repeated quote of nineteenth-century Italy as a provincial equivalent of France is to be found.

[10] On Nick Carter, see Massimo Introvigne, 'Nick Carter in Italy', *Dime Novel Round-Up*, 75/1 (2006), 12–15. On Buffalo Bill, see Matteo Pollone, 'Non solo Spaghetti: Il western italiano prima e dopo Leone', in Pollone (ed.), *Il western in Italia*, 3–22 (9–10). On early French western novels, see Luca Di Gregorio, 'Per un pugno di romanzi. L'immaginario del West di Emilio Salgari, tra "selvaggismo nero" e western americano (1896–1910)', in Pollone (ed.), Il Western in Italia, 23–36.

Overall, it appears that the emergence of American literature in late-nineteenth- and early twentieth-century Italy was determined by two factors. First, a scant and non-specialist attention on the part of literary critics, whose interest in specific authors such as Whitman and Poe was much influenced by the French literary debate. Secondly, the great popularity of works of narrative that pertained to the lower echelons of the literary canon, such as Fenimore Cooper's adventure novels and, further down, the cheap paperback fiction to be found in market stalls and news kiosks.

If we move to the genre where literature met music, the opera libretto, here, too, the influence from France is palpable. Although the use of the Italian language was still dominant in Europe and the Americas, the work of French popular fiction writers such as Victor Hugo, Alfred de Musset, and Casimir Delavigne was particularly in vogue as an inspiration for Italian operas. A third of Gioachino Rossini's work—inclusive of his masterpiece *Il barbiere di Siviglia* (1816)—were adapted from French narratives. This was also the case for other famous Italian opera composers of the following generation. A considerable number of Giuseppe Verdi's most renowned works had plots that were based on French works—from *Nabucco* (1842), to *Rigoletto* (1851), *La traviata* (1853), and *Un ballo in maschera* (1859)—and so were Giacomo Puccini's *Manon Lescaut* (1893; whose fourth act is set in New Orleans), *La Bohème* (1896), *Tosca* (1900), and *Madama Butterfly* (1904).[11]

However, even in the traditionally conservative world of opera, the influence of America began to emerge. At its start we find the case of Lorenzo da Ponte, the librettist of Mozart's Italian operas. Da Ponte spent the last thirty years of his life in New York, after fleeing from his creditors in Europe. In 1833, he was involved in the creation of the first purpose-built opera house in New York, the Italian Opera House, which opened with Rossini's *La gazza ladra* (1817). However, it was a venture quickly destined to fail—two years later—like many of Da Ponte's projects.

Mention should also be made of the peculiar genesis of Verdi's *Un ballo in maschera* (1859). Based on an earlier libretto by Eugène Scribe, Verdi's version moved the historical setting from Sweden to the North America of the colonial years in order to avoid political censorship. The American setting was therefore purely instrumental, although Verdi did exploit the dramatic potential of a setting in the New World, and, as Körner has shown in detail, the opera contributed to the image of America at the time of Italy's wars of independence.[12]

However, it was in the years following the foundation of New York's Metropolitan Opera, in 1883, that America started to compete with Europe's

---

[11] On this, see Sassoon, *The Culture of the Europeans*, 549–61. More specifically, on Rossini's relationship with French culture, see Benjamin Walton, 'Rossini and France', in Emanuele Senici (ed.), *The Cambridge Companion to Rossini* (Cambridge: Cambridge University Press, 2004), 25–36.

[12] See Körner, *America in Italy*, 164–98.

major opera houses. In 1907, the Metropolitan's board of directors decided that the time had come to hire one of Europe's most respected impresarios in order to set the opera house on an international footing. Its President, Otto Kahn, met in Paris with Giulio Gatti Casazza, impresario at Milan's La Scala, and in one single swoop he managed to hire Gatti Casazza and Italy's most famous conductor of his generation, Arturo Toscanini. The former was to remain in charge of the Met until 1935, whereas Toscanini was in New York for seven years, between 1908 and 1915. With the two, came the commissioning of an opera by Italy's then most renowned composer, Giacomo Puccini. In this case the American setting was part of the deal.

The libretto *La fanciulla del West* was set in California at the time of the Gold Rush, adapted from the near-homonymous play, *The Girl of the Golden West* (1905), written by America's most successful playwright, director, and impresario at the time, David Belasco. Puccini's opera was premiered in New York on 10 December 1910, with Italy's most famous tenor, Enrico Caruso, starring in the protagonist's role of Dick Johnson. David Belasco had been indirectly involved in the making of another major opera by Puccini: *Madama Butterfly* (1904). Despite being French in its origins—a novel by Pierre Loti—the libretto had been adapted from a derivative short story by American author John Luther Long, which itself had been turned into a successful play by David Belasco. During one of his visits to London, in the summer of 1900, Puccini had seen Belasco's play on stage. There is a sense that America (beyond the Japanese setting, Madama Butterfly's husband is an American naval officer), and America's literary world, embodied by Belasco, were by then emerging as a new source of inspiration. It should also be remembered that Puccini had already experimented with a swinging, syncopated rhythm in a band march that he had composed under commission in 1899 for the celebration of the centenary of Alessandro Volta's invention of the electric battery. For the occasion, Puccini had chosen a contemporary sound, and the piece was topically entitled 'La scossa elettrica'.

As for *La fanciulla del West*, set in a Californian gold-mining camp, the libretto followed closely the plot of Belasco's play. It is a story that adopts the traditional image of the Wild West as a land of extremes and primitiveness, but at the same time gravitates around the figure of a woman, Minnie, whose strength, intelligence and courage—she is also an Annie Oakley-style sharpshooter—turn her into a dominant, powerful character. Puccini had watched a production of Belasco's play during his visit to New York in 1907, a trip that had been financed by the Metropolitan so that he could attend the American premiere of two of his operas, *Manon Lescaut* (starring Pino Caruso and Lina Cavalieri) and *Madama Butterfly*. It was then that Puccini began to think about creating his next composition around *The Girl of the Golden West* and have it premiered at the Met. At the time, he was actually committed to an opera version of the French novel *La femme et le pantin* (1898) by Pierre Louÿs. Moreover, as his English was very poor, he had to

AMERICAN LITERATURE, OPERA LIBRETTOS, AND PRAGMATISM 141

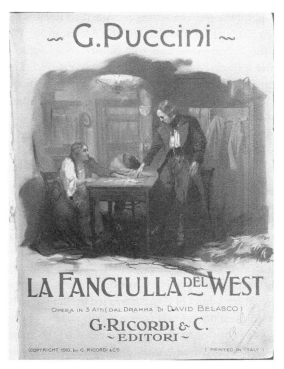

Fig. 4.1. Front cover of the first edition of the libretto of Puccini's *La fanciulla del West* (1910). (courtesy of the Weston Library, Oxford)

wait for a copy of Belasco's play to be translated into Italian before he could seriously consider the American play. The translation was completed after his return to Italy, and at that point Puccini dropped the French novel (which was turned into an opera by Riccardo Zandonai) and committed himself to *The Girl of the Golden West*.

To write an opera set in America and to present it first to an American audience was a great challenge for Puccini (less so for his two librettists, since they stayed close to the play by Belasco, who was also involved in the staging of the opera). Indeed, beyond the enthusiastic reception on the premiere's night, the comments by music critics were lukewarm. Puccini had attempted to import American melodies and rhythms within the score. His choices, however, proved to be somewhat awkward, and this did not go unnoticed. Caruso's character, Dick Johnson, although a Mexican, was associated with a cakewalk song, a type of music strictly connected with African Americans. And a Native American melody that was adopted was oddly turned into a song played by a blackface minstrel who was part of the small mining community. Neither did the opera prove particularly popular in Italy. Puccini's attempt both to explore the American musical tradition and to adopt the western setting remained an isolated case. The awkward marriage between Italy's opera tradition and the American Far West proved sterile. If the press of the Italian American community could write proudly about a premiere that had showcased the best of Italy's musical tradition with the trio of Puccini–Toscanini–Caruso, what was noteworthy was the fact that New York's Metropolitan had begun to rival Paris as commissioning venue for a prestigious premiere.[13]

However, as we will see in Chapter 5, it was not opera but a very different genre of music that marked the American presence in Europe. Jazz was an autochthonous development that was about to cross the ocean and take Europe by storm.

## 4.2 Migration to the USA in Italian literature and early cinema

The tendency either to ignore or to defend patriotically the poor conditions of Italian migrants in America's big cities was reflected in contemporary literature. This is particularly true of the pre-First World War years. Despite the fact that the late-nineteenth-century school of *verismo* was led by Sicilian writers who concentrated their narratives on provincial life, it was only at a very late stage—almost as an afterthought—that one of them devoted a novel to the subject of migration. This was Luigi Capuana's *Gli americani di Ràbbato*, a short novel published in 1912 that was aimed at a younger readership—so-called *letteratura per ragazzi*—and reached little notoriety. The novel tells the story of a barber who returns from New York to his Sicilian hometown, boasts of his newly acquired wealth, and convinces scores of his fellow citizens to travel with him back to America. Two peasant brothers decide to follow him—and the novel concentrates on them. The less mature of the two, however, Stefano, refuses menial jobs and ends up in the criminal underworld as a member of the infamous 'Black Hand'. In the meantime, a third, 9-year-old brother has joined them and, thanks to the fact that he can read and write, he can easily get a good job. But Stefano is arrested and goes to jail, and so his two brothers return to Sicily to defend his honour (they spread the lie that Stefano is prospering as a farmer) and eventually decide to stay in Sicily for good. The ending overflows with patriotic feelings, with the youngest, Menu, shouting: 'I want to be Sicilian, Italian, not a bastard American!' The novel's sociological interest is carried by the story's suggestion that artisans were an active,

---

[13] On *La fanciulla del West*, see Annie J. Randall and Rosalind Gray Davis, *Puccini and the Girl: History and Reception of 'The Girl of the Golden West'* (Chicago: University of Chicago Press, 2005); and Michele Girardi, *Puccini. His International Art* (Chicago: Chicago University Press, 2000), 259–327. On the enthusiastic reception among the Italian American community, see Kunio Hara, '"Per noi emigrati": Nostalgia in the Reception of Puccini's *La fanciulla del West* in New York City's Italian-Language Newspapers', *Journal of the Society for American Music*, 13/2 (2019), 177–94. Puccini's opera, in whose first act the miners sing a nostalgic song about their migration from Europe, played an intentional chord with the Italian American audience.

interested part in the initial wave of migration, but from a literary viewpoint it is an aesthetically average and isolated testament to the mass migration of Italians.[14]

Likewise, one would have expected writers of a socialist leaning to pay attention to such a mass phenomenon, clearly linked to the misery and exploitation of Italy's lower classes. But, again, only one case is worth mentioning. It concerns Edmondo De Amicis, author of *Cuore* (1886), the ever-popular collection of short stories that generations of Italian children were expected to read in order to absorb its sentimental patriotism. The longest story in *Cuore* is 'Dagli Appennini alle Ande', which tells the tear-jerking misadventures of a child who migrates to Latin America in search of his mother. In order to undertake his research, in 1884 De Amicis had boarded a steamer full of migrants heading to Argentina and had travelled there and back (in first class, he admitted). The result was a number of articles, the already mentioned 'Dagli Appennini alle Ande', and later the travel book *Sull'oceano* (1889). What Capuana's novel and De Amicis's short story had in common was a narrative of tragedy and nationalistic redemption.

In both stories, migration is ultimately a failure: the decision to leave is deeply regretted, the humiliations received are an insult to the humble nature of Italians, and consolation can be found only in the return to the motherland. Nationalism and literature were at the very centre of another important figure at the turn of the century: this is Enrico Corradini, a literary author, polemicist, and, later, nationalist politician whose party was to merge with the Fascist one in 1923. He too produced a novel, *La patria lontana* (1910), in which migration was once again presented as a national tragedy, necessary for Italians to regain a clear knowledge of their valour and of the need to return to the mother country, help build a stronger nation, and fulfil Italy's imperial calling.[15]

Another major writer who set four novels and more than a hundred short stories in his native Sicily, between 1884 and the First World War, is Luigi Pirandello. Despite such prolific activity, and the rural setting of most of his work during this period, Pirandello dedicated scant attention to the phenomenon of migration. Only two short stories are devoted to the subject, again, both written at a late stage: 'L'altro figlio' (1905) and 'Nell'albergo è morto un tale' (1917). In both, migration is depicted as a tragedy associated with neglect and loss: the two brothers who migrate to America in 'L'altro figlio' are portrayed by their other brother as lazy and selfish, and the tragedy of the abandoned, illiterate mother is made brutally cruel by the realization, in the course of the story, that the letters to her

---

[14] On the lack of interest in migration on the part of Italian literary authors, see Martelli, 'Dal vecchio mondo al sogno americano', 433; Emilio Franzina, *Dall'Arcadia in America: Attività letteraria ed emigrazione transoceanica in Italia (1850-1940)* (Turin: Edizioni della Fondazione Giovanni Agnelli, 1996), 2-26; and Gianni Paoletti, *Vite ritrovate: Emigrazione e letteratura italiana di otto e novecento* (Foligno: Editoriale Umbra, 2011). On Capuana's novel, see Giordana Poggioli-Kaftan, 'The "Third Space" in Luigi Capuana's Gli americani di Ràbbato', *Studi d'Italianistica nell'Africa Australe/Italian Studies in Southern Africa*, 31.2 (2018), 29-51; and Chiara Mazzucchelli, 'La Merica for Children: Emigration in Luigi Capuana's *Gli "americani" di Ràbbato*, *AltraItalia*, 1 (2019), 60-76.

[15] A similar trend is detected by Emilio Franzina in his detailed analysis of minor literature on migration published during the same period (in his *Dall'Arcadia in America*, 63-106).

sons that she had dictated to another woman had never been sent, not even recorded in actual writing. In the other short story, the migrant does not even have an identity. In Pirandello's typical evocation of existential anxiety, the character remains invisible: it is a man who has just come back from America, but all that is described is his pair of shoes, old and worn out, left outside the door of his hotel room. Before the protagonist can meet him—an old woman who wants to know what it is like to cross the ocean—the news come that the man has been found dead in his bed.[16]

A similar combination of lack of interest and negative depiction can be detected if we move to the field of cinema. Among the many films produced in the pre-First World War years—one-reel shorts as much as the first longer narratives—there is only one Italian silent film that addresses the subject. It is Febo Mari's aptly entitled L'emigrante, of 1915. The plot, once again, tells of the pain and sufferings of migration, and comes full circle with the return of the migrant to his mother country. The closing intertitle wraps up the narrative in explicit terms: 'In his old house, next to the happy couple, Antonio can forget the past and regain his lost happiness.'

A nationalistic thread is present in all these narratives. Migration is seen as an economic and moral loss that should be resisted. The same can be said for Italy's major poets at the time. At the turn of the century, the role of bard of the Italian nation was contested by two popular figures: Giovanni Pascoli and Gabriele D'Annunzio. Despite their different political inclinations—the first closer to socialism, the latter embued with the Nietzschean notion of the superior man—both addressed migration as an insult to the newly unified nation. Italian migrants were the children of a celebrated, centuries-old Latin culture, humiliated by foreign countries that were unable to recognize their virtues and their historic superiority. Both poets agreed that Italy's overpopulation—one of the established causes of migration—should be tackled through colonialist policies. Italy had a right to create its own empire overseas instead of lending its labour to foreign governments. The invasion of Libya in 1911 turned aspirations into government policy and was warmly welcome by Italy's intelligentsia. Italy's most successful silent film in those years was Giovanni Pastrone's *Cabiria* (1914), whose historical narrative of the ancient Roman Republic's war against the Carthaginians in northern Africa was to be seen as a parallel glorification of Italy's Libyan campaign. Gabriele D'Annunzio was hired to write the intertitles to the film and boasted of being the author of the film's screenplay too. The latter, however, was more of a clever escamotage on the part of Pastrone, the real author and producer

---

[16] Even in the post-First World War years, Pirandello's narrative production continued to ignore the mass phenomenon of migration. Only one short story is devoted to it, *Il Chiodo*, published in 1936, a few months before his death. On Pirandello and migration, see Sebastiano Martelli, 'America, emigrazione e "follia" nell'opera di Pirandello', in Mario Mignone (ed.), *Pirandello in America: Atti de simposio internazionale 30.10–1.11 1986* (Rome: Bulzoni, 1988), 211–35.

of the film, who used D'Annunzio's literary fame as a vehicle for adding cultural dignity to the medium of cinema, which, in those early years, was still snubbed by the intelligentsia. As for Pascoli, after his long, empathetic elegy of Italian migration—the 450 verses of *Italy* (1904)—he returned to the subject with an even stronger nationalistic fervour in his renowned speech of 1911, 'La Grande Proletaria s'è mossa' ('The Great Prolerariat is on the Move'). In his impassioned words, Italy's colonial campaign was a sacrosanct counterbalance to the humiliations suffered by Italians migrants. They had too often been treated as badly as negroes, Pascoli went on to comment, with exemplary, nationalistic lack of consideration for other ethnicities, whether in the New World or in Italy's newly conquered African colonies.[17]

This response to a social phenomenon that by the turn of the century was having a massive impact on Italian society makes one wonder whether sociologist Jeffrey Alexander's concept of 'cultural trauma' might not be appropriately used here. The denial of something that is disempowering and upsetting is at the root of Alexander's concept of 'cultural drama'. Memories of a traumatic event are transformed in order to neutralize it either through its removal or through the construction of narratives that are only partially defined by the historical event that triggered it.[18] This is relevant here, because there is a sense that the sporadic narratives created during this early phase of mass migration tended to avoid the causes that triggered the desperate act of social uprooting and overseas migration. The real event—that is, the desperate poverty and poor health among peasants in vast parts of the peninsula—was an unexplored detail at the start of the narrative. What drove the story was a nationalistic reaction to the hardships and the feelings of rejection that migrants experienced once abroad. The wrongs were all with the foreign communities who did not appreciate the influx of Italian migrants. Hence the idea of migration as a tragic mistake, a journey that should have never been undertaken. A key aspect underlined by Alexander relates to the role played by what he calls 'the carrier group'—that is, the group of people who build the narrative. They are not necessarily part of the group who suffered the trauma, and, indeed, this is our case since all narratives about migration were the product of journalists and writers who at most—such as in the case of Capuana and De Amicis—relied on their observation of the phenomenon.

Contemporary Sicilian novelist Leonardo Sciascia was to complain bitterly about this lack of representation of such a momentous social upheaval. In line

---

[17] On Corradini, and Pascoli, see Franzina, *Dall'Arcadia in America*, 127–75. On D'Annunzio, see Woodhouse, *Gabriele D'Annunzio*. On Italian literary culture and migration, see also the enlightening introductory essay by Martino Marazzi, 'Introduzione: La cultura dell'emigrazione italiana e il ruolo della tradizione', in Marazzi, *A occhi aperti. Letteratura dell'emigrazione e mito americano* (Milan: Franco Angeli, 2011), 11–22.

[18] See Jeffrey C. Alexander, 'Toward a Theory of Cultural Trauma', in Jeffrey C. Alexander et al. (eds), *Cultural Trauma and Collective Identity* (Berkeley and Los Angeles: University of California Press, 2004), 1–30.

with Gramsci's views on the detachment between Italy's educated elite and its vast semi-illiterate masses, Sciascia's judgement left no prisoners:

> Italy's ruling class, and the culture that represented it, was so occupied finding the traces of the Italian genius (Genius) in foreign lands, from the year 1,000 until the French Revolution, that they did not notice the hundreds of thousands of Italians who, stowed away like animals, continued to leave the Italian shores. They did not want to notice it, that is; they did not want to deal with it.[19]

It is topical that Sciascia's comment should come from a preface he wrote on the collection of poems on migration by a local Sicilian author. Indeed, if a firsthand story of the trauma suffered by Italian migrants has only recently been dug up by social historians looking at alternative sources such as oral literature and migrants' correspondence, poetry too has played its role. A less rhetorical picture of early migration can be found in the niche ambit of dialect literature. The Veronese poet Berto Barbarani, for example, dedicated a few poems to migration in his collection of 1897, symbolically entitled *I pitochi* (*Lice*). Pier Paolo Pasolini rediscovered Barbarani in his anthology of dialect poetry and penned a dedication in rhyme for the 1968 reprint of *I pitochi*. The quotation of the final part of Barbarani's poem 'I va in Merica' ('They leave for America') is an appropriate ending to this section:

> To hell with Italy! they swear, let's go away!
> And so they count themselves—How many of you are there?
> —Only ten who can work hard;
> the rest are women with babies in their arms,
> the rest are old men and children.
>
> But to stay here means no food, for God's sake,
> we need to make this big step;
> if winters comes with ice
> poor us, it'll make minced meat of us!
>
> —By October, heavy with bundles
> after having cursed the rich
> after having drunk a few glasses;
>
> mad and drunk in their head
> they hug each other
> and, wobblingly, they take the road!

---

[19] Leonardo Sciascia, 'Introduzione', in Stefano Vilardo, *Tutti dicono Germania Germania* (Milan: Garzanti, 1975), 5–7 (6).

## 4.3 American Pragmatism, Giovanni Papini, and the Florentine Pragmatist Club

Linked to the Romantic debate and mainly circulated in French translation, American philosophy was known in some Italian intellectual circles in the mid-nineteenth-century. It was the work of the Transcendentalist school, led by Ralph Waldo Emerson and David Thoreau. An odd but direct link with Italy was provided by Margaret Fuller. Moving from Transcendentalist circles—Emerson famously compared her to Mme De Staël by calling her a 'Yankee Corinna'—into journalism, Fuller had ended up spending three years in Italy, in 1847–50, where she became a fervent Mazzinian and took an active part in the Roman republic. Tragically, when she travelled back to America in the company of her Italian husband and newly born son, their ship sank during a storm only a few miles from the port of New York.

The later phase of American philosophy was pragmatism, founded in the late 1870s by the father of semiotics, Charles Sanders Peirce. What reached Italy was mainly its development through the work of William James, elder brother of the famous novelist. James moved pragmatism away from the scientific understanding of events, as Peirce had theorized, to an exploration of the psychology of individuals and the study of religious belief. Particularly influential was his essay 'The Will to Believe' (1896), in which he argued that a rational leap of faith can be necessary in order to achieve a goal that cannot be entirely predicted. Among the few enthusiastic Italian readers of James's work was Giovanni Papini, who, from Florence, was battling for an anti-positivistic renewal of Italian culture. Papini began to write about James's pragmatism in his iconoclastic journal *Leonardo* (1903–7), then collected his contributions in his volume *Pragmatismo* (1911), and later edited a volume of his translation of a selection of essays by William James (*Sul pragmatismo* (1918)). The two had met in 1905, at a psychology conference in Rome. Papini was by then already an enthusiastic reader of James's work, and James was equally struck by the genius of his Italian acolyte. Through Papini, James discovered that the Florentine *Leonardo* was giving voice to a small group of enthusiastic interpreters of American pragmatism, among whom was Papini's close fellow intellectual, Giuseppe Prezzolini—both in their early twenties. In the April 1905 issue of *Leonardo*, the group had published their collective view on pragmatism, signing themselves as 'The Florence Pragmatist Club' (with bold reference to Boston's so-called Transcendental Club). In this essay one finds the definition of pragmatism as a 'corridor theory'—that is, a philosophy that can lead to different developments: it was a definition that James appreciated—attributing it solely to Papini—and he mentioned it in his own writings. In the case of Papini, and similar to what had happened to him and D'Annunzio when reading Whitman, the 'corridor' of pragmatism led to its interpretation as a philosophy praising the right of a superior individual to rise above common sense and, consequently, above the masses.[20]

In the following two years, Papini and James remained in close contact. In 1906 James published a brief essay on Papini and pragmatism in the *Journal of Philosophy, Psychology and Scientific Method*, and the following year he facilitated the publication of an article on pragmatism by Papini himself in the American *Popular Science Monthly*. James was familiar with Papini's idiosyncratic interpretation of his work and did not seem scandalized by it. In fact, he was pleased to show the impact of his thought in 'poor little Italy', as he defined it. Papini's mystical tangent could represent a potential development of pragmatism, as James wrote: 'in the writings of this youthful Italian, clear in spite of all their brevity and audacity, I found [...] a tone of feeling well fitted to rally devotees and to make of pragmatism a new militant form of religion or quasi religious philosophy.'[21]

Papini had been particularly struck by James's essay 'The Will to Believe', which, alongside his readings of Nietzsche and Bergson, became part of his own praise of the 'Uomo Dio' ('Man-God') defined by his superior will, genius, intuition, and daring action. In Papini's part-factual part-mystical autobiography, *Un uomo finito* (1913), he defined pragmatism as 'a practical, optimistic and American gospel', which he had developed along a mystical, irrational tangent. When, from Trentino, young Benito Mussolini corresponded and collaborated with Papini and Prezzolini, he was so struck by their praise of American pragmatism that when, in April 1909, he presented the journal *La Voce* to his readers in Trento, he chose to define the approach of Prezzolini and Papini as 'a pragmatist philosophy'. Another, French source through which Mussolini learned about American pragmatism in his pre-First World War readings was the revolutionary syndicalist Georges Sorel, who also found James's writings inspiring in his development of a social theory that justified (violent) action in lieu of a democratic process.[22]

---

[20] The Florence Pragmatist Club, 'Il pragmatismo messo in ordine', *Leonardo*, 3/2 (April 1905), 45–7. Another striking aspect of this and other essays published in *Leonardo* was the practice of quoting passages from James and other American and British philosophers in the original English, without bothering to provide an Italian translation. It was part and parcel of Papini's intentional elitism, and, as an editorial practice, it remained an isolated case.

[21] William James, 'Giovanni Papini and the Pragmatist Movement in Italy', *Journal of Philosophy, Psychology and Scientific Method*, 3/13 (1906), 337–41 (340). On Papini and James, see Carlo L. Golino, 'Giovanni Papini and American Pragmatism', *Italica*, 32/1 (1955), 38–48; and Daniele Fulvi, '"Compagni di pragmatismo": Giuseppe Papini e William James', *Nóema*, 6/2 (2015), 18–36.

[22] Giovanni Papini, *Un uomo finito* (Florence: Libreria della Voce, 1913), 184. At p.187, Papini also suggests that he taught himself English, together with Prezzolini, as part of a never-fulfilled plan to settle in the USA to create a utopian religious community. Benito Mussolini, 'La Voce', *Vita trentina*, 13 (3 April 1909), 7; now in *Opera omnia*, ed. Edoardo and Duilio Susmel, 44 vols (Florence: La Fenice, 1951–80), ii. 53–65 (53). On Georges Sorel and on the young Mussolini, see Jo-Anne Pemberton, *Global Metaphors: Modernity and the Quest for One World* (London: Pluto Press, 2001), 34–58; Brett Colasacco, 'From Men into Gods: American Pragmatism, Italian Proto-Fascism, and Secular Religion', *Politics, Religion & Ideology*, 15/4 (2014), 541–64; and Alexander Livingston, *Damn Great Empires! William James and the Politics of Pragmatism* (Oxford: Oxford University Press, 2016), 32–42. We will return to Mussolini and American pragmatism in Chapter 6.

This interest in James's pragmatism, though passionate, was not to leave a lasting mark. After the First World War, the ever-restless Papini moved on to other philosophical pastures, and Mussolini's early interest became a distant memory, entirely replaced by the neo-idealist approach of Giovanni Gentile—a harsh critic of James. Indeed, by the 1910s, despite the occasional polemic, both Papini and Prezzolini had already come to accept Croce's and Gentile's philosophical work and had embraced it as part of their call for a regeneration of Italian culture.[23]

Croce's and Gentile's dismissal of pragmatism did not leave any space for dialogue. In his 1904 review of one of James's books, Gentile had refused to consider the author as a serious philosopher. Its incipit is self-explanatory: 'James is a psychologist and an author of great value; but, as a philosopher, he seems to be afraid of logic.' The rest of the long review was a full condemnation of James's lack of coherence, with the damning conclusion that his arguments belonged more to the personal psychology of the author than to 'his debatable philosophy'. At around the same time, Croce too expressed a dismissive view on American pragmatism.[24]

In the end, both Papini and Prezzolini moved away from James's philosophy. As we will see in Chapter 6, its influence was almost entirely denied in later years by Mussolini too, no doubt thanks to Gentile's tight grip on any philosophical definition of Fascism.

## Conclusion

The three main sections of this chapter have taken us to different fields—from literature, to opera and cinema, and finally to philosophy—and the sense of American culture emerging in Italy in a rather unsystematic, scattered fashion is somehow structurally reflected here. A small number of Italian literati—from Nencioni and the Milanese *Scapigliati*, to Cecchi and Papini—were developing a keen interest in American literature, often specifically in authors already translated and praised in France, such as Whitman and Poe. This had triggered the curiosity of some of Italy's leading authors, from Pascoli, to D'Annunzio. It was an initial, unmethodical phase that could include sudden enthusiasms, later scaled down and forgotten, as was the case of Papini's interest in James's pragmatism.

---

[23] On the convergence of the young Florentine intellectuals' nationalistic irrationalism and the neo-idealism of Croce and Gentile, interpreted as an anti-positivistic turn in Italian culture, see Norberto Bobbio, 'La cultura italiana tra ottocento e novecento', in anon. (ed.), *La cultura italiana tra '800 e '900 e le origini del nazionalismo*, 1–19.

[24] Giovanni Gentile, 'Religione e prammatismo nel James' (1904), in Giovanni Gentile, *Il modernismo e i rapporti tra religione e filosofia. Discorsi di religione* (Bari: Laterza, 1909; Florence: Sansoni, 1965), 171–90. See also Gentile's 'Prammatismo razionale' (1907), in *Saggi critici* (Naples: Ricciardi, 1921), 203–14 (205). Benedetto Croce, *Filosofia della pratica: Economia ed etica* (Bari: Laterza, 1909), 42.

At the same time, America was also making its first, more concerted appearance from 'below'—that is, as part of the increasing popularity of American culture beyond the restricted circles of the ruling elite. The literature of women writers such as Stowe and May Alcott, or of the frontier novels by Fenimore Cooper, put America on the literary map of those hundreds of thousands of readers of limited education who, at the turn of the century, were approaching literature in search of good stories, often made more vivid by illustrated editions. Below that, the adventures of Nick Carter and Buffalo Bill became an affordable literary pastime for those who would normally shy away from a high-street bookshop.

Percolations between these different levels were also possible. Edgar Allan Poe's poetry could be translated by Pascoli, and at the same time his crime and ghost stories were published by commercial publishers with few literary ambitions. Giacomo Puccini, as we saw in Chapter 2, had been a curious spectator of Buffalo Bill's Wild West show in Milan. At the same time, he was exposed to the success of Belasco's plays in London and had eventually been lured to compose and premiere an 'American' opera at the Metropolitan.

Meanwhile, the section on the representation of migration was able to address the question of the cultural effects of the sudden familiarity of the USA in the lives of millions of Italians. The distance between those who lived the actual experience and those who wrote about it was, however, patent. Nationalism had nothing to do with leaving one's country in search of a better life. If nothing else, it was a rejection of it. And, at the same time, this was the lens through which it was observed, from De Amicis, to Corradini, Mari, Pascoli, and Capuana. Return to the motherland was the dominant literary and cinematic answer. It was a narrative that added little to the knowledge of America, and even less to the knowledge of how American society was changing in the wake of the mixture of different cultures, to which the Italian migrants were bringing no small contribution.

# 5
# The First World War and the Arrival of Jazz

In the final sequence of *Good Morning Babilonia* (1987), the Taviani brothers' film about two Tuscan brothers who emigrate to the USA in the early twentieth century, Italy's entry into the First World War plays an important symbolic role. Having found employment as set designers in Hollywood—working on the Babylonian episode of D. W. Griffith's masterpiece *Intolerance* (1916)—the brothers decide to return to Italy following the outbreak of the war. Whether this mirrors historic truth on a larger scale is a moot point. In fact, more than three-quarters of migrants who were supposed to return to Italy and enlist in the army refused to do so. Once again, caution is needed before we align the thoughts and aspirations of the educated elite with those of the masses of Italian migrants at the turn of the century.[1]

More important for the present study is the fact that the late entry of both Italy and the USA in the First World War saw them fighting on the same side: for the first time, the two nations stood shoulder to shoulder. If Italians had been travelling on mass to America in search of work, now it was time for about two million US soldiers to cross the Atlantic, and for a portion of them to find themselves on Italian soil, collaborating with the Italian army, watched and marvelled at by the Italian population. If, in the 1890s and early 1900s, Buffalo Bill had brought a tiny sample of the USA to Italy, still shrouded in the legendary past of the Far West, the First World War brought the reality of the economic muscle and entrepreneurial flair of a new world power.

In her scholarly monograph on Italy and the USA during the war, Daniela Rossini suggests that we should distinguish between the different impact and interaction that the US entry into the war made on the Italian elite, on the one hand, and on the vast majority of poorly educated Italians, on the other.[2] By 1915, thanks to millions of migrants moving back and forth between Italy and the USA, or simply sending letters to relatives and friends back home, the 'American dream'

---

[1] Fewer than 100,000 migrants returned to Italy to enlist in the army between 1915 and 1917. On this, see Stefano Luconi, 'Le comunità italoamericane degli Stati Uniti e la prima guerra mondiale', *Dimensioni e problemi della ricerca storica*, 1 (2015), 91–110. On migrants' decision to return, many feared they would never be allowed back if they did not enlist, see Emilio Franzina, *Al caleidoscopio della Gran Guerra: Vetrini di donne, di canti e di emigranti, 1914–1918* (Isernia: Cosmo Iannone, 2017), 204–23.

[2] Rossini, *Woodrow Wilson and the American Myth*, 17–32.

was a familiar concept for working-class Italians. However, the upper crust of society—with a few exceptions among militant republicans, socialists, and industrialists—still retained the patronizing stereotypes with which the Italian intelligentsia had viewed America for decades. On the eve of US intervention on the Italian front, on 27 November 1917, the American ambassador in Rome commented:

> I would say that the feeling towards America is rather one of complete indifference, based for the most part on complete ignorance of what America is and represents... The great body of the people who represent Italian life make no distinction between the United States and the states of South America.[3]

This meant that diplomatic and military relations were often strained by mutual incomprehension. More than that, the US administration considered its relations with Britain and France as much more important, and this was clearly shown by the size of its commitment on the western front.[4]

Italy's sworn enemy at the time was the Austro-Hungarian Empire, which controlled two regions of Italian culture outside Italian borders, often referred to in propaganda tracts by the names of their respective main cities: Trento and Trieste. Few remember that Italy's declaration of war in May 1915 was directed solely at the Austrians, whereas Germany was declared an enemy only much later, in August 1916. The US approach was the exact opposite, and for different reasons. The so-called Sacred Egoism that led Italy to align itself with the Triple Entente had been criticized by US President Thomas Woodrow Wilson. Through the secret Pact of London, Italy's demands had gone beyond the appropriation of Italian-speaking lands, and so were contrary to Wilson's commitment towards securing a stable post-war settlement, respectful of national cultures. Furthermore, it was Germany that eventually pushed the USA into the war. Its indiscriminate submarine offensive in the Atlantic, and the revelation of its secret anti-US negotiations with Mexico, brought the USA to declare war on Germany in April 1917. It was only in December of that year that the Austro-Hungarian Empire became a US enemy as well.

This had a double effect. First, it concentrated the fighting efforts of the USA on the western front. Only a single military unit was deployed in Italy during the entire conflict. The rest of the US contingent in Italy comprised medical and propaganda corps. Secondly, the US intervention and Wilson's idealism were eventually perceived by the Italian elite as a pernicious interference in the

---

[3] Letter by Thomas Nelson Page to Edward Mandell House (an influential aid to President Wilson), dated 27 November 1917; quoted in Rossini, *Woodrow Wilson and the American Myth*, 18.
[4] See H. Stuart Hughes, *The United States and Italy* (Cambridge, MA: Harvard University Press, 1979; enlarged edn, 2013), 6–7.

political and diplomatic arrangements that had brought Italy into the war. Of Wilson's Fourteen Points announcing America's commitment to a peaceful world, in January 1918, number nine referred directly to the Italian situation: 'IX. A readjustment of the frontiers of Italy should be effected along clearly recognizable lines of nationality.' The collapse of the territorial claims by the Italian government during the Versailles negotiations was to be its clearest outcome.[5]

The following pages will address two major issues. First, more focus and detail will be added to a discussion of the cultural impact of US personnel in Italy and to the role of President Wilson in shaping the policies and image of the USA. The second section will examine a cultural bond that was to be long-standing: that of music, as the syncopated rhythms of jazz were first brought to Italian ears by the arrival of the US Army.

## 5.1 The American Way at a Time of War

In 1916, by the time of Wilson's re-election as President of the United States, his policies were well known to Americans and much discussed abroad. In Italy, however, it was mainly after the US intervention in the war that his profile as the leader of a powerful nation came into focus. Wilson's approach to international politics was both innovative and provocative to European ears: he aimed to speak directly to the people, formulating simple but appealing slogans and policies that shaped public opinion, and at the same time he became the first leader of a powerful nation who was prepared to commit his country to the principles of peaceful international collaboration. The latter meant that the USA and Italy would eventually clash on questions of post-war territorial settlement. However, one key factor kept these tensions at bay during the last phase of the war—namely, the catastrophic defeat of the Italian army at Caporetto, on 24 October 1917. The scale of the military debacle, not to mention its huge impact on morale among Italy's troops and its civilian population, demanded an immediate injection of hope and trust in the future. The USA was elected to take part in this campaign. After all, for decades, America had been imagined as a place of hope by millions of lowly educated Italians. Now that became government policy. In military and nationalistic circles, the image of the USA was scaled up and given a near-prophetic presence.[6]

---

[5] It should be noted, however, that Wilson's ninth point was initially understood, particularly by the Italian ambassador in Washington, as not necessarily a threat to the Italian claims. It was only at Versailles that the distance between Italy and the USA became fully apparent. On this, see Rossini, *Woodrow Wilson and the American Myth*; and Liliana Saiu, *Stati Uniti e Italia nella Grande Guerra 1914–1918* (Florence: Olschki, 2003).

[6] For a study of the development of the perception of the USA within nationalistic circles, see Federico Robbe, 'Da "civiltà mercantile" a "grande popolo": Il mito americano nel nazionalismo italiano durante la Grande Guerra', *Eunomia*, 4/4 (2015), 333–70.

The national press caught up with this in the following months. On the most traditional date in the American calendar, 4 July, the *Corriere della Sera* dedicated two-thirds of its front page to a celebration of US military intervention. The main article opened with a declaration by President Wilson complimenting his Secretary for War for the country's effort. The presence of the US Army in Europe had by then just exceeded one million troops. The article was followed by a propagandistic introduction to the meaning of the celebration, which, in Wilsonian terms, defined America's struggle for freedom, at its origin as much as in 1918. The article went on to describe the USA as 'the great Republic of the New World' and its military intervention as a messianic source of morale-boosting:

> [We are] galvanized by the firmness of spirit that invigorates these fighters. For it is the very same spirit with which their ancestors proclaimed their right to independence and swore to face any necessary sacrifice or even death in order to achieve it.
>
> Like a new spring of vital vigour, the youth of America penetrates the battlelines where the future of all people is defended [...] and reinvigorates our common effort in view of the enormous task that lies ahead of us.[7]

Next to these articles, a poem by Gabriele D'Annunzio, entitled 'All'America in armi', exalted, in the typically bombastic tone of his war lyrics, the ideal of liberty that Americans had fought for during their struggle for independence and were now fighting for in the battlefields of Europe. Beyond the rhetorical glorification of death as a price for the defence of freedom, a revealing aspect of the poem lies in its representation of America. The traditional, patronizing image of the USA as a country of businessmen, obsessed by money and technology, is still present in D'Annunzio's description; but, thanks to the ideal of liberty, a transformation is taking place:

> It does not add to your beauty, Republic, your immense reserves
>   of gold, nor the unending amounts that your wingless genies
>   pour in from the darkness,
> nor the swift axe that turned woods into neat cities, nor the
>   ardour of your sky-high houses, which are your cathedrals,
> nor the number of enslaved machines that produce your profits
>   and your luxuries, nor the pride that hardens and shapes
>   your race,
> but a word that the republican voice spoke in you, a word that
>   makes you the fairest.

---

[7] Anon., 'Data mondiale', *Corriere della Sera*, 4 July 1918, p. 1.

> And suddenly your gold and all your metals and all your forges
> and all your people transform into operating light.
> You are all light. Which illuminates even the darkness of your
> mines, so that your black coal becomes diamond.

Liberty was the redeeming feature of American society, it was the magic element capable of transforming a materialistic nation into an altruistic force for good. D'Annunzio was not alone in producing this narrative of moral metamorphosis: a similar, prosaic version was published a few weeks later by nationalist and diplomat Leonardo Vitetti in an article on America's role for *L'Idea nazionale*, the weekly paper of the Italian Nationalist Association. In Vitetti's words, the captains of American industry had turned themselves into army organizers—plantation-owners had become the army's officers, and its workers had turned into troops. America had turned its economic might into an insuperable war machine.[8]

Within this explosion of pro-American sentiment, even traditional, derogatory expressions referring to America had to be reformed. For example, Bologna's daily newspaper published an article entitled 'All'americana', on 6 May 1918, which warned the public that the idiomatic expression referred to in the title, normally associated with a fraudulent deal, had to be censored and turned on its head. If nothing else, 'done in the American way' in those days had to mean the absolute opposite: the epic, heroic commitment to war of an entire nation. Even mass production acquired a new, positive light, now described as a source of military superiority on the side of the Triple Entente.[9]

But what was the actual presence of the American army on Italian soil? The short and limited military collaboration between the two nations during the last months of the war meant that the US Army in Italy was used mainly for propaganda and morale-boosting purposes. Italy's defeat at Caporetto gave this an added a sense of urgency and a clear aim. This also meant that the upper echelons of the Italian army at that time became keen to enlist any help that might contribute to the war effort and particularly to restoring self-belief and military discipline. A more constructive approach to the welfare of soldiers, which, up until then, had been snubbed in Italian military circles in favour of repressive measures against all forms of indiscipline, had become official policy with the creation of propaganda units. Attached to each Italian division, the so-called P Sections were supposed to provide propaganda material, from in-house journals to collaborating with non-military associations in organizing entertainment and support to the fighting troops. It was a field in which the Americans could boast organizational

---

[8] Leonardo Vitetti, 'Le onde dell'Atlantico', *L'Idea nazionale*, 29 July 1918; quoted in Robbe, 'Da "civiltà mercantile" a "grande popolo"', 367.
[9] Anon., 'All'americana', *Il Resto del Carlino*, 6 May 1918, p. 2.

knowhow through its powerful Committee on Public Information, which had helped American society gear up for the war effort.[10]

The entire US contingent was involved in this battle for minds. Its composition was made out of four distinct parts: the American Red Cross; a fighting corps (the 332nd Ohio Regiment); a propaganda unit from the Committee on Public Information; and the representatives of the Young Men's Christian Association, whose charitable activities were given official, military recognition. Each of the four deserves some consideration relative to its importance in the perception of America on Italian soil.

The deepest mark was left by the American Red Cross (ARC). Its presence in the immediate aftermath of the defeat of Caporetto saw American ambulances operating in Italy before the USA had even declared war on the Austro-Hungarian Empire. As such, they quickly became a symbol of hope in the mighty power of the US Army, and a wishful sign of the imminent arrival of US fighting troops, which would secure Italy's military recovery and eventual victory. With the ARC already established on the French front, the first contingent of ambulances had travelled through France and entered northern Italy in November 1917. By July 1918, more units had arrived by sea through the port of Genoa, bringing the contingent to a total of 35 units operating with 360 ambulances.[11] Much to the frustration of its 1,641 voluntary personnel, the vehicles were sometimes used on off-the-front-line assignments for morale-boosting and propaganda assignments. The ARC also ran twenty-two refreshment points, all placed near the front line, where Italian troops could enjoy some rest, free food, beverages, letter-writing material, and cigarettes. Such a plentiful display did, in the mind of many soldiers, confirm the idea of the USA as a generous land of plenty, to the point that, as reported by a journalist in July 1918, soldiers would choose to refer to them with the same expression used by migrants in previous years: 'Andiamo a trovare l'America!' ('Let's go and find America!').[12]

Among the ambulance drivers were many young volunteers from the best American universities, including the 19-year-old Ernest Hemingway. His novel *Farewell to Arms* (1929) was to become the object of censorship during the Fascist period, because of its critical view of the Italian army as seen by an American ambulance driver. Hemingway was one of the many young volunteers who, before the USA had entered the war, decided to help out by joining the Red Cross.

---

[10] On the Italian unit of the Committee on Public Information, see Daniela Rossini, 'La propaganda americana in Italia durante la Grande Guerra: Guglielmina Ronconi', *Contemporanea*, 8/2 (2005), 299–310. On propaganda within the Italian army, see Vanda Wilcox, *Morale and the Italian Army During the First World War* (Cambridge: Cambridge University Press, 2016), 46–53.

[11] On the American Red Cross during the First World War, see Arlen J. Hansen, *Gentlemen Volunteers: The Story of the American Ambulance Drivers in the Great War: August 1914–September 1918* (New York: Arcade Publishing, 1996).

[12] Arnaldo Fraccaroli, 'Il grano e il sangue', *Corriere della Sera*, 21 July 1918; quoted in Rossini, *Woodrow Wilson and the American Myth*, 243.

Fig. 5.1. Ernest Hemingway in the American Red Cross uniform with Nurse Agnes Von Kurowski (centre left) convalescing in Milan after sustaining multiple wounds on 8 July 1918. (courtesy of the John F. Kennedy Presidential Library and Museum, Boston MA)

He arrived in Italy in June 1918 and was sent to the front line at the foothills of the Alps. His service was brief, since on 8 July he was wounded by shrapnel from a mortar bomb while distributing relief goods to front-line Italian soldiers. He spent the rest of his Italian campaign in a Milanese hospital, where he met and fell in love with a nurse, Agnes Von Kurowski, whom he hoped to marry until she broke off their relationship following his return to America.[13]

Hemingway was not the only young American ambulance driver with a literary future ahead of him who happened to be stationed in Italy. Another one was John Roderigo Dos Passos, whose memoirs add factual detail to the literary reconstructions. While Hemingway came to Italy directly from the USA, Dos Passos had already experienced the horror of trench warfare in the summer of 1917, as an ambulance driver on the French front, at Verdun. He arrived in Italy in December 1917, with the first contingent of ARC ambulances. Hence his frustration, once in Italy, at seeing ARC units used for propaganda parades around

---

[13] A recent collection of essays dedicated to Hemingway and his Italian writings is Mark Cirino and Mark P. Ott (eds), *Hemingway in Italy: Twenty-First Century Perspectives* (Gainesville, FL: University Press of Florida, 2017).

Italian towns. A passionate pacifist, Dos Passos recorded in a diary entry of 1 January 1918 his frustration at overhearing a half-drunken commanding officer confess the propagandist aims of the Italian campaign:

> We are here for propaganda it seems—more than for ambulance work—we will be used in the most conspicuous way possible—We must show Italy that America is behind them. [...] God, it made you vomit to hear it. So we are here to cajole the poor devils into fighting—they dont [sic] know why—they dont [sic] care why—
> Probably—from a coldly intellectual viewpoint—the most interesting feature of the Italian situation will be that here, owing to the simple-mindedness and ignorance of the Italians, all the issues are vastly simplified. The machinery of how government are run and controlled into war is more obvious—to a citizen of fairly sophisticated countries the wires will seem plain as day.[14]

Given the negative bias that educated Italians displayed towards Americans, it is paradoxically refreshing to hear a well-educated, young American profess his superiority towards Italians, whom, in the entry of the previous day, he had simply defined as 'hopeless'. Dos Passos's entry confirms that ambulance units were indeed part of the ostentation of America's rich, industrial economy. As we saw in Chapter 4, by 1918 the circulation of mechanized transport in America had reached levels that were unimaginable in the rest of Europe. Even more they were in Italy, where, outside of the big cities, cars and trucks were still a rare sight. However, the ARC did not limit itself to its ambulance services to the military. In fact, a higher proportion of its budget was spent on activities relating to the civilian population, close to the front as much as in the rest of Italy. As the map in Fig. 5.2 shows, the presence of the ARC was spread across the whole country. A total of 65 per cent of the ARC budget was invested in a national network devoted to the support of individuals and communities all over Italy. It took the form of food deliveries, medical support, financial aid, and the donation of writing materials for families with relatives at the front. The ARC provided good practice on how to combine propagandist action and material help for the newly formed propaganda units of the Italian army. For instance, unit commanders on the front line were given the opportunity to name specific soldiers who had distinguished themselves in showing discipline and commitment: the ARC would then send a small amount of money to their families. The funding arrived together with a stamped and self-addressed card, which the family could send to their relative on the front line, thus fostering good relations between soldiers, officers, and families at home, and, of course, enhancing the image of the ARC.[15]

---

[14] John Dos Passos, *The Fourteenth Chronicle: Letters and Diaries of John Dos Passos* (Boston: Gambit, 1973), 115.

[15] More detail on this and other ARC initiatives can be found in Charles M. Bakewell, *The Story of the American Red Cross in Italy* (New York: Macmillan, 1920). On the history of American ambulance

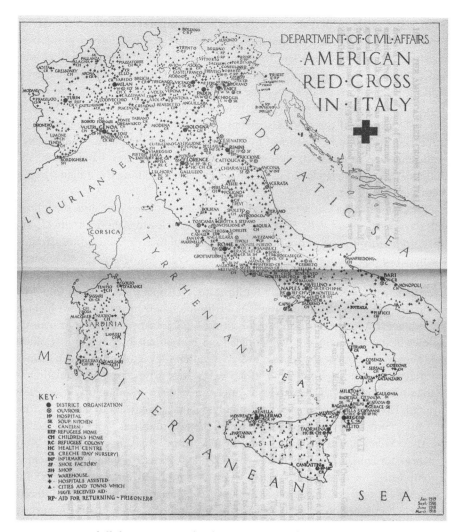

**Fig. 5.2.** Map of all the centres run by the American Red Cross in Italy in January 1919; reproduced from Bakewell, *The Story of the American Red Cross in Italy*. (courtesy of the National Library of Medicine, Bethesda, MD)

A propagandist role was also played by the only fighting unit deployed in Italy. The 332nd Ohio Regiment counted about three thousand soldiers perfectly equipped and ready for combat. In fact, it was used only once in battle, in one of the last episodes of the war. The regiment arrived, like the ambulance units, through

---

units in the First World War, see Hansen, *Gentlemen Volunteers*. More specifically, on Dos Passos and Hemingway, see the parallel biography by James McGrath Morris, *The Ambulance Drivers: Hemingway, Dos Passos and a Friendship Made and Lost in War* (Boston: Da Capo Press, 2017).

France and made its first stop in Milan. The troops paraded through the city on Sunday, 28 July 1918, and, on that morning, Milan's *Corriere della Sera* announced their arrival with an article entitled 'Per un saluto ai soldati americani di passaggio' ('Welcome to the American Soldiers Passing by'). It invited the population to join the celebration and described the late afternoon parade, which would see the troops march to the Piazza Duomo, then along via Manzoni and to the Stazione centrale. Dozens of the city's associations were involved. Along the streets, the American troops were welcomed by huge crowds, and the parade ended with a well-rehearsed celebration, with speeches by local authorities, band music, and military salutes, all enveloped in hundreds of banners joining the Italian *tricolore* with the stars and stripes of the American flag.

The *Domenica del Corriere* devoted its front cover to the event, and, the following day, the *Corriere della Sera* dedicated two articles to American affairs. The first, on the front page, announced that the head of the US Food Administration agency, Herbert Hoover (future US President, 1929–33), was going to ensure a smooth flow of goods from the USA. The second, on page 2, entitled 'Entusiastiche accoglienze ai soldati americani' ('Enthusiastic Welcome for American soldiers'), returned to the parade, describing it as a triumph of affectionate fervour by both the Milanese and the city's authorities. It narrated a cameo appearance by a US soldier of Italian origin, who was singled out by the Italian commanding officer and showered with cheers by the crowd. Given that the regiment had been formed entirely from troops from Ohio—then a US state with a small population of Italian immigrants—the presence of American soldiers of Italian origin was very limited. However, the few cases were highly publicized in order to feed the narrative of a newly found brotherhood between the two countries.[16]

After Milan and a similar parade near Verona—this time saluted by King Vittorio Emanuele III in person—the 332nd Regiment was stationed behind enemy lines, north-east of Treviso, where it continued its combat drills. The troops were ordered to march along the roads, each time wearing a different uniform combination so as to give the impression of a much greater American presence. In the recollection of its commander, Colonel William Wallace: 'Our first marches were more in the nature of triumphal processions than of stern military operations. In every city—shouting, crowds, bands, banners, flowers, speeches and parades.'[17]

It was only on 2 September that the first battalion of the regiment was assigned to a front-line position along the Piave River. It was a very quiet sector, to the

---

[16] Among the American troops who fought in the First World War, more than 100,000 were of Italian origin. The near totality of them, however, were sent to fight on the western front. On this, see Christopher M. Sterba, *Good Americans: Italian and Jewish Immigrants during the First World War* (Oxford: Oxford University Press, 2003).

[17] William Wallace, 'A Summary', in William Wallace et al., *Ohio Doughboys in Italy: Reminiscences of the 332d Infantry* (Pleasantville. NJ: Penhallow Press, 1921), 64–72 (64).

**Fig. 5.3.** Front-page illustration of *La Domenica del Corriere*, 28 (14-21 July 1918), dedicated to the celebrations of The Fourth of July in Milan's Piazza del Duomo. (courtesy of BSMC, Rome)

point that a battalion's officer described it as 'quite a drawing card for all kinds of generals, newspaper men, etc., etc. In fact we are still in the game of propaganda and Italian officers and men are brought here to get a little extra pep.'[18] Indeed,

---

[18] Quoted in Matthew J. Seelinger, '"Viva l'America!": The 332nd Infantry on the Italian Front', *On Point*, 4/3 (1998); the article is available in the National Museum of the United States Army website.

the battalion's main loss of men came from the accidental explosion of a mortar during a fighting drill, which killed seven soldiers. It eventually met action in the final, successful offensive of 27 October 1918, which the regiment joined, crossing the Piave River, on 3 November. When the American troops halted at the next natural front line, marked by the River Tagliamento, an Austrian officer on the other side asked for a parley and relayed to the commanding officer of one of the battalions that an armistice was soon to stop the war. The implicit request for a truce did not find the approval of the regiment commander, who already knew of the imminent end of the fighting. The American troops were ordered to cross the river the following morning, meeting little resistance. By the early afternoon, news came that the armistice had been signed. By then the Ohio Regiment had lost one man, and six had been wounded in combat.[19]

It should be noted that, on the propaganda front, the regiment seemed to have been successful against the enemy too. As an officer recorded with glee, when he and others questioned captured Austrian generals, it became clear that they had been convinced that the presence of the US Army was much more substantial than it actually was. Once the war was over, the 332nd Ohio Regiment was stationed for a few months in formerly Austrian areas—the city of Fiume was one of them—and eventually sailed for the USA from Genoa on 29 March 1919. Back home, before being demobilized, the regiment marched first along New York's 5th Avenue and then through the streets of Cleveland. Both parades—the one in New York being followed by a crowd estimated at 350,000 people—had been co-organized by various Italian American associations.[20]

As already mentioned, the official propaganda arm of the US administration was the Committee on Public Information (CPI). Created by President Wilson at the very start of America's involvement in the war, in April 1917, the CPI was the first government agency in the world whose entire brief was to create mass, public support through propaganda. On the home front, the CPI established a solid, enthusiastic backing for the war effort, while abroad it turned Wilson into the most prominent and respected head of state during the war years. Given that the heyday of radio was still to come, this was achieved through a persistent use of the press, other forms of printed propaganda—from posters to postcards—and through the mobilization of thousands of intellectuals and volunteers. The Committee on Public Information became a political example

---

[19] The narrative of this episode is recollected by an officer of the regiment, Bruce McFarlane, in his essay 'The Second Battalion', in Wallace et al., *Ohio Doughboys in Italy*, 59–63. It is also mentioned in the memoir of a sergeant major, Joseph Lettau, in his *In Italy with the 332d Infantry* (Youngstown, OH: Lettau, 1921), 39.

[20] On the history of the 332nd Ohio regiment in Italy, see also Francesco Brazzale, Luigino Caliaro, Andrea Vollman, *Grande Guerra, americani in Italia, nascita di una superpotenza* (Valdagno: Rossato, 2017), 69–90, 231–6.

of both the entrepreneurial spirit and the aptitude for using publicity for marketing purposes of the US economy.[21]

In Italy, a CPI unit was created in April 1918, first within the American Embassy in Rome and soon thereafter in its own premises in Via del Tritone. About fifty people worked under the direction of Charles E. Merriam, a professor of Politics from Chicago University, chosen more for his devotion to the progressive policies of Wilson—although he was a Republican—than for his knowledge of Italian culture. Thanks to his title, *Alto Commissario per l'Italia* ('High Commissioner for Italy'), he was considered as important a figure as that of the ambassador, and, indeed, Merriam had easy access to the highest echelons of the Italian establishment, from Prime Minister Vittorio Emanuele Orlando to King Vittorio Emanuele III and the then head of the army, General Armando Diaz. However, following Wilson's brief, the aim of Merriam's department was to reach the Italian people.

CPI units were organized into four departments: News, Photography, Cinema, and Speakers. The abundant funding of the CPI allowed them to organize a stream of initiatives, which delivered a vast diffusion of US propaganda, both on the front line and throughout the peninsula and main islands. The News Department worked as a press agency that distributed news items and fully-fledged articles to Italy's national and provincial press. It also commissioned specific propaganda articles: the already mentioned poem by Gabriele D'Annunzio, for example, was the result of a CPI operation. Merriam had asked the American Consul in Venice to contact D'Annunzio and commission a poem from him in celebration of Independence Day. The Italian poet was at the time busy volunteering as a fighter pilot—his famous flight over Vienna was to take place a few weeks later, on 9 August—but, never deaf to a paid commission, he found the time to pen a war poem glorifying America's intervention.[22]

The Photographic Department was similarly active, distributing free photographic material throughout the country. A few figures give a sense of the size of the operation. In its first eighteen months of existence, the Italian CPI sent out 4.5 million postcards, 360,000 propaganda pamphlets, 200,000 small USA flags, 70,000 posters of President Wilson, and 66,000 American war posters. Nearly 3,000 exhibitions based on American photographic material were organized in Italian towns. The Cinema Department distributed US-made documentaries about the war and about American life across the ocean: 420 of them were shipped to Europe. The department worked in collaboration with American film distributors, so that its propaganda material became part and parcel of the

---

[21] For a comprehensive study of the CPI as part of the war effort, see Ronald Schaffer, *America in the Great War: The Rise of the War Welfare State* (Oxford: Oxford University Press, 1991).

[22] On this episode, see Carl A. Swanson, 'D'Annunzio's "Ode all'America in armi" (IV LUGLIO MCMXVIII)', *Italica*, 30/3 (1953), 135–43.

screening of American films. The CPI also produced its own full-length feature films, which were premiered in the presence of political and military authorities.[23]

Finally, the Department of Speakers organized propaganda tours by American personalities who were capable of addressing Italian audiences in their own language. Speakers were asked to use an unflowery style—once again, Wilson was the model—which was intentionally in clear contrast with the classical rhetoric of Italian officials. Many of the speakers were Italian Americans who had reached a position of prominence. One of them was Salvatore A. Cotillo (1886–1939), a lawyer and the first Italian-born elected member of New York's State Assembly. When he toured the south of Italy in the summer of 1918, his secretary recorded the enthusiastic reception they received in every town. In Naples he delivered a speech in one of the city's main squares, the Piazza Plebiscito, in front of an estimated crowd of fifty thousand people. Cotillo's family came from the small town of Montella, in the Campania region, and when Cotillo delivered a speech in the nearest main town, Avellino, the reception they received overwhelmed both senator and secretary:

> The town was bedecked with American and Italian flags. [...] The whole population turned out to cheer us on our way to the hotel. The following day the senator was given a luncheon by the city authorities at which several stirring speeches were made of Italy's great affection for America, and her reliance on America's cooperation. [...] Wilson has certainly taken the Italian people by storm. Every place we visit we find that his name is worshipped. We have met hundreds of people who are more conversant with Wilson's speeches than I am.[24]

What impressed Cotillo most was the popularity of the USA among Italians, particularly in the south. As he wrote in his memoirs:

> The thing that impressed me most of all was the sincere, unselfish love of the Italians for America. Which they manifested on every occasion. I have no hesitancy in saying that no nation loves and worships America more than does Italy. The gratitude of the people for the aid given by us is unbounded and everywhere I went the name of America brought forth expression of reverence and respect. [...] A deep sympathy for us always existed and I might say that fully nine-tenths of the population of southern Italy recognizes America as a second fatherland.[25]

---

[23] Data sourced from George Creel, *Complete Report of the Chairman of the Committee on Public Information, 1917: 1918: 1919* (Washington: Government Printing Office, 1920).

[24] Report for Speaker's Department, 30 July 1918; quoted in Rossini, *Woodrow Wilson and the American Myth*, 122.

[25] Salvatore A. Cotillo, *Italy in the Great War* (Boston: Christopher House, 1922), 30.

Cotillo's memoirs appeared within a book on Italy during the First World War, which he published in 1922 with a short introduction by none other than General Diaz himself. In it, Cotillo boasted that America's propaganda war had been a crucial factor in the conduct of the war on the Italian front:

> If no attempt had been made by us to re-awaken and elevate the morale of the Italians, which was shaken before and after the disastrous affair of Caporetto in October, 1917, it is doubtful whether the Italians would have held together long enough to be able to withstand and defeat the Austrian blow of June, 1918. Our propaganda of enlightenment brought victory to the Allies, as surely did the successes on the battlefields.[26]

Consistent with his ties to Italy, Cotillo took a fervent, pro-Italian stance during the negotiations in Versailles.

Another prominent New York personality was Fiorello H. La Guardia, born in Greenwich Village in 1882 to Italian parents—an army bandmaster from Apulia and a highly educated mother from Trieste, who came from a distinguished Jewish family. Before the war, following the father's discharge from the US Army for health reasons, the La Guardia family had spent a few years in Trieste, where Fiorello had found work in the US diplomatic service as an interpreter (he spoke Italian, Yiddish, and Serbo-Croat), moving to various cities of the Austro-Hungarian Empire. Once back in New York, in 1906, he took a degree in law, and, by the time of the American intervention in the war, he had just begun his political career. He was unexpectedly elected to Congress as a Republican candidate, thanks to his popularity among the Italian community in East Harlem.

When the USA entered the war, La Guardia volunteered in the Army Aviation Section. He was given the rank of captain, and in early October 1917—just before Caporetto—he was dispatched to Italy to the air base in Apulia, where Italian and American pilots flying Caproni Ca.44 bombers were trained. By chance, the base was in Foggia, his father's home town. He became second in command of the training programme and managed to be involved in war operations: as a co-pilot he flew over the Austrian lines, bombing enemy positions.

On one occasion La Guardia briefly met Gabriele D'Annunzio. In his autobiography, La Guardia wrote that he mentioned the meeting with D'Annunzio during a conversation with King Victor Emmanuel III. The Italian poet had not been impressed by the American's ironic parallel between the two of them: 'You are in the Air Service, so am I. [...] You make speeches. I make speeches too. The people don't understand your Italian, but they pretend they do. They don't understand

---

[26] Cotillo, *Italy in the Great War*, 32.

**Fig. 5.4.** Fiorello La Guardia (centre front, wearing a brimless beret) surrounded by Italian and US officers; the photo was probably taken at Foggia's aviation training base, in 1917–18. (courtesy of La Guardia and Wagner Archives, New York City)

me either, but they ask what I am trying to say.' The king allegedly enjoyed the anecdote very much.[27]

Consistent with his political interests, La Guardia spent part of his time touring the peninsula as a CPI's public speaker. Despite his diminutive height, another trait he shared with D'Annunzio, he showed great oratorical skills and an energetic personality, which in later years would grant him three successive terms as Mayor of New York and the appellation 'The Napoleon of New York'.[28] A short extract from one of his speeches, complete with annotations about the crowd's response, gives a flavour of his simple, unrhetorical style:

> America joined this war not to prolong it, but to bring it to an end [thunderous applause]. They say that we are a people obsessed with money, a people without feelings or ideals. Well, it's true we have money, but we also have feelings and ideals; with this difference: that we know how to put those feelings and ideals

---

[27] Fiorello H. La Guardia, *The Making of an Insurgent: An Autobiography: 1881–1919* (Philadelphia, PA: Lippincott, 1948), 187.

[28] Among the biographies of Fiorello H. La Guardia, I referred to Thomas Kessner, *Fiorello H. La Guardia and the Making of New York* (New York: McGraw-Hill, 1989); and H. Paul Jeffers, *The Napoleon of New York: Mayor Fiorello La Guardia* (New York: John Wiley & Sons, 2002).

into practice, while others are content with singing them in the form of poetry [laughter, cries of approval].[29]

La Guardia's oratorical skills, like Cotillo's, were considered too rough in the upper echelons of the CPI—its Italian director, Merriam, complained about them in a confidential report he sent to Washington—but there is no doubt that they were effective with the Italian crowds.[30] La Guardia also acted as a diplomat, representing the US Air Force in both Paris—the headquarters of the American army—and Rome—where he became a familiar figure with the king and many senior Italian politicians.

All in all, La Guardia's profile as a second-generation Italian who had managed to be elected in Congress and was now fighting in the First World War as an aviator was influential in both Italy and America. In America it helped the image of the Italian American community as a patriotic and fully committed part of American society; in Italy it confirmed the hopes of millions of Italians who had seen relatives and friends move to America and who were probably cultivating similar dreams themselves.

A few lines should finally be devoted to the role of the Youth Men's Christian Association, the YMCA. If the American Red Cross had started to operate in France before April 1917, the commitment of the YMCA began when the USA went to war. The head of the YMCA offered the services of his association, and the YMCA was integrated into the US Army (volunteers wore the army uniform just like the ARC ambulance drivers), becoming responsible for the entertainment of troops away from the battlefield. Its first units were established in Italy in January 1918: the headquarters were in Bologna, and offices opened next to all Italian army divisions on the front as well as in Italy's main cities throughout the peninsula. Similar to what had happened in France, its denomination was not a direct translation of the American: it was called *Opera di fratellanza universale* ('House of Universal Brotherhood'), whereas its French counterpart had been called *Union franco-américaine*. Their activities involved a mixture of morale-boosting propaganda and material aid, not dissimilar to those of the ARC, with the difference that the YMCA concentrated its efforts on military units and on the entertainment of soldiers. The YMCA lavishly furnished the Italian army's network of *Case del soldato* ('Soldiers' houses') and directly ran a quarter of them. Only about two thousand people worked for the YMCA in Italy, but its presence was multiplied by its limitless supplies. Free English courses were offered to officers and soldiers. Moreover, the Italian YMCA created a screening department with about 300 film projectors—some equipped for open-air venues—and these

---

[29] Speech given at La Scala Opera theatre in Milan on 3 February 1918, later published as a pamphlet by the Italian Union of Teachers; quoted in Rossini, *Wilson and the American Myth*, 226.
[30] Report from Merriam to Creel, 25 June 1918; quoted in Rossini, *Wilson and the American Myth*, 111.

entertained millions of soldiers (nineteen million was the estimated figure between January 1918 and March 1919).[31]

Once again, the organization of the American administrative machine and the abundance of its provisions were repeatedly mentioned in formal and informal reports, particularly in the months following the Caporetto defeat. It was one more example of the 'truth of the American myth', which had been forming in the mind of millions of Italians.

The popularity of the USA, of both its army and its president, reached its peak after the end of the war, during Wilson's visit to Italy in the first week of January 1919. No foreign authority had ever been welcomed with similar enthusiasm. Whether it was in Genoa, Milan, or Rome, Wilson's appearance was constantly accompanied by excited crowds, whose reverence for the American president was entirely genuine. However, the dark clouds of the Versailles conference were already looming on the horizon. Conscious of the inevitable tensions that Wilson's stance on the Italian claims were going to create, the Italian authorities made sure he was never allowed to address the crowds in an open speech. Also, in Rome, the band of the 332nd Regiment was not allowed to take part in the parade honouring Wilson's arrival.[32] All this had the undesired effect of making Wilson even more ill-disposed towards Italy's ruling class. His internationalist idealism was to clash with the passionate nationalisms that the war had stoked. Wilson's image was to suffer from this, although, as we will see in the second part of this book, the influence of American culture continued its rise unabated.

## 5.2 Jazz Music and the the Great War

With regard to the origin of jazz music, historians today agree that in New Orleans, at the turn of the century, African American musicians were developing their sound in close contact with other ethnic communities. As has already been mentioned, the migration of thousands of Sicilian peasants to the city in the late nineteenth century had formed a class of white immigrants whose status, abode, and lifestyle were close to those of the black community. It is therefore not surprising to see the presence of Italian American musicians in early jazz bands, and nor is it provocative to state that the first published sheet of blues music, in 1908, was 'I Got the Blues' by Antonio Maggio, and that the first studio recording of a jazz piece, 'Livery Stable Blues', was made by the Original Dixieland 'Jass' Band led by Dominic James 'Nick' La Rocca. Both Maggio and La Rocca were of Sicilian

---

[31] Data sourced from YMCA, *L'opera del YMCA presso l'esercito Italiano* (1919); quoted in Rossini, *Wilson and the American Myth*, 96–9.

[32] The misadventures of the band of the 332nd Regiment during Wilson's visit is recalled in Lettau's memoirs (*In Italy with the 332nd Regiment*, 56–7). The band eventually forced itself into the parade in the Via Nazionale, breaking through the cordon of Italian soldiers in the Via Nazionale.

origin: the former's father came from the village of Cefalù, east of Palermo, and La Rocca's from Salaparuta, near Trapani. In the words of the ultimate New Orleans' jazz star, Louis Armstrong, La Rocca was 'one of the great pioneers of syncopated music', and his Dixieland band was 'the first great jazz orchestra'.[33]

Admittedly, although it is part of the story of Italian Americans in the Deep South, it would be inappropriate to say that it played a substantial part in the arrival and fortune of jazz music in Italy. To some extent this is surprising, since the Italian intellectual circle that most enthusiastically welcomed jazz as a modern form of music was that of the Futurists. Given Futurism's blend of support for experimental arts and its ultranationalism, one would have expected Futurist intellectuals to emphasize the connection between the origin of jazz and the Italian American community. The reality is that, in the years around the First World War, the local notoriety achieved by musicians such as Maggio and La Rocca had not reached the Italian public. Jazz music first arrived in Italy as part of the newfangled practices brought by the US Army.[34]

By 1917, the syncopated rhythms of ragtime and foxtrot were becoming increasingly popular in the great metropolises of north-eastern and western America: first of all in Chicago, followed by New York and San Francisco. It was inevitable that this new fashion should cross the Atlantic together with an army of soldiers whose aim, particularly in Italy, was to entertain as much as to fight. The larger army units were accompanied by a military band, and the insertion of new rhythms distinguished these bands from those of other allied armies, making them popular with the public. Most military bands performed in France, but Italy too had its share, starting with the band of the 332nd Ohio Regiment. One jazz historian mentions a three-day band symposium in Milan, on 3–5 March 1918, during which the band of the US 18th Infantry Regiment outshone the Italian and British ones with its entertaining repertoire, which included the odd syncopated rhythm. A soldier of the 332nd Ohio recalls his regimental band playing ragtime music during a visit in October 1918 by Samuel Gompers, the historic founder and later president of the American Federation of Labor.[35]

---

[33] Louis Armstrong, *Swing that Music* (New York: Longman, 1936), 9–10. Among the studies on the history of early Jazz in New Orleans in connection with the Italian community, I relied mainly on Alyn Shipton, *A New History of Jazz* (London: Continuum, 2001); Adriano Mazzoletti, *Il jazz in Italia*, i (Turin: EDT, 2004); Samuel B. Charters, *A Trumpet around the Corner: The Story of New Orleans Jazz* (Jackson, MS: University Press of Mississippi, 2009); Bruce Boyd Raeburn, 'Stars of David and Sons of Sicily: Constellations beyond the Canon in Early New Orleans Jazz', *Jazz Perspectives*, 3/2 (2009), 123–52; Shane Lief, 'Anarchist Blues', *Jazz Archivist*, 25 (2012), 34–42; and Anna Harwell Celenza, *Jazz Italian Style: From its Origins in New Orleans to Fascist Italy and Sinatra* (Cambridge: Cambridge University Press, 2017).

[34] Nick la Rocca and his band played in London for more than a year, but only in 1919–20, and they never toured in Italy. And, as we will see in Chapter 8, when jazz spread into Italy's major northern towns soon after the First World War, the role of Sicilian immigrants in the genesis of jazz in New Orleans was almost totally unknown.

[35] The Milan concert in March 1918 is mentioned by Mazzoletti in his *Il jazz in Italia*, i. 21. The visit of Gompers to the 332nd Regiment is mentioned in Lettau, *In Italy with the 332nd Infantry*, 23.

More pertinent to the history of early jazz music was the arrival in Italy of the biggest contingent of US Army ambulance personnel—70 officers and 1,641 men—in June 1918. A group of them formed the US Army Ambulance Service Jazz Band. Better known in its abbreviated denomination—the American Jazz Band—the group was formed by musicians who had been involved in a musical produced by the US Army Ambulance Service entitled *Good-Bye Bill*, which had run in New York and Allentown (the USAAS training base) in April–May 1918. Seven musicians got together during the voyage across the Atlantic in order to entertain the troops on board, and once in Italy they were allowed to form a proper musical ensemble. They were based in the northern Italian city of Mantua, headquarters of the USAAS, where the band leader, Sergeant Charles W. Hamp, was stationed. The American Jazz Band performed in front of military and civilian crowds in several Italian cities, from Milan to Rome (in the presence of the American ambassador) to Naples, and in Fiorello La Guardia's air base in Foggia. They then travelled back up the Adriatic coast, performing in Rimini, Ravenna, and Venice, where, to fulfil a vow made while crossing the Atlantic, the band tied two gondolas together and played on the Grand Canal, passing under Rialto Bridge. As a band member recalled in a letter: 'This was a new experience for the Italian people with American dance and jazz music, and although many did not understand the words of the songs, they loved their rhythms, the humour, and the lonesomeness of a blues tune.'

The defining element of this early jazz ensemble was the drum kit, something unknown to European small orchestras at the time. Its foot-operated bass drum was one more example of the innovative, nonconformist spirit of American culture. Finally, in December 1918, the American Jazz Band recorded eighteen songs in one of Milan's early recording studios, the Società italiana di fonotipia, all of which, sadly, have been lost. At the end of the month, the American Jazz Band was moved to Paris, where it continued to play, touring France, until its members were discharged and eventually returned to the USA in the summer of 1919.[36]

It was a short season, but, similar to what happened when Buffalo Bill toured Italy in 1890 and 1906, it was the first time that Italians living in the main cities had an opportunity to receive a first-hand impression of a distinctly 'American' cultural product. Another jazz band was formed by American soldiers and performed for the YMCA branch in Rome, led by an army sergeant called Griffith. It was vividly remembered by one of Italy's most talented early jazz guitarists,

---

[36] On the American Jazz Band, see chapters 5 and 6 of John R. Smucker, *The History of the United States Army Ambulance Service—1917, 1918, 1919* (Allentown, PA: USAAS Association, 1967); and Rainer Lotz, 'The United States Army Ambulance Service Jazz Band', *Vintage Jazz Mart*, 145 (2007), 2–7. The quotation is taken from a letter of an unnamed member of the band, reproduced in Smucker, *The History of the USAAS*, 131.

Fig. 5.5. The American Jazz Band, wearing Italian army helmets, presumably in Milan, 1918. (courtesy of C. B. Barlow, USAAS Section 563)

Vittorio Spina, who learnt to play the banjo while working first as an errand boy and then as a musician in the last years of the war.[37]

There were also chance contributions by individuals unconnected to established musical ensembles. In his memoirs, Sergeant Major Joseph Lettau remembers how he and his fellow soldiers of the 332nd Regiment used to spend their free time during their training period in Sommacampagna, on the outskirts of Verona:

> Then, there were the new vinos (wines) and cognacs of Italy to be tried and many pleasant evenings were spent in dingy little shops we would not think of entering at home.
>
> Others, musically inclined, struck up an acquaintance with the owner of a piano and thus amused themselves with the good old American tunes. The Italians generally liked American rag-time. We were made welcome everywhere and in turn thought highly of our hosts.[38]

---

[37] Spina's memories of his teenage experience with the YMCA jazz band are recalled in Mazzoletti, *Il jazz in Italia*, i. 12–15.
[38] Lettau, *In Italy with the 332nd Infantry*, 17.

The new rhythms of jazz music were part and parcel of the image of American lifestyle, an exciting and innovative model, which the US Army brought with it to Italy.

At the end of the war, a battalion of the 332nd Regiment was stationed in the Istrian city of Fiume, which, coincidentally, was to become the focus of Italy's frustrated territorial claims as embodied by its military occupation at the hands of Gabriele D'Annunzio. In the preceding months, on the musical front, things were much smoother. As Lettau recalls:

> The regimental band was sent for and on several nights dances were held which were greatly enjoyed. At first, the girls could not understand the American way of dancing, but it was not long before they were one-stepping and fox-trotting as if they had never danced otherwise.[39]

---

[39] Lettau, *In Italy with the 332nd Infantry*, 69.

PART 2

AMERICAN CULTURE IN
FASCIST ITALY, 1922–1943

# 6
# America as a Mirror of Modernity

The post-First World War years saw America take a leading role in the new popular narrative art *par excellence*: film. Cinema theatres became imaginary, giant telescopes through which Italians could view the world, and America in particular. By the 1920s, films could reach millions of individuals at once, every day, in a way that their main competitors—novels and theatre plays—had never achieved. Audiences across the country could acquire a vivid image (if somewhat fabricated) of contemporary America: its people, its vast expanses, its urban glamour, and its modern lifestyle.

In the world of music, too, America rose to a new prominence. From ragtime and foxtrot rhythms dominating the radio and in dancing halls, to the fight for elite appreciation through George Gershwin's compositions and jazz music, it was no longer possible to write off America as a country of naïve and uncultured nouveaux riches.

That all this should happen at a time when Italy was falling into the hands of a nationalistic leader who made 'autarky' a buzzword of his economic and cultural policies adds further distinctive colour to this period. Benito Mussolini, as we will see, approached America with the ideological flexibility that characterized his leadership more broadly. America was a friend and a model of modernity to be praised, but at the same time could also be a degenerate, materialistic, Protestant country, and ultimately an enemy during the final, more radical years of his regime. His ambivalent views reflected those of a nation. But Mussolini and the Fascist regime had another reason to think carefully about their position vis-à-vis America: if the USA was emerging as a powerful yet contested economic and cultural model for European countries, Fascist Italy was also studied and judged as a possible 'third way' between liberal capitalism and a communist state economy. This created a competitive edge of sorts, which peaked in 1933 with Franklin D. Roosevelt's 'New Deal' policies and the widespread suggestion that the American president had learnt profound lessons from Mussolini's regime.

By the 1920s the United States of America was home to millions of first- and second-generation Italian immigrants who were slowly climbing the social ladder, some very successfully so. Rejoining American politics after his contribution to the war as an aviator in Italy, Fiorello La Guardia moved from Congress to the mayorship of New York City in 1934, which he held until 1945. In San Francisco, Amadeo Giannini led the merger of his Bank of Italy with Los Angeles' Bank of America in 1929, making him one of the most powerful bankers of interwar

*America in Italian Culture: The Rise of a New Model of Modernity, 1861–1943*. Guido Bonsaver, Oxford University Press.
© Guido Bonsaver 2023. DOI: 10.1093/oso/9780198849469.003.0007

America, much welcome in Hollywood. These were also the years of the 'Latin Lover' *par excellence*, Rodolfo/Rudolph Valentino, and of the popular films directed by Frank Borzage (Borzaga) and Frank Capra, not to mention, in Chicago, the infamous deeds of Alphonse Gabriel Capone. Two questions therefore present themselves. First, how was the multicultural fabric of American society perceived in Italy now that Italian Americans were becoming a defining part of this vast democratic nation and Italy had become a dictatorship? And, secondly, to what extent did Italian Americans influence the perception of America in Italy during these years?

The six sections of this chapter build towards a comprehensive answer to these two questions. Section 6.1 looks at the development of the pro- and anti-American stance in the interwar years; 6.2 focuses on the Italian national press—both Fascist and 'independent'—and on popular illustrated magazines; 6.3 concentrates on Mussolini's views on America and on those of a number of influential individuals close to the regime. The final three sections will be devoted, respectively, to three themes that recurred in public debates on America: technology, women, and the Italian American connection.

## 6.1 Modern America in Full View

The long-standing critical stance towards American culture was based on a dualistic view. As Sassoon succinctly put it:

> All over Europe the staple clichés of anti-Americanism were not based on politics but on a contrast between quality (Europe) and quantity (America), spirit (Europe) and matter (America), man (Europe) and machine (America), tradition (Europe) and modernity (America).[1]

As we will see, this patronizing view of America continued to colour even the alleged praise of qualities such as Americans' higher standard of living or the emancipation of women. The temptation to lower the discussion to the anecdotal narrative of some 'americanata' remained constant.

The philosophical distinction between 'spirit (Europe) and matter (America)' was a strongly felt sentiment in Italy. Between Giovanni Gentile's presence at the heart of the regime and Benedetto Croce's influence among non-Fascist circles, there was a neo-Hegelian, idealist bloc that provided continuity with the pre-First World War years. This meant an open hostility towards the American pragmatism of William James, despite the interest it had generated among the influential

---

[1] Sassoon, *The Culture of the Europeans*, 942.

Florentine group of intellectuals led by Papini and Prezzolini. It is somewhat ironic to think that Fascism could have claimed to have realized the marriage between idealism and materialism that James had seen as fundamental to the development of philosophy in the twentieth century. He wrote this in 1907, at a time in which the mystical reading of his essay *The Will to Believe* (1896) had become part of Papini's and Prezzolini's nationalistic call for men of action, capable of sweeping away the rhetorical webs of Liberal Italy. Fascism's civic religion and its cult of *Il Duce* as an infallible Man-of-Will could have been presented as a claim to a pragmatist, Fascist 'third way' in the philosophical field.[2]

By the 1920s, however, the ever-restless Papini had moved on to other philosophical pastures, and, for Mussolini, the reading of James's essays must have been a youthful memory and certainly not a belief strong enough to challenge Gentile's firm control of Fascism's ideological self-image. This is symbolically revealed in the 1926 interview that Mussolini gave to the Italian correspondent of the *New York Times*, Anne O'Hare-McCormick. After mentioning William James as one of the influences on his personal philosophy, Mussolini insisted that Fascism was an entirely Italian product and suggested that the American journalist should talk to Gentile for a more detailed understanding. This is precisely what O'Hare-McCormick did, and an interview with Gentile forms the second part of her article. Gentile fully ignored pragmatism and proceeded to present the Italian, neo-idealist roots of Fascism.[3]

Indeed, when it came to American culture, Gentile inclined towards the decades-old cliché of Americanism as a soulless form of materialism, the product of a society driven by material gain and hedonistic utilitarianism. Pragmatism could be dismissed as an attempt to give philosophical shape to these sentiments, something at the antipodes of his philosophical doctrine. The distinction between European spirituality and American materialism, however defined, was recurrent in Fascist Italy and sometimes present in Mussolini's speeches too.

It was equally popular among non-militant intellectuals. Fresh from the successful world tour of his theatre company, Luigi Pirandello gave an interview to *Il Giornale d'Italia* in May 1924, in which he expanded upon his disillusionment towards the American way of life:

> I dislike mechanical progress. It adds nothing to life. [...] The fundamental error on which American life is based is the same error which, in my opinion, proves the invalidity of the democratic concept of life. I am anti-democratic *par excellence*. The masses need to be shaped, they have material needs, aspirations which are limited to practical necessities. Wellbeing for wellbeing's sake, wealth for

---

[2] James, *Pragmatism: A New Name for Some Old Ways of Thinking*, 3–40.
[3] Anne O'Hare-McCormick, 'Behind Fascism Stands a Philosopher', *New York Times Magazine*, 26 September 1926, pp. 3, 18.

wealth's sake, these have neither meaning nor value. [...] In Italy wealth would create spiritual values.

Given his anti-democratic views, it is not surprising that, a few months later, during Mussolini's dark moment following the assassination of Socialist MP Giacomo Matteotti, Pirandello decided publicly to join the Fascist party. What is indicative here is Pirandello's suggestion that wealth in America was a sterile product, in opposition to the spiritual fruits that Italian culture might produce with the same means.[4]

Six years later, in another interview, Pirandello's vision of the battle between mechanistic America and spiritual Europe acquired apocalyptic tones:

> If I were in charge of the world's destiny [...] I would suppress machines and all those who invented them! Machines devour everything, they express only the surface of life, nothing of its depth. [...] Time and space will disappear. One day we will reach such a state of mechanical exasperation that machines will perhaps be tasked with destroying themselves. Already on the streets of New York people have decided it's not worth driving anymore; the traffic is so bad that it's quicker to get out and walk. [...] Why is Europe not defending its exceptional spiritual richness? America has its own lifestyle, and that isn't a problem. We shouldn't impose laws on America, but neither should we suffer their laws. Europe must defend the millenia-old spirit that was given to her to protect.[5]

This near-Luddite vision of the dangers of technology was recurrently associated with its commercial consequence: mass production. Whenever a journalist or a traveller wanted to add a pejorative edge to his or her description of American life, negative connotations referring to mass production came to hand.

A good example can be found in the work of Emilio Cecchi, an author who will be a regular figure in this second part of the book. As a literature, art, and film critic, and as an author and journalist, Cecchi was one of Italy's most refined prose writers of the interwar years. He was also influential within Italy's film industry when, in 1931-3, he became Production Director of Italy's major film production company in Rome, Cines. Cecchi had developed an interest in American culture and taught himself English, giving him a privileged status as an

---

[4] Giuseppe Villaroel, 'Colloqui con Pirandello', *Il Giornale d'Italia*, 8 May 1924, in Ivan Pupo (ed.), *Interviste a Pirandello: 'Parole da dire, uomo, agli altri uomini'* (Saveria Manelli: Rubbettino, 2002), 248–51 (249). For an exploration of Pirandello's relationship with the regime, see Patricia Gaborik, 'Fascism', and Guido Bonsaver, 'The Royal Italian Academy', in Patricia Gaborik (ed.), *Pirandello in Context* (Cambridge: Cambridge University Press, 2023), 12–24, 56–70. On the return from his American tour, in March 1924, Pirandello had already made clear his pro-Fascist view. See Luigi Bottazzi, 'Le impressioni d'America di Luigi Pirandello', *Corriere della Sera*, 8 March 1924, in Pupo (ed.), *Interviste a Pirandello*, 221–4.

[5] Eligio Possenti, 'Colloquio con Luigi Pirandello', *Corriere della Sera*, 28 October 1930, p. 3; in Pupo (ed.), *Interviste a Pirandello*, 292–4.

Italian voice on America with first-hand knowledge of it. During and after a long stay in Berkeley as a visiting professor in 1930, Cecchi wrote a number of articles published in the *Corriere della Sera*. His lectures on Italian art were attended mainly by female students, and in describing them in an article for the *Corriere della Sera* he linked the conformity of their appearance to agricultural mass production:

> And their bodies too, slender, elastic, well formed, neither fat nor thin, had something abstract and cold about them: it was something which made one think of the apples, all identical, of the same colour, odourless, in the exhibitions of Californian fruit-vendors.[6]

With one simile, Cecchi's student cohort is diminished and portrayed as an attractive but ultimately unappealing product of mass production.

As to the role of French culture as a privileged intermediary channel for many Italian intellectuals, the interwar years were not exempt from it. Paris continued to be the first stop of every educated Italian's Grand Tour. Many stayed there for long periods; others, such as Leo Ferrero, settled there. One of the most cosmopolitan young intellectuals of his generation, Ferrero was a *trait d'union* between Piero Gobetti's liberal circles in Turin and those grouped around Florence's literary journal *Solaria*. He moved to Paris in 1928, became close to Paul Valéry, and, following an invitation by Bernard Grasset, wrote a book in French about Paris's status as a European cultural capital.[7] In Ferrero's view, Paris represented the fusion between the artistic 'Athenian civilization' that Italy had once inherited, and the more pragmatic 'Roman civilization' embodied by nineteenth-century imperial Britain. The educated French elite was, according to Ferrero, predestined to show the West the philosophical and cultural values on which they should base their own national cultures. As he wrote in the concluding pages:

> Today, people expect from the French elite the definition of the principles they must obey, the goods they must desire, the futile whims they can enjoy without shame: philosophy, politics, the arts, the salons, debauchery, the opulence of all

---

[6] Emilio Cecchi, 'E le ragazze?', *Corriere della Sera*, 13 February 1935, p. 3; then in Cecchi, *America amara* (Florence: Sansoni, 1939), 258. Cecchi had started to learn English on his own, in 1902, while at the officers' training school in Florence. On this, see Margherita Ghilardi, 'Cronologia', in Emilio Cecchi, *Saggi e viaggi* (Milan: Mondadori, 1997), pp. xxix–lv.

[7] Leo Ferrero, *Paris: Dernier modèle de l'Occident* (Paris: Les Éditions Rieder, 1932). The book was published by Rieder, since Grasset eventually declined the manuscript because of its philosophical slant. Nicola Chiaromonte wrote a long review of Ferrero's book in *Solaria* in which he praised it and at the same time contested the exclusivity that Ferrero gave to the French educated elite in their role as custodians of Western culture. Nicola Chiaromonte, 'Parigi come modello', *Solaria*, 8 (1933), 59–62.

the West respectful of the great laws or of the mysterious rules that Paris has established for two centuries.[8]

However, there were developments in the perception of America within French intellectual debates as well. As Sassoon suggested:

> When it came to cultural trends and fashions, many Europeans still looked to Paris and its artistic circles, but these, especially in the 1920s, were relatively pro-American.[9]

The Parisian openness to all forms of the avant-garde was instrumental in raising interest in American culture. Its expat intellectual circles—the so-called lost generation—became a source of interest, particularly when figures associated with it such as Francis Scott Fitzgerald and Ernest Hemingway were becoming increasing popular.

At the same time, American music and entertainment took Paris by storm. Jazz rhythms became dominant, and equally epoch-making was the sensual lure of two American women: first, the mother of modern dance, California-born Isadora Duncan, who tragically died in Nice in 1927, and, secondly, the Missouri-born 'Black Venus', singer and performer Freda Josephine MacDonald, naturalized French as Joséphine Baker. Baker was such a renowned star that, when Kra published a book on her thoughts entitled *Les Mémoires de Joséphine Baker* in July 1927, only two months later Mondadori was able to advertise its Italian translation, *Le memorie della Venere negra: Joséphine Baker*. Italy's most prestigious theatre magazine—*Comoedia*—devoted a long and positive review to the book (unsurprisingly, since *Comoedia* was owned by Mondadori), in which Baker was presented with these words:

> Today miss Baker is worshipped in Paris. Indeed, more than worshipped: Joséphine and 'blackness' have become so fashionable that she can say 'there'll be so much black (in Paris) before long that whenever you light a match you'll have to light another one, just to make sure the first one hasn't gone out'.[10]

This is not to say that France was not also a centre for the diffusion of anti-American views. When Pirandello was interviewed for the already quoted article

---

[8] Ferrero, *Paris*, 257–8.
[9] Sassoon, *The Culture of the Europeans*, 943.
[10] A. Ramades Ferrarin, 'Joséphine Baker, "Self Made Woman"', *Comoedia*, 9/9 (September 1927), 31, 48. *Comoedia* was founded by Mondadori in 1919, its title and cover layout closely inspired by its prestigious French antecedents, the daily *Comoedia* (1907) and the fortnightly *Comoedia illustré* (1908). Isadora Duncan and Joséphine Baker were preceded by another groundbreaking American dancer, Loïe Fuller, whose extravagant, free-dance performances at Paris's *Folies-Bergère* at the turn of the century turned her into a cult figure associated with the *Art Nouveau* movement.

in the *Corriere della Sera*, he was caught by the Italian journalist reading Georges Dumahel's *Scènes de la vie future* (1930), a key text of French anti-Americanism. Indeed, Pirandello expanded on Dumahel's critique of the weakness of Europeans and stated that 'Paris has become an American bazaar: hotels, shop windows, entertainment, all is prepared to welcome rich Americans'.[11]

But were Europeans passive victims of America's cultural capital? Considering that the most iconic dance costume worn by Joséphine Baker at Paris's *Folies-Bergère* featured a skirt made of golden bananas, there is a sense that, if Buffalo Bill's Wild West had represented the American *homme sauvage* in the mind of nineteenth-century Europeans, it was now African Americans and their innovations—jazz music—that had taken its place. Their African ancestry provided easy symbolism of primitivism tinted with racist connotations. Like black jazz musicians, Baker was at the same time a symbol of primitivism and modernity and, as such, provoked ambivalent reactions of awe and repulsion.[12]

**Fig. 6.1.** Josephine Baker's iconic banana skirt, *La Folie du jour*, Folies-Bergère, 1926. (courtesy of Everett Collection/Alamy Stock)

---

[11] On Duhamel, see Armus, *French Anti-Americanism*, 24–6; and Roger, *The American Enemy*, 269–97.
[12] In Italy, popular composer Dino Rulli associated Baker's name with a syncopated dance in vogue at the time, the Black Bottom, in the title of a piece he composed in 1924: 'Josephine-Black Bottom',

Primitivism, in the fine arts in particular, was a vital component of avant-garde innovation in early twentieth-century Europe. One only has to think of the work of Paris-settled Italian artist Amedeo Modigliani. The Italian Futurists also viewed contemporary American culture as symbiotic with their avant-garde praise of modernity and at the same time saw in it a fusion of the modern and the atavistic. Already before the war, one of Futurism's most gifted artists, Umberto Boccioni, when writing of 'our need to Americanize ourselves', had specified that this meant the praise of 'all the wild, anti-artistic facets of our era'.[13]

Sadly, Boccioni was not the only talented Futurist artist whose patriotism led him to volunteer, fight, and die in the First World War. Another was Athos Casarini, who had moved to New York in 1907 and from there had joined Marinetti's call for a Futurist art. Despite his initial doubts, Casarini eventually decided to return to Italy to volunteer in the Italian army as an officer, and was eventually killed in action in September 1917. Before he left for Italy, Casarini announced his decision in an article in the *World Magazine*—for which he had been working as an illustrator. Beyond his fervent praise of Italy as a civilizing nation, Casarini added an equally fervent farewell to his adopted city:

> After six years of residence in this great Futuristic city of New York I return to my country, fortified by the iron I breathed in this exhilarating atmosphere. But I am taking with me the indelible memory of thy broad streets, with their agitated crowds, the vibrant fervor of thy factories and thy constructions, of thy clear-cut lines, of thy busy rivers, of the sea that defends thee, of thy youth, thy faith, thy aspirations. O America, newest born of the immortals![14]

America was not just the closest of all Western countries to nature and to humanity's ancestral past: it was now the land of modernity too.[15]

---

thus creating a sexual innuendo. The picture was complicated at the time of Italy's invasion of Ethiopia by Joséphine Baker's public siding with Mussolini, denouncing the Ethiopian Negus as a feudal lord still imposing slavery, which the Italian occupation was going to end. See Raffaele De Berti, 'Princess Tam Tam: Josephine Baker una venere in Italia (1928–1936)', *Àgalma 22: Rivista di studi culturali ed estetica*, 22 (2011), 38–47; Roberto Dainotto, 'The Saxophone and the Pastoral: Italian Jazz in the Age of Fascist Modernity', *Italica*, 85/2–3 (2008), 273–94 (275); and Harwell Celenza, *Jazz Italian Style*, 110. On the reception and status of Joséphine Baker in France, see Jules-Rosette Bennetta, *Second Skin: Josephine Baker in Art and Life: The Icon and the Image* (Urbana and Chicago: University of Illinois Press, 2007); and Laurent Cugny, *Une histoire du jazz en France*, i. *Du milieu du XIXe siècle à 1929, Jazz en France* (Paris: Outre Mesure, 2014), 198–226.

[13] Umberto Boccioni, 'Simultaneità', in Boccioni, *Pittura e scultura futuriste (dinamismo plastico)* (Milan: Edizioni Futuriste di 'Poesia', 1914), 81–99; then in *Gli scritti editi e inediti* (Milan: Feltrinelli, 1971), 176; also quoted in Dall'Osso, *Voglia d'America*, 103.

[14] Athos Casarini, 'The Futurist Hears the Call of War: "And I am going" Says Casarini', *World Magazine*, 15 August 1915, p. 11. On Casarini, see Dall'Osso, *Voglia d'America*, 95–7; and Franco Solmi, *Athos Casarini pittore. 1883–1917* (Bologna: Alfa, 1963).

[15] On 'Americanism' and European urban culture in the early post-First World War years, see Wakeman, *A Modern History of European Cities*, 198–206.

Another Futurist who embraced the city of New York and attempted to take root in it was Fortunato Depero. Despite his Austrian birth certificate—he grew up in Trentino before the First World War—Depero developed his artistic career in Italy, joining the Futurists during a stay in Rome in 1913. By the 1920s he had become one of the movement's front-line members as a painter, author, graphic artist, and stage-, costume- and furnishing-designer, and hence a staunch promoter of the Futurists' ideal of revolutionary creativity in all walks of artistic and domestic life. At the peak of his career, in October 1928, Depero decided to move to New York. He knew no English but was counting on the support of the Italian and Italophile communities there. He rented an old hotel in Chelsea and transformed it into the Futurist House, which he hoped would become a beacon of Italian Futurism in America. Depero's initial optimism is made clear in his correspondence to Marinetti and involved, not just his plan to take the American art world by storm, but also more utopian ideas such as the foundation of a Futurist school and even a Futurist village.

Reality, however, proved much harsher. The New York art scene was difficult to break into—although Depero's paintings were positively reviewed by the influential journal *Brochure Quarterly*—and he lacked the financial solidity needed to be able to develop his plans without the help of the Italian authorities (which he sought unsuccessfully). The economic depression triggered by the Wall Street crisis of October 1929 made his prospects even worse. As a result, Depero was unable to stage a grandiose project called 'The New Babel', which would have seen him collaborate with famous Russian choreographer Léonide Massine and complete a multimedia work entitled *New York—Film vissuto* (planned as a book accompanied by two vinyl records). He did at least manage to illustrate two covers of the magazine *Vanity Fair*, to design the costumes of Massine's dancers at the prestigious Roxy Theatre on at least one occasion, and to redesign two Italian American restaurants, but the lack of continuous commissions and the meagre sales of his paintings eventually forced him to cut his losses and return to Italy. He did so in October 1930, exactly two years later, after which he reopened his Casa d'Arte Depero in his native Rovereto, which still exists today as a museum.

His writings on New York reveal, on the one hand, a sense of awe and excitement inspired by the metropolis's gigantic features and, on the other—and this is probably linked to frustration for his lack of personal success—a sharp criticism of the people's cold, soul-less, and manic manners. As Katia Pizzi concluded, his experience of New York remained, in the end, that of 'an alien'.[16]

---

[16] Katia Pizzi, *Italian Futurism and the Machine* (Manchester: Manchester University Press, 2019), 118. On Depero's New York period, see also Raffaele Bedarida, '"Bombs against Skyscrapers": Depero's Strange Love Affair with New York City: 1928–1949', *Italian Modern Art*, 1 (2019), 1–33. The entire collection of Depero's writings on New York has been reprinted as: Fortunato Depero, *Un futurista a New York* (Montepulciano: Editori del Grifo, 1990). On Depero and advertising, see Giovanna Ginex, 'Not Just Campari! Depero and Advertising', *Italian Modern Art*, 1 (January 2019), 1–28.

**Fig. 6.2.** Depero's advertising image for Campari inspired by New York's skyline (1931). (courtesy of Museo Campari, Milan)

The shift to an image of America as a model of ultimate modernity resulted in the decreasing importance of the romantic image of the Wild West. Although it remained very much alive within literary and film productions, it was no longer viewed as a vision of what America was and had ceased to be. Buffalo Bill too was by then confined to the virtual cabinets of popular history. As just mentioned, the new *homme sauvage* was the African American: Josephine Baker in France and Louis Armstrong in America. It was an image linked to

**Fig. 6.3.** New York skyscrapers, 1932; the photo, by Irving Underhill, shows lower Manhattan's piers and skyline; the tallest building, on the centre, is 70 Pine St (called Cities Service building at the time), 952 feet (290 metres) high. (courtesy of Prints and Photographs Division, Library of Congress, Washington, DC)

urban landscapes. Indeed, one could say that the Old West was entirely overtaken by the 'New East', which equally attracted and fascinated Italians. It was the urban, modern, technology-driven America that in New York City found its ultimate symbol as a futuristic land.

By the interwar years New York had established itself as the self-assured financial and cultural capital of the USA, clearly aspiring to a global role beyond the oceans. Visually, too, its rivalry with Chicago was over. Even if Chicago was still adding skyscrapers to its skyline, there was no doubt that Manhattan's had become by far the most familiar image of urban America. The vast majority of migrants in the early twentieth century passed through Ellis Island, and the port of New York was the arrival destination of just about every Italian who visited the USA in order to write about it. The gigantic sight and sound spectacle when the ocean liners slowly approached Manhattan's bustling docks was the obligatory *incipit* of any travel writing on America.

Chicago became a sort of 'Gotham city', a dark, sinister city renowned mainly for violent crime and its industrial-size abattoirs, whose near-infernal organization had famously been depicted by Upton Sinclair in his 1906 novel *The Jungle*.[17]

New York's skyline, instead, stood for a city of the mind. In his detailed analysis of journalistic descriptions, Michel Beynet noticed that, when confronted by these colossi of iron, glass, and concrete, hardly any author showed interest in the technical side of the phenomenon. Nobody seemed to find the need to describe how those buildings could reach such vertiginous heights and rarely what it meant to live and work in them.[18]

Unsurprisingly, a recurrent simile pertained to the field of geology rather than to that of technology. The peaks of Lower and Midtown Manhattan's skyscrapers reminded Italian visitors of Italy's most spectacular mountain range, the Dolomites. This also implies that the negative reaction to the aesthetics of skyscrapers, which had recurred in writings before the First World War, was now replaced by a positive attitude. In 1925, from the third page of the *Corriere della Sera*, Arnaldo Cipolla described New York's skyscrapers as a 'Dolomitic vision', after which he suggested that they should be considered as a symbolic message that Americans had built in full view of the ships of incoming migrants:

> Where 'sky-scrapers' rise up one finds the whole of America, that is to say, American progress and civilization, geometrically and harmoniously concentrated in their three dimensions. It has been said that the skyscraper has created a new architecture, made by giants, and this statement used to be laughed off by Europeans, but they were wrong. One has to judge the skyscraper in America. In our cities it would be monstrous.[19]

However, not everybody, in those years, thought that a skyscraper in an Italian town should be avoided at all costs.

A Milanese architect, whose prestigious career had developed in Latin America, thought that such a thing could be done even in the middle of Rome. And Mussolini approved. This is the mostly forgotten story of Mario Palanti, who planned and presented the detailed drawings and model for a giant skyscraper to be built next to Italy's parliament, intentionally overshadowing St Peter's dome. Thanks to the collaboration of Ottavio Dinale (an old collaborator of Mussolini and then responsible for the Fascist associations in South America),

---

[17] On the description of Chicago by Italian travellers, see Ambra Meda, 'Babilonie stellate: Immagini delle metropoli americane nella letteratura di viaggio degli anni trenta', *Forum Italicum*, 45/1 (2011), 100–23 (104–12).

[18] Beynet, *L'Image de l'Amerique*, i. 279–85, 313–14. Similarly, Beynet suggests that Italian journalists tended to discuss the mechanization of the American industry and in particular Taylorism from a rather philosophical viewpoint, hardly ever entering a discussion of how mass production works and how it differs from pre-Taylorian industrialism in Europe (ii. 643). Both aspects, he argues convincingly, were a consequence of their idealistic education.

[19] Arnaldo Cipolla, 'Grattacieli', *La Stampa*, 19 February 1925, p. 3.

the project was perused and warmly received by Mussolini when he visited its official presentation in a hall of Palazzo Chigi (then the seat of Italy's Foreign Office), on 27 September 1924. Palanti's megalomaniac plan was supposed to celebrate Fascism's seizure of power.

By then, Palanti was a successful architect living in Argentina, already famous for stylistically debatable but nonetheless prestigious high-rise buildings such as the Palacio Barolo in Buenos Aires (1923) and the Palacio Salvo in Montevideo (completed in 1928; then the tallest building in Latin America). According to Palanti, the time had come for Rome to enter the twentieth century and bear witness to Italy's Fascist era in a most spectacular fashion. The skyscraper he planned, clearly inspired by New York's Woolworth Building (1912; the world's tallest building at the time), was meant to dwarf anything that had been built in Europe. It was planned to be 330 metres tall (St Peter's stopped at 136) and to house the new Italian parliament in its gigantic base.

After the official presentation, Palanti made sure that the news of Mussolini's praise would travel far. Three days later they had reached the *New York Times*, which ran the following headline on its front page: 'Mussolini to Build Highest Skyscraper; to Rise 88 Floors, 1,100 Feet, above Rome'. The journalist seemed to have no doubts about the political value of the operation: Mussolini's decision was presented as a *fait accompli*, and the short article mentioned that the building was going to be called 'Torre Littoria' in honour of Fascism. A month later, the paper returned to the subject, this time with an illustration and an even more sensational headline—'Mussolini's Plans to Outdo the Dreams of the Caesars: The Mole Littoria'. A spectacular, full-page illustration was published by the *London Illustrated News* a few weeks later. This time, however, Mussolini was left out of the headline: 'The World's Largest Skyscraper: Rome to Outsoar New York?'[20]

How serious was Mussolini when he showed his approval? Nobody doubts that, on the day, he seemed positively impressed by this grand project. It promised, after all, to impose a most revolutionary mark of modernity directly associated with his regime, for all the world to wonder at. In the following days and weeks, however, Palanti's plan encountered the resistance and ill-concealed scorn of Italy's architects and Rome's governor, Filippo Cremonesi. After all, it took little to show that Palanti's vision fully ignored the aesthetic and logistical impact of

---

[20] On Palanti's project, see the essay by architectural historian Dietrich Neumann, 'A Skyscraper for Mussolini', AA Files, 68 (2014), 141–53. There is almost no trace of Palanti's project in Italy's histories of architecture during the Fascist years. Paolo Nicoloso mainly concentrates on Palanti's contribution to another project, the competition for the Roman headquarters of the Fascist Party, in 1934, and Emilio Gentile fully ignores the case of the Mole Littoria. Paolo Nicoloso, *Mussolini architetto: Propaganda e paesaggio urbano nell'Italia fascista* (Turin: Einaudi, 2008), 131, 134, 164; Emilio Gentile, *Fascismo di pietra* (Rome and Bari: Laterza, 2007). In English, Aristotle Kallis dwells on the project in his essay '"In miglior tempo...": What Fascism did not Build in Rome', *Journal of Modern Italian Studies* 16 (2011), 59–83 (71–3). The skyscraper's detailed plans were published in a volume printed by the then newly born Rizzoli publishing house: Mario Palanti, *L'Eternale—Mole Littoria* (Milan: Rizzoli, 1926).

188  AMERICA IN ITALIAN CULTURE

Fig. 6.4. Artist's illustration of Palanti's plan for a giant skyscraper to be built in Rome's city centre, published in the *London Illustrated News* (24 January 1925). (courtesy of Bodleian Library, Oxford)

such a colossal project in an already congested historic centre. Given that in the autumn of 1924 Mussolini was still reeling from the attacks on his prime ministership in the wake of Matteotti's assassination, it is possible that he might have cynically thought of Palanti's project as a potential source of distraction in the public debate, rather than a serious proposition. In any case, once he had registered the united resistance to the plan among the Italian intelligentsia, he allowed Palanti's vision to sink into oblivion, despite the fact that the Milanese architect repeatedly returned to Mussolini with further proposals, until he was no longer allowed an audition. As for the regime's most influential architect at the time, Marcello Piacentini, he had already manifested his opposition to the presence of skyscrapers in the historic centres of Italian towns in a short article published the year before. However, as we will see later, this did not stop him from designing Italy's first fully-fledged skyscraper in 1940.[21]

To return to the public debate on American skyscrapers, similarly split between fascination and rebuff was another *Corriere della Sera* senior journalist, Luigi Barzini, When he prefaced his son's book on New York, he defined Manhattan as 'the most stupendous and powerful phenomenon of modernity in the entire world', after which, within the same paragraph, he mentioned first the 'Dolomitic majesty' of its skyscrapers and the 'monstrous multitudes' of its people.[22] Together with the Dolomites, another image familiar to Italians was regularly used in comparisons with New York's skyscrapers—this image was of the medieval towers of San Gimignano. Emilio Cecchi produced an elaborate description of the New York skyline, comparing it to the towers of San Gimignano in an article he published in the *Corriere della Sera* on 1 March 1935, ten years after Cipolla's but with exactly the same title: 'Grattacieli'. It is a long piece, which is worth paraphrasing, since it provides another example of the ambivalent image of America that could be contained within the same text, and at the same it gives us a sense of the depth of Cecchi's culture. He starts by stating that the first to make a comparison between New York and San Gimignano was the American art historian—and personal friend of his—Bernard Berenson—after which Cecchi dwells on a number of American intellectuals in whose writings one can find harsh critiques of the skyscraper—from novelists Henry James and Waldo Frank, to art historian Nat Meyer Shapiro, to architect Frank Lloyd Wright. At the end of this long sequel of condemnations, however, Cecchi turns the table and confesses his own personal appreciation:

> And similar to what happened to Ninive and Babylon, one day mankind will come to accept that skyscrapers were a monstrous growth, a sin of arrogance worthy of Nebuchadnezzar, a madness. As for me, I am happy to have lived at a time during which these sins, this madness, were committed. Because, as much as it might only be an illusory beauty, the work of a Fata Morgana; or, to use Frank's words: a demonic beauty; how can one deny that skyscrapers are beautiful?

---

[21] Marcello Piacentini, 'In tema di grattacieli', *Architettura e arti decorative*, 2/8 (1923), 311–17. We will dwell on Piacentini in Chapter 10.

[22] Luigi Barzini, 'Prefazione', in Luigi Barzini Jr, *Nuova York* (Milan: Giacomo Agnelli, 1931), 5–7 (6).

This comment is then followed by five paragraphs of uniquely chiselled, lyrical prose describing first New York and then Chicago and San Francisco at night. The conclusion is humorously apocalyptic: 'Skyscrapers will disappear. We are happy to have made it in time to see them.' It is difficult not to be captivated by Cecchi's fascination and by his poetic language, and so, one imagines, must the *Corriere della Sera*'s readers have been at the time. New York, and by association America, seemed to provoke the ambivalent feeling of a sinful pleasure.[23]

It was a youthful sinful pleasure, one could add, if we move to another influential figure, Mario Soldati. The Italian author and filmmaker had moved to New York in November 1929. He was at the time a postgraduate art historian who had been offered a grant to study and teach Italian art at Columbia University. In later years, he described this decision as an attempt to escape from the provincialism of Italian culture. It was in New York that he met his first wife, Marion Rieckelman,

Fig. 6.5. Carlo Levi's front cover image for Mario Soldati's *America primo amore*, Florence: Bemporad, 1935. (courtesy of the Bodleian Library, Oxford)

---

[23] Emilio Cecchi, 'Grattacieli', *Corriere della Sera*, 1 March 1935, p. 3. This article became part of Cecchi's book *America amara*; then in *Saggi e viaggi*, 1121–7. On Cecchi's prose, see Paolo Leoncini, *Emilio Cecchi: L'etica del visivo e lo stato liberale* (Lecce: Milella, 2017).

with whom he had three children, although in 1931 he had to return to Italy after failing to secure a permanent job. In Rome he began to work in the film industry, at Cines, employed by Cecchi and under the wing of expert director Mario Camerini. When his marriage fell apart—Marion returned to the USA in September 1934—Soldati sat down to complete his book of essays, dedicated to his American period. The result was the already mentioned *America primo amore* (1935), one of Soldati's most popular books. Here we will concentrate on its cover, since it provides a visual equivalent of the expression 'sinful pleasure'. It was the work of his Turinese school friend, the artist and author Carlo Levi. New York's skyscrapers appear in the background, projected on a sketchy map of the USA, but what is indicative of the imagery is that the naked woman sensually lying down in the front is depicted with demonic traits. If Manhattan's skyline had come to define the ambivalent fascination of American culture—wondrous yet outlandish—Carlo Levi had captured the disturbingly sensual appeal that America projected in the interwar years. Ruth Ben-Ghiat wrote of this book as underscoring 'America's status as an emblem of deviant modernity', and both cover and text seem to confirm this.[24]

## 6.2 America in the Italian Press: Continuities and Developments

In his essay on America in Fascist Italy, historian Emilio Gentile identifies the notion of 'modernity' as key to understanding the regime's contradictory vision of the USA: 'Americanism was, for fascist culture, one of the main mythical metaphors of modernity, which was perceived ambivalently, as a phenomenon both terrifying and fascinating.' He notes that interest in American society rose steeply in the 1930s, with fifty-one books dedicated to the USA, as against only a dozen in the previous decade.[25]

This calls for a more nuanced exploration of the different phases of the phenomenon, an exercise that has been extensively addressed by Michel Beynet in his three-volume study of America in Italy's interwar years. Differently from Gentile, Beynet concentrated on the periodical press rather than on book publications.[26]

Within a study of the perception of America, Beynet's is a fruitful approach, since it can easily be assumed that newspapers and magazines reached a wider readership than books, which were rarely printed in more than half a dozen thousand copies. Benefiting from both Gentile's and Beynet's insights, and following a

---

[24] Ben-Ghiat, *Fascist Modernities*, 43.   [25] Gentile, 'Impending Modernity', 7.
[26] Beynet, *L'Image de l'Amérique*, see in particular i. 35–351, ii. 352–666, and iii. 667–722.

similar approach to that used for the pre-First World War years, I will then add a few considerations on an important sector that remained outside their study—that of illustrated periodicals aimed at a less-educated readership.

A first fact to consider with regard to America and the Italian press in the post-First World War years is the increased presence of Italian journalists. It was a rise that was proportionate to the progressive presence of the USA on the world stage, and at the same time it was facilitated by shorter times in crossing the Atlantic. This opens the space for a brief aside. While most beer-drinkers outside Italy will no doubt recognize Peroni's *Nastro azzurro*, few will remember that the name was given to the beer in order to celebrate the prize won for the then fastest westbound crossing of the Atlantic, in August 1933. It was clocked by the Italian ocean liner *Rex*: 4 days, 13 hours, and 58 minutes, at an average speed of 28.92 knots. In the pre-war years, the Blue Riband had gone mainly to either British or German ships and the westbound record decreased from eight days in 1863, to six in 1883, and eventually to three in 1937. The *Rex* was to remain the only Italian ship to figure in the Blue Riband hall of honours. It was a sign of Italy's regained capacity to compete with northern European nations, and Fascist propaganda made the most of it. Unsurprisingly, decades later, when Federico Fellini dedicated a film to his childhood memories of the Fascist years—*Amarcord* (1973)—the passing of the *Rex* off the Adriatic coast near his hometown, Rimini, was to fill one of its most poignant sequences.

As we have seen, Italy's most popular national daily, Milan's *Corriere della Sera*, stationed its first US correspondent in New York in February 1909. Felice Ferrero continued in this role until the end of 1926. His characteristic traits as

Fig. 6.6. Commemorative postcard celebrating the record-breaking crossing of the Atlantic by the Italian liner *Rex*. (author's personal collection)

a journalist—his mild anti-American conservatism and his tendency to avoid moving below the surface of the odd events he chronicled—have already been discussed in Chapter 2. When Ferrero ended his stint, the management of the *Corriere della Sera* decided to move to a more dynamic set-up. From 1927 and throughout the 1930s the USA was covered by a mixture of Italian journalists resident in America—none of them ever defined as *corrispondente*—and prestigious third-page authors who spent limited time there, such as Arnaldo Fraccaroli, Giuseppe Antonio Borgese, and Emilio Cecchi. All three left a lasting mark through their reportage on America.

At the time, Fraccaroli was the *Corriere della Sera*'s most renowned travel writer, and he was the first to replace Ferrero. He did so for an extended period, from January until November 1927, with the title of 'Inviato' (roughly translatable as 'non-resident correspondent'). Fraccaroli was a prolific author who criss-crossed the world, constantly turning his observations into articles, which were subsequently collected in the scores of books he published. His fifty-five 'Lettere americane'—as each article was pre-titled—provided material for four books, to which he later added a novel set in the USA.[27] Also a popular playwright of humorous comedies, Fraccaroli had a style as a journalist that reflected his tendency to explore the amusing potential of his odd encounters with foreign people and places. This, coupled with a never-repressed patriotism that gave his writing recurrent shades of a 'sedentary traveller',[28] could have limited his articles to an entertaining but superficial account of his experiences. In fact, Fraccaroli's imagination and well-informed opinions allowed him to move beyond a clichéd vision of America and provide stimulating insights.

This marked a great improvement from Ferrero's dullish reporting of previous years. Fraccaroli's first article, which appeared on the paper's front page, is exemplary in this respect. He narrates the traditional arrival of his ship at Manhattan's piers with an initial adherence to the decade-old snobbishness common among educated Europeans: since the fog is hiding the city from his sight, he cannot share the excitement of the American man standing next to him on the ship's deck. Initially New York for Fraccaroli is simply an 'ignoto fragoroso' (a 'thunderous unknown'). Then the first skyscraper appears, and the journalist judgement moves from defining it as 'idiotic and offensive' to being increasingly attracted by the skyline:

---

[27] Fraccaroli's travel books are *Vita d'America* (Milan: Treves 1928), *New York ciclone di genti* (Milan: Treves, 1928), *Hollywood, paese d'avventura* (Milan: Treves, 1928); and *Donne d'America* (Milan: Omenoni, 1930). The novel is *Il paradiso delle fanciulle, ovvero* American Girls (Milan: Treves, 1931).

[28] I am using the expression coined by Deleuze and Guattari in their philosophical work *A Thousand Plateaus* (1987) and developed by travel literature theoretician Chloe Chard. In brief, the viewpoint of the sedentary traveller is deeply rooted in his or her home culture, framed through a comparison with the already known, the familiar. See Chloe Chard, *Pleasure and Guilt on the Grand Tour: Travel Writing and Imaginative Geography 1680–1830* (Manchester: Manchester University Press, 1999).

And then, gradually, they are no longer monsters, but giants. When isolated among normal houses, they seem unfinished belltowers, shapeless towers: when built in groups, next to each other, they gain majesty and magnificence, they are venerable and formidable, they resemble a mountain range of palaces, Dolomitic colossi. They make one think of a gigantic human race, of legendary people led by titanic heroes.[29]

What follows is a long praise of New York's vibrant spirit and gigantic potential. Only at the very end of the article does Fraccaroli counterbalance his enthusiasm with a brief, almost sinister remark:

America transpires wealth. And from that a new economic doctrine was born: to spend, to spend in order to preserve prosperity.
Wealth comes from production, production needs continuous consumption in order to renew itself continuously. [...] This great machine is made out of a gigantic system of mechanisms.
Now a creaking sound has been heard coming from this machine.

The abrupt end evidently suspends the attention of the reader, and indeed a week later Fraccaroli picked up where he had left off with a piece explicitly entitled 'S'è udito uno scricchiolìo' ('A creaking sound has been heard'). The article addressed the issue of overproduction in the US industry and the dangers of easy access to credit. Although Fraccaroli shows himself to be far from interested in the dry economic argument, his perception of an impending crisis of the American economy sounds almost prophetic, written just two years before the Wall Street Crash.[30]

The articles that followed are devoted mainly to meetings or specific portraits of senior politicians (including President Calvin Coolidge), industrialists, and bankers. In July 1927, Fraccaroli began a slow journey towards the west coast, which eventually brought him to Los Angeles. There he devoted five articles to Hollywood, which, once again, give the measure of his professionalism. Each article concentrates on a different aspect of the film industry: its appeal to the masses, its star system (two articles), its financial viability, and its studio set-up. Put together—as he did, and expanded upon, in his book *Hollywood, paese di avventura* (1928)—his journalistic work provides a vivid and informative account of the organization of American cinema.

If there is one blind spot in Fraccaroli's eleven-month correspondence from the USA, it is his lack of engagement with the Italian American community. It is mentioned rarely and then only in passing—for example, when discussing the success of Italian restaurants in New York, or when visiting a big farm in

---

[29] Arnaldo Fraccaroli, 'Prefazione all'America', *Corriere della Sera*, 27 January 1927, pp. 1–2.
[30] Arnaldo Fraccaroli, 'S'è udito uno scricchiolìo', *Corriere della Sera*, 5 February 1927, p. 3.

California. What makes this even more noticeable is the fact that in his fifty-five pieces he devoted whole articles to the African American community (twice), Native Americans, and the Chinese community. It is as if his patriotism did not include Italian Americans or his interest as a journalist. His last piece, on 3 November, confirms this. In his overall evaluation of his American experience, he discusses the American economy and its society based on dollars and smiles, rightly predicts the future dominance of American culture—from jazz to cinema—but fails to include so much as a single line on the millions of Italians living there. If he mentions anything Italian, it is always in connection with the mother country, as in his patriotic parting lines:

'To study with passion what happens in other countries is one of the best ways to feed our great love for our own country,' said Camillo Cavour.
He actually never said that. But I say it, and it is equally true.
The great Italian ship glides majestically on the water, its three-coloured flag flapping in the wind, multitudes of passengers on its rails and decks.
—*Good bye, America!*[31]

After his long stay in the USA, Fraccaroli moved on to other countries, starting with Greece the following month. He was to return briefly to the USA, eight years later.

After Fraccaroli, coverage of the USA by the *Corriere della Sera* fell mainly in the hands of Leone Fumasoni Biondi, an aristocrat and journalist already resident in New York, who wrote dozens of articles between 1928 and 1931. Unlike his predecessors, Fumasoni Biondi revealed a clear pro-Fascist stance, which took the form of explicit mention of the regime's policies and their echoes in America. This does not mean that before him the *Corriere della Sera* was entirely free of any pro-Fascist substance in its coverage of the USA. After Luigi Albertini's dismissal as director in November 1925, the 'Fascistization' of the newspaper had become visible in its reliance on Agenzia Stefani's short press releases, which were mainly aimed either at presenting the USA as a bizarre, violent country or at highlighting positive reactions to Italy's Fascism. Crime—obviously not Italian American generated—and disasters of various kind, human and natural, were a recurrent feature. Coupled with them were generic announcements both of the enthusiastic reception in America of visitors from Italy and of the positive resonance of events in Fascist Italy, with Mussolini and his speeches often at their centre. On top of these short propaganda-slanted articles, Fumasoni Biondi was the first correspondent (although he was never given this official title) who was explicit about his political views. Typical is his article of 18 April 1930, which appeared on the paper's front page, somewhat unimaginatively entitled 'Scambi culturali e turismo:

---

[31] Arnaldo Fraccaroli, 'Good bye, America!', *Corriere della Sera*, 3 November 1927, p. 3.

Italia e Stati Uniti' ('Cultural Exchanges and Tourism: Italy and the United States'). It begins with a recognition of the great role played by the USA in recent political events, and a positive judgement on the mechanization of the country's industry. After that, the article moves to a long explanation of how Italy can export its millenia-old culture to America, now reinvigorated by its glorious post-March-on-Rome present, and ends with a call for the improvement of Italy's tourism marketing so that Americans can be better informed about Italy's everlasting culture and beauty.[32] It is unfortunate that Fumasoni Biondi should have been covering US affairs for the *Corriere della Sera* at the time of the Wall Street crisis, since his coverage of it was rather superficial and, again, politically slanted.

Given the above, it will not be surprising to learn that Fumasoni Biondi coupled his activity as a *Corriere della Sera* journalist with the job of being the Agenzia Stefani's representative in the USA. This forces us to return briefly to the history of the Agenzia Stefani, whose pre-First World War vicissitudes were reconstructed in Chapter 1. The closeness between the Agenzia Stefani and Italian governments was turned into a synergy by Mussolini with the help of his close collaborator Manlio Morgagni. Today, Morgagni is vaguely remembered as the only Fascist high official who committed suicide at the news of Mussolini's deposition on 25 July 1943. He had been a devout sidekick of *Il Duce* since the latter's interventionist turn in 1914. Morgagni helped Mussolini run his daily *Il Popolo d'Italia*, and in 1924 he was rewarded with the financial control and presidency of the Agenzia Stefani. Morgagni remained at its helm for the entire 'Ventennio', until that fateful morning in July 1943. Throughout those two decades, he made sure that Stefani's news launches were instruments of Fascist propaganda.

Within this perspective, Fumasoni Biondi was a coherent choice, beyond his limitations as a journalist. Moreover, Morgagni showed interest in US affairs and visited New York twice, in 1926 and in 1932. His confidential reports to Mussolini allow a detailed view of his impressions, first the awe in front of the great wealth and economic power, coupled with a Fascist critique of the Americans' lack of restraint and discipline, and then the shock of the devastating impact of the Great Depression, again with the pro-Fascist morale of the superior way in which Mussolini's Italy was reacting to the crisis.[33]

After Fumasoni Biondi, the *Corriere della Sera* returned to a prestigious signature. The choice fell on Giuseppe Antonio Borgese, the renowned Sicilian academic and literary author. In July 1931, Borgese had sailed to New York, where he

---

[32] Leone Fumasoni Biondi, 'Scambi culturali e turismo: Italia e Stati Uniti', *Corriere della Sera*, 18 April 1930, p. 1.

[33] On Morgagni's visits to New York, see Stefano Luconi, 'La città della Grande Depressione: Manlio Morgagni a New York, 1932', *Storia urbana*, 109 (2005), 35–50. It is interesting to note how, in his study, Luconi comes to a similar conclusion (p. 47) to the one reached in these pages: Morgagni too, when visiting New York, did not seem interested in the life of the Italian community, which by then constituted about 15% of New York's population.

had started to send pieces to the *Corriere della Sera*, roughly two a month. His residence in the USA was motivated by the invitation to spend a semester at Berkeley as a visiting lecturer. Borgese, however, had never hidden his dislike of Mussolini's regime, although his anti-Fascism had not been militant. For example, in 1925, he had refused to sign Croce's Manifesto of Anti-Fascist Intellectuals, and had continued to contribute to the *Corriere della Sera*, even after Albertini's political dismissal. The watershed came in August 1931, when Mussolini's Minister of Education introduced the oath of allegiance to the regime, which all Italian academics were asked to swear. Borgese was one of the very few—18 out of 1,251—who refused to oblige.[34]

Once he decided to go into voluntary exile, Borgese continued to teach for other American institutions, eventually holding a professorship in Italian at Chicago University. Mussolini's tolerance of Borgese—from as early as when he was teaching in Milan, when Mussolini had intervened to discourage any action against him by local Fascists—must have extended to his collaboration with the *Corriere della Sera*. As with other non-Fascist intellectuals living and working in Fascist Italy, the silent agreement was that Borgese would make no critical reference to Italian politics in his published writings. Nonetheless, readers of the paper must have felt the great difference in tone and style between Borgese's insightful comments on American society and the pro-Fascist, dull coverage by Fumasoni Biondi.

Worth dwelling on are two articles Borgese wrote in July and October 1933. The first one was dedicated to the Italian community. As a fellow Sicilian, Borgese tells us, he was welcome in their associations, which grouped migrants from the same villages or areas. The article is mainly related to one of these experiences, in which he was asked to be Toastmaster at a society's banquet. Apart from the sense of fraternity, which is unusual in a piece by a visiting Italian journalist—Borgese writes about the pleasure of listening to an old woman using the same dialect that his mother spoke—he mentions his regret at the fact that no Italian author has ever written a novel about migrants. This takes us back to a consideration that has already been put forward in the discussion of pre-First World War literature on migration—namely, the almost total lack of literary representations of the massive exodus of Italians towards other parts of the world. Borgese was aware of it, and in his article—not by chance entitled 'Un tema di romanzo' ('A Theme for a Novel')—he calls for such a novel of migration to be written. He dwells on the need for that future author to have a deep understanding, among other things, of the mixture of languages that migrants end up using: from dialects, to Italian mixed with the foreign language, to their children's full command of English. Borgese's conclusion is that he too was not up to such a difficult task, but 'it would

---

[34] On the academics' oath of allegiance, see Helmut Goetz, *Il giuramento rifiutato: I docenti universitari e il regime fascista* (Florence: La Nuova Italia, 2000). On Borgese's political thought, see Luciano Parisi, *Borgese* (Turin: Tirrenia, 2000).

be worth attempting. It could be the work, national and at the same time universal, to which the ambition of contemporary Italian writers should aspire.'[35]

The second article, entitled 'In cerca del mare' ('Looking for the Sea'), is a long, at times lyrical description of the north-eastern coast, which is typical example of Borgese's literary flair. At the same time, the description of places alternates with descriptions of people, and eventually the author reveals his intention: to show that Americans are a far more varied and interesting community than European clichés tend to allow. Then, humorously, he gives up:

> Even if, to write about these and other similar things, I were to consume ten typewriters' ribbons, I would not dislodge from one single brain the idea, so comfortable because so simple, that America is nothing other than unsophisticated luxury, dollar-grabbing and crude pleasure.[36]

Together with Fraccaroli's reports, Borgese's articles mark the highest point of the *Corriere della Sera*'s coverage of America during the interwar years.

After him, a few articles were published by Luigi Barzini Jr, son of the famous, old-guard journalist Luigi Barzini. Like his father, Luigi Barzini Jr cut for himself an equally prestigious figure as a journalist. He had spent a few years in America, since his father, after the increasing difficulties in his relationship with Albertini at the *Corriere della Sera*—Barzini Sr was a nationalist and pro-Fascist—had moved to New York in 1922 in order to found a new daily. This was the *Corriere d'America*, financed by a rich Italian American relative of the Crespi family, which controlled the *Corriere della Sera*. However, after the attempt to build a solid collaboration with its Italian opposite number had failed, Barzini's daily encountered financial difficulties, and in 1931 it was bought by Italian American millionaire Generoso Pope. Pope already controlled the historical Italian daily in New York, *Il Progresso Italo-Americano*, and he turned the *Corriere d'America* into one more instrument of his political campaigning, which included open support for Franklin D. Roosevelt at the 1932 presidential elections.[37] As a consequence of his father's American experience, Luigi Barzini Jr lived in New York as a teenager and studied journalism at Columbia University. He had started to contribute to American papers when his father's decision to return to Italy forced him to look for a career as a journalist there. His debut was the already mentioned book collecting his impressions of New York, published in Milan in 1931 with a preface by

---

[35] Giuseppe Antonio Borgese, 'Un tema di romanzo', *Corriere della Sera*, 23 July 1933, p. 3.
[36] Giuseppe Antonio Borgese, 'In cerca del mare', *Corriere della Sera*, 24 October 1933, p. 3.
[37] When still in good relations with Albertini, in 1920, Barzini had tried to convince him to be directly involved in the ownership of *Corriere d'America*. After Albertini's withdrawal, Barzini encountered huge personal debts in order to get the newspaper going, which were to haunt him for the rest of his life. On this, see Simona Colarizi, *Luigi Barzini: Una storia italiana* (Venice: Marsilio, 2017), 75–88.

his father. His enthusiasm for the city went hand in hand with a vigorous pro-Fascist nationalism, so that the final chapter, devoted to the Italian American community, started with mention of Mussolini's March on Rome as the key historical event that, according to him, changed the self-perception of Italians in America and ended with the prediction that Italians' innate genius and love of beauty would eventually turn them into the dominant race in the USA.[38]

Barzini Jr then started to work for the *Corriere della Sera*, like his father, as an 'inviato speciale' in various parts of the world. It was in such a role that he found himself in the USA between February and June 1934. His aim was to present a portrait of America slowly emerging from the Great Depression. By then, Barzini Jr's philo-Fascism had toned down, and his articles, despite his harsh critique of America, rarely opened up to a comparison with Mussolini's Italy. In his article of 15 February 1934, in which he discussed the instability of the USA, not just economically but also socially, he suggested that democracies tend to produce confusion and oversimplification, but it is a comment that remains marginal, indirect. Equally, when discussing Roosevelt's policies, Barzini does not attempt a comparison with Mussolini's policies, which, as we will see, was a recurrent feature in Fascist publications at the time.[39]

In the second half of the 1930s, the USA was covered for the *Corriere della Sera* by a number of different journalists. Emilio Cecchi was the most prestigious one of these, but the one recurring figure was Pietro Carbonelli. After writing from various parts of Europe, in May 1935 Carbonelli had taken up residence in the USA, and from there wrote the odd article until the very end of the regime. With him the *Corriere della Sera* returned to an uninspiring and clearly pro-Fascist coverage similar to that of Fumasoni Biondi. His second article, of 5 June 1935, published on the front page, set the tone: it was a defence of Italy's invasion of Ethiopia based on a parallel with the failure of US governments to improve the lot of its black community. The racist tone was hardly implicit:

> Eighty years of free cohabitation with a great, civilized people such as the American people has failed to modify the semi-barbarous and primitive psychology of the twelve million Negroes living in the United States. [...] How can one then expect that a few years of belonging to the Geneva-based League could have transformed Abyssinia, feudally closed to any breath of human progress, into a modern country that deserves a place on an equal footing with other great civilized nations?[40]

---

[38] Barzini Jr, *Nuova York*, 249–72.
[39] The following articles by Barzini are exemplary of the 1934–6 period, and all are published on the third page of *Corriere della Sera*: 'La sbalorditiva confusione americana', 15 February 1934; 'Questa è l'America', 1 June 1934; and 'Un nuovo ciclo sociale negli Stati Uniti', 10 November 1936.
[40] Pietro Carbonelli, 'L'America e la questione abissina', *Corriere della Sera*, 5 June 1935, p. 1.

Following this line, segregation in the USA was presented by Carbonelli as a commensurate reaction to the ever-impending barbarity of the black community, as was lynching (forgetting the fact that Italian migrants too had been victims of this crime). This stance takes us back to the radical racism shown by several travel authors in the late nineteenth century. Carbonelli is much closer to their viewpoint than to those expressed by his contemporaries—such as Amerigo Ruggiero, his opposite number at *La Stampa*, or Mario Praz or Emilio Cecchi—who similarly associate black culture with primitivism but also strongly condemn segregation and lynching.[41]

If the *Corriere della Sera* experimented with the juxtaposition of different voices, some more independent minded and others closer to the regime's propagandist expectations, its Turinese rival, *La Stampa*, relied on the single voice of its resident correspondent, Amerigo Ruggiero. A socialist militant in his youth, Ruggiero had moved to the USA in 1907 to join his brother, who had settled as a pharmacist there. After his first experiences as a journalist, in particular for New York's *Il Progresso Italo-Americano*, Ruggiero had volunteered in the Italian army during the First World War, after which he had returned to New York in 1922 and continued to work as a journalist, eventually becoming *La Stampa*'s resident correspondent in April 1929.

Beynet singles Ruggiero out as the Italian correspondent who more than any other went against the tendency to ignore the Italian American community. Indeed, Ruggiero dedicated a series of articles to Italian migration to America, producing facts and figures about their presence and addressing the social issues—from destitution to anti-Italian racism—that still plagued those communities. According to Beynet, it is no coincidence that Ruggiero was of southern extraction. He came from Basilicata, the southern region that, with Campania and Sicily, produced the highest numbers of migrants to the USA in the early twentieth century. Indeed, Ruggiero and Borgese, a Sicilian, are an exception among Italian correspondents in the USA, who tended to come from either northern or central Italy. A sense of empathy certainly played a role, plus, in Ruggiero's case, his past socialist militancy can be detected in his investigation into the state of the Little Italys in the big industrial towns of the north-east, as he made no effort to avoid critical remarks against the Liberal governments that failed to tackle the *Questione meridionale* ('the Southern question'). As Beynet suggests, blaming pre-Fascist governments for the state of the Italian American community was a safe way to avoid the potential political fallout of Ruggiero's

---

[41] See, e.g., the following articles: Mario Praz, 'America nera', *La Stampa*, 6 June 1930, p. 3; Amerigo Ruggiero, 'Ondata di linciaggi', *La Stampa*, 2 January 1934, p. 1; Emilio Cecchi, 'L'agape nera', *Corriere della Sera*, 23 August 1938, p. 3; and 'Gente nera che vuol essere bianca', *Corriere della Sera*, 1 September 1938, p. 3. Sadly, not far from Carbonelli's racism was that of the earlier correspondent of *Corriere della Sera*, Felice Ferrero: see, e.g., his 'L'impero dei negri', 21 October 1920, p. 3; and 'Bianchi e neri', 9 September 1924, p. 3. Beynet devotes an entire chapter on the representation of the black community, in his *L'Image de l'Amérique*, i. 392–431.

articles. Nonetheless, they stand out in the overall coverage of the USA during the interwar years, clearly informing *La Stampa*'s readers about the struggles of millions of Italian migrants. Moreover, given that by the time he became resident correspondent, Ruggiero had been living in the USA for twenty-two years, his status could well be considered as that of an Italian American journalist.

In his preface to the collection of his journalistic writings on the USA, Emilio Cecchi apologized for ignoring the Italian American community and excused himself by saying that how Ruggiero had tackled the topic was insuperable. Ruggiero too collected his correspondence in two volumes: *L'America al bivio* (1934), and *Gli italiani d'America* (1937). Other facets of Ruggiero's journalistic work will be touched upon later in this chapter.[42]

As for illustrated magazines, among the three popular ones we selected for our analysis in the first part of the book, Treves's *L'Illustrazione popolare* had closed down by 1916. This time, *L'Illustrazione italiana* and *La Domenica del Corriere* will be discussed together with a new illustrated magazine that appeared in 1923 as a monthly complement to Mussolini's *Il Popolo d'Italia*. This is *La Rivista illustrata del Popolo d'Italia*, co-directed by Mussolini's brother Arnaldo and Manlio Morgagni, who, as we saw, led the Agenzia Stefani. After the death of Arnaldo, in 1931, Morgagni took over the directorship of the *Rivista illustrata* until June 1943. Again, I have privileged two specific years in order to get a sense of any developments through the years: 1930 and 1939.[43]

In 1930, what characterizes both weekly magazines, in comparison with their pre-First World War editions, is a similar strong interest in the USA, coupled this time with a drop in the coverage of news from France. *La Domenica del Corriere*, for example, continued to show its obsession with its coverage of American *faits divers*, with an article being devoted to it in almost every single issue. 'Americanate' might have stopped being a headline of those articles, but the content and tone continued in the same vein.[44] The articles would often be rather short, dominated by an illustration that gave ample space for a condescending gaze. The images in Fig. 6.7 are typical: a Hollywood actress, Alice White, sporting the latest 'americanata' in fashion, a hat in the shape of an aeroplane; and an article criticizing two extremes of prison systems, a Romanian hard-labour camp and an American prison where life-sentenced inmates are invited to join a jazz orchestra.[45] As for France, the drop in its coverage seems to be caused by a drop of interest in French politics.

---

[42] On Ruggiero's articles on Italian migration, see Beynet, *L'Image de l'Amérique*, i. 24–6, 236–46. The cover image *America al bivio* was created by Carlo Levi, who, during his political confinement in Basilicata, in 1935–6, had befriended Ruggiero's parents.

[43] Once again, I am grateful to both Alice Gussoni for her detailed analysis of the three magazines, and Oxford's Faculty of Medieval and Modern Languages for providing the funds to facilitate this.

[44] In the meantime, 'Americanate' had also become the title of a musical variety show that toured Italy in 1931. Reference to this is in Camilla Poesio, *Tutto è ritmo, tutto è swing: Il Jazz, il fascismo e la società italiana* (Florence: Le Monnier Università, 2018), 25.

[45] Anon., 'L'aereocappellino' and anon., 'Prigioni antiche e prigioni moderne', *La Domenica del Corriere*, 32/6 (9 February 1930), 12, and 32/11 (16 March 1930), 7.

Fig. 6.7. Detail from two articles published in *La Domenica del Corriere*, February and March 1930. (courtesy of BSMC, Rome)

Indeed, in the interwar years, France too begins to be worthy of attention, mainly when something bizarre happens, or a disaster, or when something 'Italian' is taking place there, such as Italian sportsmen triumphing on French soil.

More surprisingly, when it comes to the *Rivista illustrata del Popolo d'Italia*, the dominant characteristic is that, not only does the journal devote far more photographic space to the USA than to France, but America recurrently appears as a model of modernity. Full-page illustrations of major buildings and public constructions abound, in every issue. Fig. 6.8 shows examples from

AMERICA AS A MIRROR OF MODERNITY    203

Fig. 6.8. Three photos dedicated to America's economic and architectural might in *La Rivista illustrata del Popolo d'Italia*, 15/10 (October 1930): an oilfield, a skyscraper, and a futuristic restaurant. (courtesy of BSMC, Rome)

October 1930—the three juxtaposed images all presenting American achievements related to the sphere of economics: the almost overnight creation of a large oil-extraction plant in California, the latest skyscraper in Manhattan (the Empire State Building), and a futuristic restaurant planned for Chicago's 1933 World's Fair. This is rather surprising given the heavy nationalistic tone that, as expected, dominates the pages of the *Rivista illustrata*.

The recurrence of this motif makes it clear that Morgagni—who, as we saw, had twice visited the USA—must have been rather philo-American in those years. And, knowing Mussolini's great attention to the press, in particular to the one he owned, he must have been implicitly in agreement with such practice. In the year of the invasion of Ethiopia, this was still the case. Interestingly, in the January 1935 issue of the *Rivista illustrata*, which contained two full-page photographs of impressive New York buildings, the editors could even suggest an implicit parallel with Fascism. This is the case of a replica of one of the most famous icons of the regime, the bundle of fasces. It is naturally an iconography that comes directly from ancient Rome—and in America was prominently present in Washington's Lincoln Memorial (1914–22)—but by the mid-1930s it was difficult not to think of it as somehow synonymous with Fascist Italy too. One can therefore imagine the pleasure with which the editors pointed to the presence of a new set of traffic lights in New York's 5th Avenue, which, as the photo shows in detail, sported the fasces as symbols of law and order, next to the world's then highest building.[46]

After the Ethiopian invasion, the nationalistic craze combined with the opposition of Western democracies, Roosevelt's USA *in primis*, meant that international news almost totally disappeared from the pages of the *Rivista illustrata* unless it served some nationalistic purpose of showing Italy's prestige abroad or reported some disaster, political or natural. At the same time, a rapprochement of Nazi Germany began to show. We will return to this in Chapter 10, when examining the aftermath of the anti-American turn of 1938.

Overall, it seems that during the 1920s and early–mid-1930s the journalistic debate on America was fairly open, with strong independent voices—Ruggiero, Borgese, Fraccaroli—balancing out the predictable pro-Fascist views of others. The visual space devoted to America by illustrated magazines—the *Rivista illustrata del Popolo d'Italia* included—confirmed the fascination that the country's modern and dynamic society held for Italian readers.

---

[46] The caption oddly calls the photo 'Emblemi d'America', which makes one wonder whether the reference is ironic, somehow pointing to the connections between Mussolini's economic policies and Roosevelt's New Deal, as recurrently raised by Fascist commentators in those years. One might also wonder whether such decorative style was an intentional ingratiation of New York's new Italian American mayor, Fiorello La Guardia, who had taken office a year before, in January 1934. On this last point, however, we know that this model of a two-light traffic light—called a Mercury signal because of the statuette of Mercury standing on top of the box—was introduced in New York's 5th Avenue earlier on, in 1931. It remained there until the early 1960s. On New York's historic traffic lights, see Christopher Gray, 'Mystery of 104 Bronze Statues of Mercury', *New York Times*, 2 February 1997, p. 5.

Fig. 6.9. A set of traffic lights featuring fasces decoration, next to New York's Empire State Building; photo published in *La Rivista illustrata del Popolo d'Italia*, 13/1 (January 1935). (courtesy of BSMC, Rome)

## 6.3 Mussolini, Fascism, and America

When considering Mussolini's perception of America, and that of some of the influential figures among his close associates, it is useful to make a distinction between, on the one hand, the more strictly political and economic dimension and, on the other, the more varied cultural one. The first, as we will see, developed closely in relation to both Mussolini's foreign policy and his opinion—realistic or otherwise—of Italy's position on the international stage. The cultural dimension is related more to the alternation of the opposing stereotypical views of America that preceded and coexisted with the regime. Mussolini's own views on American culture hardly remained unequivocal.

To a young Fascist in 1922—and Mussolini, at 38 years old, was relatively young then, indeed the youngest prime minister since Italy's unification—the United States of America had much to offer as an exemplary nation state. It was a country born out of a revolution, whose strong-handed leaders and immense natural resources had turned into a powerful, autarkic society, increasingly wealthy thanks to its mastery of mass production in both industry and agriculture. Moreover, the cult of youth and modernity, which, through Futurism, had become a dominant component of Fascist ideology, had an equally strong role in American society. The USA was a young, ambitious country, and so was Fascist Italy. Granted, it was a democracy, but even in this respect it was understood as different from the 'old democracies' of Britain and France. Its presidential governance was often presented as a halfway position between parliamentary democracies and the right-wing dictatorship of which Mussolini's Fascism was the rightful model. This perception was strengthened by the fact that during the early decades of the twentieth century the USA had been developing an increasingly complex interplay between state policy and private enterprise. This was the consequence, first, of Wilson's vision of America's self-defined global mission in the 1910s and 1920s, and, secondly, of Franklin D. Roosevelt's policies addressing the deep economic crisis in the early 1930s. The latter somehow created a synergy of sort with Fascism's own attempts to create a third way between capitalism and communism, based on a strict collaboration between state and private interests. It should also be noted that the crisis of American capitalism in 1929 did not destroy America's reputation as a leading economic power. As Mary Nolan suggests, 'for all its problems, America remained a model of economic modernity among regimes highly critical of its political system and cultural values'.[47]

Before his career as prime minister had even started, Mussolini showed a particular interest in ensuring that the US administration approved of his actions. A few days before the March on Rome, Mussolini paid a visit to the American embassy and in a meeting with Ambassador Richard Washburn Child disclosed his plan of action, to which he received a tacit endorsement. Child was an unusual type of diplomat. A former lawyer and fiction writer, he had worked as a journalist and political advocate during the war years, as one of the several writers employed in the US propaganda effort by the Committee on Public Information

---

[47] Nolan, *The Transatlantic Century*, 131.

(CPI). Under Wilson, Child had defended the president's strong leadership, and, as ambassador in Rome, he quickly identified Mussolini as the rising politician who could bring Italy back to social and economic stability, a necessary requirement for US investment. Child, as ambassador until February 1924, and as a journalist for the *Saturday Evening Post* in the following years, played a determining role in securing Mussolini's acceptance by the American media, and consequently by the American people.

If Child praised Mussolini as a strong leader, before the disaffection following the Versailles treaty Mussolini had praised Wilson as a strong leader internationally. On 10 October 1918, he dedicated the whole width of the front page of *Popolo d'Italia* to him. The expression used to define Wilson could come as little surprise, as Mussolini called him 'Duce supremo' ('Supreme leader').[48]

On the economic front, there was also one further reason why Mussolini's goodwill towards the USA increased: Italy's war debts. At the end of the First World War, Italy owed the US treasury 1.6 billion dollars. Finding a solution to the huge debts towards the USA accumulated by the winning countries (Britain's and France's debts were even greater), coupled with the equally thorny tasks of stabilizing European currencies and agreeing on the level of reparations to impose on Germany, gave the USA a commanding role that had to be respected. Indeed, in relation to the latter, the subsequent settlements that were agreed

Fig. 6.10. Detail of the front page of *Il Popolo d'Italia*, 10 October 1918. (courtesy of BSMC, Rome)

---

[48] On Mussolini's early contacts with members of the US administration, see Giorgio Bertellini, *The Divo and the Duce: Promoting Film Stardom and Political Leadership in 1920s America* (Oakland CA: University of California Press, 2019), 165–97. It should be added that the term *Duce* was already in use during the nineteenth century, with reference to *Risorgimento* heroes such as Giuseppe Garibaldi.

upon came with the name of the US diplomats who had hammered them out, starting with the Dawes Plan of 1924 and followed by the Young Plan of 1929.[49]

Mussolini was determined to make use of American capital in order to finance his plans both for strengthening the Italian lira and for delivering large-scale economic campaigns. As he wrote to King Victor Emanuel III only a few months after his seizure of power, on 29 June 1923:

> Given the economic and financial situation which Italy finds herself in today, there is no doubt that the return of migratory flow into the United States and cooperation with American capital represent two elements of vital importance for us.[50]

Mussolini's hopes regarding migration were to be frustrated by the anti-immigration policies of those years. The financial aspect, however, was successfully addressed. During the years 1923–8 Mussolini's economics minister, Count Giuseppe Volpi di Misurata, managed to obtain extensive loans from American banks (led by J. P. Morgan) with peaks of $111 million in 1926 and $120 million in 1928. It took the Wall Street Crash to stop the flux of money. In parallel with government action, Italy's leading car and tyre manufacturers, FIAT and Pirelli, benefited too, with loans of respectively $10 million and $4 million. All this was facilitated by the fact that the American government, led by Republican President Warren G. Harding, and after his death in August 1923 by his deputy Calvin Coolidge, had welcomed Mussolini's leadership as an eventual solution to Italy's social instability. The same could be said of the vast majority of the American press, including the *New York Times Magazine*, the *Saturday Evening Post*, and *Time Magazine*.[51]

In the early 1930s, Roosevelt's New Deal policies created much debate in Italy about the level to which US politics seemed to be taking economic lessons from Mussolini's Italy. President Roosevelt's book outlining his views on American social and economic challenges, *Looking Forward*, was quickly translated into Italian and published by Bompiani. Not only did Mussolini write a short preface to the book; he also reviewed it positively for the *Popolo d'Italia* on 7 July 1933, using the occasion to paint an image of Roosevelt as a sort of 'Mussolinian US President', rising to the challenge of fighting off decrepit democratic institutions

---

[49] On the economic relations between Fascist Italy and the USA, see Gian Giacomo Migone, *Gli Stati Uniti e il Fascismo: Alle origini dell'egemonia americana* (Milan: Feltrinelli, 1980); the war debts figures are on p. 20; English trans. *The United States and Fascist Italy: The Rise of American Finance in Europe* (Cambridge: Cambridge University Press, 2015), 2.

[50] Migone, *Gli Stati Uniti e il Fascismo*, 96 (English edn, 83). Migone does not specify the exact date of this letter, which is not included in Mussolini's *Opera omnia*. It can be found in Ruggero Moscati (ed.), *I documenti diplomatici italiani*, 7th ser., ii (27 April 1923–22 February 1924) (Rome: Istituto Poligrafico dello Stato, 1955), 68–9, n. 102.

[51] Migone, *Gli Stati Uniti e il Fascismo*, 59–74, 151–60, 179–99.

such as the Senate in order to centre legislative and executive power in his hands. In his conversations with Emil Ludwig, Mussolini already had no doubts about presenting Roosevelt as the closest a democracy could come to giving dictatorial powers to an elected leader. Beyond this, it is indicative of Mussolini's frame of mind at the time that within a period of a few months he welcomed Roosevelt's electoral victory while initially showing little enthusiasm for Hitler's chancellorship[52]

By then, however, it was clear that Mussolini's foreign policy was developing a more assertive stance, which distanced him from Roosevelt. The replacement of Dino Grandi as foreign minister in 1932 (Mussolini was to chair this ministry himself for the following four years) was the first signal that *Il Duce* was developing a new foreign policy, less supine to the American interests. Mussolini criticized Grandi for his pacifist outlook, which was too subservient to US, British, and French demands.[53]

The development of the relationship between Fascist Italy and the USA was to grow inversely, but in similar stages, with Mussolini's progressive commitment to Nazi Germany as a political and military ally. The first step came with the invasion of Ethiopia in the autumn of 1935. Until then Roosevelt had been determined to maintain cordial relations with Fascist Italy. He was hoping, like many at the time, that Mussolini could prove to be the necessary restraining force to Hitler's ambitions, and hence a vital element in maintaining peace in Europe. Another reason was related to home politics, since the Italian American community, which formed a significant part of his electorate, was mostly pro-Fascist. But Italy's defiance of the League of Nations and its eventual expulsion brought Roosevelt's tolerance to its limit. However mildly executed, the economic sanctions against Italy created a gulf that Hitler was quick to fill. The failure of Britain's and France's policy of offering concessions to Mussolini convinced the latter that

---

[52] Benito Mussolini, 'Roosevelt e il sistema', *Il Popolo d'Italia*, 7 July 1933, p. 1. Emil Ludwig, *Colloqui con Mussolini* (1932; Milan: Mondadori, 2000), 120. On Mussolini and Roosevelt, see Maurizio Vaudagna, '"Drammatizzare l'America!": I simboli politici del New Deal', in Vaudagna (ed.), *L'estetica della politica* (Rome: Laterza, 1989), 77–102; and 'Mussolini and Franklin D. Roosevelt', in Cornelis A. van Minnen and John S. Fears (eds.), *FDR and his Contemporaries: Foreign Perceptions of an American President* (London: Macmillan, 1992), 157–70. For a recent comparison of Roosevelt's New Deal and Mussolini's policies, see Wolfgang Schivelbusch, *Three New Deals: Reflections on Roosevelt's America, Mussolini's Italy and Hitler's Germany, 1933–1939* (New York: Picador, 2006); and Nolan, *The Translatlantic Century*, 117–31, 140–1. Incidentally, one should mention one further parallel between Roosevelt and Mussolini: both escaped assassination attempts by Italian anarchists who had migrated after the First World War. Michele Schirru and Angelo Sbardellotto travelled back to Italy respectively from the USA and from Belgium with the sole intention of murdering Mussolini. The Fascist Tribunale Speciale sentenced them to death, despite the fact that both had been arrested before they tried to execute their plans. The murder of F. D. Roosevelt was attempted by Calabrese migrant Giuseppe Zangara on 15 February 1933, while the recently elected president was giving an impromptu speech from an open car, in Miami. Roosevelt was untouched, but one of the five bullets shot by Zangara hit Chicago's mayor, Anton Cermak, who later died in hospital. For this, Zangara was sentenced to death and executed by electric chair on 20 March 1933. On Michele Schirru, see the fascinating portrait by Antonio Scurati in the second volume of his fictional trilogy on Fascist Italy: *M. L'uomo della provvidenza* (Milan: Bompiani, 2020), 569–74.

[53] Migone, *Gli Stati Uniti e il Fascismo*, 289–90.

he could now play a more aggressive role in international politics, and that an alliance with Hitler's Germany was the natural way forward.

The USA became less and less of a point of comparison, because Mussolini was now facing an exemplary totalitarian system in Hitler's Germany. The swift centralization and regimentation of German society operated by Hitler was to turn Mussolini from a somewhat condescending father–dictator to an understated but keen follower of Hitler's policies. This was already evident in 1934 when Mussolini asked his son-in-law to turn his Press Office of the Head of State into a culture ministry. The plans of Joseph Goebbels's Reich Ministry of Public Enlightenment and Propaganda were used as a model for the creation of the Fascist Undersecretariat of Press and Propaganda, which was eventually named Ministry of Popular Culture in 1937.[54]

If the presidency of F. D. Roosevelt had coincided with a new phase in the regime's attitude towards the USA, this does not mean that the cohabitation of different views had ended. It is indicative that, on the cusp of the comparison between the policies of Roosevelt and those of Mussolini, the latter should have felt the need to discourage such parallels. On 28 July 1933, Mussolini's Press Office sent a memo to all chief editors of Italian newspapers—one of the infamous *veline* notes through which the regime steered the press—ordering that parallels between Italian Fascism and Roosevelt's economic policies should be avoided in order not to give ammunition to Roosevelt's political enemies in the USA. It was somewhat contradictory for Mussolini to suggest that comparing Roosevelt to him would give the American president a bad name. Perhaps Mussolini was annoyed by the servilism with which his own comments on *Looking Forward* had been followed; perhaps he had decided to follow the advice of his American ambassador, who had noted the negative repercussions in America of the Italian debate; or perhaps he had decided that the time had come to emphasize the differences rather than the similarities between Fascism and the USA. The arrival of a new, highly ambitious totalitarian country in the shape of Nazi Germany was certainly a factor: it exposed the divergences between democratic nations and right-wing dictatorships. The honeymoon period between Mussolini's Fascism and America was coming to an end.[55]

---

[54] I dwell on the creation of Mussolini's culture ministry in Bonsaver, *Censorship and Literature in Fascist Italy*, 95–128.

[55] Maurizio Vaudagna discusses the reports by the Italian Embassy in Washington, emphasizing the repercussions of the Italian debate in the USA, with accusations of philo-Fascism being raised against Roosevelt, in his essay 'New Deal e corporativismo nelle riviste politiche ed economiche italiane', in Giorgio Spini, Gian Giacomo Migone, and Maurizio Teodori (eds), *Italia e America dalla Grande Guerra a oggi* (Venice: Marsilio, 1976), 101–40. For the full text of the *velina* of 28 July 1933, see Nicola Tranfaglia, *La stampa del regime: 1932-1943 Le veline del Minculpop per orientare l'informazione* (Milan: Bompiani, 1995), 232. On the potential parallels between Fascism and the USA as seen by American nationalists, see the recent work by Sarah Churchwell, *Behold, America: The Entangled History of America First and the American Dream* (London: Bloomsbury, 2018).

The Spanish Civil War, which closely followed Italy's invasion of Ethiopia, strengthened the German–Italian axis even further. Dashing the hopes of revolutionary fascists such as Elio Vittorini, Mussolini followed Hitler in welcoming General Franco's attempted *coup d'état* and in providing military help to the nationalist cause, which in the case of Italy included the engagement of about 50,000 troops. The final line was drawn by Roosevelt in his renowned 'Quarantine speech' of 5 October 1937: in his stark warning of an impending descent into world war, he did not mention individual states, but his accusation of the 'epidemic of world lawlessness' spread by 10 percent of the world population was clearly directed against Germany, Italy, and Japan. Italy's anti-Semitic legislation, the following year, brought the matter of constructive Italian–US relations to a close.

If we move on to the cultural dimension of Mussolini's view of America, historian Emilio Gentile's definition of Fascism as 'political modernism' provides a stimulating base. The notion of modernism points towards the connection between Fascism as a political movement, its self-perception as a revolutionary force, and the avant-garde movements that, at the start of the century, were questioning traditional canons and conventions in different cultural fields. The early consonance with Italian Futurism is a clear telltale sign of this. Moreover, Mussolini was no novice to the Italian intellectual and literary debate. As we saw, in his youth as a revolutionary socialist, Mussolini had been corresponding with Papini and Prezzolini and contributing to their influential journal *La Voce* (1908–16), a major catalyst in the wave of radical nationalism that swept through Italy in the pre-First World War years.[56]

Papini's peculiar interest in American pragmatism was an important factor, which, mixed with Bergson's notion of intuition and Nietzsche's *Übermensch*, brought Mussolini towards abandoning orthodox socialism and justifying a nationalistic and autocratic turn around which Fascism began to take shape. By the 1920s, Papini had moved away from American pragmatism, but this does not mean that it was not an influential part of Mussolini's youthful readings, as Margherita Sarfatti suggested in her biography of 1925. A year later, Mussolini returned to James's pragmatism in an interview with the British *Sunday Times*. The interviewer, Andrés Révész, then foreign editor of the Spanish daily *ABC*, produced a blunt question: 'Which of three influences was the most decisive in its effect upon the forming of your Excellency's character: that of Nietzsche, that of James, or that of Sorel?' Mussolini's reply deserves a full quotation:

> That of Sorel. Nietzsche enchanted me when I was twenty, and reinforced the anti-democratic elements in my nature. The pragmatism of William James was of greatest use to me in my political career. James taught me that an action

---

[56] Gentile, 'Impending Modernity', 1–9. On Mussolini and Florentine intellectuals, see Adamson, *Avant-Garde Florence*, 257–62.

should be judged rather by its results than by its doctrinary basis. I learnt of James that faith in action, that ardent will to live and fight, to which Fascism owes a great part of its success. That which Fascism has accomplished within the last six years has already made an indelible mark on history. Others will be able to deduce from the result attained the principal lines of the Fascist theories. For me the essential was to act. But I repeat, it is to Georges Sorel that I owe the greatest debt. It was that master of Syndicalism who by his rugged theories on revolutionary tactics contributed most decisively to the forming of the discipline, the energy and the power of the Fascist cohorts.[57]

Sorel too, after all, had shown enthusiastic interest in James's thought as a way to justify direct action in lieu of democratic debate. Indeed, it seems that Mussolini followed in the wake of Sorel and Papini, both of whom were particularly struck by James's essay *The Will to Believe* (1896), interpreting it as an invitation to seek action justified by self-belief. It was essentially a political, anti-democratic reading of James's essay. As philosophy historian Alexander Livingston suggests: 'Pragmatism promised spiritual powers of self-transcendence to both the individual and the nation through the pursuit of militant self-assertion.'[58]

As a fervent reader of Friedrich Nietzsche, Mussolini had welcomed the need for an *Übermensch* capable of elevating European culture to—as Sarfatti would write—'new sources of pleasure, of beauty, of ideal'. The young Mussolini had literary ambitions too. These took the shape of an anti-clerical novel, *Claudia Particella, l'amante del Cardinale* (*Claudia Particella, the Cardinal's Lover*), which was published first in instalments and then as a volume in 1910. Sarfatti described it as 'a highly-coloured romance à la [Émile] Gaboriau, with a basis reminiscent of Dumas père'. He was certainly an unorthodox Socialist.[59]

By the time of his seizure of power in 1922, Mussolini's intellectual interests had to be sidelined by politics' impelling demands on his time. Even the nonetheless political question of the cultural policies of his nascent regime remained marginal in his mind well into the late 1920s. The social and economic stabilization of the country, the defeat of any form of opposition, and the imposition of Fascism as the only political credo remained at the top of his political agenda. The cultural dimension was left to his Education Minister, Giovanni Gentile, and, more discreetly, to his close collaborator and then lover, Margherita Sarfatti. The latter was a highly educated Jewish woman whose sophisticated knowledge

---

[57] Andrés Révész, 'Special Interview with Mussolini: "Why I Broke with Socialism"', *Sunday Times*, 11 April 1926, pp. 15–16.

[58] Livingston, *Damn Great Empires!*, 38. I should also note an essay by American political scientist William Kilborne Steward, who as early as 1928 had already formed a well-focused understanding of the Sorelian and Papinian roots of Mussolini's interest in American Pragmatism: 'The Mentors of Mussolini', *American Political Science Review*, 22/4 (November 1928), 843–69.

[59] Margherita Sarfatti, *The Life of Benito Mussolini* (London: Butterworth, 1925), 156.

of contemporary art and literature was put at the service of Mussolini, sometimes taking the shape of the first draft of speeches and articles he adopted as his. She almost certainly played a part in the drafting of one of the first speeches by Mussolini devoted to the relationship between Fascism and the arts. It was delivered on 14 February 1926, at the inauguration of an exhibition by Italian artists under the keen patronage of Sarfatti, the *Novecentisti*. Borrowing the Gentilian notion of 'ethical state', Mussolini spelled out his vision of a society enriched by an organic relation between politics and art under the nationalistic aegis of Fascism.[60]

When it comes to the USA, it is a symbolic coincidence that Mussolini's first public statements should have come through the most modern forms of communication and art: radio and cinema. The former concerns a radio speech broadcast in December 1926 in which Mussolini praised the USA as a country that had found a virtuous balance between technological progress and 'the spiritual activity of the world', a fully positive view that he was to move away from in later years.[61] More revealing still is the second episode involving the medium of cinema.

During the race between Warner Bros and Fox for the launch of the first ever talking movie in 1927, the latter produced two talking Movietone newsreels that accompanied the screening of Murnau's *Sunrise* at New York's Times Square on 23 September 1927. They had both been recorded in Rome by Movietone's crew. The first was a musical piece featuring the Vatican's choir. The second featured Benito Mussolini delivering a brief message of friendship to the American people. He was the first political leader ever to appear in an American sound newsreel. This episode is important in more than one respect.

First, it shows Mussolini's readiness to embrace the latest technology and risk his reputation in appearing in an early experiment of talking movies and in breaking ground in terms of political communication.[62] Secondly, the production of the Movietone newsreel shows the degree of friendly relations between the regime and the American film industry. This had already started in the summer of 1923 with Samuel Goldwyn's production of *The Eternal City* (1924), a film adaptation of Hall Caine's eponymous novel (1901) and subsequent play. The setting had been transposed to contemporary times, shot in Rome, the protagonist

---

[60] On the relationship between Margherita Sarfatti and Mussolini, see Philip Cannistraro and Brian R. Sullivan, *Il Duce's Other Woman* (New York: Morrow, 1993); and Simona Urso, *Margherita Sarfatti: Dal mito del Dux al mito americano* (Venice: Marsilio, 2003).

[61] The radio address by Mussolini to the American people was broadcast on 14 December 1926; see its text in Mussolini, *Opera omnia*, xxii. 290.

[62] At the same time, Mussolini was more cautious about playing a direct part in filmmaking. Between 1923 and 1924, twice he refused offers by Unione Cinematografica Italiana (a consortium of eleven Italian production companies created in January 1919 to try and revive the fortunes of Italian cinema), to be involved first in the scripting of his anti-Catholic novel *L'amante del cardinale* and second in the writing of the intertitles of a remake of *Quo Vadis*. See Gian Piero Brunetta, *Storia del cinema italiano*, i. *Il cinema muto (1895–1929)* (Rome: Editori Riuniti, 1993), 278.

transformed into a black shirt leader. The then Italian ambassador in Washington, Prince Gelasio Caetani, an unreserved Fascist, had been directly involved, as was Will H. Hays, the powerful head of Motion Picture Producers and Distributors of America (MPPDA). Mussolini had given his express consent to appearing in the documentary footage at the end of the film, which marked the political 'happy ending; of the story: Fascism in power.[63] Thirdly, it signalled the international popularity of Mussolini as a new type of leader: self-assured, charismatic, energetic—he was filmed in the gardens of Villa Torlonia, wearing riding breeches—and larger than life. Unsurprisingly, American commentators regularly compared him to a film star. The fourth and final reason for the importance of this episode concerns the content of the message. Within his brief address of about 150 words, Mussolini mentioned the Italian American community twice. 'I see and recognize among you, some of your land as well as ours, my fellow citizens, who are working to make America greater' was the first mention. He then referred to them again as a living symbol of the connection between the two countries: 'I salute the Italians of America, who unite in a single love our two Nations and honour both with their work.' It showed Mussolini's clear intention to make use of the Italian American community as an instrument in the political and cultural relations between the two countries.[64]

Overall, for the purpose of this book, a question that should be asked is whether this unexpected convergence between Mussolini's political persona and the American film industry should not be treated as signalling a new phase in the cultural relations between Italy and the USA. In their recent studies, Bertellini and Erbaggio convincingly argue that the personality cult built around Mussolini by the American media in the immediate period following the March on Rome was part of a concerted plan to exploit Mussolini's outstanding personality and manners in order to present Fascism as an acceptable political movement. This involved top diplomats on both fronts and a number of people who moved between the worlds of American politics, finance, and the media. The best example of this convergence of interests was embodied by Richard Washburne Child, who, as we have already seen, moved with ease in all three camps. This is far from saying that American publicists taught Mussolini the importance of the press and of the new medium, cinema, in establishing political ideas and reputations. But there is no doubt that there was a meeting of like-minded people. John Diggins goes as far as suggesting that many Americans welcomed Mussolini since

---

[63] There was a first film version of *The Eternal City*, produced by Famous Players and shot in 1914 between Britain, Italy, and the USA. Because of its anti-Catholic content (the protagonist, a socialist, turns out to be the pope's son), the film was never distributed in Italy. The plotline of the 1923 version was purged of all references to religion, and David, the protagonist, went from being a socialist militant to a charismatic Fascist. It seems only right that Benito Mussolini should have played a part in it. On the two productions, see Muscio, *Napoli/New York/Hollywood*, 106–11.

[64] On this event, see Janet Bergstrom, 'Murnau, Movietone and Mussolini', *Film History*, 17 (2005), 187–92.

his personality and policies seemed to fuel their 'desire to see the Americanization of Italy'.[65]

As a politician, in 1922, Mussolini certainly represented a new generation, different from the stilted figures who had featured in the pre-Fascist years. The charisma generated by his unusual posturing and by his blunt, direct language was repeatedly mentioned by both opponents and followers as one of his raw qualities from as early as 1912, when he emerged as a radical voice and a promising young leader during the Socialist Congress of Reggio Emilia. Mussolini's stage presence did not go unnoticed. He was the first political leader to become a regular presence in illustrated magazines. The American film industry was fascinated too, as commented on a few years later by Charles Peden, a Fox Movietone cameraman: 'among foreign public men the best performer is Mussolini. He can always be depended on to deliver a vigorous speech extemporaneously, and pictorially he is ideal.' According to Erbaggio's calculations, between April 1925 and August 1936, at least once a month a newsreel featuring Mussolini was distributed in cinemas all over the USA by either Fox or Hearst.[66]

Mussolini's life too was ideal for an 'American-style' biographer. His humble origin and nomadic early adulthood, spiced by a number of arrests and prison sentences, lent themselves to a rags-to-riches narrative that would entice a mass public. The first one to maximize that potential was Margherita Sarfatti's official biography of 1925, opening with a brief preface penned by Mussolini himself. This time we know for certain he was the author, since the first edition included a facsmile reproduction of his manuscript, complete with cancellations and additions in the margins. In this short piece, Mussolini started by confessing his hatred for biographies and then conceded that they are part and parcel of a public persona:

> I am perfectly resigned to my lot as a public man. In fact, I am enthusiastic about it. Not just on account of the publicity which it entails—that phase of vanity lasts only from one's twentieth year to one's twenty-fifth; not just for the fame and the glory and, perhaps the bust to which one may be entitled in the marketplace of one's native village. No, it is the thought, the realization, that I no longer belong merely to myself, that I belong to all—loved by all, hated by all—that I am an

---

[65] Pierluigi Erbaggio, 'Mussolini in American Newsreels: *Il Duce* as Modern Celebrity', in Mark Epstein, Fulvio Orsitto, and Andrea Righi (eds), *Totalitarian Arts: The Visual Arts, Fascism(s) and Mass-Society* (Newcastle upon Tyne: Cambridge Scholars Publishing, 2017), 62–81; and Bertellini, *The Divo and the Duce*, 208–21. John P. Diggins, *Mussolini and Fascism: The View from America* (Princeton: Princeton University Press, 1972), 21.

[66] Charles Peden, *Newsreel Man* (Garden City, NY: Doubleday, Doran & Co., 1932), 13; quoted in Erbaggio, 'Mussolini in American Newsreels', 68. On the representation of Mussolini in text and images, see also Simonetta Falasca-Zamponi, *Fascist Spectacle: The Aesthetics of Power in Mussolini's Italy* (Berkeley and Los Angeles: University of California Press, 1997), 47–49; and Luisa Passerini, *Mussolini immaginario* (Rome and Bari: Laterza, 1991).

essential element in the lives of others: this feeling has on me a kind of intoxicating effect.

What is indicative about this passage as much as the whole preface is the fact that Mussolini focuses entirely on the impact that a biography has on the public and on himself. He seems to be solely interested in the function of the book he is prefacing, not on its content, nor on his past life as recounted in those pages. The impact caused by the book is the message. This was reflected in the narrative style adopted by Sarfatti. She showed little interest in a factual, historical reconstruction of Mussolini's life.

The first chapter of her biography sets the tone by stating that great wars produce great men, but the First World War has produced none of the kind among the major opposing nations—France, Britain, and Germany. Instead, two great figures have come out of Russia and Italy: a pernicious one, Lenin, and a positive one, Mussolini. Symbolically, D'Annunzio is mentioned but immediately dismissed as an episodic appearance. Mussolini was the New Man of humble origins and at the same time of great ancestry. The latter was based on the dubious assumption that, since there existed a *Capitano del popolo* called Mussolini in thirteenth-century Bologna, it can be presumed that Benito should be part of the same genealogical tree. The rest of the biography continued along similar lines: a bombastic glorification of the uniqueness, of the superior genius of Mussolini, from being able to repair his car in front of his dumbfounded countrymen—the prime minister repairing his car!—to his superior culture, amazing stamina, sensual charisma, and world-leading statesmanship. In the photograph of Mussolini in the frontispiece, *Il Duce* is sporting a quasi-Gioncondesque smile that chimes with this narrative of a man, who is constantly surprising the reader with his innumerable talents.[67]

Sarfatti's concluding remark—addressed directly at Mussolini—returned to his dominant image:

Mine is essentially a woman's book. [...]

From my post of advantage, bordering the turmoil, in a comparatively quiet backwater, I have noted something of the memorable occurrences of our time. The scene—*Signor Presidente,* is dominated by your figure. The landscape is lit up by the steadily rising sun of your aims and hopes—by your love for Italy and by your unswerving resolution to bring her to the attainment of her Destiny.

So may it be![68]

---

[67] It is indicative that, when the book was subsequently published in Italian by Mondadori, in 1926, this photograph was not reproduced. It was perhaps too unorthodox in presenting the leader of Fascist Italy to its own people.

[68] Sarfatti, *The Life of Benito Mussolini*, 346–7.

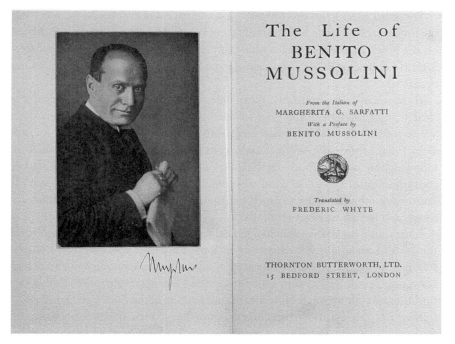

Fig. 6.11. Photographic portrait and facsimile of Mussolini's signature appearing on the frontispiece of Margherita Sarfatti's biography of 1925. (courtesy of the Bodleian Library, Oxford)

Given that both Sarfatti and Mussolini had been militant socialists in the pre-1914 years, it is a sad irony—or perhaps an intentional touch—that Mussolini should have been compared to a rising sun, *il sol dell'avvenire*.

The book was a huge success. The English edition went into a second printing within a few weeks, eventually selling about 200,000 copies. It was translated into eighteen different languages, and in Japan sales reached 300,000. The following year, when Mondadori was allowed to publish the Italian version, entitled *Dux*, it became Mussolini's most successful biography, selling in excess of a million copies, in seventeen separate editions. In the 1920s, Mussolini had become the most notorious foreign politician in Europe and in America (until F. D. Roosevelt and Hitler entered the frame in 1933). His image in the USA was also guaranteed—again with the help of Sarfatti, this time as a ghostwriter—by a stream of op-ed articles that were published by the many American newspapers attached to United Press and, later, to the Hearst press. This happened between 1927 and 1936, at the rate of one or two per month, and it allowed Mussolini to cultivate his image of 'statesman of the people' among the American public.[69]

---

[69] The composition of the articles for United Press—which Sarfatti drafted after an initial discussion with Mussolini, who then added a final revision before it was translated—was also helped by the

The series came to an end following a combination of events. On the one hand, the invasion of Ethiopia had seriously complicated Mussolini's image in America; on the other, by the mid-1930s Mussolini had decided to distance himself from Sarfatti because of her Jewish origin (as he boasted privately on more than one occasion).

However instrumental Mussolini's philo-Americanism must have been, it is clear that he thought of the USA in much more positive terms than any other Western democracy. He also had no qualms about making this explicit. As early as in 1924, he did so in a short address to the American people, published the following day on the front page of *Il Popolo d'Italia*: 'America and Italy are two countries destined to understand and complete each other. [...] It is necessary to know each other in order to work together. These two types of civilization can merge and form a superior synthesis.'[70]

At the same time, Mussolini had to deal with the traditional view of America as the land of materialistic hedonism and mass-produced consumerism that was still firmly rooted in Italy's educated elite, among influential figures such as Giovanni Gentile and also in Catholic circles. Gentile, among other things, was the ultimate authority in monitoring the publication of the *Enciclopedia Italiana*— Italy's first state-sponsored major encyclopedia—which in 1929 published its volume containing the entry 'Americanismo'. The wording was measured but nonetheless critical, presenting the praise of American culture in opposition to European traditions: 'Americanism: [...] the admiration, whether naive or reasoned, but mostly excessive, of American (United States') ideas or things; an admiration which at times even becomes a fashion, in contrast to European cultural traditions.'[71]

The same year saw the official opening of the Royal Italian Academy, the institution that Mussolini had founded in order to provide Italy with a national equivalent to the British Academy and the Académie Française. In his inaugural speech, *Il Duce* espoused a Gentilian notion of Fascist culture as an idealistic reaction to the impending materialism of contemporary times. America was not mentioned, but Mussolini's warning that contemporary society risked sinking 'in mechanization and thirst for money' made use of the two stereotypical critiques commonly raised against American society.

---

head of the United Press office in Rome, Thomas B. Morgan. Morgan was close to Margherita Sarfatti and benefited from privileged access to Mussolini. On this, see Cannistraro and Sullivan, *Il Duce's Other Woman*, 350–68. In his memoirs, Morgan distanced himself from Mussolini and gave no space to his personal relationship with him and Sarfatti. Thomas P. Morgan, *The Listening Post: Eighteen Years on Vatican Hill* (New York: G. P. Putnam's Sons, 1944).

[70] Benito Mussolini, 'Al popolo americano', *Il Popolo d'Italia*, 19 January 1924, p. 1.

[71] The text was by Jesuit historian Enrico Rosa, 'Americanismo', Treccani online, http://www.treccani.it/enciclopedia/americanismo_res-545223ec-8bab-11dc-8e9d-0016357eee51_%28Enciclopedia-Italiana%29/ (accessed 30 March 2023). (Indeed much of the entry concerns the term 'Americanism' in relation to the nineteenth-century polemics among the Catholic Church that we addressed in Chapter 2.)

Overall, Mussolini's attitude towards America reflected the ambivalent mixture of fascination and reproach that characterized the outlook of the European educated elite during the interwar years. At the same time, it is tempting to add that these two positions reflected two different 'selves' of Mussolini. On the one hand, as a revolutionary and as a self-made man, he must have seen America as a kindred nation: daring, maverick, and fearless. Mussolini's futuristic interest in technology—from cars to aeroplanes—as well as his fixation with physical activity found a natural correlative in American culture. On the other hand, as a statesman and as the leader of Fascism, he must have felt the need to critique the USA so as to appease the more conservative circles in the regime—and Gentile was part of it—and at the same time to suggest that Fascist Italy could be exemplary, superior to America with its capacity to restrain the forces of individualism and liberalism under the firm hand of the state.

When it comes to the views on America on the part of influential members and institutions forming the regime, once again one is faced with a variety of positions moving from the crudest anti-Americanism, particularly present among *Strapaese* circles attached to the journals *Il Selvaggio* and *L'Italiano*, to sympathetic attitudes linked to a disparate group, from Futurist artists, Mussolini's son, Vittorio, and the ever-present (until the early 1930s) Margherita Sarfatti. It was a dialectic cohabitation of different positions, which lasted well into the 1930s, only for the anti-American faction to become prevalent in the wake of President Roosevelt's critique of Italy after the invasion of Ethiopia. By the autumn of 1937, the party's official line was solidly anti-American, although this does not mean that expressions of praise towards the USA were suppressed.

One of the achievements of Beynet's three-volume study of America in Fascist Italy is his thorough analysis of all the major periodicals more or less formally attached to the regime. One of its striking results is that, up until the very late 1920s, there seemed to be little interest in America among authoritative journals such as *Critica fascista, Augustea,* and *Gerarchia* (this last one officially directed by Mussolini but in reality run by Sarfatti). What triggered their interest was the financial crisis of 1929 and its long-lasting impact on American society. As already mentioned, it allowed commentators to draw comparisons between Italy and the USA that predictably contained a self-complimentary tone. *Critica fascista* had the advantage of a New York correspondent in the shape of Beniamino de Ritis, a *Corriere della Sera* journalist who had been hired as editor by Luigi Barzini when he set up his American daily *Corriere d'America*. His regular pieces on the USA, some of which were published also in an independent—but equally 'fascistized'—journal, the historic *Nuova antologia*, struck a mid-course between anti- and pro-Americanism. He was among the vocal promoters of a parallel between Fascist Italy and Roosevelt's economic policies before Mussolini put an end to it. The title of his article—'Il Rubicone americano'—published in *Nuova antologia* in July 1933—only two weeks after Mussolini's review of Roosevelt's

*Looking Forward*—is in itself indicative of his argument: in a similar fashion to Mussolini's decision to 'cross the Rubicon' of the Italian Constitution by unleashing the March on Rome, Roosevelt was depicted as creating an 'authoritarian democracy' that embraced Fascism's notion of the state as the supreme ruler in every field, economy included. Like the other *Corriere della sera* journalists, De Ritis collected and published his pieces on America in three books, the title of the last one featuring the regime-friendly Italianization of New Deal into *nuovo trattamento*.[72]

Margherita Sarfatti maintained a positive outlook towards the USA, reinforced by her long stay there from March to June 1934. During her trip from coast to coast, Sarfatti benefited from the network of influential interlocutors she had built thanks to her position as Mussolini's close aid for everything American, from relations with diplomats and journalists, to their articles for the American press. In New York she could count on powerful friends. One of them was Nicholas Murray Butler, president of Columbia University and fervent internationalist (not to mention winner of a Noble Peace Prize in 1931). The two had sailed together on 21 March—he had come to Italy to interview Mussolini—on board the luxurious *Rex* ocean liner. Another friend was Marie Mattingly 'Missy' Meloney, chief editor of the Sunday magazine of the *New York Herald Tribune* and close friend of the Roosevelt family. A good part of Sarfatti's American stay was dedicated to giving interviews and lectures in which she boasted of Mussolini's achievements in both home and international affairs. By then Giuseppe Prezzolini had moved to New York, where he was director of the *Casa Italiana*. He too opened the door to Sarfatti, organizing a press conference with sixteen American journalists interested in foreign affairs. When in Washington, on 15 April 1934, she was granted a long, private meeting with the American president and his wife, Eleanor. In many ways, the American political and journalistic circles were treating her as if she were a sort of First Lady of Italian Fascism.

When Mondadori published her impressions under the title *America, ricerca della felicità* (1937), large parts had already appeared soon after her journey, in *Nuova antologia*. A central theme of Sarfatti's attempt to define America was the concept of optimism and the search for happiness, which, enshrined by the US Constitution, marked a clear connection, in Sarfatti's eyes, between the utopian ideals of eighteenth-century European Enlightenment and the formation of a national consciousness in the USA. Reminiscent of Mussolini's early expressions

---

[72] De Ritis's third book was *Stati Uniti: Dalla guerra civile al 'nuovo trattamento'* (Varese: Tip. A. Nicola, 1938). The other two were *Mente puritana in corpo pagano* (Florence: Vallecchi, 1934) and *La terza America* (Florence: Sansoni, 1937). The article 'Il Rubicone americano' appeared in *Nuova antologia*, 368 (July 1933), 227. The 'fascistization' of *Nuova antologia* took place under the editorship of Tommaso Tittoni—the seasoned liberal politician who turned to Mussolini and became the first president of the Accademia Reale d'Italia. The journal's editorial board was filled with intellectuals close to the regime, such as Gentile, Sarfatti, and the famous scientist and philo-Fascist Guglielmo Marconi.

of philo-Americanism—which she might have helped to write—Sarfatti saw American society as a place where technological advancement could be married with social progress. Within this vision, which did not prevent her from taking a critical stance, the figure of F. D. Roosevelt loomed as a gigantic embodiment of all those values. The timing of the book's publication turned Sarfatti's views into one of the last positive accounts of America to appear in Italian bookshops. According to her biographers, it was also part of Sarfatti's last-ditch attempt to convince Mussolini to favour America against the progressively closer alliance with Nazi Germany. Instrumental to this was also her racist vision of White America as a successful melting pot of European populations implicitly opposed to Hitler's single-race Aryanism. If this was indeed her aim, it did not work. It did not last long either, since the anti-Semitic legislation was to hit Sarfatti, with the quiet withdrawals of her books at the end of 1938.[73]

Among other influential members of the regime, some seemed to sense what the prevalent view on America was at a given time and somehow reflected this in their writings. The most exemplary case is that of Franco Ciarlantini. An ex-socialist militant converted to interventionism, Ciarlantini had been an early close collaborator of Mussolini, at *Il Popolo d'Italia* and later in government, although he spent much of his time travelling as a journalist and a propagandist. He was the founder and director of *Augustea* and was head of the Fascist federation of publishers until his death in 1940. Ciarlantini wrote extensively on the USA, and his writings were collected in three volumes. The first, *Incontro con il Nord America* (1929), is an enthusiastic celebration of America as a country that, like Mussolini's Italy, is united in creating wealth and happiness. Here we are very close to Mussolini's positive outlook, as condensed in his 1924 statement of Italy and America as potential halves of a superior synthesis. This positive view, however, begins to be counterbalanced in his second book of 1931 by a description of the darker side of America—its violence, its extreme liberalism, its obsession with wealth.

By the time of his third book—aptly entitled *Roma–New York e ritorno: Tragedie dell'americanismo* (1934)—the outlook is bleak. The Great Depression crash is presented by Ciarlantini as a sort of Dantesque *contrapasso* for the country's sins. At the other end of the spectrum, a section entitled 'La tradizione di Roma' is a messianic hymn to the renewed, Fascist Italy, which has returned to its universal role of moral beacon of the Western world. If Margherita Sarfatti, in her book, had come to see Roosevelt's America as the rightful continuation of the ideals of freedom and the pursuit of happiness, Franco Ciarlantini's last book had

---

[73] The effects of the anti-Semitic legislation will be discussed in Chapter 10. On Sarfatti's trip to the USA, see ch. 29 of Cannistraro and Sullivan, *Il Duce's Other Woman*. It should be added that Sarfatti, despite her progressive views in other ambits, was opposed to the integration of non-white individuals, black as much as oriental. On this see Urso, *Margherita Sarfatti*, 223–7.

done the exact opposite: to him it was Rome, now Fascist Rome, which was the leading light, and all Western countries, America included, had better follow it.[74]

A final note should be devoted to a periodical that was openly Fascist but at the same time fell well outside the official line. Mino Maccari's *Il Selvaggio* was the most vocal journal of the *Strapaese* group of militants—mainly Tuscan—who praised Italy's provincialism, its roots in rural, rough, but genuinely Italian culture. Founded in the wake of the Matteotti murder in order to defend the values of Fascist *squadrismo*, when, in 1926, Maccari decided to concentrate on cultural rather than political questions, the theme of the protection of Italian culture against foreign influence became prominent. America was identified as the biggest danger. In 1927 Maccari defined the 'Strapaesani' as those who 'save themselves from the American civilization by searching in our land for the roots of our true greatness'. The following year he warned his readers: 'Look around you, Italian, and you will see Americanism all around you, in front, to your left, right, behind you.'[75]

There was almost no *Il Selvaggio* issue, in subsequent years too, that did not attack Americanism in some form or another. America's materialism and its industrial mass production were recurrent themes, often enriched by others that were provocatively vulgar—involving pederasts and brothel-keepers—or suprematist—with reference to either Judaism or Protestantism as inferior to Roman Catholicism. Their extremism went as far as attacking 'Fascist fellow travellers' such as Marinetti, whose post-First World War development of Futurism was accused of being a Trojan horse of American values, or of leading Fascist architects Giuseppe Pagano and Marcello Piacentini, whose pan-rationalist architecture was equally attacked as Americanized. It goes without saying that Hollywood cinema and whoever praised it in Italy were straw enemies to be burnt up in flames.[76]

On the one hand, it is not surprising that virulent nationalistic journals such as *Il Selvaggio* should have turned against any form of xenophilia. At the same time, their obsession with Americanism gives a sense of the extent to which the USA was perceived as a major influence on the lifestyle of Italians. In many ways, the public debate on America and the one led by Fascist leaders and their publications somehow followed similar paths. Praise and condemnation were shared equally, and up until the mid-1930s there did not seem to be a prevailing view. The next three sections explore in more depth three themes that, in my view, are

---

[74] Beynet touches upon Franco Ciarlantini's work in *L'Image de l'Amérique*, i. 601–3. See also Gentile, 'Impending Modernity', 17–19.

[75] Orco Bisorco [Mino Maccari's pseudonym], 'Gazzettino ufficiale di Strapaese', *Il Selvaggio*, 4/13 (15 June 1927), 1; 'Gazzettino ufficiale di Strapaese', *Il Selvaggio*, 5/6 (30 March 1928), 21.

[76] On this, see Walter L. Adamson, 'The Culture of Italian Fascism and the Fascist Crisis of Modernity: The Case of *Il Selvaggio*', *Journal of Contemporary History*, 30/4 (October 1995), 555–75. See also Ellwood, *The Shock of America*, 157; and Beynet, *L'Image de l'Amérique*, i. 44–52.

central to an understanding of the perception of America as closely woven with Fascist Italy's self-image.

## 6.4 Technology as an American and Fascist Passion

The connection between modernity and technology is an obvious one. In the first decades of the twentieth century, modernity's icons were skyscrapers, fast cars, aeroplanes, and electrical and mechanical gadgets, which seemed to beam their owners into futuristic households featuring radio sets, fridges, and washing machines. In Italy, most of these goods became common, mass-owned items only in the 1950s, but they were part of the 'American dream' during the interwar years, and belonged to the part-real, part-fictional perception of America by the average Italian.

When Mario Soldati arrived in New York in 1929, he found that all the Italian Americans he met were boasting about their cars, radios, fridges, and thick Sunday papers: that was the America they had found, he wrote in a denigrating tone.[77] At the same time, when it came to building cars and aeroplanes, Italians had proven as good as their European neighbours and the USA. We have already seen in Chapter 3 how, at the start of the century, industrialists like Giovanni Agnelli and his FIAT factory had no qualms about competing with the giant manufacturers from across the Atlantic. But cars and aeroplanes were not only the leading edge of mechanical engineering. They were the stuff of dreams, as Marinetti had well understood when penning the first Futurist manifesto in 1909. All countries hailed their heroes, and Italy had its first one in the flamboyant personality of Gabriele D'Annunzio.

D'Annunzio was the symbol of the superior intellectual who could dominate technology and fly over the enemy's capital, Vienna, or pilot a high-speed boat among the Austrian fleet, or survive an aeroplane crash and write about it while still convalescent. By the 1920s, however, D'Annunzio's public persona had begun its final, descending trajectory. Mussolini was the new star, and, in many ways, he was a minor D'Annunzian figure. We have already mentioned Mussolini's passion for driving his cars through the countryside, even as a seasoned dictator, probably enjoying the startled recognition of passers-by. Aeroplanes played a big part in his life too. He took flying lessons in 1920, and Margherita Sarfatti in her myth-making biography added a spice of D'Annunzian epic by saying that he was forced to stop in the aftermath of an undescribed incident, which his then instructor later confirmed. Whether it was the accident or the increasing political

---

[77] Soldati, *America primo amore*, 49.

commitments that had the better of him, he did not give up for long. Mussolini remained determined to cultivate his passion for aviation.[78]

Within a few weeks after his appointment as prime minister, in January 1923, *Il Duce* created a royal commission for the reorganization of Italy's military and civil aviation. This brought the creation, two months later, of the Regia Arma Aeronautica—that is, a military Air Force freed from its subservient role to the Army and Navy. A bond seemed immediately to take shape between Fascism and military aviation, to the point that propagandists and journalists at the time would often refer to the Italian Air Force as the 'Arma Fascistissima' ('Super-Fascist Army'). Prestige was also regained through winning the world's most prestigious aeroplane race, the Schneider Trophy, which saw seaplanes compete once a year for the highest speed. An Italian Macchi aeroplane won in 1926, breaking the run of two consecutive wins by an American Curtiss.

However, the most iconic flying achievement of those years was the solo crossing of the Atlantic by American aviator Charles Lindbergh. Today, almost nobody remembers that the first transatlantic flight was actually completed in 1919 by two British aviators, John Alcock and Arthur Brown. What made Lindbergh's attempt so much more special was not only the fact that he faced alone a flight that, in his case, lasted thirty-three hours, but also the choice of two iconic cities as the points of take-off and landing: New York and Paris. That was the condition imposed by Raymond Orteig, the creator of the $25,000 Prize, a rich New York hotel businessman. When set up in 1919, it was considered beyond the technology of the time, and it was only in 1926-7 that a string of aviators tried and failed to make the crossing either way, five of them losing their lives.

Lindbergh's attempt seemed the most daring of them all: not only was it the first lone attempt, but he had chosen a single-engine plane, giving himself no bailout options if a mechanical problem were to strike. The landing of his plane at Paris Le Bourget, in the very late evening of Saturday, 21 May 1927, was hailed by a crowd claimed to reach a hundred thousand. Lindbergh instantly became the hero of world aviation. More than that, his feat became symbolic of all that was good about America: a daring spirit, the love of technology and speed. Cultural historians writing about US influence in early twentieth-century Europe, dwell upon Lindbergh's flight as a key moment in the European's perception of the USA.[79] The Italian press too splashed the event onto its front pages: the *Corriere della Sera* devoted half of its front page to it on 22 May, and the following day the entire front page, complete with six columns dedicated to the Italian translation of Lindbergh's article for the *New York Times*.

---

[78] Sarfatti, *The Life of Benito Mussolini*, 31-2. Richard Bosworth, *Mussolini* (London: Arnold, 2002), 140-2. Mussolini's instructor was First World War pilot Cesare Redaelli, who was the author of a memoir published by the Fascist Party: *Iniziando Mussolini alle vie del cielo* (Milan: Ufficio Storico del Partito Nazionale Fascista, 1933), 77-80, on Mussolini's crash in March 1921. See also Guido Mattioli, *Mussolini aviatore e la sua opera per l'aviazione* (Rome: Pinciana, 1935).

[79] See, e.g., Ellwood, *The Shock of America*, 106-7; De Grazia, *Irresistible Empire*, 37.

On the third day after the event, once again the entire front page of the *Corriere della Sera* was devoted to aviation, but this time with a propaganda twist. The then Italian equivalent of Lindbergh was an officer of the *Regia Aeronautica* called Francesco De Pinedo. A First World War pilot of seaplanes, he had made a name for himself internationally with a long-distance flight in 1925, which, in many steps and over seven months, had taken him from Rome to Melbourne, Tokyo, and back. Mussolini had enthusiastically supported him and had guaranteed the full financial and logistical support of the government. In 1927, the time had come to plan a similarly long flight across the Atlantic: it was called 'the Four Continents Flight', since De Pinedo's plane would fly from Europe to the west African coast, then reach South America, and eventually North America before its return to Italy. The seaplane was symbolically named *Santa Maria*. By the time of Lindbergh's flight, De Pinedo and his crew were three months into their journey and about to fly back over the Atlantic. The North American stage of the journey had been enthusiastically followed by the American and Italian press, although it was not free from controversies. During a stop in Arizona, the plane had accidentally caught fire while refuelling and was entirely destroyed. In a show of Fascist efficiency, Mussolini ordered that a replacement seaplane should immediately be sent over, to allow De Pinedo and his mechanic to continue their journey. The incident took place on 29 March, and by 5 May an Italian ship was docking in New York with a brand new replacement, appropriately called *Santa Maria II*.[80]

Fig. 6.12. Detail of the front page of *Corriere della Sera*, 24 May 1927, hailing De Pinedo's and Lindbergh's aviation feats within the same headline. (courtesy of BNC, Rome)

---

[80] The renowned *Corriere della Sera* correspondent Arnaldo Fraccaroli was in the USA at the time and closely followed De Pinedo's vicissitudes, interviewing him twice. His articles on De Pinedo's flight were published in the *Corriere della Sera* between 8 April and 17 May 1927.

At the time of Lindbergh's flight, De Pinedo had reached Newfoundland, after a stop in Montreal. He planned to cross the Atlantic with a halfway stop in the Azores islands. The *Santa Maria II* took off in the early morning of 23 May, but strong counter-winds meant that the aeroplane ran out of fuel, so that it was forced to land on the sea and was towed by ship to the Azores. It was not a short tow: the plane had embarrassingly landed about 200 miles short of the Azores. It was only eight days later that De Pinedo reached dry land. In the *Corriere della Sera* of 24 May, as one can see in the illustration, De Pinedo's flight was hailed with equal space to Lindbergh's. According to the paper, the latest news was that all was well. By ignorance or by intentional censorship on the part of the Agenzia Stefani, the news of the unfortunate forced landing had not yet reached the newspapers. The following day, the paper reported on a telegram by General Italo Balbo, head of the Regia Aeronautica, complimenting American aviation for Lindbergh's feat, and the reply by the US military attaché at Rome's embassy. This was slightly odd, since the *Spirit of St Louis* was a private plane and the US administration had played no role in the event. In any case, the military attaché promptly replied, kindly connecting Lindbergh and De Pinedo: 'Lindbergh's flight and that by De Pinedo will contribute to aeronautical progress and to the success of flying.' Below this, a longer article dwelled on Mussolini's visit to a military airport to inspect the planes and crews involved in a grand manoeuvre by the Italian Air Forces. The boastful, propagandist content of the article allows for the suspicion that somebody must have thought that Mussolini too had to be part of this glorification of Italian aviation.[81]

Flying was no doubt part of Fascism's self-identity. Its popularity among Fascist leaders was widespread, from Giuseppe Bottai to Galeazzo Ciano and Alessandro Pavolini, to the male sons of Mussolini, Vittorio and Bruno. The last four flew sorties during the Ethiopian war, but it was only Bruno who became a full-time military pilot, eventually dying in an airplane crash, on 7 August 1941, while testing the prototype of a four-engine bomber plane. Above them all, and, as an aviator, above Mussolini too, towered the figure of Italo Balbo.

As leader of the Fascist squads in Ferrara, Balbo had been a close aid to Mussolini during the March on Rome, despite his young age of 26. After he had undertaken various roles of responsibility within the Fascist Party and in government, in 1926 Mussolini asked him to become the political head of the Regia Aeronautica. At that point, Balbo had little flying experience, but he quickly made up for it—by 1928 he was a pilot and Air Force general—and soon established himself as a charismatic leader, eager to promote Italian aviation across the world,

---

[81] Anon., 'L'on Mussolini a Centocelle passa in rivista gli aviatori', *Corriere della Sera*, 25 May 1927, p. 5. Even the traditionally sombre journal *Gerarchia* dedicated a long article to Lindbergh: Armando Armani, 'Febbre di gloria', *Gerarchia*, 7/1 (January 1927), 418–21. For a scholarly article in English on De Pinedo, although concentrating on an earlier transoceanic flight see Alberto Cauli, 'Francesco De Pinedo and Ernesto Campanelli's Record-breaking Flight to Australia—Perception, Recognition and Legacy: An Account in the Australian Press', *The Journal of Navigation*, 74.2 (2021), 328–42.

and eager to be personally involved. At the time of the Lindbergh and De Pinedo transatlantic flights he began to plan a way through which Italy could raise its game to a new level.

The time had come for Italy to display its new Fascist persona through a collective show of strength. From there came the idea of 'the Italian Air Armada', as the American press called it. No nation had yet ventured in long-distance formation flights, and Balbo thought he could use Italy's expertise in seaplanes to do just that. The potential for propaganda was massive, and Mussolini fully agreed with it. The first of two 'trasvolate' took place in the Mediterranean in 1928, after which Balbo felt ready to face the ocean. A squadron of twelve seaplanes flew to South America in December 1930. The planes were the same type as had been used by De Pinedo, the reliable, two-engined Savoia Marchetti S.55. But it was mainly a dress rehearsal for the bigger formation flight that was to mark the tenth anniversary of the Regia Aeronautica. The chosen destination was the USA, more specifically Chicago, which in those days was hosting the Century of Progress International Exposition, a perfect stage for a showdown of Italian technological prowess. This time twenty-five aeroplanes were going to be involved. A media frenzy exploded before the tour had even started, with *Time* magazine dedicating one of its covers to Balbo the week before they left. The twenty-five S.55 took off on 1 July 1933, although one was lost at the end of the first stage, during the landing in Amsterdam, when one crew member was killed. After another three stops and bouts of bad weather, the giant formation reached Chicago on 15 July. The flight over the international fair—and then over New York's Manhattan four days later—was cheered by hundreds of thousands of Americans, most vocally by the Italian American community. Balbo was received as a true hero: Chicago offered him an honorary degree, a street name, a monument (to which Mussolini contributed with an ancient Roman column taken from Ostia), and a bizarre induction to the Sioux tribe as 'Chief Flying Eagle'. New York offered him a motorcade down Broadway worthy of a national hero, and the following day he had lunch in the White House with the American president. On the way back, one more plane and the life of another pilot were lost in the Azores, after which the formation eventually landed at its base on Orbetello lagoon, north of Rome, on 12 August 1933.

Biographers of both personalities agree that Mussolini was eventually annoyed by the personal success achieved by Balbo. Jealousy might have played a part, together with Balbo's tendency to speak his mind and the fact that many had begun to gossip about him as a potential future successor to Mussolini. Whatever the exact reason, three months after his return from his American glories, Balbo was ordered by Mussolini to resign his post and move to that of Governor of Libya. In itself, this could have been construed as a promotion—after all, it was an appointment created on the eve of Fascism's further expansion into Africa, with the invasion of Ethiopia the following year—but there is no doubt that the move was going to remove Balbo from the Italian and international media spotlight. He was no longer given the means to organize formation flights or anything of that sort.

Fig. 6.13. Mussolini being instructed by Balbo at the commands of a Savoia Marchetti S.62, c.1932; photo published in Redaelli, *Iniziando Mussolini alle vie del cielo*. (courtesy of BNC, Rome)

In subsequent years, his criticism of Fascism's alliance with Nazi Germany and his rejection of anti-Semitism made his position even weaker, so much so that he was never called back to the mother country. In a tragic and ironic twist of fate, Balbo was to meet his death while airborne, in Libya, when his aircraft was shot down by friendly fire on 28 August 1940 during the initial skirmishes following Italy's late entry in the Second World War.[82]

After Balbo had stepped down as head of Regia Aeronautica, Mussolini regained the role of Fascism's first aviator, sometimes appearing in flying uniform when he used military transport to reach a distant location. Propaganda announcements

---

[82] On Italo Balbo's life, see Giorgio Rochat, *Italo Balbo* (Turin: UTET, 1986); and Claudio Segrè, *Italo Balbo: A Fascist Life* (Berkeley and Los Angeles: University of California Press, 1987).

and newsreels regularly informed the public that Mussolini had piloted the plane himself. His most flamboyant act took place at the Stresa conference in April 1935. The prime ministers of France and Britain met Mussolini to agree on a statement—later named the Stresa Front—opposing Hitler's decision to rearm Germany and move away from the Versailles treaty. The conference took place on a small island of Lake Maggiore. We do not know which idea came to Mussolini's mind first, but having an international conference take place in the middle of an Italian lake was too big a temptation for his aviation interests and his flair for populist propaganda. While Laval and MacDonald arrived by train and were taken to the island via a small motorboat, Mussolini landed on the lake on board a tri-motor Savoia-Marchetti S.66 seaplane. Perhaps not by chance, he had chosen a model similar to the one used by Balbo on his historic flights, only bigger in size.[83]

For reasons of space it is not possible to devote equal attention to other technological fields in which a dialogue between Italy and the USA seemed particularly alive. However, mention must be made of the Italian car industry, since we gave space to it in Part I of this book. The figure of Henry Ford remained highly popular during the interwar years. His 1922 autobiography was translated into Italian three years later. And just about every Italian correspondent who travelled to the USA had to pay him a visit. Fumasoni Biondi, for *Corriere della Sera* defined him as 'a great dreamer who has managed to realize his dreams'. More critical was Ruggiero, for *La Stampa*, who devoted five articles to Ford and his company in December 1933. He denounced him as an autocrat who enslaves his employees and called him 'l'ultimo feudatario' ('the last feudalist').[84]

Among Italian industrialists, as we saw, Henry Ford's successes in mass-producing cars at an affordable price had a keen disciple in FIAT's founder Giovanni Agnelli. Much as he tried before the First World War, it was only with the construction of the Lingotto factory, completed in 1923, that Agnelli was properly able to organize production around Taylorist principles and a moving assembly line.[85] As for the potential presence of American cars in the Italian market, protectionist tariffs kept them away throughout the interwar years. In 1920, imported US cars paid a 36 per cent tariff plus another 35 per cent *ad valorem*, complete with a road tax that was three times more expensive than that of an Italian car. Crunch time came in 1928, when Ford decided to buy the Italian company Isotta Fraschini, as a sort of Trojan horse, and planned the creation of a new factory in Trieste. At that point Giovanni Agnelli used all his influence to try to

---

[83] On Mussolini as aviator, see also Gerald Silk, '"Il Primo Pilota": Mussolini, Fascist Aeronautical Symbolism, and Imperial Rome', in Claudia Lazzaro and Roger J. Crum (eds.), *Donatello among the Blackshirts: History and Modernity in the Visual Culture of Fascist Italy* (Ithaca, NY: Cornell University Press, 2005), 67–81.

[84] Leone Fumasoni Biondi, 'L'azione e le idee di Henry Ford', *Corriere della Sera*, 30 December 1930. On Amerigo Ruggiero see Beynet, *L'Image de l'Amerique*, i. 339–43.

[85] More on the Lingotto factory and FIAT's first low-cost car, the Fiat 500, in Chapter 9.

convince Mussolini to stop the process. The two had had good relations following Agnelli's early support of Fascism. Mussolini eventually relented and in November 1929 declared that the Italian car industry was vital to the national economy and therefore had to be protected. During the hiatus between Mussolini's decision and the implementation of the legislation—in July 1930—Giovanni Agnelli proposed a deal between FIAT and Ford. Once again, the Italian entrepreneur did not show any deference towards the American giant: the deal would have allowed him to control Ford's production on Italian soil. Ford's rejection was almost immediate, and equally final was its decision to withdraw from the Italian market.[86]

## 6.5 The American Woman, Right or (Mainly) Wrong

In Chapter 2, we noted how the emancipated lifestyle of American women had already become a regular topic of discussion in the writings of Italian journalists and travel authors throughout the decades preceding the First World War. Then, during the war years, images of women actively involved in the war effort were also emphasized by US propaganda. Victoria De Grazia, however, warns us that it would be wrong to think that the phenomenon was perceived much beyond the upper layer of Italy's educated elite, even during the interwar years.[87]

Nor was the change in lifestyle recognized among return migrants. If, when in America, women might have been employed in the manufacturing firms of the industrialized north-east, this did not mean that they were no longer expected to maintain their role of carers for the men and children of the family. Nor did it mean that their salaries were freely available to them for their own needs and wishes. Returnees did not become a vehicle of gender emancipation. Furthermore, if American women's emancipated lifestyle could be considered one of the effects of modernity, this does not mean that all Italian modernists were enthusiastically open to it. One has to register the presence of what might be called a gender block. In other words, when Italian men embraced modernity and boisterously jumped into the driving seat of cars and aeroplanes, it was all very well. If women embraced modernity through their emancipation inside and outside their homes, it was a different matter.

In both journalistic reports and fictional representations, the image of an emancipated woman was more likely to embody a critique of American modernity, rather than its praise. In the world of theatre, historian Camilla Poesio points to the fact that, when Italian playwrights used jazz music as a symbol of American

---

[86] Toninelli, 'Between Agnelli and Mussolini', 366–71. Castronovo, *FIAT*, 278, 339–45, 401.
[87] Victoria De Grazia, *How Fascism Ruled Women: Italy*, 99–102, 135–6, 207–10. See also Gigliola Gori, *Italian Fascism and the Female Body: Sport, Submissive Women, and Strong Mothers* (New York: Routledge, 2004).

degenerate society, the criticism was recurrently accompanied by the portrait of a woman losing her moral compass.[88] And when women's emancipation was debated among Italy's educated classes, there is a sense that it was mostly understood as a fashion—upper-class women at the wheel of cars and even aeroplanes—rather than a social achievement of early feminism.

A contemporary representation of these tensions can be found in a very popular film of the interwar years, *Il signor Max* (1937). Directed by Mario Camerini, the film stars a young and flamboyant Vittorio De Sica, who plays the part of Gianni, an ambitious lower-middle-class young man—owner of a newspaper kiosk—who is fascinated by the life of the upper classes. Thanks to the generosity of a rich friend, he has the opportunity of spending a holiday on a luxury ocean liner, where he pretends to be an aristocrat. While on board the luxury ocean liner, he falls in love with a glamorous, rich woman, donna Paola, and is forced to fake familiarity with the American craze that surrounds this small circle of privileged people. The linguistic dimension is introduced early on, with Gianni confessing to his friend that he had been studying English on his own, rejecting Latin and Ancient Greek, because 'What's the point of learning Greek? I thought a bit of English would be more useful'.

Gianni's aspiration, to join the life of the higher classes, is also suggested by the mise-en-scène, first with Gianni wearing an elegant suit totally in contrast with his fellow worker at the kiosk, and then with a long medium-shot in which Gianni is surrounded by two images of sophisticated, 'Americanized' beauty (see Fig. 6.14). On his left there is a book cover of the Mondadori translation of the 1935 novel by the German–American author Katrin Holland, *Camilla Bauer, Aviatrice*, and on his right there is another book cover by Mondadori, this time of the 1933 short novel by German author Josef Maria Frank, *L'adoratore di Greta Garbo*. It is only a coincidence, but in the year during which the film was shot, Katrin Holland—whose glamorized portrait dominates the book cover—had moved away from her native Germany and settled down in New York, where she began to write in English. Her novel's title, moreover, recalls the then most famous woman aviator, the American Amelia Earhart, Lindbergh's female equivalent, who also crossed the Atlantic in a solo flight in 1932. Like Katrin Holland but much more famously, Greta Garbo too was a European ex-pat who had settled in America, and the short novel by Frank is dedicated to the infatuation by a small *bourgeois*, who, like Gianni, has dreams of escaping his grey reality and, in his case, joining Garbo in her glamorous American world.[89] The two book covers, in other words, symbolize the lure of a

---

[88] Poesio, *Tutto è ritmo, tutto è swing*, 29–31.
[89] On Frank's novel, see Giuseppe Girimonti Greco, '"Adoratori" romanzeschi della Garbo: (De-)figurazioni narrative di un volto divino (1933–2007)', in Matteo Colombi and Stefania Esposito (eds), *L'immagine ripresa in parola: Letteratura, cinema e altre visioni* (Rome: Meltemi, 2008), 147–71

**Fig. 6.14.** Vittorio De Sica in a still from Mario Camerini's *Il signor Max* (Cines, 1937). (DVD screenshot)

sophisticated American lifestyle and warn us of Gianni's future betrayal of his social class and national identity. More importantly, this degenerate, foreign influence takes the shape of female modernity.[90]

Throughout the film, this topos recurs more or less overtly, with Gianni failing to play bridge, pretending to play tennis and golf, and unable to join his new 'peers' in their cocktail parties across the Atlantic. He eventually gives up and realizes that true love lies with the young Italian tutor of donna Paola's little sister—played by Assia Noris. The two abandon the philo-American and pseudo-emancipated world of the higher classes and happily begin their life together as a truly Italian couple. The regime is not mentioned at all in the film, but, given its moralistic overtones, it is not surprising that, at the Venice Film Festival, Camerini was to be awarded the prize for best Italian director, sponsored by the Ministry of Popular Culture.

(150–66). Both novels were part of the newly created series of cheap paperbacks, 'I Romanzi della Palma', by Mondadori, which relied heavily on American fiction.

[90] A very similar pattern is presented by Mattioli's film *Tempo massimo* (1934), in which an Italian man—played once again by Vittorio De Sica—is forced to follow the Americanized lifestyle of the upper-class woman with whom he has fallen in love. More on this in Chapter 9.

The connection between Americanism and Italy's higher classes was also made by Marinetti in one of his many manifestos: 'Contro l'esterofilia: Manifesto futurista alle signore e agli intellettuali' ('Against Xenophilia: Futurist Manifesto for Ladies and Intellectuals'), first published in September 1931. Famous for his sexism, Marinetti penned an invective that concentrated on the female gender. Point 11 of his manifesto left no stones unturned:

> Italian ladies from the aristocracy and upper middle class, who are infatuated by foreign customs and snobbery, are xenophiliac and therefore guilty of anti-Italianness. An example: the American snobbery of drinking spirits and the craze for cocktail parties, which are perhaps good for the North-American race, but are certainly toxic to our race. We therefore call cretin and vulgar the Italian lady who thinks it more elegant to say 'I drank four cocktails' than to say 'I ate soup'. This, unless she is under the influence of the much-envied financial superiority of foreigners, a superiority that has by now been destroyed by the world crisis.[91]

Beyond the semantic pyrotechnics of Marinetti's prose, one can note, once again, how the critique of Americanism was dressed up in female clothing.

The tendency for female emancipation to be discussed critically is certainly a fact when it comes to press coverage of America throughout the interwar years. We have already seen some examples in the previous pages when discussing the American reportages by famous journalists such as Fraccaroli and Cecchi. This is amply treated by Beynet in *L'Image de l'Amerique*, although in this case I am not entirely in agreement with his conclusions. I concur with his overall argument that Italian writers showed great interest in the lifestyle of American women. It is a recurring topic, and, in line with De Grazia's suggestion, it is treated in a self-defensive way—that is, appreciated by male authors but immediately critiqued as either excessive, ridiculous, or downright immoral. The parallel between American women and mass production is recurrent and always used in order to suggest that the widespread, better social conditions of women ultimately produce soulless conformism and hedonistic superficiality.

So, even when the purpose of the article is to praise women's emancipation—such as in Arnaldo Fraccaroli's 25 May 1927 piece entitled 'Elogio delle donne'—this is constantly neutralized by the ironies of the author, who suggests that the independence of women and their presence in the workplace turn them into bad mothers and poor housewives. In another article published two days later, Fraccaroli returned to the subject with a long description of life in a female

---

[91] F. M. Marinetti, 'Contro l'esterofilia: Manifesto futurista alle signore e agli intellettuali', *Gazzetta del Popolo*, 24 September 1931, p. 3; later inserted in his *La cucina futurista* (Milan: Sonzogno, 1932).

college symbolically summarized as 'how to build an American woman'.[92] Something similar concerns a small book that Umberto Notari dedicated to the modern woman in 1928: here, again, she is presented as the product of the 'mechanical and industrial civilization', and her power is proportionate to northern European and American men's failure to keep her under control.[93]

Emilio Cecchi even managed to go a step further. On 13 February 1935, he devoted an entire article to the emancipation of American women and managed to find the space for a theory on the subject. The power and independence of women were, according to him, the result of the weakness of American Anglo-Saxon men. Here is the crux of the argument:

> I hope not to be too generic. But, in the cult of the Virgin Mary, Catholicism has glorified the instincts of veneration that men feel towards women; some of which, if left to their own device, could degenerate. With this too, Catholicism has given us equilibrium. By idolizing the Virgin Mary on the altars, we feel freer and more at ease with women in the real world. For Puritans, this is different. Too proud to venerate the Virgin Mary's divinity, they constantly run the risk of sanctifying (or something similar) the woman in their house.[94]

Cecchi here seems to be suggesting that Italian men can control the emancipation of their female companions thanks to their Catholic exhaustion of any feeling of veneration of women. More than anything else, it seems a topsy-turvy attempt to turn Italy's civil rights backwardness into a positive value blessed by the Church. Later articles confirm Cecchi's low opinion of the other sex, at least when American.[95]

Reading dozens of articles devoted to American women, one gets the sense that Italian male journalists struggled to cope with the subject, mainly refusing to admit the gulf between the recognized rights of women in America and the far more conservative situation in Italy. The way out is often to avoid any comparison and to deride the American approach, either by mentioning some ridiculous extreme—back to 'americanate'—or by suggesting that emancipation brings a faceless lack of individuality. Even Giuseppe Antonio Borgese, arguably the most open-minded of all Italians reporting on America at the time, fell into the trap.

On 24 June 1932 he wrote on American women in an article entitled 'Grecismi dell'America' ('Greek Traits of America'). As in Fraccaroli's article mentioned earlier, the declared intention was to write in praise of American women, in this case through a comparison with the classical beauty of ancient Greece. However, once

---

[92] Arnaldo Fraccaroli, 'Elogio della donna', and 'Una città di fanciulle', *Corriere della Sera*, 25 and 27 May 1927, both on p. 3.
[93] Umberto Notari, *La donna tipo tre* (Milan: Società Anonima Notari, 1928; repr. by Milan: La Vita Felice, 1998), 14.
[94] Cecchi, 'E le ragazze?'; then in *America amara*, 258.
[95] See, e.g., Emilio Cecchi, 'Arrivano le donne', *Corriere della Sera*, 1 January 1938, p. 3.

again the widespread presence of young women eager to show their independence is seen ultimately as a sign of a lack of individuality. The American woman, suggests Borgese, 'triumphs particularly in mass showings', and the concluding simile is self-explanatory: 'If it is necessary to compare her to a flower, let us say that she belongs to the species of tulips; which, individually have little to say, but are spectacular in a flowerbed.'[96]

La Stampa correspondent Amerigo Ruggiero stands out as an exception. This is where I will have to agree to disagree with Beynet's analysis. It is true that, particularly in his first articles, Ruggiero purports to destroy all myths and stereotypes about America and shows enthusiasm towards the American working woman. However, when one reads his many articles from 1929 to the mid-1930s, it is difficult not to notice the number of times Ruggiero falls into the negative stereotypes he had proclaimed to destroy. On 24 January 1930, for example, La Stampa gave front-page prominence to an article by Ruggiero on the role of women in American society. The first few lines are devoted to a swift description of their positive influence. However, halfway down the first paragraph comes a *volta* signalled by a 'but', after which Ruggiero devotes the entire article to the pernicious effects of female dominance in various walks of American society. First, in the world of education: he mentions an article by an MIT scholar who accuses female teachers of being too rigid in their delivery of the school curriculum. By excluding them from schools, Catholic institutions fare much better. Then the critique moves to their pernicious influence in public life: pacifism, prohibitionism, and indulgence towards crime are all utopian and ultimately flawed theories that women have imposed in American society. Finally, the publishing world suffers from their presence. Gone are the times when male writers were respectful of the canon and discreet in public life. Instead, women authors are self-promoting, crave success, and make use of publicity in a similar way to the launch of an industrial product. As for the content of their writings, they fail to produce good literature owing to the fact that many women take part in the political, social, and literary life of America because these activities represent a substitute for their frustrated sexuality. In conclusion, he wrote mercilessly, it is 'aphrodisiac literature' written by sex-starved spinsters.[97]

Other articles on American women by Ruggiero display a similar alternation between praise and ruthless attacks. For example, in a piece entitled 'La donna emancipata', of 28 May 1933, Ruggiero dwells on the failure of women's emancipation in the workplace, which is presented from the start as a 'pitiful lie'. But then, two weeks later, he praises women for being better than their male counterparts in facing the challenges of the Great Depression. If it is true that, as Beynet

---

[96] Giuseppe Antonio Borgese, 'Grecismi dell'America', *Corriere della Sera*, 24 June 1932, p. 3.
[97] Amerigo Ruggiero, 'L'influenza femminile nella vita americana', *La Stampa*, 24 January 1930, pp. 1–2.

suggests, Ruggiero stands out as the most positive of Italian journalists when it comes to American women, it is equally striking how even Ruggiero must have felt the need, from time to time, to strike a blow that would contradict his positive stance. It is also politically relevant to note that when his comments were negative—the same happened for an article on lynching, dated 2 January 1934—the article would be allowed extra visibility by being promoted to the front page.[98]

A final comment should be spared for the subtopics of American women in association with sport and cinema. Had the regime been inclined towards the promotion of sport among women, it would have found an inspirational comparison with its much-debated diffusion among young American women. Instead, if a more positive attitude seemed to be prevalent in the 1920s, which led to the opening of the Female National Academy of Physical Education in 1932, in reality the regime was more preoccupied with maintaining the traditional role of women as mothers, even more so once, with the Lateran Pacts of 1929, the views of the Catholic Church had become more vocal. As suggested by De Grazia, similar to what happened across the board, even when sport was involved, sexism kicked in and the regime favoured the image of the modern sportsman as against its gender opposite. Mussolini never had any doubts on the matter. And if one thinks that Margherita Sarfatti's feminist past might have had an impact on Mussolini's views, one has to accept a substantial failure on that front. Sarfatti herself, in fact, accepted Mussolini's sexist views earlier on in their relationship. *Il Duce*'s debatable opinion of—and relationship with—women was accepted as a secondary effect of his overabundant virility and male leadership. He was an *Übermensch*, after all, in an ideological frame that did not conceive of an *Überfrau*.[99]

The connection between sport and women was to be left to the 'Americanised' domain of lifestyle among the upper classes—hence the craze for tennis immortalized in Giorgio Bassani's novel *Il giardino dei Finzi-Contini* (1962), set among Ferrara's *jeunesse dorée* during the late 1930s. At the other end of the social spectrum, the vast mass of Italian lower-class women was to be left safely distant from any kind of physical emancipation. Female hedonism and self-grooming were to be critiqued, and America provided examples of such excesses.[100]

---

[98] See Amerigo Ruggiero, 'La donna emancipata', *La Stampa*, 28 May 1933, p. 1; 'La donna americana nella bufera', *La Stampa*, 10 June 1933, p. 3; and 'Ondata di linciaggi'. Beynet's comments on Ruggiero can be found in *L'Image de l'Amérique*, ii. 502–18.

[99] Traces of Sarfatti's acceptance of Mussolini's male superiority are present in her *Life of Mussolini* too. See for example the approving tone with which she describes Mussolini's cruel treatment of a female friend as a young boy (p. 29), or the submissive tone with which she presents herself as a female author (p. 346).

[100] See for example the *velina* dated 12 July 1932, which Mussolini's Press Office passed on to the chief editors of all Italian dailies: 'In case this has not been published yet, make reference to the news from New York about women who lost their eyesight after being on a diet', in Tranfaglia, *La stampa del regime*, 177.

As for the connection between American women and cinema, the screenshot of Vittorio De Sica surrounded by the photos of two glamorous women—Greta Garbo's creating an immediate connection with Hollywood—is emblematic of another aspect. American cinema was the most powerful channel through which Italians of all classes forged an idea of American femininity. It was certainly more widespread that the reading of Italy's national dailies. Whether or not Hollywood's female stars were acting the part of 'good' or 'bad' woman, their physical appearance was always designed to trigger sensual attraction, like any other female star. This brings the question of the potential influence of American cinema in creating an image of 'American beauty' capable of competing with European models at a time when Paris would often set the trend. This book does not deal with the world of fashion, but it adds strength to our overall argument about the perception of American culture to note that, as early as 1921, a Milanese supplier of beauty toiletry can be found advertising its line of American products in the pages of one of Italy's early film magazines, *La Rivista cinematografica* (see Fig. 6.15). Linguistically, it is interesting to note the awkward Italianization of the American brand, presented as 'The American Beauty Instituto', and the fact that the advert refrained almost entirely from the use of French expressions—which dominated the fashion industry—with 'Eau de toilette' being translated into an unusual 'Acque da toiletta'. Culturally, this advert is meaningful in its indication that by 1921 a businessman would think possible to exploit the potential connection between female beauty and American cinema in order to sell US-imported goods.

The identification of Hollywood with glamorous beauty was beginning to make inroads, and a leading contributor to this phenomenon was Max Factor, Hollywood's most renowned make-up artist, whose line of beauty products became legendary in the interwar years. According to the memoirs of none other than Will H. Hays, the then tzar of American cinema, a discussion about Max Factor's wonders was part of the conversation between Edda Mussolini and Countess Vitetti, the American wife of an Italian diplomat, both of them sitting next to him at a dinner in the American embassy in Rome, in November 1936. The dinner had been organized to celebrate Hays's 1936 agreement with Mussolini and Ciano on the distribution of American films in Italy. The two women had been cheerfully chatting away in Italian over Hays's shoulder, so when he asked them for the topic of their conversation, they replied that they were discussing what they would do first if they were to visit Hollywood. Hays commented confidently that the answer must have been to meet Clark Gable. But he was wrong: 'They insisted that wasn't it at all. Finally I wormed it out of them: the very first thing they wanted was "to be made up by Max Factor"! Thus the influence of movie stars!'[101]

---

[101] Will H. Hays, *The Memoirs of Will H. Hays* (New York: Doubleday & Company, 1955), 519–20. See further on the Ciano–Hays agreement in Chapter 9.

238  AMERICA IN ITALIAN CULTURE

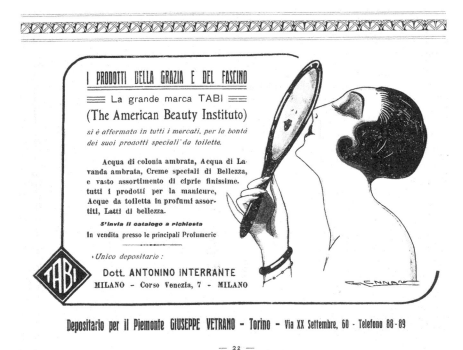

Fig. 6.15. Advert for American beauty products appearing in *La Rivista cinematografica*, 1 (1921). (courtesy of Museo Nazionale del Cinema, Turin)

A magazine of the interwar years that attempted to combine literature, Hollywood cinema, and fashion was Pitigrilli's *Le Grandi firme* (1924–38), whose penchant for highly sensual themes and illustrations made it very popular but eventually triggered its censorship and eventual closure in October 1938. By then it was directed by Cesare Zavattini as part of his leading role in the art management of Rizzoli's illustrated magazines. Also closely linked to the world of fashion was Alessandro Blasetti's 1937 screwball comedy *La Contessa di Parma*. The title makes it sound as if it was one of his historical movies, but in fact it refers to the name of the dress worn by a model who is mistakenly considered to be an aristocrat. Here America is present in the form of the inspiration provided by its then most popular comedies. When discussing it at the time, Blasetti mentioned the American stimulus offered by Capra's screwball comedies *It Happened One Night* (1934) and *Mr Deeds Goes to Town* (1936) and by Frank Borzage's *Desire* (1936).[102] Symbolically, the film features a foreign 'enemy' in the form of the French world of *haute couture*. Italian fashion seems to be entirely under French

---

[102] Alessandro Blasetti, 'I dispiaceri del regista', *Cinema*, 17 (10 March 1937), 174.

domination: this is embodied by the boss of the Turinese fashion house, named Maison Printemps (the dress in question too is actually called Comtesse de Parme), who is constantly travelling to Paris in order to observe and replicate the latest fashion. His conversation, unsurprisingly, is peppered with French words, and his advertising methods are presented as bizarre and outdated. The French umbilical cord is eventually cut by the arrival of a Milanese businesswoman. She sacks the France-obsessed boss and promotes a new marketing approach: a fashion show in the elite ski resort of Sestrières. She also happens to be the aunt of a famous footballer—sport is, once again, closely linked to modernity—who eventually marries the down-to-earth model from whom the whole comedy of errors had started. As Eugenia Paulicelli suggests in her study of fashion under Fascism, *La contessa di Parma* was intentionally conceived as an 'Americanised' vehicle for praising the modernity of the Italian urban landscape—Turin's, this time—and, more importantly, for promoting Italian fashion against its French competitors.[103]

In conclusion, beyond the realm of Hollywood, the image of American women was regularly opposed, as it ran against Fascist Italy's own categorization of women's role in society. Cultural, religious, and economic principles were raised in order to resist praise of women's emancipation *per se*. Modernity was mainly a preserve of the Fascist man.

## 6.6 Italian America and Return Migration

Once the First World War was over, Italy's political and socio-economic tensions seemed to push towards a resumption of the migration flows of earlier years. Data for 1920 confirmed this, with about 400,000 Italians migrating overseas. Mussolini's already quoted 1923 letter to King Victor Emanuel III revealed how he was hoping that this would continue in future years. On this front, however, he was to face a setback.

The progressively firmer grip on immigration by the US administration was particularly aimed at the most recent wave of migration, in which Italy played a major part. The Literacy Act of 1917 was the first step, since illiteracy was particularly high among Italian immigrants from the south. Then came the Emergency Quota Act of 1921, which fixed a quota of 3 per cent of the number of residents of each nationality as recorded in the 1910 census. As a result, the number of Italians who could be granted a visa dropped to 42,057 per year. It was patently clear that

---

[103] Eugenia Paulicelli, *Fashion under Fascism: Beyond the Black Shirt* (Oxford: Berg, 2004), 91–7. In Paulicelli's view, beyond screwball comedies, Blasetti's film takes its inspiration from so-called powder-puff films, which, by being based around the world of fashion shows, provided indirect, 'soft' publicity for beauty products and clothing.

eastern and southern European migrants—and Italians in particular among the latter group—were the target of those restrictions. The act's revision in 1924 was the final blow: by both dropping the percentage to 2 per cent and moving the year of reference to 1890, Italian migration was reduced to a trickle. This does not mean that Italians suddenly stopped migrating overseas during the Fascist years, as is often believed. Despite the near-closure of the US borders, it took more than a decade to reach a substantial reduction, from an average annual migration of 200,000 in 1926–30, to 90,000 in 1931–5 and finally a drop to about 50,000 in 1936–40.[104]

Issues of national pride and of Fascist propaganda prevented the Italian media from discussing the fact that the Emergency Quota Act treated Italy as a second-class country. However, if new immigration was impeded, there was no denying that by the 1920s the Italian American community in the USA had reached a significant size. In New York, by 1910 there were already about 500,000 Italians, either first-generation immigrants or sons and daughters of Italians who had settled there. As Foerster noted, it was an urban concentration that surpassed that of any Italian city at the time, with the exception of Naples. By 1930, the number had risen to 1,070,355, surpassing even Naples by more than 20 per cent.[105]

Mussolini turned towards making use of the Italian community abroad as a sort of fifth column that would foster commercial and political ties with the mother country. The notion of 'Italiani all'estero' ('Italians abroad') had been an established concept among Italian nationalists since the late nineteenth century. The progressive prevalence of southern Italian migrants in the early years of the twentieth century, and their tendency to settle in the Little Italys of the great urban centres in the north-east, made it easier to reach out to most of the Italian community living in America. Mussolini developed this link through the creation of a tighter connection between Italian migration and Italy's foreign policy. The incorporation of the government department that dealt with migration, the Commissariato Emigrazione, into the Foreign Ministry as early as 1923 was not just a symbolic act. It was part of an attempt to turn migration—a clear consequence of Italy's economic deficiencies—into a glorification of the Italian people, who for centuries had travelled abroad, bringing their culture and genius to other countries, from Marco Polo in China to the Italian explorers who had discovered America, to the many artists, architects, and musicians who had settled in the

---

[104] See Maddalena Tirabassi, 'Why Italians Left Italy: The Physics and Politics of Migration', in William J. Connell and Stanislao Pugliese (eds), *The Routledge History of Italian Americans* (New York: Routledge, 2018), 117–151 (124); King, *Il ritorno in Patria*, 35–6 (on migration flows post-1924); and Migone, *Gli Stati Uniti e il fascismo*, 47.

[105] See Emilio Franzina, *Gli Italiani al nuovo mondo* (Milan: Mondadori, 1995), 288; and Robert F. Foerster, *The Italian Emigration of our Time* (Cambridge, MA: Harvard University Press, 1919), 328–9. The 1930 figure is based on the US Federal Census, quoted in Luconi, 'La città della Grande Depressione', 45.

courts of Europe and beyond. It was a propaganda switch that allowed the regime to focus on reaching Italians abroad rather than tackling the endemic social and economic issues that had caused migration in the first place. In this respect, it is indicative that, when a dictionary of Fascist ideology was published in 1934, Montemaggiori's *Dizionario della dottrina fascista*, the entry for 'Migration' opened with a suggestion to look at another entry: 'Emigrazione (vedi anche Espansione)' ('Emigration (see also Expansion')).[106]

Mussolini's image as the head of state who had managed to re-establish law and order and was building a stronger Italy, worthy of its prestigious past, was at the heart of the matter. As we have already seen, the American media played a part in this, fostering a sense of national pride in many Italian Americans. Italy was no longer the indifferent country they had left: it was now a nation to be proud of, led by a Caesarian Duce, hailed and respected by the Western world. Only a few years after the humiliating conditions of the Emergency Quota Act, Italo Balbo's 1933 formation flight above the skies of Chicago and New York was a demonstration of Italy's new status. It should come as no surprise that the vast majority of Italian Americans praised Fascism for having created a new, stronger image of Italy abroad. This image was cultivated by various philo-Fascist organizations operating in the USA. There were either 'homegrown' associations, such as the powerful Italy–America Society, the many local pro-Fascist periodicals aimed at the Italian American community and, at a higher level, Columbia University's *Casa italiana*, or emissaries of the regime's Foreign Office—that is, its major consulates and propagandists who toured the country, like Luigi Villari.

The invasion of Ethiopia demanded further effort to stem the political and social tensions—the latter coming from the African American community—and this brought the creation of a federation of about 400 Italian American societies under an umbrella association, the Unione Italiana d'America, founded in July 1935 and symbolically led by the son of Gabriele D'Annunzio, Ugo Veniero. Mussolini's approval of the creation of the Centro Italiano di Studi Americani, in 1936, whose aim was to facilitate relations between Italian and American scholars and students, was part of the continuing cultural diplomacy through which the regime attempted to strengthen both its image and its ties with the Italian American community.[107]

---

[106] See Philip V. Cannistraro and Gianfausto Rosoli, 'Fascist Emigration Policy in the 1920s: An Interpretive Framework', *International Migration Review*, 13/4 (1979), 673–92. Amerigo Montemaggiori, *Dizionario della dottrina fascista* (Turin: Paravia, 1934), 285.

[107] Ugo Veniero D'Annunzio had moved to the USA in 1924 as a young engineer after working for Caproni and Isotta-Fraschini, manufacturer of, respectively, aeroplanes and cars. He settled down in New York and became a propaganda figurehead for the Fascist regime. Among the vast bibliography on the regime's cultural policies in the USA, see Philip V. Cannistraro, *Blackshirts in Little Italy: Italian Americans and Fascism, 1921–1929* (West Lafayette: Bordighera, 1999); Stefano Luconi, *La 'diplomazia parallela': Il regime fascista la mobilitazione degli italo-americani* (Milan: Franco Angeli, 2000);

More important to the interests of this book is the question of returned migrants and of their potential influence on the perception of America in their mother country. Similar to the discussion in Chapter 2 with regard to return migration before the First World War, the bibliography on the subject remains scant. The available sources are just about the same, as are the conclusions reached by experts: the 'Americani' who settled back in Italy did not have a substantial cultural impact on the communities to which they returned. Their economic impact is unquestionable, but that too remained limited to the families who had experienced migration or to the local church to which they were attached. It did not leave a lasting mark on national and regional economies, nor did it bring a solution to the *Questione meridionale*, as some politicians and economists had hoped at the turn of the century.

Culturally too, the impact was limited, and this for two main reasons. First of all, the strong ties among Italians abroad—particularly those who were concentrated in the urban centre of the north-east—their constant contact with relatives in Italy, and their widespread intention to move back after a few years, meant that their assimilation to the American lifestyle was only partial. As we will see, a recurrent comment among studies of returned migration concerns the swift 'reassimilation' into the original social and economic landscape of many returnees. The money saved in America might have allowed them to buy farmland and move to better housing, but in essence they returned to the role of peasants, and in many cases returned to a state of poverty in the midst of the economic crisis of the early 1930s. The second motive is related to the fact that, in the vast majority of cases, returnees did not go back to Italy, the country: rather, they went back to their home villages or towns, whose economy and employment opportunities had not changed since their departure. This means that professional skills and lifestyle habits that the migrant might have absorbed during their American stay were useless and therefore quickly abandoned. Many who had been working in the American construction and industrial sectors found themselves back in economically depressed areas where those activities were languishing or non-existent. Had they moved back to rapidly expanding cities such as Milan, Turin, or Rome, they would have stood a much higher chance of maximizing their American experience. Instead, the centuries-old dream of achieving better standing through the acquisition of land and the desire to return to one's own *campanile* ('belltower') proved a stronger magnet.

A much-quoted source of information about life in a migration-hit, peasant village of the Deep South is Carlo Levi's *Cristo si è fermato a Eboli* (1945). The book is based on Levi's forced confinement, owing to his anti-Fascist views, in the Basilicata villages of Grassano and Aliano, whose population had been more than

---

Matteo Pretelli, *La via Fascista alla democrazia americana: Cultura e propaganda nelle comunità italo-americane* (Viterbo: ASEI-Sette Città, 2012).

halved by transatlantic migration. Between August 1935 and May 1936, Levi became close to the local population thanks to his free offer of medical help. The book provides a vivid portrait both of a peasant community still steeped in ancient habits and of the cultural shock experienced by Levi, an educated, middle-class man from Turin. Of the few signs of modernity found by Levi among the peasants of Gagliano—the pseudo-toponym used in the book—the notion of 'America' looms largely. In line with the above-mentioned considerations, though, Levi warns us that, despite the legendary charisma of America in the minds of peasants, the 'Americani' quickly return to their old ways once they are back:

> The peasants who emigrate to America remain just what they always were; many stay there and their children become Americans, but the rest, those who come back twenty years later, are just the same as when they went away. In three months they forget the few words of English they ever learned, slough off the few superficial new habits and are the same peasants they were before, like stones which a rushing stream has long coursed over but which dry out under the first warm rays of the sun. In America they live apart, among themselves; for years they eat nothing but bread, just as they did in Gagliano, saving all their meagre earnings. They live next door to the earthly paradise, but they dare not enter.[108]

Levi then moves on to say that most 'Americani', after their reassimilation, would distinguish themselves only by occasionally revealing their bitterness at not having made it in America. The positive myth of America, in other words, coexisted with the bitter memory of the sacrifices, humiliations, and losses in the personal life of each migrant. In this case, moreover, it must be noted that it is likely that such disappointment amongst 'Americani' during Levi's stay was more pronounced following the economic depression of the previous years, which had resulted in thousands of migrants losing their jobs, particularly in the construction industry. Unsurprisingly, the image of F. D. Roosevelt as a saviour was, according to Levi, present in the home of peasants almost as often as that of the local patron, the venerated Madonna di Viggiano.

The lack of non-agricultural employment in Gagliano is also evidenced by the fact that, of all the 'Americani', only two have retained an occupation related to their former lifestyle across the Atlantic. One offers his own car for taxi services to the nearby towns but, according to Levi, only manages to do a couple of trips per week. The other one is a tailor, who, again, struggles to make a living, while back in America he used to run a shop with four assistants. Beyond that, Levi tells us that what little distinguished the 'Americani' from the rest of the population were samples of their former access to goods that in provincial Italy were still

---

[108] Carlo Levi, *Cristo si è fermato a Eboli* (Turin: Einaudi, 1945; trans. Frances Frenave, 1947), 123–4.

considered a luxury: a radio, a gramophone, gold teeth, and the odd dollar note, which was pinned to the veil of the Madonna statue when it was paraded around the streets of Gagliano.

Another interesting source of information is a sociological study that concentrates on the migrational flows between two villages of the same name, Roseto in Apulia and its eponym in Pennsylvania, which was officially given its name in 1912. Carla Bianco's study concentrates on the Italian American population that grew up in Roseto, PA, during the interwar years and compares it with the lifestyle and traditions of the population of the Italian Roseto.[109] Her findings are very much in line with Carlo Levi's observations. The similarities between the two communities are striking, fostered by the continuous toing and froing of various members of the communities. Her conclusion is that very little of the American lifestyle has been passed on to the Italian community, because, once again, the interwar generation of Roseto, PA, had in itself absorbed little. Their attachment to the motherland's traditions and culture even takes the shape of resentment towards the 'Americanization' of their children:

> In a country like the United States, where youth and modernity are venerated and age is fought strenuously by everybody, this is a community for the most pastoriented. While all adult members love their children dearly and do their best to give them the maximum support, the departure from the old patterns hurts them and appears to them as a decline in humanity which they blame on America.[110]

Paradoxically, the emancipation of American women was not seen in a particularly positive light either. Italian American husband and wife still had very separate roles and responsibilities in the house, and Bianco reports how an Italian American woman commented negatively on men who helped in the house: 'Now men are becoming more and more feminine, I think. And this, too, isn't Italian. It comes from our becoming American!'[111]

Bianco's study confirms Levi's observations also with regards to the existence of a double vision of America as a land of plenty and at the same time as a place of hard work, toil, and nostalgia. Folkloric material—songs, tales, and fairy tales—is fully shared by the two communities. America is a land of 'flowers and food' in some songs, but at the same time the most popular of all migration songs is one that speaks of suffering and death, 'Mamma mia dammi cento Lire', which was already popular in the late nineteenth century.[112]

---

[109] Carla Bianco, *The Two Rosetos: The Folklore of an Italian–American Community in Northeastern Pennsylvania* (Bloomington, IN: Indiana University Press, 1974).
[110] Bianco, *The Two Rosetos*, 233.   [111] Bianco, *The Two Rosetos*, 216.
[112] Bianco, *The Two Rosetos*, 71–6, 80, 114, 237.

All studies on the subject seem to reach the same conclusion: the cultural impact of return migrants was limited and circumscribed to the community to which they returned, often a small, peasant village whose economy remained stagnant and where opportunities for innovation were very limited. Unsurprisingly, a generation later, after the Second World War, migration returned to being the only way forward, for many Veneti in the north-east as much as for southerners, with the only difference that Italy's industrial triangle of Milan, Turin, and Genoa was by then able to absorb a substantial number of them.[113]

Finally, as for the representation of the Italian American community in the Italian press, one has to conclude that, once again, an ambivalent approach prevailed. On the one hand, as shown by our examination of the press coverage by Italy's main dailies, Italian journalists did not seem particularly interested in teasing out the many stories related to the life of the Italian American communities. The fact that exceptions could be found in the work of southern Italian authors such as Ruggiero and Borgese makes one imagine a regional bias, as Beynet suggested. This, however, would not justify the relative silence that surrounded even very successful 'northerners' such as banker Amadeo Giannini and film director Frank Borzage. The impression, rather, is that glorification of Italians abroad runs somehow contrary to the representation of migration as a loss to the motherland, which was typical in the pre-First World War period and somehow continued to exist in the nationalistic perspective of the Fascist regime. As late as May 1940, Giuseppe Bottai would still speak of migration as Italian 'blood cells' strengthening 'anaemic foreign states'.[114]

This is indirectly suggested by the type of news that the Agenzia Stefani tended to privilege. Italian American associations came to the limelight in relation to facts and events related to Fascist Italy, as when an Italian delegation visited the USA or when the motherland was celebrated, such as on Columbus Day, which the US Congress had eventually enshrined as a national celebration in 1934. If the arrival of an Italian aviator in the American skies could trigger entire front pages of the *Corriere della Sera*, the deeds of the Italian American community—from La Guardia's popularity as a politician (and despite his First World War fame as a US Army aviator stationed in Italy), to Joe Di Maggio's meteoric baseball career, or

---

[113] On return migration's cultural effect, see King, *Il ritorno in patria*, 38, 137–8; Choate, *Emigrant Nation*, 156–7. See also Francesco P. Cerase, 'Migration and Social Change: Expectations and Reality: A Case of Return Migration from the United States to Italy', *International Migration Review*, 8/2 (1974), 245–61.

[114] Keynote speech by Bottai at the 'Giornata degli Italiani nel mondo' ('Day of Italians in the World'), 19 May 1940; published in Giuseppe Bottai, *L'Italia dall'emigrazione all'impero* (Rome: Società Nazionale Dante Alighieri, 1940), 20; quoted in Matteo Pretelli, 'Mussolini's Mobilities: Transnational Movements between Fascist Italy and Italian Communities Abroad', *Journal of Migration History*, 1 (2015), 100–20 (101). Frank Borzage's father, Luigi Borzaga, had migrated from Trentino in the 1880s. The surname was probably changed at the time of his move from Pennsylvania to Salt Lake City, where Frank was born, in 1894. See Hervé Dumont, Frank Borzage: The Life and Films of a Hollywood Romantic (Jefferson NC: McFarland, 2006), 31–7.

Frank Capra's great prestige as film director—rarely went beyond the odd article in a specialist journal. Somehow it was a 'transnational Italy' that, even when successful, was not entirely welcome in the nationalistic and autarkic climate of Fascist Italy.

## Conclusion

The length of this chapter is proportionate to the importance of the public debate on America in the interwar years. Mussolini's regime was enormously ambitious in its commitment to a radical, modernizing reform of Italian society, and American culture had by then risen to the status of a model to be reckoned with. America was a mirror of modernity through which the regime could contemplate and measure its own achievements. It could even dream of seeing its own *grandeur*: as when Balbo's roaring hydroplanes flew over the skies of Chicago and New York, or when Margherita Sarfatti was received by Roosevelt as a First Lady of sorts.

At the same time, some key features of the pre-First World War image of America persisted throughout the interwar years. The cultural and religious distance through which WASP (White Anglo-Saxon Protestant) America was seen and judged by Italian commentators was still present. Paradoxically, the multicultural dimension of urban America, in which the Italian American working-class community played a prominent part, was almost an interference to this vision, and as such was left at the margins. WASP America continued to be the preferred object of observation by Italy's WICCs ('White Italian Catholic Commentators', if I am allowed to coin a counter-acronym).

Emilio Cecchi's mocking explanation of the emancipation of American women resulting from a weakness in the psychology of the Protestant man is a telltale sign of the persistence of such a mindset. Americans' industriousness and social progress were often smirked at rather than studied: together, they were yet another source of 'americanate'. The racist propensity towards African Americans—and here WASP and WICC found common ground—was also still present. If nothing else, it was made worse by Fascist Italy's need to justify the great expansion of its colonies through the suppression of Africa's last independent country.

# 7
# The Craze for American Literature and Comics, and the Plight of the English Language

When a bearer of both good and bad news comes to us, we commonly ask them to start with the bad news first. This chapter follows the same approach, so the first part will be devoted to the misfortunes of the English language—that is, the impact of the continued, widespread ignorance of this language among educated Italians during the interwar years.

In Chapter 1 we anticipated how the attempt by the then Minister of Education, Luigi Credaro, to introduce the Liceo Moderno, in 1911, was eventually suppressed by Giovanni Gentile's reform of secondary education in 1923. We will now see how foreign-language teaching was then reorganized during the Fascist years. We will also dwell on the persistence of French culture among Italy's educated elite and on its gatekeeping role when it came to approaching American literature.

The second and third sections will focus on the diffusion of American literature in Italy's interwar years. Here, the much-debated notion of the *mito americano* will need to be unpacked, historically and as a critical concept, in order to give space to a more nuanced understanding of the overall phenomenon. First, the vast popularity of American middlebrow literature in the 1920s will need more attention than has traditionally been paid to it. Secondly, we will revisit the discovery of contemporary literature in the 1930s, and the political reverberations attached to the role played by influential figures such as Cesare Pavese and Elio Vittorini, and by newly born publishing houses such as Bompiani and, to a lesser extent, Einaudi.

The fourth and final section of the chapter will return to popular culture and concentrate on comics, the printed, visual narratives which, imported from America, inhabited the mind of millions of young Italians in a similar fashion to Hollywood cinema. The first generation of America's superheroes enjoyed an astonishing popularity in the early 1930s, which the regime took years to police effectively. Their circulation was a major ingredient in the foundation of the 'Americanization' of Italian culture, which was to grow to much greater heights after the Second World War.

*America in Italian Culture: The Rise of a New Model of Modernity, 1861–1943*. Guido Bonsaver, Oxford University Press.
© Guido Bonsaver 2023. DOI: 10.1093/oso/9780198849469.003.0008

## 7.1 English for Women, French for Understanding America

If, during the decade before the March of Rome, Luigi Credaro had been the most prominent pedagogist in Italian politics, Mussolini's choice of Giovanni Gentile brought in an entirely new era. As philosophers, the two had not seen eye to eye for many years: Credaro had never spared his criticism of neo-idealism, and Gentile had replied in kind, denying the status of pedagogy—Credaro's specialism—as a science distinct from philosophy. The *carte blanche* given by Mussolini to Gentile as Minister of Education allowed the latter to wipe out the heritage and even presence of Credaro from Italy's educational policies. Apart from the suppression of the Liceo Moderno, in 1923 Gentile also suppressed the Pedagogy departments that Credaro had introduced in the faculties of Philosophy and Letters and had Credaro replaced as Deputy President of the Consiglio Superiore della Pubblica Istruzione, the ministry's high commission on education.

Finally, Credaro's moderate policies as Commissario straordinario per la Venezia Tridentina—to which he had been appointed in 1919 with the role of helping the harmonization among different ethnicities in the newly annexed, former-Austrian territories in the north-east—were fully reversed. The effects were pernicious, particularly in Alto Adige, better known as South Tyrol. The province was almost entirely steeped in Germanic culture—only about 3 per cent of the population spoke Italian at the time of its annexation to Italy—and Credaro had been careful in negotiating the introduction of the Italian administration. However, he was forced to resign in October 1922, only a few days before the March on Rome, and the dominant figure became that of ultra-nationalist Ettore Tolomei. For years, Tolomei had been the obsessive advocate of the 'Italianization' of South Tyrol, which the Fascist government proceeded to implement, starting with the school system and the forced Italianization of German surnames and toponyms.[1]

Gentile's 1923 reform of Italy's secondary education confirmed the Liceo classico in its dominant position. It was the only secondary school that gave access to the faculties of Humanities and Law; hence it remained the course of study chosen by Italy's ruling classes. The study of foreign languages was confirmed as deeply steeped in the classics, with Ancient Greek and Latin being taught in all five years, whereas the study of a foreign language, French, was limited to the first

---

[1] On Credaro and Gentile, see Marco Antonio D'Arcangeli, 'Giovanni Gentile–Luigi Credaro: Due protagonisti a confronto fra "pubblico e privato"', in Giuseppe Spadafora (ed.), *Giovanni Gentile: La pedagogia; La scuola* (Rome: Armando Editore, 1997), 461–78. D'Arcangeli rightly dwells on the undeserved neglect of the figure of Credaro as a groundbreaking pedagogist in Italy's history of national education (pp. 463–5). On Credaro's and Tolomei's policies in South Tyrol, see Sergio Benvenuti, *Il fascismo nella Venezia Tridentina (1919-1924)* (Trento: Società di studi trentini di scienze storiche, 1976). I am grateful to my former D.Phil. student Jamie Green, whose groundbreaking study on South Tyrol has meant I have been steeped in the cultural history of my home region.

two years. English or German could be studied in the Liceo scientifico, but its limited access to university education turned it into a very unpopular choice (only 5,492 students in 1925–6 as against 55,333 attending the Liceo classico). As for the suppression of the Liceo moderno—which the entry in the *Enciclopedia italiana* was to define as a 'grave threat to classical education'[2]—the baton of the teaching of modern languages was passed on to a new creation: the Liceo femminile. There, together with French, female students were given the choice of a second foreign language in the last three years, either English or German.

With the Liceo femminile, gender and sexism were formalized in one fell swoop. Gender was implicit in the decision to create a Liceo for girls only. Private institutions for the girls of Italy's nobility and upper bourgeoisie had naturally been in existence for decades, mostly run by religious orders and called Educandati. However, this was the first time that an Italian government set up a similar institution, different from the Scuole magistrali, which had been specifically created for the professional formation of primary-school teachers. The sexist dimension was linked to the fact that the Liceo femminile gave no access to university education. It was conceived as a finishing school for young women from wealthy backgrounds who were supposed then to move on to a comfortable life as wives and mothers. Giuseppe Prezzolini, in a private letter, referred to Gentile's Sicilian origin and dismissed the Liceo femminile as 'a mistake by a Sicilian who's oblivious of modern life'.[3] If Prezzolini's Tuscan dig at a Sicilian intellectual can be ignored, the reference to modern life makes sense if one thinks that, for example, physical education in the Licei femminili had been replaced by lessons in dance. As was suggested in the previous chapter in relation to the emancipation of women under Fascism, there is a sense that Fascist lawmakers, despite their aims to modernize Italy, did not include the female sex in their plans. Moreover, Gentile's disregard for women's role in society was even worse than Mussolini's and Marinetti's.

When still writing as a philosopher and a pedagogist, in May 1918, Gentile had written a public letter to the then Minister of Education, published on the front page of Bologna's newspaper, *Il Resto del Carlino*. In the letter Gentile condemned the deterioration of Italy's secondary-school education. According to him, this was mainly due to the invasion of hundreds of thousands of new students coming from the lower classes. The original text of the letter, much longer than the published version, developed this thought with an open reference to female students,

---

[2] See the 1934 entry 'Liceo-Ginnasio', in Giovanni Gentile (ed.), *Enciclopedia italiana* (Rome: Istituto dell'Enciclopedia Italiana, 1934), https://www.treccani.it/enciclopedia/liceo-ginnasio_%28Enciclopedia-Italiana%29/ (accessed 1 December 2021), the so-called Treccani.

[3] Letter by Giuseppe Prezzolini to A. Casati, 30 June 1924, published in A. Casati and G. Prezzolini, *Carteggio*, ii. *1911–1944* (Rome: Edizioni di Storia e Letteratura, 1990), 453; quoted in Eleonora Guglielman, 'Dalla "scuola per signorine" alla "scuola delle padrone": Il Liceo femminile della riforma Gentile e i suoi precedent storici', in M. Guspini (ed), *Da un secolo all'altro. Contriibuti per una 'storia dell'insegnamento della storia'* (Rome: Amicia, 2004), 155–95.

who were now 'invading' university classes too. His low opinion of women's potential could not be more explicit:

> either secondary schools (and I am thinking in particular of classical schools, cradle of all the substance of true, national culture) regain their ancient characteristics [...] or schools will fall from a precipice. And the first sign will be this: that they will be abandoned by men, attracted by more advantageous and virile careers: and they will be invaded by women, who now are crowding our universities, and who, it must be said, do not have, nor will they ever have, either that animated originality of thought, or that firm spiritual energy, which are the superior, intellectual, and moral forces of humanity, and which have to be the cornerstone of schools aimed at shaping the superior spirit of the country.[4]

It is possible that the scissors of the newspaper editor cut this passage in order to help Gentile and *Il Resto del Carlino* avoid the accusation of misogyny. If so, Gentile did not seem to agree, since he proceeded to insert the entire text of his letter, including this passage, in a book published the following year. A reverberation of Gentile's sexism can be found in the norms attached to the directorship of each Liceo femminile: it was to be assigned to a man, thus precluding women from a career within the Ministry of Education.[5]

Another example showing how widespread among the Italian intelligentsia was an abrupt distinction between men's and women's potentials comes from an interview with Luigi Pirandello on 8 May 1924. Asked for his thoughts about women writers, he replied:

> This is another difficult subject. In general I don't think much of them. I like Grazia Deledda a lot. Literary women in any case shouldn't be thought of as women. Women are passive, whereas art is active. This doesn't mean that there can't be an active feminine spirit. But then it is not a woman.[6]

In the end, the Liceo femminile proved a fiasco. Despite the fact that the reform planned the opening of ten Licei in Italy's major towns, only seven actually

---

[4] Giovanni Gentile, 'Esiste una scuola in Italia? Lettera aperta a S. E. Berenini', *Il Resto del Carlino*, 4 May 1918, pp. 1–2. The full text was published in Giovanni Gentile, *Il problema scolastico del dopoguerra* (Naples: Ricciardi, 1919), 3–15 (8).

[5] This point was openly criticized during the parliamentary debate on the reform. See Guglielman, 'Dalla "scuola per signorine"', 32. On the Fascist reform of secondary education, see also Jürgen Charnitzky, *Fascismo e scuola: La politica scolastica del regime (1922–1943)* (Florence: La Nuova Italia, 1996).

[6] Giuseppe Villaroel, 'Colloqui con Pirandello', *Il Giornale d'Italia*, 8 May 1924, in Pupo (ed.), *Interviste a Pirandello*, 249. Pirandello's reference to Grazia Deledda is controversial, since in 1911 he had written a novel, *Suo marito*, which was based on the much-gossiped drive for success and notoriety by Grazia Deledda's husband and literary agent, Palmiro Madesani. Pirandello's publisher at the time, Emilio Treves, had refused the manuscript in order to respect Deledda's private life, and the novel came out with the small Florentine publisher Quattrini.

opened, and by the school year 1926/7 two had already closed down and the total number of students was risible, at 97. Gentile by then had left the Ministry of Education, and his successor quietly decided to put an end to the project. By 1928 all Licei femminili had ceased to admit students.

One of the most critical voices was that of Piero Gobetti. He sarcastically called the reform 'the school of landladies, the school of servants, the school of sycophants', and, with reference to the Liceo femminile, he commented that it was 'symptomatic and symbolic of the dominant psychology at the time of the Fascist advent'. He was right in suggesting that the reform revealed a nationalistic and conservative outlook that was also to prove a step back in the knowledge of modern foreign languages among Italy's educated elite.[7]

The reform had obvious repercussions in relation to first-hand knowledge of English-speaking cultures, American included. A telltale sign of this concerns the most prestigious figure among Italian literati, who, in the 1930s, commanded a new interest in American literature: Cesare Pavese. He was one of the few young Italians who in the 1910s had chosen to attend the Liceo moderno section at his local Liceo in Turin. Thanks to this, Pavese developed an interest in American literature and was to become one of the very few Italians of his generation who obtained a degree with a dissertation on the subject—on Whitman's poetry. As we will see, this was to give him a leading edge over other 'Americanisti' like Elio Vittorini, whose knowledge of English remained limited to the point that he would sometimes read American novels in their French translation and have his friend and ghost-translator, Lucia Rodocanachi, provide a first draft of translation, which he would then polish and publish as his own.[8]

The lack of progress in Italy's educational policies concerning modern languages meant a similar status quo in the cultural debate. The 'French connection' dominated the discussion on American literature in the interwar years too. Incidentally, it was present even on the occasion of Pavese's dissertation, since his supervisor—strange to say—was a professor of French literature, Ferdinando Neri, then editor of the journal *La Cultura*, to which Pavese was to contribute. And, even in terms of resources for the study of American literature, in a letter dated 29 November 1929, Pavese lamented their almost complete absence, in Turin and in the rest of Italy. That letter was the first one addressed to his Italian American friend Anthony Chiuminatto, a young musician who had been employed to teach English at Pavese's Liceo. It was Chiuminatto who, by then back in the USA, provided Pavese with precious advice on the meaning of slang

---

[7] Piero Gobetti [signed as: \*\*\*], 'La scuola delle padrone, la scuola dei servi, la scuola dei cortigiani', in *La Rivoluzione liberale*, 2/13 (8 May 1923), 53.
[8] Vittorini's dependence on Rodocanachi was revealed only in the 1990s, after her private papers became open for study. On this, see Franco Contorbia (ed.), *Lucia Rodocanachi: Le carte, la vita* (Florence: Società editrice fiorentina, 2006); and, in English, see Bonsaver, 'Vittorini's American Translations: Parallels, Borrowings and Betrayals', *Italian Studies*, 53 (1998), 68–97.

expressions found in his readings of American contemporary novelists. Those exchanges had already started during Chiuminatto's four-year stay in Turin, as Pavese commented in his unpolished English:

> Perhaps you don't even assume what usefulness had for me your little lessons of American spoken. Yet I keep those jottings carefully, and scanty as the expressions and words I could put down, yet as I read modern American authors, I feel more assured, bolder in understanding them, more in touch with their mood of living and thought. And all comes from your lessons of language![9]

Less fortunate was another Piedmontese 'Americanista' of that generation whom we have already met: Mario Soldati. He was born into a wealthy family of Turin's upper bourgeoisie in which—Treccani's entry on Soldati tells us—'French and Turinese were normally spoken; less so Italian'. Following the family tradition, Soldati went to a Liceo classico, so when, in 1929, he boarded a ship taking him to New York, he had no knowledge of English. Indeed, during his sailing across the Atlantic, his conversations in a foreign language mainly involved his newly acquired companionship with a Sicilian aristocrat, with whom, oddly, he used to converse in French. As he wrote in *America primo amore*, within a few months his English had grown to a point where he could now talk with 'the elegance of Pope or Addison'. This—one would hope self-ironic—comment is part of the book's early section entitled 'Italo-americani'. There, Soldati compares his sophisticated upbringing with the rougher traits of an Italian American family, and is forced to retreat into the memories of his days in Turin, as exemplified through a poem by Baudelaire.[10]

French was to remain the one and only modern language known by the vast majority of Italian intellectuals during the entire Ventennio. This included one journal that, in order to reach an international readership, was written entirely in French. Soon after the end of the First World War, when the two Tuscan mavericks of Italian culture, Ardengo Soffici and Giovanni Papini, decided to address the rest of the world, they founded the journal *La Vraie Italie*, directed and mostly composed by the latter, which he defined as an 'Organ of Intellectual Connection between Italy and other Countries'. From its first issue, published in Florence in February 1919, the journal's objective was very clear: to convince Italy's war allies of the need to maintain the promises of territorial gains, as stated in the Treaty of London. As a probable act of diplomacy, the first issue contained an article in

---

[9] Letter by Pavese to Chiuminatto, 24 November 1929, in Mark Pietralunga (ed.), *Cesare Pavese and Antonio Chiuminatto: Their Correspondence* (Toronto: Toronto University Press, 2007), 25–7 (26). On Pavese's early American studies, see Antonio Catalfamo, 'La tesi di laurea di Cesare Pavese sul Walt Whitman e i suoi studi successivi sulla letteratura americana', *Forum Italicum*, 47/1 (2013), 80–95. On the genesis of Pavese's thesis, see Lawrence G. Smith, *Cesare Pavese and America: Life, Love, and Literature* (Amherst, MA: University of Massachusetts Press, 2008), 135–9.

[10] This episode has already been commented upon in the Introduction. See the entry 'Mario Soldati' in vol. xxiii of Treccani's *Dizionario biografico degli italiani*.

which the journals' editors professed their support of Wilson's internationalist approach. The journal's tone, however, reflecting the frustration for the failures of Italian diplomacy at the negotiating table, became more and more jingoistic. This provoked a critical reaction in French intellectual circles, which convinced Papini to take a more diplomatic tone. The journal was eventually closed down in May 1920. In his farewell piece entitled 'Adieux', Papini lamented that the journal had fallen short in its aim of influencing the foreign elite, as evidenced by the fact that three-quarters of both their readership and their subscribers were Italian.[11]

Once Papini and Soffici moved on to another of their ambitious but often short-lived periodicals, the latter developed his vision of a pan-Latin brotherhood to one of a Mediterranean brotherhood led by Italy. This was the ideological core at the heart of the magazine *Rete mediterranea*, founded by Soffici in March 1920. This time Soffici went entirely on his own: he would write all the articles, and, indeed, his biographer defined it as 'the journal of loneliness'.[12] Once again, nationalism loomed large within its pages, and what is particularly interesting for the scope of this book is to note Soffici's quasi-obsession with praising Italy's culture in opposition to that of France. The importance attached to the classical tradition—in many respects this journal is a clear signal of the Florentine avant-garde intellectuals' so-called return to order—allows Soffici to present Italy's primacy over France. At the same time, almost as a symbolic compromise between the two cultures, Soffici identifies the recently deceased poet and critic Guillaume Apollinaire as the father-figure of his new vision. Apollinaire's Italian roots—he lived in Rome as a child—become instrumental in presenting him as an Italian spirit who foresaw the much-needed marriage between classicism and modernity, which Italian intellectuals can now take forward. Eventually, *Rete mediterranea* was destined to an even shorter life than *La Vraie Italie*. By December of the same year, it ceased to exist. This time one could argue that the short life of the periodical was somehow the result of the pace with which the political and social debate had been moving towards a crisis, followed by the rise of Mussolini's Fascism.

Albeit from a distance because of his reclusive personality, Soffici was an enthusiastic supporter of the Fascist seizure of power, and he even moved from Tuscany to Rome in December 1922. He was soon disappointed by the lack of radical changes in the life of the nation, but he remained a genuine supporter of Mussolini after he returned to his Tuscan home village. In April 1925 he signed Gentile's manifesto of Fascist intellectuals, and he collaborated on Maccari's periodical *Il Selvaggio*, which represented the views of the 'Strapaesani', the radical Fascists who favoured Italy's traditional provincial culture, as against the 'Stracittadini', who favoured a more urban and cosmopolitan vision of Fascist

---

[11] On this journal, see the introduction and the annotations on all issues of the review in Stefania de Carlis (ed.), '*La Vraie Italie*' *di G. Papini* (Rome: Bulzoni, 1988). See also Giladi, 'Les Écrivains florentins d'avant-garde et la France', 229–34.

[12] Simonetta Bartolini, *Ardengo Soffici: Il romanzo di una vita* (Florence: Le lettere, 2009), 15.

Fig. 7.1. Front page of the second issue of Giovanni Papini's *La Vraie Italie* (March 1919). (courtesy of CIRCE, University of Trento)

Italy. Among the latter, we find one more example of the role of French as the international language of culture for the Italian elite.[13]

In 1926, the periodical *900: Cahier d'Italie et d'Europe* was founded by Massimo Bontempelli and Curzio Malaparte and directed by the former. *900* was

---

[13] On *La Vraie Italie* and *Rete mediterranea*, see Bartolini, *Ardengo Soffici*; and Simona Storchi, 'Ardengo Soffici's *Rete mediterranea*: The Aesthetics and Politics of Post-War Modernism', *Annali d'italianistica*, 33 (2015), 321–40.

composed entirely in French and symbolically set up with two assistant editors, one based in Rome and the other in Paris. The two founders were both rising figures in Italy's literary circles and at the same time could not have been more different in personality, with perhaps the only common trait being their open support of Mussolini's regime. Indeed, Malaparte's collaboration lasted for only four issues, after which, with his renowned intellectual nonchalance, he moved to the opposite front and became a fierce critic of *900* from a 'Strapaesano' viewpoint. What interests us, however, is their initial justification behind the choice of French. The topic was tackled by Bontempelli in two of his long notes at the end of the first issue. Whereas for Papini and his *La Vraie Italie* the reason was external—that is, it was an effort to reach an international audience—Bontempelli produced an internal logic. Asking Italian authors to translate their thoughts and works into a foreign language was an exercise in forging a thought capable of travelling through different cultures. It was an exercise that Bontempelli did not see as anti-nationalistic, since he believed—and here a political dimension entered his second reflection—that Rome's mission as ancient capital of Western thought had to continue, even now that its heritage had moved first to northern Europe, and more recently to America. Italians had to retake a leading role in the development of a new civilization in the twentieth century. Despite his mention of the USA as the new frontier of Western civilization, Bontempelli did not find the need to justify his choice of French. It was an obvious fact: French was still the international language of culture. As he had explained in an article that preceded the publication of the journal:

> I hope that in ten years' time it will be possible to write *900* in Italian. For the time being, if I wrote it in Italian, it would be read by 1,000 Italians and 50 foreigners; in French, it will be read by the same 1,000 Italians plus 5,000 foreigners.[14]

Finally, Bontempelli's attempt to create a European locus of literary discussion meant that his journal would welcome foreign contributions as much as Italian ones. The most prestigious one was the publication of an extract from James Joyce's *Ulysses* in the first issue. Expecting an English text to be read in French translation by an Italian readership was, as we have seen, not unusual, and, given that the Italian translation of the entire novel had to wait until 1960, it was a worthy initiative, indicative of Bontempelli's determination to keep at the front of the modernist movement.

As for his idea of American culture, Bontempelli touched upon it in the fourth issue of *900*. In a long note dedicated to defining the difference between Futurism and his 'Novecentismo', Bontempelli listed six reasons, and the fifth one related to

---

[14] Massimo Bontempelli, 'Perché "900" sarà scritto in francese', *Il Tevere*, 18 May 1926, p. 3.

an accusation he shared with the Futurists, that of 'américanisme'. It was an accusation that he dismissed, as 'it came from people so obtuse that one should not even talk about it'. From whatever camp it came, it is odd that such accusations should have been levelled at *900*, given that the previous three issues did not contain anything that could be judged as 'pro-American'. Perhaps this was due to 'Americanism' being used as near-synonym of 'modernity', as noted in Chapter 5, which was indeed a recurrent topic in Bontempelli's notes. In any case, what Bontempelli went on to reveal is an idea of America rooted in a romanticized past. The Futurists, he wrote, praised America as a 'mechanical civilization', whereas he admired Americans' 'spiritual virginity', their 'Homeric soul'. Given this view and returning to Bontempelli's Euro-centric vision of Western culture, it is not surprising that the only time in which he dwelt on a specific element of American culture—jazz music—he should have praised it as a primitive art that was going to find its sublimation only when 'from the barbaric mixtures of jazz-bands will be born the Mediterranean music of the new century'.[15]

To return to the role of France as a channel through which American culture entered Italy, this was still a fact in the 1930s. Pavese himself came to this conclusion when he wrote the following in 1932:

> Beyond doubt, contemporary north American authors were revealed to us by the French, in particular through the KRA publishing house and the 'Nouvelle Revue Française'. The importance of this fact has not been properly recognized yet, although our reviewers often get their information quickly from Michaud's *Panorama*, after which they protest against the Italian malpractice of always looking to Paris.[16]

Pavese's words were echoed by those of Lorenzo Montano (pen name of Danilo Lebrecht), a key figure in the acquisition of English and American literature by Mondadori. He masterminded the popular 'Gialli' series of crime fiction, which started in 1929, and the prestigious 'Medusa' series of novels in translation, born in 1933—more on both later. In a letter to Arnoldo Mondadori, written in 1931, he admitted that most foreign authors became popular in Italy only after their work had been translated into French:

---

[15] Massimo Bontempelli, 'Analogies', *900: Cahiers d'Italie e d'Europe*, 4 (Summer 1927), 8–13 (12); and 'Morale du Jazz', *900: Cahiers d'Italie e d'Europe*, 2 (Winter 1926-7), 173–5 (175). On *900* as an attempt to project Italian culture abroad, see Rosario Gennaro, 'Una guerra italiana combattuta a Parigi: Bontempelli, *900* e i suoi avversari', *Incontri*, 34/2 (2019), 86–99.

[16] Cesare Pavese, 'Romanzieri americani', *La Cultura*, 11/2 (April-June 1932), 408–9. The reference to Régis Michaud concerns his book *Littérature américaine* from the series 'Panoramas des littératures contemporaines' (Paris: Éditions Kra, 1930). On the influence of Michaud's studies on American literature in Italian intellectual circles, see Dunnett, *The 'Mito Americano' and Italian Literary Culture*, 384–6.

Indeed, we can see that, in Italy, they [non-French foreign novels] normally become popular once they have been translated into French, sometimes years after they have reached popularity all over the world apart from France. I will just quote the two examples of Thornton Wilder's *The Bridge of San Luis Rey* and Sinclair Lewis's *Babbit*, which became well-known works among the reading publics of Britain, Germany, Scandinavia, etc., at least four or five years before the French, and subsequently the Italians, decided to translate them.[17]

The importance of France in the creation of a critical viewpoint vis-à-vis America was detectable in the pages of the prestigious journal *Nuova antologia*. Its issue of April 1928 contains an article by French critic Étienne Fourniol entitled 'L'America nella letteratura francese del 1927', which provided the Italian readership with an overview of three recent books on America published in France. What is particularly striking is that when, a year later, one of Fascist Italy's most esoteric philosophers, Julius Evola, published an article in the same magazine on the materialistic limitations of American capitalism and Soviet bolshevism, his analysis of the USA was almost entirely filtered by his reading of one of the three French books on America that Fourniol had reviewed the year before: André Siegfried's *Les États-Unis d'aujourd'hui* (1927).

A similar case concerns Fascist propagandist Franco Ciarlantini, who, in 1933, when writing in the pages of his periodical, *Augustea*, about the USA following the election of Roosevelt, explicitly used a recently published French book—André Maurois's *Chantiers américains* (1933)—as his main guide to an understanding of contemporary America. A final example concerns literary critic Aldo Sorani, whose book *Il libro italiano* (1925) had polemically raised the issue of the limited popularity of contemporary Italian literature. When it came to discussing the supposed 'invasion' of American literature, Sorani based his considerations around the French literary debate, starting from a critical comment by the President of the Académie Goncourt, Rosny Aîné. In the world of literary criticism, Paris was, as Pascale Casanova has suggested, 'the Greenwich meridian of literature'.[18]

---

[17] Letter by Montano to Mondadori, 6 May 1931, in Claudio Gallo, 'Carteggio inedito tra Lorenzo Montano e Arnoldo Mondadori: Alle origini del "Giallo" e di alcune collane Mondadori', *Atti Accademia Roveretana degli Agiati*, VIII.II.A (2002), 181–226 (231). I am grateful to Sara Sullam for alerting me to this correspondence. I refer to her article for more information on how Montano, from his Mondadori office in London, was consciously trying to rival the gatekeeping role of the French publishing industry: Sullam, '(Middle)browsing Mondadori's Archive', 185–6. A similar approach was attempted by Augusto Foà and his literary agency ALI. On this see Anna Ferrando, *Cacciatori di libri: Gli agenti letterari durante il fascismo* (Milan: Franco Angeli, 2019), 27–128.

[18] Étienne Fourniol, 'L'America nella letteratura francese del 1927', *Nuova antologia*, 7/158 (April 1928), 370–81; 'Julius Evola, 'Americanismo e bolscevismo', *Nuova antologia*, 7/165 (May 1929), 110–28. Franco Ciarlantini's article is 'Il compito di Roosevelt', *Augustea*, 9/5 (1933), 131–2. On *Nuova antologia*, see Beynet, *L'Image de l'Amérique*, i. 82–3, 92–3. Aldo Sorani, 'L'offensiva letteraria americana', *La Stampa*, 21 September 1928, p. 3. Pascale Casanova, 'Paris, méridien de Greenwich de la

On a more general level, the importance of the French viewpoint in Fascist Italy was noted even by a renowned anti-Fascist who lived abroad, Gaetano Salvemini. In his *Mussolini diplomatico* (1932), Salvemini commented on how the French press was by far the most influential foreign source of information in Fascist Italy:

> The damage is not so relevant as long as critiques [of the Fascist regime] appear in British, American, or German papers: very few Italians can read English, even fewer German. But in Italy all people with even a mediocre education will read French. For this reason all that is written in French is immediately known in Italy. It is natural, therefore, that articles by left-wing French papers have the power to put Mussolini and his friends in a state of frenetic exasperation.[19]

In literary circles, the dependence on the French intellectual debate was explicit. When collecting his interwar critical writings, Sergio Solmi admitted that France, for his peers, was 'the window onto the world'. The most influential French literary review at the time, the *Nouvelle Revue française*, was followed assiduously and incessantly quoted. If there was competition among the most outward-looking Italian journals of the 1920s and 1930s—from Milan's *Il Convegno* to Florence's *Solaria*—it was the attempt to look and read like the Parisian *NRF*.[20]

In the meantime, American literature became more popular at different levels. Now promoted by a powerful publisher such as Mondadori, the craze for American fiction became widespread among Italy's bourgeoisie. This is a defining fact of the late 1920s. An epoch-making shift in the publishing industry was beginning to take place: French literature was slowly losing its dominant role in Italian bookshops.

This can be exemplified with the data produced in an extensive statistical study of the translations into Italian from different languages conducted by Jean-Pierre Viallet.[21] His analysis produces much data and food for thought, and the most

littérature', in Christophe Charle and Daniel Roche (eds), *Capitales culturelles, capitals symboliques* (Paris: Éditions de la Sorbonne, 2002), 289–96.

[19] Gaetano Salvemini, *Mussolini diplomatico* (Paris: Éditions Contemporaines,1932), 42–3.

[20] Sergio Solmi, *Scrittori negli anni: Saggi e note sulla letteratura italiana del 900* (Milan: Il Saggiatore, 1963), 11–2. On the influence of the *Nouvelle Revue française*, see Anne-Rachel Hermeter, 'La *NRF* de Paulhan et l'Italie: Regards croisés (1925–1940), in Jean-Yves Guérin (ed.), *La Nouvelle Revue française de Jean Paulhan (1925–1940 et 1953–1968)* (Paris: Éditions Le Manuscrit, 2006), 45–64. On the exemplary role played by the *NRF* for the 'Solariani' group, see Sergio Briosi, *Il problema della letteratura in 'Solaria'* (Milan: Mursia, 1976), 15–16, and Gilbert Bosetti, 'Les Lettres françaises sous le fascism: Le Culte de la "NRF" dans l'entre-deux-guerres face à la francophobie fasciste', in *Mélanges de l'École Française de Rome*, 98/1 (1986), 383–432.

[21] Jean-Pierre Viallet, 'Statistiques et histoire des relations culturelles franco-italiannes: L'Example des traductions (1932–1938)', in Jean-Baptist Duroselle and Enrico Serra, *Il vincolo culturale tra Italia e Francia negli anni trenta e quaranta* (Milan: Franco Angeli, 1986), 246–94. Viallet's data on translations from English do not distinguish between British and American publications.

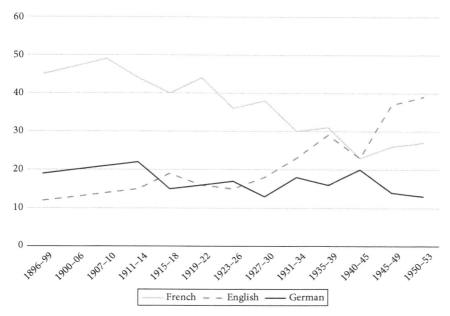

**Fig. 7.2.** Translations from French, English, and German, 1896–1953. (data from Viallet, 'Statistiques et histoire des relations culturelles franco-italiannes')

important and visually striking statistic for us, particularly if presented in a graph, concerns the number of translations into Italian, from the beginning until the mid-twentieth century. Fig. 7.2 traces the number of titles that were translated from French, English, and German. Noteworthy is how, at the start of the century, French literature had a prevailing position, with more than twice the number of translations from its language compared to others. Then, throughout the decades, German stayed at the lowest level, with a trough and peak connected with, respectively, anti-German sentiment in the First World War and pro-Nazi attitudes in the Second World War. More impressive is the constant crisis of French, which stabilized only in the 1950s, after losing almost 50 per cent of its presence in Italy's publishing industry. A mirror-opposite is the trend of translations from English, which rose slowly in the early decades and then shot up from the second half of the 1920s onwards. The drop caused by the anti-British and anti-American policies of the regime during the Second World War shows merely as a blip that was immediately recovered in the post-war years.[22]

---

[22] For a study of translated literature in periodicals that, for the 1930s, confirms the trend suggested in the Fig. 7.2, see Fabio Guidali, 'Tradurre in "roto": Periodici popolari e letteratura straniera (1933–1936)', in Anna Ferrando (ed.), *Stranieri all'ombra del Duce: Le traduzioni durante il fascismo* (Milan: Franco Angeli, 2019), 87–103. For a detailed reference work for the interwar period, see Christopher Rundle, *Publishing Translations in Fascist Italy* (Oxford: Peter Lang, 2010).

## 7.2 The Fortune of American Literature in the 1920s

Literary historians have recently thrown significant new light on the history of American literature in Italy's interwar years. The critical narrative that dominated until then was that of the so-called *mito americano*, closely related to the translations produced in the 1930s and early 1940s. 'The decade of translations', Pavese's definition coined soon after the war, became proverbial to the point that many critical works adopted it as a chronological watershed.[23] The correction of recent years was made possible by a simple but fundamental switch from intellectual to social history: from a history of the influence of American literature on Italian authors, to a study of the fortune of American literature in Italy's bookshops and booksellers' stands. This switch invited literary historians to extend their studies to the 1920s and reconstruct the vast popularity of middlebrow American literature there and then.

As we will see, these two historical narratives are not mutually exclusive. To a large extent, what is at work is a coda of the 'two-nation' effect that we noticed in the pre-First World War decades—that is, a differentiation between the widespread interest among lowly educated readers in the fictional work of American authors such as Jack London, and the later canonization of American literature among highbrow circles thanks to the critical work of Pavese, Vittorini, and others in the 1930s. The first was market-driven inasmuch as it responded to a growing readership asking for affordable books that told adventurous and action-packed stories. America's Wild West was the perfect setting for these stories. The second was the result of a process of critical appreciation by the above-mentioned authors, who were, not by chance, key editors in publishing houses such as Bompiani, Einaudi, and Mondadori, which brought American literature into their prestigious series of foreign literature.

A useful tool for our overview of American literature in the post-First World War years is the table of published translations provided by Valerio Ferme. We have already referred to it in Chapter 4 for the pre-First World War years, and, in comparison with those years, it is interesting to note that some American authors remained popular in subsequent years. I am referring in particular to Edgar Allan Poe and Mark Twain, together with the by then 'classics' of middlebrow literature, Harriet Beecher Stowe's *Uncle Tom's Cabin* and Louisa May Alcott's *Little Women*, both of which had by then entered the genre of *letteratura per ragazzi* ('young adult fiction').[24]

---

[23] Cesare Pavese, 'L'influsso degli eventi', 5 February 1946, but published posthumously in *La letteratura americana e altri saggi* (Turin: Einaudi, 1951), 245–8.

[24] Ferme, 'Appendice'. For the 1920s, see also Francesca Billiani, *Culture nazionali e narrazioni straniere* (Florence: Le Lettere, 2007, in particular appendix B, 'I successi e le novità editoriali degli anni Venti', 309–28.

What immediately strikes the eye is the growing popularity of American literature that can be measured in both the number of books, and the number of different authors, being translated. If, during the years 1921–5, an average of about ten American books and seven different authors were being translated into Italian every year, by 1928 this trend had grown to fifty books by fourteen different authors. Within this surge of interest, Jack London emerges head and shoulders above the rest. Two of his novels were first translated into Italian in 1924: by the following year the corpus had grown to eight, and by 1928 it had reached the astonishing figure of thirty-four. As one can imagine, some titles—also because of the relaxed legislation on copyright in Italy up until 1928—were competitively published by more than one house. This indirectly confirms the craze for his work.

The Italian translation of London's first two books, in 1924, allows a first insight into the phenomenon. First of all, a quick look at what was happening in neighbouring France confirms our previous, general considerations. By the time London's most famous novels—*The Call of the Wild* (1903) and *The Sea Wolf* (1904)—arrived in Italy, they had already been translated into French. Indeed, London had seen publishing success in France during his lifetime (he died in 1916). The choice of these two novels for London's Italian debut is not surprising, but it followed different patterns somehow related to the novels' different content. *The Sea Wolf* had benefited from the great popularity achieved by its predecessor, but in itself is a more complex literary work. London's philosophical preoccupations are embodied by two of the three main characters, who happen to be intellectuals: Humphrey Van Weyden, a literary critic, and Maud Brewster, a poetess. Their unexpected involvement in the cruel and violent world of captain Wolf Larsen, aboard his ship *The Ghost*, adds a meta-literary dimension that is part of the reason why this novel was to become less popular as an adventure story, and even less so as young adult fiction, compared to *The Call of the Wild*. This fits with their Italian translation's history. London's masterpiece was translated and edited by Gian Dàuli for the Modernissima publishing house, founded in Milan in 1919, which specialized in translations of foreign fiction and aimed at a middlebrow market. *The Sea Wolf*, on the other hand, was translated by none other than Giuseppe Prezzolini, whom we have already met as one of the most influential intellectuals among Florentine circles at the start of the century.

To concentrate on Prezzolini first, his appreciation of American culture dates back, as we saw in Chapter 4, to his interest in William James's pragmatist philosophy in the early 1900s. As a passionate auto-didact, Prezzolini had acquired a good reading knowledge of English, given that at that time he was already able to quote James's essays in the original. Moreover, in 1905, in the midst of a religious crisis, Prezzolini and Papini had planned to emigrate to the USA: Prezzolini seemed prepared to abandon his wife in order to do this, but the plan was eventually cancelled, and Prezzolini resumed his restless life between Perugia,

Florence, and Milan.[25] It was a crisis from which Prezzolini and Papini were to emerge with a new determination, which, among other things, produced *La Voce*, the already discussed influential periodical that was to count Mussolini among its passionate readers and as an occasional contributor.

America remained an interest of Prezzolini's, to the point that, soon after the war, when his family's wealth, invested in government bonds, was quickly devoured by high inflation, among the paid jobs he found when moving to Rome, in 1919, was that of editor and journalist for the Italian branch of New York's Foreign Press Agency. He was to fulfil his dream of a move to the USA in 1929, as director of Columbia's *Casa italiana*, but the translation of *The Sea Wolf* predates this move. In the summer of 1923 Prezzolini was at Columbia for a cycle of lectures on Italian literature. His English must have benefited greatly from the prolonged stay in New York, and it was at that time that he worked on the translation of London's novel. In this respect, even if Prezzolini did not have Pavese's deep interest in American literature, he provided one of the earliest cases of a leading Italian intellectual devoting his time to the translation of contemporary American fiction. The choice of *The Sea Wolf* is also a signal of a move towards more sophisticated forms of narrative.

The translation of *The Call of the Wild*, on the other hand, is more typical of the rising popularity of American adventure literature throughout the 1920s. Moreover, critics today agree that Gian Dàuli's role during this decade was a central one. Dàuli (his real name was Giuseppe Ugo Nalato) came from a small bourgeois family from the Veneto and followed his restless adolescence with a flight to Liverpool in 1903, as a 19-year-old, where he was to remain for three years, learning the language and fostering his literary interests. On his return to Italy, he moved to Rome, determined to develop a career in publishing and translation from English, helped by his wife, the American Edith Carpenter, herself a translator. His larger-than-life personality brought him to Milan after the First World War, where he continued his publishing ventures, wrote fiction, and became director of a small publishing house, Modernissima, in 1920, which he committed to the publication of Jack London's entire fictional work. Dàuli's daring ambitions coupled with his poor commercial skills tended to end in financial woes, which Modernissima too suffered, facing bankruptcy in 1927. The publishing house—founded in 1919 by Icilio Bianchi, the son of a *Corriere della Sera* journalist—specialized in the translation of foreign fiction, and Dàuli became very vocal about the need to move towards good, professionally made translations from the original in opposition to the poor translations published in those years, often hastily translated from French. This was advertised within the

---

[25] Echoes of this crisis can be found in Giuseppe Prezzolini, *Diario 1900–1941* (Milan: Rusconi, 1978), 70–1; and in the posthumously published correspondence with his first wife: *Diario per Dolores*, ed. Giuliano Prezzolini and Maria Cristina Chiesa (Milan: Rusconi, 1993). As already mentioned (in footnote 22), Papini referred to this in his autobiographical novel, *Un uomo finito*, p. 187.

paratext of Modernissima books too, to the point that a young Cesare Pavese read one of those appendixes and wrote to Dàuli on 12 March 1930, offering his services, and suggesting the translation of work by Sherwood Anderson and Sinclair Lewis. Dàuli never answered Pavese's letter; thus a historical meeting, of minds at least, between these two important figures never took place.

Dàuli boasted a leading role in the introduction of contemporary foreign fiction—in 1928 he translated London's other very popular novel, *White Fang*— but at the same time he was troubled by the failure of some of his many initiatives, including the creation of his own, short-lived publishing house. Some stability was provided by Enrico Dall'Oglio, who employed him as director of the Corbaccio series 'Scrittori di tutto il mondo', which Dàuli had developed with Modernissima. The two, however, eventually ended their collaboration, in 1934, after which Dàuli's activity as a publicist became more and more marginal, detached from the big publishing houses, which in the 1930s came to dominate the market of foreign fiction.[26]

As for the work of Jack London, beyond its popularity as adventure fiction, one should also note a political dimension. London was a radical socialist thinker, and some of his work reflected this, in particular the dystopian novel *The Iron Heel* (1908). The book tells the story of a capitalist oligarchy taking over the US government but eventually being overturned by a people's revolt that ushered in a new era called the 'Brotherhood of Man', a utopian, socialist world that remains clouded in a distant future. The novel's reception in America was rather lukewarm, but it will not come as a surprise that a film adaptation was produced in 1919 in the post-revolutionary climate of Soviet Russia.

In Italy, its first translation was produced by the Monanni publishing house in 1928 (while, for record's sake, we should note that the French translation dates back to 1923). Monanni, a small, Milanese publishing house, had been founded in 1909—then called Società Editoriale Milanese—by two Tuscan anarchists, Giuseppe Monanni and Leda Rafanelli. A fiction writer and an anarchist militant, Leda Rafanelli had met Benito Mussolini in Milan, and the two had had a prolonged love affair, ending with Mussolini's interventionist conversion, in 1914, which Rafanelli passionately opposed.[27] The Monanni catalogue contained a number of left-leaning political works, which were to earn the publishers the opposition of both Fascist militants and the police forces after October 1922. Monanni survived until 1933 by adapting to the political climate, stopping the

---

[26] On small publishing houses active in the 1920s, particularly in Milan, see the paradigm-shifting work edited by Ada Gigli Marchetti and Luisa Finocchi, *Stampa e piccola editoria tra le due guerre* (Milan: Franco Angeli, 1997). See also Billiani, *Culture nazionali e narrazioni straniere*, 77–148; and Ferrando (ed.), *Stranieri all'ombra del Duce*, which contains an essay on Dàuli by Elisa Marazzi: 'Dalle carte di un mediatore. Gian Dàuli e l'editoria milanese', 123–37.

[27] Leda Rafanelli published an account of her relationship with Mussolini soon after the war: *Una donna e Mussolini* (Milan: Rusconi, 1946). On Mussolini's relationship with Rafanelli, see Cannistraro and Sullivan, *Il Duce's Other Woman*, 130–2, and Bosworth, *Mussolini*, 91–5.

publication of so-called subversive works and moving towards the regime's expectations with works linked to Fascist syndicalism or the translation of Gustave Le Bon's and Friedrich Nietzsche's work, both favourite readings of Mussolini.

Censorship problems, however, continued to come from the publication of Russian and American novels, which were accused of being implicit vehicles of socialist propaganda. London's *The Iron Heel*, in particular, was singled out by two police raids, in 1929 and 1931, as a book that was constantly found in the bookshelves of suspected anti-Fascists and, as a communist militant confessed, was circulated as part of the induction of new militants into revolutionary ideas. The second raid included a visit to the publishing houses, and it produced the seizure of, respectively, 790 copies of *Il tallone di ferro* from Monanni, and 160 from Dàuli's Modernissima. The political controversies related to the political content of *The Iron Heel*, however, had no impact on the circulation of London's adventure novels. They continued to remain highly popular, and the publication of new titles continued well into the 1930s. During 1936 alone, sixteen works by London were newly printed either in competition with existing translations or as new titles.[28]

As for the critical reception of American literature, the 1920s saw a new generation of critics who shared a characteristic that we associated with their pre-First World War predecessors—that is, they were non-specialists who cultivated it as an aside to their studies in English literature and who mainly published their work in the form of articles for non-academic periodicals. Carlo Linati and Mario Praz were the most prominent figures. Linati's interest in American literature came second to his passion for Irish and English literature, a passion that he developed during a journey to the British islands in 1913. He alternated his critical work with his own narrative production. His occasional pieces on contemporary American literature were published in *Corriere della Sera*. The first, dated 10 July 1925, was based on a meeting with Ezra Pound, who introduced Linati to the work of the circle of American 'expats' working in Paris, which Pound had just left to settle down in Rapallo, where he was going to live during the interwar years. Ernest Hemingway is mentioned, together with a number of other figures who did not achieve literary fame. From the very start, Linati addressed the Italian literati's resistance to taking American literature seriously and vouched instead for this young generation, which, in Paris, was absorbing avant-garde techniques and promising to forge a new approach to realism. In a later article, Linati introduced Italian readers to a still unknown nineteenth-century American

---

[28] I dwell on the history of the Monanni publishing house during the Fascist years in Bonsaver, *Censorship and Literature in Fascist Italy*, 32–9. The 1936 data are extracted from Ferme, 'Appendix', 227. On the political dimension of Jack London's translations, see Beynet, *L'Image de l'Amérique*, iii. 899–939.

author, Herman Melville. When he wrote about him, on 15 April 1927, no work by Melville had ever been translated into Italian. Indeed, Linati discussed Melville first by introducing the recent French translation of his first novel, *Typee* (1846; *Un Eden cannibale* (1926)), and then by concentrating on *Moby Dick* (1851), which by then had not seen a French translation either. This was to arrive the following year, after which Cesare Pavese famously took on the task of providing an Italian translation, published in 1932.[29]

The case of Sinclair Lewis confirms Linati's importance as an intellectual pioneer. His article, entitled 'Un cronista del Middle West', published in July 1927, presented Lewis as America's greatest fiction writer, concentrating in particular on his most popular novels, *Main Street* (1920) and *Babbitt* (1922). At that time, Lewis's work was unknown in Italy; and, as Montano had commented in his letter to Mondadori, the French publishing industry had also been slow in recognizing its value. The award of the Nobel Prize for Literature in 1930 unleashed a translation rush to catch up with his work. *Babbitt* was translated into both French and Italian in that year (Gian Dàuli published it for Modernissima), and eight of Lewis's novels were then translated into French and five into Italian in the following two years.

The surprise conferment of the Nobel Prize on Sinclair Lewis is arguably one of the causes behind the watershed between the 1920s and the 1930s. What Lewis's work came to represent—and the character of George F. Babbitt and his beloved city of Zenith became proverbial in this respect—was a harsh critique of American society. The timing of Lewis's award could not have been better. The financial collapse of Wall Street and the following economic depression turned *Babbitt*'s cold-blooded demystification of the American Dream by middle-class, provincial Americans into an almost prophetic work of literature. This generated an interest in other contemporary writers who similarly challenged the mores of American society. Among them, we find the authors chosen and translated by Cesare Pavese, Elio Vittorini and others in the 1930s. It was a move that, in Italy, met with an open door from the political viewpoint too, since, as we saw earlier, a competitive feeling towards the USA was somehow present within the regime. If there was often criticism of the high number of translations from American literature, the books that depicted America critically were, one could say, less unwelcome.

But before we move on to the 1930s, we need to dwell on the other leading figure in the critical discovery of American literature: Mario Praz. Differently from Linati and from Emilio Cecchi—the other 'americanista' whom we considered in Chapter 6—Mario Praz followed a professional journey in academia: following his degree in Law, he converted to literature and privately developed his knowledge of the English language. After undertaking a few prose and poetry

---

[29] Carlo Linati, 'Tra cannibali e balene', *Corriere della Sera*, 15 April 1927, p. 3.

translations from English, in 1923 Praz moved to England—first on a scholarship, quickly followed by the post of lecturer in Italian at Liverpool University and then the position of professor at Manchester—where he was to stay for eight years. His first translations from English authors came out in those years, and as an academic, he developed a scholarly knowledge of European literature that was to peak with his influential *La carne, la morte e il diavolo nella letteratura romantica* (1930; translated in 1933 as *The Romantic Agony*).

In 1934, Praz returned to Italy to take up the Chair of English Literature at Rome University. During his period in Britain, he had developed an interest in contemporary American literature, thanks also to his acquaintance with T. S. Eliot, whose *Waste Land* (1922) he was to translate into Italian in later years. In 1926, Praz wrote in praise of Anita Loos's best-selling novel *Gentlemen Prefer Blondes* (1925), and his defence of the literary value of the book for its social critique of contemporary America influenced its Italian translation by the Bemporad publishing house, in 1928, which added Loos's sequel, *But...Gentlemen Marry Brunettes* (1927), the following year.[30]

At that time, Praz had also started his collaboration with *La Stampa* as a literary critic. He was the first to devote a critical study to a then young and still untranslated Ernest Hemingway. He wrote about him on 13 June 1929, a long article in which Praz offered the translation of almost the entirety of the short story 'Cat in the Rain' (from *In Our Time* (1926)) and provided a stylistic appreciation of Hemingway's narrative technique. Apart from his characteristic ironic remarks—such as his suggestion that Hemingway's apparent lack of erudition works in his favour, since, as a consequence, his boxers do not suffer from Pirandellian existential languors and his matadors do not think of Mithraic rites when killing their bulls—Praz's analysis is extremely well focused, and well exemplified by his translation. At the same time, one can also find the seeds of Hemingway's future problems with Fascist censorship. Praz makes no secret of Hemingway's low opinion of the conduct of the Italian army in the First World War and of the more recent rise to power of Fascism.

Coincidentally, three months after Praz's article, Hemingway published *A Farewell to Arms*. The book was to prove his first bestseller in America and the cause of his blanket ban in Fascist Italy. The novel's anti-war sentiment, its vivid description of the ignominious retreat of the Italian army after defeat at Caporetto, was at loggerheads with the nationalistic and military fervour of Fascist Italy. Hemingway, moreover, had already publicly shown his disregard for Mussolini in an article he had published for the *Toronto Daily Star*, in January 1923, after meeting *Il Duce* together with other correspondents at the Conference of Lausanne, in Switzerland. But if Hemingway's belittling portrait of Mussolini published in a

---

[30] Praz, '"Gentlemen Prefer Blondes".

distant Canadian daily might have gone unnoticed, Praz's article had the double effect of, on the one hand, introducing the innovative qualities of Hemingway's narrative and, on the other, ringing an alarm bell as to the political 'incorrectness' of his political thinking, which *A Farewell to Arms* quickly confirmed. As we will see, Hemingway's anti-Fascist militancy in the Spanish Civil War was to raise the issue to an even higher level.[31]

## 7.3 The literary *mito americano* in the 1930s

In an influential early monograph on the *mito americano*, Dominique Fernandez carefully distinguished between what he defined as the 'the learned myth of intellectuals' and the 'popular myth' of earlier years. The latter is then set aside, since Fernandez openly intended to concentrate on the intellectual history of the discovery of American literature by Italian authors.[32]

In later year, what was a fully justified methodological approach became a recurrent trend among Italian literary historians. There was also a political dimension to this. The fact that both Pavese and Vittorini had been anti-Fascists and enthusiasts of American literature at the same time somehow entangled these two issues and formed a historiographic knot. To challenge it and to try to unravel it risked the accusation of attempting to belittle the fight against Fascism by Italian intellectuals. As a consequence, for years, interest in American literature in the 1930s somehow became synonymous with covert anti-Fascist militancy, and little was done in order to throw documented and complicating light on this issue.[33]

Beyond these introductory considerations, I will not dwell on a fully-fledged reconstruction of the critical debate on American literature in Italy from the postwar years until the twenty-first century. There are a number of recent works that

---

[31] Mario Praz, 'Un giovane narratore americano', *La Stampa*, 13 June 1929, p. 3. The selfexplanatory title of Hemingway's article was 'Mussolini, Europe's Prize Bluffer', published in the *Toronto Daily Star* on 27 January 1923. Praz returned to Hemingway's work in a post-war essay for *Partisan Review*. On that occasion, he remarked the dependence of Italian intellectuals on the French literary debate: 'literary vogues usually did take more than five years to reach us in the twenties, and usually came via France'; in 'Hemingway in Italy', *Partisan Review*, 15/10 (1948), 1086–1100 (1086).

[32] Dominique Fernandez, *Il mito dell'America negli intellettuali italiani dal 1930 al 1950* (Caltanissetta and Rome: Sciascia, 1969). The book was translated from French and was never published in the original. Fernandez, today an established literary critic and novelist, member of the Academie Française since 2007, is an Italianist by education: before his 1969 book, he had written his doctoral thesis on Cesare Pavese, which was published by Grasset in 1967.

[33] Personally, when, in the late 1990s, I worked on a monograph on Elio Vittorini, I was surprised by the number of available archival sources that had been left untapped for decades. Literary historians had relied mainly on Vittorini's own reconstruction of his trajectory from an enthusiastic Fascist to a Communist partisan; the same with the genesis of his interest in American literature. One of the few voices that, in Fernandez's years, rose against this prevailing trend was Alberto Asor Rosa in his first book, *Scrittori e popolo: Il populismo nella letteratura contemporanea* (Rome: Samonà e Savelli, 1965; then Turin: Einaudi, 1988).

have thoroughly accomplished this. Among those written in English, the most comprehensive, and one that I have already quoted, is *The 'mito americano' and Italian Literary Culture*, by Jane Dunnett. When useful, other critical works will be mentioned in the following pages. Here, however, I will simply return to the fundamental point stated earlier—that is, the perception that the 1930s exhibit a different kind of interest in American literature.

In many ways, what had been simmering in previous years comes to the boil, and this is the recognition that America had produced a literary tradition that was not just worth the time of literary historians, but was contributing in a substantial way to the development of contemporary Western literature. This new perception was the result of developments within both American and Italian society, which in different ways had their effect on the two countries' literary production. When Praz wrote about Anita Loos's *Gentlemen Prefer Blondes*, in 1926, he alerted his readers to a self-critical turn among contemporary American authors. Their depiction of the 'American Dream' was becoming increasingly sour, and demystifying. The Wall Street crisis and the following Great Depression fuelled this process by exposing dangerous imbalances in the American economy and by bringing social inequalities to the fore.

Across the Atlantic and over the Alps, in Italy too one can detect signs of change. By the second half of the 1920s, Italy was entering a period of relative stability under the by-then secure dictatorship of Mussolini. We have already seen how the nationalistic policies of the regime—economic as much as social and cultural—began to promote a sense of self-confidence in Italy's status as a European nation. By the early 1930s, Roosevelt's New Deal's policies could be smirked at as an American plagiarism of Mussolini's economic 'battles' for the betterment of Italy. If we now zoom in onto the literary debate, one can see signs of changes there too. Praz's article was published in *La Fiera letteraria*, and this literary weekly itself, founded by Umberto Fracchia in Milan, in December 1925, and featuring from its first issue the collaboration of prestigious authors such as Pirandello and Ungaretti, was a sign of new things to come. As Fracchia stated in its opening editorial, *La Fiera letteraria* was a literary journal aimed at moving away from the past—the 'stupid and adorable nineteenth-century') and instead face Italy's boisterous cultural scene—hence the title of the journal—and address a mass readership while avoiding elitist tones.[34] Politics was outside the remits of the journal, but a symbolic bow to the government was presented in the most prominent article in the first issue: an interview with Mussolini's Law Minister, Alfredo Rocco, about the new legislation on copyright in the arts and letters. The symbolic description of the dusty nineteenth-century furniture of the ministry as against the dashing figure of the young and clear-minded minister was clearly meant to draw a political equivalent to what *La Fiera letteraria* intended to be in the cultural debate.

---

[34] Umberto Fracchia, 'Esistere nel tempo', *La Fiera letteraria*, 1 (13 December 1925), 1.

Another journal that signalled a change in Italy's literary circles is Ugo Ojetti's *Pegaso*, founded in 1929, in Milan again. In Chapter 2, we dwelt on Ojetti as a young literary and art critic travelling to the USA during the summer of the Spanish–American war of 1898. Since then, his promises as a journalist and critic had been maintained, culminating among other things in the directorship of *Corriere della Sera* in 1926. Mention of this introduces the political dimension of Ojetti's work. As a nationalist and an old friend of Gabriele D'Annunzio, Ojetti had welcomed the seizure of power by Mussolini, and, although never militant, had accepted various appointments that signalled his support for the regime. In 1925, Ojetti was one of the signatories of Gentile's Manifesto of Fascist Intellectuals. As we saw, at the end of that year, the director of *Corriere della Sera*, Luigi Albertini, had been ousted by the daily's owners because of his open opposition to Fascism. Because of this, the appointment of Ojetti as the first director of the new pro-Fascist phase of the *Corriere della Sera* carried an obvious political weight. Ojetti, however, was not at ease in the role of chief editor of a daily and left in December 1927, after less than two years. He returned to the gentler rhythms of his critical work and soon he founded a sophisticated monthly review on literature and the arts, *Pegaso*, printed in his adopted city, Florence.

If *La Fiera letteraria* had started with an impressive line-up, Ojetti's *Pegaso* did the same and confirmed his status as one of the most respected intellectuals in Fascist Italy. A quick scroll through the authors appearing in its first issue (see Fig. 7.3) shows that each one of them was an eminent figure in his or her field. Fracchia too appeared in it, in his less well-known guise as a novelist. Ojetti's contribution to the first issue was an open letter to Mussolini in which—through a blend of erudition and obsequious reverence—he repeatedly praised *Il Duce*'s wisdom in allowing the arts to be judged on their merits alone.[35] Instead, the task of setting the journal's tone was left to the prestigious pen of Giovanni Papini. His sardonic overview of contemporary Italian literature took no prisoners, but what is notable is, on the one hand, his initial identification of good literature with the French language (peppered with two citations in French) and, on the other, the crisis in Italian society as coming from the craze for sport, illustrated magazines, and cinema, which he associates with English-speaking countries. The essay concluded with a typical nationalistic tirade by Papini. This time the target was Italian intellectuals who had lost their way because of their exchange of 'Italic genius' for constant imitation of foreign fashions. However, while the conclusion one could have expected from such premises was that Anglo-American literature was to be avoided at all costs, Papini seemed to have forgotten about that side of his argument. Instead, he wrote: 'What is most toxic to Italian writers is the dominant influence of the French', somehow implicitly suggesting that even the craze for Anglo-American culture was a derivation of a French cultural trend. This final point by Papini was, probably unintentionally, mirrored by the review section of

---

[35] Ugo Ojetti, 'Lettera a S. E. Benito Mussolini', *Pegaso* 1 (January 1929), 89–92.

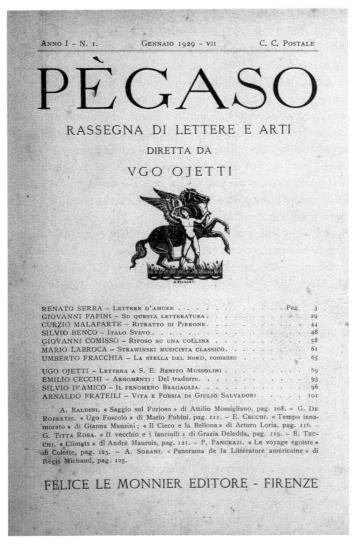

Fig. 7.3. Cover of the first issue of Ugo Ojetti's *Pegaso* (January 1929). (courtesy of Fondazione Alfred Lewin—Biblioteca Gino Bianco, Forlì)

the journal. Of the eight books reviewed in the first issue, three were French publications, one of which was Régis Michaud's *Panorama de la littérature américaine*. In other words, while Papini criticized Italy's dependence on the French literary scene, the review section of the same issue devoted almost half of its space to French publications and made the French–American connection explicit through the review of Michaud's book. What is notable about the latter is the emphasis on Michaud's appreciation of contemporary American fiction for the same reasons suggested by Praz in his article on Anita Loos. Here was a new generation of American writers who were producing 'a protest literature [...] a literature of non-conformity, of critique, sometimes of full dissatisfaction with America'. To this one should add that the first issue of *Pegaso* also included a short article by Emilio Cecchi on translation. Once again, the discussion started from a French precedent—this time an essay by André Gide in the *Nouvelle Revue française* of the year before—which Cecchi used to develop his own view of the craze for Anglo-American literature. The tone was a positive one, or, better, Cecchi criticized Italian publishers for the debatable quality of many hastily prepared translations, while at the same time he confirmed the importance of keeping up to date with recent literary production in English.[36]

Overall, both journals confirmed the signs of a new attitude towards American literature, a recognition of its importance, while at the same time reflecting on the mediatory role played by French culture. By 1929, the founder and head of Italy's biggest publishing house, Arnoldo Mondadori, had caught up with the trend. It is in this year that Mondadori moved in to create a new series based on the translation of mainly American crime fiction: 'I Gialli', an epoch-making series so popular that it ended up coining a new meaning for the colour yellow in the Italian language. By the 1930s, 'giallo' became a synonym for 'romanzo poliziesco'—that is, crime fiction—and both the series and the term's usage are still alive today. Determined to beat smaller publishing houses at their own game, Mondadori made full use of its printing powerhouse. Not only were 'I Gialli' published at the industrial rhythm of one every week: in order to maximize sales, Mondadori had them sold in newspaper kiosks all over Italy. The same sale strategy was adopted with another series of affordable paperbacks, created in 1932 and called 'I Romanzi della Palma'. Mondadori's commercial instinct left no stones unturned in targeting a clearly middlebrow market, dominated by female readers. The brightly coloured cover illustration taking up the entire surface, the low price clearly highlighted near the novel's title, the cheap quality of both cover and paper, the insertion of illustrations to accompany the story, all made these books resemble a closer relative to the illustrated magazines sold in newspaper kiosks than to anything that one would find in respectable bookshops. The series's first title promised sensual atmospheres with a translation of *Ex-Wife* (1929) by American author Ursula Parrott (embarrassingly misspelled with only one 't' on the Mondadori cover (see Fig. 7.4)). Its film adaptation, *The Divorcee* (1930), won the female lead, Norma Shearer, an Oscar, making the novel even more popular; unsurprisingly, a photographic portrait of the Hollywood actress dominated the front cover.

The use of photo portraits of beautiful young women, often Hollywood actresses, created a clear connection between this series of novels, the glamorous

---

[36] Aldo Sorani, 'Régis Michaud, *Panorama de la Littérature américaine*, Kra, Paris, 1928', and Emilio Cecchi, 'Del tradurre', *Pegaso*, 1 (January 1929), 125–9 (127) and 93–5.

**Fig. 7.4.** Front cover of the first novel published in Mondadori's 'I Romanzi della Palma' series, 1932. (author's personal collection)

world of Hollywood, and the many illustrated magazines that were battling for the new mass market of readers. Mondadori added a final touch by colour-coding the level of 'adulthood' of the plot through a coloured dot that appeared on the spine of each Palma novel, thus resembling the age limitation norms for cinema screenings: blue was for everybody, whereas a red dot categorized 'novels that should not end up in anybody's hands', as a note in the inside cover mysteriously explained. In 1938, conscious of its prevailing female readership, Mondadori created a third colour code: unsurprisingly, pink for women's novels.[37]

Once he had invaded the middlebrow market, Arnoldo Mondadori proceeded to create a more sophisticated series of foreign novels in translation: this was called 'La Medusa', and it started its publications in 1933. Initially, it proposed contemporary European authors: it opened with Alain-Fournier's novel *Le Grand Meaulnes* (1913), and, before it offered an American novel, it published three French, three German, and two British ones. The ninth title of the 'Medusa' series

---

[37] On Mondadori's 'Romanzi della Palma', see Enrico Decleva, *Arnoldo Mondadori* (Turin: UTET, 2007), 179–82.

was a translation of Pearl S. Buck's *The Good Earth* (1931). In February of the same year, Enrico Piceni, Head of the Press Office at Mondadori, director of 'I Romanzi della Palma', and editor in charge of translations from English, received a letter from a young Sicilian author offering his services as a translator. It was Elio Vittorini, who had by then settled down in Florence, where he worked as a contributor both to *Solaria* and to *Il Bargello*, the paper of the provincial Fascist federation, which its founder, Alessandro Pavolini, a rising leader of the regime, had turned into a respected publication. Piceni proposed the translation of D. H. Lawrence's *St Mawr* (1925), for the 'Medusa' series, which Vittorini completed with the discreet help of the already mentioned Lucia Rodocanachi. Vittorini's enthusiasm for both English and American literature grew to the point that a couple of years later he was employed by Mondadori as a consultant, often able to select the novels he would translate. It should be added that Vittorini's interest in translation was partly related to his financial situation. His correspondence at the time is full of remarks about his need to earn a living in order to support his family (his second son was born in 1934), and, indeed, he welcomed his first translations as a useful extra source of earning.[38]

Vittorini's first American translation was a collection of short stories by Edgar Allan Poe published under the title *Racconti e arabeschi,* in 1936. However, the American authors whose recognition in Italy was to a large extent the result of Vittorini's translations are William Saroyan, William Faulkner, Erskine Caldwell, and John Steinbeck. In 1938, he published translations of Saroyan's short stories in the magazine *Omnibus* and in *Letteratura*, the journal founded by Alessandro Bonsanti after the closure of *Solaria*, all of which ended up in Mondadori's 'Medusa' volume *Che ne sembra dell'America?* (1940).[39] Vittorini translated a short story by William Faulkner in 1938, followed by *Light in August* (1932), another 'Medusa' title that he had proposed in 1936 and on which he had been working since the following year. As for Erskine Caldwell, after translating some of his short stories, Vittorini worked on his novel *God's Little Acre* (1932), published in 1940, by which time he had started to collaborate with another publisher, Bompiani, and indeed the novel came out under his editorship for that house. Steinbeck too he translated for Bompiani, with the novel *Tortilla Flat* (1935) as their first collaboration in 1938.

Before we move over to Bompiani, however, it is important to tackle the question of the potential influence of American fiction on Vittorini's own literary

---

[38] On Enrico Piceni at Mondadori in the 1930s, see Antonella Di Spalatro, *Censura e politca editoriale: Enrico Piceni alla Mondadori negli anni trenta* (Rome: Lithos, 2021). On Vittorini, I refer to my monograph, *Elio Vittorini: The Writer and the Written* (Leeds: Northern Universities Press, 2000; London: Routledge, 2017), 21–34.

[39] The texts were selected from Saroyan's four collections: *The Daring Young Man on the Flying Trapeze* (1934), *Inhale and Exhale* (1936), *Little Children* (1937), and *The Gay and Melancholy Flux* (1938).

production. There is no space here for a detailed analysis, but the briefest answer would be that the influence is detectable in both style and content. Vittorini's interest in contemporary American fiction had a clear formal dimension. The dialogue-based, paratactic prose style around which Caldwell, as much as Steinbeck and Hemingway, notably based their narrative technique was absorbed by Vittorini, and it marks a stylistic watershed from his earlier work up until the mid-1930s. The development is so marked that it includes the revision of a novel that Vittorini had written in previous years.[40] Indeed, reviewers of his late 1930s and 1940s novels—I am thinking in particular of *Conversazione in Sicilia* (1938–9) and *Uomini e no* (1945)—regularly mentioned this, sometimes in praise, more often as a criticism.

Vittorini explicitly dwelt on this matter in an article he published in English, in the first issue of the *American Quarterly*, in 1949 (written during the months in which the English translation of *Conversazione in Sicilia* was about to be published). The focus of this piece is on the influence of American novelists on his generation. A number of writers are quoted, from Moravia to Bilenchi, Pavese, and others, after which Vittorini concentrates on an unnamed one whose description entirely befits Vittorini himself. At that point, the case about the influence of American fiction starts from a critique of the 'prosa d'arte' that was in vogue at the time, exemplified by the intricate yet flowing rhythms of Emilio Cecchi's prose style. The passage deserves ample quotation:

> One didn't write 'he said' or 'she said', but something like this: 'In a long whispering that seemed like the cheek of a cloud come from the farthest horizons of their infancy, he enveloped her in the following words...' [...] Something quite different was needed by our young writers. [...] They were getting notable results, when one of them, having learned English, began to translate and publish the short stories and novels of contemporary Americans in order to make a better living than he had been able to make as a workman. What American writers? Hemingway, Faulkner, Ring Lardner, Saroyan, Steinbeck, Cain, and Erskine Caldwell. [...] But it was on Hemingway that the attention of our young man was fixed, and on some of the functional qualities which all the Americans, independent of their artistic stature, seemed to have in common. [...] His translations, through which he was himself finally formed (like the Latins who were formed by translating from the Greeks, although living in Rome as romans), constituted a decisive factor in the Italian literary revolution of the years between 1930 and 1940. In them was finally found the authorization to write 'he said,' or

---

[40] This is Vittorini's first novel, *Il garofano rosso*, first published in instalments in 1933–4 and then revised for Mondadori in 1937–8. For example, Vittorini aimed at a simplification of the dialogues through the replacement of more sophisticated expressions with the 'American-style' repetition of 'he said', 'she said'. On this, see Raffaella Rodondi, *Il presente vince sempre: Tre studi su Vittorini* (Palermo: Sellerio, 1985), 132–35; and, in English, chapter 7 of Bonsaver, *Elio Vittorini*.

'she said,' as, once upon a time, the fourteenth century author of the *Novellino* had written and as Boccaccio had written—and it was a *modern* authorization. It was also an anti-Fascist authorization, in a certain sense. Just the kind that our young men needed in order to turn away from the last academic prejudices and welcome without further reservation the vital promptings of their rage and of their love.[41]

The final point in this passage deserves a comment: The idea that the influence of American novelists was somehow a vehicle through which Italian authors could regain the directness and simplicity of fourteenth-century Italian fiction writers is fascinating, although somehow odd in the fact that it was not adopted by other writers of his generation nor ever developed further by Vittorini. Perhaps it was more of a self-defensive comment to avoid the risk that contemporary Italian authors abroad would be judged simply as an offshoot of their American peers. Moreover, one should note that the final mention of the anti-Fascist dimension of an interest in American literature is left to a fairly emphatic but vague level, simply built on the assumption that, by going against dominant trends in literary circles, one would take a political stand too. More recent work on the period has shown that the situation was not as clear-cut. For example, an anti-intellectual element was present in Fascist literary as much as in political circles and, indeed, the early fictional work by Moravia and Vittorini had been praised by a number of Fascist journals at the time.

When it comes to the style of Vittorini's fiction in those years, I would suggest a dual influence, each detectable in his work of the 1930s and 1940s. When Vittorini wrote *Conversazione in Sicilia*, fresh from his disillusionment following Italy's intervention on Franco's side in the Spanish Civil War (for Vittorini, a so-called revolutionary Fascist, this was the ultimate sign that Mussolini had no intention of returning to his radical, near-socialist positions of 1919), contemporary American fiction showed him ways of being critical of his own country. The realistic mode could not be chosen for the simple matter of censorship, so Vittorini adopted and multiplied Saroyan's slightly surreal, prophetic register as a way to hide his critique. The result was one of the very few genuinely modernist novels produced in Italy's interwar years. When it came to writing *Uomini e no*, in the early 1940s—and by then Vittorini had made the decision to join the underground network of the Communist Party—the impression is that Vittorini had decided to move in the direction of a more complex, choral form of narrative, closer to the composite narrative structures of Faulkner's fiction. It was a move that was not to prove fruitful. *Uomini e no* was popular at the time because it was the very first novel about the Italian Resistance, published only a few

---

[41] Elio Vittorini, 'American Influences on Contemporary Italian Literature', *American Quarterly*, 1 (1949), 5–6.

months after the end of the war, in 1945. But its complex narrative technique never convinced its reviewers and readers. Vittorini too was never particularly fond of this novel. However, beyond its critical reception, it was a sign of his search for new narrative approaches, which his meeting with American literature had triggered.

As for questions of content, Vittorini, differently from Pavese, never invented an American setting; nor was America discussed by any character in his fictional work. The only, brief exception is indicative of his perception of America as something 'other' (he, too, had never been to America). In *Conversazione in Sicilia*, the protagonist is called Silvestro Ferrauto, a name that is symbolic of his identity crisis, split between his Sicilian, rural origin—Silvestro, as 'coming from the woods'—and the big, industrial city in the north where he has settled down—Ferrauto, a composite of 'iron' and 'automobile'. While travelling by train back to Sicily, in search of his roots, Silvestro meets a small family of Sicilian peasants, whose misery forces them to eat the produce of their land that they are unable to sell, oranges. Silvestro tries to connect with them by praising the cheese he is eating, saying 'no cheese is as good as ours'. The Sicilian husband, however, is unconvinced and comments that Sicilians never eat in the morning. After which a question follows: 'Are you American?' Silvestro reflects on the question, coming from a peasant who sees Silvestro's relative wealth as alien to his lifestyle, and resignedly answers: 'I'm American. I've been American for the last fifteen years.' What follows is a short conversation between the two, in which the peasant wants Silvestro to confirm his vision of America as a fabulous, rich land, whereas the latter is forced to run with his lie, but at the same time initially resists such a view by telling the peasant that not everybody is rich and that there is unemployment in America too. But the peasant insists, and Silvestro eventually gives up, the first-person narrative adding the following comment:

> I could have told him no, that sometimes even I didn't eat in the morning, and that I knew many people who didn't eat perhaps more than once a day, and that all over the world it was the same, but I couldn't speak ill to him of an America where I had never been and that, after all, wasn't even America, was nothing real, concrete, but his idea of the kingdom of heaven on earth. I couldn't do it, it wouldn't have been right.

Silvestro takes pity on the peasant's desperate need to believe in an opulent America and gives up his criticism. By implication, the vision of America as a land of plenty is a projection of desires rather than a factual reality. The *mito americano* is in the Italian mind, and Vittorini's protagonist does not share in its naïve, uncritical vision.[42]

---

[42] Elio Vittorini, *Conversazione in Sicilia* (Milan: Bompiani, 1941), 15–16, 19. On Vittorini's translations within the bigger picture of his entire generation, see Edoardo Esposito, *Con altra voce: La*

Moving back to the interwar years, if 1929 was the year of Mondadori's 'I Gialli' series, it was also the year in which one of his most valued managers decided to create his own publishing house, Valentino Bompiani. Coming from aristocratic stock—his father was an army general—Bompiani was employed by Mondadori in 1924 as a young, personal secretary, and quickly rose through the ranks to become an esteemed editor in contemporary fiction. That was the niche on which the Bompiani publishing house was to concentrate and prosper. One of his first commercial and critical successes was the humorous novel *Parliamo tanto di me* (1931), by a then little-known Cesare Zavattini, whom we will find later on as a writer in the comics industry and, more importantly, as a publicist with a keen eye on Hollywood cinema. As for American literature, we should note first of all that Bompiani had a good knowledge of English thanks to a long stay in Britain as apprentice manager at a Nestlé factory. Translations of American works appeared early in his catalogues: the first title was the 1930 translation of a travel book by maverick journalist and world traveller Richard Halliburton, *New Worlds to Conquer* (1929); this was followed by a non-academic history of the USA by American-naturalized author Hendrik Willem van Loon, *America: The Story of America from the Very Beginning up to the Present* (1927).

Incidentally, Valentino Bompiani was one of the protagonists in the publishing world of those years whose post-war memoirs were influential in the creation of the short circuit between American literature and anti-Fascism mentioned earlier. In his *Via privata* (1973), he would often dwell on his games of hide and seek with Fascist censors. Archival sources, however, suggest a slightly different story, closer to that of his old employer, Arnoldo Mondadori, who would cultivate his personal acquaintance with Mussolini in order to negotiate in advance the publication of books that would probably fall under the axe of Fascist censorship. This implied the occasional return favour to the regime, such as, for example, the publication by Bompiani of the two volumes of Adolf Hitler's *Mein Kampf* (1925), whose Italian translation rights were owned by Mussolini himself. The first of the two volumes was widely publicized when its launch in 1934 coincided with Hitler's first official visit to Italy.[43]

In any case, Bompiani's commitment to the publication of contemporary American novelists came at a later stage, coinciding with the beginning of Vittorini's close collaboration with him. This became a fully-fledged operation in 1938, concentrating first on John Steinbeck. Cesare Pavese was hired to translate *Of Mice and Men* (1937), followed by Vittorini's translation of *Tortilla Flat*. At the same time, Bompiani continued to publish lighter, non-fictional works by

---

*traduzione letteraria fra le due guerre* (Rome: Donzelli, 2018). All quotations from *Conversazione in Sicilia* come from the published translation, *Conversation in Sicily*, trans. Alane Salierno Mason (New York: New Directions, 1951), 12, 15.

[43] On the Italian translation of Hitler's *Mein Kampf*, see Giorgio Fabre, *Hitler's Contract: How Mussolini Became Hitler's Publisher* (London: Enigma, 2006). On Bompiani and censorship, see Bonsaver, *Censorship and Literature in Fascist Italy*, 129–36, 221–30.

American authors, such as Dale Carnegie's best-selling self-help book, *How to Win Friends and Influence People* (1936).

As for Cesare Pavese, by the time he was hired by Bompiani, he was already an established translator of American fiction. His first commission was part of the rush for translations of Sinclair Lewis's novels. Pavese translated his first one, *Our Mr Wrenn* (1914), which Bemporad published in 1931. What followed was the vastly more challenging *Moby Dick or the Whale* (1851), by Herman Melville, published in 1932 by Carlo Frassinelli, a Turinese printmaker and friend of his. In 1932, Frassinelli also published Pavese's translation of Sherwood Anderson's *Dark Laughter* (1925). Pavese then continued his American work with Mondadori, concentrating on John Dos Passos's work: between 1934 and 1938 he signed the translation of the first and third novel composing Dos Passos's trilogy, *USA: The 42nd Parallel* (1930) and *The Big Money* (1935). At this point, it might come as a surprise that, so far, almost no mention has been made of the Turinese publishing house with which Pavese is traditionally associated, Einaudi. The reason is that, like Bompiani, Einaudi also developed its catalogue of contemporary American fiction at a relatively late stage. Moreover, it never committed to it in a meaningful way.

Giulio Einaudi, son of Luigi Einaudi, a prominent liberal economist and senator, was part of the circle of young Turinese intellectuals that had coalesced around the charismatic presence of their Italian and Latin literature teacher at the Liceo, Augusto Monti. Pavese was also one of them. A former close collaborator of Piero Gobetti, whose outspoken opposition to Mussolini had ended in his self-exile and death in France, in 1926, Monti acted as a bridge between the early opposition to Fascism in Turin and the organization of underground militancy attached to the liberal, anti-Fascist association, Giustizia e Libertà, founded in Paris in 1929. Giulio Einaudi was 21 when he decided to create a publishing house, in 1933, and many of his collaborators came from his close circle of school friends. Their catalogue initially developed around non-fictional, scholarly works, much under the shadow of Giulio's father. Then, in May 1935, the publishing house risked being prematurely closed when its offices were raided by the police. An informer, who had an introduction into Turin's literary circles, had revealed the anti-Fascist activities of many of Giulio's friends and collaborators. Leone Ginzburg, the most militant among them, had already been arrested the year before as a member of Giustizia e Libertà and condemned to two years in prison (from which he still managed to exert his influential role as editor). But this time almost two hundred people were arrested and, among them, four key figures in Einaudi's editorial team. Giulio Einaudi and Luigi Salvatorelli were released a few days later with no charges, but Massimo Mila (more on him later for his interest in jazz music) received a seven-year prison sentence and Pavese one year in confined residence. The survival of the Einaudi publishing house was to a great extent the consequence of Mussolini's instrumental tolerance towards prestigious figures of liberal culture such as Benedetto Croce and Giulio Einaudi's father, Luigi.[44]

Contemporary American fiction entered the Einaudi catalogue only after the creation of the series 'narratori stranieri tradotti', directed by Pavese, in 1938. In that year, Einaudi also published Angelina La Piana's *La cultura americana e l'Italia*, a scholarly study on the interest in Italian culture of American literati in the eighteenth and nineteenth centuries. However, the first translations from English, by Pavese himself, were of British classics, first Defoe's *Moll Flanders* and then Dickens's *David Copperfield*. It was only in 1940 that, again in Pavese's translation, Einaudi published Gertrude Stein's first novel, *Three Lives* (1909). This takes us into the war years, the chronological span that will be the subject of our final chapter. Here, one can only note that, despite his keen interest in contemporary American literature, Pavese did not seem particularly committed to making this a distinctive trait of his Einaudi series. This is probably due to the fact that, in its early years, Einaudi remained a fairly small publishing operation, so that most of the translation rights for American authors in vogue at the time ended up in the more entrepreneurial hands of Bompiani and Mondadori.

Just as for Vittorini, though, it is important to consider the extent to which American fiction shaped Pavese's own creative practice as a literary author. The majority of critical studies on the subject point in the direction of language and setting, rather than narrative technique. Pavese's first collection of poems, *Lavorare stanca* (1936), is often picked as showing the clear influence of Pavese's American models. First, there is the focus on ordinary, mundane characters and their daily, small rebellions against their humdrum life, through alcohol, sex, violence. They remind us of Praz's description of Hemingway's characters: ill-fated people who ignore the anxieties of a Pirandellian kind. And similarly unsophisticated and colloquial is the language with which they are described, and the language with which they communicate. This is what Pavese explicitly found to be characteristic of Sinclair Lewis, in his first critical essays on contemporary American fiction, in 1930. The general malaise that Lewis depicted in the life of George Babbitt and that was a recurrent trait in the pre- and post-Depression literature produced by the 'lost generation' became a feature of Pavese's literary work too. 'Middle West e Piemonte' is the title of Pavese's following essay on Sherwood Anderson, and here the title itself makes explicit how Pavese saw a social parallel between America and Italy—as a result of modernity and urbanization—which had to find its literary equivalent.

---

[44] The identity of the police informer became known in the post-war years: it was Dino Segre, a popular author of risqué novels under the pen name of Pitigrilli. On Einaudi's history, see Gabriele Turi, *Casa Einaudi: Libri uomini idee oltre il fascismo* (Bologna: Il Mulino, 1990); and Luisa Mangoni, *Pensare i libri: La casa editrice Einaudi dagli anni Trenta Agli Anni Sessanta* (Turin: Bollati e Boringhieri, 1999).

Pavese's fiction in the 1940s was a repeated attempt to absorb the lesson of the Americans, from *Paesi tuoi* (1941) to his last novel, *La luna e i falò* (1950). In the latter, beyond the neorealist theme of Italy's civil war at the end of the Second World War, the protagonist's attempt to make sense of his life and of his relationship with the people and land in which he grew up, and the America he migrated to, is evocative of similar representations in American novels of the interwar years. The sudden explosions of uncontrolled violence, the ties to a land that is averse to human life, a sense of helplessness that characters embody rather than express in words—all this reminds us of the settings and plots by authors such as Caldwell, Faulkner, Hemingway, and Steinbeck. When the protagonist's memories take us back to his years spent in America, it is difficult not to read those pages as a homage to American fiction: at night, under the cold light of an indifferent moon, the American dream appears shattered by the cruel reality of a land where everything is temporary, fragile, dull, and grimy. It is an atmosphere that is reminiscent of the provincial California described by James Cain in his *The Postman Always Rings Twice* (1934), a novel that Pavese never translated, although in 1946 he confessed that Cain was the American author that had probably influenced him more than any other.[45]

Pavese's conclusion, when dwelling on the importance of American literature for his generation of writers, still rings true today:

> Those who didn't stop after leafing through the pages of a dozen or so of surprising books that came out from across the Atlantic, but shook the plant so that its hidden fruits would fall, and rummaged around in order to find its roots, they quickly understood that the creative richness of that people came not so much from the theatrical search of scandalous and, after all, easy social assumptions, but from an austere and already one-century-old aspiration to force the whole of daily life into language. [...] In other words, that culture seemed to us an ideal place to work, and to search, a hard-earned and hard-fought search, and not just the Babel of clamorous efficiency, of neon-floodlit cruel optimism that blinded the naïve ones and, spiced with some Roman hypocrisy, would have been accepted even by some of our provincial Fascist leaders.[46]

---

[45] Pavese's essay on Lewis and on Sherwood Anderson appeared in *La Cultura* (September 1930, and April 1931); both in *Saggi letterari* (Turin: Einaudi, 1951), 9–34, 35–50. Pavese's comment on Cain can be found in 'L'influsso degli eventi' (*La letteratura americana e altri saggi*, 222–3). Among the vast bibliography on Pavese and America, see Daniela Brogi, 'Tra letteratura e cinema: Pavese, Visconti e la funzione Cain', *Allegoria*, 64/2 (2011), 176–95; Fabio Ferrari, *Myths and Counter-Myths of America: New World Allegories in 20th-Century Italian Literature and Film* (Ravenna: Longo, 2008), ch. 3; Marie Kokubo, 'L'influenza della letteratura e del cinema americano nei personaggi di *Lavorare stanca* di Cesare Pavese', in Hideyuki Doi, Katsuo Hashimoto, and Takeo Sumi, Sobunsha (eds), *Per i sessant'anni del professor Tadahiko Wada* (Tokyo: Sobunsha, 2012), 5–23.

[46] Pavese, 'Ieri e oggi', *L'Unità*, 3 August 1947; then in *Saggi letterari*, 173–5 (174).

AMERICAN LITERATURE AND COMICS    281

This perception of the 'darker side' of American culture is linked in Pavese's writings to recurrent references to its musical output: the melancholic sound of blues, rather than jazz. Blues as a musical expression of a fatalistic acceptance of one's mortality, the loss of everything, enters Pavese's own writing, turning it into an expression of his own personal anxieties.[47]

At a more general level, one could wonder about the extent to which Italian neorealist literature was influenced by the American fiction of the interwar years. One of its protagonists, together with Vittorini and Pavese, is Italo Calvino. He wrote explicitly about his early discovery of American fiction and in particular of Hemingway's narrative technique. For a second time, this takes us to a chronological span that is outside the study of this book, so I will limit myself to a single consideration related to what has just been said of Pavese.

When Calvino sat down to write a novel about his experience as a Communist partisan in the mountains of his native Liguria, he explicitly chose to invent the story of a group of partisans who were everything but schoolbook freedom fighters. He also decided to move his personal experience on to a different level by focusing the novel on an invented little boy, Pin, who is confused, conflicted, and struggles to make sense of the tragedy surrounding him. In order to counterbalance this un-hagiographic representation, Calvino introduced the chapter on Commissario Kim, a committed partisan, which provided an ethical edge to the story. Only, when Calvino asked Pavese and Vittorini to read the first draft of the novel (all three were at the time working as editors at Einaudi, and Calvino saw his two older colleagues as literary father figures), both suggested he should eliminate that chapter. Calvino's preoccupations—he was then a militant member of the Italian Communist Party—convinced him to leave the chapter in, and, despite that, *Il sentiero dei nidi di ragno* (1947) was still criticized in some militant leftwing circles. Only in 1964, when writing the preface to a new edition of the novel, did Calvino admit that Pavese's and Vittorini's suggestion had probably been wise, but by then it was too late to change.

Beyond the anecdotal interest of this episode, I would argue that Calvino's representation of the partisan war followed a process of, let us call it, 'lost-generation Americanization' of the plot, whereby, despite the clear political and ethical dimension of the fight against Nazi-Fascism, all characters are somehow enveloped in an atmosphere of unease, of undefined but pervasive physical and psychological turmoil. Calvino's ragged partisans, with their idiosyncratic personalities and brutal manners, their daily lives filled with lice, dirt, and the odd, sudden spark of desire or hatred, are closer to the protagonists of, not just the

---

[47] In his study of the presence of jazz in twentieth-century Italian literature, Giorgio Rimondi dwells on Pavese's connection with jazz and blues music, which had come to him through his teacher Massimo Mila. Giorgio Rimondi, *La scrittura sincopata: Jazz e letteratura nel Novecento italiano* (Milan: Bruno Mondadori, 1999), 137–40. See also Franco Bergoglio, 'Pavese, Mila, Gramsci. Letteratura, jazz e antifascismo nella Torino degli anni trenta', *L'impegno*, 20.2 (2000), 40–51.

Spanish partisans of Hemingway's *For whom the Bell Tolls*, but also of a Caldwell or a Steinbeck novel than to anything Italian literature had produced in the interwar years.

Whether or not literary critics will continue to call it the 'decennio delle traduzioni', one can still argue that the interest in contemporary American fiction shown by Italian authors who were to become leading figures in contemporary Italian fiction makes the 1930s a different phase from the previous decade. This is a generation of writers whose own creative work was deeply influenced by American contemporary fiction. Moreover, the involvement of prestigious publishing houses in the 1930s as against the smaller and financially frailer operations of 1920s publishers elevated the critical discussion and circulation of contemporary American fiction. The young Calvino was one of the first to benefit from it.

## 7.4 The American Comics' Craze: 1932–1938

Up until the early 1930s, comics in Italy had a limited circulation, mainly addressing a children's readership. No Italian daily regularly featured comic strips, as had become common in other countries, particularly in the USA, since the late nineteenth century. The first Italian magazine for children to include the odd comic strip among pages mainly devoted to illustrated and full-text fairy tales and adventure stories was *Il Novellino*, founded in 1899. At the start of the century, comic strips became the dominant feature of the *Corriere dei Piccoli*, created as a Sunday supplement of the *Corriere della Sera*, but also sold separately. The front page of its first issue, of 27 December 1908, presented a full transfer of its American model: a page from the comic strip *Buster Brown*—then inserted in the newspapers of the Hearst group. The only difference, apart from the protagonist's name being changed to Mimmo, was the replacement of the texts in speech balloons with a rhyming couplet at the foot of each panel. Several cases of transfer followed, from *Happy Hooligan* (in 1910) to *Bringing up Father* (in 1921) and *Felix the Cat* (in 1926).

In the following years, comic strips began to appear in other dailies, mainly with weekly inserts dedicating one or more pages to young readers. The use of foreign comic strips—mainly British and American—was the norm, although a number of original stories by Italian authors quickly became popular and featured on the front page of *Corriere dei Piccoli*. One of them was *Bilbolbul*—an African child, present from the first issue—and *Il Signor Bonaventura*—the magazine's most popular character, a happy-go-lucky, Chaplinesque character introduced in 1917. The striking, visual characteristic of comics in Italian papers was the use of rhyming couplets, traditionally eight-syllable *ottonari*. It was a practice with its roots in the European tradition.

*Max and Moritz* (1865), by Wilhelm Busch, was a German illustrated tale which historians of comics consider the Ur-father of the genre. It tells the story of two children whose seven pranks and final punishment are narrated in rhyming, eight-syllable couplets. *Max and Moritz* was widely influential on early American comics too—such as *The Yellow Kid* (1895) and *The Katzenjammer Kids* (1897)— although both quickly moved to the use of speech balloons. At the start of the century, popular French comic strips such as *Bécassine* and *Les Pieds nickelés* were still using bottom texts, but in prose. *Corriere dei Piccoli* somehow merged the latest American production with the oldest tradition in the use of texts.[48]

According to Italian comics historian Leonardo Becciu, the literary dimension of bottom texts in rhyme was symbolic of a resistance on the part of the Italian press towards replicating the 'visual' and 'colloquia' dimension of American comics, and more specifically their speech balloons. It was an attempt to defend the privileged value of language and add literary dignity to a new medium that, like cinema, was perceived as an unsophisticated form of narrative.[49] This was the fate of all other American comics imported in those early years. Their Italianized names were *Arcibaldo e Petronilla* (*Jiggs and Maggie*), *Fortunello* (*Happy Hooligan*), *Checca* (*Maud*), and the already mentioned *Katzenjammer Kids*, which became *Bibì e Bibò*.

The condensation of dialogue and sounds in the original illustrations into a rhyming couplet at the bottom of the panel had the predictable effect of making those narratives rather stilted and more strictly pedagogical, since the third-person, rhyming narrative provided a moralistic frame to the tale. It could be described as a case of 'engineered' transfer. The *Corriere dei Piccoli* was to dominate the Italian market up until the early 1930s.

The Fascist regime tried to compete with it with the launch of *Il Balilla*, in February 1923, which by 1925 had become the children's weekly supplement of *Il Popolo d'Italia*. Its format was clearly modelled on the *Corriere dei Piccoli*, complete with rhyming couplets, which were kept until the mid-1930s. Its equivalent for girls was created in 1927, named *La Piccola italiana*. However, the dominant educational and political element of these periodicals was the cause of their scarce popularity.

In the meantime, the comics industry had developed in other European countries, taking the shape of children's magazines and so-called annuals, yearly publications collecting comics that had already been published in newspapers

---

[48] On the history of early comics, see Thierry Smolderen, *The Origins of Comics: From William Hogarth to Winsor McCay* (Jackson, MS: University Press of Mississippi, 2014).

[49] Leonardo Becciu, *Il fumetto in Italia* (Florence: Sansoni, 1971), 29–32, 179–96. It was only in 1939 that *Corriere dei Piccoli* opened up to the use of balloons in some of its strips, but always accompanied by rhyming couplets. And only in 1968 did the *Corriere dei Piccoli* fully convert to the use of balloons.

Fig. 7.5. Front page of a 1928 issue of *Corriere dei Piccoli*, featuring a story of Signor Bonaventura, its text in rhyming couplets below the images. (courtesy of Bernd Zillich, Munich)

and magazines, often concentrating on one single set of characters. In Britain, the development of the picture story and the cartoon in the nineteenth century had found its prominent place in both serious and comic illustrated magazines (most famously *Punch*). Equally, the comics market had been cultivated in particular by the Amalgamated Press of Alfred Harmsworth (the media mogul and future founder of the *Daily Mail* and the *Daily Mirror*), which became a dominant force, nationally and internationally, at the end of the nineteenth century. Its

Fig. 7.6. The head title of Lucio l'Avanguardista (Rob the Rover) as it appeared on p. 3 of *Jumbo*'s first issue of 17 December 1932. (courtesy of giornalepop.com)

comics, *Comic Cuts* and *Illustrated Chips*, both created in 1890, quickly adopted the American format of speech balloons and featured a combination of British and US imported characters.

Mention of British comics is relevant, since the start of a new phase in Italian comics began with the creation of a comic, *Jumbo*, launched in December 1932 by a Milanese publisher, which featured a combination of Italianized American and British comics. Indeed, the title came from the front-page story of Jumbo, a British comics' character (originally a friend of the very popular Tiger Kid). Even more interesting was the Italianization of another popular British character in the pages of *Jumbo*, Rob the Rover. In order to make the young protagonist's exotic adventures a source of national pride, the publisher, Lotario Vecchi, decided to change its name to Lucio l'avanguardista and had the drawings touched up so that Lucio would appear in a black shirt and would sport a Fascist salute in the story headline. The Avanguardisti were the members of the paramilitary Fascist association for boys between the ages of 14 and 18, so this gave a sense, not just of the political correctness of the publisher, but also of the attempt to place the magazine in a different market from *Corriere dei Piccoli*. If the layout of *Jumbo* was inspired by its rival, its self-definition as 'Settimanale illustrato per ragazzi' ('Illustrated Weekly for Boys') clearly marked the differentiation.[50]

As for the use of bottom text versus speech balloon, *Jumbo* followed the British practice of a combination of both. Rhyming couplets, therefore, were abandoned for brief prose narratives at the foot of the panel, and this added one more striking novelty to the magazine. The head title of *Jumbo* made it very apparent that Vecchi's source of inspiration had been the British magazine *The Rainbow*—again owned by the Amalgamated Press—which featured the stories of Jumbo and Tiger Kid.[51]

---

[50] An excellent history of comics during the Fascist period is Fabio Gadducci, Leonardo Gori, and Sergio Lama, *Eccetto Topolino: Lo scontro culturale tra Fascismo e Fumetti* (Rome: Nicola Pesce Editore, 2011). But see also Juri Meda, *Stelle e strips: La stampa italiana a fumetti tra americanismo e antiamericanismo, 1935–1955* (Macerata: EUM, 2007); and Caterina Sinibaldi, 'Between Censorship and Innovation: The Translation of American Comics during Italian Fascism', *New Readings*, 16 (2016), 1–21.

[51] According to Becciu, *Jumbo* reached a circulation of more than 300,000 copies (*Il fumetto in Italia*, 78).

Vecchi's early lead, however, was soon challenged by Nerbini, a small Florentine, family-run publisher. The father, Giuseppe Nerbini, was a socialist who had followed Mussolini in his interventionist turn and had become a militant fascist. The catalogue of their publishing house reflected this development. But it was his son Mario who became the protagonist of Nerbini's involvement and rose to a position of dominance in Italy's comics industry. Only two weeks after the publication of *Jumbo*, Nerbini distributed its new comic, whose title has a more familiar ring to it: *Topolino*. By then, Walt Disney's most famous character, Mickey Mouse, was rocketing in popularity all over the world following the launch of the first animated short films, first among them *Steamboat Willie* (1928) and *Plane Crazy* (1928). By 1932, morning screenings of Mickey Mouse's shorts had become a regular feature in cinemas all over Italy's main cities. Moreover, comic strips featuring Topolino had sporadically appeared in Italian papers too, more or less copyright-cleared. Nerbini's magazine, on its debut, lacked the legal rights to use Mickey Mouse's images (and, indeed, as Fig. 7.6 shows, the first drawings were an unsophisticated replica of the original), but a deal was quickly secured with Italy's representative of Walt Disney's comics.

Beyond featuring Mickey Mouse's stories, Nerbini's magazine was a more traditional product compared to Vecchi's *Jumbo*. It contained educational rubrics and full-text short stories plus the use of rhyming couplets in Mickey Mouse's stories (although speech balloons were later added to them). However, the popularity of Mickey Mouse—which in 1933 was also the subject of a radio programme on Italy's national radio called 'Le avventure di Topolino'—guaranteed the magazine's huge success. Nerbini understood that American comics, if more expensive to acquire, constituted the cutting edge, particularly in the subgenres of adventure and super-hero stories, both of which proved extremely popular among Italian teenagers. Nerbini's acquisition of the recently launched story called 'Tim Tyler's Luck' (1928) was turned into 'Le avventure di Cino e Franco' and from December 1933 it added to the popularity of *Topolino*.

Most American comics—Walt Disney's included—were distributed throughout the world by the powerful King Features Syndicate. Their representative in each country therefore had great influence on the development of the local comics industry. In the case of Italy, this was Guglielmo Emanuel, an experienced journalist, who had been a foreign correspondent for the *Corriere della Sera* during Luigi Albertini's years. Emanuel was one of the few journalists who had followed his director when Albertini had been ousted because of his anti-Fascist stance, and he resigned from the paper in November 1925. Emanuel then began to work for American and British press agencies, and, in the summer of 1931, he took up the role of director of the Italian office of the King Features Syndicate.[52]

---

[52] The date of Emanuel's employment at King Features Syndicate (KFS) is clarified by Mauro Canali in his *La scoperta dell'Italia: Il fascismo raccontato agli americani (1920–1945)* (Venice: Marsilio, 2017),

Fig. 7.7. Front page of *Topolino*'s first issue, 31 December 1932. (courtesy of Leonardo Gori, private collection)

One aspect that Emanuel recurrently touched upon in his correspondence was the fact that, in America, those stories were often published in dailies and were targeted at an adult readership. This could easily be seen through the romantic adventure stories, the odd sexual innuendo in the dialogues, and the voluptuous shapes of the female characters' physique. Oddly, despite Emanuel's attempts,

199, 233. At the end of July 1931, he was asked to replace Valerio Pignatelli, who had represented KFS in Italy since 1928.

those stories found their place in magazines aimed at adolescents, but could never break into Italy's dailies, apart from their young adults' supplements. In a sense, Italian adolescents in the interwar years went from being treated like children during the years of *Corriere dei Piccoli*'s near-monopoly to suddenly being thrust into the adult world with the adventurous and sensual stories of the American comics published in Nerbini's magazine. Whether this 'misplacement' was one of the reasons behind its wild popularity among Italian teenagers is an easy guess to make.

Thanks to his eager correspondence with Emanuel, Nerbini was able to secure the most popular stories produced in the USA. In 1934, he went on to create a new magazine that was to steal the thunder entirely from Vecchi: *L'Avventuroso: Grande settimanale d'avventure*. Featuring a full transfer of the latest generation of American comics—apart from the translation of the texts—it was an immediate success. The most famous character was Flash Gordon, created in January 1934 by Alex Raymond, and reaching Italian readers with the first issue of *L'Avventuroso* on 14 October 1934. In his case the name was initially Italianized as 'Gordon Flasce', but the awkward surname was dismissed a few issues later. Nerbini even dared to present a crime story series inspired by hard-boiled American novels such as Dashiell Hammett's *The Maltese Falcon* (1930) without translating its English title: 'Radio Patrol'. Three months after its debut, *L'Avventuroso* added another new American character that was to become a classic in the history of the genre: Mandrake, the aristocratic-looking lone investigator, always followed by Lothar, his charismatic, gigantic black servant. Mandrake kept his American name, although generations of Italian young readers (including the author of this book) were to pronounce it following the Italian literal pronunciation, hence something like 'Mandrache'.

Other weekly comics mushroomed in the mid-1930s, produced by Nerbini and other publishers, Vecchi included, who responded to *L'Avventuroso* with his *L'Audace: Viaggi-sports-avventure* (note the use of an Anglicism in the plural). Their popularity convinced even the Catholic Church—in continuous competition with the regime for the 'souls' of Italy's youth—to create its own comic featuring more morally appropriate adventures stories. This was *Il Vittorioso*, launched in December 1936, owned by Azione Cattolica, the Church's youth association. It would be too burdensome here to trace the individual histories of each one of them, but it will suffice to say that—as an example of the impact of the American 'craze' of those years—between 1935 and 1938, there were more than thirty weekly comics for sale in Italy's newspaper kiosks.[53]

---

[53] On the history of individual magazines, see Gianni Bono's encyclopedic work *Guida al fumetto italiano*, 2 vols (Milan: Epierre, 2003). On *Il Vittorioso*, see Ernesto Preziosi, *Il Vittorioso: Storia di un settimanale per ragazzi 1937–1966* (Bologna: Il Mulino, 2012).

AMERICAN LITERATURE AND COMICS    289

Fig. 7.8.  Front page of *L'Avventuroso*'s first issue of 14 October 1934, featuring a Flash Gordon story. (courtesy of Donald at annitrenta.blogspot.com)

One of them, curiously, was French: it was *Hurrah!* The reason behind this is that one of the most entrepreneurial publishers of periodicals in 1930s France was an Italian, Cino Del Duca. After creating a small publishing house in Milan—Casa Editrice Moderna—in 1929, which specialized in middlebrow fiction and periodicals (he was also to publish three popular comics: *Il Monello*, *L'Intrepido*, and *La Risata*), Del Duca decided to move his operations to Paris in 1932. There was a political motivation attached to this, since, as a former socialist militant,

Del Duca had never hidden his anti-Fascism, and this was creating difficulties for his business (whose Italian branch was to fold in 1941). In France he established another publishing house, similarly dealing in popular magazines and children's comics, and he managed to become a prime player when the 'American comics craze' hit France too. To a large extent, he did in France what Nerbini had done in Italy, and *Hurrah!* was the French equivalent of *L'Avventuroso*. Because of his Italian operations, Del Duca was also a competitor in Italy, although his attempts to distribute some of his French publications, like *Hurrah!*, met the opposition of Italian publishers, since it created the double publication of the same American comic strips, whose copyright was held by Del Duca for France while it was held by Nerbini or Vecchi for Italy.[54]

Nerbini also broke new ground in publishing annuals, called 'Albums', which presented comics in a different editorial format, often following the horizontal layout of the comic strips as published in America. However, his dominance in this first phase of the introduction of American comics to a readership combining both children and teenagers received a major blow when a bigger and even more dynamic publisher entered the frame. Similar to what had happened in the popular niche market of middlebrow fiction, this turned out to be Arnoldo Mondadori.

It is not clear when the negotiation started, but by March 1935 the director of Walt Disney Enterprises–Italy and Arnoldo Mondadori were ready to sign a contract that gave the latter the right to publish all comics strips created by the Disney company. It should be noted that, in the summer of 1935, Walt Disney went on a European tour, Italy included, with his brother Roy and their respective wives, so it might well be that, prior to travelling, the Disney corporation concentrated on revisiting its contracts in the countries Walt Disney was about to visit. Indeed, the tour combined a mixture of holiday and business. In Italy, Disney's arrival in Milan on 13 July 1935 was immediately followed by a trip to Lake Como, where the Disneys had been invited to spend a day with Arnoldo Mondadori at his villa on the lake shore. Subsequently, on 16 July, Walt Disney met the managers of Italy's leading music company, Ricordi, in order to sign a contract for the use in Disney's film productions of works by famous Italian composers. Rome was the next stop. There, on 20 July, the Disneys met Galeazzo Ciano, then Minister of Press and Propaganda, who accompanied them to Mussolini's private residence in Villa Torlonia, where they met the wife and children of Mussolini but not *Il Duce* himself.[55]

---

[54] On Del Duca, see Becciu, *Il fumetto in Italia*, 104–8. During the Nazi occupation, Del Duca joined the French Resistance and was later decorated by the French government with the *Croix de Guerre*.

[55] On Disney's Italian tour, see Didier Ghez, *Disney's Grand Tour: Walt and Roy's European Vacation—Summer 1935* (New York: Theme Park Press, 2013), pp. 69–86. Romano Mussolini, in a post-war interview, remembered meeting the Disneys as a child, at Villa Torlonia, but, indeed, he does not mention his father as being present. The text of the 1995 interview can be found as an appendix in Gadducci, Gori, and Lama, *Eccetto Topolino*, 403–7.

Business-wise, Mondadori's agreement was in apparent contradiction of the contract signed by Emanuel and Nerbini only two years before. Indeed, a compromise was eventually found so that Nerbini, on top of a generous lump sum of 300,000 lire provided by Mondadori, was allowed to continue to print Disney 'Albums', while the rights to the use of Topolino as the head title of a magazine and to publish any new Disney material was passed on to Mondadori. In order to make this patently clear, Mondadori founded an *ad hoc* company named Edizioni Walt Disney–Mondadori, which, in August 1935, took over the weekly magazine *Topolino*, now entirely composed of Disney comics. Displaying his industrial might, Arnoldo Mondadori then proceeded to flood the market with his own Disney albums, published every fortnight. His entry into this niche market and the development of a 'Disney craze', fuelled by the world success of Disney's first animation film, *Snow White and the Seven Dwarfs* (1937), had the effect of eroding the sales of other comics. Even Nerbini's jewel, *L'Avventuroso*, progressively lost its readership, and in 1943 was taken over by Mondadori itself.

The huge success of American cartoons between 1932 and 1938 caught the regime censors with their guard down. This was also due to the creativity of publishers, who quickly learnt to replicate and Italianize those exotic characters, adding whenever possible a reference to Fascism. This was not necessarily a cynical act: the published photographs of Mario Nerbini either in a black shirt or in the company of Fascist leaders such as Alessandro Pavolini—the most prestigious exponent of Fascism in Florence—are signs of sincere militancy. He could also count on the support of Giovanni Gentile, an equally powerful figure in the Florence of the Fascist years.[56]

Mondadori too had been supporting Mussolini and his Fascist squads since their first skirmishes back in 1919. The tension was not so much between Fascism and anti-Fascism as between the cultural expectations of a totalitarian regime and the commercial opportunities unleased by the discovery of a highly profitable new market—teenage magazines—which had been totally untapped until 1932. Naturally, protests from a pedagogical and moralistic viewpoint were raised in those years, but, if nothing else, they were stronger in Catholic circles than in Fascist ones, where the dynamism, violence and 'superman-ism' of American adventure strips were more likely to trigger enjoyment rather than scorn. Moreover, as mentioned earlier, both the Church and the regime had actually joined the frame with their own comics featuring 'American-influenced' stories and characters. This had created an Italian industry whose role went well beyond that of importing popular American comics. The competition among the many

---

[56] On Nerbini's political connections, see Gadducci, Gori, and Lama, *Eccetto Topolino*, 26–30, 142–5. In 1936, Gentile wrote to Mussolini to support Nerbini's plea for a meeting with *Il Duce* (p. 144).

magazines on the market was such that Italian artists and authors were asked to join in and create 'American-looking' replicas.

The case of the western genre is the most exemplary. Similar to what happened in the early years of cinema, Italian-made westerns were created *ex novo*. A notable example is that of 'Ulceda: La figlia del Gran Falco della prateria', written and drawn by Guido Moroni Celsi and making its debut in a Mondadori magazine in June 1935. Freely inspired by Salgari's western trilogy of 1908–10, it told the story of the daughter of the chief of a native American tribe. However, the real protagonist of the story became Vittorio Ranghi, a young and dashing Italian immigrant who had left his motherland to work in his uncle's Brasilian farm. The first issue defined him as a type of audacious Italian, like those 'that today's Italy has forged in little more than a decade'. As Fig. 7.9 shows, the very improbable move of the setting to South America did not prevent Moroni Celsi from taking full inspiration from orthodox western settings in the Far West, complete with the appearance of a Grizzly bear.[57]

This fostered the development of an 'Italian school' of American comics, particularly within Mondadori, which produced copyright-protected, in-house stories featuring Disney's most popular characters, from Mickey Mouse (Topolino) to Donald Duck (Paperino) and Pluto (Pippo). Moreover, the Mondadori comics needed extra material of the adventure story type, and, again, Italian artists and authors stepped in with their own 'American-looking' creations. Some replicated American types and settings (particularly with crime stories), others took inspiration from European middlebrow fiction, from Dumas's three musketeers to the adventure novels of Emilio Salgari, in order to add some Italian—sometimes openly philo-Fascist—flair to their stories. In all cases, however, the American style of cinematographic visuals and balloon dialogues dominated. Among them were two artists who were to become cult figures in the Italian comics industry of the post-Second World War years: Rino Albertarelli and Walter Molino. In 1936 Arnoldo Mondadori appointed Cesare Zavattini as editorial director of all his illustrated periodicals and comics. He too became involved in the writing of adventure stories set in exotic and even extraterrestrial places, two of which were turned into comics by Molino.[58]

The historic *Corriere dei Piccoli* eventually joined the American craze too and gave front-page prominence to the stories of Formichino, which one should probably translate as 'Mickey Ant', since the character, drawn by Florentine artist Roberto Sgrilli, was clearly copied from Disney's mouse and sported speech

---

[57] On the intentional vagueness of geographical and historical references in Italian western comics, see Matteo Pollone, 'L'anonimo fondale dell'avventura: Lo spazio astratto del fumetto western italiano delle origini (1935–1965)', *Between*, 8/15 (2018), 10–11.

[58] On this, see Gadducci, Gori, and Lama, *Eccetto Topolino*, 246–302; and Luca Boschi, Leonardo Gori, and Sergio Lama, *I Disney italiani* (Bologna: Granata Press, 1990).

Fig. 7.9. Copy of the twentieth instalment of the comics story 'Ulceda', by Guido Moroni Celsi, published in Mondadori's weekly *I Tre Porcellini*, on 16 October 1935. (courtesy of giornalepop.it)

balloons (see Fig. 7.10). Formichino was a lead comic character of *Corriere dei Piccoli* from 1936 to 1941, and it was so popular that it was resurrected in the 1950s.

The regime's relative toleration stopped almost abruptly in 1938. Comics were included in the raft of directives through which, throughout that year, Mussolini tried to regiment Italy's Fascistization once and for all. By then, the invasion of Ethiopia and the Spanish Civil War had made it clear that the honeymoon between Mussolini and America had come to an end, and the convergence with

294   AMERICA IN ITALIAN CULTURE

Fig. 7.10. Detail from the front page of *Corriere dei Piccoli* of 9 June 1940, featuring the 'Mickey-Mouse-inspired' character of Formichino. (author's personal collection)

Nazi Germany was dominating the political landscape. Voices against the crudeness and 'non-Italian' look of US-imported comics had also begun to dominate in Fascist circles. As head of the Ministry for Press and Propaganda (soon to be renamed Ministry of Popular Culture), Dino Alfieri expressed his disapproval of the 'American craze' in the comics industry when speaking to the Senate on 21 May 1937. He stated the need to move away from American models, and for the government to show a firmer hand in shaping the industry. It was, therefore, not a total surprise when the 1938 directives hit the comics industry too.[59]

As we will see in Chapter 10, despite his Fascist militancy, Mario Nerbini proved too small a player to resist the change. At the other end of the spectrum, Arnoldo Mondadori made full use of his long-established relationship with Mussolini. Skilfully, he managed to save his interests, to the point that Disney comics continued to entertain the Italian youth right through the years of open war against the USA.

---

[59] On the build-up to the censorial directives of 1938, see Francesca Mazzarini, 'Storia "non breve né facile": La "bonifica della stampa per i ragazzi"', *Storia e problemi contemporanei*, 28/2 (2001), 33–50.

# 8
# Dancing to Jazz on Fascist Airwaves

Italian Futurists loved jazz music, at least up until the late 1920s. They appreciated it as a 'primitive' art springing from the ancestral rhythms of the African American community—and this they shared with other modernist avant-gardes. But they also loved it as the sound of the New World, the 'cooler' jazz coming out of the modern metropolises in the north-east—Chicago, New York—played predominantly by all-white orchestras and danced in elegant ballrooms frequented by the upper classes. The tension between these two sentiments was not perceived as problematic, and it was not felt as such in America either.

Had the Futurists been the only channel through which jazz entered Italy, it would have remained an elite form of culture, much loved by avant-garde intellectuals, much despised by upper-class conservatives, and fully ignored by the rest of the population. Instead, jazz's syncopated rhythms became more and more popular, thanks to the new technologies of mass entertainment: film and radio. Going to the cinema had, by the mid-1920s, become a popular pastime, and the sound of jazz—and of its predecessor, ragtime—came to people's ears, most often inadvertently, through the accompanying music of the comical shorts by Charlie Chaplin and Buster Keaton, or through the first Disney films. The radio, particularly in Italy, remained an elite domestic object, but at the same time more and more people could listen to it in bars and other public places. However nationalized and controlled by the Fascists, the EIAR proved more than open to American rhythms, whether imported or home-grown.

Indeed, Italians did not just listen to jazz music: they played and composed it too. The availability of sheet-music versions and vinyl recordings allowed local musicians and bands quickly to catch up with the new fashion. Those living in the big cities added the odd encounter with American jazz musicians touring Europe: black musicians too, most famously when Sam Wooding and his Chocolate Kiddies performed in Milan and Rome, in December 1926, or when Louis Armstrong played in Turin on 15–16 January 1935.

There is also an Italian American connection. One should actually say 'Sicilian American', since migration to New Orleans was almost entirely a Sicilian affair—hence the contribution of the Italian community to the music scene in early twentieth-century Louisiana came specifically from that island. As already mentioned in Chapter 5, both the first printed sheet of blues music and the first vinyl recording of jazz were produced by Sicilian Americans. In 1908, Antonio 'Anthony' Maggio, barber, musician, and anarchist, heard an African American play a song on his guitar. Later on, Maggio composed a piece for piano based on that song and called it 'I got the Blues'. Its immediate popularity when played by his five-man orchestra at Fabacher's Restaurant in New Orleans convinced him of the need for a print version. Whilst Maggio's intrusion in the history of blues music remained occasional and derivative, a more central role was played a few years later by Dominic James 'Nick' La Rocca, son of a Sicilian immigrant who had played the trumpet in his village brass band back in Salaparuta, in the hills of western Sicily. Born in New Orleans in 1889, La Rocca was the leader of another five-man orchestra called the Original Dixieland 'Jass' Band, which moved north and made its name in Chicago and New York, finally recording the foxtrot song 'Livery Stable Blues' in February 1917. It was the first vinyl recording of jazz music, which was followed by other popular songs such as 'Tiger Rag', recorded in the same year.[1]

The still-debated question of the contribution of Italian American musicians to the development of jazz in its early years is beyond the remit of this book. More relevant is to assess whether this Sicilian–American connection played a role in the assimilation of jazz music in Italy during the interwar years. This topic too will be addressed in this chapter, followed by the overarching question of how the Fascist regime negotiated the popularity of jazz rhythms on its airwaves and in the dance halls of Italy's major cities.

## 8.1 Jazz from Above: The Futurists

In a short, autobiographical piece published in 1926, Filippo Tommaso Marinetti defined himself as follows: 'Marinetti was born in Alexandria of Egypt: he was given in care to a black wet-nurse who pumped black, Jazz-Band frenzy and boxer's stamina into his blood.' The two English expressions used by Marinetti in the original Italian ('Jazz-Band' and 'boxeur') reveal his uneasy relationship with that foreign language: in a similar way to other Italian intellectuals in the 1920s, Marinetti used the expression 'Jazz-Band' as a synonym for 'jazz music'; furthermore, the expression 'boxer' is adopted through its French loanword, 'boxeur', with the spelling adapted to a Francophone user. But, more importantly, this description is typical of the Futurists' enthusiasm for jazz music as a raw, explosive expression of vitality that they totally embraced.[2]

Marinetti was not particularly interested in music, and there is a sense that his recurrent but superficial references to jazz throughout his literary production in

---

[1] It was only after its 1917 recordings that La Rocca called his ensemble 'Jazz Band', conforming to the established form of the neologism.
[2] Filippo Tommaso Marinetti, 'La nutrice sudanese', *Le grandi novelle*, 1926; quoted in Rimondi, *La scrittura sincopata*, 72. The use of 'jazz band' as a synonym for 'jazz music' is noted, among others, by musicologist Luca Cerchiari in *Jazz e fascismo* (Palermo: L'Epos, 2003; then Milan: Mimesis, 2019), 13.

the 1920s are little more than part of the overloaded baggage of similes and metaphors with which he incessantly declared his urge to embrace modernity and dispose of any form of tradition. Jazz was an alternative to the norm in music, and it was also a Dionysiac invitation to let go, to let the instinct prevail. In Marinetti's *Vulcano*, a theatre piece that Pirandello's company staged at Rome's Teatro Valle in March 1926, the two protagonists look back at their passionate world tour and describe their love life as 'syncopated love like black people's dances!', their hearts 'still dancing the jazz-band of New York'.[3]

In *Jazz Italian Style*, Harwell Celenza informs us how, as early as 1913, an American journalist wrote an article in a San Francisco daily paper on the term 'jazz', oddly calling it a 'Futurist word'.[4] This, however, concerns the vague use of the expression "futurist" in America, rather than how the Futurists themselves perceived jazz music. The word 'jazz' does not feature in any of the early Futurist manifestos dedicated to music: neither in the 'Manifesto dei musicisti futuristi' and its appendix 'La Musica futurista. Manifesto tecnico' (1911), nor in 'Abbasso il Tango e Parsifal!' (1914), nor in the 'Manifesto della danza futurista' (1917). In the latter, Marinetti made only one passing reference to an American dance— 'We, Futurists, prefer Loie-Fuller and black people's cakewalk'—within a text that contained the usual welter of name-dropping, and described three types of Futurist dance that had nothing to do with jazz or its associated dances. Marinetti's passing reference to cakewalk mirrors that made by another Futurist artist, the painter Umberto Boccioni, in 1914: 'It is this passionate love of Reality that makes us prefer an American cakewalk dancer to hearing the Valkyrie, that makes us prefer the news of a day caught on film to a classic tragedy.'[5] So, where did this knowledge of the African American cakewalk come from? Once again, the answer is: Paris. As recently pointed out in the first volume of Laurent Cugny's monumental history of jazz in France, the cakewalk was made popular in France at the time of the *Exposition Universelle* of 1900. Indeed, in 1903, pioneering French filmmaker Georges Méliès made a film entirely based around this dance, entitled *Le cake-walk infernal*, featuring two black dancers. And in 1908 Claude Debussy published his suite for solo piano whose sixth and final movement was called 'Golliwogg's cakewalk'. Marinetti and Boccioni had both lived in Paris in the pre-First World War years.[6]

---

[3] Filippo Tommaso Marinetti, *Vulcano: Otto sintesi incatenate* (1926); in *Teatro*, iii (Rome: Bianco, 1960), 137–206 (177).

[4] Ernest J. Hopkins, 'In Praise of Jazz: A Futurist Word which Has Just Joined the Language', *Bulletin*, 5 April 1913, p. 7; quoted in Harwell Celenza, *Jazz Italian Style*, 28–30.

[5] Boccioni, 'Contro il paesaggio e la vecchia estetica', in Boccioni, *Pittura scultura futuriste*, 26–7; quoted in Harwell Celenza, *Jazz Italian Style*, 50.

[6] Cugny, *Une histoire du jazz en France*, i. 94–104. According to Mazzoletti, in the pre-First World War years Italy was almost entirely cut off from the first European encounters with American music, and, he concludes, 'the result was a delay of about twenty years compared to the rest of Europe' (*Il jazz in Italia*, i. 1 (see also pp. 16–20)).

The fictional New York memories of the protagonists of Marinetti's *Vulcano* are suggestive of a different story. The interest in jazz music was part of the Futurists' passion for urban nightlife, and the one led by the wealthy elite in New York was becoming more and more of a model. New York's roaring years, so vividly brought to life by the fiction of Anita Loos, Scott Fitzgerald, and others, were typically portrayed by the odd night visit to a jazz club or the frenzied excitement of the foxtrot being danced late into the night. Indeed, in the Futurists' capital cities— Milan and Rome—the arrival of jazz music was closely related to nightlife among the elite. Futurist painter Giacomo Balla was personally involved in the creation of a nightclub called Bal Tic Tac, which opened in Rome, in the winter of 1921–2 (its name sounding like a Futurist variation on the historic Parisian venue founded in 1904, called Bal Tabarin, which is also the source of the Italian loan 'tabarin', much in vogue in the interwar years, to indicate a cabaret-style nightclub). When jazz historian Adriano Mazzoletti interviewed the venue's bandleader, Ugo Filippini, the latter recalled the exclusive atmosphere, mixing young aristocrats and avant-garde artists, and an electric sign at the end of the entrance corridor which said: 'If you do not drink champagne, get out!'[7]

A few months later, another Futurist artist, Fortunato Depero (who, as we have seen, was to move to New York in 1928), opened a restaurant–cabaret space inside the exclusive Hotel Élite, in Rome, entitled Cabaret del Diavolo. Despite the Futurists' self-proclaimed rejection of the past, the venue was organized on three levels inspired by the three *cantiche* of Dante's *Divine Comedy*. Furnishing, wall paints, tapestries, and marionettes were designed entirely by Depero. These venues, however, did not play just American rhythms. When the Futurists staged their performances, their attraction to the mechanical noises of modern life would often lead to a deafening cacophony of sounds inspired by Luigi Russolo's Futurist manifesto, 'L'arte dei rumori', of 1913, which prophetically asked composers to open up to the mechanical noises of contemporary life.[8] In this respect, the drum kit and spectacular live performances were the defining elements of the relationship, if any, between Futurism and jazz. The drum kit was the rhythmic heart of any jazz band, providing a modern, machine-like, driving urgency to music which the Futurists found very appealing. The clownish movements and costumes associated with the cakewalk and with the theatrical gesturing of jazz musicians on stage struck a note with the Futurists' own desire 'to scandalise the bourgeosie' in their own performances.

---

[7] Mazzoletti, *Il jazz in Italia*, i. 56 (on how Filippini cut his teeth as a jazz musician in Paris, see also pp. 18–20).

[8] On Luigi Russolo, see Mark A. Radice, '"Futurismo": Its Origins, Context, Repertory, and Influence', *Musical Quarterly*, 73/1 (1989), 1–17 (6–14). The essay makes no connection between Futurist musicians and jazz, concentrating instead on the innovative contributions of Futurism's main composers, Francesco Balilla Pratella and Luigi Russolo.

The term 'jazz' made its official appearance in a Futurist manifesto in the 1924 essay entitled *La musica futurista*. Its author was Franco Casavola, a young composer who had enthusiastically joined the movement following an invitation from Marinetti in 1922. He presented it at the Primo Congresso Futurista, which took place in Milan on 24 November 1924, and it filled the first four pages of the December issue of the movement's monthly, *Il Futurismo: Rivista sintetica illustrata*. In its introduction, after declaring the ultimate sterility of all contemporary European composers—from Debussy to Stravinsky—and praising the creative role of the performer, Casavola identified jazz music (still awkwardly defined as 'Jazz Band') as an inspiring innovation, thanks to its emphasis on improvisation:

> Jazz Band represents today the practical—although incomplete—realization of our principles: the individuality of the voice of its instruments, which blend for the first time sound elements of different origins; the persistence of its bold and necessary rhythms constitute the basis of Futurist music. Let us give each voice, in singing, a liberating, improvising individuality: the new music will be born creating unexpected, inimitable relations, and it will be rich and profound like the soul of the crowd.

In the rest of the manifesto, jazz music is no longer mentioned, but what is worth dwelling on is how Casavola identified jazz partly with improvisation. He supported it as a liberating approach that would free European music from the shackles of traditional rhythms, traditional instruments, and fixed performances. Indeed, Casavola had contributed to a multimedia Futurist production at Bragaglia's Casa d'arte, on 2 June 1922. He was the composer of the music score for *Ballo meccanico futurista*, which included the revving sound of two motorcycles. This was closer to the Futurists' praise for industrial noise, which Luigi Russolo had developed into the production of *ad hoc* noise-making machines (called 'intonarumori'), for which he had also devised an appropriate music notation. Casavola's approach to music lent itself to the integration of Russolo's machines with traditional instruments. For example, 'Danza dell'elica' (1924), a ballet created by Marinetti for which Casavola composed the music score, was written for flute, clarinet, violin, kettledrum, and Russolo's wind machine.

All the same, Casavola did not become a champion of improvisation in his own creative work. He composed pieces featuring various syncopated variations, among them a song for piano and voice entitled 'Fox-Trot Zoologico', and an instrumental piece for piano called 'Tango viola', from the suite *Cabaret epilettico* (1925), which, halfway through the piece, moves to a syncopated melody in a major key, thus creating an appealing tension between the melancholic mood of the tango in a minor key and the syncopated sections, suggesting the feel of a ragtime.[9] Indeed, his reluctance fully to embrace a radical approach pushed him in the opposite direction. In 1927, Casavola decided to break away from Futurism and any form of experimental music and return to tradition. The result was an opera, *Il gobbo del califfo*, close to the traditional style of Pietro Mascagni, which was successfully premiered at Rome's opera house in 1929 before it went to Milan's La Scala.

On the whole, it seems that the relationship between the Futurists and jazz music was a peculiar one. On the one hand, there is no doubt that the Futurists were among the first Italian intellectuals to see jazz as a paradigm-shifting force in the world of music. Their involvement in the nightlife musical scene in Milan and Rome was equally part of the history of the arrival of jazz in Italy. At the same time, judging from the actual work of Italian composers linked to Futurism— from Pratella, to Russolo and Casavola—it is difficult to consider jazz as a form of music which was adopted and practised by them beyond the odd experiment or touch of syncopation. Casavola's 'return to order' in 1927 was also a rejection of jazz that somehow closed the door on the matter. Indeed, the honeymoon between Futurism and jazz did not survive for long after his departure.

Another front-line Futurist who broke ranks, in an even more spectacular fashion, was Anton Giulio Bragaglia. He was an avant-garde playwright, theatre-set designer, photographer, and filmmaker living in Rome (his father was then artistic director of Cines, Rome's leading film production company). Bragaglia was one of the earliest adherents to Futurism, publishing in 1911 his essay *Fotodinamismo futurista* (an invitation to use photography in order to represent movement), experimenting with film and promoting a number of events in Rome, particularly through his already mentioned Casa d'arte, which Bragaglia founded in 1918 with his brother Carlo Ludovico. Moreover, like Balla and Depero, Bragaglia too was involved in the management of a nightclub, La gallina a tre zampe, which opened in 1922 and whose band regularly played jazz. Once Marinetti had moved to Rome, in 1925, the two would often appear shoulder to shoulder, leading Futurist performances in all forms of art, often blending them in more or less successful ensembles. Both were also staunch Fascists. In the autumn of 1926, Bragaglia was a vocal contributor to the debate on Fascist art that took place in the pages of *Critica fascista*, demanding that the regime should get rid of the old generation and allow young artists to revolutionize the arts as the Fascists had revolutionized politics.[10]

Bragaglia's cultural interests tended toward the visual arts. However, in 1929, he published a book devoted entirely to jazz. Its cover, as can be seen from Fig. 8.1,

---

[9] I am grateful to composer Gioacchino Balistreri for his assistance in analysing the rhythmic and melodic characteristics of this interesting piece by Casavola.
[10] Anton Giulio Bragaglia, 'Lo stile è l'epoca', *Critica fascista*, 22 (15 November 1926), 417–18.

**Fig. 8.1.** Front cover of Anton Giulio Bragaglia, *Jazz Band* (1929). (courtesy of Museo Nazionale del Cinema, Turin)

did not necessarily suggest a critical view, with a caricature of a cheerful, black drummer in a dark tie. But its content, beneath Bragaglia's long narratives in lyrical prose, and his many asides discussing other forms of dance (about which he had already written extensively), boiled down to a condescending, racist attack on jazz music. On page after page, scorn is woven into the fabric of the book, denouncing the fashion for jazz as the invasion of an animalistic, degrading, Africa-originated form of entertainment that proud Italians should reject. The following passage is a good example of Bragaglia's 'Marinettian' prose-style, with its blend of xenophobic and pro-fascist elements:

> The poses of Anglo-Saxon snobism, the Americanism and the devilment of negroes, and the traditional Paris-ism, are still dominant, together with crazy orchestras. As a result, in these Fascist times, the degeneration which hides the aesthetic and pedagogic value of dance could no longer be tolerated. And today, calling for Italian dances, it is understood that feet will move in urban style, with elegance and class, without any kind of animal rage, not even when imitating animals.[11]

[11] Anton Giulio Bragaglia, *Jazz Band* (Milan: Corbaccio, 1929), 31–2.

What triggered such a publication? Musicologist Luca Cerchiari recently devoted an essay to the issue, and its title is self-explanatory: 'How to make a career by writing against jazz.'[12] According to Cerchiari, both Bragaglia's Casa d'arte and the Teatro degli Indipendenti (the latter created in 1922) were constantly at risk of becoming victims of the Fascists' imposition of law and order, repressively introduced after Mussolini's move towards a full-blown dictatorship in 1925, and regularly called for—when it came to Roman nightlife—by the Vatican. Indeed, in 1926 the Teatro degli Indipendenti was temporarily shut down and then reopened thanks to the direct intervention of Mussolini himself.[13] It is possible, according to Cerchiari, that Bragaglia might have been advised to show his allegiance to the regime with a publication that supported its nationalist vision. As we will see later, in 1928 a number of fascist journals had started a xenophobic campaign against jazz. In this respect, Bragaglia's *Jazz Band* was a welcome contribution to it. No documentary evidence supports this interpretation, but there does not seem to be any other explanation, and, Cerchiari adds, it is probably not by chance that, in later years, Bragaglia benefited from a number of official appointments. These peaked with the directorship in 1937 of the Teatro delle Arti, a newly created theatre in Rome financed entirely by the government (it was housed within a building owned by the Corporazione dello spettacolo), which Bragaglia headed until the fall of the regime. Whatever the reason behind it, it is difficult to disagree with Cerchiari that Bragaglia's *Jazz Band* is a surprising publication, 'unusual and, to today's eyes, ridiculous.'[14]

Marinetti's cultural–political trajectory in the 1930s was similar to that of Bragaglia, if on a different scale. In the same year of the publication of Bragaglia's *Jazz Band*, Marinetti accepted appointment to the aristocratic circle of the first thirty members of the newly formed Reale Accademia d'Italia. This was in itself an extraordinary volte-face on the part of an avant-garde intellectual whose image had been built entirely on his rejection of tradition, famously urging the destruction of academies and museums. Marinetti took it as recognition of his historical role in the 'Fascist revolution', and this probably made him more prone towards accepting Mussolini's expectation of a more nationalistic and autarchic approach. The result was an increasingly acritical adherence to Fascist cultural policies. With regard to music, the Italian dimension of the origin of jazz never played a

---

[12] Luca Cerchiari, 'How to Make a Career by Writing against Jazz: Anton Giulio Bragaglia's *Jazz Band* (1929)', *Forum Italicum*, 49/2 (2015), 462–73. Mazzoletti too suggests a similar motivation behind Bragaglia's sudden jazz-phobic stance (*Il jazz in Italia*, i. 186–8).

[13] On this, see Patricia Gaborik, *Mussolini's Theatre: Fascist Experiments in Art and Politics* (Cambridge: Cambridge University Press, 2021), 99–100.

[14] Cerchiari, *Jazz e fascismo*, 116. In Bragaglia's defence, it should be said that his closeness to government circles and his attacks on jazz did not prevent him from continuing his promotion of contemporary theatre, which included work by American playwrights such as Eugene O'Neill and Thornton Wilder, even in the late 1930s, when anti-Americanism was official policy. On Bragaglia and American theatre, see Gaborik, *Mussolini's Theatre*, 96, 111, 165–7.

part in Marinetti's appreciation; hence, when the regime's racist tendencies became more and more official policy, Marinetti fell in line and expressed his regret for having once liked 'negro rhythms'. His first formulation of these new sentiments appeared in a 1934 manifesto, this time written together with musician Aldo Giuntini and entitled 'Manifesto futurista dell'aeromusica: Sintetica geometrica e curativa' ('Futurist Manifesto of Aeromusic: Synthetic Geometric and Therapeutic'). In its pages, the two authors colourfully condemned what was left of the popularity of jazz music, devoting to it a specific entry in the manifesto:

> (e) we condemn the imitation of jazz and of black music, by now killed by rhythmic uniformity and by the absence of inspired composers, a long Puccinian lamentation asthmatically broken up by punches and syncopated tam-tams of trains and railtracks.[15]

The passing reference to Giacomo Puccini is somehow obscure, since, although the composer's attention to jazz was known—we mentioned it in Chapter 4 and will return to it later on in these pages—it is difficult to imagine how Italian jazz could be defined as a 'Puccinian lamentation'.[16]

However, it was in 1937 that Marinetti's U-turn was completed, with a manifesto the title of which was explicit: 'Contro il teatro morto. Contro il romanzone analitico. Contro il negrismo musicale' ('Against Dead Theatre. Against Long Analytical Novels. Against Musical Negroism'). Co-authored with Futurist playwright Bruno Corra, the manifesto clearly showed its political allegiances by mentioning Mussolini three times within the first ten lines. This in itself was something of a novelty within the 'genre' of Futurist manifestos. When it came to music, Marinetti admitted his own youthful error, in his usual pyrotechnic prose style:

> In order to create space for living Italian musicians and living creators of home-grown comedy, we fight both the lugubrious humour with its black pills coming from the North and the funereal asthma of what could be called musical negroism, an obstinate moaning melopoeia, syncopatedly broken up by piston-like songs and dances for which we had hopes twenty-five years ago but which we no longer believe can let originality flourish.
>
> Instead, the weight of gloomy monotony oppresses the halls of nightclubs and luncheon dances, where everybody feels suicidal whenever the band leader, believing he is a new man because he is not using his baton, abandons himself to

---

[15] Filippo Tommaso Marinetti and Aldo Giuntini, 'Manifesto futurista dell'aeromusica: Sintetica geometrica e curativa', *Stile futurista*, 1/2 (August 1934), 1–4.

[16] Perhaps Marinetti was thinking of concessions to jazz by Puccini, such as the presence of a scoring for saxophone in his 1923 opera *Turandot*.

neurasthenic gestures with pederastic hands in order to manufacture mechanically false gaiety among the musicians.
Enough enough enough.
Better better cry hooray and bring on the tarantella played by the virile musical instruments from the Gulf of Naples.[17]

At a closer look, even the language of the manifesto reveals the inner contradictions of Marinetti's new stance. Given the Futurists' glorification of the machine, it is ironic that he should ridicule jazz while describing its music as 'piston-like' and its musicians' smile as 'mechanically manufactured'—that is, using a lexis that Futurists traditionally associated with positive values. Equally, the final praise of traditional folk music seems almost tongue-in-cheek, given Marinetti's much-repeated disdain for forms of popular culture that projected a clichéd image of Italy. Was he trying to suggest that his anti-jazz stance was only a veiled bow to the regime's cultural policies? Whether or not Marinetti was sending a cryptic message to his disciples or, as Pier Paolo Pasolini cruelly opined, he was simply revealing his lack of intelligence, there is little doubt that he had decided that jazz music could no longer be listed as a 'Futuristic' product of modern life.[18]

The 1930s saw the Futurists follow the Fascist regime in its growing intolerance of American culture. However, the syncopated rhythms introduced by jazz musicians continued to be popular in Italy's dance halls and on its airwaves, thus showing that the popularity of jazz went far beyond the Futurists' early enthusiasm.

## 8.2 From Ballrooms to Airwaves: The Fortunes of Jazz in the Interwar Years

One American witness to Rome's nightlife in the early 1920s was none other than Francis Scott Fitzgerald. He was there for two weeks in June 1921 and then for a whole three months in the winter of 1924–5. The second stay is the one of more interest to us. From his base on the French Riviera, where he had moved in April 1924 in order to finish *The Great Gatsby*, Fitzgerald drove to Rome, together with wife Zelda and daughter Scottie. The plan was to spend a 'warm quiet economical winter in Rome' in order to save on their lavish expenses and to rest after the tension of finishing his major novel.[19] They stayed first at the Hotel Quirinale on the

---

[17] This manifesto was published in *La Gazzetta del Popolo*, 22 October 1937, p. 3.
[18] Pier Paolo Pasolini's trenchant comment on Marinetti can be found in 'Alcuni poeti', *Tempo illustrato*, 5 April 1974; then in Pasolini, *Descrizioni di descrizioni* (Turin: Einaudi, 1979), 190–1. On jazz and Futurism, see also David Chapman, *Jazz italiano: A History of Italian Syncopated Music 1904–1946* (Newcastle upon Tyne: Cambridge Scholars Publishing, 2018), 20–30.
[19] The quotation comes from the autobiographical and posthumously published short story that Fitzgerald devoted to his stay in Rome: 'The High Cost of Macaroni', *Interim*, 4/1–2 (1954), 3–15 (6); quoted in Caterina Ricciardi, 'Scott Fitzgerald in Rome', *RSA Journal*, 10 (1999), 29–46 (36).

Via Nazionale (about a hundred yards from Bal Tic Tac) and then at the Hotel des Princes near Piazza di Spagna. The fact that in those months the American film crew of the Hollywood runaway production of *Ben Hur* was also in town meant that Fitzgerald's nightlife was not as quiet as predicted, although, in his correspondence, he repeatedly expressed his low opinion about what little night entertainment Rome could offer.

On 20 December 1924, at the end of an alcohol-fuelled night out, Fitzgerald got into a quarrel with a taxi driver and eventually punched a by-stander who was trying to calm the situation and who turned out to be a policeman in civilian clothing. Fitzgerald was treated to a police beating—these were the months between the assassination of Socialist MP Giacomo Matteotti, in Rome, and Mussolini's eventual resorting to dictatorship with his parliamentary speech of 3 January 1925, and so tension among police forces must have been very high—and spent a few hours in an Italian jail. This autobiographical episode was later fictionalized in a short story and occupied two chapters of his last novel, *Tender is the Night* (1934). In the latter, the narrative describes the protagonist's visit to a nightclub before the incident happened. The place is called Bonbonieri, which is likely to refer to La Bombonnière, a Roman nightclub open in those years in Via del Pozzetto, near the Trevi Fountain. As regards music, Fitzgerald briefly introduces the figure of the band's leader, described by the narrative voice as a 'Bahama negro' whom the protagonist, already drunk, treats with disrespect. Strangely, though, Fitzgerald decides to describe the band as playing a waltz when the protagonists enter and not an American dance.

According to Mazzoletti, some of the key iconic figures of early jazz in Italy played at the La Bombonnière in the early 1920s, such as the Italians Ugo Filippini and Mario Escobar, and the Americans Mons Smith and Jocelyn Frisco Bingham. Among the musicians who played in Filippini's bands in the early 1920s there was Jack Russell, a clarinettist from the Caribbeans. Given that Russell was famous for his musical talents as much as for his heavy drinking, it is a possibility that Fitzgerald might have met him and subsequently used him as a model for his musician at the Bonbonieri.[20]

Beyond the anecdotal value of this episode—and despite its scant information about the musical scene—I chose to dwell on it at the start of this section since it touches upon a number of aspects that are central to a discussion of the circulation of jazz in interwar Italy. Like Bal Tic Tac, La Bombonnière opened in the winter of 1921–2, and this indicates that the Futurists were part of a general trend, with new venues mushrooming all over the historic quarters of the capital,

---

[20] The Bonbonieri episode unfolds in chapters 22 and 23 of part II in *Tender is the Night*. On this, see also Kirk Curnutt, 'Of Mussolini and Macaroni: Hemingway, Fitzgerald, and Expatriate "Italianicity"', in Rena Sanderson (ed.), *Hemingway's Italy: New Perspective* (Baton Rouge, LA: Louisiana State University Press, 2005), 75–89. For reference to jazz at the Bombonnière, see Mazzoletti, *Il jazz in Italia*, i. 56, 63–4, 67–75; on Jack Russell, pp. 122–3.

Fig. 8.2. Ugo Filippini's Black & White Jazz Band in a photograph taken at Rome's La Bombonnière, in October 1922; Filippini is standing on the far left. (courtesy of Adriano Mazzoletti, Rome)

catering for the entertainment of the upper classes, as indicated by the fact that many of them were housed in top-class hotels. In her then popular 1925 travel book on Rome, American author Clara Laughlin, when dropping a tip about the best place to listen to American dance music, suggested a visit to the exclusive Hôtel de Russie, whose celebrated jazz band also routinely played at the Grand Hotel at Rocca di Papa, in the Alban hills, south of the city.[21]

The French name of the venue referred to by Scott Fitzgerald, and the presence of foreign musicians, are also symbolic of, once again, the role of Paris as a beacon of new fashions, and of the transnational dimension of the dissemination of jazz in Europe, which, from the start, saw the circulation of musicians of different nationalities, mainly toing and froing between the northern capitals of Europe: Paris, for sure, but equally important were London and Berlin. Italy's main cities, even the northern and more progressive Turin and Milan, played a secondary role, often featuring only at the end of the European tour of American jazz bands, and always for no more than a day or two. But those contacts with the big northern European metropolises, however sporadic, proved vital.

Moreover, Scott Fitzgerald's mention of a jazz band playing a waltz can be seen as a warning about the need to define what was understood then as 'jazz music'. As Italian jazz historians agree, the so-called hot jazz played in New Orleans, which gave ample space for improvisation by individual instruments, was mainly

---

[21] Clara Laughlin, *So You're Going to Rome!* (Cambridge, MA: Riverside Press, 1925; repr. 1928), 355–6.

unknown in the 1920s. To Italian musicians, jazz largely meant the new, syncopated rhythms coming from America through a number of recordings and a few concerts by mainly white American bands that had started to tour Europe. Some of them were formed by musicians who had served in the Army and were part of that first wave brought by US Army bands, which allowed them to stand out from their European counterparts. Any melody could be turned into a syncopated, 'jazzy' tune. We have already mentioned Casavola's 1925 tango, which cleverly moved in and out of a syncopated melody. Another story of musical metamorphosis concerns a slow, melancholic tango, composed in 1928 by an Italian pianist working in a Viennese band. The song is recognized today as a jazz classic: 'Just a Gigolo'. Leonello Casucci wrote the music, Austrian librettist Julius Brammer added the lyrics, and the song—'Schöner Gigolo, Armer Gigolo'—became popular all over Europe. However, when it reached America, the lyrics were rewritten (not just translated, given that the Hussars' officer of the original text was conveniently turned into a decorated army veteran from the French army) and the song was performed in 1931 by Bing Crosby and, more importantly, by Louis Armstrong. The latter decided to double its tempo, turning its second half into a typical one-step, and since then it has become an iconic jazz piece, peaking—and here the circle somehow closes with an Italian American end—when Louie Prima turned it into a juke-box hit in 1954.[22]

All this is to say that what defined the sound of jazz bands in 1920s Europe was mainly their syncopated rhythms, which opened up a whole spectrum of different dance styles. It was a tempo hammered by the beating heart of each jazz band, its drum kit, while the melodies were enriched by those shining new instruments coming from America, the banjo and the saxophone. If musicians went to jazz venues in order to listen and understand as much as possible about the techniques used by more experienced players, most of the public were there to dance. And for this reason the odd tango and waltz had to be part of the repertoire of bandleaders, no matter how popular the foxtrot had become. And popular it was. Memories of the First World War were still fresh when, in February 1920, the illustrated magazine of Rome's main daily, *La Tribuna*, devoted an entire page to the new fashion: 'fox-trott', as they spelled it. The title of the article (see Fig. 8.3) defined it as 'supreme dance!', its illustration taught its main steps, and the text hailed it as a 'sporty' dance, with quotes from a French magazine's interview with the popular singer and dancer Mistinguett, who confirmed its fame in Paris.[23]

The foxtrot came from pre-First World War America, and it was initially danced to ragtime tunes. As already mentioned, to most Europeans, jazz was understood as the well-orchestrated, improvisation-free, syncopated, foxtrots by all-white orchestras. Paul Whiteman conducted the most popular one, which

[22] On 'Just a Gigolo', see Mazzoletti, *Il jazz in Italia*, i. 92; and Harwell Celenza, *Jazz Italian Style*, 65.
[23] Geppi Cipriani, 'Fox-trott, ballo sovrano!', *La Tribuna illustrata*, 28/8 (22–9 February 1920), 6.

Fig. 8.3. 'Fox-trott, ballo sovrano!', article in Rome's *La Tribuna illustrata*, 22–9 February 1920. (courtesy of Digiteca, BSMC, Rome)

carried his name and surname (an odd surname for a musician who became famous for domesticating jazz as played by Louisiana's black musicians). Many of the songs Whiteman recorded became great hits, which entered the repertoire of jazz bands all over Europe, such as 'Whispering', first recorded in 1920, or 'Mississippi Mud', whose 1928 version saw his orchestra feature the trio of the Rhythmic Boys, led by Bing Crosby. The song gained visual fame in the 1930 iconic film *King of Jazz*, which celebrated Whiteman's status as a musician. Indeed, the title refers to Whiteman himself, as he was often so called by journalists, although most jazz historians today are keen to clarify that he was more a great bandleader who made jazz music popular and was open to other genres too. Undoubtedly, his place in music history is assured by his commission of an orchestral piece for jazz band and piano by the then young George Gershwin. The result was *Rhapsody in Blue*, which Whiteman premiered in New York on 12 February 1924, with Gershwin at the piano.

Nightlife entertainment and dance were associated with jazz in its 'straight' version played by orchestras in the north-east, and so it was in Italy too—hence the connection with nightclubs in all the big cities of central and northern Italy. The south of the peninsula, despite the key contribution by Sicilian migrants to the origins of jazz in Louisiana, remained more faithful to the traditional rhythms and venues closer to the model of waltz-dominated, nineteenth-century Viennese dance halls. Indicative of this is the fact that, if the first jazz magazine published in Italy, in 1926, was *Jazz Band*, edited in Venice by musician Augusto Febeo, and mainly dedicated to the promotion of Italian bands and to vinyl recordings, its almost homonymous *Il Jazz Band*, founded in the Apulian city of Bari the following year, was a literary magazine solely collecting short stories set in the sensual underworld of nightclubs. The first story in the first issue, predictably entitled 'Jazz Band', was authored by Mura (Maria Volpi), the popular Milanese author of middlebrow fiction whose 1934 novel, *Sambadù amore negro*, was to trigger a radical shake-up in Fascist censorship. 'Jazz Band' is somehow related to the novel, since it similarly depicts a—in this case only potential—love story between an Italian woman and a charismatic African American. The protagonist, Nellina, dances passionately with him to the rhythm of foxtrots and charlestons, only to realize later that he is the star of the evening, as he tells her before walking on stage: 'Jazz, Miss Nellina: I am the celebrity fresh from Paris.'[24]

As Mura's story reminds us, the foxtrot was not the only dance associated with jazz. Others became fashionable at different times, such as the shimmy, the Charleston, and the black bottom. The foxtrot, however, remained the most popular throughout the interwar years. Its popularity and the beginning of its circulation among all social classes are suggested by a short article published in the *Corriere della Sera* on 13 September 1921. It reported an episode of small crime related to a brawl at a dancing venue. What is interesting to us, however, are the introductory lines of the article, which describe the venue as organized by a socialist association and frequented by 'young workers and proletarian girls' who were there to dance the foxtrot.[25]

---

[24] Mura, 'Jazz Band', *Il Jazz Band*, 1 (January 1927), 8–9.

[25] Anon., 'Aggrediti dopo il ballo', *Corriere della Sera*, 13 September 1921, p. 5; see Mazzoletti, *Il jazz in Italia*, i. 44. The popularity of the foxtrot was to last until the arrival of rock'n'roll: symbolically, when Decca distributed Bill Haley and his Comets' greatest hit, 'Rock around the Clock', in 1954, the song was labelled on the vinyl itself as 'Fox Trot'.

**Fig. 8.4.** Front cover of the music sheet of 'Villico Black Bottom', a song composed by Dino Rulli and C. Bruno, 1928. (author's personal collection)

Another example of the popularity of American dances is related to a song composed by Dino Rulli—a prolific composers of popular music (we have already encountered his 'Josephine-Black Bottom' in Chapter 6). In 1928 Rulli composed the music for another 'America-inspired' song, this time entitled 'Villico Black Bottom'. The lyrics tell the story of a provincial Italian village taken over by the craze for black-bottom dancing, starting with the image of a shepherd who has ditched his flute for a saxophone (as illustrated in the song's music sheet), followed by women wearing sexy clothes and ending with the following lines: 'With this American disease | everywhere has become a nightclub.'

A key figure in the arrival of jazz in Italian nightclubs was Arturo Agazzi, better known with his art-name Mirador, which he also used to name his venues and bands. Mirador had worked in the nightclub industry of 1910s London, eventually becoming an impresario. There he witnessed many performances by American jazz musicians and was able to bring some to Milan, after he had moved there in 1918. A jazz enthusiast, he was also a skilled drummer, although he preferred to take a back seat and organize events rather than be involved in the nitty gritty of hours of live playing on stage (he features in the photograph taken at

La Bombonnière in 1922 (Fig. 8.2): he is the one in the background, on the right of Filippini). Mirador's first Milanese venue opened in December 1918: it was near Sempione Park and carried his name. It featured a quintet that included three Americans—violinist Eddie Solloway and pianists Mons Smith and Mary Smith (they were a married couple). During that winter of 1918–19, the city of Milan not only offered the first jazz venue in Italy; it also featured the first dance school to advertise lessons in foxtrot and one-step. The fact that, by the winter of the following year, jazz and foxtrot had become so popular that they deserved a full-page article in the illustrated magazine of Rome's most important daily gives us a measure of the speed with which this new fashion had been spreading across northern and central Italy. Not that jazz did not have its detractors too. The very same *La Tribuna illustrata* published a short article in October 1919 that spared no racist slur in order to ridicule the music. Signed with the pseudonym 'Campman', it described jazz as an African American dance—'it is a dance for negroes, for savages, for monkeys'—and ended in a crescendo with the following definition: 'a saltarello [a medieval folk dance] for cannibals'.[26]

Mirador was involved in the arrival of jazz in Rome too. Foxtrot had already made its appearance as part of the repertoire of violinist Umberto Bozza's orchestra, which played at the fashionable Apollo nightclub, in Via Nazionale. It was an all-Italian band that regularly offered traditional dance music, but, thanks to Bozza's earlier years in Paris, was up to date with the latest American fashion. From his band came violinist Ugo Filippini, whose talent was spotted by Mirador, who asked him to form his band and play at La Bombonnière. Mirador was also responsible for bringing Ellie Solloway and Mons and Mary Smith to Rome and for helping to form a first network that allowed musicians to move between the venues of Rome and Milan, but also Florence, Genoa, Turin, and summer resorts for the elite such as Viareggio, Sanremo, and Venice Lido. From Mirador's early bands also came other influential musicians, such as one of Italy's first saxophone players, Carlo Benzi, himself later a bandleader; Carlo Benzi Jazz Band Ambassadors toured Italy's major venues and, in 1924, even Switzerland and France.[27]

Many of these musicians had received a thorough classical training; hence they were highly respected for their skills and professionalism. At the same time, if nightclubs and dance schools had opened their doors to jazz, Italy's music schools—the Conservatori—remained entirely alien to it. Throughout the interwar years (and well after the Second World War) the only way to learn the techniques of jazz instrumentalists was to copy their performances either from records or from watching their appearances on stage. Another channel of contact

---

[26] Campman, 'Commenti alla vita: Dallo "jazz"', *La Tribuna illustrata*, 27/40 (5–12 October 1919), 7. See Mazzoletti, *Il jazz in Italia*, i. 26–7 on Mirador; on Campman, p. 35.

[27] On Benzi, see Mazzoletti, *Il jazz in Italia*, i. 64–8, 143–6; and Chapman, *Jazz italiano*, 20–2.

**Fig. 8.5.** Carlo Benzi and Milietto Nervetti (second and fourth from the left) on their arrival in New York, in 1928. (courtesy of Adriano Mazzoletti, Rome)

between Italian musicians and their American counterpart was provided by the dance orchestras working on the ocean liners criss-crossing the Atlantic. Italian bandleaders and individual musicians took advantage of that option, since it gave them the opportunity of a few days in New York, totally free, to attend the most fashionable jazz venues. Carlo Benzi was one of them. There were also cases of 'return-migrant musicians'—that is, Italian musicians who migrated to the USA, were involved in the jazz scene there, and then recrossed the Atlantic to became prominent jazzmen in their homeland. Among them were banjo player Michele 'Mike' Ortuso, from Apulia, trombonist Armando Manzi, from Abruzzo, and Saxophonist Pietro 'Pete' Corona, from Piedmont.[28]

Beyond dance halls, nightclubs, and cinemas, another channel for the circulation of jazz music was the radio. However, in this respect Italy lagged behind northern European countries. As Forgacs and Gundle remind us:

> By 1934, after ten years of regular transmissions, there were still only 440,000 licensed subscribers, just over one percent of the population compared with five million at the same time in Germany and nearly six million in Britain, and the majority were in the North and in the cities and towns.[29]

---

[28] See Mazzoletti, *Il jazz in Italia*, i. 111–17, 297–9.
[29] Forgacs and Gundle, *Mass Culture and Italian Society*, 169.

Even by 1939, when the number of subscribers reached one million, radio sets in Italy remained a status symbol of the wealthier classes. At the same time, since radio broadcasts could be listened to in public places—bars, restaurants, or through government-sponsored initiatives—the actual number of listeners was probably much higher than statistics suggest.

Italy's broadcasting history starts in August 1924 with the creation of the Unione Radiofonica Italiana (URI), which was the result of a merger between Guglielmo Marconi's Radiofono and the Italian branch of the US company Western Electric, which specialized in the construction of radio sets. In this initial phase, the regime seemed happy to allow private enterprises to take the lead. In this instance there was the guarantee of Marconi's enthusiastic support of Mussolini, which the latter was to acknowledge by making him president of the Royal Academy of Italy in 1930 (a position he held until his death in 1937). However, the slow development of the wireless as a mass medium eventually brought it under state control. In November 1927, the URI was renamed the Ente Italiano Audizioni Radiofoniche (EIAR)—the consonance with the Fascist battle cry of D'Annunzian origin—Eia Eia Alalà—making it a welcome acronym—and by 1933 it was entirely controlled by the regime.[30] In the 1930s, the regime also imposed the production of affordable radio sets—the Radio Rurale and the Radio Balilla—with the aim of reaching communities and families living in the countryside. The relatively late use of radio as a mass medium of propaganda—the first politically explicit programme was *Cronache del regime*, which started in January 1934—meant that entertainment was at the very centre of its output.

Dance music was much in evidence, and, particularly in the early years, it opened and closed daily transmissions. Live music was also preferred to recorded music, and this provided opportunities for orchestras, working either in the URI/EIAR's studios or from their traditional public venues. URI's weekly magazine—then called *Radio Orario*—published the schedule of programmes of the then only station in Rome, starting from January 1925. Each day, programming started in the late afternoon, at 5.15 p.m., with half an hour of *musica leggera* provided by pianist Mario Escobar's orchestra at the Hôtel de Russie, which, as we have seen, was renowned for its American repertoire. Indeed, starting from 2 February 1925, the daily schedule showed, following the half-hour of the 'Orchestrina del Hôtel de Russie', another three-quarters of an hour entitled 'Jazz Band', which presumably involved the same orchestra now moving to a full-blown jazz performance. Symbolic of the novelty of this music is the fact that, within the detailed schedule of the entire week, the programme was misspelled 'Yazz Band' five out of seven times. By the following week, however, the wording 'Jazz' was firmly established.[31]

---

[30] The consonance between the EIAR and D'Annunzio's battle call is commented on by Alberto Monticone in his monograph *Il fascismo al microfono* (Rome: Studium, 1978), 37.

[31] The entire archive of *Radio Orario*—which became *Radiocorriere* as of January 1930—is publicly accessible in the Italian state television's digital archive, Radio Teche.

Was the regime involved in the promotion of jazz music on the Italian airwaves? A key player in the development of radio in the 1920s and early 1930s was Costanzo Ciano, who was Minister for Communication throughout those years. Thanks to his past as a decorated officer in the Italian navy, and to his reputation as an authoritative but balanced nationalist conservative, he had Mussolini's full support. Ciano favoured new technologies and was central both to the progressive nationalization of radio broadcasting and to the government's effort to popularize it. An indication of the internal debate within the regime comes from Ciano's proposal to Mussolini for the names of the members of the EIAR's new Comitato di Vigilanza, in 1928: among others, Ciano suggested the appointment of world-renowned conductor Arturo Toscanini, which Mussolini refused to accept, replacing him with the composer Pietro Mascagni, who was openly philo-Fascist and of more conservative views. Toscanini, who, as we have seen, had worked at New York's Metropolitan for seven years—from 1908 until 1915—was more open to foreign influences than Mascagni, who had made his vitriolic dislike for jazz public on more than one occasion.[32]

This would suggest that Mussolini favoured a more conservative and nationalistic vision of music. At the same time, and this is possibly not a coincidence, it was in 1928 that a number of Fascist periodicals—from Bottai's *Critica fascista* to Mussolini's *Il Popolo d'Italia*—started to publish critical views of jazz, presenting it as a foreign fashion that had to be kept at bay. The following is an extract from an article by Carlo Ravasio, a leading Milanese Fascist journalist:

> It is heinous and insulting for tradition, and therefore for the race, to put back in the attic violins, mandolins, and guitars in order to blow into saxophones and bang on kettledrums following barbarous melodies that exist only for the fashionable magazines. It is stupid, it is ridiculous, it is anti-Fascist to go into ecstasy over the umbilical dances by a half-caste or to follow like fools any 'americanata' from across the ocean![33]

'Americanata', as we can see, was still a fashionable expression in the interwar years. Moreover, with the benefit of hindsight, it is ironic to add that the end of

---

[32] On Mascagni's low opinion of jazz, see Mazzoletti, *Il jazz in Italia*, i. 119–20. After his appointment, Mascagni attacked the presence of jazz on the Italian airwaves with an article published in *Il Popolo d'Italia*, on 3 August 1929. That year he was also appointed to the Reale Accademia d'Italia, together with Marinetti. Mascagni reiterated his profound dislike for jazz when interviewed by *Radiocorriere*, in the first issue of 1930, which also congratulated Arnaldo Mussolini—Benito's eldest brother—on his appointment as Direttore Generale of the EIAR. Arnaldo, though, did not exert particular influence on the EIAR: the death of his son, in the summer of that year, distanced him from his political responsibilities; he was to die of a heart attack the following year, on 21 December 1931.

[33] Carlo Ravasio, 'Fascismo e tradizione', *Il Popolo d'Italia*, 30 March 1928, p. 3. For more examples, see Mazzoletti, *Il jazz in Italia*, i. 183–5, 188–9. It should also be noted that, at the other end of the political spectrum, Antonio Gramsci, in a letter to his sister-in-law written from prison on 27 February 1928, revealed an equally negative opinion of jazz, considered by him a sign of the progressive 'Africanization' of European culture.

the article presented a poetic image of tradition by referring to Mussolini rocking the cradle of his newly born under an oak that he himself had planted years before. Other snobbish and xenophile parents, Ravasio concluded, would surround themselves with 'misses and pretty boys in order to stroke them to the sound of a cacophonous American jazz-tune!'. Ironically, the newly born was Romano Mussolini, who, as already mentioned, was to become a professional jazz musician in the post-war years.

In response to such attacks, other voices rose in defence of jazz, among them that of another important figure in Italy's classical music circles, Alfredo Casella, who deserves some introduction here. An infant prodigy, Casella was born in 1898 to a family of musicians, who moved from Turin to Paris in order to broaden Alfredo's musical horizons—indeed, he was to mix with the likes of Ravel and Debussy. An accomplished pianist, composer, and conductor, Casella returned to Italy in 1915, to lecture at the prestigious Accademia di Santa Cecilia, in Rome, although he was often on tour abroad, including America. He went there twice, first in 1921 and again in 1927, this time with a three-year contract as conductor of Boston's Symphony Orchestra. It is during the final months of his stay in Boston that Casella wrote four articles devoted to the classical music scene in the USA and one on jazz. On his return, he also published an open letter to Mascagni. Careful to avoid the accusation of lacking nationalistic spirit, Casella praised jazz as a most innovative approach to music—comparing improvisation to other twentieth-century avant-garde techniques in art and literature—and fully condemning Mascagni's narrow views on contemporary music, jazz included.[34]

What was the effect of this cultural battle on the EIAR's programming? By January 1929, the EIAR could boast of another two radio stations (Genoa and Naples), and a close look at their now-overlapping schedules, as published in *Radio Orario*, shows that jazz was still present. Milan kept its one-hour slots of jazz music, explicitly named 'Eiar-Jazz', Rome stopped its own slot but had foxtrots as part of its dance-music programmes (and so had Genoa), while Naples finished its transmissions with half an hour of jazz entitled 'Trasmissione Jazz Trocadero'. Once again, one is drawn to the conclusion that if, on the one hand, nationalistic and conservative circles stirred up recurrent waves of xenophobia, on the other, there were equally strong circles praising modernity, youth, and a more cosmopolitan outlook, able to raise a counter-debate, and defend spaces such as the one held by jazz music on the EIAR's airwaves.

Both factions, however, lived in permanent expectation of Mussolini's approval of their respective stances. And here we have the missing piece of the jigsaw, since

---

[34] Casella's articles on American music and his letter to Mascagni were published in *L'Italia letteraria*, between 1 September and 15 December 1929, and subsequently collected in his book *21 + 26* (Rome: Augustea, 1931). With regard to the origin of jazz, Casella too makes no mention of the contribution by the Italian American community in New Orleans.

there is no evidence of *Il Duce* having a strong opinion on the matter. In the more than six hundred pages that constitute the notes on Yvon De Begnac's many conversations with Mussolini during the mid-1930s, cultural questions are constantly discussed: American literature is commented upon, American cinema is mentioned more than once, but there is never any discussion about American music. Similarly, in his conversations with Emil Ludwig of 1932, music is discussed, and its national character too, but, once again, no mention is made of what came from America. The only documented comment comes from an extract from an interview that Mussolini gave to United Press journalist Webb Miller, which was published in *Il Popolo d'Italia* in 1937. The central topic of the interview concerned Mussolini's capacity to stay healthy and alert despite the enormous demands on his time after fifteen years as head of state in charge of various ministries. Mussolini therefore was asked to talk about his daily routine and diet. When it came to his free time, he spoke about his reading habits, then, when moving on to theatre and music, he continued:

> I do not have much free time to go to the theatre where I prefer lyrical and joyous music, the combative and personal lyricism of Verdi and Wagner and the playfulness of Rossini. You will not be surprised if I tell you that I have no antipathy for jazz; as dance music, I find it entertaining.[35]

With this rather diplomatic concession to his American interviewer, Mussolini maintained a balance by showing openness towards jazz while at the same time marginalizing it as entertaining dance music. It is a comment that is in line with his attitude towards the arts in general—that is, demonstrating a certain openness towards contemporary, groundbreaking movements, while at the same time avoiding a full embrace and preferring instead to preside over a variety of practices. It reminds one of Marinetti's decade-long wait for the official recognition of Futurism as Fascist art *par excellence*, which Mussolini never conceded. With jazz, too, it seems as if *Il Duce* wanted to avoid being labelled as either a firm supporter or an opponent. Beyond this, we have no proof that he developed any particular interest in jazz.[36]

---

[35] Webb Miller, 'Ho fatto del mio organismo un motore costantemente sorvegliato e controllato che marcia con assoluta regolarità', *Il Popolo d'Italia*, 6 March 1937; then collected in Mussolini, *Opera omnia*, xxviii. 136–9. Yvon De Begnac, *Taccuini mussoliniani* (Bologna: Il Mulino, 1990). Ludwig, *Colloqui con Mussolini*.

[36] Harwell Celenza devotes a section to this topic entitled 'Mussolini's Musical Interests' in *Jazz Italian Style*, 75–81. There, statements such as 'thanks to Mussolini's initiatives, jazz became a symbol of national identity during his years in power' (p. 73) or 'he incorporated it [jazz] into Italy's cultural policy' (p. 81) are left unsubstantiated, lacking documentary evidence to support them. In this respect, Mazzoletti's *Il jazz in Italia*, Cerchiari's *Jazz e fascismo*, Poesio's *Tutto è ritmo, tutto è swing*, and Chapman's *Jazz italiano* offer a more convincing reconstruction, showing the inner contradictions and the cohabitation of a variety of views concerning jazz and avoiding any suggestion that Mussolini might have played a central role in it.

In the meantime, jazz had established itself as a new musical craze across different media. This is well summed up in the lyrics of a song that was part of a variety show led by one of Italy's most popular comedians at the time, Totò:

> A gramophone here, a radio set there!
> and music is everywhere
> inside houses and in the streets
> and no Christian is safe from
> the mad American rhythm
> Jazzband!!! Jazzband!
> You gave us mechanical songs
> Jazzband! Jazzband!
> Even Movietone joined in!
> The guttural sound on the radio
> The frù frù sound from the records
> natural voices
> are no longer the fashion…
> Jazzband! Jazzband!
> epilepsy
> and frenzy, that's what you are![37]

Further evidence that jazz was holding on to its place come from the 1935 issue of the EIAR's annual publication. Statistical data concerning radio programming during the previous year were published in an illustrated table: and the image representing the most popular genre—'Musica leggera e da ballo' ('Pop and Dance Music')—featured a black musician playing a saxophone. In the same publication, the EIAR's officials publicly defended jazz, stating that it was a music much favoured by the youth and should therefore have its place. The reference to the youth of Italy is indicative, since there is little doubt, that even within the households of both Mussolini and Ciano, jazz was much loved by the younger generation. Whenever asked about his passion for jazz, Romano Mussolini, *Il Duce*'s youngest son, who became a respected jazz pianist in the post-Second World War years, would answer that he discovered jazz through the records that his elder brother Vittorio and his sister Edda brought home. The former even wrote some jazz reviews for the monthly magazine *Il Disco*, in 1934–5, but Edda in particular seems to have possessed a good collection of records. In April 1930, she married Galeazzo Ciano, Costanzo's eldest son, who joined his father in a stellar political

---

[37] Bel Amì, *Il Grand'Otello* (1933); quoted in Pasquale Iaccio, *Vincere! Vincere! Vincere!: Fascismo e società italiana nelle canzoni e nelle riviste di varietà, 1935–1943* (Rome: Ianua, 1981), 31. Iaccio devotes one chapter of his monograph to the reception of jazz music in Fascist Italy (pp. 31–53) and he too makes no mention of Mussolini's potential role in it.

career, encouraged by Mussolini, which led to his becoming head of the ministry of culture (in its earlier denominations from 1933 to 1936) and then foreign minister until the autumn of 1942. Edda and Galeazzo were known for their sophisticated and 'modern' lifestyle, which included playing golf and throwing grand parties, where one can imagine foxtrots featuring prominently. Overall, it seems that the fortune of jazz in Italy was subject to a generational tug of war played at different levels and with different results during the Fascist years.[38]

Jazz historians regularly refer to the fact that on 5 November 1935—in the same year as the EIAR's public defence of jazz, and in the heated weeks following the League of Nations' economic sanctions against Italy's invasion of Ethiopia—the Ministry of Press and Propaganda distributed a memorandum to all chief editors of Italy's newspapers (one of the infamous *veline*) in which they were warned that its deputy head, Dino Alfieri, was about to introduce a raft of cultural directives as a reprisal for the League's sanctions:

> The Hon. Alfieri then stated that he is studying a plan that will see a ban on all Italian performances of foreign comedies and operas, whose authors belong to nations adopting sanctions against us; in the meantime he has begun by ordering the radio not to broadcast any English jazz and other English music.

Dino Alfieri was deputy head of the Ministry for Press and Propaganda, which was headed then by Galeazzo Ciano himself. How are we supposed to interpret this initiative, which ambiguously presented jazz as an 'English' phenomenon? In its awkwardness, the memo made a distinction that was to play an important part in the fate of jazz during the last years of the regime. The ban could be interpreted as being aimed at jazz music played and sung by English-speaking musicians and singers. Jazz had to go if it was a foreign fashion; but it could stay as long as it was played by Italians and sung in Italian. Was Ciano behind this initiative of his deputy? Probably not, since he was in Ethiopia in those months, serving as an Air Force officer, in accordance with Mussolini's expectation that his younger ministers should take an active part in the war. Alfieri at the time was, *de facto*, acting Minister of Culture. Moreover, seven months later, Mussolini was to decide, unexpectedly, to move Ciano from the Ministry of Press and Propaganda to the Foreign Office, and to promote Alfieri to be head of the culture ministry. This might indicate that Mussolini appreciated Alfieri's stronger hand and found it in tune with a

---

[38] On Vittorio Mussolini's reviews for *Il Disco*, see Benedetta Zucconi, 'Esordi della riflessione discografica in Italia: *Il Disco. Bollettino discografico mensile (1933-37)*', *Forum Italicum*, 49/2 (2015), 474–90 (487). To my knowledge, Mussolini never commented on his son's interest in jazz. In De Begnac's conversations, Mussolini talks about the intellectual work of his eldest son, commenting on his activity as director of the film magazine *Cinema*, but makes no reference to his interest in music (De Begnac, *Taccuini mussoliniani*, 423). On Edda Mussolini/Ciano, see Harwell Celenza, *Jazz Fascist Style*, 77.

Fascist state that was building a colonial empire, was strengthening its autarchic policies, and was now at loggerheads with the democratic nations of the West.

The bizarre content of the *velina*—Italy reacting to an economic embargo by banning 'English' jazz from its airwaves—makes one think of a knee-jerk reaction by the ministry possibly triggered by Mussolini's annoyance and request for immediate retaliation across all ministries. Alfieri was known as a rather wooden, directive-following executor, so it is very unlikely that he would have taken any initiative unless he was prompted from above. In the field of censorship, it was, after all, *Il Duce*'s explicit irritation in April 1934 that provoked the sudden change in the organization of book censorship, which we mentioned earlier.[39]

As for the impact of Alfieri's directives, the EIAR's magazine comes to our help again. The change was, indeed, substantial, but a closer look reveals that by then jazz had already been somehow marginalized. Foxtrots and other American steps were played within dance and so-called light-music slots, but all the programmes explicitly devoted to jazz had already disappeared more than a year earlier.

It all seems to have started at the end of January 1933, which is when jazz programmes disappeared from the networks of the EIAR's major stations. The week before, America had featured prominently in *Radiocorriere*, with three long articles devoted, respectively, to 'Americanismo' (presented in a positive light), to a live concert from Turin featuring American music directed by American composer and conductor Werner Janssen, and to the conductor of New York's symphonic orchestra, Walter Damrosch, and his four-year, educational tour all around the USA in order to introduce music to every provincial corner of the country. This was accompanied by the usual presence of American music in the EIAR's schedules, which, as well as Janssen's concert, featured three jazz programmes broadcast from Bari, Florence, and Palermo. However, the following week, the word 'jazz' was almost entirely removed from the weekly schedule. America, in any form, also disappeared from the articles of *Radiocorriere*. Coincidentally, a short, anonymous article entitled 'La musica leggera e le radio-orchestre' briefly tackled the topic of jazz on the EIAR's airwaves. After declaring the impossibility of pleasing all listeners when it came to jazz music—starting with those complaining about its presence—it noted that the EIAR had four orchestras, each one specializing in one musical genre. Number 2 was the jazz orchestra conducted by Gino Filippini (no relation to Ugo Filippini, but a jazz musician himself); hence, every time the diction 'Radio Orchestra no. 2' appeared on the schedule, listeners should know what to expect. Again, it is interesting to

---

[39] The text of the *velina* can be found in Tranfaglia, *La stampa del regime*, 187. In his memoirs, Giorgio Pini, chief editor of *Il Popolo d'Italia* and long-standing close collaborator of Mussolini, dwelled on this characteristic—that is, on Mussolini's outbursts, which his ministers were often too keen to turn into political directives. Giorgo Pini, *Filo diretto con Palazzo Venezia* (Bologna: Cappelli, 1950), 89–90. On Alfieri's political figure, see Philip V. Cannistraro, *La fabbrica del consenso: Fascismo e mass-media* (Rome and Bari: Laterza, 1975), 130–4.

note that the full schedule of other orchestras was normally included, specifying composer and title of the pieces being played, but not for orchestra no. 2.[40]

Once again, it is possible to imagine that a clash had been followed by yet another compromise. Perhaps the cause this time was the excessive attention to American music during the previous week, but documentary evidence is lacking. From February 1933 onwards, jazz continued to be played by Filippini's Radio Orchestra 2 and within programmes of recorded music (called 'Dischi', which by then were beginning to compete with live music), but their presence was toned down, certainly in the pages of *Radiocorriere*. At a more general level, this is probably linked to the fact that the EIAR was becoming increasingly politicized. As we saw, it was between 1927 and 1933 that the regime completed the nationalization of the radio—and therefore its output began to be judged for its contribution to Fascist propaganda. The issues of *Radiocorriere* indicate a progressive presence, during 1932, and a sudden expansion in 1933, of propaganda articles devoted to Fascism, sometimes not at all connected with radio programmes. The year 1933 was important in the history of the EIAR: the creation of the Ente Radio Rurale, in June of that year, whose role was to spread the wireless medium throughout rural Italy, gave further impetus to the propagandist aims of the medium in Fascist hands. This went hand in hand with a nationalist propensity and a degree of xenophobia.

One other possible factor was the publication of a manifesto by ten Italian composers denouncing contemporary music and defending Italy's nineteenth-century Romantic tradition. The manifesto was published on 17 December 1932, simultaneously in the *Corriere della Sera*, *La Stampa*, and *Il Popolo d'Italia*, with the title 'Manifesto musicale'. Signed by prestigious composers such as Ottorino Respighi, Ildebrando Pizzetti, and Riccardo Zandonai, it asked Italian musicians to reject recent trends and to be faithful, instead, to their nineteenth-century heritage. It did not mention jazz but specifically attacked contemporary composers Gian Francesco Malipiero and Alfredo Casella. The latter, as we have seen, had been a public supporter of jazz. The prestige of the signatories might have carried some weight within the EIAR.

A clear stepping-up of Fascist propaganda in the pages *of Radiocorriere* took place in the summer of 1933, following Italo Balbo's formation flight over the Atlantic. In Chapter 6 we discussed the cultural impact of Balbo's flight in the creation of an image of Italy as a modern country capable of competing—at least in terms of image—with the USA. The editors of *Radiocorriere* responded to this with unprecedented fervour: not one but four issues were devoted to Balbo's flight, each time occupying the whole front cover. The first one (Fig. 8.6) is particularly symbolic: in futurist style, it depicts Balbo's hydroplanes flying over the

---

[40] Radio Orchestra no. 2 was based in Milan and had been formed in January 1933. Anon., 'La musica leggera e le radio-orchestre', *Radiocorriere*, 9/4 (22–29 January 1933), 14.

**Fig. 8.6.** Front cover illustration of *Radiocorriere*, 9/30 (23–30 July 1933). (courtesy of Biblioteca Nazionale Centrale, Florence)

skyscrapers of Chicago and New York. Its caption clarifies the visual symbolism: 'Escorted and protected by the stellar light of our Homeland, which, thanks to Fascism, has regained the tenacious and patient power of Rome, the Italian wings roar victorious over the skies of America.' The Italy versus USA connection continued the following week with a cover photo of the iconic Goodyear airship flying over the Italian Pavillion at Chicago's international fair, and, the following week, it featured Balbo delivering a speech in front of an array of radio microphones dominated by the acronyms of NBC and EIAR (see Fig. 8.7).

The role played by the EIAR in keeping its listeners abreast with the progress of Balbo's flight expedition is possibly one of the early examples of radio providing a better service than newspapers, whose reports, the following day, were always lagging behind. In a sense, it is possible that the huge propaganda effort relating to Balbo's flight and the role played by the radio were instrumental in augmenting the expectation that the EIAR should become a stronger voice in support of the regime. Symbolically, from then on, the cover illustrations of *Radiocorriere* were regularly devoted to images of marching soldiers, Fascist celebrations, and generic nationalist images.

As far as music is concerned, jazz continued to be present both within the repertoire of the EIAR's no. 2 orchestra and in programmes based on vinyl records.

**Fig. 8.7.** Front cover illustration of *Radiocorriere*, 9/32 (6–13 August 1933). (courtesy of Biblioteca Nazionale Centrale, Florence)

For example, the debut of Gershwin's *Rhapsody in Blue* on the Italian airwaves dates to 1 March 1933, as part of an evening programme transmitted from Milan called 'Dischi di musiche modernissime'. That week, *Radiocorriere* devoted its front-cover illustration to a quartet of country music players—vaguely described in the caption as 'four actors from American radio'—and then a full-page article entitled '"Radiocity" comincia a vivere', devoted to the Rockefeller's Center (known as 'Radiocity', since it housed companies attached to the Radio Corporation of America, such as NBC).

All explicit references to jazz disappeared from the EIAR's schedules, starting from the last week of March 1934. This time, again, an article in *Radiocorriere* had hinted at the upcoming change within the rubric entitled 'La Posta della Direzione' ('The Chief Editors' Mailbox'). Among the selection of letters appearing in the 18–26 March 1934 issue, three out of seven concerned jazz. Two of them condemned it resolutely, but a third one offered a full defence. Written by a 'radioascoltatrice' ('female radio listener') living in Bologna, the letter argued that the EIAR should not be deterred by the fact that not everybody likes jazz, and concluded with a question: 'Is it too much to ask for half an hour per week of authentic jazz?' The editorial reply allows a useful insight into the EIAR's ambiguous policies:

> With music recorded by English and American jazz bands, the EIAR fills much more than the half an hour per week you request, thus showing an enviable sense of discretion, and if this is not evident, it is only because we do not follow the practice of several foreign radio stations, which create specific programmes that bunch together those pieces, instead of mixing them with others. [...] At the moment, the problem of dance music is under review, and we hope to solve it once and for all.

The self-compliment about their 'discretion' in inserting jazz in the EIAR's schedule, coupled with the final admission that the issue is under review, makes one think that the editors were discreetly warning the EIAR's jazz fans that, from then on, they might have to look for their preferred music within the general programmes of *musica leggera*. This is indeed what happened from the following week onwards. It is also indicative that jazz should be associated with dance music, once again giving the impression that jazz was mainly understood as orchestra-played, dance-hall material.

In the months to follow, if the front-cover illustration of *Radiocorriere*'s issue of 23–29 September 1934 could still contain the small image of a duo of jazz musicians playing saxophone and banjo, the stations' schedules were entirely 'purged' of any reference to jazz. At the other end of the cosmopolitan versus national spectrum, the presence of Italian folk music had substantially increased.

From the end of March 1934, therefore, jazz on the Italian airwaves was left to the capacity of the EIAR's programmers and musicians to keep the genre within their 'light-music' schedules. If Filippini's Radio Orchestra no. 2 had been marked as a jazz Radio Orchestra in the early 1930s, by March 1934 the distinction between differently numbered orchestras was also abandoned. Instead, music programmes would be announced without a specific reference to the orchestra performing them.

On 16 March 1934, the Annual General Meeting of the EIAR had taken place in Rome, and its coincidence with the sudden change in the company's schedule makes one think there might have been a connection between the two events. So, what was announced at the meeting? *Radiocorriere* devoted three pages to it, with a long extract from the report by the company's Board of Directors. Indicatively, the text was juxtaposed with four square blocks displaying in bigger typeface a quotation from a speech by Mussolini (with no specific relation to the radio) and two photographs of crowds listening to a speech, with the caption to the latter clarifying the connection: '*Il Duce*'s words stirred deep feelings and enthusiasm in everyone...'. The report itself, after a long section devoted to the many technical innovations introduced in the previous months, moved on to an analysis of the EIAR's 'artistic activity'. When it came to orchestras, the report mentioned a reshuffle of the ensembles, which involved 'appropriate selections and substitutions' in order to increase their efficiency. This meant that the standing arrangement of having four, clearly distinguished Radio Orchestras was coming to an end. As for non-musical programmes, the EIAR was going to 'expand and accentuate the journalistic character of our schedule in order to bring it closer to current events, to daily life, and to the climate of Fascism'. Within this climate, there is little doubt that any foreign fashion—jazz included—was going to be marginalized.[41]

The only way jazz could survive was through its 'Italianization'. Alfieri's *velina* of November 1935, announcing the boycotting of 'English jazz' on Italian radio, was part of this process. Moreover, if, in November 1935, Alfieri was informing all newspapers of his nationalist stance, three months earlier an even more strongly worded memorandum had been sent by the EIAR'S director, Raoul Chiodelli, to the company's programmers and orchestra conductors, informing them of the decision to stop all kind of 'music with a negro character—negroes' popular songs or their imitations, etc.—and dance music with refrains sung in English'.[42] This suggests that, on the eve of Italy's invasion of Ethiopia, the regime was preparing its people for the African military adventure, and one of the exercises was to purge the nation's airwaves of any 'African' presence. It was not just happening on the wireless. In August 1935 newspapers were told to avoid publishing images of the defeat of Italy's heavyweight champion, Primo Carnera, who on 25 June 1935 had been knocked out in six rounds by the African American boxer Joe Louis. The fight, which took place at New York's Yankee Stadium in front of more than 60,000 people, had been a national embarrassment, given Primo Carnera's high profile as a great Italian (physically, too, he was more than 2 metres tall) and the regime's use of him for propaganda purposes.[43]

Even during that period of nationalist fervour, however, there was enough will in some EIAR quarters to defend jazz. Turin, where the administrative headquarters had moved in 1930 (from Milan), where *Radiocorriere* was published, and where Cetra, EIAR'S record company, had been founded in 1933, was the site of strongest resistance. In July 1935, a British jazz bandleader, Claude Bampton, had been contracted to conduct the Turinese orchestra, which was called Cetra, as it also recorded for the company's label. Only a month later, he was sacked, allegedly because of Chiodelli's disapproval of his appointment.[44] Politics seemed to have overridden the EIAR's artistic choice. But only a year later, in October 1936, the Turinese orchestra was put into the hands of Giuseppe 'Pippo' Barzizza, another renowned jazz bandleader. Of Genoese origin, Barzizza was one of those young Italian musicians who had learnt jazz first hand when working for Italian cruisers crossing the Atlantic. Barzizza turned into Italy's Paul Whiteman (indeed,

---

[41] Anon., 'Rassegna annuale dell'attività artistica e tecnica dell'Eiar', *Radiocorriere*, 10/13 (25 March–1 April 1934), 5–7.
[42] Chiodelli's memorandum is discussed by Mazzoletti in *Jazz in Italia*, i. 328.
[43] Tranfaglia, *La stampa del regime*, 108, 109, 177.
[44] On Bampton, see Mazzoletti, *Il jazz in Italia*, i. 328–9.

he was sometimes similarly called 'the King of Italian Jazz'). He was a most popular jazz conductor, a multi-instrumentalist, and a composer, famous for his recordings as much as for his live broadcast and concert tours. His orchestra Cetra, which he conducted all through the last years of the regime, became a guarantee that his well-orchestrated, syncopated rhythms were to remain on the EIAR's airwaves despite the up and downs of jazz in the eyes of the regime. Yet another compromise had been reached: jazz at the EIAR was allowed to live on in the hands of an Italian conductor.

Barzizza was not the only jazz bandleader who came into his own in the mid-1930s. Another who was equally influential was Gorni Kramer. He did not work much for the radio, but his love for jazz was partially determined by it. As he remembered in many interviews, thanks to a wireless set in his house, he was able to listen to an American station that, in its short-wave schedule, used to broadcast Duke Ellington's band live from New York's legendary Cotton Club. The son of a musician, Kramer formed his first jazz band in 1934, in Milan, by which time he was already renowned as an innovative accordion player. His capacity quickly to learn and perform the latest jazz pieces coming from America made him famous in the recording studios too. Most importantly, Kramer composed some of the most iconic 'jazzy' songs of Italy's late 1930s, from 'Crapa pelata' (1936) to 'Pippo non lo sa' (1939). Both those songs became immensely popular on Italy's airwaves and in music halls (and remained so in the post-war years). They displayed Kramer's genius in creating an appealing balance between ear-catching melodies and a sophisticated use of syncopated rhythms and

**Fig. 8.8.** 'Pippo' Barzizza as conductor of EIAR's Orchestra Cetra in the late 1930s. (courtesy of Adriano Mazzoletti, Rome)

instrumental jazz solos. His songs were performed by the most popular singers of those years.

The best-known version of 'Pippo non lo sa' came from the Trio Lescano, formed by three sisters of Dutch origin who Italianized their names when they settled in Italy in 1935. Their choral virtuoso singing was much influenced by their American equivalent, the famous Boswell Sisters, from New Orleans, who had by then become international stars. Kramer's 'Crapa pelata' is instead exceptional for its musical qualities. It shows Kramer's sophisticated adoption of some characteristic traits of the latest jazz sounds from America: from its roots in Duke Ellington's swing to 'hot' traits such as the use of humming, scat-vocal, and the succession of individual instruments improvising around the same melodic line. At the same time, the superimposition of the lyrics taken from an old nursery rhyme in Milanese dialect adds a specific Italian flavour to the song. Some of Kramer's songs were also sung by Italy's 'crooners' of the time, Alberto Rabagliati and Natalino Otto, whose connections with America deserve fuller mention.[45]

Milanese Alberto Rabagliati started his career as an actor, winning a competition as a Rodolfo Valentino's lookalike in 1927 (Valentino had died the year before), which saw him travel to Hollywood with the prospect of replacing the Italian film star. He spent four years in Los Angeles, but his acting career proved a fiasco. During these years he formed a passion for jazz music, developed his talent as a singer, and on his return to Italy joined 'Pippo' Barzizza's orchestra. By the mid-1930s he had become one of the most popular male voices on the Italian radio, to the point that, in 1941, he had his own radio show called 'Canta Rabagliati'. His persona was fully associated with American, 'jazzy' rhythms, and his firm popularity throughout the mid- and late 1930s is proof of the strength of the public appreciation for American syncopated rhythms.[46]

Natalino Otto, on the other hand, was born on the outskirts of Genoa and, like Barzizza, had worked on the transatlantic liners sailing between his home town and New York. In 1935, he even sang for an Italian American radio station there and became friends with the Italian American jazz violinist Joe Venuti, then one of the star soloists in Paul Whiteman's orchestras. Back on the Italian mainland, Otto joined Gorni Kramer's orchestra, with which he recorded many popular records. Otto was never able to rival Rabagliati's exclusive position at the EIAR, but his success as both a live performer and a recording artist—mainly for Cetra's

---

[45] On Barzizza, see Chapman, *Jazz italiano*, 31–6. On Kramer, see Cerchiari, *Jazz e fascismo*, 30–4; and, on the Trio Lescano, see Harwell Celenza, *Jazz Italian Style*, 148–9, 177–8, 182–3; and Gabriele Eschenazi, *Le regine dello Swing: Il Trio Lescano: Una storia fra cronaca e costume* (Turin: Einaudi, 2010).

[46] Rabagliati wrote a memoir of his Hollywood stay: *Quattro anni fra le 'stelle': Aneddoti e impressioni* (Milan: Giovanni Bolla, 1932). See also Muscio, *Napoli, New York, Hollywood*, 163–5.

main competitor, Fonit—ensured his position as Italy's 'other' popular jazz singer.[47]

Barzizza, Kramer, the Trio Lescano, Rabagliati, and Otto were popular household names. Thanks to them, and to scores of other jazz bands and singers, the syncopated rhythms of American descent remained popular on Italy's radio and dance halls throughout the 1930s, despite the increasing intolerance of the regime and the volte-face of the Futurists. As we will see in Chapter 10, the overall picture was to degenerate in 1938, when foreign music—and jazz in particular—became the target of what Di Capua defines as a full-blown 'campaign for musical autarchy'.[48] By then, however, jazz had become too popular and too widespread to be totally eradicated. What the regime could do was to mark a clear distinction between foreign and homegrown jazz, and then proceed to remove the former. Some propagandists were even to suggest the adoption of the neologism 'gez' as the appropriate, Italian-spelled word for jazz produced in Fascist Italy.

## 8.3 Echoes of Italian American Jazz

This section is not devoted to the contribution by the Italian American community to the origin of jazz, starting from New Orleans. The questions addressed here are different ones. They concern the level of awareness that there was, in interwar Italy, of such a contribution, and the extent to which it influenced the popularity of jazz in Italy.

A close look at the documented evidence leads to a brief answer to both questions: very little. The role of Italian American musicians is almost never mentioned in the scores of articles on jazz published in Italy throughout the 1920s and 1930s. As already suggested, the Futurists too—despite their obsessive nationalism—never mentioned it in their writings. Marinetti was probably not even aware of it, since all his references point to jazz as a primitive sound brought to life by black musicians. In his history of Italian jazz, Mazzoletti is very explicit about this: 'Even if a few records by ODJB [La Rocca's Original Dixieland Jazz Band] were available in Italy soon after being issued in the USA, nobody took any notice.'[49] According to him, this went hand in hand with the widespread ignorance in Italy about the New Orleans roots of jazz music.

As Harwell Celenza rightly points out, it is a historical fact that the presence of Italian musicians on the New Orleans jazz scene of the 1910s was pointed out in an article published in 1919 and written by the Italian consul there, Bruno

---

[47] On Natalino Otto, see Harwell Celenza, *Jazz Italian Style*, 142–8.
[48] Giovanni Di Capua, *Faccetta nera: Canti dell'ebbrezza fascista: Saggi critici, testi, spartiti, commenti* (Valentano: Scipioni Editore, 2000), 38.
[49] Mazzoletti, *Il jazz in Italia*, i. 74.

Zuculin. But this unique case remained unmentioned by all those who wrote about or played jazz in the following years. A first example: when composer and musicologist Fernando Liuzzi (who taught music aesthetics at Rome University) wrote a long article on the jazz question for a 1927 issue of *Nuova antologia*, whenever he referred to the origins of jazz, he made no mention of an Italian American contribution. A second example concerns another musicologist, Giacomo Del Valle de Paz, son of the composer Edgardo, who discussed the origins of jazz in an article he wrote for the music monthly *Il Pensiero musicale* in 1928. His view is critical both of jazz as a music form and of its popularity in France, as is sadly summed up in this one sentence: 'jazz in France can by now count on a number of historians, aestheticians, technicians and propagandists: it could not have been more lucky on Latin soil, this bastard son of Afro-Americans!' Del Valle de Paz too, when dealing with its origins, never mentions a possible involvement of other communities in New Orleans, whether Italian or French–Creole. Interestingly, the article ends with a parallel between the improvisation in jazz and in the Italian Commedia dell'Arte tradition, but steers clear of any mention of a possible Italian contribution to the origins of jazz.[50]

A third example concerns the entry for 'Jazz' in the prestigious *Enciclopedia italiana*. Contained in the volume published in 1933, the entry was signed by composer Ildebrando Pizzetti. Once again, the history of the genre is identified solely as 'the musical art of America's negroes'. A fourth example concerns another publication of 1933, the famous list of 500 exoticisms that *Gazzetta del Popolo* journalist Paolo Monelli polemically published for Hoepli. The entry on 'jazz' goes on for two pages and contains an attempt at a history of the origin of jazz. Differently from the *Enciclopedia italiana*, Monelli concentrates on the bands of white musicians that emerged from New Orleans and moved to Chicago and New York, but, despite this, he makes no mention of a potential involvement of the Italian American community. A fifth and final example concerns journalist and jazz music connoisseur Angelo Nizza, who had travelled throughout the USA exploring the jazz scene, which he then covered in three articles published by *La Stampa* in the winter 1933–4. Despite the fact that Nizza met some of the prominent Italian American musicians at the time—Joe Venuti, Eddie Lang, and others—he never attempted to treat jazz as a genre in any way 'belonging' to the Italian American community. At the same time, he presented a sophisticated explanation of jazz music, distinguishing between its 'hot' and 'straight' schools.[51]

---

[50] Harwell Celenza, *Jazz Italian Style*, 7–8, 36–40. Fernando Liuzzi, 'Jazz e anti-jazz', *Nuova antologia*, 251 (January 1927), 70–6. Giacomo Del Valle de Paz, 'Critica del jazz', *Il Pensiero musicale*, 8/9–11 (September–November 1928), 132–4 (132).

[51] Paolo Monelli, *Barbaro dominio* (Milan: Hoepli, 1933), 176–7. See, in particular, Nizza's article entitled 'Che cosa è il jazz', *La Stampa*, 9 December 1933, p. 6. Angelo Nizza, also a librettist and a lyricist, did work for the EIAR on several occasions: he was co-author of the already mentioned programme 'Le avventure di Topolino', in 1933. He also covered Armstrong's 1935 Turin concert for *La Stampa*.

Similarly, among Italian Fascist circles and in the dozens of articles published by the EIAR's magazine in defence of jazz, there was never any attempt to praise it in connection to the role played by Italian Americans during its early years. For instance, a full-page article of *Radiocorriere*, of February 1933, entitled 'Il "jazz" e la sua storia', dwelled on the origin of jazz in Louisiana and did not contain a single line on the involvement of the Italian community. Another historical overview of the origin of jazz, published in July 1934, centred on the distinction between 'hot' jazz played by African American bands and the domesticated 'white' jazz embodied by Paul Whiteman's band and made no mention of Italian musicians. Similarly, a month later, another article briefly returned to the subject, defining jazz's roots as 'negro-American' and, more importantly, when mentioning the presence of Italian American musicians among American contemporary jazz bands, doing so with a very different emphasis: 'The most important jazz bands have among their members a good number of Italians. Their genius is such that they are able to adapt to the rather heavy reins of syncopation, which is saying something.' In other words, Italian American musicians were praised for their capacity to adapt to the rhythms of jazz rather than for being the makers of that sound.[52]

In his *Jazz Band* of 1929, Bragaglia obviously did not touch upon the Italian contribution to the birth of jazz, given that the entire book is a tirade against the genre as the product of—in his words—the primitive, vulgar, and animalistic black community of America. More indicative is that a similar indifference should be shown by two other, much more knowledgeable books on jazz that were published in Italy in later years, respectively in 1937 and 1938. These are *Il Jazz: Dalle origini ad oggi* by Augusto Caraceni, and *Introduzione alla vera musica di jazz* by Ezio Levi and Gian Carlo Testoni. By then, the invasion of Ethiopia had accelerated Italy's racist policies in the colonies. Hence, to bring together African American and Italian American musicians as part of the origin of jazz would have been a politically awkward move. Indeed, both authors stayed well away from it. Caraceni—a journalist who had written on jazz for Rome's daily *Il Messaggero*—made no mention of the presence of Italian American musicians in Louisiana and commented on the Italian contribution only as part of the later development of jazz once it reached Chicago and New York, where the white communities—Jewish, Irish, and Italian—began to add their own flavour to it. Levi and

---

[52] G. M. Ciampelli, 'Il "jazz" e la sua storia', *Radiocorriere*, 9/7 (12–19 February 1933), 13; Massimo Soria, 'Chiaroscuro del jazz', *Radiocorriere*, 10/31 (29 July–4 August 1933), 17; anon., 'Spigolature del jazz', *Radiocorriere*, 10/32 (August 1934), 17. Harwell Celenza's suggestion that Zuculin's comments on Italian Americans being involved in the early jazz scene 'inspired many Italians, including the Futurists and Mussolini, to embrace the music as a "native" art form' (*Jazz Italian Style*, 40) remains unsubstantiated. Rather, Zuculin's article does not seem to have had any influence on the debate at the time. It remained unmentioned, until Mazzoletti commented on it in his history of jazz, praising it for its importance as an insight into the early jazz world of New Orleans, but without making any assumption as to its influence on the knowledge of jazz that was taking shape in Italy at the time. Zuculin's article—'Musiche e danze americane', *La Lettura*, 19/8 (August 1919), 599–600—is reproduced in its entirety by Mazzoletti in *Il jazz in Italia*, i. 29–33.

Testoni—two jazz critics involved in the Milanese scene—had a more nationalistic approach—indeed, the book is dedicated to Vittorio Mussolini—but only in so far as expressing their desire that Italian jazz musicians should embrace the 'hot' tradition of jazz and therefore take inspiration from the African American school, rather than the 'straight' jazz played by the big orchestras in the north-east. They too, however, did not venture to mention a connection between the origins of jazz and Italian American musicians. If there is one aspect that these two monographs have in common (and that allows Caraceni to present his book as the first Italian book on jazz, totally ignoring Bragaglia's), it is their attempt to present jazz music as a groundbreaking musical genre that goes well beyond its connection with modern dance and nightclub entertainment.[53]

Levi and Testoni were two jazz critics who in 1935 founded the Circolo del jazz hot, an association that supported instrumental jazz as a serious form of music, to be listened to rather than danced to, and it sponsored its own band, the Orchestra del Circolo del jazz hot. Once again, it was an initiative inspired by Paris: the Hot Club de France had been created there in 1932 and, similarly, had its orchestra called the Hot Club orchestra (later Quintette du Hot Club de France), and even published its own magazine, *Le Jazz Hot*. Levi and Testoni's public mention of Mussolini's son in the book's dedication was probably an attempt to ensure some political 'protection' within the already mentioned internal tug of war pro/against jazz in Fascist circles. The two knew Vittorio Mussolini, since all three had contributed to the Milanese music magazine *Il Disco*. Ezio Levi, of Jewish origin, left Italy after the introduction of the anti-Semitic legislation, a few months after the publication of the book, and went to live in the USA.

Ironically, had Mussolini and his circle been genuinely interested in the Italian American scene in the USA, they would have faced the intriguing and potentially embarrassing news that in its midst was a musician called Nick Musolino—sometimes misspelled Mussolini. A trombonist, Musolino played in a popular jazz orchestra of the 1920s, the Coon-Sanders Original Nighthawk Orchestra. Based in Kansas City, this all-white orchestra became nationally famous thanks to a radio programme that, starting in December 1922, broadcast its late-night performances. Listeners were asked to phone, write, or telegraph so that they could hear their suggestions acknowledged and played on the same night. Nicholas L. Musolino was born in Quincy, the self-called 'gem city' on the Mississippi River, where his father had a fruit and produce business.[54]

The existence of Musolino, like that of most Italian American musicians, was ignored by Italian journalists either travelling to America or resident there during

---

[53] Augusto Caraceni, *Il jazz: Dalle origini ad oggi* (Milan: Suvini Zerboni, 1937). Ezio Levi and Gian Carlo Testoni, *Introduzione alla vera musica di jazz* (Milan: Magazzino Musicale, 1938). On Caraceni, see Cerchiari, *Jazz e fascismo*, 115–18.
[54] On Nick Musolino, see the brilliantly researched history of Coon-Sanders' band: Fred W. Edmiston, *The Coon-Sanders Nighthawks: 'The Band that Made Radio Famous'* (Jefferson, NC: McFarland & Co., 2003), 112–13, 128, 150–9, 329.

the interwar period. If some had their Italian American identity hidden by an Anglified name—such as guitarist Eddie Lang (Salvatore Massaro) or composer Harry Warren (Salvatore Antonio Guaragna)—many others kept their surname, which was often of Sicilian origin. Beyond the already mentioned Nick La Rocca and Joe Venuti, there were others, such as drummer Tony Sbarbaro and clarinettists Tony Parenti and Leon Roppolo, accordionist Guido Deiro, and trumpeter Frank Guarente. There is no doubt about the wealth of Italian American talent on the jazz music scene. However, journalists who spent a prolonged time in America tended to centre their writings either on reference to the roots of jazz among the African American community or on descriptions of dance halls where jazz music was feverishly enjoyed by the urban, all-white elite, recalling Scott Fitzgerald's parties in *The Great Gatsby*, with little or no mention of individual musicians.

Something similar, after all, was taking place on a broader scale. As argued in Chapter 5, during the interwar years there was still a tendency among Italian commentators to marginalize the presence and importance of millions of Italian migrants in the USA. It was another America that they were looking for: an 'Other' America, different, distant, whether it was the open spaces of the Far West and of the Deep South, or the futuristic megalopolises of the north-east. The image of jazz partook of these two extremes, having been born in the violent lands of Louisiana, and matured in the giant cities whose skyscrapers pointed to the future of humanity. The sons and daughters of Italian immigrants were present in both, but perhaps embarrassingly so. In Louisiana, they rubbed shoulders with the black community, because they were the white community closest to them, socially and economically. In New York and Chicago, the Italian community was certainly rising up the social ladder, but, with a few exceptions, Italian journalists and authors seemed more interested in the White Anglo-Saxon Protestant America, which still dominated the upper echelons of society. So, when it came to jazz, Italian Americans almost never featured in the picture, neither as musicians nor as dance-hall *habitués*, whether in Harlem's Cotton Club or Manhattan's Broadway theatres and luxury hotels.

In the end, New Orleans' Consul Bruno Zuculin's article of August 1919 remained an isolated contribution during the entire interwar period. Caraceni's two chapters on the origin of jazz in his *Il jazz dalle origini a oggi* make no mention of the Italian community in New Orleans. Indicative of a potential case of self-censorship is the fact that, when touching upon the earliest jazz record, Caraceni does register the original Dixieland 'Jass' Band's 1917 recording as the first ever, but strikingly omits to mention the fact that the group was led by Nick La Rocca.[55] Beyond that, the historical fact that La Rocca's band performed in

---

[55] Caraceni, *Il jazz*, 44. Caraceni did know of La Rocca's existence, since his name is briefly mentioned in a list of famous early jazz composers, on p. 101. Other Italian American musicians are mentioned among others in the book, but never with reference to their ethnicity.

London for an entire year, the very year Zuculin's article was written, and never went to Italy, adds to a sense of detachment between the very first generation of Italian American jazz musicians and post-First World War Italy. Later on, direct contact between Italian American jazzmen and Italian musicians who met them either in New York or during the former's European tours increased the creative ties between the two communities. However, in the mind of Italians, Fascist or not, as much as in the minds of Italian music journalists throughout the interwar years, the origins of jazz coincided with the history of the African American community in the Deep South.

As for the appreciation of Italian American jazzmen, Fascist propaganda was eventually to move in the opposite direction, at least in the realm of cinema. Pietro Redi, known in America as Peter Reed, a successful composer of jazz songs, is the fictional protagonist of Carmine Gallone's film *Primo amore* (1941): the success and glamour Reed had achieved in America is left behind when he comes back to Italy and finds his true inspiration in the folk tradition of Italian music and in the love of an Italian girl, as against the American femme fatale, jazz singer Jane Blue.

By the final years of Fascism, all things American, jazz included, had become propaganda material. By then, Mussolini and his regime were in an irreversible collision course against its icon of modernity, the United States of America.

# 9
# The Lure of Hollywood

During the interwar years, cinema was the field in which the presence and influence of American culture was at its strongest. This was the effect of a double cause. On the one hand, the crisis of the Italian film industry, following the collapse of the European markets and its partial restructuring in line with the war effort during the First World War, meant that Italy's capacity to produce its own repertoire of films spiralled to staggeringly low figures. If, in its pre-First World War heydays, Italian film production companies were capable of producing and exporting hundreds of films per year—and about 200 were still produced in 1920—by the second half of the 1920s the industry's nosedive was nearing its complete collapse, with only eight films being produced in 1930 and two in 1931.[1]

By then, Mussolini was nearing the end of his first decade in power, and this fact alone signals the regime's initial lack of interest in this cultural industry. On the other hand, the 1920s saw America reach a position of absolute dominance in the European film market. Hollywood became a paradigm, a model, as Victoria De Grazia put it:

> America's movie industry offered an entirely new paradigm for organizing cultural production on industrial lines: what Fordism was to global car manufacturing, the Hollywood studio system was to promoting a mass-produced, internationally marketed commodity.[2]

Moreover, it was not just a question of technical supremacy. As Geoffrey Nowell-Smith suggests, it was also part of a radical change in Western culture:

> The triumph of Hollywood in the 1920s was a triumph of the New World over the Old, marking the emergence of the canons of modern American mass culture not only in America but in countries as yet uncertain how to receive it.[3]

---

[1] Associazione nazionale industrie cinematografiche audiovisive (ANICA) data on Italian film production, tabled in Daniela Manetti, *'Un'arma poderosissima': Industria cinematografica e stato durante il fascismo, 1922–1943* (Milan: Franco Angeli, 2012), 62.

[2] Victoria De Grazia, 'Mass Culture and Sovereignty: The American Challenge to European Cinemas, 1920–1960', *Journal of Modern History*, 61/1 (1989), 53–87 (56).

[3] Geoffrey Nowell-Smith, 'Silent Cinema, 1895–1930: Introduction', in Geoffrey Nowell-Smith (ed.), *The Oxford History of World Cinema* (Oxford: Oxford University Press, 1996), 2–5 (4).

As far as cinemagoers were concerned, it was a welcome invasion, since the aesthetic quality of American films and their depiction of the many wonders of American society made them most attractive to their eyes and minds. Hollywood's average share of the Italian market between 1926 and 1938 was about 75 per cent. This means that, for the millions of Italians who embraced film as their favourite form of narrative and free-time entertainment, going to watch a movie was often equal to consuming an American product.[4]

This experience was shared by both Italy's lowly educated masses and its ruling elite. A number of Italian intellectuals who grew up in the interwar years remember American cinema as by far their most memorable experience as young cinemagoers: from Cesare Zavattini to Federico Fellini, Attilio Bertolucci, Italo Calvino, Umberto Eco, and Leonardo Sciascia. In a post-war interview, Zavattini said: 'I must confess that in those years I had no knowledge of Italian cinema; cinema for me was already American cinema, only American cinema.' Calvino was not far from that view: 'I haven't said it yet but I thought it was implicit: cinema for me was the American one, what came out of Hollywood at the time.' Attilio Bertolucci's opinion was only more highbrow: 'Don't stone me to death, but Griffith, Chaplin, and Keaton are to cinema what Tolstoy, Dickens are to the novel.'[5]

The regime's eventual heavy investment in strengthening the Italian film industry and in turning it into a propaganda tool took years to kick in. By 1938, Italy's fiction film production was still below fifty films per year, a fraction of what the distribution industry needed to feed an ever-increasing market. In the same years, Mussolini had discovered that cinema was 'the most powerful weapon' in the war for the minds of Italians (an expression he had borrowed from Lenin). Hollywood was both an industrial model and a powerful competitor: hence a degree of ambivalence and the formation of different camps within the Fascist regime. By the end of the 1930s, incapable of competing with American cinema in a square fight, and in line with his Nazi ally, Mussolini was to accept that protectionism was the only answer.[6]

---

[4] See 'Appendix C: Percent of American Films Shown in Italy between 1920 and 1940', in James Hay, *Popular Film Culture in Fascist Italy: The Passing of the Rex* (Bloomington, IN: Indiana University Press, 1987), 253.

[5] Zavattini's 1979 interview is quoted in Vito Zagarrio, *Cinema e fascismo: Film, modelli, immaginari* (Venice: Marsilio, 2004), 209. Italo Calvino, 'Autobiografia di uno spettatore', preface to Federico Fellini, *Quattro film* (Turin: Einaudi, 1974); repr. in Italo Calvino, *Romanzi e racconti* (Milan: Mondadori, 1994), iii. 27–49 (33). Attilio Bertolucci, 'Che emozione quando Fay Wray lanciava violette nello stivale di Von Stroheim', *La Repubblica*, 20 August 1976; repr. as 'Il cinema che ho amato', in Attilio Bertolucci, *Riflessi da un paradiso perduto: Scritti sul cinema* (Bergamo: Moretti & Vitali, 2009), 49–51 (50). Gian Piero Brunetta dwells on this generational phenomenon in his *Il ruggito del leone: Hollywood alla Conquista dell'impero dei sogni nell'Italia di Mussolini* (Venice: Marsilio, 2013), 17–26.

[6] The slogan 'La cinematografia è l'arma più forte' ('Cinematography is the most powerful weapon') was painted as a backdrop on the site of Cinecittà when its construction was officially started by Mussolini on 29 January 1936. On this, see Stephen Gundle, *Mussolini's Dream Factory: Film Stardom in Fascist Italy* (New York and Oxford: Berghahn, 2013), 19.

In the interwar years, the Fascist regime was not alone in its late recognition of the cultural importance of the production and consumption of films. The critical appreciation of film by Italian intellectuals was a late occurrence too. Once again, the inspiration came from over the Alps, this time in the form of a number of publications: Louis Delluc's 1921 book on Charlie Chaplin, and the renowned 1926 issue of *Cahiers du mois*, entirely dedicated to cinema. When the most prestigious Florentine journal, *Solaria*, responded to *Cahiers du mois* with its own cinema issue, in 1927, a different attitude was there for all to see. If the French magazine had produced the first collective discussion on the importance of film, the majority of the 'Solariani' responded with a condescending dismissal, treating it as a minor art with little potential other than that of competing with the second-rate market of cheap adventure and sentimental narrative. One of the few voices against this trend was that of Antonello Gerbi, who addressed this in an erudite and humorous essay in the pages of the Milanese journal *Il Convegno*. Beyond him, only a few voices rose against this elitist stance.[7]

In the same period, a committed filmmaker and then a genuine militant fascist, Alessandro Blasetti, founded his own film journals—first *Lo Schermo*, in 1926, and the following year *Cinematografo*—through which he hoped to pressure the Fascist government into protecting the Italian film industry. Blasetti also complained about American productions in Italy, accusing them of exploiting Italian skills, again asking for the Fascist government to intervene. But it took years before Italy could boast of a raft of high-quality film periodicals such as *Cine-Convegno* (an offshoot of *Il Convegno*), *Lo Schermo*, *Cinema*, and *Bianco e nero*, all founded between 1933 and 1937—the last three being a product of the regime's eventual involvement.[8]

Similarly, the first scholarly monograph on cinema was Ettore Margadonna's *Cinema ieri e oggi*, published in 1932, eleven years after Delluc's. And, still in 1932, in his official speech at the Italian evening of the Venice Film Festival—then in its very first year—Gino Rocca (playwright and theatre critic at *Il Popolo d'Italia*)

---

[7] Antonello Gerbi, 'Teorie sul cinema (A proposito di un "Cahiers du mois")', *Il Convegno*, 7/10 (October 1926), 766-81. *Il Convegno* was the first cultural magazine to devote a section on cinema, starting from May 1927. It also benefited from the collaboration of Ettore Margadonna, who, as we will see, proved to be one of the most committed and insightful film critics of his generation. A pro-cinema view came from Leo Ferrero, 'Dialogo sull'ombra', *Solaria*, 2/3 (March 1927), 23-30. Beynet notices how, when Italian intellectuals wrote about cinema, in the 1920s, they often referred to the critical debate in France in apologetic terms, as a justification for taking this art seriously. See Beynet, *L'Image de l'Amérique*, iii. 806-8.

[8] *Lo Schermo* was founded in 1935 by the Fascist journalist and politician Lando Ferretti under the auspices of the then Ministry of Press and Propaganda. The connection with Blasetti's defunct *Lo Schermo* of 1926 was only symbolic. Blasetti did not contribute to its first issue, despite the fact that it was openly presented as an initiative coming directly from the regime and showcased contributions by renowned figures such as Luigi Freddi, Luigi Chiarini, and Corrado Pavolini. The latter, an author and brother of the politician and future Minister of Popular Culture, Alessandro Pavolini, was to accompany Vittorio Mussolini during his 1937 trip to Hollywood.

was defining cinema as 'humanity's mechanical toy', presenting it as a technology-born offshoot of theatre, still in search of its own identity.[9]

It goes without saying that there had been a critical debate on cinema during the silent movie period too, from Anton Giulio Bragaglia's theories to comments by literary figures such as D'Annunzio and Pirandello. Equally, there were a few film magazines aimed either at distributors and cinema managers or at the growing viewing public. At the same time, Brunetta agrees in dating the birth of the professional film critic in Italy to the early 1930s, when Italy's major newspapers began to employ intellectuals such as Mario Gromo (who had contributed to the *Solaria* issue with a short, surprisingly condescending view on cinema) and his collaboration with *La Stampa*, which, from January 1933, started to devote an entire weekly page on cinema.[10]

Mention of the Venice Film Festival reminds us that, by the early 1930s, Italy was leading the way at least in the field of film festivals. Cannes opened only seven years later, in 1939, in order to offer an alternative to the Axis-led politicization that had dominated at Venice the year before. In the early years of the Venice Film Festival, the line-up presented the cream of American films, some of which were to become classics, such as King Vidor's *The Champ* (1931) and Frank Capra's *It Happened One Night* (1934). In 1935, Hollywood won the most prestigious awards: Vidor's *The Wedding Night* for best director, and Clarence Brown's *Anna Karenina*, starring Greta Garbo, won the Mussolini Cup for best foreign film.

In the four sections of this chapter, the first one will explore the channels through which millions of Italians came to watch American films and read about them. It will also look at the impact of the first Hollywood runaway productions, which put the Italian and American film industries in direct contact. The second will examine the regime's attitudes and policies towards American cinema. Differently from jazz music, here Mussolini's opinion was expressed on more than one occasion, and so was that of two key figures who pulled the Italian industry in opposite directions: Mussolini's son, Vittorio, a keen film critic and an aspiring producer of clear philo-American tendencies, and the Fascist tzar of Italian cinema, Luigi Freddi, head of the Direzione Generale per la Cinematografia since its creation in 1934, and a staunch promoter of national production.

---

[9] Ettore Margadonna, *Cinema ieri e oggi* (Milan: Editoriale Domus, 1932). Part of the book is constituted by articles Margadonna had been writing for *Comoedia* since February 1930. Gino Rocca's speech is quoted in Filippo Sacchi, 'La serata italiana al Festival del Lido', *Corriere della Sera*, 12 August 1932, p. 5.

[10] Gian Piero Brunetta, *Storia del cinema italiano (1895–1945)* (Rome: Editori Riuniti, 1979), 447–8. Beynet too concludes that the Italian daily press paid little attention to cinema until the late 1920s. The already discussed visit to Hollywood by Arnaldo Fraccaroli for *Corriere della Sera*, in August 1927, marks a clear development in that respect (Beynet, *L'Image de l'Amérique*, iii. 747–9). On the development of film criticism in Italy and on its dependence on the French intellectual debate, see Fabio Andreazza, *Identificazione di un'arte: Scrittori e cinema nel primo novecento italiano* (Rome: Bulzoni, 2008), 140–82.

The third section—articulated in different subsections—will assess the ways in which the Italian film industry responded to the practices and style of Hollywood cinema during the interwar years. The fourth and final one will return to a topic already tackled for the years before the First World War: film representations of migration to the Americas. Some brief, concluding remarks will tie back together the various threads of this long but necessary discussion of American cinema in Fascist Italy until 1938.

## 9.1 American Cinema in Italy

In the early 1920s, the Italian film industry could still boast of its past glories as a producer of epoch-making films such as Pastrone's *Cabiria*. However, at the other end of the production and consumption chain—that is, the distribution and screening network—Italy lay behind leading European countries. By 1933, it had a total of about 2,250 cinemas, and not even half of them were wired for sound. Germany, in comparison, despite the post-war economic depression, had reached 5,267 by 1928. There was also a geographical differentiation, considering that cinemas were mainly concentrated in urban centres and that the majority of them were in the north of the country.[11]

This means that the Italian market was proportionally less important to the American majors. A telltale sign of such a situation is the fact that, in the early post-First World War years, France and Germany hosted respectively seven and five American distribution subsidiaries, whereas Italy only had one, created by Fox in 1919.[12] Despite their small footprint in Italy, American film companies deployed their marketing strategies in order to maximize their lion share. The few film magazines of the early post-war period—such as the weekly *Al cinema* (1922–30) or the monthly *Figure mute* (1919–20)—were mostly composed of adverts, interspersed with the constant editorial lamenting the crisis of the Italian film industry, or presenting—rather than critically discussing—individual films. Many adverts were by Italian companies, and the name of the Italian female star *par excellence* of those years, Francesca Bertini, appeared prominently, although by 1921 she had decided to take a break from her acting career, which included refusing a generous contract from William Fox to move over to Hollywood.

The advertising pages of those magazines featured American productions too. The October 1919 issue of *Figure mute*, as an example, contained fourteen pages (out of ninety-eight) filled with adverts of American films, in which the Universal

---

[11] Figures from James Hay, 'Appendix A: Number of Motion Picture Theatres in Italy, 1928–1937', in Hay, *Popular Film Culture in Fascist Italy*, 251; and Corey Ross, 'Mass Culture and Divided Audiences: Cinema and Social Change in Inter-War Germany', *Past & Present*, 193 (2006), 157–95 (160).

[12] Data sourced from company reports and tables in Bakker, *Entertainment Industrialised*, 251.

Fig. 9.1. First page of an article signed 'Metro Goldwin' (*sic*) devoted to MGM's film *The Midshipman* (1925), in *Comoedia*, 5/8 (August 1926). (courtesy of BNC, Rome)

catalogue featured prominently. It is also interesting to note that, when Italy's most prestigious theatre magazine, Mondadori's *Comoedia,* began to publish the odd article on cinema, starting in September 1925, it would often feature heavily illustrated, enthusiastic descriptions of American productions, which had clearly been written—and paid for—by those companies' press offices. Some were oddly signed with the name of the film production company itself. The article partly reproduced in Fig. 9.1 is a four-page piece devoted to MGM's film *The Midshipman* (1925)—*Il guardiamarina*—directed by Christy Cabanne and starring Mexican star Ramon Novarro. The text, signed 'Metro Goldwin' (*sic*), narrates the making of the film, with frequent praise for its grand-scale collaboration with the US Navy. *The Midshipman* was shot at the Naval Academy in Annapolis and involved thousands of navy sailors and officers as extras, various warships, and scores of hydroplanes. American President Coolidge was even present at some of the shooting, boasted the article.

The year before, Ramon Novarro had also been the leading man in another box-office hit by Metro-Goldwyn-Meyer, *Ben-Hur: A Tale of the Christ* (1925). This other film—as already mentioned in Chapter 9 in relation to Scott Fitzgerald's stay in Rome—was initially shot in Italy. Before becoming a film, *Ben-Hur*, like Edward Bulwer-Lytton's novel, *The Last Days of Pompeii* and its fortunate pre-First World War film adaptations, had been a popular nineteenth-century historical-come-religious novel, by Lewis Wallace, which in this case had also been turned into a successful Broadway play. Furthermore, it was not the first American production shot in Italy. As we saw with George Kleine, in Chapter 3, the temptation of coming to Italy and benefiting from its combination of skilled labour, great locations, and low cost of living had already been taken up with the creation of the American–Italian Photo Drama company, back in 1914. Other ventures followed. Between 1914 and 1926, thirteen films were shot in different Italian locations, either produced by American film companies or led by an American filmmaker. The latter was the case of Herbert Brenon, who, during his ten-month stay in Italy in 1919–20, directed three films. They were all produced by Unione Cinematografica Italiana (UCI) in an attempt to add international flavour to Italy's film production. At the same time, the impending crisis of the Italian film industry meant that it was mainly American production companies that were taking the lead. Whether this meant more financially successful enterprises is a different story.[13]

During the early years after the First World War, Europe at large was eyed by the American film industry as a potential site for their productions. In 1921, Fox invested in the creation of an Italian subsidiary in Rome, as the leading American film industry paper, *Exhibitors Herald*, boasted in a long article dedicated to the eighteen-year anniversary of the foundation of Fox Film (see Fig. 9.2). Despite its optimistic promotion as Willam Fox's latest enterprise, however, only one film came out of Fox's Italian studio. This was *Nero* (1922), directed by James Gordon Edwards, an old hand of toga dramas (the year before he had directed Fox's *The Queen of Sheeba*, filmed in California). *Nero* was one of many historical films set in classical times, and it is clear that the choice of Italy for its staging was partly an attempt to exploit Italy's prestigious record in this genre, of which William Fox was a great admirer. Analogously to what was going to happen with *Ben-Hur*, costs spiralled during the Italian shooting, and, despite its relative box-office success, the film made a loss; hence Fox decided to withdraw its industrial footprint from Italy altogether.[14]

The interest in Italy by American filmmakers is also testified to by an article that Charles Rosher—the cinematographer involved in the Italian shooting of

---

[13] See Muscio, *Napoli/New York/Hollywood*, 100–56. See also Di Chio, *Il cinema americano in Italia*, 74–9; and Brunetta, *Il ruggito del leone*, 27–46.

[14] Gordon Edwards shot a few scenes of another historical–religious drama, *The Shepherd King* (1923), in Italy, a film that shared a cast with *Nero*. However, the search for spectacular biblical landscapes meant that most of *The Shepherd King* was then shot in the Middle East. On this, see David J. Shepherd, *The Bible on Silent Film: Spectacle, Story and Scripture in the Early Cinema* (Cambridge: Cambridge University Press, 2013), 205–11. On *Nero*, see Muscio, *Napoli/New York/Hollywood*, 118–25.

Fig. 9.2. *Exhibitors Herald*'s article of 21 January 1922 celebrating the eighteen-year anniversary of Fox Film; the photographs on the left show Fox's studios, respectively, in New York (top and mid-right), Rome (mid-left), and Los Angeles (bottom-right); the small photo in the centre of the right page features the bungalows purpose built as dressing rooms for stars at Fox studios in LA. (courtesy of MHDL, Wisconsin Center for Film and Theater Research)

another half-forgotten Italian American film production, *Sant'Ilario* (1922)—published in the *American Cinematographer* of September 1922. Entitled 'An Analysis of the Film Industry in Italy', the introductory lines of the article give a clear-headed, American-style-worded image of the state of Italian cinema:

> Ten years ago those interested in the cinema looked to Italy for new ideas in the art. Now Italy is not leading but following.
>
> Films there resemble the champion pugilist who has suffered defeat and, although trying to 'come back', does not have the confidence in himself he once enjoyed.[15]

In the paragraphs that followed, Rosher's analysis touches all the points that film historians list with today's power of hindsight as the reasons behind the crisis: the

---

[15] Chas (Charles) Rosher, ASC, 'An Analysis of the Film Industry in Italy', *American Cinematographer*, 2/9 (15 September 1922), 7–9 (7). On Sant'Ilario and Chas Rosher, see Muscio, *Napoli/New York/Hollywood*, 115–18.

consequences of the First World War, lack of funding, the non-rationalized and fragile organization of the industry, its dependence on one-man, one-film projects, and its ageing infrastructure. Equally unfortunate was, in his view, the outdated aspiration for big, historical canvases while lacking attention to questions of storytelling and characterization. We will return to this last point, since it is an indicator of where some of the influence of American cinema might have entered Italian filmmaking.

The geographical move from Kleine's venture in Turin, in 1914, to Fox's in Rome in 1919 is also emblematic not so much of the fact that Turin was losing its leading role in the Italian film industry (it had not, by then) but of the reality that, while Kleine was interested only in a partnership with Italian filmmakers, Fox's interest was equally driven by location—Rome, which embodied the lure of historical, still-standing classical buildings. Indeed, the Colosseum featured in a number of American films shot at the time, from *The Eternal City* (in both the 1914 and 1923 versions) to Fox's *Nero* in 1922. However, what Kleine had been looking for was to be found less and less there. Rosher's article gave a clear warning to American filmmakers about Italy's by-then outdated infrastructure. Location and the professional skills of individuals, actors in particular, were outstanding, he admitted, but the work of an American cinematographer was made very difficult by the lack of the latest generation of hardware, lighting gear in particular. Even basics such as easy access to electricity inside the studios was not to be taken for granted, plus, he complained, Italians were not used to the tight, factory-like rhythms of American productions, and so the planned savings, due to lower costs of labour, were quickly burned up in longer shooting times and constant delays.[16]

If William Fox understood this early enough, it seems that nobody had paid attention to Rosher's article at Goldwyn. *Ben-Hur* promised to be a more monumental enterprise than *Nero*, hence the stakes were even higher. The theatrical version of *Ben-Hur*, which had opened on Broadway in November 1899, had already been a mammoth operation in its genre. The iconic chariot race at the heart of the plot was staged with eight horses galloping on a hidden treadmill, while a painted landscape of the Circus Maximus whirred in the opposite direction. Bringing such a scene to a film shot on location certainly opened up wondrous opportunities for an ambitious film company. However, it equally raised the level of commitment to great heights, to shooting plans in a foreign country

---

[16] The Italian film industry's negative differential in terms of technical facilities and knowhow compared to the American one was highlighted by filmmaker Anton Giulio Bragaglia in an article for *Critica fascista* in 1926. Bragaglia came up with the suggestion that a team of young, bright apprentices in various aspects of filmmaking should be sent to Hollywood for a couple of years in order to learn about the latest techniques and hardware. Bragaglia, 'Lo stile è l'epoca'; discussed by Brunetta in *Storia del cinema italiano*, ii. *Il cinema del regime (1929–1943)* (Rome: Editori Riuniti, 2001), 161–2.

that proved impossible to stick to, and that almost turned the film into a colossal production fiasco.

With a flight of the imagination inspired by detailed insight into what had happened, silent-film historian Kevin Brownlow likened the production of *Ben Hur* to 'a Dunkirk of the cinema: a humiliating defeat transformed, after heavy losses, into a brilliant victory'.[17] Once Goldwyn had eventually earned the film rights to the novel, the decision to shoot in Italy was apparently taken by the company's powerful head scenarist and only female executive, June Mathis. The film crew and some of its cast moved to Rome in the autumn of 1923, but the construction of the two key scenarios—the Circus Maximus (whose bottom half was built outside Porta San Giovanni while the upper half was a painted miniature) and the sea battle, which required thirty ships to be built at Anzio—quickly went behind schedule, so that shooting did not start until the following year. By then Goldwyn had merged with Metro and Mayer to form the giant Metro-Goldwyn-Mayer, and the triumvirate at its head did not like the first footage that was sent over by director Charles Brabin. However, despite the disappointing first results and the worrying production delays, MGM decided to stick to the project and, indeed, reinforce it with a new director, Fred Niblo, and a new leading actor, Metro's rising star Ramon Novarro, who took the part of Ben-Hur from the hands of George Walsh. By then the film had been in production for over a year. The sea battle, which was shot in September 1924, was the one in which the skills of Italian artisans were shown at their best, with the complete reconstruction of a seaworthy Roman trireme and a pirate galley. The actual shooting proved chaotic, since the trireme, rammed by the galley, burst into flames more quickly than expected. Dozens of panicking extras threw themselves into the sea, and three of them were assumed to have drowned until they turned up the following day, having been rescued by a passing boat.[18]

Eventually, in January 1925, *Ben-Hur*'s cast and crew were taken back to Hollywood. The replica of Circus Maximus was rebuilt, this time in Culver City, and the iconic chariot scene was shot again. Sadly, it was now the turn for scores of American horses to be injured and put down for the sake of the realistic vividness of the big chariot pile up at the end of the scene. This time, forty-two cameras were used to film the scene from every possible angle, ten of them hidden around the corner of the racetrack where the main accident was going to take place. *Ben-Hur* proved that, technically, there was no reason for any American production to move to Europe. A better strategy was to lure the best European

---

[17] Brownlow, *The Parade's Gone By*, 386.
[18] More than ten years later, an article in *Cinema* was still boasting of Italy's great skills at creating real-size historic ships as against the American use of miniatures. The article was based on the comparison between two movies, Warner Bros' *Captain Blood* (1935) and the Italian *Il corsaro nero*, then in production by Artisti Associati, based on Emilio Salgari's popular 1898 novel. See Maria Cecchi, 'Quando il trucco ha torto', *Cinema*, 1/6 (1936), 216.

directors and actors to America. Coincidentally, when Louis B. Mayer went to Italy to follow the doomed shooting of *Ben-Hur*, in October 1924, he then continued his journey to Germany, where he signed up director Mauritz Stiller and his protégée, a young Swedish actress called Greta Garbo.[19]

In relation to the production of *Ben-Hur*, one should mention the fortunate migration to Hollywood of an Italian cinematographer, Silvano Balboni, whose American experience was later to benefit the technical set-up of Cinecittà. Balboni had started his career in the 1910s, working for one of Turin's film production companies—Pasquali e C.—and in the first years after the war had been involved in first British and then American productions. While employed as one of the cinematographers for the Italian leg of the production of *Ben-Hur*, Balboni entered into a relationship with MGM's June Mathis. The two got married in Los Angeles on 20 December 1924. There, Balboni continued to work on a number of American productions as cinematographer; he also directed two films for First National Pictures, the studios to which Mathis had moved after the fiasco of *Ben-Hur*'s production in Italy. However, after Mathis's sudden death, on 26 July 1927, Balboni decided to return to Italy. He was eventually hired as Ispettore Generale at Cinecittà in 1937.[20]

According to some film historians, the Italian production of *Ben-Hur*, on top of all its problems, had the pernicious effect of contributing to the crisis of the Italian film industry, since it more or less monopolized studio sets and the best technicians for a whole year. Whether or not this effectively amounted to a *coup de grâce*, it is equally reasonable to ask whether this direct contact between two film industries contributed to any lessons being learnt on the Italian side. The answer, as De Grazia suggests, might be linked with the person of Stefano Pittaluga.[21]

From the start, in his native Genoa, back in 1907, Pittaluga had worked in the business of the distribution of films. He developed this into a fully-fledged, national company after his move to Turin and the creation of the Società Anonima Stefano Pittaluga (SASP) in March 1919. By the early 1920s, Pittaluga's company was distributing Italian and foreign films—he was the exclusive distributor for Warner Bros—along the entire peninsula, directly controlling over a hundred cinema theatres in most of Italy's major cities and, in total, serving two-thirds of the entire national network of movie theatres. His fortunes went in the opposite

---

[19] On the production of Ben-Hur and on Mayer's trip to Europe, see Brownlow, *The Parade's Gone By*, 386–414; and Charles Higham, *Merchant of Dreams: Louis B. Mayer, MGM, and the Secret Hollywood* (New York: Sidgwick & Jackson, 1993), 75–88.

[20] On the relationship between Mathis and Balboni on and off the film set, see Ivan St Johns, 'Fifty–Fifty: June Mathis Meets the Perfect Collaborator—and Marries him', *Photoplay*, 30/5 (October 1926), 46, 123–4. More on this later on in this chapter. See Balboni's biographical entry in Alessandro Gatti (ed.), *I cineoperatori: La storia della cinematografia italiana dal 1895 al 1940 raccontata dagli autori della fotografia*, i (Rome: Edizioni AIC, 1999), 86–7.

[21] De Grazia, 'Mass Culture and Sovereignty'. See also Libero Bizzarri and Libero Solaroli *L'industria cinematografica italiana* (Florence: Parenti, 1958), 28.

direction from those of the production industry, so that, when UCI went into liquidation (the *coup de grâce*, in its case, was the disastrously unpopular remake of one of Italy's glories from the pre-war years, *Quo Vadis*), in the autumn of 1926, Pittaluga was in a position to step in and take it over, beating Paramount to it thanks also to a huge loan from the Banca Commerciale Italiana. It was the first time that an Italian entrepreneur had had the opportunity to create a vertical system of production, distribution, and exhibition at national level, in a fashion resembling that of an American major.

Furthermore, given his formation as a distributor, it is not surprising that Pittaluga should have been particularly open-minded towards foreign film production. With the arrival of sound, the following year, Pittaluga invested heavily in the updating of the Cines studios in Rome (which were part of UCI). Interviewed by the *Corriere della Sera*, in April 1929, he was asked for his opinion of this 'new American devilry': sound films. Pittaluga, who had visited a sound cinema theatre in London the year before, had no doubts in defining it as a revolution that Italy had to live up to. By then he could announce that his company was hard at work, and, indeed, by 1930 Pittaluga–Cines (as it was formally called from 1928) could boast the same RCA Photophone sound equipment used in Hollywood.[22]

At the same time, Pittaluga tried to impose an American-style rationalization of film production, marketing, and distribution. Publicity, for example, raised above 1 per cent of the entire budget of Cines film productions, in an attempt to move towards the 2–10 per cent invested at the time by the American majors.[23] Pittaluga's efforts did not bring about a renaissance of the Italian film industry but they turned Cines into a profit-making company and a clear leader in Italy. From the new Cines studios were to emerge Italy's first two sound films. The first was Gennaro Righelli's *La canzone dell'amore* (1930), a film that, like America's first talkie, Alan Crosland's *The Jazz Singer* (1927), featured a musician among the protagonists and hence a dominant, intra-diegetic music score. The second one was Alessandro Blasetti's *Resurrectio* (1931), which, once again, had a composer at its centre, plenty of music, and even a jazz band. Tellingly, the appearance of the jazz band was in tune with the director's heavily nationalistic viewpoint, since it accompanied the appearance of the 'bad' female character, the selfish former lover who brings the composer to the brink of suicide, while his compositions are faithful to the classical tradition.

The shooting of Blasetti's film started before that of Righelli's, and it is an open question whether the delays in the former's production were the result of

---

[22] Anon., 'L'arte italiana e il cinema parlante nel parere di un competente', *Corriere della Sera*, 30 April 1929, p. 3.
[23] Data provided by Marina Nicoli in her essay 'Entrepreneurs and the State in the Italian Film Industry, 1919–1935', *Business History Review*, 85 (Winter 2011), 775–98 (780).

Pittaluga's intention to 'premiere' in the world of sound cinema with *La canzone dell'amore*, a more commercial film (although artistically less sophisticated), which carried the added literary publicity value of being a free adaptation from a novella by Pirandello. *La canzone dell'amore* was constructed around a heavily sentimental storyline and a final happy ending, which, in fact, wreaked havoc on Pirandello's text. It tells the story of a young woman who is prepared to sacrifice her career and her love life in order to look after the baby her dead-in-childbirth mother has had out of wedlock. She eventually gives the baby away to his rich and contrite father and is saved from suicidal desperation by her loyal fiancé. Furthermore, Righelli went overboard in order to depict Rome at its best, from long panoramic shots of classical monuments at the start, to the cutting-edge modernity of rationalist buildings, particularly in the form of the recording studio (the fiancé is a composer), showcasing Italy's alleged technological advancement. The film was shot in three different languages—dubbing, as we will see, was still to come—but the French and German versions did not travel far, although the production was eventually a profit-making one. The film reached the USA the following year, within a limited regime-sponsored distribution in cinemas catering for the Italian American communities.[24]

*La canzone dell'amore* was one of the three films produced by Pittaluga-Cines in 1930, out of the eight produced in Italy in that year. The dominance of American films can be condensed in two statistics: in 1930, Pittaluga alone managed the distribution of 98 American film, out of a total of 234.[25] It is a figure that is even more impressive if one considers the odd circumstances in which imported films found themselves. With the arrival of sound, the response of the Fascist government was to ban the use of foreign languages in Italian screenings. Admittedly, this policy was announced only in October 1930, which is why it hit the distribution of American films mainly in the following year, whose total, in the case of Pittaluga, fell indeed from 98 to 50. It was a response that was nationalistic and protectionist (as it indirectly boosted the revenues of the few Italian sound films such as *La canzone dell'amore*), but it was also pragmatic, considering that at the time only a tiny fraction of Italian cinemas were equipped with sound. This forced foreign films to be recut with the addition of a raft of intertitles in

---

[24] According to Nicoli, the film cost around three million lire, and its box-office return eventually amounted to about four million (Nicoli, 'Entrepreneurs and the State', 789). On the distribution of Italian fiction films in 1930s' USA, see Roberto Vezzani, 'Fascist Indirect Propaganda in 1930s America: The Distribution and Exhibition of Italian Fiction Films', *Italianist*, 38/2 (2018), 156–73. The novella by Pirandello that ends with the suicide of the protagonist (an ill-tempered 18-year-old man rather than the film's beautiful young woman) and the death of his little brother is entitled 'In silenzio' (1905, then collected in the homonymous volume in 1923).

[25] Nicoli, 'Entrepreneurs and the State', 791. Società Italiana degli Autori ed Editori (SIAE) data from their published statistics: *La vita nello spettacolo in Italia nel decennio 1924–1942* (Rome: SIAE, 1935). On the figures of film distribution in 1930, see Elaine Mancini, *Struggles of the Italian Film Industry during Fascism, 1930–1935* (Ann Arbor, MI: UMI Research Press, 1985), 66.

order to make up for the lack of sound dialogues. In many cases, it totally destroyed the narrative flow and musical value of films, such as in King Vidor's *Halleluiah* (1929) or Sam Taylor's adaptation of Shakespeare's *The Taming of the Shrew* (1929), featuring two great stars of the day, Mary Pickford and Douglas Fairbanks.

This situation lasted for about two years, until adequate dubbing technology was developed. Before this happened, one of the American majors, Paramount, had responded with a jaw-dropping reaction: in 1930 it created its own studios in France—taking over and rebuilding one of the historic studios of French cinema, in Joinville, a suburb of Paris—where it initially started to 'remake' American films with foreign actors, in fourteen different languages. Italian was one of them, and Mario Camerini was hired to direct the Italian versions. It was a near-megalomaniac project, although one should remember that Paramount had amassed funds it was forced to invest in France as a result of French legislation on foreign film distribution. By 1931, hit by the world's recession, Paramount reduced the number of languages to three (French, German, and Spanish) and by 1933 it wound down the whole operation, since dubbing was solving the problem much more cheaply. Even the use of Joinville as a dubbing centre quickly became useless, since various nations—Italy was not alone in this—imposed the rule that dubbing had to take place in the country of distribution.[26]

The Fascist government legislated on dubbing in October 1933, thus adding a small boost to the Italian film industry, which began to employ hundreds of actors and technicians in this niche sub-industry. This provided the added bonus to the regime of making censorship of specific dialogues possible. Censorship authorities could ask for certain lines to be changed, sometimes even involving the identity of a particular character. With regard to American productions, the most memorable and extreme example is that of Archie Mayo's *The Adventures of Marco Polo* (1938), which, in order to be allowed distribution in Italy, forced United Artist to accept total reshaping of the identity of the protagonist, played by Gary Cooper, whose swashbuckling character took too much dignity away from the Italian historic figure. Marco Polo was then turned into a very improbable Scottish explorer hired by the Venetians, as even the film's title clarified: *Uno scozzese alla corte del Gran Kan*.[27]

As for Cines, one of the reasons why it did not develop into the equivalent of an American major is mainly due to Pittaluga's reluctance to invest in such a

---

[26] On Paramount's venture in Joinville, see Colin Crisp, *The Classic French Cinema, 1930–196* (Bloomington, IN: Indiana University Press, 1997), 173–5, 279–80; and, on multiple-language films in general, see Ginette Vincendeau, 'Hollywood Babel: The Coming of Sound and the Multiple-Language Version', in Andrew Higson and Richard Maltby (eds), *'Film Europe' and 'Film America': Cinema, Commerce, and Cultural Exchange 1920–1939* (Exeter: University of Exeter Press, 1999), 207–24.

[27] On Fascist censorship through the dubbing of foreign films, see Jean A. Gili, *Stato fascista e cinematografia: Repressione e promozione* (Rome: Bulzoni, 1981), 33–7; and Carla Mereu Keating, *The Politics of Dubbing: Film Censorship and State Intervention in the Translation of Foreign Cinema in Fascist Italy* (Oxford and Bern: Peter Lang, 2016).

348  AMERICA IN ITALIAN CULTURE

**Fig. 9.3.** American and Italian theatrical release posters of Archie Mayo's *The Adventures of Marco Polo* (1938). (courtesy of Mauro Maspero, Cantù)

high-risk enterprise as the production of films. Distribution and screening ensured a much more manageable source of profit. Bakker's study of the crisis of the European film industry would suggest that Pittaluga was right in being cautious, since it was in the vastly increased costs in film production in the 1920s—hence the need for huge amounts of capital in order to be able to absorb eventual losses—that lay the incapacity of European companies to compete with the increasingly more capital-robust majors across the Atlantic.[28]

Comparative figures concerning production budgets, published in 1934 by economist Raffaello Maggi, suggest that Italian productions were not only on a much smaller scale compared to Hollywood. There was also a clear difference in the apportioning of funding in one particular department: scripting. According to Maggi's figures, on average, American film productions in the 1920s spent 12 per cent of their budget in the initial phase of development of the screenplay. Italian productions (German ones too, for that matter) spent one-quarter of that, 3 per cent. However approximate these figures might be, they seem to suggest that the lower quality of Italian film narratives in those years—of which *La canzone dell'amore* was a good example—were partially the result of too superficial a dedication to the creation of a sophisticated narrative.[29]

[28] Bakker, 'The Decline and Fall of the European Film Industry', 310–12, 337–43.
[29] Raffaello Maggi, *Filmindustria-Riflessi economici* (Busto Arsizio: Pianezza, 1934). Maggi's work is discussed by Nicoli, in 'Entrepreneurs and the State', 792–3. More recently, Bakker comes to a

It was, after all, a weakness that the Italian film industry had already shown in its more prestigious phase before the First World War. It was also a known factor to those who had read the series of articles dedicated to the organization of film production in Hollywood that Tito Antonio Spagnol—a journalist and aspiring filmmaker—wrote for *L'Italia letteraria* in the summer of 1931. A journalist, by then self-exiled in France, Spagnol had tried his luck in Hollywood in 1929, where he had lived for more than a year. The climax of his attempts was a brief collaboration with Frank Capra as assistant director on the set of his Columbia production *Dirigible* (1931). After his return to Italy, Spagnol went back to journalism. He also injected his American experience into a novel, *Roma–Hollywood e ritorno*, which was published first by Rizzoli's weekly *Lei*, in 1934, then in *Cinema illustrazione* (1938–9), and eventually as a volume. We will return to the novel in the following chapter, but more important here is to highlight the detailed knowledge of the organization of Hollywood studios shown by Spagnol in his 1931 articles. Collected today in a single text, the five instalments run for more than twenty pages and provide a clear delineation of the various phases of American film production, which see the collaboration of different departments in the development of a treatment into a fully-fledged script and eventually into a film.[30]

When comparing Hollywood's working practices with the Italian ones, as done by Maggi, Spagnol identifies a weakness in the attention paid in Italy to the preparation of a script:

This detailed, patient and astute work of balancing, distributing, of rhythmical effects, cannot be improvised nor done in a rush, as it happens among us, where producers often expect an individual to jot down in a couple of months two or three hundred pages of a typescript. The dreary emptiness, the excessive verbosity, the lack of movement, the lack of invention and situations, all of which one can find in all our films, have their principal if not only cause in this disgraceful system. One only need to make a comparison to realize it.

Take any minor American film and one of our big ones. Forget about the treatment and instead analyse each one of the about six hundred scenes that form the fabric of film, and make a note of all the ones that are repetitive, mere filler,

---

similar conclusion with regard to the French and British industry: the share of budgets relating to the cost of 'creative inputs' (script, director, actors) was proportionally one-third higher in the USA than in France and Britain. Bakker, 'The Decline and Fall of the European Film Industry', 323. See also his *Entertainment Industrialised*, 229–71; and Mancini, *Struggles of the Film Industry*, 95–6.

[30] Tito A. Spagnol, 'Idee e metodi americani', in Spagnol, *Hollywood Boulevard* (Turin: Aragno, 2006), 45–67. The text was originally published in five instalments of *L'Italia letteraria* (29–33) between 19 July and 16 August 1931. Spagnol's role as assistant director in *Dirigible* is not officially recognized, since he left before the film was finished. As proof of this event, however, Orio Caldiron inserted a reproduction of the Columbia contract and a letter by Frank Capra thanking him for his collaboration in the volume he edited, Tito Spagnol, *Hollywood Boulevard* (Turin: Aragno, 2006), 19, 23.

patches over nothing. The poverty of our films will shockingly appear, and it is no use masking it with different shots or other expedients with which our directors try to give weight or new blood to them.[31]

In the original Italian, Spagnol's siding with American cinema is revealed linguistically too, given his reference to the figure of the film director through the use of the English loanword *direttore* as against the mainstream, French-derived *regista*, from *regisseur*.[32]

One can imagine Stefano Pittaluga reading with interest Spagnol's detailed study of the internal organization of a Hollywood studio. His articles, however, came out too late for that to happen. In the aftermath of a surgical operation, Pittaluga's entrepreneurial drive at Cines came to an abrupt end with his death, on 4 April 1931, at 44 years of age. The company's headship then fell into the hands of Ludovico Toeplitz, the representative of Cines' major financing bank, Credito Commerciale. Toeplitz, lacking knowledge of the film industry, decided to appoint as production director one of the few Italian intellectuals who combined an interest in film with a good first-hand knowledge of Hollywood. This is a well-known figure in the pages of this book: Emilio Cecchi.

Whether or not Cecchi had read Spagnol, under his watch the artistic level of Cines's productions improved, thanks to his involvement of literary figures capable of more sophisticated scripting work, such as the young Mario Soldati and the revered Pirandello, who was asked to be directly involved in the production of Cines's films (he was the lead scriptwriter of *Acciaio* of 1933), instead of his novellas simply being used as a mine for debatable free adaptations. Cecchi also ensured the service of some of the then best directors: from Blasetti to Brignone (back from a spell of work in Germany), Camerini (fresh from his experience with Paramount at Joinville), and the young Goffredo Alessandrini, who had been assistant director to Blasetti, and who later worked in Hollywood for MGM, in 1932, and then returned little more than a year later to resume his activity in Italy.[33]

In 1932, Cines increased its production, opened up to documentaries thus competing with the government-controlled LUCE institute, and contributed to

---

[31] Spagnol, 'Idee e metodi americani', 51–2.

[32] Mario Soldati, too, in those years, stuck to the use of *direttore* as against *regista* in his book on filmmaking (published under the pseudonym Franco Pallavera): *24 ore in uno studio cinematografico* (Milan: Corticelli, 1935; only in 1985 was the book reprinted by Sellerio as Soldati's). The use of a pseudonym was due to fact that, at the time, Soldati did not want his growing literary reputation to be dented by the authorship of a commercial book on cinema.

[33] Alessandrini was a near mother-tongue speaker of English thanks to the British tutor who looked after him, as a child, during the eight years in which his family lived in Egypt, where his father, an engineer, was responsible for the construction of a dam. During his short period at MGM, he also worked as scriptwriter and scenographer. On Alessandrini's American experience, see his long interview with Francesco Savio in *Cinecittà anni trenta: Parlano 116 protagonisti del secondo cinema italiano, 1930–1943* (Rome: Bulzoni, 1979), i. 6–56.

the celebrations of Fascism's Decennale della Rivoluzione with a mild propaganda fiction film, *L'armata azzurra* (1933). Directed by Righelli, the film featured three officers of the Italian Air Force, whose presence were an excuse for plenty of footage of formation flying, military operations, and stunning aerobatics. However, Cines's most successful production lay in the genre of romantic comedies. Its best combined critical and commercial success came with Camerini's *Gli uomini che mascalzoni* (1932), starring a young Vittorio De Sica playing the part of a modest driver who turns up in his boss's car in order to impress a young woman. Mario Soldati was one of the three scriptwriters involved.[34]

The duo's partnership continued and produced another box-office hit, this time in the wake of Hollywood's new sentimental comedy subgenre, the so-called screwball comedy, where the man's masculinity is challenged by an emancipated, powerful woman. Frank Capra's *It Happened One Night* (1934) is considered one of its early masterpieces, made famous by the sharp repartees between a down and out journalist and a rich heiress, played respectively by Clark Gable and Claudette Gilbert. This film can be put in parallel with the plot of Camerini's and Soldati's *Il signor Max* (1937)—newspaper kiosk owner meets noble young woman—with the difference that, while the American film thrived on the woman's authoritative *savoir faire*, the Italian one stuck to a more traditional vision, where the woman's superiority is only class related. Indeed, the happy ending of *Il signor Max* is the product of another character, the poor-but-honest childminder looking after the noblewoman's young sister, who eventually provides the male protagonist with a passive, subservient woman with whom he falls in love.

In this respect, the Italian comedies of these years seem to treat female characters in a manner that echoes the misunderstandings concerning female emancipation when journalists and travel writers reported on American women, as discussed in Chapter 6. They were often represented as, yes, professionally independent, and sometimes boldly so (such as the female protagonist of *L'armata azzurra*, who drives her own luxurious car), but the plots constantly praised those who showed emotional intelligence, humbleness, and passion towards the male protagonist, inevitably leading to their happy marriage to him. This is the case of another of Camerini's successes at the time, *Darò un milione* (1935), starring De Sica once again, but this time the fruit of the collaboration with a different rising star of scriptwriting, Cesare Zavattini. Anna—played by Assia Noris, Italy's leading female star at the time—is a humble woman who understands and loves the male

---

[34] On Cines during the Toeplitz–Cecchi management, see Brunetta, *Storia del cinema italiano*, ii. 231–53; and Mancini, *Struggles of the Italian Film Industry*, 57–98. Mario Soldati too wrote on Hollywood cinema, and his 1935 book on filmmaking (*24 ore in uno studio cinematografico*, more on this later) constantly referred to American cinema. See also Mario Soldati, 'Il segreto di Hollywood', *Pan*, 2/4 (December 1934), 551–65.

protagonist—a millionaire whom Zavattini symbolically gave the English name 'Gold'—for what he is and not for what he has.[35]

Cines did not produce *Darò un milione* nor *Il signor Max*. Sadly, the Italian company had by then been hit by yet more crises. First of all, the Toeplitz–Cecchi management had not lasted long. The continuous financial troubles had seen its replacement by the end of 1933. But the company's final blow came with a devastating fire at the Cines studios during the night of 25 September 1935. Production came to a halt, and Cines was not to re-emerge as a production company until 1942. The near destruction of Rome's historic studios of Via Veja, near the Via Tuscolana, prompted the construction of a brand new structure, further down the same street, which was to take the name of Cinecittà. This marked the irreversible commitment in cinema production on the part of the Fascist government, hence, given the political implications of this new phase, the following section will privilege the angle of the regime's perception of—and policies concerning—the American film industry.

## 9.2 Fascism and American Cinema

When Mussolini took office as prime minister, in October 1922, the tensions caused by President Wilson's refusal to play along with Italy's territorial demands, at Versailles, were, if not forgotten, certainly put aside. Mussolini's cordial disposition towards President Harding's administration and America in general was partly fuelled by the need to convince them to adopt a benevolent approach towards the thorny questions of Italy's war debt. This is possibly one of the reasons why, even if Mussolini had decided to take a more active role in forging the regime's cultural policies in its early years, it is unlikely that he would have attacked American interests in the film industry.

A further reason was that cinemagoing was understood as a form of escapist entertainment, which did not need to be steered for a political purpose. Mussolini too was a regular consumer of films in his free time, at least in the 1930s, as testified by his regular visits to the screening room within the compound of his residence, in Villa Torlonia's park, where he watched movies together with family and friends. Each Tuesday evening Mussolini was shown the latest LUCE newsreels, and then, on another evening, normally on Fridays, one feature film, often chosen

---

[35] *Darò un milione* was one of the few Italian films that was distributed in the USA. It did not receive good reviews, but it triggered a Hollywood remake by Twentieth Century Fox, which was equally unsuccessful. On this, see Forgacs and Gundle, *Mass Culture in Italian Society*, 209. On Assia Noris, see Stephen Gundle's chapter, emblematically entitled 'Everybody's Fiancée: Assia Noris', in Gundle, *Mussolini's Dream Factory*, 166–83. More generally, on the role of women in Fascist Italy as against the mirror of American female emancipation, see De Grazia, *How Fascism Ruled Women*, 98–102, 207–10.

by Freddi in order to elicit Mussolini's opinion (as happened with Chaplin's *Modern Times*, in 1936, of which Mussolini approved apart from the scene of cocaine-snorting in prison, which was cut). Those private screenings were organized in the film theatre of the Istituto Internazionale di Cinematografia Educativa (IICE), headed by Luciano De Feo, which had its main site in the grounds of Villa Torlonia park.[36]

As for protectionist measures, by 1927 the only imposition on the Italian film market was that all cinemas had to screen at least one Italian film for every ten in the programme. It was hardly a heavy-handed policy, and, in a way, it was a pragmatic one, given that by then the Italian film industry would have struggled to meet any target beyond 10 per cent of the market.

As late as 1931, one of the most influential Fascist leaders in the cultural sphere, Giuseppe Bottai, could make the following statement in parliament, confident of reflecting the regime's policies on cinema:

> I rarely go to the movies, but I have always noticed that, invariably, the general public gets bored whenever cinema tries to educate them. The general public wants to be entertained, and it is precisely in this field that, today, we want to help the Italian industry.[37]

In other words, the regime could perhaps be convinced to do more in order to address the financial struggles of the industry, but there did not seem to be any interest in experimenting with the propaganda potential of cinema. As we have already seen, the political dimension was considered to be limited to its direct representation through the newsreels, which the Istituto LUCE had firmly controlled since the mid-1920s. Fiction meant entertainment, and, if the Americans were the best at doing it, so it was only logical that they should be due the biggest slice of the market.

As Schnapps convincingly suggested in his study of the 1932 exhibition for the tenth anniversary of the Fascist revolution, it is only around that time that Mussolini—and Margherita Sarfatti behind him—and other Fascist leaders moved towards the idea of the state as a ruling presence in the cultural debate.

---

[36] See Luigi Freddi, *Il cinema*, 2 vols (Rome: L'Arnia, 1949); repr. in single vol. as *Il governo dell'immagine* (Rome: Gremese, 1994), 183–90 (189 on Chaplin). Luciano De Feo, the founder of Istituto LUCE, was often present at the screenings and sat next to Mussolini. On De Feo, see Fiamma Lussana, 'Luciano De Feo direttore dell'Istituto LUCE', *Studi storici*, 56/4 (2015), 935–61. In his memoirs, Mussolini's long-time personal waiter, Quinto Navarra, confirmed Mussolini's keen interest in screening movies (*Memorie del cameriere di Mussolini* (1946; repr. Milan: Longanesi, 1972), 198–200).

[37] Giuseppe Bottai, 'Dichiarazioni a favore della legge', *Lo Spettacolo italiano*, 7 (July 1931); quoted in Ben-Ghiat, *Fascist Modernities*, 79. Bottai was then head of the Ministero delle Corporazioni and his intervention was part of the parliamentary debate relating to a law in support of the Italian film industry, to which he had contributed with a report and a bill proposal entitled 'Disposizioni a favore della produzione cinematografica nazionale' (as reported in the February 1933 issue of *Lo Spettacolo italiano*, 59–61).

There had been a run-up to it with the debate on defining Fascist art, which Giuseppe Bottai had hosted in the pages of his review, *Critica fascista*, during 1926 and 1927, and which had brought most—certainly Bottai—to the conclusion that Italian Fascism promoted a sort of benevolent pluralism in the arts that respected the creative genius of individual artists. It was a neo-idealistic, Crocean–Gentilian notion of art, which was to create a strong differentiation with Nazi Germany and in particular with Hitler's narrow-minded vision. This approach also allowed Mussolini not to distribute labels of 'Fascist art', as some of his followers—Marinetti *in primis*—would have hoped and lobbied for years to receive.

When it came to the 1932 exhibition, however, decisions had to be taken, and here Margherita Sarfatti, helped by Marcello Piacentini—the regime's architect *par excellence* (on whom we will concentrate in Chapter 10)—showed their *savoir faire* in helping chief organizers Dino Alfieri and Luigi Freddi produce a working compromise between different tendencies. The 'modernist' school was the prevalent one, starting from the rationalist avante-garde design of the exhibition's entrance. The neoclassical façade of the Palazzo delle Esposizioni was turned into a proto-brutalist, bunker-like stylization with four gigantic, black *fasci* jutting out in front of the expanses of a plain, dark blood-red wall.[38] From the cultural debate concerning the Mostra came the first grand experiment in propaganda filmmaking in Fascist Italy. This is *Camicia nera* (1933), Giovacchino Forzano's debut film, a LUCE production, whose script had received an award during a competition held under the aegis of the Mostra.[39]

The film—part-fiction part-documentary—aimed at showing Italy's metamorphosis from a poor, war-battered nation into an industrialized, modern country enthusiastically supporting its *Duce*. It must be added that the film proved to be everything but an artistic milestone. Soviet propaganda films were clearly an inspiration, but *Camicia nera* failed to fuse its overtly political aim—boldly presented with avant-garde effects such as multiple over-impressed images and complex editing—with the narrative line of the poor peasant who becomes a prisoner of war, loses his memory because of shell shock, but then happily returns to a renewed Italy under Mussolini's leadership. The government, which had financed its production through the Istituto LUCE, eagerly organized its premiere in three different capitals of Europe and in Italy's main cities, on 23 March 1933. Despite the raft of obediently positive reviews on the day—Mario Gromo's for *La Stampa*

---

[38] The façade was the work of the collaboration of rationalist architects Adalberto Libera and Mario De Renzi. See Terry Kirk, *The Architecture of Modern Italy*, 2 vols (New York: Princeton Architectural Press, 2005), ii. 88–92.

[39] Forzano was by then an already well-established author of novels, librettos, and plays, two of which, *Campo di Maggio* (1930) and *Villafranca* (1932), had seen the collaboration of Benito Mussolini. Among the participants to this competition there was also an American poet, Ezra Pound, who collaborated on the script by an unknown author from Liguria, Ferruccio Cerio. On this, see Gian Piero Brunetta, 'Il sogno a stelle e strisce di Mussolini', in Maurizio Vaudagna (ed.), *L'estetica della politica: Europa e America negli anni trenta* (Rome and Bari: Laterza, 1989), 173–86.

is a masterclass in reluctant enthusiasm—the film was quickly recognized for its limitations in Fascist circles too, its rhetoric being overstated and clumsily presented.[40]

The failure of *Camicia nera* proved the risks of investing in fiction film, however munificently funded by the state. Four years had to pass before Mussolini would give the green light to a further, similar experiment. In the meantime, however, a new player had joined the international stage, one that was to influence the development of Fascism's official position towards American cinema: Nazi Germany. Joseph Goebbel's culture ministry quickly imposed the importance of propaganda and of the centralization and regimentation of culture as a necessary step towards totalitarianism. In March 1933, only two months following Hitler's appointment as head of government, Goebbels began to turn his ministry, the newly named Ministry of Public Enlightenment and Propaganda, into a powerful machinery, which either nationalized or regimented every single sector of the culture industry, one by one.

Goebbels's first official visit to Italy took place in May 1933. On the one hand, he wanted to learn more about the quasi-religious glorification of the leader that was the core of Fascist propaganda, but at the same time he intended to showcase the progress already made by his ministry. His then opposite number, Gaetano Polverelli, head of Mussolini's Press Office, wrote a memorandum in which he noted the need to move in a similar direction. Mussolini must have been similarly impressed, since, on 1 August 1933, he appointed his son-in-law, Galeazzo Ciano, then a young diplomat, as the new head of his Press Office. The department quickly grew in size and role, becoming first Undersecretariat for Press and Propaganda in 1934, then Ministry for Press and Propaganda in 1935, finally to be renamed Ministry of Popular Culture in 1937. It should be noted again that, when Ciano worked on expanding his ministry, he had a plan of his German counterpart on his desk. Not by chance, the Italian ministry ended up having an internal organization that resembled that of Goebbels's ministry.[41]

With specific regard to the film industry, the situation in the two countries was rather different. Since 1917, the German industry had been consolidated into a giant consortium, UFA, which dominated film production and distribution.

---

[40] Mario Gromo, 'Il film del decennale: "Camicia nera"', *La Stampa*, 24 March 1933, p. 3. On the unsuccessful international distribution of the film, see Benedetta Garzarelli, 'Cinema e propaganda all'estero nel regime fascista: Le proiezioni di *Camicia nera* a Parigi, Berlino e Londra', *Dimensioni e problemi della ricerca storica*, 2 (2003), 147–65; repr. in Garzarelli, *Parleremo al mondo intero: La propaganda del fascismo all'estero* (Alessandria: Edizioni dell'Orso, 2004). On its circulation in Britain, see Pierluigi Ercole, '"The Greatest Film of the Fascist Era": The Distribution of *Camicia nera* in Britain', *Alphaville: Journal of Film and Screen Media*, 6 (Winter 2013), 1–14.

[41] On the evolution of the Press Office of the Head of Government into the Ministry of Popular Culture, see Cannistraro, *La fabbrica del consenso*, 106–10; and Bonsaver, *Censorship and Literature in Fascist Italy*, 95–128. The parallels between Goebbels's ministry and its Italian equivalent, with specific reference to cinematography, are touched upon by Manetti, *'Un'arma poderosissima'*, 78–80.

By the time the Nazis seized power, UFA was in the hands of media entrepreneur and nationalist politician Alfred Hugenberg; hence its political alignment was assured. Indeed, by March 1933, all Jewish employees were dismissed. Hugenberg had even entered Hitler's first cabinet as economy minister but, disgruntled for his lack of autonomy, resigned six months later. Goebbels brought UFA under government control through state-financed shareholding companies, and eventually, in 1941, with further mergers, UFA was officially presented as state-owned.[42]

In Italy, Mussolini's regime until then had simply regulated the Italian film industry. Protectionist legislation in 1927 and 1931 had given financial oxygen to the sector, but, apart from the Istituto LUCE, Mussolini had stayed clear from investing state funding into such a volatile industry. The fiasco of *Camicia nera* in 1933 had confirmed the point. However, the organization of cultural policies as a consequence of the creation of the Ministry of Press and Propaganda included a division whose specific duty was to monitor and direct the film industry: the *Direzione Generale per la Cinematografia*, created in September 1934. At its head, Ciano appointed Luigi Freddi, a 39-year-old militant journalist at *Il Popolo d'Italia*, who, beyond his involvement in the Mostra della Rivoluzione, had some first-hand experience of the Hollywood system. He had spent two months there after travelling the USA as a correspondent, following the deeds of the Italian aviators on which we dwelled in Chapter 5.[43]

The fact that, after his return, in February 1934, Freddi presented to Mussolini a detailed report on the American studio system, suggests that by then he had already been lined up for a position in relation to cinema. In his role as divisional head, Freddi proved a very influential figure, keen to maximize the political impact of film production and at the same time being respectful of the industry's commercial and artistic needs. With regard to American cinema, Freddi was equally a moderate of sort. On the one hand, he was well aware of the need to learn from the most successful industry in the field, and—following public demand—to allow widespread distribution and exhibition of American films. On the other, his firm nationalism constantly inclined him towards taking measures that would defend Italy's film industry, allowing it to grow and progressively seize a bigger slice of the market.

Whether Freddi possessed a refined understanding of the aesthetics of filmmaking is a moot point. When it came to propaganda films, his low opinion

---

[42] On UFA's history, see Klaus Kreimeier, *The UFA Story: A History of Germany's Greatest Film Company, 1918–1945* (Berkeley and Los Angeles: University of California Press, 1999).

[43] Luigi Freddi had published a book based on his correspondence work for *Il Popolo d'Italia*, entitled *Altre terre* (Florence: Corbaccio, 1933). The pages dedicated to America denote a rhetorical nationalism (Italian migrants are corrupted by American greed, pp. 23–4), which becomes open racism when he visits Dakar on his journey back to Italy (pp. 141–61). On Freddi's collaboration with Alfieri in the creation of the Mostra della Rivoluzione Fascista, see Stone, *The Patron State*, 134–42.

of Blasetti's *Vecchia guardia* (1934) against his full support for Gallone's *Scipione l'Africano* (1937) makes one think that political considerations were perhaps clearer in his mind than artistic quality. But he certainly was a charismatic and efficient organizer. As the key person behind the state-sponsored restructuring of the Italian film industry, the main question to be asked in this chapter is the extent to which he looked at Hollywood as a model.

Considering the crucial message of his inaugural speech in 1935—'The State regiments. The State helps. The State rewards. The State controls. The State promotes'[44]—there is little doubt that Freddi's Gentilian notion of the state as supreme value was at loggerheads with Hollywood's cult of private entrepreneurship. At the same time, Freddi followed Mussolini's vision of a totalitarian state that allowed private industry to thrive within the well-guarded boundaries created by the regime. In other words, it was a question of finding a way of reinforcing the film industry so that it could rival its European and, mostly, American competition, while avoiding an expensive and high-risk nationalization of the sector. Freddi was also vocally opposed to any form of heavy-handed interference in the artistic process. Nazi Germany was for him an example of how a thriving national film industry could be damaged by an overly invasive political presence. He made this explicit in a report he submitted to Alfieri, this time on returning from a visit to Germany, in 1936.[45]

A close collaborator of Freddi was Luigi Chiarini, a versatile figure as director, critic, and cultural organizer. Chiarini was made head of the Centro Sperimentale di Cinematografia, founded in 1935, the first, big commitment to the film industry at large on the part of the Fascist government. A smaller cinema school had already been active since 1932, thanks to the initiative of Alessandro Blasetti and Anton Giulio Bragaglia, which in some way was one of the few tangible outputs of the debate on Fascist culture promoted by Bottai the year before. However, Freddi and Chiarini brought the school to a higher level, not just in terms of visibility and dimensions, but also through the ambition of creating a new generation of film experts in both practice and theory of filmmaking. In this respect the Centro Sperimentale was in line with Gentile's reform of secondary education: all students had to follow humanities courses on aesthetics, history of cinema, art, and music, irrespective of their professional specialization. Structurally, if there was a model here, it was the Moscow Film School, with the idea of a centre whose teachers came from the leading edge of contemporary filmmaking. Led by Chiarini, Blasetti and Umberto Barbaro, the Centro Sperimentale was thought of as a hub attracting the best practitioners in each branch of filmmaking. When the new site

---

[44] Quoted in Brunetta, *Storia del cinema italiano*, ii. 45.
[45] The report is reproduced in its entirety as an appendix in Cannistraro, *La fabbrica del consenso*, 458–64.

was built on the outskirts of the city, along the Via Tuscolana, it could also boast some of the best facilities in the world. The ambition was sealed with the creation of a professional film magazine, *Bianco e nero*, which began its publication in 1937, again under the leadership of Chiarini.[46]

Almost across the road from the Centro Sperimentale, another gigantic facility had taken shape: Cinecittà. After the partial destruction of the Cines studios in September 1935, Freddi grasped the opportunity to provide Italy with a competitive edge in studio facilities too. When the architect in charge, Gino Peressutti, began work on the project, Freddi provided him with the plans and data about Hollywood studios that he had put together during his stay there. During the early months of Freddi's directorship, the Italian ambassador in the USA, Augusto Rosso, had also visited the studios of Freddi's favourite major, MGM, in order to pass on information, making no secret that Hollywood was being used as a model. Meanwhile, in Italy, the American trade consul, John McBride, was also being consulted. At the same time, Peressutti visited other European studios—his favourite ones were the London Film studios, built in 1935, although he admitted that its set-up was not exemplary, since it privileged indoor shooting as a consequence of the weather. Rome's climate was closer to that of Los Angeles.

Under Freddi's close supervision, construction went on at breakneck speed. In little more than a year the studios were ready. Inaugurated by Mussolini on 28 April 1937, Cinecittà was the most modern and the biggest film studio in Europe. It was almost one-third bigger than UFA's. As economic historian Barbara Crespi concludes, the overall planning of Cinecittà, accurately separating the facilities relating to different production phases and allowing for several films—up to five—to be produced concurrently, was based on Hollywood. The ample space dedicated to film stars was a telltale sign: each of the nine *teatri di posa* ('studios') was equipped with an adjacent two-floor building offering ten dressing rooms and two flats adequately called *appartamentini per divi e dive* ('small flats for male and female stars'). Moreover, following Cines's lead, some of the technology was American—together with French, German, and Italian hardware—and the role of technical supervisor (Ispettore generale) went to the already mentioned Silvano Balboni, a cinematographer who had worked in Hollywood for four years. Back in Italy, Balboni was involved in the planning stage of Cinecittà, and, indicatively, when it was under construction, he wrote a long article for *Bianco e nero* describing with plenty of technical detail the lighting equipment used in Hollywood studios.[47]

---

[46] On the Centro Sperimentale di Cinematografia, see Manetti, 'Un'arma poderosissima', 134–41.

[47] Barbara Crespi, 'Cinecittà: Utopia fascista e sogno americano', in Caldiron (ed.), *Storia del cinema italiano*, v 128, 133–6. Judging from Freddi's list of the equipment that was relocated from Cinecittà to either Venice or Germany after 8 September 1943, the American manufacturers were Bell & Howell and Movado, and the sound recording system was RCA's Photophone, as recorded in the credits of the films produced at Cinecittà in those years. On the consequences of the fire at Cines and its connection

The parallel with Hollywood was constantly raised at the time, even by regime-integrated figures such as Luciano De Feo, whom we have already met as head of LUCE (until 1928) and of the Istituto Internazionale per la Cinematografia Educativa (IICE). In an editorial for his journal, *Cinema*, De Feo praised Cinecittà, adding the regular caveat that its American make-up—euphemistically called 'learning from Californian industrialists'—was necessary in order to facilitate the creation of a clearly Italian product, and concluding: 'There is no intention to imitate the "genre" of others: in industry as in artisanship, from the same materials and machinery, different peoples have produced totally different artefacts.' Equally emblematic was the fact that De Feo's two-page editorial was accompanied by a large illustration featuring the reproduction of a selection of telegrams by leading figures in world cinema sending their congratulations on the inauguration of Cinecittà. Eight out of nine of them, all written in English, came from Hollywood: from Columbia Pictures, to Warner Bros and Twentieth Century Fox, from director Frank Capra to actress Kay Francis and others. Only the ninth, written in Italian, came from German industrialist Carl Friedrich von Siemens.[48]

When Mussolini came to inaugurate Cinecittà, four films were already in the making. One of them was the ill-fated *Scipione l'Africano*, but on this occasion Mussolini also visited the set of another production. It was *Luciano Serra pilota* (1938), yet another aviation-themed film, directed by Alessandrini. It was obviously a staged act. When Mussolini entered the studio, he was welcomed by his 20-year-old son Vittorio, who had been involved in the film's treatment and was working as supervisor (collaborating with 30-year-old assistant director Roberto Rossellini: the two were later to work together on another aviation film: *Il pilota ritorna*, in 1942). Alessandrini recalled being introduced by Vittorio to *Il Duce*, who complimented him for his recent *Cavalleria* (1936), and asked where he could stand so that he could follow some of the shooting.[49] This episode provides us with a narrative cue for the smooth introduction of the figure of Mussolini's son, Vittorio, whose role in the potential 'Americanization' of Italian Fascist cinema was of similar importance to that of Freddi. The editorial by De Feo had

---

with the creation of Cinecittà, see Bizzarri and Solaroli, *L'industria cinematografica italiana*, 35–8. On Cinecittà, see, among others, Lucilla Albano, 'Hollywood: Cinelandia', 219–32. Silvano Balboni, 'Note 5', *Bianco e nero*, 1/4 (April 1937), 71–3.

[48] De Feo, then chief editor of *Cinema*, wrote this in an editorial in the issue entirely dedicated to the opening of Cinecittà: 'Editoriale', *Cinema*, 2/20 (25 April 1937), 299–301. The following article in the *Cinema* issue was a detailed, illustrated description of the logistics of Cinecittà, written by Peressutti himself: Gino Peressutti, 'Cinecittà', *Cinema*, 2/20 (25 April 1937), 302–6. See also Brunetta, *Il ruggito del leone*, 82–7.

[49] See the already mentioned interview in Savio, *Cinecittà anni trenta*, i. 6–56 (55–6). On Roberto Rossellini, see Gianni Rondolino, *Roberto Rossellini* (Turin: UTET, 1989), 34–8. Rondolino adds that Vittorio Mussolini also appeared as co-director of Aquila Films, the production company behind *Luciano Serra pilota* (p. 35).

mentioned Vittorio twice, confirming his influential presence, despite his young age, in this key phase of the development of Italy's film industry.

By the time Cinecittà opened its doors, Vittorio Mussolini had already left his mark, with an oft-quoted article in one of the first issues of De Feo's *Cinema*, in September 1936. The article was entitled 'Emancipazione del cinema italiano', and its subtitle provokingly asked: 'Does "European" Cinema Exists?'. The answer was tantamount to a 'yes, but that is not what we should aspire to'. In his article, Vittorio Mussolini strongly wrote in favour of moving away from the by-then-stilted European tradition—whether French or German—and fully embracing the American way. The first lines could not be clearer on this point:

> I will say straight away that, in this article, I propose to demonstrate, as frankly as possible, that it would be very dangerous and damaging for the reinvigorating Italian film industry to follow European production, instead of trying to find the way and method to emulate that of America.[50]

America is a young country, continued Mussolini, while Europe is very old, and, thanks to Fascism, Italy is closer in spirit to the former. He repeatedly spoke of 'Italian youth', thus presenting his viewpoint as representative of his generation and clearly stating that they much preferred the open spaces, the action, the beautiful bodies, and lively sense of humour of American cinema to the 'trite, double-entendre farce' of French cinema or the 'heavy bricks of a clear philosophical–political–cerebral kind' from Germany. As a visual exemplification, a page-and-a-half composite illustration gave an example of the difference between American and European cinema (see Fig. 9.4). The dynamism of American cinema was represented by cues to its westerns, glamorous comedies, and musicals. The French–German one was illustrated with reference to theatrical, in-door, bourgeois settings, while the Italian images, symmetrically to the American ones, were dedicated to a stage photo from Blasetti's *Vecchia guardia* (1934), a still from Alessandrini's *Cavalleria* (1936), and photo of a group of young people that—unless a colleague shall find out its connection to a specific film—seems to be a generic archival image of young people welcoming some event, symbolically representing Vittorio's generation.

The final line of the article, coming from the son of *Il Duce*, used a manifesto-like but almost sinister first-person plural: 'We have warned: let's not tag along behind today's European cinema.'[51]

---

[50] Vittorio Mussolini, 'Emancipazione del cinema italiano', *Cinema*, 1/6 (25 September 1936), 213–15.

[51] Two months later, literary author Giorgio Vigolo added his opinion, in *Cinema*, with an article symbolically entitled 'Roma e Hollywood'. After boldly suggesting that the choice of California for the seat of American cinema was mainly due to its similarities with the Italian landscape, Vigolo dwelt on the enormous influence of American cinema as a beacon of 'Americanism' all over the world. However, he argued, the construction of Cinecittà was soon going to give Italian cinema the same chance to

Fig. 9.4. Illustrations accompanying Vittorio Mussolini's article 'Emancipazione del cinema italiano', *Cinema*, 1/6 (25 September 1936). (courtesy of Cineteca, Bologna)

When he wrote the article, Vittorio Mussolini was still a 19 year old, fresh from his Liceo classico studies. His persona, however, was quickly taking public shape. As a student, with his friend Ruggero Zangrandi—who was to write a much-quoted book in the post-war years about his move from Fascist to anti-Fascist militancy—Vittorio had founded a militant journal called *La Penna dei ragazzi* (later more dignifyingly renamed *Anno XII—Rivista della giovinezza*). The journal was benevolently followed by *Il Duce*—his house hosting the journal's improvised editorial office—and he later invited Zangrandi to write for *Il Popolo d'Italia*. In the pages of their journal, Vittorio wrote about jazz and cinema, already showing a passion for American culture.[52]

---

build a similar source of imagery to be consumed abroad. Giorgio Vigolo, 'Roma e Hollywood', *Cinema*, 10 (24 November 1936), 373-4.

[52] It might have been a small journal, but, when Vittorio Mussolini commented negatively on Giovacchino Forzano's film on Napoleon, *Campo di Maggio* (1935), to whose script *Il Duce* had informally collaborated, news travelled all the way across the Atlantic and reached Hollywood's daily. Anon., 'Mussolini's Son Pans Father's Film', *Hollywood Reporter*, 7 May 1935, p. 6. Zangrandi's book is *Il lungo viaggio: Contributo alla storia di una generazione* (Turin: Einaudi, 1948); repr., in an enlarged version: *Il lungo viaggio attraverso il fascismo* (Milan: Feltrinelli, 1961).

According to Zangrandi's biographer, Vittorio even shot an amateur short film together with his brother Bruno and some school friends, which he had scripted himself. It was called *Lo sceriffo tremendone* and, we are told, was a tongue-in-cheek homage to the western genre. Vittorio confirmed his passion for American cinema in a late interview he gave in 1982, boasting, among other things, of having watched King Vidor's *The Big Parade* (1925) eight times. After leaving school, however, Vittorio had joined the Italian Air Force and, together with his younger brother, had become a pilot and volunteered in the Ethiopian war. By October 1935, he was flying bombing sorties against the Ethiopian army (about which he boasted in his book *Voli sulle ambe*, published two years later), and, on his return to Rome, the following spring, he began to study law.[53]

Things were moving very quickly for Vittorio Mussolini. It is at this time that he decided to move his interest in cinema to a higher level, and he was quickly allowed to express his opinions to the nation thanks to his closeness to Luciano De Feo. As we have seen, the Mussolini family were, in a manner, next-door neighbours to De Feo's institute, where they watched films on a weekly basis. Vittorio was often present with his friends. In the summer of 1936, De Feo had founded a fortnightly journal, *Cinema*, which was published in Milan by Hoepli (a publishing house particularly close to Mussolini) but whose administration was based a few yards from Mussolini's Villa Torlonia, with the 'technical assistance' of De Feo's institute. Luigi Freddi was a member of the journal's Comitato Direttivo—hence the initiative was a well-integrated part of the regime's progressive involvement in the film industry.

The fact that, for his very first article for *Cinema*, Vittorio should have been allowed such prominence speaks volumes about his father's influence. Similar to that of *Bianco e nero* a year later, the aspiration of *Cinema* was to present itself as the product of professional and scholarly knowledge on the film industry. However, since Vittorio had set his heart on joining the frame, a spotlight was prepared for him, even if he was by then little more than a passionate filmgoer. It is even reasonable to suspect that De Feo's creation of a journal in July 1936 might have been connected to a suggestion by Mussolini senior. After all, when Mussolini's brother, Arnaldo, had died, on 21 December 1931, *Il Duce* had him immediately replaced as chief editor of *Il Popolo d'Italia* by his brother's son, Vito, then a 19 year old himself. Vito did not actually show much interest in journalism—and indeed the 'real' chief editor was Giorgio Pini; nonetheless he remained in post until the implosion of the regime in July 1943. Within this perspective, it is possible that Mussolini might have thought that the time had come for his eldest son to take a position of responsibility. And if cinema was his

---

[53] The interview is quoted in Orio Caldiron, 'Le ambiguità della modernizzazione negli anni del consenso', in Caldiron (ed.), *Storia del cinema italiano*, v. 3–34 (24–6). Zangrandi's biography is Aldo Grandi, *Fuori dal coro: Ruggero Zangrandi, una biografia* (Milan: Baldini & Castoldi, 1993), 35.

passion, so be it. As we will see, Vittorio was to take over as chief editor of *Cinema* only two years after its foundation, in October 1938.[54]

At that point *Cinema* became more and more the sounding board of the young filmmakers who surrounded Vittorio, some of whom were to become leading figures in post-war Italian cinema, such as Michelangelo Antonioni, Giuseppe De Santis, Carlo Lizzani, and Luchino Visconti. In one of his conversations with Yvon De Begnac, which took place after Vittorio had taken over the editorship of *Cinema*, Mussolini commented on his son's involvement as follows:

> My son Vittorio has created a cinema magazine, 'Cinema', whose editorial staff is formed entirely by young men with excellent expertise in the humanities. Some of them are often my guests during the private screening of films to be distributed, both Italian and foreign. I listen to them. I listen to their opinions. I understand that the irreverence of their words is, more and more, the guarantee of independence of judgement. I do not know how much these young men love the revolution which I started. But I feel that they consider it to be the only way out of global conformism.[55]

**Fig. 9.5.** Benito Mussolini standing next to his son Vittorio (on his right) during a visit to the construction site of Cinecittà, in 1936. (courtesy of Mitchell Wolfson Jr Collection, Genoa)

---

[54] Moreover, starting with the issue of 10 March 1938, *Cinema* began to be presented in its contents list as Organo della Federazione Nazionale Fascista degli Industriali dello Spettacolo, the Fascist trade union of show-business industrialists.

[55] De Begnac, *Taccuini mussoliniani*, 423.

The fact that Mussolini should think of *Cinema* as his son's journal could simply refer to Vittorio's clear mark in his editorship in 1938, but it could also be a telltale sign of the extent to which the journal was thought of as a forum from which Vittorio had been allowed to express his thoughts ever since its very first issues, back in 1936.

What interests us here, though, is the impact of Vittorio Mussolini in relation to the debate concerning the potential model posed by Hollywood at a time of radical developments in the Italian film industry. There is little doubt that he was determined to become a vocal supporter of closer ties between American and Italian cinema. His debut article of September 1936 had the tone of a manifesto. But how did it echo within the four walls of Luigi Freddi's office at the Direzione generale per la cinematografia? First of all, Freddi had very little consideration for De Feo. In his memoirs he just about ignores his existence, to the point of not mentioning him once in the chapter entirely devoted to the Istituto LUCE, which De Feo had created and directed until 1928. Instead, Freddi dwells at length on the institute's debts, its disorganization, and its inefficiency.[56]

De Feo's support for Vittorio Mussolini's ambitions was an unwelcome interference in Freddi's own plans to lead the Italian film industry. Indeed, when it comes to the chapter of his memoirs devoted to Vittorio Mussolini, Freddi introduces it as *una grana* ('a hassle'), which he had to sort out, and ends it by quoting a report he sent to Mussolini in which he explicitly refers to De Feo as a laughable incompetent. It should be apparent by now that Freddi's reconstruction of events is rarely free from an apologetic self-representation. In this case, however, we can rely on the counter-narrative of the events penned by Vittorio Mussolini, and, more importantly, on many other sources and specific scholarly studies on the subject.[57]

After his debut in *Cinema* in September 1936, Vittorio Mussolini continued to write on the subject, adding a different medium, equally if not more authoritative: *Il Popolo d'Italia*. From there, in his weekly piece on cinema, on 23 April 1937, he announced that, in order to put his money where his mouth was as a critic, he was going to enter the frame as a film producer. He was referring to *Luciano Serra*

---

[56] Freddi, *Il governo dell'immagine*, 227–30. Freddi operates a similar 'denial' of De Feo, once again failing to recognize De Feo's role, this time as the creator of *Cinema*. Instead, he wrongly wrote that the journal was founded by Vittorio Mussolini (p. 141).

[57] Freddi's chapter in his *Il governo dell'immagine*, 141–55. Vittorio Mussolini's long memoir of the event appears in his *Vita con mio padre* (Milan: Mondadori, 1957), 70–88. The main scholarly sources about this affair are Giovanni Sedita, 'Vittorio Mussolini, Hollywood and Neorealism', *Journal of Modern Italian Studies*, 15/3 (2010), 431–57; and the chapter devoted to it in Thomas Patrick Doherty, *Hollywood and Hitler, 1933–1939* (New York: Columbia University Press, 2013), 122–36. I have also relied on Higham's book on Louis C. Meyer: Higham, *Merchant of Dreams*, 264–6, 271; Richard Lewis Ward, *A History of the Hal Roach Studios* (Carbondale, IL: Southern Illinois University Press, 2005), 100; and the articles devoted to it in *the Hollywood Reporter* and in *Variety*. A very informative but non-academic reconstruction of Vittorio's involvement in the film industry can be found in Antonio Spinosa, *I figli del duce* (Milan: Rizzoli, 1983), 150–65.

*pilota*, which, as we have seen, was one of the very first films in production at Cinecittà. The following week his piece was devoted to the American film industry: this time, however, Vittorio Mussolini poured scorn on those in Hollywood, Charlie Chaplin included, who supported various initiatives to denounce General Franco's war against the Republican government. The second part of the article returned to the Italian situation, and to American dominance: in March 1937, out of 220 films reaching Italian cinemas, 173 were American. What could be the solution to this long-standing problem? The answer came in his following piece of 6 May: beat the Americans at their own game:

> I am more and more convinced that, in order to do this, one needs, at least at the start, to learn the trade and follow the example of the Americans. Once the catapult is anchored on a solid commercial base and we have acquired the *made-in-USA* fluidity in film narrative that the heavy heads of European directors are unable to learn, it will be possible to talk of Fascist cinema.[58]

This time, Vittorio Mussolini decided to go a step further: what better way to learn the American way than to enter into co-production with one of Hollywood's most renowned studios?

The opportunity came Vittorio's way rather fortuitously. The idea of creating a synergy with an American studio in order to produce film versions of famous Italian operas had come from another young Italian who was well connected within the regime. This was Renato Senise, nephew of the then deputy chief of the Italian police, Carmine Senise (who was to become chief after the death of his superior, Arturo Bocchini, in November 1940). The young Senise already had a reputation as an unruly character: his police records tell us that he was twice sentenced to *confino* ('police-monitored confinement'). At the same time, he was also registered as a police informer. In 1933 he had moved to the USA and again had been involved in shady activities (he was in contact with New York mafioso Vito Genovese, later accused of being involved in the 1943 murder of the prominent anti-Fascist Carlo Tresca). Through an associate of his, Senise had got to know Hollywood producer Hal Roach (then at the peak of his fame with his comedy films featuring Stan Laurel and Oliver Hardy) and convinced him to allow him to take the lead in the plan of creating an Italian American company with the aim of producing films in Cinecittà based on Italian operas.[59]

---

[58] Vittorio Mussolini, 'Primi piani', *Il Popolo d'Italia*, 29 April 1937, p. 3; and 'Funzioni della Cinecittà', *Il Popolo d'Italia*, 6 May 1937, p. 3. The earlier article is 'Si gira', *Il Popolo d'Italia*, 23 April 1937, p. 3.

[59] According to *Variety*, Renato was the son of late Vincenzo Senise, Director General of Rome's Teatro dell'Opera. See anon., 'Il Duce's Phone Call to Vittorio in H'wood Climaxed Italo–US Idea: Too

Hal Roach enthusiastically involved MGM through Louis B. Mayer, and in June 1937 gave the green light for Senise to go back to Italy in order to ensure the necessary support from the Fascist government. Thanks to his uncle's recommendation, Senise was allowed to meet the then Minister of Popular Culture, Dino Alfieri, who showed interest in the project. Given Alfieri's *modus laborandi*, it is almost certain that he did not commit without having secured Mussolini's approval. In fact, the project seemed to land at the door of the Mussolini household at exactly the right time, for both political and personal reasons. Politically, it offered the possibility to establish good relations with Hollywood at a time when Mussolini's public esteem in the USA had greatly suffered, first from the invasion of Ethiopia, and then from Italy's involvement in the Spanish Civil War, together with the progressive military and political alignment with Nazi Germany and Imperial Japan. The personal dimension was entirely related to Vittorio's involvement in the film industry, which in those very weeks was finding its first big challenge in the production of *Luciano Serra pilota*. Indeed, Vittorio was involved in the series of meetings that followed, some of them taking place at Mussolini's summer house of Rocca delle Caminate (a medieval castle that the local administration had donated to *Il Duce* in 1927). Hal Roach travelled to Italy expressly and was present at the meetings. As for the necessary financial backing, Roach managed to get MGM involved, while the Mussolini surname was a sufficient guarantee in ensuring a generous credit line to Vittorio's newly formed production company—ERA Film—from the Banca Nazionale del Lavoro, whose director joined the meetings too.[60]

It was at that point that the decision was reached to create an *ad hoc* company called RAM Pictures (the acronym standing for Roach and Mussolini) and slowly

---

Much Opposition to Roach Plan', *Variety*, 125/5 (13 October 1937), 5, 52. It should also be noted that this was not the first time that an American producer had shown an interest in making use of the Cinecittà studios for his own productions. This was Walter Wanger, an independent producer like Hal Roach—and an associate at United Artists—who, before Cinecittà was even completed—had signed an agreement for producing a colour film there. The agreement was announced in October 1936, but a few months later Wanger was to have second thoughts and walked away from the agreement. In Italy, this was announced by *Cinema* in an anonymous article entitled 'Gli americani in Italia', 8 (25 October 1936), 300.

[60] However much Vittorio Mussolini's involvement in the business deal with Hal Roach seems fortuitous, it must be noted that on 16 November 1936 the *Hollywood Reporter* had already published a short article in which it announced that Vittorio was going to spend six months in Hollywood so that he could learn the trade before taking a position of responsibility in the management of Italy's film industry. The article does not mention any sources, but, even if it might have been based entirely on gossip, it is indicative of the widespread perception of Vittorio Mussolini as an important player. Anon., 'Indicate Duce Jr for Italy's Pic Top', *Hollywood Reporter*, 16 November 1936, p. 3. I am particularly grateful to Charles Leavitt for providing me with a digital copy of all the Mussolini-related articles in the *Hollywood Reporter* at a time when Covid 19 made it impossible for me to access the archival holdings. ERA Film's first production was Camillo Mastrocinque's odd *noir* film *L'orologio a cucù* (1938), set in nineteenth-century Italy, co-scripted by Mario Soldati and starring Vittorio De Sica.

to cut Renato Senise out of the deal in order to give Vittorio full control. One can easily imagine the reasoning behind this decision. However, the brutality of it was to backfire, since Senise, armed with a signed contract with Roach, was to take the latter to court.

The *Hollywood Reporter* splashed the news of what it called 'the biggest motion picture deal of the year' with a front-page article, on 15 September 1937, whose headline ran in large-print characters: 'Roach's $6.000.000 Deal'. The next step was for Vittorio to travel to Hollywood to publicize the deal. In his memoirs, Vittorio remembers talking to his father about his plans to travel to America and receiving his approval on *Il Duce*'s birthday: it was therefore 29 July 1937. An extended visit to the USA by the son of Italy's *Duce* was a high-profile public-relations event, and each step had to be carefully planned. Disruption from anti-Fascist groups in both New York and Los Angeles could be predicted.

When the Italian liner *Rex* arrived in New York, on 23 September, the American press reported Vittorio's arrival accompanied by Hal Roach. It mentioned the presence of Renato Senise too, although his existence was conveniently removed by Vittorio when it came to writing his memoirs. They also reported the presence of groups of Italian American anti- and pro-Fascists, which the police made sure to keep separate at all times. Vittorio was spared the embarrassment of an anti-Fascist demonstration by the authorities having him disembark at a different dock. Nonetheless, when at his hotel, Vittorio remembered seeing groups of protesters standing outside the entrance. He was constantly escorted by an FBI agent (an Italian American called Giusti, he remembers, who boasted of having grown up in the same neighbourhood as Al Capone), and when he left for the airport to fly to Los Angeles, he received a full police escort complete with siren-hooting police motorbikes. It was clear that the US administration was keen to avoid any political embarrassment, particularly so since President Roosevelt had plans to meet *Il Duce*'s son himself.

Vittorio stayed in Los Angeles, as a guest in Hal Roach's home, for about three weeks, until 6 October. By the end of his stay, the RAM project had quickly become a dead duck. Roach and Mayer had massively underestimated the amount of heated disapproval that a commercial deal with *Il Duce*'s son would trigger. The Anti-Nazi League for the Defence of American Democracy, led in Hollywood by high-profile stars such as Fredric March and James Cagney, left no stone unturned. There were protests outside Roach and MGM studios, and a whole advertising page of the *Hollywood Reporter* was twice turned into a denunciation of the affair, on 21 September and on 4 October (see Fig. 9.6).[61]

---

[61] The second page, not reproduced here, was signed by the Motion Picture Artists Committee, and it presented a self-damning quotation from Vittorio Mussolini's memoir *Voli sulle ambe*: 'I had anticipated terrific explosions, such as in the American films, whereas the huts of the Ethiopians, made as they are of clay and brushwood, do not offer the bomber any satisfaction.'

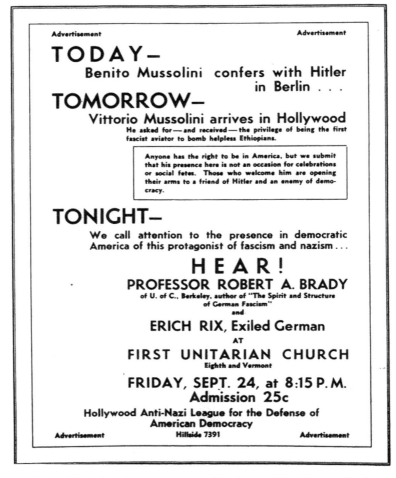

Fig. 9.6. Copy of the advertisement page used by the Anti-Nazi League for the Defence of American Democracy to protest against Vittorio Mussolini's visit; *Hollywood Reporter*, 21 September 1937, p. 8. (author's personal collection)

The first party to backtrack was MGM. During Vittorio's stay, behind the public-relations show of his visits to Fox's studios and various meetings with the philo-Fascist faction at Hollywood—which included Tyrone Power and Walt Disney—and a plush birthday party (Vittorio's twenty-first) thrown at Roach's house, the negative fallout of the deal was constantly reported to Louis Mayer, who eventually came to the decision that MGM had to pull out. News of the court case that Renato Senise was about to bring against Hal Roach—which the *New York Times* and the *Hollywood Reporter* announced on 6 October—was the

Fig. 9.7. Signed photograph by Shirley Temple after her meeting with Vittorio Mussolini at Fox Studios, Hollywood, October 1937 (from Vittorio Mussolini's memoir, *Vita con mio padre*; courtesy of BNC, Rome)

final straw. Hal Roach quickly followed suit. He decided that it was best for him too to take the hit of the cancellation of the contract and move on. The formal steps were taken only after Vittorio's departure, but this was only a question of diplomacy. Literally, the day after he left Los Angeles, the *Hollywood Reporter* splashed out with a front-page article whose headline could not be clearer: 'Roach–Italy Deal Cold. Bitter Opposition to Tie Up with Mussolini Kills Plan; Il Duce's Son Starts for Home'.

The final step of Vittorio's journey, after a brief stopover in San Francisco, was a visit to Washington, following an invitation to the White House from the Roosevelt family. Both the Italian ambassador in Washington and the American ambassador to Italy were present, thus adding weight to the occasion. The official reason was to reciprocate the courtesy with which *Il Duce* had received Roosevelt's wife and son during their visit to Rome the year before. At the same time, Roosevelt was keen to exploit the occasion, in order to confirm his intention to meet Mussolini and, with him, to try and find an agreement on how to steer European politics towards a peaceful balance. Vittorio duly reported Roosevelt's proposal, but the meeting never took place. Italy's drift towards Nazi Germany was by then reaching a point of no return.

Following the meeting at the White House, which took place on 11 October, Vittorio Mussolini returned to New York, and after a few more days he eventually embarked on the *Rex* on 16 October 1937, never to return to America. His company, ERA Film, received due compensation from Hal Roach—about half a million lire—so he was able to continue his activity as producer. ERA's most successful production was to be the comedy *Grandi magazzini* (1939), exploiting the by then winning formula of Camerini director with Vittorio De Sica as male lead. This did not prevent the company from eventually folding in 1942.

In the end, the grand plan of a close collaboration between Hollywood and Cinecittà lay in tatters, victim of the political developments of the post-Spanish Civil War years. It is worth speculating whether the deal would have gone ahead had the anti-Fascist group in Hollywood failed to raise its profile, turning it into a PR disaster for both Roach and MGM. The fact that the meeting between Vittorio Mussolini and President Roosevelt went ahead, despite protests taking place in Washington too (and by then it was clear that the RAM project was dead in the water), makes one suspect that there would have been enough goodwill in both Hollywood and Washington to allow the project to take off. Apart from its commercial dimension, RAM could have provided that closer connection between the USA and Fascist Italy that Roosevelt still hoped to foster.

As for Vittorio's 'American education', his subsequent career as film critic and producer does not exactly suggest that he became a paladin or a paradigm for a new, 'American' way of doing cinema, however much he might have considered it himself. ERA Film never had the size and financial clout to create its own studio system nor to have a vertical presence within the film industry. With the debacle of RAM, Vittorio Mussolini missed his big chance to become a central player. As director of *Cinema*, he continued to exert his influence, and more will be said in the next chapter about his activity during the last years of the regime; but he quickly understood—most likely helped by his father's advice— that the time for overt pro-American views had gone. Indeed, it did not take long. When the reforms of the Italian film industry kicked in, in 1938, triggering the disengagement from the Italian market of most of Hollywood studios, he was quick to declare from the pages of *Cinema* that he fully endorsed the regime's policies: 'Personally and politically, I am glad that American films— produced in that Jewish–Communist centre which Hollywood is—will no longer enter Italy [. . .]'. The rest of the editorial was emblematically peppered with anti-American statements, as if Vittorio wanted to make it clear once and for all that his philo-Americanism had come to an end. In line with the introduction of the anti-Semitic legislation, the vocabulary also fell in line with the new trend: it was Jewish–Communist Americans from which Italy had to protect itself.[62]

Freddi wrote a long report to Mussolini about the RAM affair, which is reproduced in its entirety in his memoirs. He does not specify the date on which he wrote it, but its content allows us to guess that it was penned at an early stage,

---

[62] Vittorio Mussolini, 'Un momento critico', *Cinema*, 58 (25 November 1938), 307.

most likely during the first days of Vittorio's trip to the USA, before news of the implosion of the deal had reached Rome. Freddi also tells us that, the day before Vittorio's departure, he had met Mussolini and had tried to convince him to cancel the trip, to which Mussolini had replied that it was too late to stop it. Freddi makes no connection between this meeting and his report, but it is likely that the latter was written, either to convince Mussolini to stop the trip or in the following days as a detailed explanation of his opposition to it. What is revealing about this text, beyond the accusations of naivety and unprofessionalism directed at De Feo, is the fact that it shows the extent to which Freddi was entirely left out of all negotiations. The target of Freddi's vitriolic comments is De Feo, but, knowing the closeness between De Feo and the Mussolini family, it is patent that the matter had been conducted almost as a family affair—including meetings in *Il Duce*'s house—and Freddi had been entirely sidelined.

This takes us to two considerations. First, Freddi's position as the tzar of the Italian film industry was not as strong as he would have liked us to think in his post-war memoirs. The RAM affair took place in the autumn of 1937. By March 1939 Freddi was replaced as head of the Direzione Generale per la Cinematografia, and only a year later he re-emerged as president of *Cinecittà*, a position that, however prestigious, was equivalent to demotion. It is likely that Freddi's vociferous complaints about the RAM affair might have started the descending trajectory of his meteoric career within the regime. Secondly, it is unthinkable that 19-year-old Vittorio should have been allowed to enter deep in negotiations with powerful figures in Hollywood without the approval of his father. Freddi was an obstacle to it, and his long, whingeing, and bureaucratically detailed report to Mussolini probably backfired, if nothing else. Indeed, the report has a distinct 'Jiminy Cricket' feel to it (in the crude spirit of Collodi's version, not Walt Disney's), and it makes one wonder how Freddi could not have predicted that Mussolini might have felt personally accused of incompetence—and certainly his son Vittorio indirectly was—and would therefore react negatively to it.

In the end, if RAM folded thanks to the opposition of anti-Fascist groups in Hollywood, its beginning can be best understood as the result of the personal power of a dictator, able to impose an improvised, high-risk venture for the simple reason that his son was involved. According to the *Hollywood Reporter*, there was also a negative coda that concerned MGM. As the newspaper announced in a front-page article entitled 'Duce Intensifies US Ban', MGM had just been denied permission to create its own first-run exhibition circuit throughout Italy. According to the anonymous journalist, the move was 'believed to be in retaliation for treatment accorded to Vittorio Mussolini by certain Hollywood elements'. The news must have come directly from Rome, since the article quoted a long passage from an article by Telesio Interlandi, who had recently attacked the presence of American studios in Italy in a front-page editorial for his militant

Fascist daily *Il Tevere*. His article, boasted Interlandi, had been written following a personal meeting between him and *Il Duce*.[63]

Finally, it is important to try and define Benito Mussolini's role in the history of American–Italian relations in the film industry beyond the specific case of RAM. *Il Duce*'s interest in watching movies and his anecdotal likes and dislikes concerning individual American films or actors are well documented, but, equally, in the early years in power he showed very little appetite for getting his government involved. His only concern was political and, as such, was directed at newsreels. This was one more field in which American cinema had been taking the lead. When Luciano De Feo created the Sindacato istruzione cinematografica (SIC) in 1924, his intention, as the denomination suggested, was to specialize in documentary filmmaking as an educational medium. One of the early productions was dedicated to Mussolini as prime minister, and the latter was quick to realize the propaganda potential of this genre. SIC was progressively nationalized through the injection of capitals from various state-controlled institutions, and, by November 1925, the more attractively renamed Istituto LUCE (L'Unione Cinematografica Educativa)—allegedly following Mussolini's suggestion—was established as the government's official film propaganda department. The following year the projection of newsreels was made compulsory in all Italian cinemas. Once it got up to speed, LUCE was able to produce four 'cinegiornali' a week, which, as we saw, Mussolini was invited to preview each Tuesday at Villa Torlonia. Foreign material was bought in, mainly from the USA, in order to add international flavour to the overall coverage. Initially, this was also due to the scarce production capacity of LUCE. Indeed, four out of six features that constituted the very first LUCE newsreel, of June 1927, were made by MGM. They included Lindbergh's flight across the Atlantic and the flooding of the Mississippi River at New Orleans. On average, one Hollywood-made feature appeared within every LUCE newsreel until 1940.[64]

Their content would focus on specific events, sometimes featuring extravagant acts that confirmed the cliché of America as the land of eternal children, such as odd contests like a rubber-horse race in a swimming pool or a competition for the ugliest man in town. The Italian features, instead, tended to be celebratory, showcasing the regime's achievements in all fields of Italian society, regularly featuring *Il Duce* as a much-adored figure. According to Freddi, who devotes an entire chapter to Mussolini's views on cinema,[65] *Il Duce* was critical of the poor quality of the Italian production, sometimes asking for modifications and cuts.

When it came to fiction films, Mussolini was a spectator like any other and, in his first years in power, he never committed his government to more than the odd

---

[63] Anon., 'Duce Intensifies US Ban', *Hollywood Reporter*, 18 November 1937, pp. 1, 14. Telesio Interlandi's editorial is 'Contro il cinema italiano', *Il Tevere*, 20–1 October 1937, p. 1.
[64] Hay, *Popular Film Culture in Fascist Italy*, 94.     [65] Freddi, *Il governo dell'immagine*, 183–91.

protectionist policy in aid of the Italian film industry. Nor did he seem interested in using it to promote his own public image, despite his early debut in one of Fox's early sound newsreels in 1927, as we saw in Chapter 6. The structural changes of 1934, with the creation of the Direzione Generale per la Cinematografia, were enormous, but it should be remembered that they happened as part of the overall centralization of the culture industry that the regime undertook in the wake of a similar development in Nazi Germany. In other words, cinema was one of the fields subjected to the attempt to regiment cultural production: it was only one of seven direzioni that also dealt with the press (Italian and foreign), propaganda, tourism, theatre/music, and the radio. During that phase Mussolini seemed entirely happy with Ciano taking the lead, and he showed no particular interest in the field of filmmaking.

Mussolini's direct interest in cinema as a propaganda tool is a later development, which becomes tangible only in 1937 with the opening of Cinecittà and the second attempt at a grand propaganda film with *Scipione l'Africano*. The latter was the first film production that Mussolini visited in an official capacity and that was widely covered by the national press. By then the Ministry of Popular Culture was in the hands of Dino Alfieri, whose philo-Nazi stance was made clear by his close collaboration with Goebbels, which flourished after their meeting at the Venice Film Festival of September 1936. Many reciprocal visits and joint decisions marked their good relations, which continued even after Alfieri's appointment as Italian ambassador in Berlin in May 1940.[66]

Even in this respect, the fact that Vittorio Mussolini was allowed to go ahead with his American project shows the extent to which Mussolini had decided to enter the stage and dictate his will. Indeed, it was not the first time that Alfieri's views had been silenced by *Il Duce*. Mention of the visit by Goebbels in September 1936 is appropriate, since it is in the following weeks that Alfieri experienced the crushing weight of the Mussolini's will. Following his talks with Goebbels, Alfieri, helped by Freddi, introduced new legislation aimed at strengthening the grip of

---

[66] Goebbels's published diary starts only in 1939, but it is interesting to note that, in its entry for 2 November 1939, on the news that Alfieri had been replaced by Pavolini as Minister of Popular Culture, Goebbels should have penned the following, laconic comment: 'I am sorry about Alfieri. He was very useful to us.' The diary proves that the two met frequently during Alfieri's stint in Berlin as Italian ambassador. However, Goebbels's consideration for Alfieri took a deep nosedive in the spring of 1941. Here is his entry for 28 April 1941: 'Alfieri has lost a lot of his reputation. [...] A typical misfit! Besides which he is unreliable in his work, absent-minded, fickle, and without capacity for hard work. Things will surely not go well for him.' And on 3 May he recorded: 'Alfieri is scatter-brained and stupid. It is difficult to make him understand anything.' In Joseph Goebbels, *The Goebbels' Diaries, 1939–1945* (London: Hamilton, 1982), 37, 338, 346. Galeazzo Ciano, as foreign minister, was only slightly more polite when, chronicling in his diary his discussions with Ribbentrop in April 1942, he noted that Alfieri 'understands little of what he hears, but is always nodding in approval', in Ciano, *Diario 1937–1943* (Bologna: Cappelli, 1948); repr. in *Diario 1937–1943* (Milan: Rizzoli, 1980), 614. On the development of the alliance between Nazi Germany and Fascist Italy, initially under the umbrella of the German-led International Film Chamber, created in 1935, see Mino Argentieri, *L'asse cinematografico Roma-Berlino* (Naples: Sapere, 1986).

**Fig. 9.8.** Goebbels and Alfieri during the former's visit to the Venice Film Festival, in September 1936. (anonymous photo; courtesy of Wikimedia Commons)

the state on the film industry and helping to reduce the domination of American movies in Italian cinemas. This time Mussolini took an interest and blocked Alfieri's plan. With regard to this episode, we have a peculiar American witness in the shape of Will H. Hays, the most powerful political figure in interwar Hollywood.

As chairman of the Motion Pictures Producers and Distributors of America (MPPDA) since its foundation in 1922 and thanks to his close collaboration with US governments, Hays had become a key figure in the American film industry and acted as its ambassador abroad. During the months of Galeazzo Ciano's expansion of his ministry, in 1934, Will Hays had secured American interests with the so-called Ciano–Hays agreement, which guaranteed US exports to Italy— that is, 250 films a year. Two years later, however, with the ministry and cinema policies in the hands of Alfieri and Freddi, the political climate had changed in view of their intention firmly to curb the dominance of Hollywood, however popular their films were. A raft of legislation was introduced in October 1936, massively reducing the import of American films to forty-two per year and cutting the amount of profits that Hollywood was allowed to take out of the country to eight million lire, which meant a huge cut of about 80 per cent. When the news reached America, Will Hays was asked to use all his diplomatic weight in order to try and buck the trend. Ciano had by then moved to the position of foreign minister, but Hays, rightly sensing that he could find in him and in his father-in-law, *Il Duce*, a more benevolent interlocutor, made sure they would both be involved in the negotiations. Hays set sail for Italy on the *Conte di Savoia*, on 7 November 1936, accompanied by his wife (the couple were later to visit the pope, who personally thanked him for the moralization of American cinema through the Hays code of 1930) and various MPPDA staff. The American embassy in Rome opened its doors to him and gave him an office so that he could be shown as representing the will of the State Department too. Alfieri and Freddi were present at the first meetings and were judged by Hays as little more than high-level bureaucrats standing in his way:

> Alfieri I met several times. One other quasi-government man, Luigi Freddi, became a bit of a problem because he kept trying to get into the negotiations, in which he had no official part. His title was Direttore Generale per la Cinematografia. This Freddi, known as the film director of the Italian Propaganda Ministry, was the man who only five months later signed for Italy a pact with Germany and Japan creating an anti-Hollywood bloc. [...]
>
> This Alfieri turned up to be quite a boy. He looked like a Peoria whisky salesman and jumped around as lively. He was undoubtedly ambitious but apparently close to the Duce.[67]

Eventually the negotiations boiled down to a face-to-face meeting with *Il Duce*, thanks also to a telegram from Roosevelt that Hays managed to trigger. After having listened to Hays's defence of the status quo and calls for future collaboration now that Cinecittà was about to be opened, Mussolini conferred with Ciano over the phone (Alfieri was present but, according to Hays, 'had sat there not saying a word') and offered a compromise. The ceiling of American imports would be brought back to 250 and the export of profit would be capped at a much higher level, from eight million lire to twenty million lire. Hays found the deal better than he had hoped. He happily shook Mussolini's hand and went back to the American embassy, where everybody celebrated the success of his diplomatic mission.[68]

To us, this episode is one more example of Mussolini's interference in the management of Italy's film industry during the mid-1930s. This time he was helped by Ciano, who, as former minister and Alfieri's former boss, must have thought he had every right to sideline both Alfieri and Freddi. The big clampdown on American imports had been avoided, although, as we know, Hays's

---

[67] Hays, *Memoirs*, 511–20 (515–16).
[68] The meeting between Mussolini and Hays is discussed by Brunetta in his *Storia del cinema italiano*, ii. 334–5.

diplomatic success was going to last less than two years. By September 1938 the so-called Legge Alfieri brought the situation back to where he had tried to put it in 1936. How come this time Mussolini showed no opposition to it? Or perhaps the question should be rephrased as follows: what had changed in those intervening twenty months?

This takes us back to the opening of Cinecittà, in April 1937, and to the involvement of Mussolini's son in what could have been the first major collaboration with the American film industry. It is likely that the RAM fiasco and the embarrassment of having his son metaphorically kicked out of Hollywood by the anti-Fascist, pro-Spanish Republic lobby had convinced Mussolini too that America was no longer a place to do business, certainly not Hollywood. In the meantime, the ties with Nazi Germany were strengthening in every sector. And protectionism became the weapon, as Ellwood rightly suggests, 'to restore the balance of cultural power and to domesticate the beast'.[69]

The summer and autumn of 1938 saw a radical development of Fascism's cultural policies across different fields. As one of such developments, the anti-American steer in the management of the film industry can be best understood if placed within that bigger fresco. It is for this reason that the discussion will continue in the following chapter. Before then, however, it is necessary to consider the influence of American cinema on the Italian film industry and on Italian culture at large.

## 9.3 Hollywood's Mark in Interwar Italy

Of the four sections of this chapter, this one is the most challenging, since it is one thing to trace the historical presence of American films in Italy and the actions of Italian filmmakers and politicians with respect to it, but a very different one to try and understand where and how Italy's film industry was replicating something specifically American. As we will see, there are a number of cases worth deliberating, and, for clarity's sake, I will tackle them by distinguishing between, adopting Bourdieu's lexis, questions of economic and cultural capital. Hence, first we will look at issues concerning the organizational/industrial dimension of filmmaking. Secondly, we will delineate the artistic influence of American film production through the discussion of five different cases. It goes without saying that it is a separation that is simply instrumental to the structure of the critical discourse.

### 9.3.1 Hollywood Studios as a Model

Victoria De Grazia's delineation of the defining traits of the American film industry is, in its conciseness, a good point of departure:

---

[69] Ellwood, *The Shock of America*, 111.

The American cinema stood for major economies of scale, capital-intensive technologies, and standardization; it favored an action-filled cinematographic narrative focused on the star and pitched to a cross-class audience. Its promoters were professionals who were formed outside of traditional centers of culture, within the industry, and who were closely attuned to the problem of marketing their products.[70]

It is imaginable that in the post-First World War years, when the European markets reopened, this quickly became the perception of Hollywood, the more so after the introduction of sound, which gave the American film industry a golden opportunity to flex its muscles—that is, to show its huge reserves of economic capital. Perhaps the only missing detail from De Grazia's definition—probably implied in 'major economies of scale'—is the vertical presence of the Hollywood majors in the distribution and exhibition of films. In a developing market such as cinemagoing in the interwar years, those were stable sources of revenue, which could be used to counterbalance high-risk investments in production.

With sound, the cost of filmmaking soared, and so did the potential losses if a particular film proved a fiasco, as many did. Standardization was the industrial answer, but film producers soon discovered that finding a 'standard' capable of producing successful films day in day out was as elusive as the alchemic formula for making gold. Nonetheless, confident of its primacy in mass production in just about every industry, the USA was at the forefront in its attempt to rationalize film production and develop the structures needed to provide a constant flow of artefacts, with quality being planned and controlled at the highest possible level. The industry's relocation from New York to Hollywood added the opportunity to create brand new facilities that reflected its potentials and ambitions. It was an organization that treated the film director as an important but not necessarily pivotal component of film production. As we will see, there were vital exceptions to this trend, but, overall, there was a sense that the artistic, creative dimension of filmmaking had to be as planned and as commercially savvy as possible, and directorship and acting came into it too.

Rationalization also meant developing a marketing branch capable of ensuring maximum presence in the public sphere, particularly through the press. The spectators' instinctive attraction towards the physical features of actors and actresses rather than the invisible presence of the director meant that the emphasis had to be put on the former—hence the development of what came to be called the star system. The world of theatre had known and exploited the fame of individual performers for centuries, and Italy was no exception to this, particularly in the late nineteenth century, when figures such Francesca Bertini, Lyda Borrelli, and Eleonora Duse were theatre divas well before cinema caught up with them. But, once again, America led the way in its industrial-scale approach to the challenge.

---

[70] De Grazia, 'Mass Culture and Sovereignty', 61.

378   AMERICA IN ITALIAN CULTURE

Advertising, a key characteristic of 'the American way', as so often noted by Italian travellers, was the powerful tool to ensure that the production investment would maximize its returns.

In Italy, the American majors began to develop their marketing strategies in the second half of the 1920s. At the start of this chapter, we saw an example from 1926, which shows how they would not just place their advertisements in the Italian press but also buy space for feature articles singing the praises of individual films. From their branch offices in Italy also came their own publicity magazines, starting with the *Bollettino della Fox Film Corp.*, in 1928, followed by MGM's *La Voce del leone* in 1930. By then, Pittaluga had already adopted this strategy with the creation of its own magazine. This was the heavily illustrated *Bollettino Edizioni Pittaluga*, whose issues, starting in 1927, run for more than fifty pages and imitated American movie magazines rather than the traditional, shorter Italian *bollettini* produced by film companies. Naturally, the journal paid equal attention to foreign films distributed in Italy by Pittaluga. The example illustrated here comes from a 1929 issue, and it advertises an American production entitled *Naughty Nanette* (1927) in the original, which was turned into *Holliwood* [sic] *terra di sogni* for the Italian audience, exploiting the fact that the entire plot is set in the capital of American cinema (it is the story of a young aspiring actress fighting her way up in the business). Note the invasive and creative set-up of images in Fig. 9.9, in which, in the style of American movie fan magazines—*Photoplay* and

Fig. 9.9. Two-page advertisement of Meehan's *Naughty Nanette* (1927), in *Bollettino Edizioni Pittaluga*, 3/8 (August–September 1929), 16–17. (courtesy of Biblioteca Luigi Chiarini, CSC, Rome)

*Motion Picture Magazine* being the most popular in the 1920s—images occupy more than half of the space dedicated to the news item.

Italy developed its own range of fan magazines. Most were independent of the movie industry, but at the same time—and just like their American counterparts—benefiting from a close collaboration with production companies, which meant receiving a constant flow of publicity material and, equally important, the possibility of interviewing or at least receiving spicy information about leading actors. Among them were *Cine-Sorriso illustrato* (1924–30) and *Cine-Cinema* (1925–7), but Italy's most popular one was the weekly *Cinema illustrazione* (1926–39) almost entirely devoted to stars and Hollywood cinema. By the 1930s, despite a string of different chief editors, who changed almost yearly, it had reached a circulation of about 300,000 copies.[71]

*Cinema illustrazione* was owned by the Rizzoli publishing house, which, together with Mondadori, led the modernization of Italy's press with the introduction of rotopress machinery, which allowed the reproduction of good-quality photos. In the 1930s, Angelo Rizzoli became interested in cinema. In 1934, he founded his own production company, Novella Film (its name derived from Rizzoli's then most popular magazine, *Novella*), which produced the already mentioned *Darò un milione* (1935), directed by Camerini. In 1938, Rizzoli also took over the publication of *Cinema*, in the year in which Vittorio Mussolini became its chief editor. Indeed, like Arnoldo Mondadori, Angelo Rizzoli had constantly remained on good terms with circles close to the regime in order to facilitate the development of his business.[72]

As for *Cinema illustrazione*, if Rizzoli's ownership might have made it particularly favourable towards its own productions, it was anything but an in-house publication. In fact, Rizzoli made sure it concentrated on American cinema and was staffed with the most promising film journalists of the time, some of whom were also involved in scriptwriting. Ettore Margadonna was one of them, and another one was Cesare Zavattini. The two were to be linked in an operation that is emblematic of *Cinema illustrazione*'s aim to replicate American fan magazines. As both confessed in the post-war years, they used to publish fake interviews with famous American stars, pretending to be American journalists in Hollywood while using published interviews as a source of information.[73]

---

[71] The circulation figure is provided by Beynet, *L'Image de l'Amérique*, iii. 873.

[72] Rizzoli also became a major stakeholder in ERA Film, Vittorio Mussolini's production company. On Angelo Rizzoli, see Enzo Biagi, *Dinastie: Gli Agnelli, i Rizzoli, i Ferruzzi-Gardini, i Lauro* (Milan: Mondadori, 1988). After the takeover of *Cinema*, the Rome-based journal was advertised in the pages of *Cinema illustrazione* as its 'sorella maggiore' ('older sister').

[73] Margadonna confessed this in his long interview with Francesco Savio, in 1974. Savio, *Cinecittà anni trenta*, ii. 714–27 (716). Zavattini's articles have been collected and published as a volume: Cesare Zavattini, *Cronache da Hollywood* (Rome: Editori Riuniti, 1996). On Zavattini, see Giorgio Bertellini, 'Strabismi culturali: Zavattini e gli Stati Uniti', in Alberto Ferraboschi (ed.), *Zavattini oltre i confini: Reti, pratiche, ricezione* (Reggio Emilia: Biblioteca Panizzi, 2020), 97–113. The practice of faking

**Fig. 9.10.** Vittorio Mussolini and Mario Camerini (third and sixth from the left) accompany Angelo Rizzoli (in the middle, wearing a hat) during his visit to the Cinecittà studios as reported in the 12 October 1938 issue of *Cinema illustrazione*. (courtesy of Cineteca, Bologna)

Another element that shows a strict parallel between Italian popular film magazines such as *Cinema illustrazione* and their American counterparts was the use of stars as vehicles in order to create a two-way relationship with the (mainly female) readership. On the one hand, stars were presented as glamorous figures, whose physical beauty and interesting lives—both on and off screen—would invite a sense of escapist identification. On the other, readers were constantly lured with the illusion of the possibility that they too could enter the world of cinema. Competitions for aspiring actors and actresses were a constant feature. In 1930, for example, *Cinema illustrazione* asked readers to send in their portrait photographs, which a committee would select and publish every week, ready for the public vote. The winners' photos would be passed on to unspecified film production companies, which were free to consider or ignore them. Interestingly enough, next to the rules of the competition, an issue presented a section called 'Indiscrezioni', which contained brief entries about the humble lives of Hollywood stars, from Jack Holt having worked as a farmhand in California to King Vidor

---

articles written in the USA was adopted in 1937 by another Rizzoli magazine, *Omnibus*. On this, see Manuela Di Franco, 'US Culture and Fascist Italy: The Case of *Omnibus* (1937–39)', in Bonsaver, Carlucci, and Reza (eds), *Italy and the USA*, 123–39 (127–8).

having attempted a career as a journalist, for years writing articles that no paper would publish. The section ended with the cheering line: 'Today all these people are celebrities!'[74]

As for the covers of *Cinema illustrazione*, throughout the years the magazine stuck with full-page colour photographs of female stars, once again copying its American counterparts, with the only difference being that *Photoplay* and *Motion Picture Magazine* would concentrate on close-up face shots, as against *Cinema illustrazione*'s alternation of close-ups with the odd full-body shot. The Italian magazine would also continue to adopt a more conservative layout, with a framed picture separated from title and headlines, resembling the traditional style—in use of font too—of Italian illustrated magazines such as *Domenica del Corriere*. Naturally, it goes without saying that there was a cross-national dimension to this phenomenon, which concerned the reciprocal influence of popular movie magazines of other countries. The Italian *Cine-Cinema*, for example, was derivative from the French weekly *Cinémagazine*. There is little doubt, however, that in the interwar years American film magazines were the most influential, not the least because they were closest to the common object of attention: Hollywood.[75]

In his memoirs, Luigi Freddi wrote that he was personally against the cult of stars, preferring to aim at a rotation of Italian actors taken from the educated middle classes so as to offer a range of respectable Italian types. Evidence suggests that his stance was more of a nationalistic opposition to Hollywood stars rather than anything else, since, after all, the set-up of Cinecittà under his supervision, as we have seen, gave privileged space to 'dive e divi', and, when Freddi became a producer himself with the resurrected Cines, in 1942, he went about hiring established stars like any other producer in search of commercial success. By the 1930s, the idea of the star system as a major vehicle in the marketing of films had simply become a fact. Cesare Zavattini recalled the statistical predictability with which pasting the photo of a popular film star on the front cover of Rizzoli's literary weekly *Novella* meant an automatic increase in sales.[76]

The front covers of *Cinema illustrazione* regularly alternated photos of Hollywood stars with their Italian equivalent, from Isa Miranda to Assia Noris,

---

[74] See anon., 'Siete voi fotogenico?', and anon., 'Indiscrezioni', both in *Cinema illustrazione*, 5/52 (24 December 1930), 15. *Photoplay* had run its first photographic competition, called 'Beauty and Brains', as early as 1916. The winners were invited to spend twelve days in New York, on an all-expenses-paid visit, complete with screen tests with a major studio. On the role of fan magazines in creating a two-way relationship in the promotion of film stars in the interwar years, see Elizabeth Ezra and Ana Salzberg, 'The Screen Test 1915-1930: How Stars Were Born', *Celebrity Studies*, 8/3 (2017), 477–88.

[75] On this, see Raffaele De Berti, 'Rotocalchi cinematografici e modelli di vita hollywoodiani nell'Italia fra le due guerre', in Raffaele De Berti (ed.), *Immaginario hollywoodiano e cinema italiano degli anni trenta* (Milan: CUEM, 2004), 75–104. See also Gaylyn Studlar, 'The Perils of Pleasure? Fan Magazine Discourse as Women's Commodified Culture in the 1920s', in Richard Abel (ed.), *Silent Film* (New Brunswick: Rutgers University Press, 1999), 263–97.

[76] On Freddi as a producer, see Gundle, *Mussolini's Dream Factory*, 49–50. Cesare Zavattini, *Io: Un'autobiografia* (posthumously edited by Paolo Nuzzi) (Turin: Einaudi, 2002), 68.

**Fig. 9.11.** A selection of 1930s covers from *Motion Picture Magazine* (February 1931), *Photoplay* (January 1933), and *Cinema illustrazione* (August 1932 and September 1933). (courtesy of Media History Digital Library, Wisconsin Center for Film and Theatre Research; and Cineteca, Bologna)

Doris Duranti, and others. Male stardom too was cultivated in the interwar years: Vittorio De Sica, above all, but, if he represented the more ordinary, benevolent face of Italian masculinity, Freddi was eager to encourage the popularity of other leading actors whose attitude and appearance would embody the type of the 'new Italian' forged during the years of Fascist rule. One of them had already reached fame by then through the unpredictable metamorphosis from black slave in Pastrone's *Cabiria* to First World War hero, always carrying the name Maciste, which became a film brand in itself. This was Bartolomeo Pagano, whose career extended into the early years of Fascism and developed into an intriguing symbiosis with the regime's obsession with projecting an image of masculine power, which Mussolini so often impersonated through his theatrical poses and his 'shows of strength'. The latter, particularly when he appeared bare chested, either harvesting wheat or skiing down a slope, created a clear-to-all parallel with Pagano's stage appearance. Mussolini was the Maciste of Italian politics, as much as in later years Primo Carnera was to become the Maciste of Italian boxing.[77]

At the same time, more conventional male stars were needed, capable of competing with Hollywood types such as Douglas Fairbanks and Ramon Novarro, and the younger generation of sound-film, stars from Gary Cooper to Cary Grant, Clark Gable, and others. The closest one to an image of Italian masculinity that would fare well in Fascist circles was Amedeo Nazzari. Unsurprisingly, Nazzari starred in many propaganda films of the 1930s—for example, playing first the part of a cavalry officer in Alessandrini's *Cavalleria* (1936) and then that of the daring aviator in his *Luciano Serra pilota* (1938). Nazzari's rise to Italian fame was confirmed by *Cinema*'s readers in the 1939 poll, which saw him top the male star list with nearly four times more votes than any other actor.[78]

Beyond these traits, the key question regarding the film industry remains: did any Italian studio resemble something similar, in both size and range of operation, to a Hollywood studio? The short answer is none. Stefano Pittaluga's involvement in production, distribution, and exhibition during his management of Cines (1926–31) was as close as Italy got to a rationalization of film production by a private entrepreneur. However, his sudden death brought the process to a halt. Under the headship of Toeplitz and Cecchi, Cines undoubtedly raised the quality of its output, but it was a short season, abruptly interrupted by the fire that destroyed its studios in September 1935.

Paradoxically, after Cines's demise, the Italian government became the only potential candidate. Here, though, it is on the production front that the problems lay. The two propaganda films financially supported by the regime—*Camicia nera* (1933) and *Scipione l'africano* (1937)—were both fiascos, which convinced Freddi to find other, indirect ways of helping the production of Italian films. Cinecittà and the Centro sperimentale per la cinematografia provided a solid base from which private companies could benefit, but they were facilities rather than autonomous agents. Then there was the nationalization of distribution under ENIC, in 1938,

---

[77] For an in-depth study of Pagano's acting career, see Jacqueline Reich, *The Maciste Films of Italian Silent Cinema* (Bloomington, IN: Indiana University Press, 2015). The other silent era star whose image has been linked to Mussolini is Rudolph Valentino, whose career, however, was entirely developed in America. On him, see Giorgio Bertellini, *The Divo and the Duce*.

[78] The results were announced in the 10 February 1940 issue of *Cinema*. Second was Fosco Giachetti, followed by De Sica. Giachetti also featured in various propaganda films as an Italian army officer. On Nazzari and Giachetti, see Gundle, *Mussolini's Dream Factory*, 184–223.

which gave the state full control of the substantial and constant revenues coming from this operation. However, by then Freddi was on his way out, and Alfieri, as minister, had a vision of the Italian film industry that did not include raising the quality of its production. The emphasis, as we will see in the next chapter, was instead on quantity—that is, on replacing the missing American films by the four Hollywood majors that had walked away.

Finally, if direct collaboration between American and Italian companies might have been a vehicle for the exchange of working practices, this proved an infertile ground. The return to higher standards with Cines–Pittaluga and then Cinecittà presented an opportunity, which was attempted and lost with Roach–Mussolini's RAM. After that, politics took over: the official anti-Americanism introduced by Alfieri in the late 1930s made any form of collaboration impossible. Germany became the default interlocutor.

### 9.3.2 Action and Narrative Dynamism in Hollywood Films

If we move now to questions of cultural capital, the discussion shifts to films as artefacts, and the key question concerns any American influence on Italian film-makers during the interwar years. As we have seen, when describing the American film industry in 1931, Tito Spagnol warned about the need to follow Hollywood in paying adequate attention to the creation of sophisticated scripts. This, however, as he repeated more than once, did not mean that American directors were simply professionals who meticulously delivered the film envisaged in a detailed script. The best ones were allowed a high degree of freedom, particularly so if their previous work had proved critically and commercially successful.[79]

Spagnol did not mention any names, but, with hindsight, King Vidor, Frank Borzage, and Frank Capra come first to mind. A step higher were those who had managed to create their own companies and thus be in control of the entire production process. For the 1920s, two names are inevitable: Charlie Chaplin and Walt Disney. The length of this section reflects the need both to proceed with caution and to add a few examples of individual cases in which American cinema played a role in the creative work of Italian filmmakers.

Today's dominant genre of 'action film' did not have a fixed label in the interwar years, but it nonetheless defined a particular characteristic of early American cinema. Called 'Adventure film' or, ironically, 'Swashbucklers', these were action-packed films in which a male hero fought battle after battle, against all odds, always to emerge victorious in front of piles of defeated enemies. The historical setting could be anywhere, from ancient Rome to Louis XIV's France, a pirate

---

[79] Spagnol, 'Idee e metodi americani', 57–60.

haven in the Antilles, a First World War battlefield, the Wild West, or an urban setting infested by gangsters. A beautiful heroine to be saved often added the sentimental thread that made the happy ending even more uplifting. Nineteenth-century popular fiction provided the inspiration for many scripts. In the pre-sound years, Douglas Fairbanks became the embodiment of this genre through iconic film such as *The Mark of Zorro* (1920), *The Three Musketeers* (1921), *Robin Hood* (1922), and *The Thief of Bagdad* (1924). Gary Cooper and Erroll Flynn were to take over in later years. Other actors came to be identified with a particular subgenre, such as Tom Mix as the ultimate western hero, a role taken later by John Wayne. Those adventure films displayed narrative qualities that did not go unnoticed by Italian film critics. As Di Chio shows, complimentary comments related to the dynamism of their plots and acting can be found in Italian magazines such as *La Vita cinematografica* and *La Cine-gazzetta* going back to the pre-World War One years.[80]

With the arrival of sound came music, and musicals quickly became a new genre, where the actions of dancers and singers gave birth to another genre in which American cinema dominated. Here the star of Fred Astaire shone above all others. However, once again, it was not just a matter of individual genius. What struck was the capacity of Hollywood cinema to produce dynamic displays involving complex sets and hundreds of extras moving in unison.

American adventure films and musicals were the kind of films Vittorio Mussolini referred to when he wrote in 1936 about the need for Italian cinema to emancipate by looking west, over the Atlantic. The Italian public loved American films, and not just their stars, he added. They were attracted by 'the narrative flow and editing of American films'. From here came Vittorio Mussolini's definition of this precise quality of American cinema:

> Our public, who crowd cinema theatres, and our youth in particular love things to be clear, with no asides, entertaining, full of life and movement. [...] The American public, after all, loves films with wide horizons, they feel the vastness of big problems, are attracted by that child-ike, happy sense of adventure, and if this youth comes to them from their lack of centuries of history and culture, of philosophical systems and laws, it is certainly much closer to our bold generation than to that of many European countries. And American production, although entirely made in the USA, has never forgotten the European markets: Hollywood is too full of 'people of foreign extraction' and of foreigners for its production not to have an international character, independent from the economic calculations towards better exploitation.[81]

---

[80] Di Chio, *Il cinema americano in Italia*, 93–6.
[81] Mussolini, 'Emancipazione del cinema italiano', 213.

Perhaps Freddi was not far from the truth when he criticized Vittorio Mussolini for being vague and sometimes contradictory in his writings on cinema. This long quotation is vague in defining the technical characteristics of American cinema. The argument quickly drifts away from dynamism and vast open spaces to questions related to the roots of American culture—the recurring story of American childishness, in this case rescued by the presence of foreign, culture-rich, new blood. Also, the parallel between American youth and Italian *giovinezza* introduced a political dimension to the discourse, which, however, added nothing to a definition of American filmmaking.[82]

But what about Vittorio Mussolini's own filmmaking? By the time he wrote that article, he was about to be involved in the production of *Luciano Serra pilota*. According to one of his friends at the time, Mussolini on one occasion drew a direct connection between the structure of a typical American western and 'his' *Luciano Serra pilota*. He allegedly said: 'The airplanes correspond to the 7th cavalry, the Ethiopians to the Indians, Errol Flynn could be substituted for Amedeo Nazzari without changing anything.'[83] The suggestion of a parallel between the film and the western genre certainly counts for the 'action' sequence of the film, in the second half. It also confirms that American westerns were seen as a model by colonial filmmakers, as Ruth Ben-Ghiat suggests.[84]

Furthermore, this parallel does not end the potential connections between *Luciano Serra pilota* and Hollywood movies. If the second part of the film contains an action-packed, western-style story of conflict in the 'Wild South' of Ethiopia, the first half presents us with a number of other topoi indicating a specific attempt at reproducing—while ideologically criticizing—other recurring features of American cinema. When Luciano Serra's wife walks out on him because of his lack of a sufficient income, the former-First World War pilot spends his evening in a Grand Hotel's ballroom, in whose glitzy atmosphere he meets a rich American couple, Tom and Nathalie Thompson. The wife is a platinum blonde who puffs smoke from a cigarette while flirting with Serra, and the husband ends up offering him a contract that takes him away from his family. Despite being told by his father-in-law that this job is taking him to 'il paese dei dollari' ('the land of the Dollar'), the on-screen caption takes us from 1921 to 1931, and inexplicably we discover that ten years later Serra is working in South America. His boss is now Mr Braun, who turns out to be a circus owner. The whole scene is

---

[82] Freddi, *Il governo dell'immagine*, 141–2.

[83] Dario Zanelli, 'Quando Vittorio Mussolini dirigeva "Cinema"', in Mariella Furno and Renzo Renzi (eds), *Il neorealismo nel fascismo: Giuseppe De Santis e la critica cinematografica 1941–43* (Bologna: Compositori, 1984), 107; quoted in Tad Gallagher, *The Adventures of Roberto Rossellini: His Life and Films* (New York: Da Capo Press, 1998), 61.

[84] Ruth Ben-Ghiat, *Italian Fascism's Empire Cinema* (Bloomington, IN: Indiana University Press, 2015), 88–90, 210–11. According to Ben-Ghiat, the features that distinguished Italian empire films and detached them from the Hollywood model were the investment in location shoots and the integration of documentary conventions. *Il pilota ritorna*, however, is not exemplary of these traits, as against, for example, colonial films such as Camerini's *Il grande appello* (1936).

designed to be a caricature of 'American' business—loud, chaotic, but 'modern' through the presence of advertising, cars, aeroplanes, radio interviews, and the publicity stunt of Serra delivering a lion by aeroplane. In the placards advertising 'Circo Braun', it is tempting to see an assonance with 'Circo Barnum', America's most famous circus.

Cinematically, the beginning of the South American sequence is also worth mentioning: it starts not with an establishing shot but rather with a long take of a medium shot showing the passing of a number of advertising placards that only later do we realize are carried by a marching line of circus employees. It is an unusual opening, which evokes a distant parallel with King Vidor's non-established, opening sequence of the couple going on their honeymoon in *The Crowd*, which similarly starts with a tilting shot of a placard that only later do we realize is part of the announcement of their train journey. In terms of *mise en scène*, the world of advertising and the circus also play a role in *The Crowd*, with the very symbolic presence of a sandwich man dressed up as a clown, whom the protagonist pities at the start of the film, only to become one of them at the end.

Without trying to read too much of a direct link between the two films, it is at least worth noting that the most prominent members of the circus crowd welcoming the arrival of Serra's plane are clowns who all happen to wear a very similar conic-shaped white hat and clothing to that of Vidor's clown. No doubt this was typical of American clowns at the time, but the similarity is nonetheless intriguing. I will add just one more thread that seems to link the two films: plotwise, both have as protagonist a married man who is about to ruin his family life because of his ambitions. There the parallel ends, though, since their reciprocal redemption takes place in a totally different way: Vidor's John Sims eventually accepts his Babbitesque ordinariness, whereas Alessandrini's Luciano Serra heroically dies in battle when the film turns into the action film we mentioned before. Later on in this chapter we will return to Vidor's popularity among Italian filmmakers, but we have already seen how Vittorio Mussolini himself boasted of having seen his films several times over. This is not about the potential influence of a single film but rather about how American productions of the 1920s and early 1930s provided examples of a narrative flow that the audience loved and from which Italian filmmakers needed to draw inspiration if they wanted to replicate the sophistication of Hollywood's visual narratives.

Vittorio Mussolini's call for particular attention being paid to the dynamism of American films was not an isolated one. Before him, in his 1932 monograph, Margadonna had identified it as the essence of American cinema:

Action, strength, movement, these are the psychological qualities which, little by little, become moral values. [...] Given that cinema is nothing other than action and movement, it is already present in the blood of the American people.[85]

---

[85] Margadonna, *Cinema ieri e oggi*, 49.

The western genre is considered by Margadonna as the exemplary projection of this vitalism, with a narrative formula that, in different clothing, can be found in American gangster films and in American comedies. Furthermore, Margadonna too picks out King Vidor as one of the most groundbreaking examples of American cinema. *The Crowd* is considered in parallel with Sinclair Lewis's *Babbitt* as an example of a narrative piercing the bubble of the American dream before the Wall Street crisis and the Depression years.[86]

Four years later, in the issue of *Cinema* that followed Mussolini's article, the discussion was continued by two influential critics, Aldo Debenedetti and Alberto Consiglio, with an article entitled 'Il senso dell'avventura'. They began by presenting cinema as the art *par excellence* of the twentieth century, following sculpture in classical times, painting in the Renaissance, and music in the nineteenth century. And cinema—they added—is movement, and movement is action, which has defined cinema from its very start. After this *incipit*, the two critics quickly dismiss French and German films and proceed to praise American cinema. Porter's *The Great Train Robbery* (1903) is the first example, followed by a whole page dedicated to images of King Vidor's western *The Texas Rangers* (1936). The praise of movement and adventure is then developed through the example of Frank Capra's *It Happened One Night* (1934) and the comedies of Emil Lubitsch, to return eventually to King Vidor and his *Our Daily Bread* (1934). Despite the contradiction of having dwelled on directors whose culture is not a Protestant one—Frank Capra in particular—the two critics come to a concluding sentence that suggests that this religious mind frame is at the root of the connection between American cinema and action:

> For a Puritan, salvation can be gained only through good deeds (hard work, the moral struggle for success): hence an obsessive, adventurous dynamism of 'doing'. This explains how Vidor has managed, with utmost seriousness and commitment, to inject a sense of adventure in his films.[87]

In many ways, this article was an attempt by Debenedetti and Consiglio to add substance to Vittorio Mussolini's claim about American cinema's superiority in bringing to the screen a sense of adventure and a dynamism that were part and parcel of early twentieth-century culture. Alessandrini's *Luciano Serra pilota*, with the help of Vittorio Mussolini's supervision, is an example of a film that tried to replicate that rhythm.

---

[86] Margadonna, *Cinema ieri e oggi*, 78, 125.
[87] Albero Consiglio and Aldo Debenedetti, 'Il senso dell'avventura', *Cinema*, 7 (10 October 1936), 263–6.

### 9.3.3 American Comic Films

Movement and action were also paramount in American comic films. The leading comedians of the interwar years worked from Hollywood: from Buster Keaton to Ben Turpin, the duo of Stan Laurel and Oliver Hardy, Rose Langdon, and, last but certainly first in magnitude, Charlie Chaplin. If D. W. Griffith can be remembered as the first American director who was able to impose his artistic vision on the production of a film, Charlie Chaplin is the one who managed to emulate him and achieve fame on a much wider scale. The two were co-founders of United Artists, in 1919, with the difference that Griffith's directorial career was by then coming to its final, less successful trajectory, whereas Chaplin's was to continue rising, making him the most popular filmmaker of the interwar years. As already mentioned, French film critics had been quick to recognize this with the first monograph on Chaplin, published by Louis Delluc in 1921. This was instrumental in the discovery of Chaplin in Italy, and a clear linguistic marker of this is the use in Italy of the French name coined to define 'the Tramp'—Charlot.[88]

Going back to the 1927 issue of *Solaria* devoted to cinema, if there is one thread connecting the many differing views it is the acknowledgement of Chaplin as an exceptional figure and the need to treat him as an 'artist', rather than as a filmmaker or a comic actor. However, it is only in 1931 that an in-depth analysis of his work was published in Italy. Signed by Margadonna, it appeared on *Comoedia* on the eve of the distribution of Chaplin's *City Lights*. After admitting the late discovery of Chaplin by Italian critics (and prefacing his own views with those of, not one, but five French critics—from Delluc to Cendrars, Poulaille, Galtier-Boissière, and Benda), Margadonna identified the originality of Chaplin's work in having used the comic image of 'The Tramp' as a vehicle through which to develop a wider vision of humanity. In this, he added, Chaplin distinguished himself from other comedians in the same way Molière distinguished himself from the playwrights of his generation.[89]

---

[88] The French nickname Charlot was coined at the time of the distribution of Chaplin's first Keystone film: *Kid Auto Races at Venice*, in February 1914, renamed in France and Italy as *Charlot ingombrante*. Since then the title of almost every single film featuring Chaplin as the legendary tramp was rendered in French and Italian using the word 'Charlot', even if the original title did not mention the protagonist's name. For example, *The Champion* (1915) was distributed in France and Italy as *Charlot Boxeur*. On the relationship between Chaplin and French film culture, see Libby Murphy, 'Charlot Francais: Charlie Chaplin, the First World War, and the Construction of a National Hero', *Contemporary French and Francophone Studies*, 14/1 (2010), 421–9. On Delluc's groundbreaking work, see Donna Kornhaber, '*Charlot* as Cinema: Louis Delluc and Charlie Chaplin at the Dawn of Film Criticism', *Film History*, 27/2 (2015), 140–59.

[89] Ettore Margadonna, 'Chapliniana', *Comoedia*, 13/2 (February–Marcch 1931), 21–4; repr. in Margadonna, *Il cinema degli anni trenta*, ed. Fabio Andreazza (Florence: Le Lettere, 2013), 96–103. Margadonna's daring comparison with Molière as, implicitly, a way to ennoble film as an art was somehow in line with Delluc's provocative comparison with Beethoven at the start of his 1921

Margadonna also touched upon Chaplin's presumed Jewishness, or, better, he took it for granted and spoke of it as part of his creative persona. It is important to mention this because one has to register that, sadly, Chaplin was sometimes the object of anti-Semitic attacks by Italian critics. It happened, for example, in a long, derogatory article published by Marco Ramperti in *La Stampa* on 19 January 1933. Symbolically entitled 'Chaplin contro Charlot', the article was a malevolent attempt at suggesting that, behind the endearing image of Charlot, hid an amoral, greedy, vain Jewish filmmaker.[90]

More central to this chapter is to gauge what impact Charlie Chaplin might have made as a potential model for Italian filmmakers. And the short answer is very little if one thinks in terms of an Italian equivalent. The most popular comedians at the time, Ettore Petrolini and Antonio De Curtis (better known as Totò), very much retained their own peculiar traits, which had little of the slapstick dynamism of Chaplin's cinema. Petrolini's fully-fledged cinema debut with Blasetti's *Nerone* (1930) was a filmed theatrical performance, and before his premature death in 1936 there were no signs that he would develop an original filmmaking style. Totò, instead, entered cinema rather late, in 1937, and did not share Chaplin's inclination either towards physical comedy or towards the making of stories that, as Margadonna had understood, went beyond their comical dimension, as *Modern Times* (1936) and, later on, *The Great Dictator* (1940) would show. Closer to Chaplin in spirit and in his writing was Cesare Zavattini, although he always remained behind the scenes. Zavattini's involvement in cinema was also a late affair, but in many interviews he confessed his deep admiration for Chaplin. When asked about his views on cinema during the interwar years, Zavattini replied: 'I entered cinema with a type of imagination which was somehow connected to the masters at the time; under my page there was always Charlie Chaplin.' And when Francesco Savio asked him to expand on Chaplin as a model, Zavattini defined it as follows:

> his influence was extremely elementary, it translated inside me into something like a need which—within my great limitations—already existed

---

monograph on Chaplin. Alberto Consiglio and Giacomo Debenedetti also wrote on Chaplin in one of the first issues of *Cinema*: 'Chaplin Charlot', *Cinema*, 6 (25 September 1936), 224–7.

[90] Marco Ramperti, 'Chaplin contro Charlot', *La Stampa*, 19 January 1933, p. 3. Ramperti also wrote regularly for *Cinema illustrazione*. When *Bianco e nero* devoted its attention to Chaplin's *Modern Times* with comments by different critics running for fifteen pages in its April issue of 1937 (pp. 78–93), beyond the repeated praise, there was also criticism, linked to his alleged Jewish origin: l.c. (presumably Luigi Chiarini), in his 'Considerazioni generali', hailed Chaplin (calling him 'Charlot' throughout the article) as a great filmmaker, but at the same criticizing him for his typically Jewish individualism and his critique of modernity (p. 81); more positive is u. b. (presumably Umberto Barbaro) in his 'Charlot regista e attore', which, however, begins with a paraphrase of four critical comments, two of which touch upon Chaplin's perceived Jewishness and anti-Catholic stance (p. 86). On the intriguing history of Chaplin's presumed Jewishness, see Holly A. Pearse, 'Charlie Chaplin: Jewish or Goyish?', *Jewish Quarterly*, 57 (2010), 38–41.

in part: that is, clarity, simplicity, the cinematic syntax, a sense of humour which is internal, mysterious [...]

Indeed, it takes little to see the Chaplinesque dimension in many of Zavattini's short stories and in his novel *Totò il buono* (1943), which provided the narrative thread that was later turned into the script of De Sica's post-war masterpiece *Miracolo a Milano* (1950). However, as the dates suggest, this is an influence that matured in later years, beyond the remit of this chapter, and, as Zavattini suggests, it acted at a deep level, rather than in a specific one related to cinematic technique: to him, Chaplin was an example of an artist who had managed to impose his imaginary, non-realistic vision on his filmmaking, and obtain commercial success beyond the regimented formulas of Hollywood studios.

### 9.3.4 King Vidor

If Charlie Chaplin remained an influential but distant figure, the director who more than any other recurs in the words and practice of Italian filmmakers of his generation is King Vidor. In his detailed analysis of the early neorealist films by Rossellini and De Sica, Chris Wagstaff comes to the following suggestion:

> Certainly, one sometimes gets the impression that the 'institution of neorealism' wilfully forgets that other good films had ever had anything profound or ethical to say about war before 1945, least of all American ones. If Pina's pursuit of the truck carrying away Francesco were 'intertextually' linked to Mélisande's pursuit of Jim's truck [in the *Big Parade*], the implications could be deemed profound.[91]

Wagstaff's suggestion of a direct link between a scene of Vidor's *The Big Parade* and Rossellini's *Rome Open City* is not just intriguing. More can be said if one thinks of parallels with De Sica's early neorealist work. First, there is the thematic resemblance between Vidor's *The Champ* (1931) and De Sica's *Sciuscià* (1946) in the love for horses on the part of the young protagonists of both films. Then there is the humiliation of the jobless father being comforted by his young son—linking Vidor's *The Crowd* (1927) with *Bicycle Thieves* (1948)—to which one could add their respective final scenes in which the protagonist is swallowed back into the crowd, thus becoming, visually, everyman. A parallel is even more apparent in Vidor's *The Champ*, whose entire plot is built around a young boy showing more maturity than his confused father, a similarity with the plot of *Bicycle Thieves* which

---

[91] Christopher Wagstaff, *Italian Neorealist Cinema: An Aesthetic Approach* (Toronto: University of Toronto Press, 2008), 166.

extends to the physical resemblance between the look and manners of Vidor's Jackie Cooper and the Italian child then chosen by De Sica, the little Enzo Staiola.[92]

In the post-war years, Vidor and De Sica actually worked together, when the former came to Italy to shoot the film adaptation of *Farewell to Arms* (1957). De Sica played the part of the protagonist's Italian friend, Maggiore Rinaldi. According to Vidor, when the two met, De Sica 'threw his arms around me and said, "Oh, *The Crowd*, *The Crowd*! That was what inspired me for *Bicycle Thief* [sic]".[93] Given that De Sica did not speak English, it is likely that Vidor's memory is not entirely faithful. However, what is important to underline is rather the perception of Vidor's mastership as a director of realistic narratives in the interwar years, which De Sica and Rossellini, both in their formative period in those years, might have absorbed. They were not alone in doing this.

Alessandro Blasetti's film magazine, *Cinematografo*, contained a rubric called 'Films americani', and, in his first issue of March 1927, it opened with a full-page review of Vidor's *The Great Parade*. In later years, Blasetti was to confess: 'I admired Fritz Lang. But my admiration fell more towards King Vidor.'[94] All major figures among Italian film critics and filmmakers in the 1930s hailed Vidor's realism as the result of his capacity to create unpretentious narratives about the 'common man'. The first, unreserved praise came from the author of Italy's first monograph on cinema, Ettore Margadonna. It came both in his book and in the shape of a long article specifically on Vidor written two years before for *Comoedia*.[95]

In his 1930 article, Margadonna concentrated on *Halleluiah* (1929), Vidor's film on the African American community living in the cotton plantations of the Deep South (a reality Vidor knew well from his youth spent in Galveston, Texas). Once again, we witness the importance of the French intellectual debate: Margadonna traces the critical debate on Vidor's film back to its reception following a Parisian screening: hence there are long quotations from the enthusiastic comments by two literary figures, André Gide and Pierre Drieu La Rochelle. The literary dimension is equally dominant in Margadonna's views on Vidor in the way his films are compared to literary works: *The Crowd* (1928) evokes a comparison with Verga's *I Malavoglia*, and *Halleluiah* with D'Annunzio's *Trionfo della*

---

[92] Wagstaff touches upon parallels between De Sica's *Bicycle Thieves* and Vidor's *The Crowd*, although he makes no reference to *The Champ*, where resemblances are equal if not even more pronounced. Wagstaff, *Italian Neorealist Cinema*, 393-4.

[93] These are Vidor's words in a 1971 interview by Nancy Dowd, as part of the American Film Institute Oral History project; quoted in Brownlow, *The Parade's Gone By*, 298.

[94] Mario Bruni, 'La grande parata', *Cinematografo*, 1 (6 March 1927), 11. Savio, *Cinecittà anni trenta*, i. 112. On the critical reception of Vidor's early film, see Francesco Bolzoni, 'Vidor visto dall'osservatorio italiano', in Sergio Toffetti and Andrea Morini (eds), *La grande parata: Il cinema di King Vidor* (Turin: Lindau, 1994), 174-88.

[95] Ettore Margadonna, 'King Vidor, poeta della sua terra', *Comoedia*, 12/8 (8 August 1930), 17-21; repr. in *Il cinema degli anni Trenta*, 60-8. We should note that Emilio Cecchi, too, when writing about the films produced in 1931, identified Vidor's *Halleluiah* as the best of that year. See Emilio Cecchi, 'Cinema 1931', *Scenario*, 1/2 (1932), 5-10; repr. in Cecchi, *Fra Keaton e Visconti*, 135-40 (138).

*morte*. Even more striking is Margadonna's confession of a particular affinity with Vidor, since both are 'southerners' in their respective countries and in their outlook. Margadonna came from the Abruzzi region, and his consideration reminds us of the way southern journalists—as we saw in Chapter 6—revealed a particular affinity with the other, lower strata of American society, Italian migrants. Indeed, both Verga and D'Annunzio are southern authors too, and one is tempted to see this as an important factor in Margadonna's mind rather than for any stylistic and thematic parallel with Vidor's work, which, in the case of D'Annunzio, is tenuous. One also gets a sense of how important the reference to literature is in order to add artistic dignity to film. Here, Margadonna dwells on the connections of *Halleluiah* with two novels: *Holiday* (1923) by Waldo Frank, and *Porgy* (1925) by Edwin Du Bose Heyward (from which came the play and eventually the musical *Porgy and Bess*, with Gershwin music, in 1935). Margadonna praised these attempts by white American intellectuals to enter the underworld of African American communities in the south through a stark realism that avoids the temptations of a benevolent, patronizing view 'from above'. The literary dimension is central again when Margadonna tackles Vidor's work in his monograph. *The Crowd* is considered the cinematic equivalent to Sinclair Lewis's *Babbitt* for its capacity to portray the dark side of the American dream.

A second, long analysis of Vidor's cinema came from an unexpected front—that is, from one of the most loved and feared personalities among the *Strapaese* movement: Leo Longanesi. In the January–February 1933 issue of *L'Italiano*, Longanesi published a long attack against the literary rhetoric of Italian cinema and its poor attempts to imitate foreign films. Only, when it came to providing an example of how cinema can focus on everyday life and bring it to the screen, Longanesi had no doubts: Vidor's style in *The Crowd*, and even more in *The Champ*, were the models to follow. Longanesi's enthusiastic comment in the final part of his essay deserves to be read in full:

> With *The Champ*, King Vidor affectionately goes back to a motif of the old American repertoire of the boxing narrative, showing how a good film can be made without resorting to the latest teachings of German and Russian cinematography, which by now dominates in Hollywood. *The Champ* is an American film *par excellence*, in its technique, in its actors, and in its *mise en scène*. All is resolved with a naturalness that does not hide fiction. The film unrolls smoothly, making the audience forget that they are sitting in a theatre. King Vidor does not make use of his skills as a *metteur en scène* in order to show photographic variations on a theme: he does not insist on detailed descriptions of locations, and he does not use cinematographic tricks in excess, such as Mamoulian does, for example. He hides behind his actors, with the only preoccupation of guiding them towards an extraordinary and poetic interpretation of the plot. Every detail is studied in detail, but each shot, each cut, and the infinite other technical

resources do not impose themselves on the public. The story is developed without expressionistic touches, without insistence, with a tranquil rhythm. We had not seen a film of this value for a long time, simple, free from the new mystery of the subconscious. We have really been bored by the avant-garde! King Vidor manages to move us, with no trick, eventually! [...]

The whole film moves on with extreme sensibility and discretion, the final scene included. The suffering of Thing [the young protagonist] is represented through a few magnificent, irresistibly moving shots, brought about through the small gesture of the child and his lament, which fills the little room where the old champ is lying: 'I want the Champ!'[96]

During the weeks of the publication of Longanesi's article, Vidor came to the attention of two other influential figures. The first was Cesare Pavese, who, in his 1933 essay on Dos Passos, briefly admitted that his interest in Dos Passos was derived from the shock of watching *The Crowd* and the fact that he had heard of a connection between Vidor's film and the narrative of Dos Passos.[97] The second was one of the historic figures of early Italian film criticism, Alberto Consiglio. His contribution was published in *Cine-Convegno* of April 1933: a thirteen-page-long essay in which he analysed Vidor's narrative and cinematic technique. Together with D. W. Griffith and Chaplin, Consiglio presented Vidor as a groundbreaking filmmaker, representing a strong American trend in his unfiltered, naturalistic approach. Vidor's realism, according to Consiglio, was the product of an almost naïve approach:

The principal virtue of King Vidor consists, indeed, in the frankness of his American spirit, in the naïve abandonment with which his works show their qualities and defects. The calm and contained unfolding of his stories finds a spiritual correspondence in the extreme simplicity of his technique, as in his poetic inner vision. [...] the gaze of his lens is anthropomorphic, direct, realistic [...][98]

Consiglio's Crocean aesthetics takes him to considerations that are more theoretical than technical. However, in his use of the term *antropomorfo*, it is difficult not to recall the much-quoted 1943 essay by Luchino Visconti, 'Cinema antropomorfico'

---

[96] Leo Longanesi, 'L'occhio di vetro', *L'Italiano*, 17–18 (January–February 1933), 74–81 (79–81). Mida and Quaglietti rightly inserted an abridged version of this essay in their volume as an example of the early debate on realism in cinema, which was to lead to the neorealist debate in the post-war years. Massimo Mida and Lorenzo Quaglietti (eds), *Dai telefoni bianchi al neorealismo* (Bari and Rome: Laterza, 1980), 118–20.

[97] Cesare Pavese, 'John Dos Passos e il romanzo americano', *La Cultura*, 12/1 (January–March 1933); repr. in Pavese, *Saggi letterari*, 105.

[98] Alberto Consiglio, 'I registi: King Vidor', *Cine-Convegno*, 1 (25 April 1933), 37–50.

in which he declared his commitment to realism and which is considered as an early call to arms before the neorealist turn in Italian cinema.

Emblematically, Visconti's article was published in *Cinema*, by which time Vittorio Mussolini's young filmmaking friends had taken over its editorship, and it appeared next to the translation of a 1925 essay by René Clair (from *Cahiers du mois*) and an article dedicated to King Vidor.[99] The juxtaposition was symbolic, indicating the roots of Visconti's praise of a socially rooted realism in the poetic realism coming from the French school of René Clair and Jean Renoir, and in the anti-hero naturalism—for lack of a better label—that characterized King Vidor's early cinema. The link between American and French cinematic realism had already been tackled by Visconti's two co-scriptwriters—Mario Alicata and Giuseppe De Santis—in another article for *Cinema*, two years before, when the production of *Ossessione* was at its beginning. Within the call for Italian cinema to take inspiration from its literary *verismo* tradition, Vidor was once again presented as a leading example, more than that of the French directors, who, according to them, had failed to exploit the tradition of nineteenth-century Naturalism. Finally, 'verismo americano' was an expression that had already been used by Renato May in his eighteen-page-long formal analysis of a single film by Vidor, *Halleluiah*, published in *Bianco e nero*, in 1937. May was a young film critic who was then attending the directors' course at the Centro Sperimentale and who was later to become one of its lecturers.[100]

If key figures of Italian neorealism—from De Sica and Pavese to Alicata and De Santis—had expressed their admiration for Vidor's cinema, film historians seem to have missed a most indicative homage that came from Cesare Zavattini, back in 1933. The reason behind its scarce recognition is the fact that it is contained in one of those articles for *Cinema illustrazione* in which Zavattini faked being a correspondent in Hollywood. Under the pseudonym of Giulio Tani, Zavattini pretended to be present at a gala evening at the legendary Ambassador Hotel, during which, rather unrealistically, he finds the time to question a score of directors, from Fitzmaurice to Mamoulian, ending with Vidor. Each director is allowed one thought, and, when it comes to Vidor, his words have a familiar ring to them:

---

[99] Luchino Visconti, 'Cinema antropomorfico', *Cinema*, 173–4 (25 September–25 October 1943), 108–9. Visconti's article was followed by René Clair, 'Senso primitivo nel cinema' (pp. 110–11) and Giulio Di Stefano, 'Appunto sul Vidor minore' (pp. 112–13). By then Vittorio Mussolini had fled to Germany, and the directorship of *Cinema* had been taken over by Mario Corsi. Visconti's article can be found in Mida and Quaglietti (eds), *Dai telefoni bianchi al neorealismo*, 177–9.

[100] Mario Alicata and Giuseppe De Santis, 'Verità e poesia', *Cinema*, 6/127 (10 October 1941), 216–17. The two were to return to the subject with a second article entitled 'Ancora di Verga e del cinema italiano', 6/130 (25 November 1941), 314–15. By then, *Our Daily Bread* (1934) was another film by Vidor that was judged as exemplary. When asked about what kind of American films interested his group of young collaborators at *Cinema*, Pietro Ingrao answered with only one example: Vidor's *The Crowd*. Interview by Vito Zagarrio, reproduced in Zagarrio, *Cinema e fascismo*, 278; unfortunately, the date of the interview is unspecified. Renato May, 'Allelujah!', *Bianco e nero*, 1/10 (31 October 1937), 82–100 (83).

> The kind of film I'd love to do? Well, as you know, we, poor directors, have to suffer Tantalus' punishment. We have all we need to make our dreams come true, but we cannot do it because of the public and, in the first place, because of producers. We cannot do what we want, but what we are allowed to do. My ideal film would describe a day in a man's life, from the moment he gets up to when he goes to bed: I am talking about an ordinary man. The length of the film should correspond to the length of my hero's day. And all should be faithfully reproduced.[101]

Zavattini makes Vidor spell out his own vision of the cinematic *pedinamento* ('tailing') of ordinary characters, which a dozen years later was to become his most iconic definition of his idea of Italian neorealism.[102]

A final note on the reception of King Vidor's films takes us to a recent study by Raffaele De Berti. Among the cheap paperback publications on cinema circulating in those years, there were literary adaptations of famous films produced by a Milanese publisher, 'Gloriosa' Vitagliano, which in 1926 created a journal called *Le Grandi Films* (each issue dedicated to one single film), followed by a book series called 'Romanzo-Film' the following year. De Berti's analysis of the volumes concerning Vidor's *The Big Parade* and *The Crowd* (respectively published when the films were distributed, in 1927 and 1928) shows that both contained a rewriting that was strongly anti-American. The American soldier GI of *The Big Parade* is turned into a French–American (his name moving from Jim Apperson to Robert Beaumont), thus making his presence on the French front appear like a return to his homeland. Also, when Apperson/Beaumont's ship docks in the French port of Brest, in an episode entirely absent from the film, the French–American of the literary version is welcomed by French, British, and Italian soldiers (something similar happens later on in the novel, with an invented dream in which allied soldiers are described). In other words, *The Big Parade* is subjected to a treatment that reflects the criticism received in Europe at the time, generated by the fact that Vidor's film showed only American soldiers without paying any attention to the wider horizon of the allied forces fighting on the French front. When it comes to *The Crowd*, here the literary narrative insists on a very negative image of New York and of the immoral costumes prevalent in American society, from alcoholism to divorce. What seems to emerge, overall, is a tendency to move the literary narratives away from a reading that might favour a positive image of America.

---

[101] Giulio Tani [Cesare Zavattini], 'La beneficiata dei direttori: Da Fitzmaurice a King Vidor', *Cinema illustrazione*, 8/22 (31 May 1933), 14. The article is mentioned by David Brancaleone in a recent biography of Zavattini: *Cesare Zavattini's Neo-Realism and the Afterlife of an Idea: An Intellectual Biography* (New York: Bloomsbury Academic, 2021), 29. Part of the article is also reproduced (albeit wrongly dated) in Cesare Zavattini, *Selected Writings*, ed. Brancaleone, 2 vols (New York: Bloomsbury Academic, 2021), ii. 5–7.

[102] See, e.g., Cesare Zavattini, *Neorealismo ecc.* (Milan: Bompiani, 1979), 83.

Without wanting to read too much into this (it might simply be the result of the nationalistic views of the individuals at the helm of 'Gloriosa' Vitagliano), it shows how a certain resistance towards American culture could be fought indirectly through a 'corrected' narrative that retold the film plot. On an even more general level, it is also indicative of how, among low- and middlebrow readers, the importance of cinema was such that it sustained the production of commercially viable literary adaptations of the most popular films, among which were King Vidor's films.[103]

### 9.3.5 Hollywood Comedies

So far we have touched upon the subgenre of the screwball comedy when considering Camerini's *Il signor Max*, in Chapter 6. For a wider overview, we benefit from the specific work on American comedies and interwar Italian cinema by film historian Vito Zagarrio, whose argument is built on earlier considerations by James Hay. Zagarrio argues that the Italian comedies of the 1930s—from Camerini's *Gli uomini che mascalzoni* (1932) to Raffaele Matarazzo's *Giorno di nozze* (1942)—adopted the American model as a form of social reconciliation, which offered a light-hearted, benevolent representation of class division ultimately resolved by the inevitable happy ending. It was a vision that was welcomed by the regime, since, apart from its commercial success, it provided an image of Italy as a modern and to some extent emancipated country—through its representation of social mobility and the odd working woman. At the same time, it emulated the American model as a narrative vehicle, as Vittorio Mussolini had asked for in his 1936 article.[104]

Zagarrio dwells on a number of Italian films where the source of inspiration is easily traceable. The successful duo Camerini–De Sica has already been discussed with respect to more than one film, and, once again, it might be worth remembering that Camerini benefited from first-hand experience when directing for Paramount during his spell at their French studios in 1930–1. Indeed, Zagarrio pays particular attention to *Gli uomini che mascalzoni...* (1932), which, unsurprisingly perhaps, is the first feature film Camerini directed for Cines–Pittaluga after his return to Italy. The scriptwriting phase saw Camerini collaborate with the 'America-experienced' Soldati and the seasoned playwright Aldo De Benedetti (whose earlier theatrical work had often seen De Sica in the role of the male lead). However, beyond the

---

[103] Raffaele De Berti, *Il volo del cinema: Miti moderni nell'Italia fascista* (Milan and Udine: Mimesis, 2012), 112–23.
[104] Zagarrio's essay is entitled 'Il modello americano e la commedia anni Trenta', in his *Cinema e fascismo*, 75–89. An English-written, succinct version of Zagarrio's essay entitled 'The First Comedy, Italian Style: Blasetti, Camerini, De Sica' has subsequently appeared in Peter Bondanella, *The Italian Cinema Book* (London: Palgrave Macmillan, 2013), 58–65.

value of the script—which arguably falls within the American subgenre of 'shyster comedies'—Zagarrio's emphasis is on Camerini's achievement in adding a sense of movement and dynamism to his camera work and editing.[105] This takes place by constructing a parallel picture of Milan, as Italy's most modern metropolis, and the natural beauty of its northern province—the lakes—which are nonetheless traversed by the protagonists with a sense of urgency and speed. Zagarrio— and Hay before him—note that Camerini's narrative technique, in providing a renewed image of contemporary Italy, was explicitly appreciated by Italian film critics at the time. The Milanese papers were both surprised by and proud of Camerini's depiction of their city. Here is one example from *Corriere della Sera*:

> Camerini, who directed the film, has managed to identify and pick out with extreme finesse those unmistakable characteristics of the image and dynamism of Milan, to give us effortlessly, and without those documentary excesses that sometimes reduce everything to a few postcard shots of famous monuments, Milan's colours and its industriousness.[106]

Another film on which both Hay and Zagarrio dwell is the much less successful comedy *Non c'è bisogno di denaro* (1933), directed by Amleto Palermi. Here the model is Frank Capra's *American Madness* (1932), which also unravels the plotline of a bank nearing bankruptcy. This time, however, one should add that Palermi's film was actually a remake of a German comedy, Carl Boese's *Man braucht kein Geld* (1931)—hence the influence came from two different directions. This is an important reminder of the constant transnational, reciprocal nature of influences, particularly in those early years of sound films, when, as we have seen, it was still common practice to shoot different versions for different national audiences (indeed, in the same year, the German scriptwriters also worked on a French remake, entitled *Pas besoin d'argent*). The German comedy, however, has a distinctly expressionistic set in its *mise en scène*, which is totally lost in Palermi's film, which is visually closer to its American counterpart.[107]

Beyond questions of plotline—after all, if society's reconciliation through a short-circuiting of high and low classes is typical of American screwball comedies, one could argue that that is a topos belonging to comedy all the way back to ancient classical times—it is more by looking at the narrative technique of Italian

---

[105] The protagonist of Camerini's film has something of the conman of American shyster comedies in the fact that he presents himself as an upper-class man by pretending that the car he is driving is his. On the American shyster comedies in the early 1930s, see Andrew Bergman, *We're in the Money: Depression America and its Films* (New York: Harper Colophon, 1971), 18–29.

[106] Filippo Sacchi, 'La serata italiana al Festival del Lido'. See also Enrico Roma, 'I nuovi film: Gli uomini che mascalzoni', *L'Illustrazione italiana*, 7/42 (19 October 1932), 12; and Maria Montesano, 'Gli uomini che mascalzoni!', *Cinema illustrazione*, 7/33 (17 August 1932), 8–9.

[107] Zagarrio, *Cinema e fascismo*, 87; Hay, *Popular Film Culture in Fascist Italy*, 90–1.

directors that we get a sense of a new, more dynamic approach linking it to their American counterparts. Speed is present, not only in relation to the characters' movement in space but also in the succession of events presented on screen. Another example coming from the Cines studios is Mario Mattoli's *Tempo massimo* (1934). The unexpected event at the start of the story—which traditionally opens up the mixing of different social classes and triggers comical effects—could not be presented in a more dramatic way: a woman in a parachute lands next to the fishing boat of the astonished male protagonist. The metonymies of modernity are all there: the emancipated woman, the roaring aeroplane, and later her smoking and drinking, her passion for sport—constantly linked with speed and movement, from skiing to horse-riding, to cycling—and her preference for jazz music. The dusty professor and mummy's boy—once again played by a flawless Vittorio De Sica—has to 'modernize' himself and embrace the reckless and sensual lifestyle of millionaire and bon viveur Sandra, the emancipated woman who has literally dropped into his life.

Here two American directors come to mind. First, Frank Capra and his *It Happened One Night* (1934, but released ten months before Mattoli's film): the ending of both films uses the same trope of the 'wrong' wedding being spectacularly interrupted and true love triumphing. The other director is German 'ex-pat' Ernst Lubitsch, who had settled in Hollywood in the early 1920s. The smooth sexual innuendos and amoral plots of Lubitsch's pre-Hays code comedies could not be followed entirely in Fascist Italy, but Mattoli seems to be following a similar approach in the representation of the 'Americanized' characters surrounding Sandra. Two of them indicatively boast English nicknames, Bob and Jack, and the latter plays ragtime as soon as, uninvited, he lays his fingers on Professor Bensi's grand piano. Lubitsch's directorial style had a more theatrical feel compared to Vidor's or Capra's, as a result of his heavily studio-based approach. However, once again one only has to follow the camera work and the unaffected acting in Lubitsch's films such as *Trouble in Paradise* (1932) or *Design for Living* (1933), particularly through the presence of active, working women who get things done their way rather than being passive objects of sensual beauty, to see how Italy's early sound films were trying to catch up with a model that offered both daring plots and a more sophisticated film style.

Cinematically, Mattoli seems closer to Capra in his use of open-air location, the high tempo of his editing, and the instinctive search for comical effect through the short-circuiting of high and low: see, for example, at the very start of *Tempo massimo*, the parallel between the cow being milked by a peasant and the upper-class mummy's boy having to drink his milk with an added dose of cod liver oil, to the consternation of the cow itself. Mattoli was not new to American culture. Before his premiere as a filmmaker, he was the director and producer of a very popular variety show, Za-Bum, which toured Italy throughout the late 1920s and early 1930s. What distinguished the Za-Bum show was the use of a jazz band on stage, entirely made of African American musicians. In *Tempo massimo*, music plays an important role—the film's theme song reached some popularity—and once again, jazz was associated with the 'modern', urban world in opposition to the traditional, provincial lifestyle of the protagonist, identified with a melodic, traditional music score. At the end of *Tempo massimo*, hoping to impress Sandra, Professor Bensi plays the melodic song he has composed for her, but this time in a ragtime tempo. At this point, however, the narrative trajectory of the Italian comedy is reaching its moralistic ending—be Italian and marry a proper Italian—and, indeed, she ignores him, and the film takes a diegetically and stylistically debatable turn in which Professor Bensi runs away and descends into the world of working-class life. Dialect all of a sudden makes a distinct appearance (it is the 'genuine Italians' who are talking), and, after some odd jobs and a slapstick, mad run through Milan's city centre on a clearly marked Lancia bus, Sandra is eventually convinced to abandon her foreign, dishonest fiancé, and the two protagonists finally agree to return to his home villa in the beautiful surroundings of Lake Como. As De Berti rightly concludes, *Tempo massimo* presents 'a set of samples of American modernity, ironically adapted to Italy'.[108]

After this successful premiere, Mattoli visited Hollywood, the following year, and like Vittorio Mussolini, was taken for a tour of the Fox studios, where he met Shirley Temple among others. According to Mattoli, though, he did not feel at ease there, and, when he was offered a contract, he refused and travelled back to Italy.[109]

A scene from Mattoli's *Tempo massimo* provides us with an ideal cue for moving to the final aspect of filmmaking in relation to American culture that we are about to consider. Towards the end of the film, among other things, Professor Bensi finds a job in the most American of advertising jobs: he becomes a sandwich man walking around Milan's city centre with a placard strapped to his back. One immediately recalls the similar fate of King Vidor's protagonist in *The Crowd*. It is possible that the inspiration could have come from that direction. However, even more emblematic is the product being advertised on the placard. It is a cinema theatre publicizing its screening of animation movies for children, and the image dominating the placard is a drawing of the world's most famous mouse, Mickey Mouse.

[108] Raffaele De Berti, 'Figure e miti ricorrenti', in Caldiron (ed.), *Storia del cinema italiano*, 294–311 (306).
[109] The interview with Mattoli takes place in the documentary *Mattolineide* (1978), extracts of which are available as an extra feature in the DVD version of *Tempo massimo*. In the only monograph devoted to Mattoli, there is a brief mention of Mattoli's visit to Hollywood, which simply confirms what Mattoli says in the filmed interview, without adding the precise dates of his stay other than saying that it took place in 1935. Stefano Della Casa, *Mario Mattoli* [Il Castoro Cinema], (Florence: Nuova Italia, 1990), 14.

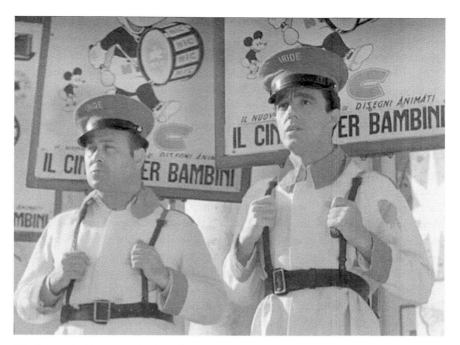

Fig. 9.12. The impoverished Professor Bensi (Vittorio De Sica) and his butler (Camillo Pilotto) in Mattoli's *Tempo massimo* advertising Mickey Mouse cartoons (1934). (DVD screenshot)

### 9.3.6 Disney's Cartoons

Animation is a niche area into which Italian film historians rarely venture when it comes to the interwar period for the simple reason that Italy's film industry produced very little in that field. With regard to the perception of American culture, however, it is necessary to devote a few paragraphs to it. If Nerbini's and then Mondadori's *Topolino* became widely popular as a comics magazine only in the early 1930s, by then Walt Disney's film animations had already entered cinema theatres all over the world. The first ones were distributed in the USA in 1928, and by the following year they had reached Italy's first run cinemas in Italy's major towns.[110]

It was a novelty closely linked to music—Disney's first animation shorts formed his Silly Symphony series—and so their distribution in Italy was linked, for their full version, to the few cinema theatres that had upgraded to sound. Provincial and second-run cinemas had to content themselves with either a silent screening

---

[110] According to Hay, the first Italian cinema theatre that presented Disney's cartoons as a regular feature was the Corso in Milan, in July 1929. Hay, *Popular Film Culture in Fascist Italy*, 82.

or one accompanied by live music deprived of the comical sound effects and animalistic squeals that came with the original sound score. The already mentioned 1933 radio programme called *Le avventure di Topolino* added to the popularity of Mickey Mouse in Italy. Its authors were Angelo Nizza and Riccardo Morbelli, and their stories were an inventive offshoot with no connection to the actual Disney production. The character of Topolino is a rich millionaire living in a big metropolis, and his servant is a black man who is constantly reprimanded by his master because of his stupidity and clumsiness.[111]

The following year, Nizza and Morbelli went on to create another popular radio programme, *I quattro moschettieri*, this time based on Dumas's novel and sponsored by Italy's food giants Buitoni–Perugia. Once again, it was freely developed by the authors: the four musketeers have the Commedia dell'Arte's character of Arlecchino as their servant, and the setting is in contemporary times so that the five can easily travel to distant countries such as Russia and the USA.[112] The reason for its mention here, despite its non-Disney derivation, is the fact that, in 1936, the radio programme was turned into a film based on marionettes provided by the historic Milanese puppet-makers Fratelli Colla. The press close to the regime at the time hailed it as an example of how Italy could compete with American cartoons through the development of an art that has deep roots in Italian culture. The film, however, did not prove popular and, indeed, was to remain a unique attempt at a film production based on marionettes. What is particularly interesting about its alleged anti-American stance, though, is the fact that the story featured two comical characters, two loafers called Fric and Froc, who were a clear replica of Stan Laurel and Oliver Hardy (who at the time were known in Italy as 'Cric e Croc'). Their resemblance was not just physical: their dialogues, too, imitated the American–Italian accent with which Laurel and Hardy's comic shorts had historically been dubbed in Italian.[113]

The American traits of the narratives initially created for the radio by Nizza and Morbelli, as against the praise given to them as a product of Italy's 'own' modernity, takes us back to the ambivalent reception of American culture in Fascist times. That the critic of *Cinema* should refer to the characters of Fric and Froc as 'of a completely original taste and humour' without mention of their

---

[111] The sound file of two 'Avventure di Topolino' is still available on the website of Radio 2 at https://www.raiplayradio.it/programmi/leavventureditopolino-radiofantasie/ (accessed 6 January 2023).

[112] Beyond the radio programme, which was broadcast at the prime time of Sunday mid-afternoon and lasted until 1937, *I quattro moschettieri* triggered a number of other Buitoni–Perugia-sponsored initiatives, from print publications to one of the earliest sticker albums, which became so wildly popular that it offered the narrative line to a comedy, *Il feroce Saladino* (1937), directed by Mario Bonnard and written by none other than film critic Ettore Margadonna.

[113] See, e.g., Rita Zanini, 'I quattro moschettieri: Un film di marionette', *Cinema*, 8 (25 October 1936), 314; and Mario Gromo, 'I quattro moschettieri', *La Stampa*, 30 March 1937, p. 5. Extracts of the film featuring Fric and Froc are available at https://www.youtube.com/watch?v=6SNBZO4mH3Y (accessed 10 December 2022).

Fig. 9.13. Poster advertising the film *I quattro moschettieri* (1936). (courtesy of Cineteca, Bologna)

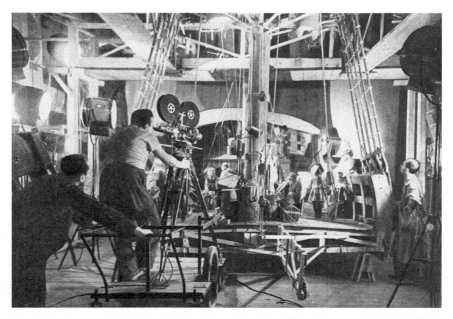

Fig. 9.14. A stage photo taken during the production of *I quattro moschettieri* (1936), which accompanied the review in *Cinema* of 25 October 1936. (courtesy of Cineteca, Bologna)

obvious resemblance to the Hollywood comedians is bizarre and at the same time indicative of a nationalistic attempt to hide the obvious.

It is roughly at this time that Walt Disney arrived in Italy as part of his European tour, which, as we have seen, had a business reason too. In July 1935, Disney first went to Milan to sort out his contracts in relation to comics and music. He then descended on Rome to address political matters. There, his meetings were mainly of a diplomatic kind, since the distribution of Disney's films was at the time autonomously managed by United Artists. On 20 July, Walt Disney and his group were accompanied by Galeazzo Ciano and his wife Edda Mussolini to Villa Torlonia, where he met Rachele Mussolini and Edda's excited younger brother and sister. In the evening, they were joined by Luigi Freddi and taken to the Italian premiere, at the prestigious Barberini cinema, of the Hollywood film *We Live Again* (1934), directed by Mamoulian, followed by the screening of three Disney cartoons. Benito Mussolini did not meet Walt Disney, although the latter was given a signed photograph of *Il Duce*, still held in Disney's archives.[114]

What emerged from Disney's conversations with the press, which followed every step of his journey, were his plans to move towards full-length animation films. Disney had already identified the fairy tale of *Snow White and the Seven Dwarfs* as the first one of the series, but during his Italian tour he mentioned *Pinocchio* as the probable second film in line. The production of *Snow White* started soon after Disney's return to America, ending with its distribution in early 1938. Two more years were to pass before *Pinocchio* saw the silver screen. However, few remember that, at the time of Disney's visit to Italy, a newly formed Italian animation company was hard at work, trying to beat him and produce the first full-length cartoon version of Collodi's Italian masterpiece. When Walt Disney spoke about his intentions, in July 1935, work was already under way, in Rome, so it is possible that there is no direct connection between Disney's own ambitions—which only in those months began to be known publicly with regard to *Pinocchio*—and the Italian production. The coincidence is nonetheless remarkable.[115]

The Italian project came from within the editorial staff of *Marc'Aurelio*, then Italy's highly popular satirical magazine, founded in Rome only a few years earlier, in 1931. Three of their caricaturists—Raoul Verdini, Mameli Barbara, and Gioachino Colizzi—were the creative unit behind the project. Funding came from a brother of Alfredo Rocco, Mussolini's Minister of Justice, who had paved the way for the establishment of the dictatorship with his constitutional reforms

[114] Ghez, *Disney's Gran Tour*, 80–4.
[115] According to Ghez, it is only in July 1935 that Walt Disney began to pick *Pinocchio* from among the famous children's stories he was considering. It is, therefore, possible that it was during his Italian journey that Disney became more interested in Collodi's book. Ghez, *Disney's Grand Tour*, 86. Among the Italian press coverage of Disney's visit to Italy, see m.g. [Mario Gromo], 'Dietro lo schermo', *La Stampa*, 23 July 1935, p. 3. Raffaello Patuelli, 'Walt Disney', *Lo Schermo*, 1 (August 1935), 24–6.

Fig. 9.15. Work at CAIR's studio for the production of *Le avventure di Pinocchio* (1935); the walls feature enlarged cut-outs from the animation film. (courtesy of Archivio Romolo Bacchini at Wikipedia Common)

of 1926. Ferdinando Rocco was interested in cinema, and this coalesced in the plan to create Italy's first animation company. It was called Cartoni Animati Italiani Roma (CAIR), and it was based in an improvised studio in Rome's city centre. According to the memoirs of one of the protagonists, it was a rather makeshift operation, with barely any of the equipment and staffing required by such an ambitious plan. The *Marc'Aurelio* caricaturists provided the key drawings for each scene from Collodi's *Le avventure di Pinocchio*, after which others added the in-between positions and another small group created the backdrops. The film was planned to be produced in colour, although it never moved from its black-and-white prints. The coordinator and director of the project was Romolo Bacchini, a film director, mainly of the pre-First World War years of Cines.[116]

Work started in the very first months of 1935, as witnessed by a visit to CAIR by *La Stampa*'s film critic Gastone Bosio. And, by September, the film magazine *Cineomnia* hosted a full-page advert that publicized *Le avventure di Pinocchio* as an 'italianissimo film' ('a most Italian film'—the use of the superlative was a Futuristic feature that recurred frequently in Fascist propaganda) nearing its worldwide distribution. This advert appeared in subsequent issues of *Cineomnia* until December 1935. Considering the political identity of the magazine—*Cineomnia* was directed by Luciano De Feo, and, indeed, it stopped its

---

[116] Mario Vergher, 'Il Pinocchio incompiuto', *Animazione*, 3 (2001), 34–5. The article is based on a long interview with Mameli Barbara.

publication when De Feo moved on and funded the more ambitious *Cinema* in 1936—it makes one wonder whether the persistent advertising of the film was an attempt to raise interest in Fascist circles. In its third version, the advert specifically mentioned that, for the production of the planned 150,000 drawings, CAIR needed an investment of more than one million lire.[117]

One is left wondering what De Feo might have thought of this venture, and whether Freddi and Mussolini were ever consulted about it. The political help that might have come from Alfredo Rocco was complicated by the fact that, throughout those months, the lawmaker's health was in a grave state: he died of leukemia on 28 October 1935. It should also be added that CAIR was not the only initiative relating to cartoons born in that year. In January 1935, the Istituto LUCE had begun its own production of short cartoons, which were supposed to add an entertaining commentary to political events (one, for example, was dedicated to the regime's campaign of reclamation works). Gastone Bosio dwelt on it in a long article for *La Stampa* illustrated with two stills from one of LUCE's first cartoons. In his article, Bosio commented that the quality of LUCE's black-and-white cartoons was in no way comparable to that of Disney's productions, but it nonetheless represented a promising start. To all intents and purposes, CAIR was not an offshoot of LUCE's initiative. However, it adds to the impression that, in those months of the restructuring of the Italian film industry, thought had been given to this particular niche of filmmaking.[118]

Reminiscent of these comments about the LUCE cartoons, in his interview Barbara confessed that the quality of the few scenes of *Le avventure di Pinocchio* that were put together was very low, given the lack of proper sequencing of the characters' movements. It was the typical of the effects that one connects with the early cartoons produced in the 1920s. After all, if it had taken Walt Disney sixteen years before he felt he was ready to produce a full-length film, it must have been overambitious of CAIR to consider a similar attempt with no previous experience and with an improvised enterprise. Bacchini admitted that his previous experience was limited to two shorts that had never been distributed. Eventually, the publicized request for extra funding for this 'italianissimo' film must have fallen on deaf ears, since the announced completion of the film in 1936 never took place. CAIR folded, and the project entered near-oblivion in the histories of Italian cinema.

When Disney's first full-length animation was premiered on 21 December 1937, the regime's anti-American turn was still distant enough to allow for an enthusiastic

---

[117] Gastone Bosio, 'Pinocchio sullo schermo', *La Stampa*, 12 February 1935, p. 6. The first advert appeared in *Cineomnia*, 3/13 (20 September 1935), 16. Stills from the animation were presented, strangely with no text attached to them, on three other pages of the issue. The same happened in the following issue (5 October1935), this time with four pages with the odd still from the film, whereas the issue of 5 December contained only the publicity on p. 6.

[118] Gastone Bosio, 'Disegni animati italiani', *La Stampa*, 29 January 1935, p. 6.

**Fig. 9.16.** Still from the animation film *Le avventure di Pinocchio* (1935). (courtesy of Archivio Romolo Bacchini at Wikipedia Common)

reception. When *Snow White and the Seven Dwarfs* reached Italy, in the summer of 1938, Lando Ferretti's regime-financed *Lo Schermo* devoted its cover image and an adulatory review to the film. At the Venice Film Festival, it received the special prize Gran Trofeo d'Arte, while, symbolically, *Luciano Serra pilota* and Leni Riefenstahl's sport documentaries, *Olympia 1* and *Olympia 2*, shared the Coppa Mussolini award for Best Film.[119]

The choice by Disney for this particular fairy tale from the Grimms' collection for his first full-length feature was never justified, other than with reference to the popularity of the tale. However, Disney's visit to Italy in July 1935 can add some revealing information on the genesis of the film. In a long review of the film by Dario Sabatello for *Cinema illustrazione*, the journalist revealed that, at the time of Walt Disney's visit to Italy, he was head of United Artist's press office in Rome and therefore had the task of escorting Disney during his visit there. After the gala night at the Barberini theatre, Disney asked Sabatello to find out about the critical response to one of the cartoons presented. What distinguished it from the others was the fact that its characters were humans. It was an operatic tale entitled 'The Goddess of Spring' (1934) in which—along the lines of the myth of Persephone—a fairy is brought to the underworld by the devil himself but eventually returns to her faithful group of dwarves and brings back life to earth. Nobody recognized the veiled reference to the Grimms' tale, and, worse, as Sabatello reported to

---

[119] Vincenzo Turco, 'Un liberatore: Walt Disney: "Biancaneve e i sette nani"', *Lo Schermo*, 7/16 (July 1938), 23–5.

Fig. 9.17. Front cover of *Lo Schermo* of July 1938 dedicated to Walt Disney's *Snow White and the Seven Dwarfs*. (courtesy of Cineteca, Bologna)

Disney, very few people liked it. Walt Disney told Sabatello that it was a first experiment towards the full-length tale of *Snow White* but confessed that they were still battling with the challenge of mixing humans with Disney's typical animalistic world. Indeed, if one compares the 1934 cartoon with *Snow White*, one gets a distinct sense of the long development process that the physical features of the human protagonists underwent, testimony of Disney's accurate preparation of the huge step he was about to make (not just in terms of the length of his films but also with the introduction of fully-fledged human characters). According to Sabatello, the production of *Snow White* cost about thirty-five million lire, an amount that was simply far beyond the scale of what the Italian film industry could afford at the time, with or without state intervention. At the same time, Sabatello could dwell on the fact that even *Snow White* contained a trace of the presence in Hollywood of Italian Americans. The voice of Snow White was that of Adele Caselotti, a second-generation migrant, born in Connecticut, whose Italian father was a singing tutor at New York's Metropolitan Opera.[120]

[120] Dario Sabatello, 'I sette nani e Biancaneve', *Cinema illustrazione*, 13/23 (8 June 1938), 4–5. On the 1934 cartoon, see Devon Baxter's detailed analysis '"The Goddess of Spring" (1934)', in the online platform *Cartoon Research*, https://cartoonresearch.com/index.php/walt-disneys-the-goddess-of-spring-1934/, posted 21 September 2016 (accessed 11 December 2022).

In the light of Walt Disney's slow build-up to his first full-length animation film, the improvised attempt by CAIR shows an ambition that was destined to remain unfulfilled. De Feo's indirect involvement and the creation of a few cartoons by the Istituto LUCE suggest that in the mid-1930s thought must have been given in Fascist circles to the possibility of developing an Italian cartoon industry. However, the implosion of the *Pinocchio* project, despite the company's links to the regime, suggests that somebody—probably somewhere high up in the hierarchical pyramid—must have decided that trying to compete with America in this particular field was too big a challenge.

## 9.4 The Power of the American Dream

When discussing Alessandrini's *Luciano Serra pilota*, mention was made of the awkward narrative move from the protagonist being offered a job by Mr Thompson, the US owner of an airline (thus the departure for the 'paese dei dollari'), to, ten years later, surprisingly finding him working for the owner of a circus in Latin America. The US years of Serra's fictional emigration were entirely deleted. In many respects, something similar happened to the cinematic representation of Italian migrants in the USA during the interwar years. Beyond the humiliation of the door being shut to Italian migration with the anti-immigration legislation of 1921 and 1924, and beyond Mussolini's early praise of the natural friendship between Fascist Italy and America thanks to the presence of millions of Italian Americans, the representation of migration to the USA remained a near-ignored topic in both literary and film narratives. Specifically in relation to cinema, however, there are two aspects that deserve to be examined.

The first concerns the parallels between the political dimension and the cinematic one. If, to migrate, was still seen in negative terms by the Fascist government as it had been by its Liberal predecessors, then, with almost no exception, the films that depicted it preferred to set their stories in places other than the USA. This might be a result of the strength of the American dream, understood as 'US American'. In other words, it must have seemed much easier to represent failure and disillusionment when they took place in, say, Latin America or a neighbouring country like France or, across the Mediterranean, in North Africa, than somewhere in the USA. I am referring to films such as Forzano's *Camicia nera* (1933), with its Tunisian setting, Brignone's *Passaporto rosso* (1935) set in Argentina, *Il grande appello* (1936) with its Gibuti migrants, and the just-mentioned *Luciano Serra pilota* (1938), where the migrant to the USA is immediately moved over to Latin America.

A common trait was also the generational gap. In most cases, the betrayal had been the result of the older generation, who had left before Italy was Fascist—that is, when it was a less attractive homeland. The youth of Italy, on the other hand, knew better, and so they reversed their fathers' decision. The sacrificial deaths of the father in both *Il grande appello* and *Luciano Serra pilota* could not have been more symbolic. A variation on the theme of the generational gap is provided by *Passaporto rosso*. Here it is the son who initially rejects his Italian identity, only to see the light at the start of the First World War, in time to die as a hero on the Italian front.

If the representation of migration as a tragedy and a mistake to be redeemed by the return to the motherland took the shape of dramatic narratives excluding the USA, when it came to comedies almost the exact reverse took place. A regular topos was that of the American millionaire—sometimes of Italian origin—who, after a number of comedy-of-errors experiences, discovers the great values of Italian life. A cluster of these films were produced in the early 1930s. The first was a Cines–Pittaluga comedy on which Mario Soldati collaborated as a co-scriptwriter. Directed by Nunzio Malasomma and entitled *La cantante dell'opera* (1932), the film is set in Venice, and tells the story of an opera singer from a humble background who begins a relationship with an American millionaire but then has to live through her initial lie of being from an aristocratic family.

The same Cines–Pittaluga produced a second comedy entitled *Due cuori felici* (1932), directed by Baldassare Negroni. This time the source text was an Austrian light opera that had just been turned into a German film production entitled *Ein bißchen Liebe für Dich: Zwei Glückliche Herzen* (1932) directed by Max Neufeld. The original music by Paul Abraham, a Hungarian musician, was kept in all versions, particularly the lead song, 'How do you do, Mr Brown', which provides a narrative thread to the story. Mr Brown is an American millionaire who arrives in Europe to visit the local branches of his automobile industry, and 'How do you do, Mr Brown?' is the catch phrase that the employees are taught to learn by heart so that they can welcome their English-speaking boss. An interesting, nationalistic variation on the Italian version is that we are told that Mr Brown is the Americanized version of the Italian 'Bruni'—so we are made to understand that the successful car manufacturer is a second-generation Italian migrant.

Given that we dwelt on the parallel between the car and film manufacturers in Chapter 3, we should complement it with a very brief update here. As already mentioned, Giovanni Agnelli's dream to imitate Henry Ford's mass-production plants had eventually come to fruition with the inauguration of Turin's Lingotto factory in 1923. The factory was in itself a model of architectural modernity. It was a modernist five-storey building that sported a spectacular flat roof with a test track for the newly built vehicles that were assembled through an upward moving assembly process. It became a shopwindow for Italian industrial technology and design. In the same year, the leading exponent of modernist architecture, Le Corbusier, referred to the Lingotto in his manifesto book *Vers une architecture* as an example of the achievements of contemporary industrial culture. And when Mussolini first visited it, on 25 October 1923, in the speech in which he nervously addressed a crowd of FIAT workers, many of whom had opposed Fascism, he

**Fig. 9.18.** FIAT's Lingotto factory in Turin, designed by Giacomo Matté-Trucco and completed in 1923. (courtesy of Archivio Storico FIAT, Turin)

praised the Lingotto as a symbol of 'European and world supremacy'.[121] However, more years had to pass before Agnelli could boast of an originally designed, affordable car. It was only in 1936 that FIAT's Lingotto began to churn out thousands of Fiat 500s. Thanks to this little, relatively inexpensive vehicle, Italy's lower middle class could finally afford to buy their first car. Today everybody remembers it as the Fiat 'Topolino', a nickname it received because of its tiny size and of its protruding main lamps, which reminded people of Mickey Mouse's ears. However, this homage to American popular culture was never intentional. It does not appear in the company's paperwork, nor was it ever used when advertising the car. A journalist used it first, after which it was quickly adopted by the public.[122]

As to whether there was a link between FIAT's Lingotto and cinema, as one can expect, a number of newsreels were produced at the time it was built. What merits particular mention is the fact that Hollywood also took an interest. A Paramount crew visited the factory in 1931 and shot a short film concentrating on cars circling around the roof track. Its captions are in both English and Italian, so it was probably shown in Italian cinemas as much as in American ones.[123]

---

[121] Le Corbusier, *Vers une architeture* (1923); English trans. *Towards a New Architecture* (London: Architectural Press, 1987), 287. On the Lingotto project, see Kirk, *The Architecture of Modern Italy*, ii. 57–62.

[122] On the history of Fiat 500, see Castronuovo, *Fiat*, 236–64.

[123] On the Lingotto as a cultural icon, see Cristiano Buffa and Peppino Ortoleva, 'Lingotto, luogo, simbolo', in Carlo Olmo (ed.), *Il Lingotto: 1915-1939: L'architettura, l'immagine, il lavoro* (Turin: Allemandi, 1994), 151–92.

**Fig. 9.19.** A 1938 photo from FIAT's archive celebrating the arrival in New York of a Fiat 500 to be sold in the USA. (courtesy of Archivio Storico FIAT, Turin)

To return to car manufacturer Mr Brown/Bruni in the musical comedy *Due cuori felici*, it is unlikely that the insertion of his Italian descent had anything to do with Italy's proudly renovated car industry. However, it was part of a trend in Italian comedies connecting Italian migration with American wealth. It almost goes without saying that the lead song 'How do you do, Mr Brown' was, unsurprisingly, a foxtrot.[124]

The following year saw another comedy starring an American millionaire—or at least someone who is perceived to be such. This is Palermi's *Non c'è bisogno di denaro* (1933). Once again this was a remake of a German play, but in this case the American returning migrant has not actually made any money: his presence and his embodiment of the American dream are enough to make people return to the bank he is allegedly trusting with his money. The same happens, a few years later, with Gennaro Righelli's *Fuochi d'artificio* (1938), but with the difference that this time the source is an Italian homonymous play by Luigi Chiarelli, and a twist of fate turns the down-and-out returning migrant into a real millionaire, but only once he is back in Italy. A key comic element of these films is the gullibility of

---

[124] On this film, see Francesco Savio, *Ma l'amore no: Realismo, formalismo, propaganda e telefoni bianchi nel cinema italiano di genere (1930–1943)* (Milan: Sonzogno, 1975), 89, 149–50; and Hay, *Popular Film Culture in Fascist Italy*, 86, 88.

people who are so enchanted by the American dream that they believe it to be real even when it is patently not so. Aesthetically, the film was considered a fiasco by both *Bianco e nero* and *Cinema* because of the lack of depth of each character, despite the presence of Italy's most charismatic male lead, Amedeo Nazzari, in the part of Gerardo di Jersay (the protagonist, whose bizarre surname and manners make him closer to the satirized upper-class individuals of Camerini's *Il signor Max* rather than to a semi-illiterate migrant).[125]

If the notion of the American dream plays a part in these films, it should not come as a surprise that Hollywood would feature in it. The love adventures of a glamorous American actress in Italy is at the centre of Guido Brignone's *Per uomini soli* (1938), a comedy that is entirely based on the perception of America as a source of both attraction and moralistic rejection. The plot features a Hollywood actress and an Italian opera singer who are made to fall into the love trap concocted by her secretary and his manager. By the end of the film, however, the Italian realizes that his Italian fiancée is much better than the fickle American goddess Herta Garbin (who, as her name suggests, was sketched around Greta Garbo). It is an ending à la *Signor Max* that once again adds a nationalistic line to the plot.[126]

Finally, between the two thematic trends that we have considered in these pages—the tragedy of migration and the comedy of the American millionaire— there are two films that, for different reasons, fall between the stools. The first takes us back to the silent era. It is one of the Maciste films or, better, Pagano's first Maciste film after his return to Italy from a year's work in Germany, in 1923. The production of *Maciste e il nipote d'America* (1924) leaves us in no doubts about its US American slant, since part of the film was shot on the brand-new ocean liner *Duilio*—owned by Navigazione Generale Italiana—which inaugurated its Genoa– New York round trip with the film crew on board. The fact that this was overtly mentioned in the film's publicity is a good example of a peculiar kind of product placement in the early years of cinema.

By that time, Maciste's films were produced by FERT, a Turinese film company that Pittaluga part-financed and that was eventually taken over in 1925 and renamed FERT-Pittaluga. Sadly, the film is lost, so it is impossible to analyse the representation of Maciste and his Italian American nephew in New York other than through what we are told by the literature on the film. The plot sees Maciste as the owner of an Import–Export company, who crosses the Atlantic as part of his attempt to marry his beloved daughter, Liliana, to his 'American' nephew,

---

[125] Gino Visentini, 'Fuochi d'artificio', *Cinema*, 3/59 (10 December 1938), 360–1; anon., 'Fuochi d'artificio', *Bianco e nero*, 3/3 (March 1939), 72–3. On *Fuochi d'artificio*, see also Hay, *Popular Film Culture in Fascist Italy*, 91.

[126] Critics were not sympathetic about the limitations of this film. From the pages of *Film*, Paola Ojetti (daughter of Ugo Ojetti) wrote that it was simply embarrassing that a renowned director such as Brignone should have been involved in a project of such poor quality. Filippo Sacchi's comment for *Corriere della Sera* was equally damning. Paola Ojetti, 'Per uomini soli', *Film*, 2/13 (1 April 1939), 2. Filippo Sacchi, 'Per uomini soli', *Corriere della Sera*, 10 April 1939, p. 4.

Vittorio. Both of them, however, are already in love with somebody else, and after various engineered encounters taking place on the ship, the two couples are eventually blessed by Maciste. As for the social and economic background of Italian uncle and American niece, the few stills available seem to suggest that they are both wealthy, and, more than anything else, the film does not seem to be exploring the question of migration *per se*. As Jacqueline Reich reminds us in her analysis of this film, the figure of speech of 'lo zio d'America' ('the American uncle') was a popular way to refer in jest to some enriched distant relative who had made it in America. In this case the trope is inverted, since Maciste happens to be a rich 'Italian uncle', but it does not seem that either the scriptwriter—Giovacchino Forzano—or the director Eleuterio Ridolfi was interested in weaving any nationalistic thread into the plot. One should also remember that these were films produced in quick succession—Pagano acted in four Maciste films in 1924—so the scripts were hardly the product of a long process of elaboration.[127]

The concluding paragraphs go to a 1936 film that, on the one hand, faced head-on one of Hollywood's most typical genres, the gangster film, and, on the other, turned on its head the potential, deleterious connection with Italian American crime. This is Raffaele Matarazzo's *Joe il rosso* (1936), adapted from a play by Dino Falconi, who also contributed to the script. The plot tells the story of a young woman, Marta, who meets a French aristocrat on her way to New York—once more on a luxury ocean liner. The two fall in love and get married. Only then, however, does Marta discovers that the American uncle who has provided for her upbringing after her parents' death is actually a member of the local mob. In this case we have a proper 'American uncle', although it is an embarrassing one. Marta valiantly offers Stefano di Sandelle-Lafitte, her newly-wed husband, a divorce, but he disagrees: he loves her, and, as long as his family does not know about her uncle, all will be fine. Only, when the two are back at the husband's family's palace on the French riviera, the mystery of a stolen painting brings Uncle Joe straight into the aristocrats' mansion, and so the comedy of errors begins.

The clever turn on the part of Falconi is that, not only does Joe turn out to be a loveable character as against the snobbishness and corruption of the French aristocrats. In actual fact, the film is intentionally vague when it comes to the protagonists' nationality. Marta is presumably Italian, but this is never made explicit, and, given that all French characters have Italian names and French surnames (in line with the Italianization of first names required in Fascist Italy), we cannot be entirely sure. Plus, her uncle's surname turns out to be Mark: he is Joe Mark, called 'Red Joe' because of the colour of his hair. So there is a strong indication that he might be an Irish rather than an Italian American gangster (but, if so, how come he speaks fluent Italian?). It is a vagueness that is instrumental in more than

---

[127] Reich, *The Maciste Films*, 192–4 (193). On this film, see also Vittorio Martinelli's notes in his *Il cinema muto italiano, 1924–1931* (Turin: Nuova ERI, 1996), 40–4, which inform us that it was the only film partly shot in the USA of this entire period.

one way. First it must have deflected possible attacks—coming from the censors too—that the film dwells on the taboo topic of Italian American crime. After all, the 1932 box-office hit *Scarface* directed by Howard Hawks and Richard Rosson had not been allowed to be distributed in Italy because of its explicit reference to the Italian American mafia, specifically Al Capone. Secondly, the French setting adds an exotic touch, which moves the strong ridicule thrown at the aristocracy on to another nationality. It is almost as if the film expects its audience to suspend their disbelief and enjoy the story, despite its many contradictions.[128]

Cinematically, the film begins with an attempt at a typical American gangster film, with a roughly edited, chaotic scene of a car chase and shooting all the way to an airport in San Francisco (again, we are never told why this mafioso of New York should end up there). However, once the story moves to the aristocrats' French mansion, the setting and the rhythms become those of a traditional play

**Fig. 9.20.** Front cover of *Cinema illustrazione* dedicated to the main cast of Matarazzo's *Joe il rosso* (1936); from the bottom left, clockwise: Armando Falconi, Luigi Pavese, Luisa Garella, and Emilio Petacci; *Cinema illustrazione*, 11/43 (21 October 1936). (courtesy of CSC, Rome)

---

[128] The ambivalent and improvised geographical setting of *Joe il rosso* is exemplary of what Mino Argentieri detects as a typical trait of 1930s Italian comedies set abroad. See Mino Argentieri, 'Autarchia e internazionalità', in Caldiron (ed.), *Storia del cinema italiano*, 148–65 (153). On *Joe il rosso*, see also Zagarrio, *Cinema e fascismo*, 85–6.

or, if nothing else, a parody of a detective film, with Joe turning into the investigation's chief. Despite the fact that the film received lukewarm reviews, *Cinema illustrazione* devoted its front cover to it, with an unusual photo portraying the four characters of the film. The two-page piece that accompanied it contained a long article by the playwright Dino Falconi, who dwelled on a chance encounter during a voyage to the USA. Aboard the by-now-almost-proverbial ocean liner, he befriended a very jovial character, who, thanks to a few extra drinks on the last night of the trip, confessed to him that his wealth came from his involvement in the illegal alcohol trade. The play was an attempt to build a story around this character. Presumably, Falconi must have met this person during a journey between Italy and the USA, so it is likely that he was an Italian American rather than an Irish American. Nonetheless, the playwright must have decided to invent a safer Irish–American background of sorts, and the final touch, in order fully to neutralize the topic of his play, must have been the French setting.[129]

The conclusion one reaches from this overview of migration as a theme in Italian films produced before 1938 is that the Italian American community was hardly ever at the centre of the attention. Latin America was preferred for serious dramas, and the topos of the rich American millionaire was exploited in comedies in a rather superficial way. No films were made that tried to explore the reality of Italian Americans in the USA, despite the high-profile position that some of them had reached, and despite the regime's attempts to connect with the Italian 'colony'—as it was called—as a fifth column for the promotion of Fascism on American soil.[130]

Indicatively, when migration and the world of cinema met in one film, *Due milioni per un sorriso* (1939), the background of the rich migrant was a Latin American one. Written by the experienced duo who also directed the film together, Carlo Borghesio and Mario Soldati, the film tells the story of a successful Italian migrant who decides to return to Italy and invest in the production of a film so that he can find a young actress whose smile can remind him of a blissful moment he experienced before he left. The migrant's country of provenance is not important, since the film is set entirely in Italy, but it is nonetheless odd that, despite Soldati's knowledge of the USA and the immediate connection that everybody would have made between cinema and Hollywood, the scriptwriters should have decided to invent a Latin–American millionaire. It was one more

---

[129] Dino Falconi, 'Joe il rosso raccontato dal suo soggettista', *Cinema illlustrazione*, 11/43 (21 October 1936), 4–5. Among the reviews, see f.s. [Filippo Sacchi], 'Joe il rosso', *Corriere della Sera*, 19 November 1935, p. 5.

[130] A film of this kind was produced in Nazi Germany. It was Luis Trenker's *Der Kaiser von Kalifornien* (1936), which depicted the life of the historical German-born Swiss migrant Johan 'John' Sutter, who migrated to California during the gold rush and was the founder of the city of Sacramento. The film received the Coppa Mussolini at the Venice Film Festival of that year.

proof that the representation of the USA and its Italian American community remained outside the interests of Italian filmmakers.[131]

## Conclusion

The length and breadth of this chapter have allowed us to address the different facets of the perception and elaboration of Hollywood cinema in interwar Italy. When addressing a case of denial of the American influence on an Italian film, I defined it as 'a nationalistic attempt to hide the obvious'. In many ways, this expression could be used as a *fil rouge* that connects all the sections of this chapter. Luigi Freddi, Vittorio Mussolini, and Tito Spagnol were more explicit than others in admitting the need to learn lessons from Hollywood. At the same time, the first two were quick to realign their views along a nationalistic perspective. This is understandable, considering that the reins of the restructuring of the Italian film industry, in the mid-1930s, were entirely in the hands of the regime. The nationalistic discourse dominated the Italian media—hence any discussion of foreign influence had to be treated with caution and peppered with euphemisms.

When it comes to the film industry, historians have probably underestimated the importance of the RAM affair and the impact on *Il Duce* of the humiliation suffered by his son in the autumn of 1937. Vittorio Mussolini, Hal Roach, and MGM were about to trigger a major collaboration between Hollywood and Cinecittà. If it finished in a public fiasco, it was as a consequence of the action taken by the anti-Fascist groups in Los Angeles. Equally important, as late as 1937, Benito Mussolini still seemed pleased for his son to conduct serious business with Hollywood, despite the political tensions following Italy's invasion of Ethiopia, two years before. The marriage between Hollywood and Cinecittà failed because America walked away, not Fascist Italy. Within this perspective, it should not come as a surprise if, the following year, *Il Duce* was eventually ready to take on board Alfieri's request to introduce harsher rules against American cinema.

This does not mean that, below the surface, American cinema did not continue to provide stimuli and challenges to Italian filmmakers. Vittorio Mussolini's journal *Cinema*, as we will see in the next chapter, was to remain a stolid defender of the need to look firmly across the Atlantic, and to address the obvious.

---

[131] For an interview with Borghesio and Soldati about the making of the film, see C. (*sic*), 'Come abbiamo fatto "Due milioni per un sorriso"', *Film*, 2/38 (23 September 1939), 9. The film marked the beginning of Soldati's career as a director.

# 10
# American Culture in Fascism's Final Years, 1938–1943

By the autumn of 1938, Mussolini had begun to transform the Fascist regime into something nastier. The diary of Galeazzo Ciano—*Il Duce*'s closest and most trusted collaborator at the time—offers an insight into Mussolini's mind. His patronizing attitude towards Hitler, palpable in his words and actions up until 1935, slowly morphed into respect and, eventually, admiration. His visit to Nazi Germany in September 1937 convinced him of the need to step up Italy's pace of Fascistization. In four years Hitler seemed to have accomplished more than Mussolini had achieved in fifteen years of Fascism. Hitler's visit in May 1938 became Mussolini's chance to show his fellow dictator that Italy too was ready for the New Order. Only two months previously he had ordered the Italian army to adopt the marching step used in imperial Rome for military parades. Given that its modern equivalent, the goose-step, was strongly associated with the German army, particular emphasis was placed on the historical root—hence its name, *passo romano*.[1] It was one of the three reforms through which—as Mussolini boasted in a speech to the Fascist party leadership on 25 October 1938—he had 'thrown three punches' at Italy's bourgeoisie, the other two punches being, first, the replacement of the courtesy form *Lei* with the allegedly more Italian *Voi*, and, secondly, the defence of the purity of the Italian race.

The sheer fact that Mussolini could present these three on an equal footing gives a chilling sense of how little he must have considered the devastating impact that the anti-Semitic legislation would have on Italy's Jewish community, a large proportion of which had supported him throughout the preceding years. Mussolini had decided that the time had come for a show of strength and rigour. This was already clear in his mind during the summer of 1938. In a diary entry dated 10 July, four days before a group of regime-prone scientists was allowed to publish their 'Manifesto della razza', which kickstarted the campaign in public, Ciano penned these disturbing words following a conversation with Mussolini:

---

[1] On the connection between the *passo romano* and the German goose-step, which Mussolini had admired when SS and party units marched for an hour in front of him during his stay in Berlin, on 25 September 1937, see Christian Goeschel, *Mussolini and Hitler: The Forging of the Fascist Alliance* (New Haven: Yale University Press, 2018), 81–3.

> A first sign of the upcoming clampdown will be the bonfire of Jewish, Masonic, and Francophile writings. Jewish authors and journalists will be banned from all activities. [...] From now on, the revolution needs to leave a mark on the lifestyle of Italians, who need to learn to be less 'nice' in order to become hard, implacable, detestable, i.e. masters.[2]

Beyond the barbarous, historical weight of these words, and to return to the sphere of interests of this book, it is notable that Ciano should have thought of Francophile writings as part of the pernicious 'foreign' influence on Italian Fascist culture. In fact, the *bonifica libraria* ('book reclamation') that followed the legislation had nothing anti-French about it. The real targets were Jewish literature and Jewish authors (together with translators and employees of publishing houses, at all levels), to whose persecution the Italian publishing industry silently complied.[3]

Ciano's expression probably referred more generally to any foreign influence, but it is indicative nonetheless that he should have thought of France as, once again, the main mark of the alleged xenophilia of Italian intellectuals. As for America, an earlier entry by Ciano, dated 6 September 1937, a few days before Mussolini's official visit to Germany (and his son Vittorio's disastrous trip to Hollywood), leaves no doubts about *Il Duce*'s thoughts:

> *Il Duce* vented against America, a country of negroes and Jews, a disrupting element of civilization. He wants to write a book: Europe in the year 2000. The races that will play an important role will be the Italian, the German, the Russian, and the Japanese. All other populations will be destroyed by the acid of Jewish corruption.[4]

This was not an isolated comment. Mussolini seemed increasingly to have converted to a vision of international politics focused through a simplistic lens of race. Consequently, the multiracial make-up of the USA was seen as a clear sign of inferiority: corrupted from above by affluent Jews and from below by former slaves. It was an outlook that made a close alliance with Nazi Germany a natural development. Moving towards Hitler's end of the ethical spectrum, Mussolini began to think of anti-Semitism as a political measure aimed at preparing Italians for their future role as a master race.

---

[2] Ciano, *Diario: 1937–1943* (1948), 207; repr. in *Diario 1937–1943* (1980), 156.
[3] The few exceptions need to be remembered: Benedetto Croce and Giovanni Laterza, who wrote directly to Mussolini to protest; and Angelo Fortunato Formiggini, who committed suicide on 29 November 1938 to protest against the order that he should change name and ownership of his publishing house because it carried his Jewish surname. The same was to happen to the prestigious publishing house Treves, which was taken over by the 'Aryan' Aldo Garzanti. On the *bonifica libraria*, see Giorgio Fabre, *L'elenco: Censura fascista, editoria e autori ebrei* (Turin: Zamorani, 1998), 169–90, and Bonsaver, *Censorship and Literature in Fascist Italy*, 169–91.
[4] Ciano, *Diario 1937–1943* (1980), 34.

As for resisting American culture, the racist–autarkic turn of 1938 was mainly targeted at the enormous popularity of Hollywood. It was not, however, the only field in which the anti-American stance became more vocal. From journalism, literature, and music to the by-then-established mass medium of the radio, the USA became more and more the object of racially tinted denigration. The drive to this was entirely political. Mussolini had taken a course that saw military intervention and opposition to the 'old democracies' become the only diplomatic tool, right in the wake of Hitler's obsession with the necessity of a world war. Hitler arrived at this in September 1939, and Mussolini followed suit on 10 June 1940, when the European war seemed at an end.

Franklin D. Roosevelt, in his quickly reshaped speech given at the University of Virginia on that very day, called it 'a philosophy of force'—after which, without mincing his words, he added: 'On this tenth day of June, nineteen hundred and forty, the hand that held the dagger has struck it into the back of its neighbor. The expression 'stab in the back' had been used by French President Paul Reynaud in a letter that Roosevelt had received a few hours earlier. Roosevelt had been advised to leave such an inflammatory metaphor out of his speech, but he reinserted it in his own handwriting when he gave the last touches to the text. It was a point of no return. Although the declaration of war between Italy and the USA had to wait until 11 December 1941, Roosevelt's condemnation of Mussolini's decision had put the two countries on a collision course.

The cultural war between the two, however, had already broken out in the autumn of 1938. Cinema was the most contested ground, and the first concerted attack took place on that front. American culture was resisted and censored in a most forceful way. At the same time, pockets of 'pro-Americanism', together with the inescapable continuation of the long-wave influence of American culture, make the picture more varied and intriguing. The first part of this chapter will be devoted to a few general questions related to the regime's attempted management of American culture next to the widening shadow of Nazi cultural policies. The press response, with a coda devoted to two aspects that have arisen in previous chapters, aviation and architecture, will also be explored. Both are connected to the image of modernity that the Fascist regime was attempting to project both on the nation and on the outside world.

The second part will look at the development of foreign-language policies and at the circulation of American literature and comics magazines. The two final parts will tackle music and cinema. This is a chapter in which the various cultural fields that have thus far been examined separately come together to give a sense of the impact of the anti-American turn across the whole cultural spectrum. The implosion of the regime in July 1943 marks the end of our analysis, by which point, direct contact with American culture had become a harsh reality. It was brought by the advancing Allied armies with the invasion of Sicily. A very different battle then began to be fought.

## 10.1 American Culture and the New Order

By the late 1930s, the regime's international cultural policies began to be hammered out in parallel with—and often in response to—the vision of a European New Order under Nazi rule. Joseph Goebbels was its prime maker, developing it for Hitler, who, unlike Mussolini, had limited interest in cultural policies. Within this vision, if France and Great Britain were given the role of decrepit liberal democracies, the USA had the added sin of being the country that embodied the evil forces of unbridled consumerism and a multicultural society that threatened local and national values. In the progressively more globalized world of the early twentieth century, American culture was projecting itself as a transnational force helped by its unrivalled capacity for mass production and for the attractiveness of its artefacts, from Hollywood films to jazz music and Coca Cola bottles. This had to be stopped.

As we have seen, a nationalistic, xenophobic stance within more conservative Fascist circles had always existed, and the *Strapaese* movement with periodicals such as *Il Selvaggio* and *L'Italiano* had been a strong voice in the public debate since the mid-1920s. However, Mussolini's interest in presenting Fascism as a revolutionary movement that supported revolutionary approaches in the arts— reinforced by the Futurists and by the modernist taste of Margherita Sarfatti— had preserved a tolerant and sometimes enthusiastic outlook towards cultural renovation, even if the stimuli came from abroad. Jazz music was a case in point: debated, contrasted, but ultimately all-pervading when it came to Italy's *musica leggera* of the interwar years.

Mention of jazz music is indicative of the divide between Fascist and Nazi cultural policies. The latter had categorized it from a racial viewpoint, together with other art forms, as a degenerate form of art (*Entartete Kunst*), the product of black negroes and white Jews. To the Italian Futurists, jazz was—at least until the 1930s—part of their search for a break with tradition combined with the feel of modernity that the urban version of jazz radiated from New York and Chicago. Some of these differences remained throughout the final years. As late as October 1942, when Goebbels organized an 'international' conference in Weimar, inviting literary authors from all over occupied Europe, the Italian Minister of Popular Culture at the time, Alessandro Pavolini, decided to send an Italian delegation that was anything but in line with Nazi conservatism. His choice, among others, fell on two outstanding literary figures in his home town of Florence who were known for their formal experimentation, and who were both translators from English: Eugenio Montale and Elio Vittorini. Montale eventually turned the offer down, but not Vittorini, who attended, with Giaime Pintor, another young intellectual at the margins of Fascist orthodoxy. Overall, even during the war years, Fascism's cultural policies insisted on showing off their specific brand of—to borrow Marla Stone's expression—'aesthetic pluralism'.[5]

At the same time, the racial question had been taking shape in Fascist Italy too. Margherita Sarfatti's progressive marginalization is indicative of Mussolini's change of mind. In December 1936, Mussolini instructed Giorgio Pini, chief editor at *Il Popolo d'Italia*, to avoid contributions to the paper from Jewish authors. Margherita Sarfatti was one of them. By 1936, Mussolini had already told her to step down from her role as director of *Gerarchia*, the political monthly he had founded. Despite her influential role as one of his closest advisers on cultural matters throughout the 1920s, by the mid-1930s she had become a source of embarrassment. On 23 September 1938, Bottai recorded in his diary a conversation with Mussolini that touched upon Sarfatti and the Jewish question. With no hint of regret, Mussolini apparently said the following words:

> I too had a Jewish friend: Sarfatti. Intelligent, fascist, mother of a true hero. Nonetheless, five years ago, sensing that one day we would have to deal with the Jewish problem, I made sure to get rid of her. I had her fired from 'Popolo d'Italia' and from the direction of 'Gerarchia'... though with proper severance pay, you understand.[6]

The final step of Sarfatti's discreet dismissal was to allow her to travel to Latin America—after a few months in Paris—where she was to live until the war had ended. Her intended destination was actually the USA, but Roosevelt's State Department had other thoughts. Despite the fact that she had been received by the American president during her US trip, in April 1934, only four years later the growing tension between the two countries had turned her into a *persona non grata*.[7]

Sarfatti's fall from grace is indicative of Mussolini's growing racial preoccupations as well as of his progressive leaning towards the more nationalistic, anti-modernist cultural policies that were firmly established in Nazi Germany. Anti-Americanism was part of this, and Alfieri's close collaboration with Goebbels was, as we have already seen in the field of cinema, a natural development of it. This does not mean, however, that Mussolini was renouncing his own dominion in cultural matters, but rather that he was still intent on maintaining a distance between him

---

[5] Marla Stone, *The Patron State*, 61. On the Weimar conference of October 1942, see Ben-Ghiat, *Fascist Modernities*, 179–80. On this specific event, literary historian Mirella Serri has dedicated a monograph concentrating in particular on Giaime Pintor, entitled *Il breve viaggio* (Venice: Marsilio, 2002). More generally, for a parallel between Nazi and Fascist cultural policies, see Benjamin G. Martin, *The Nazi–Fascist New Order for European Culture* (Cambridge, MA: Harvard University Press, 2016), in particular ch. 5.
[6] Giuseppe Bottai, *Diario 1935–1944* (Milan: Rizzoli, 1982), 134.
[7] Cannistraro and Sullivan, *Il Duce's Other Woman*, 425–6, 520–32.

and the Nazi ally. The government reshuffle of 31 October 1939 is a telltale sign in this respect. The heavily pro-Nazi Dino Alfieri was replaced by the more feisty and independent-minded Alessandro Pavolini. Only a few weeks before, Pavolini had turned 36. With him, together with Galeazzo Ciano at the Foreign Office (also 36) and Giuseppe Bottai (44) at the Ministry of Education, it looked as if Mussolini had finally entrusted a new generation with the cultural leadership of the country.

Once Italy entered the war, eight months later, Nazi–Fascist rule over continental Europe seemed inevitable. This marked the beginning of an open cultural war between Nazi Germany and Fascist Italy. Bottai, the most intellectually ambitious of the three young leaders, was particularly active in this respect, and his creation of the cultural journal *Primato*, founded in March 1940, had been a clear attempt to rally all the forces of Italian culture, including those that had been at the margins. It was a response to the need to project Fascism's cultural 'primacy' across its entire sphere of influence: the Mediterranean and the Balkans. Bottai's diary leaves no doubt about his strong belief in this mission, and the invitation of Vittorini, Montale, and Pintor to the Weimar conference suggests that Pavolini too supported this attitude. This created windows of opportunity and cultural openings that could allow a certain, positive attitude towards American culture to be retained.

For example, in order to rival the popularity as a propaganda tool of the German illustrated magazine *Signal* (1940–5), Mondadori was given extra funding to develop his own illustrated magazine, *Tempo* (1939–43)—based substantially on the American model of *Life*—and have it printed in seven different European languages. Arnoldo Mondadori's eldest son, Alberto, then 25 years old, was given the directorship of the magazine. Among his closest collaborators was the ever-present 'pro-American' Cesare Zavattini. The ambiguities and ambivalence towards American culture that we have witnessed throughout the interwar years thus persisted, albeit to a lesser degree, in the final years of the regime.[8]

### 10.1.1 The De-Americanization of the Press

The quantity and tone of press coverage of American affairs from 1938 onwards are a good indicator of the anti-American turn of those years. As a daily, the *Corriere della Sera* stopped sending its most renowned correspondents to America, as it had done throughout the interwar years. Pietro Carbonelli, who, as we saw in Chapter 6, was a mediocre and negative-minded journalist, was given the official role of correspondent in residence. The only recognizable signature of

---

[8] On *Tempo*, see Decleva, *Mondadori*, 238–44, 256–9. Bottai's *Primato* too was published by Mondadori.

some notoriety was that of Luigi Barzini Jr, a pro-Fascist whose writings on America in the mid-1930s were distinctive for their balanced tone and sense of humour. When he returned to the USA in 1939, his tone had changed entirely. After covering Italy's invasion of Albania in April 1939, Barzini was sent to New York, where he wrote a number of derogatory pieces on various 'americanate'. From the ludicrous multiracial mix of minor criminals seen during a visit to a police station (predictably multiracial, but with no Italian Americans under arrest), to the greed of American businessmen obsessed with possessing gold reserves, to Harvard students eating live goldfish as a joke: the propagandistic tone of these articles is incomparable with Barzini Jr's articles of five years earlier.[9]

Emilio Cecchi, too, made himself available when, during the summer–autumn of 1938, the *Corriere della Sera*'s chief editor, Aldo Borrelli, asked him to write a few articles on anti-African American racism in the USA. His tone was more sober than that of Barzini Jr, but the political intent was there for all to see. After the autumn of 1938, a journalistic piece on the USA was required to carry political undertones.[10]

When it comes to illustrated magazines, Leo Longanesi's *Omnibus* was conspicuous for showing interest in American affairs, alternating derisive and more balanced views. Its approach to American topics might have survived the new directives of the regime, but the magazine's fusion of American-style graphics and corrosive journalism proved too critical and unregimented, with the result that in February 1939, following yet another scandal (this time due to an irreverent article about Leopardi and Naples), Longanesi was told by the Milanese Prefecture that Alfieri, as Minister of Popular Culture, had ordered the closure of the magazine. Mussolini too, despite his long-standing recognition of Longanesi's genius, approved the decision. Mussolini also resisted Rizzoli's attempt to save the magazine by transferring its editorship. Times were no longer appropriate for the impertinent tones of *Omnibus*.

As for the *Rivista illustrata del Popolo d'Italia*, the pro-American stance, present until the early 1930s, had entirely disappeared. In this case the watershed had been marked by the invasion of Ethiopia. From 1935 on, the *Rivista illustrata* had become an inward-looking magazine, dedicating the vast majority of its coverage to the glorification of Italy's natural, architectural, and artistic beauties and to the country's industrial and military might. It is indicative, for example, that when, in

---

[9] See his articles on the third page of *Corriere della Sera* of 8 July, 20 September, and 1 October 1939. Before his journey to the USA, Barzini Jr had already published a strongly anti-American piece dedicated to the pernicious impact of American capitalism and lifestyle on European countries, openly mentioning Mussolini as an example of a statesman who had managed to counteract this influence. Luigi Barzini Jr, 'Il successo, scopo della vita: La colpa è dell'America', *Corriere della Sera*, 6 April 1939, p. 5.

[10] On Cecchi's articles and, more generally, on the anti-American stance of 1938 in the Italian press, see Pierluigi Allotti, *Giornalisti di regime: La stampa italiana tra fascismo e antifascismo (1922–1948)* (Rome: Carocci, 2012), 40–2, 96–9.

April 1936, Luigi Freddi wrote a seven-page-long, pedantic article on cinema, going through every single stage of the production and distribution of a film, American cinema was given not a single mention. Even when addressing Italy's distribution network as dependent on foreign imports, Freddi somewhat oddly mentioned it as a relic of the past, with no reference to Hollywood's continuing dominance. It was more of the same 'nationalistic denial of the obvious'. And when, in the September issue, a short article tackled the topic of foreign films at the Venice film festival, it began with a note about the disappointing quality of Hollywood films and ended with praise of German cinema.[11]

If we move to the *Rivista illustrata* of the post-1938 years, the only discernible change is the increased attention given to Fascism's military power. As for international news, Italy's 'posto al sole'—its colonies in Libya and the Horn of Africa—dominated. If other countries were covered, it was only in relation to some indirect praise of Italy's superiority. The issue of November 1938 is exemplary in this respect. If contains a rare image of America, but, tellingly, only as part of an advert by an Italian company that operated cruise liners in the north Atlantic (see the image on the left of Fig. 10.1). What dominates the issue are jingoistic celebrations of the anniversary of Mussolini's seizure of power and the propagandist glorification of Fascist Italy. The only article devoted to international news concerns the Munich agreement of 30 September 1938, which allowed Hitler to pursue his territorial claims in the Sudetenland. Mussolini and Hitler unsurprisingly appear shoulder to shoulder in the main accompanying photo (see the image in the centre of Fig. 10.1). The article described the two leaders as 'I Dittatori' pitted against the 'Governi democratici', and Mussolini was hailed as the dealmaker of the agreement. Given that in a section of this chapter we will be returning to the topic of architecture, it is also worth mentioning that, among the final forty-two pages devoted to 'Autarchia', showcasing various images of Italy's industrial autonomy, a two-page spread was devoted to an industrial skyscraper. This is the fascio-shaped tower of SNIA's newly built cellulose plant in Torre di Zuino, in the north-east of Italy. The 54-metre-high tower called Torre Littoria was doubled in 1940, and it survived the war, though its axe-shaped glass section was modified in order to remove its evident Fascist symbolism. When Mussolini inaugurated the plant, in September 1938, Marinetti dedicated a long poem to it, published as an example of 'aero-poetry'.[12]

When it comes to the *Domenica del Corriere* and *L'Illustrazione italiana*, the inward, 'autarkic' view was similarly prevailing, with perhaps the only difference

---

[11] Luigi Freddi, 'Il cinema', *Rivista illustrata del Popolo d'Italia*, 14/4 (April 1936), 67–73. LP, 'Il cinema straniero alla Mostra di Venezia', 14/9 (September 1936), 48–9.

[12] Full-page advertisement of Società di Navigazione Italia; anon., 'Nasce una nuova Europa'; Aldo Pasetti, 'Torre di Zuino, capitale della cellulosa'; *Rivista illustrata del Popolo d'Italia*, 17/11 (November 1938), 3, 63–5, 125–8. Filippo Tommaso Marinetti, *Gli aeropoeti futuristi dedicano al Duce Il Poema di Torre Viscosa* (Milan: Officine Grafiche Esperia, 1938).

426  AMERICA IN ITALIAN CULTURE

**Fig. 10.1.** From the November 1938 issue of *Rivista illustrata del Popolo d'Italia*: from the left, full-page advertisement of Società di Navigazione Italia; first page of article on the Munich agreement; first page of article on SNIA Viscosa. (courtesy of BSMC, Rome)

that the military dimension was less pronounced. America had by then disappeared entirely from the magazines' front cover. In odd articles, however, the *Domenica del Corriere* continued in its fondness for 'americanate', from Californian policemen using 'motorized skateboards' in their patrols, to a Philadelphia man who fails to commit suicide and takes a shopkeeper to court because of the poor quality of the rope he sells, and back to California with a woman who is so good at imitating a donkey's bray that even donkeys fall for it.[13]

On the other hand, a characteristic of *L'Illustrazione italiana* is its interest in cinema, which sometimes ended up covering Hollywood, not always in a negative light. Disney's *Snow White and the Seven Dwarfs*, which, after its Italian premiere at the Venice film festival, was screened in Italian cinemas over the Christmas holiday, received a glowing review in January 1939. A month later a complimentary three-page article was devoted to a gigantic water park in Florida (Marineland park, opened in June 1938), which was also used by Hollywood studios for underwater shooting. And, finally, there were regular positive mentions of Hollywood films and stars throughout the year. This is probably linked to the fact that, despite the withdrawal of four major studios, a good number of Hollywood films continued to be distributed in Italian cinemas.[14]

Overall, the impression is that the Italian press progressively sidelined American culture rather than attacking it full on. Anti-Semitic innuendos were certainly present, but this was a trait that, sadly, many Italian journalists felt they needed to include in their articles regardless of their topic. The correlative to this attempted, slow eclipse of American culture was the increasing, positive attention paid to Nazi Germany.

## 10.1.2 The Promise of Technological Supremacy: Aviation

If, in the early 1930s, the sight of Balbo's formation flights in American skies was a powerful sign of Fascist Italy's refound strength, by the time the Second World War put this to the test, the situation had changed substantially. The role of aviation in the final years of Fascism can be seen through reference to two episodes that together show the detachment between self-image and reality that had been taking place. The first concerns New York's World's Fair, inaugurated on 30 April 1939. The Italian pavilion consisted of a monumental building, typical of the 'Stile Littorio', of which the SNIA tower was one example. The very first exhibition that one entered was dedicated to Italian technology, and in particular to aviation.

---

[13] Anon., 'Monopattini a motore'; Y, 'La corda dell'impiccato'; X, 'Cifre e fatti singolari', *Domenica del Corriere*, 41/3 (8–14 January 1938), 14; 41/4 (15–21 January 1939), 4; 23 (28 May–3 June 1939), 4.
[14] Adolfo Franchi, 'Elogio di Biancaneve e i sette nani'; Marcello Girosi, 'Marineland o la terra del mare', *L'Illustrazione italiana*, 41/1 (1 January 1939), 16; 45/6 (5 February 1939), 255–7.

On a wall, a big chart illustrated the thirty-three world records that Italian aviation had broken. It also informed visitors that the total of records broken by all other nations in the world combined came to the suspiciously meagre figure of twenty-three.[15] The selection of world records chimed with the fact that, up until the eve of the Second World War, Fascist propaganda was still boasting about the might of Italian aviation: 'l'Arma Fascistissima' ('the Most Fascist Army'), as it was usually referred to. But was that still the case? This takes us to the second episode, which concerns one particular time and place: North Africa, June 1940. As we saw in Chapter 6, beyond Mussolini's own connection with aviation, it was Italo Balbo who had captured the public imagination with his formation flights across the world. However, his 'promotion' to Governor of Libya in January 1934 had been judged by many as a punishment: it was the confinement to a distant colony of a popular Fascist who had shown potential to outshine his own leader.

Balbo showed discipline and busied himself with the economic and administrative reforms that should have seen Libya become an integral part of the Italian empire. In later years, Balbo was also opposed to Mussolini's pro-Nazi and anti-Semitic drift, to the point that he openly spoke against the anti-Semitic decree during the meeting of Fascism's Grand Council on 6 October 1938. When the war broke out, Libya—because of its border with British Egypt—was instantly transformed into a theatre of war, and one might have expected Balbo to return to a position of notoriety, returning to those *beaux gestes* that had made him famous (and infamous) even before he was an aviator, as a Fascist leader in the Po valley city of Ferrara. Instead, his fortune took a tragic twist. On the afternoon of 28 June 1940, less than three weeks after Italy's declaration of war, Balbo was in the cockpit of a three-engine bomber. Together with a second plane, he arrived above Tobruk's airfield, unannounced, soon after a bombing raid by British aeroplanes. The Italian defences in the port mistook the sudden appearance of the two bombers for a second wave of attack, and Balbo's plane was shot down in flames.

Had he survived, it is unlikely that Balbo would have led the Italian air forces into a glorious African campaign. His death shortly preceded another failure. If Fascism had been rightly proud of Italy's air forces and, thanks to Balbo, had used it as a propaganda tool over American skies, by the late 1930s it had failed to keep up with technological progress. Italy's warplanes were no match for the latest generation of British and American planes. In 1940, in the Mediterranean skies, the difference was easy to spot. A Hawker Hurricane MkII was capable of a speed of 342mph and was armed with eight machine guns; Italy's direct competitor was the Fiat CR42, a biplane that could only produce a speed of 237mph and was armed with just two machine guns shooting at a reduced rate through the propeller, like a standard First World War fighter. As Narciso Pillepich, a veteran CR42

---

[15] See the long article on the Italian pavilion, written in fervent pro-Fascist terms by Luigi Barzini Jr: 'L'Americano e sua moglie al padiglione italiano', *Corriere della Sera*, 3 June 1939, p. 3.

pilot, admitted, when they engaged Hurricanes—and, even worse, Spitfires—in the sky over Malta, nobody thought of shooting down the enemy. Survival was their only target. By then l'Arma Fascistissima was far from being a paradigm of modernity.[16]

A case in point that connects our two episodes is the story of a two-engine aeroplane, the Breda Ba.88, which in 1937 broke two world speed records and was therefore much hailed by the Italian press.[17] However, when the plane was converted for military use, it became clear that speed, its only outstanding feature, was heavily compromised by the weight of the added armament. Despite this, it was produced in series and ended up on the North African front, where its lack of manoeuvrability became so evident that all planes were quickly grounded and used merely as decoys. The prestige that the display of Balbo's aeroplane formations and the breaking of speed records radiated across the world in the

Fig. 10.2. Airmen of SAAF 7 Squadron toy with a part-dismantled Breda Ba.88 left behind by the Italian Air Force in a North African airstrip, in 1942. (photo by Capt. Robert Abbot Fenner; courtesy of his sons Bill and Bob, and of Tinus le Roux)

---

[16] Conversation between Narciso Pillepich and the author. Pillepich flew Fiat CR42 fighters in North Africa and over Malta. He is mentioned in Christopher Shores, Giovanni Massimello and Russell Guest, *A History of the Mediterranean Air War 1940–45*, i. *North Africa* (London: Grub Street, 2012), 28, 55. For a detailed technical history of Italy's warplanes in the 1930s and early 1940s, see Jonathan Thompson, *Italian Civil and Military Aircraft, 1930–1945* (Fallbrook, CA: Aero Publishers, 1963).

[17] See, e.g., the *Corriere della Sera*, which, on 10 December 1937, published a photo of the aeroplane under the headline 'Nuovo primato dell'ala fascista', when the Ba.88 broke the world speed record for flights over 100 km and 1,000 km. The following day, the article was followed up with a second, longer one.

interwar years was of little use now that propaganda had to face the harsh reality of the North African battlefield. The Ba.88 arrived in Libya in August 1940, after Balbo's death. By then, however, Balbo had already grounded the mono-engine model of Breda's light bomber plane, the Ba.65, which had similarly proved to be well below operational needs. Again, one is left to speculate whether, if Mussolini had allowed Balbo to stay as head of the Italian air force in the mid-1930s, the Fascists might still have been able to claim in 1940 that they were a leading developer of the ultimate modern machine. The end result was that Mussolini failed to ensure Italy's leading edge in aviation when it was most needed. Its iconic role in Fascism's self-image of the early 1930s had degenerated into a source of embarrassment. Improved models were introduced in the following years of the war, but only once Alfa Romeo had been licensed to produce the far superior German liquid-cooled engine DB601, and in numbers that were pitifully inferior to those that the American and British aviation industries were able to field.

### 10.1.3 Fascist Skyscrapers

In Chapter 6, we dwelt on Palanti's project of a giant skyscraper towering over the Roman skyline. In the autumn of 1924, Mussolini fleetingly considered it, despite—and perhaps because of—its megalomaniac size. Palanti's career as an architect had developed far away from Italy, in South America, but there is no doubt that Mussolini could also count on a generation of home-grown, talented architects, some of whom were fervent Fascists, raring to contribute to the construction of a new Rome. Our question here is whether anything in their work implied a direct or indirect response to the challenge America offered in its most powerful architectural icon—the one that, in the minds of millions, defined American modernity: the skyscraper.

Most European cities did not try to emulate the USA in the construction of similar high-rise buildings in their historic centres. Even Berlin, the most modernity-prone of European capitals, made no attempt to compete, either before or after Hitler's seizure of power. Fascist Italy, however, did engage, well beyond Palanti's failed project. This was mainly due to the meeting of two minds: Marcello Piacentini, Italy's most influential architect of the interwar years, and Mussolini, who trusted the former and allowed him to shape the architectural image of Fascist Italy.

Piacentini's father, Pio, was a renowned Roman architect who had designed the neoclassical Palazzo delle Esposizioni (opened in 1883), which, as we saw in Chapter 9, had been refashioned in a modernist style in order to host the 1932 Exhibition of the Fascist Revolution. Marcello Piacentini had been centrally involved in this reshaping project. Indeed, although he had followed in his father's footsteps and had worked with him, Piacentini had soon started to embrace contemporary trends. His modern interpretation of Italy's Baroque style was successful in competing for a number of government buildings, peaking in the construction of the new Roman headquarters of the Banca d'Italia (1916–18), opposite the Italian parliament. In 1915 Piacentini travelled extensively through the USA: in San Francisco he was responsible for the Italian pavilion at the Panama–Pacific exhibition, after which he spent a few weeks in the north-east, visiting Chicago, Buffalo, New York, and Washington. Piacentini's interest in the use of steel frames and concrete for the construction of high-rise buildings became clear when he (unsuccessfully) competed against the best American and European architects for the design of the Chicago Tribune Tower in 1922.

Piacentini was initially opposed to the idea of skyscrapers in an Italian urban setting, but when a few years later Mussolini entrusted him with the full remodelling of one of Brescia's historic squares, Piazza della Vittoria, he must have thought that the time had come for an Italianized, first *grattacielo*, or *rubanuvole*, as skyscrapers were alternatively called in an attempt to render the English neologism into Italian. This was the 57-metre-high Torrione INA (INA being the insurance company that financed the building), then Europe's highest steel-framed building. When Mussolini turned up to inaugurate it in November 1932, he refused to take one of the four lifts and, in proper Fascist fashion, walked up the staircase all the way to the top. The use of bricks on the outer structure was derived from the use of terracotta cladding following the Chicago school skyscrapers of the early twentieth century. It was a style that worked well within the context of an Italian historic town. Despite the commercial use of the building, Piacentini also gave the design an Italian/Fascist spin by invoking the image of a medieval tower, a symbol of secular power that the Fascist regime was to implement in all its urban projects, whether it was new towns founded in recently reclaimed areas of Italy or in the reshaping of colonial towns now in Italian hands. Indeed, the expression *Torre* became almost a synonym for 'skyscraper' in many subsequent projects. In 1934, the symbolic height of 100 metres was almost reached with the Torre Littoria, built in Turin and designed by Armando Melis de Villa. The initial plan was for the skyscraper to host the Turin headquarters of the National Fascist Party, but financial constraints put it entirely under the control of another insurance company, the Reale Mutua Assicurazioni. It was Piacentini who eventually broke through the 100-metre ceiling with Genoa's Torre dell'orologio or Torre Piacentini, a commercial building completed in 1940, which was 108 metres high. At the time it was Europe's highest building. Its design took Piacentini back to his early compromise between a Chicago-style skyscraper and a medieval-tower image, this time made more Italianate by the imitation of the two-coloured horizontal strips of early medieval buildings (part of the so-called *stile neo-romanico* much in vogue at the time).

Piacentini's Torre dell'orologio was a direct, Italian response to American modernity. By then, Piacentini was involved in another challenge, one that was on

**Fig. 10.3.** Marcello Piacentini's Torrione INA in Brescia (1932), on the left, and his Torre dell'orologio or Torre Piacentini in Genoa (1940), on the right. (courtesy, respectively, of Wolfang Moroder and of Lidio Ferrando)

a much larger scale and that took place on the outskirts of Rome. The project, known as EUR42 (an acronym for Esposizione Universale Roma 1942), envisaged the creation of a new district that was intended to host an international fair. For obvious reasons the fair never took place, and some of the buildings were not completed until the post-war years. Marcello Piacentini was asked by Mussolini to supervise the entire project. By then he had become a central figure in Italian architecture, both professionally and politically. Mussolini's admiration had seen Piacentini join Pirandello and Marinetti in the 1929 list of the first appointed members of the Accademia d'Italia. Piacentini was also the founder and co-editor of the journal *Architettura e arti decorative* (1921–31), which in 1932 was renamed *Architettura* and, under his sole editorship, became the official journal of the Sindacato Nazionale Architetti. Given that all projects concerning urban redevelopments were either directly financed by the government or under strict political control, conformism to the regime was inescapable. As Kirk put it: 'Refusal to join the Fascist party and syndicate effectively ended an architect's career.'[18]

Piacentini was at the centre of this system of power and patronage, so there is no denying his political role. As for his vision as an architect, his was a position of compromise between the extremes of the Rationalist school inspired by the Bauhaus avant-garde and the moderates who pursued a more orthodox neoclassical approach.[19] It was a vision that provided the perfect encapsulation of Fascism's ideal of a fusion between modernity and Italy's classical past. Piacentini also saw himself as a team player. The creation of the new site of *La Sapienza* university in Rome, inaugurated in 1935, saw the collaboration of a team of young architects under his supervision, one of whom was Gio Ponti, who designed the Mathematics School building. Another of Piacentini's most gifted fellow architects was Giuseppe Pagano. The two, together with Cesare Valle, designed the Italian pavilion at the 1937 Exposition Internationale des Arts et Techniques Appliqués à la Vie Moderne in Paris (Fig. 10.4).[20]

The design and construction of the Italian pavilion in Paris were the first major government-sponsored project delivered after Italy's invasion of Ethiopia and Mussolini's proclamation of the empire in his speech of 9 May 1936. The pavilion was also built in the same year in which government film propaganda made its greatest attempt to link Fascist Italy with its ancient Roman past, with *Scipione l'Africano* (1937). It was an 'imperial' mood to which Piacentini and Pagano responded by concentrating on the purity of the classical paradigm, stripped from the eclectic interpretations of the Medieval and Renaissance/Baroque style of previous years. Their monumental example of fusion between neoclassicism and Rationalism established a model that, once sedimented in the expression 'Stile Littorio', was to dominate public buildings projects until the fall of the regime. It also became the defining stylistic trait of EUR42.[21]

---

[18] Kirk, *The Architecture of Modern Italy*, ii. 84.
[19] The Rationalist school was organized around the Movimento Italiano per l'Architettura Razionale (MIAR), founded in 1928, which had Giuseppe Terragni as one of its most creative minds. His was the groundbreaking design of the Casa del Fascio built in Como between 1932 and 1936. Terragni knew Margherita Sarfatti well, and he designed the monumental tomb for her son Roberto, in 1934, built on the location where he had died in combat in the First World War.
[20] Giuseppe Pagano and Gio Ponti, respectively editors of the magazines *Casabella* and *Domus*, had a major innovative influence in domestic architecture. Pagano eventually fell out with Piacentini, whom he considered too moderate and manipulative. Later, after the re-establishment of the Fascist regime, in October 1943, Pagano's opposition saw him arrested and finally interned in a Nazi concentration camp, where he died in 1945. Gio Ponti, on the other hand, became one of Italy's most renowned architects and designers in the post-war years.
[21] On the role of the 1937 Italian pavilion, see James J. Fortuna, '"Un'arte ancora in embrione": International Expositions, Empire, and the Evolution of Fascist Architectural Design', *Modern Italy*, 25/4 (2020), 455–76. On the 'Stile Littorio' and on Piacentini's role in shaping Italian interwar architecture, see Nicoloso, *Mussolini architetto*, 169–270; Aristotle Kallis, *The Third Rome, 1922–1943: The Making of the Fascist Capital* (Basingstoke: Palgrave Macmillan, 2014), 106–97; and, by the same author, 'Futures Made Present: Architecture, Monument, and the Battle for the "Third Way" in Fascist Italy', *Fascism*, 7 (2018), 45–79.

Fig. 10.4. The Italian pavilion of Marcello Piacentini, Giuseppe Pagano, and Cesare Valle at the 1937 International Exposition in Paris. (courtesy of La Photolith, Wikipedia Commons)

Undoubtedly, the EUR42 project was meant to put the final rubber stamp on this vision, and provide a world-renowned architectural image of Fascist power and Fascist aesthetics. For this reason, in the post-war years, the EUR district was to become a somewhat taboo area in Rome—an ideal location for fairs and congresses and yet at the same time haunted by its identification with Mussolini's regime. But what were the project's concerns with high-rise buildings? The final plan of EUR42 did not excel in that respect. It was more of a horizontal display of Fascist monumentality, which seems closer to Alfred Speer's designs for Berlin than to Piacentini's inclinations. Indeed, according to Speer's memoirs, when Hitler visited Rome in May 1938 and perused the EUR42 model, he concluded that it was not particularly innovative: which was good, he added, since it left Nazi's primacy unchallenged. It was naturally a biased view but one that contained a grain of truth.[22]

Had Hitler and Speer seen what the group of Italian architects initially led by Giuseppe Pagano had offered Mussolini in their first set of drawings, in April 1937, they would have realized the extent to which the Italian architects were hoping to be allowed to take a much more groundbreaking, almost futuristic approach. Figures 10.5 and 10.6 show a bird's-eye view of the initial plan, which

[22] Alfred Speer, *Spandau. The Secret Diaries* (London: Collins, 1976; originally published in German, 1975), 126.

AMERICAN CULTURE IN FASCISM'S FINAL YEARS 435

**Fig. 10.5.** Bird's-eye view of the initial project for EUR42 presented to Mussolini by Marcello Piacentini and his collaborators on 28 April 1937. (courtesy of BNC, Rome)

**Fig. 10.6.** The model of the initial version of EUR42 showing the four central skyscrapers along the main axis of the complex. (courtesy of BNC, Rome)

included four 'open-air' skyscrapers along the main axis of the complex, as the detail from the model shows. It was a vision that was light years ahead of the conservative style of Alfred Speer.[23]

In the end, however, despite his initial approval, Mussolini changed his mind. According to Speer, again, the cause was a long conversation with Hitler during Mussolini's visit to Germany, in September 1937. This is at least what Hitler boasted:

> Hitler proudly related how he had won Mussolini over, during the latter's stay in Munich, to the new German architecture. He boasted of having given him a lecture on modern architecture, and said that the Duce was now convinced that the designs of his official architect, Piacentini, amounted to nothing. At the 1940's World Fair's in Rome, Mussolini had said, he would show what he had learned in Munich and Berlin.[24]

Regardless of the historical accuracy of this memoir penned by Speer more than ten years later (and the wrong reference to EUR42 warns us about its precision), it is a fact that, on his return from Germany, Mussolini had acquired a personal vision of EUR42 that was very different from the early proposals masterminded by Pagano. In December 1937, he asked Piacentini to take the lead and to stay within the more conservative modernist interpretation of classical architecture that Piacentini, Pagano, and Valle had developed in the Stile Littorio. The result was a complex dominated by references to the classical tradition. This caused a violent rift between Pagano and Piacentini that was never repaired. If the four skyscrapers of Pagano's plan might have given a sense of Fascist Italy competing with the skyline of Manhattan, in the end EUR42 was closer to Nazism's austere classicism.[25]

Within the 4 kilometres of the project site coordinated by Piacentini, the most iconic building was the Palazzo della Civiltà Italiana. Piacentini was the overall supervisor, but its main designers were three architects, among whom Ernesto La Padula—then 35 years old and leader of the Italian Rationalist school—had the main role. Through the construction of a steel-framed inner core, the building

---

[23] The designs were published in the journal of the Fascist Syndicate of Architects, *Architettura*, directed by Piacentini, in the April 1937 issue (pp. 181–92). The two illustrations appear on pp. 187 and 192. Unusually, given that *Architettura* normally concentrated on Italy only, the journal had published a long, factual article on New York's skyscrapers in a previous issue: anon., 'Grattacieli', *Architettura* (April 1932), 189–93. Piacentini's earlier reservations seemed to have disappeared.

[24] Speer, *Spandau: The Secret Diaries*, 126. The quotation is part of the entry for 3 March 1949, pp. 124–6.

[25] On this, see Nicoloso, *Mussolini architetto*, 208–22. For a parallel study of Speer's and Piacentini's architecture, see Sandro Scarrocchia, *Albert Speer e Marcello Piacentini: L'architettura del totalitarismo negli anni trenta* (Milan: Skira, 1999; 2nd edn, 2013). On EUR42, see also Maurizio Calvesi, Enrico Guidoni and Simonetta Lux (eds), *E 42: Utopia e scenario del regime* (Venice: Marsilio, 1987); and Gentile, *Fascismo di pietra*, 123–71.

**Fig. 10.7.** The Palazzo della Civiltà Italiana of Giovanni Guerrini, Ernesto La Padula, and Mario Romano in Rome's EUR district, 1940. (author's personal collection)

could support a delicate outer façade in Travertine limestone, entirely built on the repetition of a stylized Roman arch. The building was nicknamed 'il Colosseo quadrato' ('the square Colosseum') because of the intentional similarity created by both the lines of arches and the use of Travertino. The building's height, at 68 metres, hardly qualifies the Palazzo as a record-breaking skyscraper, though it must be said that the original design proposed not six but nine floors, which would have extended its height well above 100 metres and would have made it Europe's tallest building. Eventually the committee, led by Piacentini, settled for a reduced height that was more in tune with the entire project, but nonetheless allowed the Palazzo to stand out as by far the tallest building at EUR42. It was inaugurated on 30 November 1940, and, had the world avoided a Second World War and had Rome's Universal Expo taken place in 1942 as planned, the Palazzo della Civiltà Italiana would probably have been praised as the Fascist response to America's modernity. It was not an emulating attempt, but a 'European' elaboration, capable of showing how Fascist aesthetics was able to blend leading-edge high-rise steel frame construction with Europe's best claim to superiority over the USA: its centuries-old history.

The phrase sculpted into all four sides of the Palazzo, above the top floor, left no doubt as to the nationalistic and myth-making purpose of the building. If Italians were a people of poets, artists, heroes, saints, thinkers, scientists, and travellers, then their final virtue was the most symbolic one: *trasmigratori* ('transmigrators'). Fascism's Italians were no longer a people of migrants, no longer masses of poor peasants crossing the Alps and the oceans in search for a better life. They were something much more virile, charismatic, mythological: in impeccable D'Annunzian style, the double connotation of *trasmigrare*, alluding to the cyclical migration of birds and to the religious notion of the migration of the soul after death, elevated decades of economic migration to the timeless level of an epic voyage. In many ways, the Palazzo della Civiltà Italiana stands as an icon of Fascism's aesthetics: its constant tension between *Romanità* and modernity, soaked in pompous nationalistic rhetoric.[26]

A final, ironic twist relating to the development of urban skylines in both Fascist Italy and America came in the form of the giant metallic arch that was meant to dominate the EUR42 landscape. Designed in 1937 by Rationalist architect Adalberto Libera, and much praised by Piacentini, the modernist Monumental Arch was intended to be like a gigantic gate spanning the avenue

Fig. 10.8. Detail of the top section of the Palazzo della Civiltà Italiana in Rome's EUR district, 1940. (author's personal collection)

---

[26] For a detailed history of the project, see Alessandra Muntoni and Maria Silvia Farci, 'Palazzo della Civiltà Italiana', in Calvesi, Guidoni and Lux (eds), *E 42: Utopia e scenario del regime*, 353–70. The initial drawings by Guerrini, La Padula, and Romano are held at MOMA, in New York.

that formed the axis connecting Rome's historic centre, the EUR42, and the sea. With a span of 330 metres and height of 170 metres, it would have provided a contemporary response to the Eiffel Tower, which had acted as a gateway to the 1889 Exposition Universelle. A technically challenging and expensive part of EUR42, Libera's arch was built as a scale model for structural tests in the summer of 1940, but in the end—and most probably because of the massive amount of metal that it would have required—the arch was never built.[27]

However, only a few years later, a very similar shape emerged on the other side of the Atlantic: in St Louis, Missouri. This was part of the city's project to build a memorial in honour of Thomas Jefferson near the bank of the Mississippi River. As the design competition specified in January 1945, it was to be 'one central feature: a single shaft, an arch or something else that would symbolize American culture and civilization'.[28] The selection process was completed in 1947, and the winner emerged as the Finnish American architect Eero Saarinen, who had proposed a design of a metallic arch similar to that designed by Libera.

Fig. 10.9. On the left, the official poster promoting EUR42, featuring Adalberto Libera's arch; on the right, Eero Saarinen's Gateway arch designed for the Jefferson Memorial in 1947 and completed in 1965. (courtesy, respectively, of BNC, Rome, and of Hendrickson Photography/Shutterstock)

---

[27] On the arch project, see Antonella La Torre, 'Arco monumentale', in Calvesi, Guidoni and Lux (eds), *E 42: Utopia e scenario del regime*, 467–70.
[28] These were the words used by Luther Ely Smith, chairman of the Jefferson National Expansion Memorial, during a meeting on 4 November 1944. Quoted in Sharon A. Brown, *Administrative History: Jefferson National Expansion Memorial* (Washington: National Park Service, 1984), ch. 4; available online in the Jefferson National Expansion website (accessed 15 December 2022).

The disconcerting resemblance was flagged up by the chairman of the powerful National Fine Arts Commission, Gilmore D. Clarke, in a letter dated 24 February 1948 to William Wurster, a fellow architect and a member of the commission for the Jefferson Memorial. Clarke did not accuse Saarinen of plagiarism but rather questioned the appropriateness of building a monument to American culture that so closely resembled a design produced in Fascist Rome. Saarinen denied any connection with Libera's arch, and the commission fully endorsed his vision of the monumental arch as a symbolic gate, as already represented in ancient architecture, avoiding Roman triumphal arches and instead citing the example of the still-standing giant archway at Ctesiphon, Persia's capital. This might well have been the case. However, given the fact that Libera's arch featured prominently in both the EUR42 plans and in the poster that promoted the exhibition before it was cancelled, it is surprising that it should have escaped the attention of an architect specializing in urban planning who knew European architecture well (Saarinen had spent two years in Europe, in 1934–6). Saarinen's arch was eventually completed in 1965, standing 192 metres high, and it has now become St Louis's most popular icon.[29] Mention of it in these pages is not an attempt to insist on the potential derivation of one project from another. Rather, it is to confirm the sophistication and creativity reached by Italian modernist architecture in Fascist Italy. If Manhattan's skyline was the ultimate icon of American modernity, a finished EUR42, its skyline dominated by the Palazzo della Civiltà Italiana and by Libera's arch, would have provided an ambitious Fascist counter-image.

## 10.2 American Tales in the Fascist War

This second section moves over to questions of language and literature. In 1939, as the new Minister of Education, Giuseppe Bottai proposed a radical reform of the teaching of modern languages. He was also involved in the *bonifica* ('reclamation') of Italian literature triggered by the anti-Semitic legislation. Pressure was put on Italian publishers to reduce their dependence on lucrative translations; American literature became an obvious target, but, as we will see, it could still be protected. Something similar happened to comic books, whose dependence on US imports had to be stopped. The following three subsections examine what happened in each of these fields.

---

[29] On the construction of St Louis's Gateway to the West, as the arch is known as, see W. Arthur Mehrhoff, *The Gateway Arch: Fact and Symbol* (Bowling Green, OH: Bowling Green State University Popular Press, 1992); pp. 17–28 are dedicated to the connection of the arch with ancient culture; Clarke's criticism is mentioned but quickly dismissed as 'frivolous' (p. 18). More recently, the connection between Libera's design and St Louis's gate has been discussed by Jobst Welge in his essay on Fascist triumphal arches: 'Fascism *Triumphans*: On the Architectural Translation of Rome', in Lazzaro and Crum (eds.), *Donatello among the Blackshirts*, 83–94 (92–3).

## 10.2.1 The Modern-Language Teaching that Never Came

As we have seen, among the members of Mussolini's 1939 cabinet, Bottai was the most determined in his efforts to ensure that the regime prepared the country for its future role as an empire ruling over the Mediterranean. Benevolent post-war historians have seen his involvement of Italy's young intellectuals through *Primato* as indicative of a tolerant and open-minded approach. However, his diary and his determination to take the anti-Semitic legislation to its extreme consequences, give a different picture.[30]

First and foremost, Bottai was keen to show Mussolini his ultimate loyalty, and hopefully to regain his full trust after the humiliation of having been relieved of his position of Minister for the Corporations in 1932. His subsequent appointment as Governor of Rome had seemed to him a relegation, to which he preferred volunteering in the Italo-Ethiopian war. After his return he was appointed Minister of National Education, a position that, again, Bottai considered distant from the front line of government action. At the same time, as the most intellectually minded of all Fascist leaders, he set about adding his mark to Gentile's reform of Italy's education system. Bottai's Carta della scuola was approved by the Grand Council on 19 January 1939. The autarkic and imperial mood was reflected in Bottai's glorification of the Latin language as a most formative vehicle for the minds of the future ruling classes. It was the only foreign language to be taught in the Scuola media, the unified three years of school for all students who would attend a *liceo* and then university. At the same time, when it came to secondary schools, Bottai made it clear that he intended to give more emphasis to modern languages: 'the truth is that it is unthinkable to have a humanistic study entirely based on ancient values, without a similar commitment to the modern world.'[31]

One modern language had to be taught in all secondary schools. However, when it came to university courses, the only mention of a degree in modern languages involved students from the Magistrali schools (teacher-training schools, mainly attended by girls), who were given access to degree courses in Foreign Languages and Literatures taught in the faculties of Economics, not Humanities.[32] Apart from women being once more singled out as the intended recipients of the study of modern languages, the concept that the subject should be taught in an Economics faculty demonstrates Bottai's interest in languages' connection to the world of commerce. In the end, it took Bottai more than a year to turn the Carta into a decree, submitted on 1 July 1940, by which time Italy had entered the war, and so most of Bottai's reforms were never implemented. The new programmes

---

[30] On the reaction to the anti-Semitic legislation in Italy's academic and government circles—including Bottai's—see Roberto Finzi, 'La cultura italiana e le leggi antiebraiche del 1938', *Studi storici*, 49/4 (2008), 895–929.
[31] Giuseppe Bottai, *Carta della scuola* (Milan: Mondadori, 1939), 43 (point XI of the Carta).
[32] Bottai, *Carta della scuola*, 88.

for secondary schools were presented in April 1942 but never adopted. At least two universities, however, created modern-languages degree courses inside their Economics department: Padua and Pisa, whose courses continued well into the post-war years.[33]

If Bottai's reform of Italy's school system was overtaken by other, more pressing matters during the war years, the publication of the Carta della scuola coincided with an autarkic and philo-German turn. Since 1934, a monthly journal called *Le Lingue estere* had fostered discussion of the pedagogy and techniques of foreign-language teaching, aimed principally at independent language schools. Published in Milan and founded by Bruno Galzigna, a D'Annunzian nationalist, there was no doubt about the political leaning of the publication. A recent study of this journal identifies 1938 as the key year during which the journal adopted a pro-German approach that remained dominant until the journal's temporary suspension in 1943–5. *Le Lingue estere* began to devote article after article to the teaching of German and to the theories of German linguists in defence of the purity of their language. This tendency peaked in the March 1941 issue, in which a chart allegedly showing the relative importance of all major European languages presented German as the most prestigious. English was third, and French—fresh from the country's military defeat—was a distant fifth.[34]

But how realistic was the aspiration that German should become more important in Italy's school curricula? Even a partial increase of German teaching in state secondary schools would have been very difficult to achieve in the short term, since the Italian educational system produced insufficient numbers of German teachers. Fascist leaders involved in education, if nothing else, seemed to be aware of the problem. The pact of cultural collaboration between Fascist Italy and Nazi Germany signed by foreign ministers Galeazzo Ciano and Georg von Mackensen on 23 November 1938—preceding by a few months the militarily and economically binding Steel Pact of 22 May 1939—was a clear sign of political will. Bottai and Alfieri were at Ciano's side during the ceremony. However, in the long article signed by none other than Alessandro Pavolini, which occupied three-quarters of the *Corriere della Sera*'s front page the following day, the future Minister of Popular Culture specified that, in the field of German teaching in Italian secondary schools, the target was to make it equal to that of English (whereas Germany's commitment was to make Italian equal to French in the teaching of Romance

---

[33] Modern Languages were available as a degree course in some Faculties of Letters and Philosophy, but it is indicative that Bottai's Carta made no mention of this. The creation of such courses within Economics was probably designed to allow Magistrali students to go to university to study languages, while at the same time keeping them separate from students coming from Licei. On this, see Stefano Rapisarda, 'A proposito dello studio delle lingue straniere in epoca fascista', *Le Forme e la storia*, 8/1–2 (2015), 705–14.

[34] Valentina Russo, *Le lingue estere: Storia, linguistica e ideologia nell'Italia fascista* (Rome: Aracne, 2013), 65. For a comparison between the linguistic policies of, respectively, the Fascist and the Nazi regimes, see Gabriella Klein, *La politica linguistica del fascismo* (Bologna: Il Mulino, 1986), 143–57.

languages). It was a realistic and, after all, easily achievable target, since the teaching of English in secondary schools was still very limited.[35]

The year 1939 also saw the birth of another linguistics journal open to a readership of non-specialists, but of a much higher calibre than *Lingue estere*. This was *Lingua nostra*, directed by Bruno Migliorini and Giacomo Devoto, with the editorial help of Federico Gentile (son of Giovanni Gentile, who controlled Sansoni, the journal's publisher). Migliorini had recently returned to Italy to take the newly created chair of the History of the Italian Language at Florence University. Bottai had supported both the creation of the chair and Migliorini's appointment and, indeed, had asked Migliorini to contribute to his *Critica fascista* with a number of articles published in 1937-8. Thanks to the scholarly and apolitical approach of Devoto and Migliorini—which came to be defined as *neo-purismo*—*Lingua nostra* provided a moderate approach to the xenophobic wave that had been sweeping both through the Italian press and among scholars attached to the Accademia d'Italia. The latter had been given the task by *Il Duce* of creating the definitive vocabulary of the Italian language. American-English neologisms were among their favourite targets.

This 'purist' turn resulted in a series of government decrees, which ranged from prohibiting the use of foreign words in naming public places (December 1938), to prohibiting the use of foreign names for Italian children (July 1939), to prohibiting the use of foreign names for any commercial or professional activity (December 1940). At the same time, lists of foreignisms to be converted were published regularly by the Accademia d'Italia, and in June 1943, just before the fall of the regime, Paolo Monelli published his new edition of *Barbari domini*, containing an annotated list of 650 foreignisms that had been unnecessarily absorbed by the Italian language. Suggested replacements included *coda di gallo* for 'cocktail', which did not last, or *bistecca* for 'beefsteak', which did, and others that existed alongside the foreignism in later years, such as *pugile* for 'boxer'.[36]

The practice of Italianizing first names of foreign personalities—Guglielmo Shakespeare most famously—even extended to the surname of American musicians, when, after 1939, the restrictions on foreign music gave radio programmers and jazz bands inspiration for memorable names such as Luigi Braccioforte (Louis Armstrong), Beniamino Buonuomo (Benny Goodman), and a Latin-American-sounding Carmelito for Hoagy Carmichael. Classics of American early jazz continued their life with Italian titles, such as 'St Louis Blues', which became

---

[35] Alessandro Pavolini, 'Politica della cultura', *Corriere della Sera*, 24 November 1938, p. 1.
[36] On this, see Virginia Pulcini, 'The English Language and Anglo-American Culture in Twentieth Century Italy'; and Massimo Fanfani, 'A Century of Americanisms', both in Bonsaver, Carlucci and Reza (eds.), *Italy and the USA*, 31-46, 232-45. In Italian, see Klein, *La politica linguistica del fascismo*, 113-41. On *Lingua nostra*, see Massimo Fanfani, 'La prima stagione di *Lingua nostra*', in Matteo Santipolo and Matteo Viale (eds.), *Bruno Migliorini, l'uomo e il linguista* (Rovigo: Accademia dei Concordi, 2009), 25-96.

'Le tristezze di San Luigi', as famously sung by the Trio Lescano. There were also attempts at the Italianization of the word 'jazz', but even the two alternatives apparently popular in Tuscany, of *gez* and *gezze*, never took root.[37]

Giuseppe Bottai resisted this xenophobic craze. In February 1942, when presenting future school programmes for 1943–4 to school authorities and publishers, he commented on his decision that Italian secondary-school students should study not one but two modern languages. It was a bold initiative that would have revolutionized Gentile's reform of 1923. It would also have allowed a long-term realignment of the relative importance of French, English, and German, most likely to the advantage of German. However, as the world war entered its final phase, it remained the expression of a wish that was never fulfilled.[38]

After the war, Italy's educational system retained Gentile's reform, improved by Bottai's unification of the three years of junior secondary schools. As for modern languages, if the fiasco of Gentile's *Licei femminili* and Bottai's policies—however blocked by the war—signalled the need for a new approach, in practice very little changed. Beyond a small dose of French in the *Licei classici*, and the increasing importance of the *Licei scientifici*, where English found more space, modern languages continued to be taught mainly to girls, this time in private *Licei linguistici* run by religious orders.

As for Bottai, in the early hours of 25 July 1943, at the last meeting of Fascism's Grand Council, he had voted in favour of the motion to deprive Mussolini of the command of the army. By the evening, the vote had triggered the implosion of the regime, and Bottai went underground, hid in Rome, and managed to escape the wrath of his former fellow Fascists when Mussolini's regime was reinstated. Once the capital was occupied by the Allied forces in June 1944, Bottai fled to Algeria, where he joined the French Foreign Legion under the name André Bataille. Following the amnesty of November 1947, Bottai eventually returned to Italy, where he spent his last years writing for *abc*, a political magazine he founded in Rome in 1953.

### 10.2.2 Fascism's Last Stand against American Literature

If from language we move to the literary field, a first consideration concerns the impact of the 'anti-bourgeois' turn of 1938 on the publication of foreign literature, and on American fiction in particular. As we have seen in previous chapters,

---

[37] See Anna Tonelli, 'La "sana musica italiana". Divieti e censure fasciste contro jazz e fox-trot', *Storia e problemi contemporanei*, 28 (2001), 17–31.

[38] On Bottai's presentation of the new programmes for 1943–4, see Agostino Severino, 'I nuovi programmi per l'insegnamento delle lingue straniere', *Le Lingue estere*, 9/4 (1942), 84–5; and anon., 'Bottai dà le direttive per i nuovi testi scolastici', *Corriere della Sera*, 19 February 1942, p. 3. More generally, on the development of Bottai's position towards Nazi Germany, see Nicola D'Elia, *Giuseppe Bottai e la Germania nazista: I rapporti italo-tedeschi e la politica culturale fascista* (Rome: Carocci, 2009).

by the late-1930s the popularity of American literature was widespread, from cheap paperbacks bought in newspaper kiosks to sophisticated hardback series sold in high-street bookshops. The head of the press and publishing directorate at the Ministry of Popular Culture was then Gherardo Casini, a Tuscan journalist and militant Fascist who co-edited *Critica fascista* with Bottai. Casini was considered a rather benign figure—one who was reasonable and always ready to consider the needs of the publishing industry. This was a welcome situation for Italian publishers, particularly after the 26 March 1938 circular that formalized the full centralization of the government's control on translations. From 1 April, no translation could be published without previous authorization by Casini's directorate. Was this the beginning of a xenophobic purge? There is little doubt that Casini was keen to use his powers to favour the publication of Italian literature and limit what he had termed in a letter of 3 February 1938 Italy's 'persistent subjection to certain foreign cultures'.[39] The correspondence by Mondadori and Bompiani with their respective editors in charge of foreign translation suggests an increased difficulty in receiving the ministry's authorization. It is not the case that the publication of foreign books came to a halt, though; quite the opposite. Ferme's chart of translations published during the Fascist period shows that 1940 was the year with the highest number of translations of American literature: fifty four, which was only equalled in 1930, but with a smaller number of authors then, seventeen in 1930 versus twenty-two in 1940.[40] Numbers obviously dropped substantially with the declaration of war in 1941, but the fact that the Italian publishing industry was allowed to keep to its customary levels of translations from English in 1939 and 1940 confirms the perception of Casini's office as not being particularly draconian in its approach.

One should also take into account the impact of the anti-Semitic legislation. The so-called book reclamation that followed the legislation in the late autumn had the perverse effect of diverting attention from the issue of foreign publications. It also confused matters. Keen as ever to show his determination, as early as 12 August 1938 Bottai had already surprised all school authorities by sending an order that all textbooks authored by Jews should be withdrawn in view of the upcoming new school year. Only, how were the authorities supposed to know the religious faith of their textbooks' authors? Two weeks later Bottai had to eat his words and send a second circular telling them to hold off until a list of Jewish authors had been compiled. The list of more than nine hundred names of 'unwelcome authors', the vast majority being Jews, was eventually circulated only in April 1942. This means that, for more than three years, the situation remained one of uncertainty, with a sense of an emergency taking place and at the same time the possibility of continuing normal dealings between publishers and

---

[39] Quoted in Fabre, *L'elenco*, 67.  [40] Ferme, *Tradurre è tradire*, 227.

government as much as possible. Different subcommissions coordinated by Alfieri's Ministry of Popular Culture were supposed to look at the 'reclamation' of different sectors of the Italian publishing industry, and, in practice, their respective speeds in formulating a position were the determining factor behind the delivery of this policy.

Casini described the *bonifica* with these rhetorical words: 'to adjust literature and art, on the one hand, and the culture of the people and the young, on the other, to the aspirations of the new Italian soul and to the needs of Fascist ethics.'[41] It was a rather vacuous way of dressing up an order by Mussolini, who had single-handedly cancelled five years of Fascism's supposedly more sophisticated approach to cultural policies vis-à-vis their Nazi allies. Race had become a yardstick through which to measure the value of art and literature. More barbarously, it was a yardstick used to measure not just artefacts, but people. All publishing houses were asked to get rid not just of all their publications authored by Jews, but equally of all staff of Jewish origin, editors and translators included.

As far as foreign publications were concerned, the sector that, already by November 1938, seemed ready for 'reclamation' was that of children's literature. At the end of a conference held in Bologna in November 1938, surprisingly presided over by Marinetti, the concluding statement committed the sector to the 'total exclusion of all foreign importation, both in terms of written and illustrated material and in terms of spirit'.[42] By May 1939, Alfieri could boast that in that sector the defence of Italy's youth from pernicious foreign influence had been accomplished. We will not dwell here on the humiliating and hypocritical consequences of this purge, since it did not target American literature in a significant way.

More generally, translations became central to the *bonifica* once Pavolini had been installed at the head of the Ministry of Popular Culture. A few months after the war had broken out, the new minister expressed his intention to impose a limit on translations similar to that in the cinema sector. The initial proposal of a draconian quota of 10 per cent of translations for every 90 per cent of Italian publications was counter-argued by the publishing industry, strategically delayed with promises for data to be collected—possibly with the complicit involvement of Casini—and eventually adjusted, with a settlement for a more lenient quota of 25 per cent (one translation for every three Italian books). By that time it was the spring of 1942, and, once again, it is easy to imagine how limited its effect was. Other signals allow us to understand that exceptions and favours were made along the way, particularly in a sector that saw many translations from American

---

[41] Report by Casini to Alfieri on the first meeting of the central commissions of 13 September 1938; quoted in Rundle, *Publishing Translations in Fascist Italy*, 172. On the *bonifica libraria*, see Fabre's detailed monograph, *L'elenco*. In English, see Bonsaver, *Censorship and Literature in Fascist Italy*, 169–220, and Rundle, *Publishing Translations in Fascist Italy*, 165–206.

[42] See Fabre, *L'elenco*, 187–9.

novels. Mondadori's popular 'Gialli' series was excluded from any calculation, since it was bizarrely categorized as a periodical. Because of this, Mondadori had rarely bothered to ask for authorization to publish (a situation that was formalized only in March 1941). Unsurprisingly, the Florentine publisher Nerbini, whom we met in Chapter 7 as a keen competitor of Mondadori in the field of comic books, decided to emulate their Milanese arch-rival in the field of crime fiction and in 1940 created a crime fiction series unashamedly called 'I romanzi dal disco giallo'. Their covers closely resembled those of the Mondadori's 'Gialli' series, featuring novels by American authors such as Dashiell Hammett, Carolyn Wells, and British-expat Edgard Wallace. Nerbini's way to keep the authorities at bay was to alternate an Italian author for every foreign one, hence adopting a self-made quota of 50 per cent. A very similar strategy was adopted by the newly formed publishing house Alpe (founded in Milan in 1939), whose series 'I nuovi gialli' rode the wave of Mondadori's successful leadership, publishing nineteen novels between 1940 and 1941, only two of which had been written by an Italian. The fact that both Nerbini and Alpe started a crime-fiction series based heavily on American authors in 1940 clearly indicates that, at least within the sector of cheap paperbacks, the *bonifica* was far from the strict purge it was purported to be. The axe on paperback crime fiction fell only in July 1941 with the announcement by Casini's directorate that all publications of such books had to stop. Mondadori and Alpe complied with the directive, but, intriguingly, Nerbini did not. Their *Romanzi del disco giallo* continued to be published. They were finally listed in the total ban on crime fiction that was introduced in April 1943. By then, Fascist Italy was on the verge of collapse, and indeed Italian libraries hold copies of Nerbini's 'Gialli', which were published right up until July 1943.[43]

When it comes to American literature during the war years, the most frequently discussed case is that of Vittorini's anthology of American fiction, *Americana*. As Bompiani's chief editor for foreign literature, Vittorini had already supervised similar anthologies of German and Spanish literature. The American anthology, however, was his own product, on which he had been working since 1939. By the time the volume was ready to be submitted to Casini's directorate for his approval, the political situation had taken a turn. Vittorini had to rely on his good relationship with the new minister, Pavolini. The two had been on good terms since Vittorini's contributions to *Il Bargello*, the Florentine Fascist weekly that Pavolini had founded in 1929. When Bompiani discussed the publication of the American anthology directly with Pavolini and received a cold reply, the next move was to plan a meeting between Pavolini and Vittorini himself. The latter travelled to Rome, and the two met in December 1940. Pavolini appreciated both the visit and the proofs of the book, which Vittorini had brought with him in order to add

---

[43] On the last raft of directives against crime fiction, see Rundle, *Publishing Translations in Fascist Italy*, 190–7. On Alpe, see Patrizia Grazia, *Editori a Milano (1900–1945)* (Milan: Franco Angeli, 2013), 37–9.

weight to the issue of the financial damage that a last-minute withdrawal for the hefty volume would cause. However, Pavolini was not moved. After the meeting, he wrote to Bompiani to reiterate the fact that the time was not right for a prestigious publication to be devoted to a country that was wholeheartedly supporting Italy's war enemies. Bompiani did not give up; he continued to try to convince Pavolini to lift the ban or compensate him for the financial loss (which Pavolini had offered to do on a different occasion). In the end, a compromise was found. Pavolini was ready to give his *imprimatur* following Bompiani's proposal to replace the introductory comments by Vittorini with a general introduction by Emilio Cecchi (who had been appointed to the Accademia d'Italia in May 1940). Cecchi, in other words, had been tasked with doctoring the literary slant of the volume, so that American fiction could be discussed as a representation of America's debatable cultural and social mores.

The *Americana* episode is emblematic of the place of American literature in the last years of the regime from both a political and a literary viewpoint. Politically, it showed that the regime's de-Americanization of the book sector was a rather convoluted affair. Given that it took more than a year for Bompiani to obtain the go ahead, it is even possible that Mussolini might have been consulted on the matter. Alfieri would almost certainly have done so. As far as we know, Pavolini too, on at least one occasion, had had the humiliating experience of having to bow to the will of *Il Duce*. It had happened in June 1940, when the minister decided to use the scarcity of paper as an excuse to close down Croce's historic journal *La Critica*. His publisher, Giovanni Laterza, knew Mussolini's wish to show the world his tolerance towards the greatest intellectual of pre-Fascist Italy, so he complained directly to Mussolini, who immediately ordered Pavolini to revoke his decision.

*Americana* eventually reached the bookshops in December 1942, in time to benefit from the traditional boost of Christmas sales. By the following January, Bompiani was already able to proceed to its second print run. The volume did not trigger any particularly negative reaction in the press. In May 1943, Vittorini and Bompiani commented with some relief on a benevolent review by poet and critic Ezra Pound, who by then was living in the coastal town of Rapallo, near Genoa, fully committed to supporting the Axis cause. At the same time, Bompiani warned Vittorini that Pound's review was potentially dangerous, since it focused political attention on the book. The cause of its fall from grace, however, came in the shape of an anonymous complaint dated 26 June 1943, which reached the Ministry of Popular Culture. The attack was not just aimed at *Americana*; it expressed the author's outrage at the fact that, while Italy suffered allied bombing, publishers such as Bompiani and Mondadori were allowed to continue to circulate in translation American and British books that had 'contributed to "educating" our youth about American frivolity and immorality'. By then, Casini had been replaced by his former deputy and hardliner Fernando Mezzasoma (who was to become

Minister of Popular Culture in Mussolini's Nazi-monitored government of 1943–5); and Pavolini had been replaced as minister by the old militant Gaetano Polverelli in Mussolini's final, desperate government reshuffle of February 1943. The anonymous note triggered Polverelli's rage and received the approval of Mussolini, who scribbled 'Yes, it is time to end this' in a handwritten note of approval. This was happening on the eve of the Allied invasion of Sicily and of the eventual implosion of the regime on 24 July, so it is probable that Polverelli's decision to have the book removed from all Italian bookshops was lost in the chaos of the impending collapse. Indeed, *Americana* was still advertised in the back of Bompiani's books as late as February 1944.[44]

To wrap up these comments on the political importance of the *Americana* case, one could argue that a climate of moderate tolerance of American fiction persisted even during the war years. The ban on paperback publications of July 1941 limited its visual presence in newspaper kiosks and market stalls, but at the same time it allowed high-street publishers such as Bompiani and Mondadori to continue to benefit from the popularity of American literature. In his introduction to a post-war reprint of the original volume of *Americana*, Claudio Gorlier offers some sales figures that speak for themselves: the first print of Steinbeck's *Uomini e topi* (*Of Mice and Men*) and *Il pian della Tortilla* (*Tortilla Flat*), published respectively in 1938 and 1939 by Bompiani (and translated by Pavese and Vittorini), went on throughout the war years to, respectively, forty-six and forty reprints, with totals of 238,000 and 256,000 copies sold. No Italian book at the time could remotely compete with those figures. From this came the insistence with which publishers justified their need to continue to publish American fiction in order to be able to use those profits to promote less popular Italian publications. It was, after all, a pragmatic approach that ruled Fascist policies. The publishing industry and Italian literature had to be supported, and, if this meant showing tolerance towards the American 'craze', so be it.[45]

From a literary viewpoint, *Americana* left a mark of a different type. Gorlier sees it as an attempt by Vittorini to present a personal vision of American literature entirely emancipated from French cultural discourse. Umberto Eco defined it as a 'pure intertextual dreamlike vision'. Others saw modernity in the way it used photographs attached to the text as a parallel narrative, which resembled the style of Longanesi's *Omnibus* (in which Vittorini published articles on American literature). The photographs also reinforce the decision to move away from a typical representation of both American modernity (there is not a single picture of a skyscraper) and Hollywood glamour. They are equally distant from the

---

[44] The most recent account in English of *Americana*'s censorship can be found in Rundle, *Publishing Translations in Fascist Italy*, 197–205.

[45] Claudio Gorlier, 'L'alternativa americana', in Elio Vittorini, *Americana: Raccolta di narratori* (Milan: Bompiani, 1984), pp. vii–xv (xi).

derisory depiction of some 'americanata' typical of illustrated magazines. The volume shows an everyday America, which appears in those photos, accompanied by lyrical captions that add to their visionary value. Vittorini's original comments to each section of the anthology add to this: American literature is seen as an example of a collective narrative of the everyday, of the ambitions and disillusionments of an entire people, forged in a realistic prose whose deliberate simplicity acts as a glue binding life and literature. As Pavese put it in his letter of 27 May 1942 in which he thanked Vittorini for having sent him an unbound copy of the original, uncensored volume:

> I think you'll be pleased to hear that we are all with you against Cecchi. His introduction is a felonious act—politically and critically—and all the merit and the sense of *Americana* depends on your notes. [...] Now, we must scream that they are enlightening exactly because they are narrative, a novel if you like, invention. [...] It is not by chance nor by prevarication that you start with your abstract furies, since their conclusion is, unsaid, your *Conversation in Sicily*. In this sense they are a great achievement: you brought in them the tension and the shrills of the discovery of *your own* poetic history, and since this history of yours was not a pipe dream but friction with world literature (that world literature which is implicit, in its universality, in the American one—have I understood well?), the result is that a century and a half of America is condensed in the essential evidence of a myth that we all shared and that you narrate to us.

Pavese had understood well. Vittorini's abstract furies (a cryptic, recurring expression in *Conversazione in Sicilia*) signalled the link between his discovery of American literature and his own literary production: it was less an emulation of the stylistic traits of American contemporary fiction than an attempt to forge a new social contract between a literary author and his readers. In this respect, *Americana* should be seen as the highest point of the appropriation of America by a generation of young Italian authors—Vittorini, but also Pavese and others—who saw it as a symbol of their own need to move to other ways of connecting their literary world with the social and political reality of their times.[46]

In his letter, Pavese used the expression *canagliesca* ('felonious') to define Cecchi's newly added introduction. It was a harsh, but ultimately accurate description. The visionary dimension of *Americana* was taken to pieces and softly ridiculed. Cecchi dismissed the interest in American literature in the very first paragraph of his introduction: 'signs of a fashion, even more of an infatuation, rather than the result of intelligence and taste'. Then it was the turn of Vittorini's 'narrative' approach, still evident despite the removal of all his comments. Cecchi commented

---

[46] Pavese's letter can be found in the second edition of *Il mestiere di vivere* (Turin: Einaudi, 1990), 238. Gorlier, 'L'alternativa americana', p. ix. Eco, 'Il modello americano', 11.

that a more philologically accurate edition, boring but useful, should be considered in a future reprint. As for the selection of contemporary authors: Jack London is overrated; Sinclair Lewis is absent, not just because he is a Jew, but because his work lacks depth; Hemingway is puzzlingly defined as 'a product of the shrewder impressionist culture from northern Europe, with probable Hispanic–Mexican grafts'. Finally, the worst consequence, in Cecchi's mind, was the deluge of imitations that the American craze had triggered among Italian fiction writers, of such bad quality that 'you don't know whether to laugh or cry about it'. The concluding comments take us back to the recurring critique of American society as barbarous: 'From one end of the anthology to the other, the spectacle of life which we is offered is tragic, horrendous. [...] a paganism of mere violence, lacking any trace of happiness.' The anthology's literary value, according to Cecchi, could be found in its sociological representation of America, so much so that Frank Norris's *A Deal in Wheat* (1903) should be considered akin to a financial handbook on speculation in America, and William Faulkner's *That Evening's Sun* (1931) 'says more on the obscenities of racial promiscuity [...] than the report of a lynching'. The reference to the 'obscenities of racial promiscuity' was a nod to Fascist Italy's racist spirit, which must have been welcome in government circles.[47]

A concluding note on the protagonists of the *Americana* case. In 1943 Cecchi made a further contribution to the anti-American, racist attitude with his collaboration on the scripting of *Harlem* (1943), Gallone's propaganda film, on which we will dwell later. After the collapse of the regime in July 1943, Cecchi remained in Rome and stayed there until the end of the war without taking any side. Vittorini, on the other hand, had allowed his growing anti-Fascism to become militant. After his short imprisonment as a Communist during Badoglio's stuttering interregnum in the summer of 1943, Vittorini went underground and eventually became responsible for the Milanese edition of *L'Unità* after the arrest and murder of its editor, Eugenio Curiel, on 24 February 1945. In those very last months of the war, in the same city, Pavolini experienced the inevitable end of his return to Fascism's violent roots as commander of the infamous Fascist paramilitary troops, the Brigate nere. He followed Mussolini in his final desperate attempt to reach Switzerland and was captured after running out of bullets on a rock in Lake Como. He was quickly sentenced to death by firing squad and eventually hanged upside down, together with Mussolini and others, from the roof of a disused petrol station in Milan. There, in Piazzale Loreto, fifteen partisans had been executed by the Fascists the year before and left there all day as a public warning. When it came to Mussolini's and Pavolini's fate, it is a tragic irony that this

---

[47] Cecchi, 'Introduzione', in the 1984 edition of Vittorini, *Americana*, 1037–52 (1052). On Cecchi and racist culture in interwar Italy, see Bruno Pischedda, *L'idioma molesto: Cecchi e la letteratura novecentesca a sfondo razziale* (Turin: Aragno, 2015).

dreadful spectacle should have been filmed by the cameraman of a US army unit freshly arrived in Milan.[48]

After the war, Cecchi returned to a position of pre-eminence in Italy's literary debate. His lack of collaboration with the Fascist regime in the agonizing period of the Social Republic of Italy and his initial opposition to the regime in 1925 when he had signed Croce's anti-Fascist intellectuals' manifesto guaranteed his safe reinstatement as a leading literary figure, one who was also involved in Italy's film industry. In 1947 he became an appointed member of the Accademia dei Lincei, the academy that regained its position as Italy's most prestigious historic academy (Mussolini's Royal Academy ceased to exist with the regime's fall). Bompiani, in the meantime, had published the original edition of *Americana*. Cecchi's introduction of 1942 was abandoned and forgotten, until the already mentioned edition of 1984 put it in an appendix as a historical memento. Pavese's comment too was left in darkness for decades. When, after his death in 1950, Einaudi produced the first edition of his diary entitled *Il mestiere di vivere* (1952), which contained the text of his letter to Vittorini, the line in which he criticized Cecchi was omitted. It became public only when the uncut version of Pavese's diary was republished in 1990.[49]

### 10.2.3 The End of American Comics (except Disney's)

The regime's crackdown on comics proceeded along similar lines to that on literature. On the one hand, the stiffening of the regime's cultural policies in 1938 triggered anti-American measures, and, on the other, there was the continuation of a pragmatic approach, open to tolerance and exceptions. The correspondence between the publishers' representatives and Guglielmo Emanuel, agent of the King Features Syndicate (KFS) in Italy, shows the degree to which all players counted on benevolent relations with the Ministry of Popular Culture in order to smooth out any resistance to American imports. However, already in the first months of 1938, there was a collective perception that the situation was worsening.

In April 1938, Mondadori decided to drop their exclusive right to the KFS comic strip 'King of the Royal Mounted', justifying it to Emanuel as in line with the 'wishes of the Ministry of Popular Culture, which tends to de-Americanize the character of children's magazines'. The expression 'wishes' instead of 'orders'

---

[48] The documentary footage was shown on Italian national television only in 1994. On the public debate sparked by the event, see Robert A. Ventresca, 'Mussolini's Ghost: Italy's *Duce* in History and Memory', *History and Memory*, 18/1 (2006), 86–119.

[49] See Pavese's diary entry for 27 May 1942 (p. 217 in the 1952 version, and p. 238 in the 1990 one). The same omission is present in the 1966 collection of Pavese's correspondence published by Einaudi. In English, the letter has been translated in the cut version in Cesare Pavese, *Selected Letters 1924–1950* (London: Peter Owen, 1969), 217.

or 'directives' is somehow emblematic of the relative flexibility of the system in previous years. The tune, however, seems suddenly to have changed when, on 19 July 1938, Alfieri sent a circular to all publishers peremptorily giving them three months to purge all imported American comics from their publications. If fully implemented, such a directive would have brought many publications to a grinding halt, with Mondadori's *Topolino* in prime position. Alfieri began to come under gentle pressure from different directions: from the American embassy to Arnoldo Mondadori knocking at Mussolini's office door. Before three months had passed Alfieri was already taking a more tolerant line. By September, Vecchi was able to boast that the minister had agreed to allow his publications to contain up to 30 per cent of imported material.[50]

Arnoldo Mondadori, as usual, managed to get one over all his competitors. As we have seen, having a direct line with Mussolini was a privilege the publisher never tired of using. His large investment in the Edizioni Walt Disney–Mondadori required swift and resolute action. When the commission for the *bonifica* first met on 13 September 1938, the question of children's literature was part of the agenda. This potentially included comics too, an industry that by then had reached enormous proportions. According to an official estimate by Casini, the weekly circulation of comics magazines had risen to 1,600,000 copies. No draconian decision had yet be taken, but, two months later, at the already mentioned conference on children's literature, Marinetti (who was also a member of the *bonifica* commission) came to the conclusion that Italian children had to be saved from any foreign influence. A week later, Alfieri circulated yet another declaration of inflexible resolution, but this time with an important caveat:

> Full abolition of all the imported material from abroad, with the exception of Walt Disney's creations, which distinguish themselves for their artistic value and for their substantial morality, and suppression of all those stories and illustrations which are inspired by foreign production.

In his correspondence preceding this circular, Alfieri made it clear that the order behind this exception had come directly from Mussolini.[51]

---

[50] The quotation comes from a letter by Cesare Civita (Mondadori) to Guglielmo Emanuel, dated 19 April 1938; quoted in Gadducci, Gori, and Lama, *Eccetto Topolino*, 163; on Alfieri's directive and, more generally, the comics industry's reaction to the worsening of the situation in 1938, see pp. 149–77. See also Mazzarini, 'Storia "non breve né facile"'.

[51] Circular of 16 November 1938; quoted in Gadducci, Gori, and Lama, *Eccetto Topolino*, 187. On *Il Duce*'s involvement, see Mazzarini, 'Storia "non breve né facile"', 38; and Gadducci, Gori, and Lama, *Eccetto Topolino*, 192–200. On the critique of American comics at the Bologna conference, see Meda, *Stelle e strips*, 117–31; and Caterina Sinibaldi, 'Dangerous Children and Children in Danger: Reading American Comics under the Italian Fascist Regime', in Christopher Kelen and Björn Sundmark (eds), *The National in Children's Literature: Nations of Childhood* (New York and London: Routledge, 2012), 53–67 (62–64).

Given that Mondadori had exclusive rights to most of Disney's printed production, it is not difficult to imagine the level of scorn triggered by this directive. Nerbini made an explicit, malignant reference to 'exceptions' in a note to the readers of *L'Avventuroso*, when the magazine was free-falling towards its eventual takeover by Mondadori. The circular was also a double-whammy for most publishers, since it suggested that even Italian productions could be banned if 'too-America-inspired'. Arnoldo Mondadori proved once again to be perfectly equipped to weather the storm. Instead of lamenting the loss of American superheroes, Mondadori turned the restriction into an occasion for welcoming the introduction of new stories based on Italian characters: from the young Venetian noble Daniele Marchi, and his German friend Franz Schmidt, to the army officer Capitano Giorgio Cannonieri, whose adventures were based on an autobiographical novel by the same Giorgio Cannonieri about his experience in Ethiopia (unsurprisingly published by Mondadori). Even better, Alessandrini's film *Luciano Serra pilota* (1938) was turned into a comic strip drawn by Mondadori's most gifted artist, Walter Molino. Vittorio Mussolini's supervision of the film was mentioned in capital letters on the comic's header.[52]

As for the potential suppression of comics invented in Italy but inspired by American models, a number of exceptions, again, were allowed. By the end of 1938, Vecchi had decided to move out of the comics business and allowed Mondadori to take over his popular magazine, *L'Audace*. Its arrival completed Mondadori's portfolio with a magazine specifically targeted at adolescents. *L'Audace* contained a comic strip of clear American derivation that survived the censorial axe: as the title suggests, *Sulle frontiere del Far-West* was set in the American Wild West. However, as the header specified, the title was also a homage to the homonymous first novel of Emilio Salgari's western trilogy (published in 1908–10); the comics could therefore be defended as the creation of Italian artists based on an Italian source, despite the setting.

Beyond such exceptions, pressure to replace American comics with in-house productions gave a strong incentive to Italian artists—surely a welcome outcome in the eyes of the regime. A small publishing house in Milan, Vittoria, responded with the creation of an Italian American character who proved popular for years to come: Dick Fulmine. If the film *Joe il rosso* (1936) had addressed the taboo topic of the Italian American mafia through a character with a vague Irish connection, Dick Fulmine presented an even better solution: forget about Italian American crime, Fulmine was an Italian American cop from Chicago, fighting criminals who embodied the racial varieties that the regime expected to fight: first among them the black Cuban Zambo and the 'sordid Jew' Abramo Levi. Fulmine's fellow Italian Americans were honest, innocent victims. The character

---

[52] Giorgio Cannonieri, *La mia avventura tra gli Arussi* (Milan: Mondadori, 1937). On both Cannonieri and *Luciano Serra pilota*, see Gadducci, Gori, and Lama, *Eccetto Topolino*, 285–7.

first appeared in March 1938. According to its creator, Carlo Crossio, it was based on the face of Gary Cooper with an added prominent jaw, which Cossio attributed to himself but which everybody else connected with Italy's most famous prominent jaw at the time, that of *Il Duce*.[53] The final touch was a gigantic body inspired by Italy's most famous boxer at the time, whom we have already met: Primo Carnera. Unusually for a policeman, Dick Fulmine mainly fought with his fists. He was a boisterous character prone to move from words to punches, whose ironic call before a fight—'Fatevi sotto, piccioncini miei!' ('Come on down, my little pigeons')—was more reminiscent of a Fascist *squadrista* than of an American cop. Fulmine's surname, Pestalozzi, confirmed the parallel (*pestare* being a colloquialism for 'beating up'). During the war years, the character of Dick Fulmine developed in line with the times. His American first name was dropped, so that he became to be known just as Fulmine. Then, unlike his historical fellow Italian Americans—who did not cross the ocean to enlist in the Fascist army—Fulmine joined the war effort and appeared as an Italian soldier. The character was so popular that his stories continued to be published after the war, well into the 1950s, when he returned to his original name, Dick Fulmine, and his enemies stopped resembling racial types.

In the end, the relative success of Alfieri's draconian directives brought the new minister, Pavolini, to summon all publishers involved in the publication of comics in November 1941. He informed them that the time had come to rid their periodicals of American material entirely. Then, the following month, a new directive addressed the American style of all comics: the use of speech balloons was prohibited. From the following year, all Italian comics, imported or not, had to return to the old tradition of placing any speech or caption below the illustration. Arnoldo Mondadori fought back and was once again successful. He sent a letter to Pavolini on 11 December 1941—ironically on the very day on which Italy declared war with the USA—in which he thanked him for allowing him to continue the publication of Disney comics in *Topolino*.[54]

The situation, however, kept worsening. The need to face the progressive scarcity of paper during the war years meant a cut of about 50 per cent of children's periodicals. By May 1942, it was Pavolini's turn to announce to the Fascist parliament that a complete purge of American comic strips had been achieved. This time, Mondadori's space for manoeuvre had been reduced to the absolute minimum. He was forced to replace Disney's Micky Mouse with an unappealing anthropomorphic equivalent called Tuffolino. The only concession was that he was allowed to keep the masthead 'Topolino'.

[53] Claudio Carabba, *Il fascismo a fumetti* (Rimini: Guaraldi, 1973), 53–6. On Dick Fulmine, see also Becciu, *Il fumetto in Italia*, 109–11; and Claudio Bertieri, 'Fumetto & moschetto: I comics italiani di guerra', in Mino Argentieri, *Schermi di guerra: Cinema italiano 1939–1943* (Rome: Bulzoni, 1995), 201–38.

[54] Forgacs and Gundle, *Mass Culture and Italian Society*, 115.

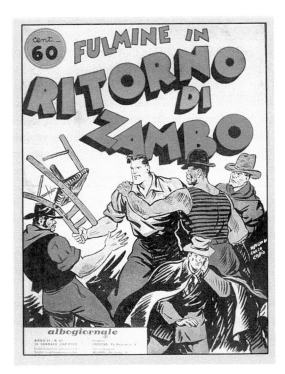

**Fig. 10.10.** Cover of a 1940 album dedicated to Fulmine, published by Vittoria. (courtesy of giornalepop.it)

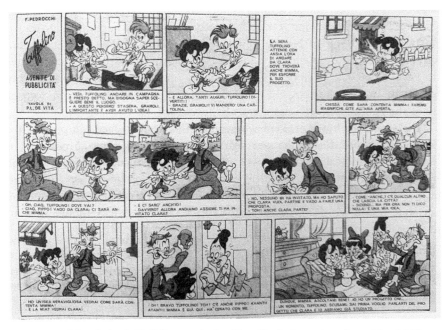

**Fig. 10.11.** Mondadori's Tuffolino replacing Topolino's characters, from May 1942, with anthropomorphic equivalents of Mickey Mouse, Goofy, and Minnie. (courtesy of Donald at annitrenta.blogspot.com)

A final note takes us to a contemporary novel by Umberto Eco. In his autobiographical *La misteriosa fiamma della regina Loana* (2004), a large part of the protagonist's recollection of his childhood in Fascist Italy—Eco was born in 1932—is devoted to his love of American comics. The novel also contains vivid colour reproductions of the front cover and internal details of books and magazines. Among them there is the front page of a Nerbini illustrated story magazine, *Buffalo-Bill: L'Eroe del Wild West*. This series was based on *The Buffalo Bill Stories* created back at the start of the century and translated into many different languages. But Eco refers to a particular series, published in 1942, in which Nerbini, evidently in a last attempt to avoid the censor's axe, adopted the metropolitan legend of the Italian origin of Buffalo Bill. The legend is somehow related to an Italian migrant who amassed a fortune in Philadelphia, first in the fur trade and then in banking. His name was Domenico Tambini, and in his later years he happened to meet and become a friend, and banker, of William 'Buffalo Bill' Cody. From then on, the fame of the latter was sometimes confused with the Italian origin and the past as a hunter of the former. At least this is what happened to some Italian journalists. The fact that Tambini came from Faenza, a small town in Romagna, Mussolini's home region, added interest to this story during the Fascist period. In any case, Nerbini's last-minute 'de-Americanization' of Buffalo Bill—through an illustration in which Buffalo Bill himself reveals his Italian identity as Domenico Tambini, from Faenza—was not successful. The magazine was suppressed. Once more, no other publisher seemed to be as successful as Mondadori in bending the regime's directives to his own interests.[55]

Mention of Nerbini's case in Eco's novel prompts us to examine how Eco depicts the influence of American comics in the development of the social conscience of a young boy growing up in the final years of Fascism. The fictionalization of the protagonist's encounter with American comics had already found an earlier theorization in an essay by Eco written more than twenty years earlier. In 'Il modello americano', Eco wrote of the influence of various superheroes—from Flash Gordon, to Mandrake and even Mickey Mouse—as examples of individuals who were fighting against tyranny, corruption, and intolerance, and as such provided Eco's generation with models that were certainly non-Fascist, and potentially even anti-Fascist. But was that really the case? Cultural historian Natasha C. Chang has recently taken Eco to task in an essay that identifies an implicit revisionist content in Eco's position. In her view, the emphasis on American comics produces two facile assumptions: first, that Fascist propaganda was entirely neutralized by the counterculture of American imports; secondly, that those young individuals, like Eco, who were fascinated by American comics

---

[55] A biographical study by a local historian has recently been devoted to the figure of Domenico Tambini: Bruno Fabbri, *Buffalo Bill di Romagna: Storia di Domenico Tambini e della sua misteriosa eredità* (Poggio Rusco: MnM, 2020). The reproduction of Buffalo Bill's 'revelation' of his Italianness in Nerbini's comic appears on p. 156.

developed—whether consciously or not—an anti-Fascist stance that allowed them to resist the influence of the regime's propaganda. The dangerous consequence of all this, according to Chang, is that we fall into the revisionist trap of treating Fascism as a 'second rate dictatorship', farcical more than deadly.[56] This refers in particular to a concluding thought by the protagonist of Eco's novel:

> Curious, I said to myself, falling asleep over Buffalo Bill's latest adventure: I was raised on adventure stories that had come from France and America; but had then been naturalized. If this was the nationalistic education that a boy received under the dictatorship, it was a fairly mild one.[57]

Eco would certainly have been horrified at the idea of being labelled a revisionist. And Chang's final opposition between contemporary historians who struggle to unveil Italy's Fascist past and those like Eco and others (Silvio Berlusconi is mentioned as part of this group) who somehow write Fascism away by implying that it was not such a deleterious regime after all is debatable. Where a point in defence of Eco needs to be made is that he is referring to the regime's failure to manipulate the circulation of comics, and not to Fascism as a political phenomenon. This is what distinguishes him from right-wing revisionists. At the same time, Chang is right to argue that the implicit anti-Fascist content of American comics is a topic to be treated with caution. What Fascist censorship no longer tolerated about American comics was the fact that they depicted non-Italian superheroes and distracted the youth from their duties and drills as young members of the Fascist state. And what young Italians loved about them was their cutting-edge modernity, in stylistic terms as much as in the treatment of the stories, whose protagonists lived through adventures set in exotic places and full of sensual encounters. Politically, one can argue that the individualistic lifestyle of most American comic heroes and their occasional fight against dictators from far away countries and planets was at loggerheads with Fascist ideology, whether it glorified the state against the individual, or *Il Duce*'s dictatorship against democracy. The extent to which young Italians reading those comics were aware of their political reverberations is a moot point. But they were certainly facing an exciting, imaginary world where the superheroes' arch-enemies were often war-obsessed dictators in uniform.

## 10.3 Broadcasting Jazz after the Last Autarkic Turn

American music—or, better, jazz—was another target identified by Fascist propagandists during the anti-bourgeois campaign of 1938. Mussolini's *Il Popolo d'Italia*

---

[56] Natasha V. Chang, 'Forgetting Fascism: Memory, History, and the Literary Text in Umberto Eco's *La misteriosa fiamma della regina Loana*', *Italian Culture*, 26/1 (2008), 105–32.
[57] Eco, *La misteriosa fiamma*, 145; trans. from the English edn, trans. Geoffrey Brock (London: Vintage Books, 2006), 144.

took an early lead in that year. On 4 March 1938, when the front and internal pages were still devoted to the recent death of Gabriele D'Annunzio, an anonymous article entitled 'Anche la musica costa quattrini' ('Even music costs money') and whose subheadline exploded in an 'Autarchia!', appeared in the page dedicated to news from Milan. A reader had sent in a letter of complaint about the fact that a prestigious Milanese dance hall, the Odeon, had two orchestras, both of which persevered in exclusively playing foreign music. The anonymous author fully concurred with the complaint and added that the impact of such practice was not just cultural but financial too, since royalties for the songs being played went to foreign companies. At the same time, the author surprisingly did not complain about jazz itself: 'With regard to dance music, Italy can boast several jazz composers who are not inferior to the Americans.' In other words, the popularity of the foxtrot and other jazz-related dances was by then considered an irreversible sign of the times. What was needed, just as for comics, was its 'de-Americanization' through the promotion of Italian producers and artefacts. The article triggered a campaign that in the following weeks and months became increasingly prominent in the pages of *Il Popolo d'Italia* as much as in other periodicals. On 7 February 1939, the newspaper could compliment itself for the result of its campaign for the Italianization of music: as the article announced, after months of pressure from the paper, and in line with the reforms within the film industry, foreign *musica leggera* had eventually been marginalized to 20 per cent of both sheet music publication and live performance.[58]

The tone of the discussion could also be more brutal. On 19 February 1939, *Il Popolo d'Italia*'s occasional page 3 column called 'La Radio' hosted a vitriolic, racist attack on Italian jazz musicians too. It claimed that the paper was still receiving hundreds of letters by young Italians complaining about xenophile music being broadcast that musicians 'devout of any fantasy or good taste compose along the lines of American congenital idiocy'. A few lines later, the author—who had already written in favour of the campaign on previous occasions—reminded readers that jazz music is 'one of the strongest and most precise Jewish weapons' aimed at killing the artistic taste of millions of Italians. It was a rhetorical attack, since the accusation remained vague and did not specify individuals, but, published in the regime's daily, it was nonetheless a threatening sign. It also indicated that the anti-Semitic legislation had added a distorting effect, whereby the clear connection with African American culture—and we saw in Chapter 8 how much it was used to vilify jazz music—had now been exchanged for the allegedly Jewish influence on jazz. If one leafs through the pages of *Il Popolo d'Italia*—or indeed of other Italian newspapers—printed in the months following the anti-Semitic legislation, it feels as

---

[58] Mauro Janni, 'Verso la realizzazione delle nostre proposte', *Il Popolo d'Italia*, 7 February 1939, p. 3. On the campaign against foreign music—mainly intended as American jazz—see Di Capua, *Faccetta nera*, 35–40.

if the peppering of anti-Semitic slurs, however elusive and groundless, was an expected ingredient whenever 'foreign' music was being criticized.[59]

EIAR's broadcasting schedules from early 1938 onwards show clearly how jazz music had been marginalized, despite the fact that syncopated rhythms continued to be part and parcel of dance-hall music and *musica leggera* programmes. By the time the war had broken out, any mention of foreign music and musicians was limited to countries within the sphere of the Axis powers. Italian jazz musicians had to exert caution and mediate discreetly. However, within those parameters, they were allowed to continue to work and even to reach the highest levels of popularity. The master in this game proved to be Alberto Rabagliati. We have already met him in Chapter 8 as a popular singer in 'Pippo' Barzizza's band. In October 1941, EIAR allowed him to have a late-evening programme in his own name, 'Canta Rabagliati', which, if nothing else, added further American glamour to his persona. A programme built entirely around a star singer was unheard of in Italy. Even more surprising was the fact that a programme such as this one should be created around a singer whose style and repertoire were based entirely on swinging, syncopated rhythms. Furthermore, the commercial sponsor of the programme was ENIC, the regime's controlled company, which in 1938 had been given full control of the distribution of films in Italy. It was a sponsor that in one stroke gave Rabagliati the safety of explicit government endorsement and the aura of a film star. How did he manage to achieve that?

The fact that his patron, 'Pippo' Barzizza—himself a jazz enthusiast—was by then head of EIAR's most important music ensemble, the Orchestra Cetra, certainly guaranteed Rabagliati a level of protection. The potential film career that Rabagliati was attempting to promote in those very months was another factor. Ten years after his failed try at becoming an actor in Hollywood, Rabagliati had returned to the world of cinema in 1940, this time essentially playing himself, a swinging, dance-hall singer. He featured in two musical films directed by Carlo Ludovico Bragaglia (and co-scripted by the ever-present Cesare Zavattini): first *Una famiglia impossibile* (1940) and then *La scuola dei timidi* (1941). The first of the two films was produced by Consorzio Cinematografico EIA, which, despite its Fascist-sounding acronym ("Eia Eia Alalà" was the war cry coined by D'Annunzio and later adopted by the Fascists), was a company with strong American connections: until 1938 it was responsible for the distribution in Italy of all films produced by Columbia Pictures, plus the ever-successful Disney cartoons and films. Both films

---

[59] Mauro Janni, 'La Radio – Musica leggera moderna', *Il Popolo d'Italia*, 19 February 1939, p. 3. The 'Semitic turn' was in line with Italy's Nazi ally, which considered jazz as part of the 'degenerate' culture fostered by Jewish intellectuals. At the same time, jazz proved to be useful when German broadcasting went on the offensive and produced propaganda channels aimed at listeners in enemy countries. Jazz was then considered a Trojan horse, and Nazi radio could boast its own American jazz orchestra. On this, see Will Studdert, *The Jazz War: Radio, Nazism and the Struggle for the Airwaves in World War II* (London: I. B. Tauris, 2017); and Horst J. P. Bergmeier and Rainer E. Lotz, *Hitler's Airwaves: The Inside Story of Nazi Radio Broadcasting and Propaganda Swing* (New Haven: Yale University Press, 1997).

Fig. 10.12. Detail from *Radiocorriere* containing the publicity of Rabagliati's solo programme, *Radiocorriere*, 17/48 (29 November 1941), 12. (courtesy of BNC, Florence)

with Rabagliati failed to become box-office hits, but one can imagine that the decision to create a radio programme entirely based around him was a strategy to develop a commercial synergy between film and music. The fact that it should have come with the publicized sponsorship of ENIC leaves no doubts as to the fact that, at least within the circles of ENIC's management, Rabagliati's jazzy style was not considered an embarrassment. Probably the contrary. A recent essay on Rabagliati returns to the question of how 'anti-Fascist' or 'non-Fascist' the content of Rabagliati's songs was, particularly the self-ironic 'Quando canta Rabagliati' (1941), in which there is specific mention of antagonism between his singing style and that of Tito Schipa, a more politically correct popular singer at the time. The author, Dario Marinelli, comes to the conclusion that it would be naïve to think of those songs as implicitly anti-Fascist. Rather, they found a clever way to remind listeners of the originality of jazz music while appearing—through self-irony—to be belittling it. One can also imagine the promotion of Rabagliati and his films as linked to the replacement of American musicals in the years of ENIC monopoly of film distribution.[60]

---

[60] Dario Marinelli, 'Da Yeah a Ueee senza passare dal MinCulPop. Strategie di coesistenza e resistenza del jazz italiano durante il fascismo', *California Italian Studies*, 4/1 (2013), 1–15. Rabagliati's

Rabagliati's solo radio programme in the winter of 1941 was to remain an exception that lasted for only two months. However, it is an important exception, since, once again, it shows how government directives were sometimes sidelined through *ad hoc* concessions and allowances. If Rabagliati was the 'de-Americanized' face of Italian jazz, then it almost begs a daring parallel. If, in 1938, calling the Nazi army's goose-step *passo romano*, in order to 'de-Germanize' its nature, was supposed to fool the Italian people into thinking of its late adoption by the Italian army as an 'autarkic' move, one is left wondering whether avoiding the word 'jazz' and excluding foreign musicians from EIAR's airwaves was enough to fool Italians into thinking that jazz music was an Italian phenomenon. Rabagliati's use of scat singing and his body language, directing the rhythm by wagging his index finger, clearly revealed his American models. It is almost as if the regime counted on the possibility of making things different simply by saying that they were different. Once again, this takes us back to the expression 'nationalistic denial of the obvious' mentioned in earlier chapters.

Whether or not Italians fell for all of this, it seems that, in its final years, Fascism based much of its propaganda strategies on make-believe. It was a visionary approach prone to fairground-style exaggerations and tall tales to be obediently received. At the same time, underneath this vault of propaganda statements, many people continued to live their lives in ways that lay outside the regime's image of the country.

Another example of a contradiction in terms relates to the most popular singing ensemble of the Fascist years, the Trio Lescano. Their repertoire featured different musical genres, but their clear derivation from Louisiana's Boswell Sisters meant that many of their lyrics were sung to the rhythms of jazzy scores. Their most popular hits—'Pippo non lo sa' and 'Tulipan'—were syncopated songs, the latter being a cover of a greatest hit by the American Andrew Sisters, another popular singing trio from America. Once they had been spotted by EIAR's artistic manager, Carlo Prato, their career was built under the auspices of the government's radio and its complementary recording company, Cetra, which managed their records. In many ways they were the female counterpart to Rabagliati, often appearing accompanied by 'Pippo' Barzizza's orchestra. Once their Hungarian surname was Italianized from Leschan to Lescano (they grew up in Holland, but their father, a trapeze artist, came from Hungary), their foreign origin did not seem to represent a problem. After all, even one of Italy's most famous 'Italian' actresses, Assia Noris, was not Italian (raised in France, she was the daughter of Russian ex-pats). The Trio also appeared in the odd movie, the most memorable being Giacomo Gentilomo's *Ecco la radio!* (1940), a film,

programme ran every Monday from 20 October 1941 until 29 December, from 9.40 to 10 p.m. Just as had happened in Hollywood, Rabagliati's film career did not take off. He featured in another two films, in 1943—one directed by Bragaglia again and featuring a budding star, Anna Magnani (*La vita è bella*)—but again they did not prove popular. His artistic fame remained confined to the field of music, and that is how he is remembered today.

as the title suggests, that was created as a publicity vehicle for EIAR and the regime's attempts to widen its audience.

In 1942 the three singers were granted Italian citizenship and continued to perform, often in morale-boosting events, until the end of 1943. In their case, they were also hiding a 'racial secret' in the fact that their mother Eva, who accompanied them throughout their professional career, was of Jewish faith. This did not mean that the Trio was in breach of the law. Their own case had already been officially cleared in November 1939, thanks to the fact that their father was not Jewish and that they had been baptized. However, their mother—as a Jewish foreign national who had arrived after 1919—should have left the country within three months of receiving the notification. The daughters managed to help her avoid this fate, thanks to a benevolent attitude from the authorities, probably smoothed by their notoriety and their many friends within the regime and the royal family in Turin (they were friends of one of the sons of King Victor Emanuel III, Umberto).

Following the devastating Allied bombing raids in the winter of 1942–3, the Trio's mother, Eva, was evacuated to a small village in the Piedmontese pre-Alps, which they visited regularly. After the summer of 1943 and the restoration of Fascist power under Nazi control, the Trio continued to perform, but their situation was made much more precarious by the absence of some of their old friends and patrons (Umberto had followed his father in his escape to Allied-controlled southern Italy on 9 September 1943) and the increased risk of a potential malevolent exposure of their mother's case. Their situation came to a surprising head on a late evening in November 1943. The place is familiar to us: it was the 'Teatro Grattacielo', the theatrical venue built inside Piacentini's Chicago-style skyscraper in Genoa, the Torre dell'orologio. The theatre was still popular, despite its vicinity to the city port—the target of many Allied bombing raids—because the skyscraper boasted one of the safest air-raid bombing shelters in Genoa, and theatre tickets-holders were automatically allowed in in case of an alarm. The Trio Lescano was due to perform there. What we know is that the three singers were arrested when they were about to walk on to the stage and taken to the Fascist militia's headquarters.

The Lescanos' post-war recollections of the event provided differing versions, or, rather, they all started with a German army captain: only, in one version he accused them of being Jewish and in another of being Allied spies. The latter version had the risible explanation that their song 'Tulipan' contained a cryptic message to the Allies (if nothing else, it is possible that the song might have ignited the wrath of the German officer, as it was a cover of a famous American hit). We do not even know for sure how long they were kept in prison—versions range from a few days to a month. Eventually they were released and could safely return to Turin. However, it was time to vanish. As of 1 December 1943, a directive instructed that all Jews had to be interned in concentration camps, thus making their mother's situation even more dangerous. The trio left Turin and joined her, eventually hiding in Val d'Aosta, near the Swiss border. Their mother, Eva, escaped persecution, but after the war she found out that many members of her family in Holland had disappeared in Nazi concentration camps.[61]

Unlike Rabagliati, after the end of the war the Trio Lescano was not allowed back on national radio, despite the fact that their records continued to sell. The damning reason is probably linked to the fact that, back in 1942, thankful for receiving their Italian citizenship, they had written to Mussolini to ask to be made members of the Fascist Party. Their wish was fulfilled in April 1943, and, given that the news was made public, it was probably considered proof of their collaboration with the regime. A long tour in Latin America became the only way to continue their performing career. There they lived for a few years until the group split in 1952.

Overall, however, de-Americanized, jazz rhythms dominated Italian light music programmes until the very end of Fascism. As we will see in the next section, a jazz musical was even produced in the spring of 1943, starring one of Italy's most gifted jazz musicians, Gorni Kramer.

## 10.4 The War on Hollywood

When it comes to the film industry, a clear watershed was provided by the government decree that, on 4 September 1938, gave ENIC a monopoly in the distribution of all foreign films. It was the so-called Legge sul monopolio, which triggered the boycott of four majors—Fox, MGM, Paramount, and Warner Bros—who decided that the conditions imposed by the regime made the Italian market no longer worth their attention. The decree was not a ban, nor was the reaction to it a full boycott by Hollywood, but its effect was nonetheless enormous, largely because of the disincentive triggered by the fact the ENIC increased the fees that had previously been set by American companies. The number of American films in distribution dropped from 162 in 1938 to 64 the following year.[62]

It was a brutal strategy that Luigi Freddi had tried to avoid, but his influence was by then on the wane—he had left the Direzione Generale in March 1939— and Mussolini was closer to Alfieri's pro-Nazi views, asking for stronger measures. As Brunetta reminds us, it was also the climax of a campaign by the magazine *Film*, a weekly born in January 1938 and very close to the Direzione Generale per la Cinematografia (it was part-financed by the Ministry of Popular Culture). Indeed, its first issue, published in a broadsheet format, had opened with an

---

[61] On the Trio Lescano, see Eschenazi's monograph *Le regine dello Swing: Il Trio Lescano*.
[62] This data are based on Rome's area, as collected by SIAE's annual publication (*Lo spettacolo in Italia*), and discussed by Lorenzo Quaglietti, 'Cinema americano, vecchio amore', in Argentieri (ed.), *Schermi di guerra*, 307–27 (312). For a detailed analysis of the impact of the decree on the American film industry, see Di Chio, *Il cinema americano in Italia*, 211–14.

editorial by Vittorio Mussolini dedicated to the Italian film industry's need to raise its capacity to compete with that of the Americans. These were the months preceding the distribution of Alessandrini's *Luciano Serra pilota*, and, unsurprisingly, the whole of the third page was devoted to a long, illustrated article by the director himself, singing the praises of the film that Vittorio Mussolini was so valiantly supervising.[63]

An interesting statistic concerns the number of cinema tickets sold nationally before and after the decree. The growing trend continued—from about 343 million tickets in 1938, to 354 in 1939, and 364 in 1940—thus suggesting that the disappearance of a large part of American first-run films did not impact on the popularity of cinema as a leisure activity.[64] Italians simply learned to live with less of Hollywood entering their lives. The press helped in this, with a distinct move towards an anti-American stance. A first example of this stance was a long article on couples in cinema, which was first published in *Cinema* and a few weeks later, in a shortened version, in *Cinema illustrazione*. It is very unusual to find an article published by two film magazines that were theoretically in competition with each other. In this case, the reason can be easily seen as political, given that they came out close to the announcement of the *Legge sul monopolio*. In the article, using the same couples in different films was judged to be 'an aberration of the star system'. However, when it came to the specifics, the mainly negative portrayal of Hollywood couples—particularly in the second version—was redeemed by the example of a 'good' couple, which, unsurprisingly, was an Italian one. It was the duo of Vittorio De Sica and Assia Noris starring in Camerini's *Darò un milione* (1935) and *Signor Max* (1937). Camerini was complimented specifically, and, given that the only American director who had received a positive comment was King Vidor, a parallel of sorts was created between the two. The illustrations accompanying the reduced version for *Cinema illustrazione* were concentrated in a single frame, with the De Sica–Noris image at the end, thus creating a narrative of sorts whereby the Italian couple appeared as the saving grace in the trend. The caption beneath the photo was the only complimentary one, presenting the duo as 'a simple and humane couple'. The implicit effect was that of presenting De Sica and Noris as an antidote to the glamour and artificiality of the American couples (Fig. 10.13).[65]

---

[63] Brunetta, *Storia del cinema italiano*, ii. 20–1. Vittorio Mussolini, 'Anno nuovo, vita nuova?', and Mino Doletti, 'Si gira "Luciano Serra" in Etiopia', *Film*, 1/1 (29 January 1938), 1, 3. Mino Doletti was *Film*'s chief editor.

[64] Data from the 1955 Annuario Statistico della SIAE, quoted in Brunetta, *Storia del cinema italiano*, ii. 24. The trend is confirmed by the data provided by Luigi Freddi, based on ENIC's box-office returns—which grew from 67 million lire in 1937–-8 to 77 million and 81 million in the following two years. Freddi, *Il governo dell'immagine*, 299.

[65] Osvaldo Campassi, 'Le coppie', *Cinema*, 3/52 (25 August 1938), 119–22; and 'Coppie', *Cinema illustrazione*, 13/38 (21 September 1938), 5.

466  AMERICA IN ITALIAN CULTURE

**Fig. 10.13.** Osvaldo Campassi, 'Coppie', *Cinema illustrazione*, 13/38 (21 September 1938), 5. (courtesy of Cineteca, Bologna)

An even more anti-American article on couples in cinema was published by *Cinema illustrazione* two months later, this time adding the ever-recurrent signifier of American immorality: divorce. The anonymous article entitled 'Falsa vita di Hollywood' quoted the writings of two American celebrities—Joan Crawford and Ria Gable (then wife of Clark Gable)—both discussing their respective marriages and both heading for divorce. The rest of the page, with no accompanying text other than the photos' captions, was entitled 'Tre coppie dello schermo tedesco' and featured stills from three UFA productions. The fact that the image of the first couple—Käthe von Nagy and Willy Fritsch in Robert Stemmle's *Am Seidenen Faden* (1938)—showed them on their fictional wedding day provided the perfect visual counterpart to this juxtaposition of Hollywood's sinfulness and German moral orthodoxy.[66] By then, actresses working in Italian or German productions were also beginning to replace Hollywood actresses on *Cinema illustrazione*'s front covers. The 23 November issue featured one of the iconic divas of UFA's late-1930s films, Swedish femme fatale Zarah Leander, Goebbels's intended answer to the 'Americanized' Marlene Dietrich and Greta Garbo.

The most symbolic expression of the paradigm-shifting impact of the anti-American stance of late 1938 came from the regime's official film periodical, *Bianco e nero*. The entire issue of February 1939, edited by two leading figures at the Centro Sperimentale di Cinematografia, Luigi Chiarini (who was also deputy director of the journal) and Umberto Barbaro, was devoted to a general assessment of filmmaking. The issue was thought of as an anthology of writings about the idea of cinema, and its contents page was organized by nationality. The proportion of pages given to each nationality was therefore in itself symbolic. First came the Italians with 71 pages, then the Germans with 39, followed by shorter sections devoted to British (28), French (9), and Russian cinema (17). Hollywood was nowhere to be seen. Such a blatant exclusion could not go unmentioned, and indeed it was argued head-on by Luigi Chiarini in his short preface to the issue.

The text began with a strong attack against those who think of cinema as an industrial phenomenon: 'cinema needs healthy ideas more than technical and financial means'. From this came the exclusion of American cinema, since 'in that country cinema is an eminently and exclusively industrial fact'. The issue was de facto presented as a European answer to Hollywood's industrial and marketing strategies:

> We are firmly convinced that the fortune of American cinema is due to a phenomenon of skilful publicity and that the day in which the European public will get used to appreciating a cinematographic work of a deeper and more serious content, of a higher artistic form, the gods of Hollywood's Olympus will face a quick twilight. In Italy, God willing, the recent monopoly decree—which is of the highest spiritual value, since under the Fascist regime every economic measure, thanks to the corporatist organization, is linked to an ethical and social premise—will contribute to speeding up the public's detoxification from the subtle venom of 'made in USA' films.[67]

---

[66] Anon., 'Falsa vita di Hollywood', and anon., 'Tre coppie dello schermo tedesco', *Cinema illustrazione*, 13/47 (23 November 1938), 6.
[67] Luigi Chiarini, 'Prefazione', *Bianco e nero*, 3/2 (1939), 5–7 (5).

**Fig. 10.14.** 'Falsa vita di Hollywood', *Cinema illustrazione*, 13/47 (23 November 1938), 6. (courtesy of Cineteca, Bologna)

The 'European' answer was then skilfully reduced by Chiarini to the Axis powers, since, as he explained, even the British and the French invoked the intervention of state and authoritarian solutions, 'indicating as a model the initiative of the totalitarian regimes, and specifically Fascist Italy and Nazi Germany'. The preface then twice cites the essay by Goebbels included in the issue, praising its clarity, expertise, and courage. The ending of the preface confirmed the idealistic, 'mystical' notion of cinema as a tool in the hands of political power:

Cinema must fatally move towards that mission of being a bearer of civilization and culture that is its destiny. We firmly believe that, in order to accelerate this move, the more specific contribution will have to come from the authoritarian countries that more than others have the force to act, but, above all else, have the faith in a mission of civilization.

Being an anthology, this issue of *Bianco e nero* can be examined through the lens of the rationale of the selection and the collective narrative that emerges from it. As the contents page shows (Fig. 10.15), Luigi Freddi, as the journal's director and

LUIGI CHIARINI: *Prefazione* . . . . . . . . PAG. 5

## ITALIANI

| | | |
|---|---|---|
| LUIGI FREDDI: *Arte per il popolo* . . . . . . | PAG. | 11 |
| GIOVANNI GENTILE: *Prefazione a « Cinematografo »* . . . | » | 13 |
| MASSIMO BONTEMPELLI: *Cinematografo* . . . . . | » | 15 |
| F. T. MARINETTI: *Primo manifesto per la cinematografia futurista* | » | 21 |
| TELESIO INTERLANDI: *Chi ha paura del cinema politico?* . . | » | 26 |
| EMILIO CECCHI: *Il film a colori* . . . . . . | » | 29 |
| SEBASTIANO A. LUCIANI: | | |
|     *Che cosa è il cinematografo* . . . . . . | » | 31 |
|     *Che cosa è il film* . . . . . . . | » | 34 |
| ALBERTO CONSIGLIO: *Cinema come arte pura* . . . . | » | 38 |
| RICCIOTTO CANUDO: *L'estetica della settima arte* . . . | » | 47 |
| EUGENIO GIOVANNETTI: *Il cinema come fatto estetico* . . | » | 60 |
| LEO LONGANESI: | | |
|     *L'occhio di vetro* . . . . . . . . | » | 74 |
|     *Clima cinematografico* . . . . . . . | » | 76 |
|     *Polemica nel cinema* . . . . . . . | » | 78 |

## TEDESCHI

| | | |
|---|---|---|
| GIUSEPPE GOEBBELS: *Discorso alla Reichsfilmkammer* . . | PAG. | 85 |
| HANS RICHTER: *Prefazione a « Filmgegner von Heute - Filmfreunde von Morgen »* . . . . . . . . | » | 106 |
| BÉLA BÁLÀZS: *Il film a colori* . . . . . . | » | 114 |
| GEORG WILHELM PABST: *Servitù e grandezza di Hollywood* . | » | 118 |

Fig. 10.15. Detail of the contents page of *Bianco e nero*, 3/2 (February 1939), 181. (courtesy of Cineteca, Bologna)

reigning tzar of Italian cinema, was given the first word. It was an extract from a speech he had made in 1934 at the start of his directorship of the Direzione Generale per la Cinematografia. Interestingly, and predictably, Freddi stressed the need for an efficient fusion of artistic and industrial dimensions in cinema. This put him somehow at loggerheads with Chiarini's preface, which only a page before had argued for the primacy of ideas over 'technical and financial means'. The final sentence of Freddi's piece left no doubts about this misalignment: the quality of Italian cinema had to be improved, not simply through the 'perfect fusion of ethical and aesthetical factors; but equally from a solid economic frame, coming from an intelligent and conscientious industry'.

The second piece in the issue is a short text by Giovanni Gentile. The presence of the regime's neo-idealist philosopher in the unusual role of film theoretician added further rubberstamping to Chiarini's call for attention to be paid to ideas rather than technical matters. In Gentile's words, the technical dimension had to be entirely absorbed by art, which is the single, finite expression of the spirit. As for the following Italian essays, they all fell within the dominant neo-idealist view of cinema as pure art. Only the last one, like Freddi's, stood out as an exception.

Leo Longanesi's contribution had originally appeared in 1933: it was an extract from the long essay in *L'Italiano* on which we dwelled in Chapter 9. The brief introductory lines in *Bianco e nero* presented Longanesi's contribution as important because it called for a return to 'Italian settings and situations, free from the empty and silly obsession (which is called commercial but which has often brought financial ruin to producers) of a servile and derivative imitation of American film'. This was true, but when it came to proposing a model, as we have seen, the last two pages of the essay concentrated on one director and one film: King Vidor and *The Champ*. In other words, the Italian section of the *Bianco e nero* issue that had excluded American cinema in fact finished with strongly worded praise of an American director and his realistic portrait of American life.

What are we to make of these eighty pages of Italian film criticism, fully in line with Chiarini's demand for a neo-idealistic discussion of ideas about cinema, apart from the opening essay by Freddi asking for a better organization of Italy's film industry (and everybody knew what he thought of Hollywood studios as a model) and Longanesi's extended encomium of American film? An intriguing ingredient to be added to this is the fact that both Freddi and Longanesi were removed from their respective positions shortly after the publication. The February issue of *Bianco e nero* was still in Italy's newspaper kiosks when Longanesi was told to close down *Omnibus* because of its persistent irreverence. And, by March 1939, Freddi had been replaced as head of the Direzione Generale per la Cinematografia. In his memoir, Freddi described the event as a resignation, citing a long letter that he sent to Alfieri on 19 February 1939, once again lamenting the lack of organization and efficiency of the film industry.[68] Within the same pages, however, Freddi had described Alfieri as 'naïve' and had mentioned his failure in getting Mussolini to listen to him. This leaves the possibility open that his resignation was requested rather than offered. After the implosion of Vittorio Mussolini's film production deal with Hal Roach in 1937 and the haughty tones of Freddi's report to *Il Duce* about the whole affair, it is not surprising that the relationship between the two should have cooled somewhat. Moreover, eight months passed between Freddi's resignation and his appointment as head of Cinecittà, making it difficult to think of this move as a planned development in his role as head of the regime's film policies. Obviously, this is far from suggesting that the odd presence of Freddi's and Longanesi's essays in *Bianco e nero* was the cause of or had anything to do with the sudden crisis in their respective careers. However, one is left wondering whether this strange macro-narrative of the Italian section was intentional—and at this point one could imagine a discreet role being played by the issue's co-editor, Umberto Barbaro, who was no longer an open supporter of the regime—or whether the choice of Freddi's and Longanesi's essays was simply an awkward attempt to show the 'openness' of the intellectual debate in Fascist Italy.

The rest of the issue contains no more surprises, apart from the slightly odd fact that Goebbels is the only foreign contributor whose first name is Italianized, with a slightly comical-looking 'Giuseppe Goebbels' next to all other foreign contributors, including Hans Richter and Georg Pabst. Goebbels's piece is a long speech that stretches over twenty pages, entirely dedicated to his efforts to raise the quality of German films. Only mild anti-American sentiments can be found in his suggestion that the perception in Germany of the superiority of American films is simply due to the fact that only the best American products reach Europe. Of a similar tone is the short essay by Austrian director Georg Wilhelm Pabst, entitled 'Servitù e grandezza di Hollywood', which, on the one hand, attacks Hollywood for its lack of esteem for the creative role of the film director but, on the other, praises the professionality to be found in each individual sector of film production. The British section contained only a single essay by film historian Paul Rotha (from his book *Documentary Film* (1936)), which praised authoritarian nations—Goebbels's ministry in particular—for their interest in educational film-making as against the entirely commercial drive of American cinema. And, in the French section, film director René Clair is represented with a 1925 piece from *Cahiers du cinema* in which he calls for government intervention in regulating the quality of film production. The final section, left to the Russians, was limited to a collection of extracts from the by then canonic essays on film editing and narrative construction by Pudovkin, Eisenstein, and Timoshenko (whose work was particularly followed and promoted by Umberto Barbaro).

---

[68] Freddi, *Il governo dell'immagine*, 252–4.

Overall, this issue of *Bianco e nero* confirms how, even following the monopoly decree and the anti-American turn of September 1938, it was difficult to rein in different views with respect to cinema. On the one end of the spectrum we see Chiarini's orthodox line and his imperious rejection of American cinema, and at the other end Longanesi's praise of an American film as the ultimate model of realism. Unfortunately we lack any documentation concerning the preparatory material for this anthology, so the question of whether this tension was intentional or involuntary cannot be answered.

Beyond the fact that the two dissenting voices of Freddi and Longanesi found themselves in difficult waters in the following months, what confirms the momentum of the anti-American trend is the presence of an essay by Emilio Cecchi in the subsequent issue of *Bianco e nero* entitled 'Stanchezza del cinema americano'. As one can see from the contents page, a very short essay by Cecchi had been present in the anthology, but it was only a brief and not particularly memorable note about the arrival of colour in film. It was not much, considering that the biographical introduction had described Cecchi as 'the most refined and elegant of all Italian essayists'. Instead, the essay in the March issue of *Bianco e nero* spanned over seven pages and gave him a better chance to expand on the subject, leading one to wonder whether it might in fact have been intended for the previous issue. The essay moved from the reported drop in cinema tickets in the USA in the first semester of 1938 to a discussion of what might have caused such a crisis. Cecchi firmly believed that it was due to the diminishing quality of American films. Despite the recent success of *Snow White and the Seven Dwarfs*, Disney too was presented as incapable of reproducing the quality of yester years.

Film stars, too, were under attack, their wages drying up the empty coffers of the 'Big Four'. Cecchi did not specify who the 'Big Four' were, nor did he admit that it was an unusual expression, since the American press would not normally talk in those terms (and if nothing else there were five big major studios in those years). Cecchi was obviously referring to the four majors that, because of the hit on their own distribution networks, had walked away from the Italian market entirely (RKO did not). It was a modification of a figure of speech for the eyes and mind of the Italian readership. 'The Big Four' were guilty of rejecting Italy and were now suffering some sort of Dantesque *contrapasso* with a drop in their internal sales. In actual fact, the fifth of the 'Big Five' had been suffering similar losses too, but Italians did not need to know. Moreover, it would not have chimed well with an anonymous note towards the end of the issue that maliciously informed the reader that an unmentioned Italian newspaper had recently made a typo when referring to the four American companies as the 'Pig Four'. 'We like the allegory', concluded the note, 'and it might not even have been a typo'.[69]

---

[69] Emilio Cecchi, 'Stanchezza del cinema americano', and anon., 'Note. 3', *Bianco e nero*, 3/3 (1939), 13–19, 59–60.

After this dig at Hollywood, however, there was still space left for a positive view of American cinema. The entire book reviews section was dedicated to a single, long review of the French translation of an anthology of writings by a number of Hollywood figures: *Silence! on tourne:. Comment nous faisons les films*, edited by Nancy Naumburg. The review agreed that American films were on average of superior quality thanks to the better organization of their production; it praised the professionality and collaboration by different experts at each stage of film production as it emerged from the anthology, and ended with the following—'Freddian' one could say—sentence: 'In conclusion, it is a useful book which should be read by those who intend to make industrial cinema in Italy'. It was yet another example of opposing views being contained within the two covers of *Bianco e nero*.[70]

As for the ripple effect of the journal's call for a discussion of ideas about cinema, the May issue of *Bianco e nero* contained four long extracts from articles that had commented on the previous issue. By then the journal's director was no longer Luigi Freddi but his successor, Vezio Orazi, a Prefect with no experience of the film industry who had been put at the head of the Direzione Generale per la Cinematografia. The fact that the defenestration of Freddi from the directorate should have passed with not a single line of recognition, and that the handover at *Bianco e nero* should have been marked only by a brief and unaffectionate message at the bottom of the very last page, is an indication that the handover had been unexpected and possibly less than amicable.[71]

The four articles—from Florence's daily *La Nazione*, Turin's *La Stampa*, and *Il Dramma*, and the journal *Lichtbild-Bühne* (Germany's oldest illustrated film magazine)—all praised the anthology and paid particular attention to Goebbels's speech. The German article, entitled 'Eine frühere Rede Dr Goebbels findet in Italien Verbreitung' ('A Former Speech by Goebbels Is Distributed in Italy'), was entirely reproduced in the original, with no Italian translation. There was not a single mention of the absence of American cinema or of the odd presence of Longanesi's essay. In other words, the press, according to *Bianco e nero*'s selection, had responded only to the anti-American, pro-Nazi side of the anthology.[72]

Emilio Cecchi continued in his critique of American cinema with an essay entitled 'Letteratura americana e cinematografo', published in a December 1939 issue of *Cinema*. The essay started with the admission that New York had replaced Paris in the minds of Italians: 'as Paris used to be, New York is today the Mecca of

---

[70] FP, 'I libri', *Bianco e nero*, 3/3 (1939), 62–4 (64). FP almost certainly stands for Francesco Pasinetti, a young filmmaker and assistant editor of *Bianco e nero*.

[71] 'As of this issue, the direction of the journal passes to the Fascist Vezio Orazi, Director General for Cinematography. To comrade Luigi Freddi, who has directed this journal since its birth, goes the grateful farewell of *Bianco e nero*'. On Vezio Orazi, see Manetti, *'Un'arma poderosissima'*, 100; and Gili, *Stato fascista e cinematografia*, 57–8. After his replacement by Eitel Monaco, in 1941, Orazi returned to his work as Prefect. He was killed in an ambush by Tito's partisans near the city of Zadar, in Croatia, on 26 May 1942.

[72] Anon., 'Rassegna della stampa', *Bianco e nero*, 3/5 (1939), 85–96.

xenophiles all over the world. Those who cannot travel there by ship will travel there via a book.' Coherent with his notion of cinema as a minor art compared to the 'noble art' of literature, Cecchi argued that contemporary American literature had been subjected to the influence of cinema and had suffered by adapting itself to the jargon of poor film scripts.[73]

The editorial line of *Cinema*, however, was in those months quickly changing as a result of the stronger presence of the group of young film enthusiasts around Vittorio Mussolini. Cecchi's anti-American critique was more the exception than the rule. Two months after *Bianco e nero*'s anthology, in May 1939, *Cinema* produced an issue that was almost a counter-reply. In lieu of its normal editorial, it courageously hosted an article by Will Hays, which protested against Italy's monopoly decree and other protectionist policies in other countries. The following article seemed more orthodox, with the headline 'Timori per Pinocchio: Che avverrà di Pinocchio nei cartoni di Walt Disney?' ('Fears for Pinocchio: What will Happen to Pinocchio in Walt Disney's Cartoon?'). In fact, its author, Domenico Purificato (a young painter and film enthusiast who was to take over the directorship of *Cinema* after Fascism's implosion in July 1943), used the news of Walt Disney's choice of *Pinocchio* for his next full-feature cartoon, on the one hand, to express the concern that the cartoon adaptation would move away from the original story (as it partially did), but, on the other, to express the joy that Disney should have chosen an Italian story, and to confirm the journal's full trust in Disney's genius. The use of the first-person plural on the part of Purificato was symbolic, particularly in passages praising Disney such as this one: 'each one of us has faith in him; and one can expect a fanciful approach superior even to Collodi's.' Thirdly, an article entitled 'Influenza di Hollywood' by famous British intellectual Winifred Bryher—patron of the 'lost generation' writers in 1920s Paris and co-founder of the film magazine *Close Up*—identifies two major contributions by American cinema in its technological primacy and its capacity to unify different ethnicities in the USA. Fourthly, not one but two further articles appeared with English words in their headlines: 'Girls' and 'Filosofia del Gag', both dedicated to cinematic features—variety shows and gags—in which American filmmakers were seen as masters. Fifthly, the section 'Galleria' was devoted entirely to a adulatory profile of an American actor, James Stewart, Capra's lead actor in box-office hit comedies such as *You Can't Take it with You* (1938) and *Mr Smith Goes to Washington* (1939), which was still in production at the time. There is little doubt that this issue of *Cinema* was a daring reply to Chiarini's call for an anti-American stance in *Bianco e nero*.[74]

---

[73] Emilio Cecchi, 'Letteratura americana e cinematografo', *Cinema*, 4/84 (25 December 1939), 374–5 (374). A long extract of the article was republished in *Bianco e nero*, 4/2 (1940), 83–4.

[74] Will Hays, 'Dare e avere'; Domenico Purificato, 'Timore per Pinocchio'; anon., 'Girls'; W. Breyer, 'Influenza di Hollywood'; Amedeo Agri, 'Filosofia del "Gag"'; Puck, 'Galleria: LIXI James Stewart', *Cinema*, 4/69 (10 May 1939), 289, 290–1, 297, 298–9, 300–1, 306–7. In his analysis of film journals in

This editorial line continued right into the war years, though never again in such obvious tones. The role of Vittorio Mussolini, in this respect, was vital. Despite the setback of the Italo-American venture of RAM Pictures, he was still involved in film production through ERA and ACI (he brought Jean Renoir to Italy, in 1939, for a film adaptation of *Tosca*, and was behind the production of three war films, one of which was 'his' *Un pilota ritorna* (1942), which he asked Roberto Rossellini to direct). But, more than that, his status as '*Il Duce*'s son' allowed him a degree of freedom, which he exerted to the maximum, extending it also to the group of young filmmakers that was becoming increasingly vocal within the pages of *Cinema* as much as in their first productions. Visconti's *Ossessione* (1943) was to be the climax of this trend, and by then one could argue that the disciples were turning against their young master himself. Vittorio Mussolini was conscious of the need to find a diplomatic balance between his pro-American stance and the regime's directives. A good example of this can be found in his editorial of 25 November 1939, entitled 'Importazione ed esportazione cinematografica'. On the one hand, the article returned to his recurring theme of the need for the Italian film industry to raise the quality of its products; on the other, while saying that he disagreed with those—critics and public—who would like to see American cinema back, he admitted that he had always argued that American cinema was superior to European cinema.

More compromising statements were left to the 'young Turks' who surrounded him. The 28-year-old Michelangelo Antonioni, for instance, then a young film critic recently arrived in Rome from his provincial Ferrara, wrote an article for the 25 February 1940 issue of *Cinema* in which he praised American cinema for its capacity to give realistic credibility to moral types. The title of the article was 'La scuola delle mogli' ('The School for Wives'), and, indeed, Antonioni dwelt on the most vilified American topos, that of the fragility of marriages, and turned it upside down in order to show that ordinary married women in American cinema tend to embody an image of moral strength. Frank Capra's comedies provided the example, and Myrna Loy and Maureen O'Sullivan were the American actresses who best fitted this role. Surrounding Antonioni's essay in the same issue were four other articles on Hollywood.[75]

---

the war years, Quaglietti agrees that *Bianco e nero* and *Cinema* were at different ends of the critical spectrum when it came to Hollywood cinema. Quaglietti, 'Cinema americano, vecchio amore', 318–21.

[75] One was Emilio Ceretti's 'Rimorso dei comunisti di Hollywood', which informed *Cinema* readers that the left-wing militant craze among Hollywood filmmakers had come to an end (obviously with no mention of their role in the RAM fiasco of 1937). Emilio Ceretti is an important figure in relation to American culture. A journalist and a translator from English for Mondadori, he is also remembered for creating in 1936 the Italian version of one of the most American of all board games: Monopoly. Italianized as *Monòpoli* (pronounced with the accent on the second syllable, as in English) and featuring references to Milan's street plan, the game became widely popular in Italy's middle- and upper-class homes.

Reference to the importance of contemporary literature in film productions and the call for more realism in the choice of locations in Italian films were the recurring Trojan horses through which a parallel with American cinema was introduced. In the *Cinema* issue just considered, for example, a long essay by Umberto De Franciscis, entitled 'Scenografia vera', called for local colour in the setting of Italian films, offering as a model the success of American western films in imposing an unequivocally American landscape. The same could be said, it argued, for the urban setting of comedies such as Frank Capra's *Mr Deeds Goes to Town* (1936). As for literature, the *Cinema* issue of 10 May 1941 opened with an editorial by Vittorio Mussolini (hidden by the acronym 'TSM', which stood for the anagram Tito Silvio Mursino), which, once again, called for more realistic settings following the American example:

> Look at the Americans (an eternal, by now tiresome comparison), how they have managed to make us familiar with their country, their customs, their whole way of thinking, so much so that if we were to find ourselves in New York, nothing would surprise us, not even if we were sitting on the window-sill at the 14th floor of the Waldorf-Astoria, seeing underneath us the immense metropolis with its human herd at pasture.[76]

Mussolini's editorial was followed by the translation of a literary essay by one of the most popular American fiction writers at the time, William Saroyan. The essay praised the sense of sight in general terms, but Saroyan's initial reference to the special 'eye' of a film camera and the accompanying, unrelated but large illustrations from Howard Hughes's daring film *The Outlaw* (released only in 1943 because of censorship issues) turned this literary piece into, once more, an indirect praise of American cinema.

Eventually, with the declaration of war in December 1941, even *Cinema* had to tone down its pro-American stance, first and foremost in a clear drop in the number of articles directly or indirectly devoted to the subject. In the first issue published after the outbreak of war, Vittorio Mussolini dedicated his editorial to the subject. The tone was obviously nationalistic and radiated self-confidence in Italy's capacity to win the war, both on the battlefield and in cinema theatres. Once again, however, and contradicting himself, Mussolini could not refrain from admitting the superiority of American cinema in representing everyday reality. It was a balancing exercise that was proving increasingly difficult for him to maintain. More importantly, the editorial did not go unseen. Alessandro Pavolini, then Minister of Popular Culture, protested against the

---

[76] TSM [Vittorio Mussolini], 'Constatazioni', *Cinema*, 6/117 (10 May 1941), 297.

tone of the article and warned Vittorio Mussolini against publishing such unorthodox pieces in the future.[77]

But Vittorio's young collaborators at *Cinema* were not willing to bow to pressure, as the next issues showed. In February, Massimo Mida wrote an article praising American culture for its capacity to connect the worlds of cinema and sport. And the call for better realism in Italian cinema continued to provide an excuse to return to the topic. The issue of 25 July 1942 is exemplary in this respect. It presented a two-pronged attack. First Tito A. Spagnol heavily criticized a recent Italian comedy by an old-guard director, Guido Brignone's *Turbamento* (1942), accusing Brignone of having failed to create credible contemporary characters. And here the attack included the accusation that he had tried and failed to copy the rhythm and style of American comedies. It was then the turn of Antonio Pietrangeli to praise the stark realism of a new film then in production, Visconti's *Ossessione* (1943), a film adaptation of an American novel that had been uprooted and immersed in the crude reality of rural life in the Po valley. Pietrangeli, as we know, was part of the crew that helped Visconti write and shoot the film, together with other contributors to *Cinema* such as Mario Alicata, Giuseppe De Santis, and Gianni Puccini. The importance of this film for the entire *Cinema* group is easily discernible from the number of times in which stills from the film in production appeared in the odd issue of the journal throughout 1942 (including the front-cover photograph of the 25 July and 10 November issues) up until the film's premiere in April 1943.[78]

The production of *Ossessione* takes us to an aside that, for the last time in this book, concerns the ever-recurring role of France as a channel in accessing American culture. It was not the first time that James Cain's raunchy novel *The Postman Always Rings Twice* (1934) had been brought to the silver screen. The first time had been in France with Pierre Chenal's *Le Dernier Tournant* (1939). Chenal had already thought about moving the setting away from Cain's California to the deserted beaches of Provence, with the city of Marseille providing the urban equivalent of Cain's Los Angeles. It is not clear whether Visconti had seen Chenal's film during his long stay in France. Unfortunately, he was never asked this question. The historical narrative, reconstructed from various sources, is that Visconti received the French translation of the novel directly from Renoir, who also passed on an unfinished film treatment. By open admission of one of the scriptwriters—De Santis—none of the crew knew English well enough to be able to read the novel in the original. It was only once the production arranged its headquarters in Ferrara (Visconti's own equivalent to Los Angeles) that the group

---

[77] Vittorio Mussolini, 'Nuova situazione', *Cinema*, 6/132 (25 December 1941), 381. On Pavolini's reaction, see Sedita, 'Vittorio Mussolini, Hollywood and Neorealism', 444–5.

[78] Massimo Mida, 'Quadrato americano', *Cinema*, 7/136 (25 February 1942), 102–4. Tito A. Spagnol, 'Una serata al cinema', and Antonio Pietrangeli, 'Analisi spettrale del film realistico', *Cinema*, 7/146 (25 July 1942), 378–9, 393.

struck up a collaboration with a local intellectual who had a copy of the original American novel and offered to help with the dialogues. This was 26-year-old Giorgio Bassani, who, in the post-war years, was to become one of Italy's most famous novelists with *Il giardino dei Finzi-Contini* (1962).[79]

Beyond the issue of the French filter through which Visconti and his collaborators approached *The Postman Always Rings Twice*, it is also enlightening to read a late essay by Giuseppe De Santis devoted to the production of the film. Beyond confirming that the writing of the script had been based on the French translation of the novel, De Santis indirectly reveals the strong 'French roots' of his literary culture through a number of telltale details. First he describes the characterization of lead actress Clara Calamai as directly inspired by the women of Modigliani's adopted home (Paris, so to speak). Then he refers to the cultural models of both Visconti and Libero Solaroli (the film's producer) as passionately French; after which he dwells on the choice of Ferrara, describing it as the most French of all Italian cities. The final touch is his comment that the film was inspired by 'la grande tradizione del cinema francese' ('the great tradition of French cinema').[80]

There is no doubt that, in the *Cinema* group's quest for realism, the contemporary examples by Jean Renoir, René Clair, and Marcel Carné presented French contemporary cinema as a stimulating presence. Equally, however, the recurring term of comparison was American cinema (and, by 1941, Renoir had produced his first Hollywood film, *Swamp Water*). Was De Santis intentionally removing the American dimension in order to distance the film from the 'pro-American patron' of the group, Vittorio Mussolini? In a recent essay, Giovanni Sedita dwells on the removal of the memory of the role played by Mussolini on the part of many of the young filmmakers whose post-war careers had only to benefit from such an operation. At the same time, as Sedita himself recognizes, Mussolini had been instrumental on the 'French front' too, since, by inviting Renoir to come to Italy and direct *Tosca*, he had indirectly triggered a first-hand encounter between a leading French director and those young *Cinema* contributors who had not had Visconti's privilege of an extended stay in France.[81] Film historians have tended to follow Visconti's mention of the relationship with Renoir as key to the choice of this film, but at the same time no critic has ever considered *Ossessione*'s potential connection with Chenal's *Le Dernier Tournant*. This is not to diminish the groundbreaking value of Visconti's film, which, for example, in its cinematic focus on the male body of Massimo Girotti was entirely novel. If nothing else, a close comparison with Chenal's film would reveal how the French film's conventional representation of gender is closer to the post-war Hollywood adaptation by

---

[79] On the genesis of the film, see Lino Micciché, *Visconti e il neorealismo: Ossessione, La terra trema, Bellissima* (Venice: Marsilio, 1990), 21–68.

[80] Giuseppe De Santis, 'Quando Visconti girava Ossessione tra Ferrara e Pontelagoscuro e io,...', *Bologna incontri*, 14/4 (April 1983), 23–32.

[81] Sedita, 'Vittorio Mussolini, Hollywood and Neorealism', 443–4.

Tay Garnett (*The Postman Always Rings Twice* (1946)) and had nothing in common with Visconti's daring approach.[82]

However, within the pages of this book, the case of *Ossessione* prompts two considerations. First, the presence of an American novel as the source of the most innovative film of the final years of Fascism is a signal of how much the literary and cinematic dimensions interacted in keeping 'the American craze' alive, despite the regime's repeated attempts to silence it. Secondly, the French connection behind the film shows the extent to which French culture was still active as a go-between for Italian intellectuals interested in American culture. As for the reception of the film within Fascist circles, Sedita shows how *Ossessione*—in this respect very like the publication of Vittorini's *Conversazione in Sicilia* in 1941—was not unanimously condemned; in fact, a number of militant papers praised it as a groundbreaking piece of filmmaking. As for the Mussolini family, according to De Santis, Vittorio did not like *Ossessione* and allegedly commented: 'This is not the real Italy'. Il Duce, however, was also given a private screening of the film, in the company of Pavolini, as Minister of Popular Culture, and both approved of the film, the former allegedly saying: 'It's an original work which has its reason to be. Some will protest, but it doesn't matter'. Indeed, the film was not subjected to any form of central censorship (apart from the removal of a few seconds in which Fascist militia men unintentionally appeared in the background of a shot) and was premiered on 31 March 1943. Unsurprisingly, the most vociferous protests came from Catholic authorities, scandalized not just by the debauched elements in the plot but also by the fact that the scriptwriters had maliciously introduced a parish priest who was more interested in going fishing and hunting with his friend than looking after the moral upbringing of his flock.[83]

In the end, even *Cinema* had to conform to the regime's anti-American propaganda demands. The issue of 25 February 1943 contained two articles, both professing the ultimate rejection of American cinema. The first was more moderate, written by neorealist-director-to-be Carlo Lizzani. He argued there was a need to move away from the American yardstick in judging the success of Italian productions. The second was a propaganda piece entitled 'Il cinema americano contro l'intelligenza europea'. Its author said he was fresh from a trip to Istanbul, where he had been able to sample the most recent American films. The poor

---

[82] For a critical reading of *Ossessione* and gender representation, see William Van Watson, *Luchino Visconti's (Homosexual) Ossessione*, in Jacqueline J. Reich and Piero Garofalo (eds), *Re-Viewing Fascism: Italian Cinema 1922–1943* (Bloomington, IN: Indiana University Press, 2002), 172–93. In 1946, the producers of Chenal's film took Visconti to court with the accusation of plagiarism, which was eventually quashed. According to Miccichè, it is not even clear whether Visconti had seen the film. On both see Miccichè, *Visconti e il neorealismo*, 26.

[83] Giuseppe De Santis, 'Visconti's Interpretation of Cain's Setting in *Ossessione*', *Film Criticism*, 3 (1985), 22–32. The reactions of both Mussolini and Pavolini are quoted in Arrigo Petacco's biography of Pavolini: *Il superfascista: Vita e morte di Alessandro Pavolini* (Milan: Mondadori, 1999), 96–7. Visconti confirmed the story about Il Duce's positive response in the post-war years. See Luchino Visconti, 'Vita difficile del film "Ossessione"', *Il Contemporaneo* (24 April 1965), 7–8. On the presence of American and French influences in the production of *Ossessione*, see in particular Charles L. Leavitt, *Italian Neorealism: A Cultural History* (Toronto: Toronto University Press, 2020), 28–31.

performances of European directors and actors working in Hollywood, he concluded, was a direct consequence of a plan by Jewish producers to stifle the creative spirit that distinguished European art.[84]

Beyond the intellectual and political debate, to what extent was America still present in Italian cinemas following the decree of 4 September 1938? We have already mentioned the quantitative decrease in the distribution of American films. It was a sudden drop, which the Italian film industry was called to counterbalance with a proportional increase of its production, complemented by other imports from friendly countries such as Germany and Hungary. The annual production of Italian films did increase substantially, from 64 films in 1938 to the zenith of 114 in 1940, before the war effort caused a downward trend. This increased production was expected to serve two purposes, a political and a commercial one. The USA had to be the target of war propaganda, particularly after December 1941, and at the same time the market needed films capable of meeting the spectators' years-long familiarity with genres and settings that were dominated by American cinema. Even better if the two goals could be achieved in one fell swoop.

Nunzio Malasomma's *Cose dell'altro mondo* (1939) tackled head-on one of the most distinguished subgenres of American crime movies of the 1930s: prison films. The film is set in an American penitentiary, but the scriptwriters—including Giacomo Debenedetti and Sergio Amidei—tried to achieve a difficult fusion with the more conventional comedy of errors set in a wealthy bourgeois environment. The squalor and violence of real prisons is nowhere to be seen. First the family of the prison chief is forced to pretend to be convicts, and then the three alleged criminals who had escaped turn out to be a prison captain and his family. The prison, in other words, is more a narrative feature than a realistic setting. The starring role of Amedeo Nazzari, who, as we will see, featured in so many of these films, was not enough to save the film from oblivion. Critics were unanimously scathing.[85]

Despite the fiasco of his first 'American film', a year later, Malasomma was asked to direct a second attempt. This time the tentative American setting proposed by *Dopo divorzieremo* (1940) was that of New York's shopping mall attendants (although the film was almost entirely filmed inside their surprisingly luxurious flat), and, as the title suggests, the narrative thread was the recurring theme of the ease with which Americans walk in and out of a marriage. Amedeo Nazzari led the cast once again. This time the source was an Italian play that Malasomma and

---

[84] Carlo Lizzani, 'Vie del cinema italiano'; Emilio Ceretti, 'Il cinema americano contro l'intelligenza europea', *Cinema*, 8/160 (25 February 1943), 103, 116–17.

[85] On this film, see, e.g., Francesco Càllari, 'Cose dell'altro mondo', *Film*, 2/50 (16 December 1939), 2; and Giuseppe Isani, 'Cose dell'altro mondo', *Cinema*, 4/84 (25 December 1939), 393. Both Càllari and Isani mentioned Stan Laurel and Oliver Hardy's *Pardon us* (1931), their first full-length feature, as a prison film of a totally different, much superior quality.

Amidei had adapted for the screen. Jazz tunes added to the American urban tone, helped by the odd poster or placard in English. Apart from that, the externals were limited to medium shots, so that the studio reconstruction of New York could be contained and the characters all spoke in perfect Italian, with no concession to the English language other than for the names of characters—to the extent that, when the two protagonists get married, they walk under a welcoming sign saying 'Viva gli sposi' incongruently written in Italian. Amedeo Nazzari plays the part of Phil Golder, a lazy but talented violinist who by the end of the film becomes the successful director of a nightclub orchestra. This gives the director the chance of a welcome change of scene, with Nazzari conducting a fast and furious foxtrot sung in Italian ('C'è un'orchestra sincopata' by Cesare A. Bixio), moving his hands in Rabagliati style. The moral compass of the film, however, is strictly orthodox, with the foxtrot being followed by a slow, romantic tango, and the rebellious fiancée, played by a brilliant Lilia Silvi, eventually tamed. At the very end of the film, after being spanked by Phil, she promises to be good, affectionate, and obedient, after which she smilingly swoons in his arms. This time the critics were more positive, and Malasomma ended up directing a Spanish remake of the film entitled *El marido provisional* (1940).[86]

Another 1940 film showed the return of Mario Camerini to a screwball comedy, starring his wife Assia Noris, this time with the ever-present Amedeo Nazzari in lieu of Vittorio De Sica (who was by then beginning to think of his own career as a director). *Centomila dollari* (1940) was set in Budapest but featured an American millionaire who offered the vast sum in the title to an already engaged young woman (an orphan working as a telephone operator in a Grand Hotel) on the condition that she have dinner with him. The film started with a sudden event bringing together the two protagonists from different social backgrounds in a similar vein to Mattoli's *Tempo massimo*. In that case it was a woman parachuting herself and landing next to the rowing boat of the male protagonist, this time the 'modern woman' athletically throws stones to a church bell to make it ring, but, on one occasion, misses and breaks the windscreen of the millionaire's car. Predictably, the two eventually fall in love and the final sequence is clearly inspired by *Tempo massimo*. In both cases the woman is set to marry the rival until the male protagonist literally gatecrashes the scene—at the wheel of a pullman in the case of Vittorio De Sica, and with an ambulance in that of Amedeo Nazzari. When watching these films, and comparing them with their American models, one gets a sense of the rightful criticism coming from contemporary young critics such as Tito Spagnol, who, as we saw, denounced the scripts as underdeveloped

---

[86] Complimentary film reviews were published by *Cinema*, 5/104 (25 October 1940); and *La Stampa* (1 November 1940). The production company was Excelsa Film, a recently founded subsidiary of Minerva Film, the historic film distribution company founded in 1912 by Antonio Mosco and Costantino Potious. Five years later, Excelsa produced one of the most iconic films of Italian neorealism: Rossellini's *Roma città aperta*.

(and, indeed, dialogues are never consistently crisp and witty), or Antonio Pietrangeli, who attacked the artificiality of the settings, inventing glamorous but improbable mise-en-scènes.

Old-guard director Carmine Gallone tried to respond with a film—*Primo amore* (1941)—that included long takes of a documentary nature showing peasants working in the fields or following a religious procession in the mountainous landscape of Abruzzo. Here the American theme was linked to the fact that the male protagonist is an Italian musician who had become a famous jazz composer in America, but, having returned to Italy, converts to writing Italian melodies and falls in love with an Italian woman. Equally symbolic was his rejection of an American femme fatale (and jazz singer) who had followed him to Italy. The nationalistic plot was as unconvincing as the melodramatic tones of the suffering Italian woman played by an over-languorous Valentina Cortese. This tale of a near-religious clash between the amoral sophistication of American culture and the genuine purity of Italian traditions more than justified the mocking tone with which Diego Calcagno reviewed it for *Film*, dwelling on the adjective *galloniano*, which, after the fiasco of *Scipione l'Africano*, could hardly be used as a mark of guaranteed quality.[87]

The year 1942 brought two screwball comedies partially shot in Cinecittà: Raffaello Matarazzo's *Giorno di nozze* and Alessandro Blasetti's *Quattro passi fra le nuvole* (on which Cesare Zavattini worked as a scriptwriter). In the latter, the clash came in the form of a well-to-do salesman from northern Italy who meets an abandoned pregnant woman from the south. She convinces him to accompany her to her father's farm and to pretend that he is her husband to avoid being thrown out of the house. The tone here is dramatic, and even the final resolution—the salesman, subtly played by Gino Cervi, reveals his true identity but at the same time manages to convince the young woman's father to look after his daughter—leaves the bitter taste of a social reality that, though resolved in this case, leads most often to despair and brutal exclusion. The film has a no direct connection to American cinema or American settings. However, like Visconti's *Ossessione*, which was shot in the same year, it provides a convincing portrait of daily life in a corner of Italy, something that the young *Cinema* critics had been calling for, citing as model the capacity of American cinema and literature to narrate the 'real' America. Indeed, Giuseppe De Santis enthusiastically welcomed *Quattro passi fra le nuvole*, defining it as the realization of 'a poetics that we have been wishing for for a long time'.[88]

Entirely derivative of the American genre par excellence—the western—was a comic film starring popular comedian Erminio Macario, released in time for the Christmas holiday of 1942. To consider it as an ancestor of the Spaghetti westerns

---

[87] Diego Calcagno, 'Sette giorni a Roma', *Film*, 5/11 (14 March 1942), 6.
[88] Giuseppe De Santis, 'Quattro passi fra le nuvole', *Cinema*, 8/157 (10 January 1943), 27.

of the post-war years is too generous a link, since the film (lost today) was probably closer to the parodies one could find in comic films at the time from the likes of Buster Keaton. Indeed, Macario, after years of successful vaudeville shows—one of them was called 'Follie d'America'—had created the 'character' of Macario, which in some ways was an Italian equivalent to Charlie Chaplin's Tramp: the poor, wide-eyed, naïve little man who always manages to get by thanks to his instinctive wit. The title, after Puccini's opera, was *Il fanciullo del West*, but the plot had nothing to do with it, since it was based on the rivalry between two families brought to an end by Macario's character. *Cinema* wrote benevolently about Macario when the film was still in production, and, perhaps not by chance, in the same issue Osvaldo Campassi published a long article on the history of Hollywood westerns. Only in the concluding remarks, Campassi orthodoxically commented that the latest generation of American westerns—from King Vidor's *The Texas Rangers* (1936) to John Ford's *Stagecoach* (1939)—revealed a crisis of the genre.[89]

Films set in an imagined America continued to be produced until the regime's implosion in July 1943. Three such films were released in the final few months of 1943. Two were co-written and directed by Guglielmo Giannini, the playwright and journalist whom we have already met as co-scriptwriter in *Joe il rosso*. Early in 1943, Giannini had premiered as a film director with a propaganda crime film, *Il nemico* (1943). It was based on his play of a double murder that is eventually revealed as caused by a spy who used a transmitter hidden in a grand piano. The film was lukewarmly reviewed, but it must have been good enough for the producers to give Giannini the go-ahead for a sequel of cheaply produced crime films, shot in Cinecittà. Mindful of his 'American experience' in *Joe il rosso*, Giannini wrote and directed two other crime films, both set in an imaginary New York. The first, *Grattacieli* (1943), was unusually short—sixty-nine minutes—and entirely set in the luxurious top-floor apartment of a gangster called Jim Mayer Flynn, who turns out to be the murderer (though he is himself killed in the film's final scene). The improbability of both the film's setting and the plot were taken to pieces by the critics. Nevertheless, Giannini marched on with a second feature, *Quattro ragazze sognano* (1943), which featured a similar cast, this time with a young woman who manages to avoid being swindled out of an inheritance by a crooked lawyer thanks to a down-and-out but warm-hearted gangster symbolically called Al. In a similar way to *Joe il rosso*, the figure of an Italian American gangster was made acceptable through his characterization as a benevolent and entertaining figure. The film was released during the early days of Marshal Badoglio's interim government, on 5 August 1943.

---

[89] Enrico Morovich, 'Due soggetti per Macario', and Osvaldo Campassi, 'Vera essenza dei film della prateria', *Cinema*, 7/152 (25 October 1942), 610, 614–16. Giuseppe De Santis reviewed the film after his release, praising the director's—Giorgio Ferroni—camera work but criticizing the repetitive nature of Macario's comic gags—in *Cinema*, 8/159 (10 February 1943), 87.

A more significant film of 1943 that presented an American setting was *Harlem*, a Cines production shot in Cinecittà and directed by Carmine Gallone. The New York setting was introduced through the use of documentary footage of the city, accompanied by the syncopated rhythms of a jazz orchestra. It was a much more sophisticated approach compared to cheap productions such as *Dopo divorzieremo*, where the only concession to an external take of New York had been the enlarged photograph of a skyscraper appearing behind the back of a character. The team of scriptwriters, beyond the regular Sergio Amidei and Giacomo Debenedetti, saw the return of Emilio Cecchi to the company he had directed in the early post-Pittaluga years. Propaganda features were present in every twist of the cumbersome plot. First, we have an Italian migrant arriving in first class: no longer a semi-illiterate peasant, Tommaso Rossi (played by Massimo Girotti, fresh from his lead role in Visconti's *Ossessione*) is an architect and a skillful amateur boxer. Then we witness the fight between his brother, an honest Italian American businessman, and the seedy and cruel world of gangsters (clearly presented as non-Italian American). And, finally, we have the long sequence of the boxing match between the Italian hero and an African American that is meant to reverse the historic memory of Carnera's embarrassing defeat in 1935 against Joe Louis. *Harlem* ends with the gangsters murdering the brother, who, before breathing his last, tells Tommaso to leave behind the corruption of America and return to their fatherland.

How did critics respond to it? Beyond the praise of most of the Fascist press—well drummed up by Cines and the Ministry of Popular Culture—the specialist journals had other views. *Cinema* expressed its doubts with a long review by Giuseppe De Santis, published in May 1943. De Santis started by quoting a number of Hollywood films that had provided a stereotypical view of Italy. After that came the predictable volta: *Harlem* had done the same with America, and De Santis proceeded to list a number of superficialities through which the film had mimicked American life. He expressed his surprise that Emilio Cecchi should have been among the scriptwriters. How could such a fine, first-hand connoisseur of American life be satisfied with such a two-dimensional portrait? A month later, it was the turn of *Bianco e nero*, which, surprisingly, dedicated a three-page review of the film by another 'young Turk' who normally wrote for *Cinema*, Antonio Pietrangeli. It was the last issue of *Bianco e nero* before a four-year hiatus in the wake of Fascism's collapse. Pietrangeli started the piece with a famous 1922 quote by D. W. Griffith provocatively saying that the public has the collective mind of a 9 year old and that all that is needed for success is a gun and a girl. One could have predicted that the review was about to say that *Harlem* was that kind of film: popular with an unsophisticated audience. Initially the review seemed to move in that direction, even mentioning the audience standing up when following the most heated parts of the film. In fact, at that very point Pietrangeli turned the review into a brutal attack that makes it almost incredible that *Bianco e nero*'s director—the Luigi Chiarini who seemed so close to the regime—should have allowed it to be published. The second part of the review made no prisoners, and Cecchi was once again attacked in even more negative terms:

> The America we find in this story is artificial, re-churned a hundred times [...] The film's authors have in brief wanted to give the audience a surrogate of those American films whose fascinating atmosphere is still so attractive to them. Hence the personality, moves, and lives of the 'baddies', the situations, their developments, the solutions, are all copied from American models. And it is surprising to find that, among the scriptwriters of this kind of film, there should appear the name of academy-member Emilio Cecchi, allegedly an expert on things over the Atlantic. Which is the real America for him? That of Faulkner, Caldwell, Anderson, Hemingway, or that of Forde, Ledermann, and Hillyer? The master of the giant and sophisticated chinoiserie of erudite editorials—this social plague that one day or another, God willing, will quickly disappear—has signed off once again a script that is awkward, meaningless, full of cumbersome contradictions and sentimental falsettos so dear to the soppy stupidity of so many spectators.[90]

Beyond the personal views of Pietrangeli, the presence of such an article in *Bianco e nero* makes one think of a bigger picture of internal dissent. Luigi Freddi, then president of both Cinecittà and Cines, was heavily involved in the production of *Harlem*. He had spotted the short story around which the script was built and was keen to turn it into the ultimate propaganda film. It was an attack on American society that at the same time built on Hollywood's tradition: gangster movies and filmed sport events. It was also meant to be the film that eventually told a positive story of Italian migrants in the USA. However, despite Pavolini's initial approval, there had been resistance inside the Ministry of Popular Culture once the ministry fell into the hands of Polverelli. In the weeks before the release, Freddi wrote directly to Mussolini to make sure the film was not stopped, praising it as a sophisticated work of cinematic art (yet another example of Freddi's debatable taste in film aesthetics). Perhaps in some quarters it was feared that the film would provoke a similar propaganda fiasco to Gallone's *Scipione l'Africano*, or perhaps the idea of digging up Carnera's defeat, with mention of the Ethiopian war (now that the colonies were lost), was considered inopportune. Knowing Polverelli's *modus laborandi*, it is very unlikely that he should have taken any initiative towards a major project without Mussolini's consent. It is, therefore, possible that doubts about the value of Freddi's production were coming from *Il Duce* himself. In any case, the momentum was such that the film was screened on

---

[90] Antonio Pietrangeli, 'Harlem', *Bianco e nero*, 7/6 (June 1943), 32–5.

20 April 1943 to a group of distributors before reaching Italy's first-run cinemas the following week.[91]

Returning to *Bianco e nero*'s scathing review, one might wonder whether Pietrangeli was allowed space and a free rein in order to teach Freddi and Cines a lesson. Or was there a bigger picture? By the spring of 1943 the cracks within the regime were appearing—some accepting the inevitability of a military surrender to avoid a ground war on the Italian peninsula—and perhaps the film was seen as a vicious attack against the USA at a time in which more diplomatic means had to be used? Or perhaps it was Mussolini's own views—it had been planned that *Harlem* would be privately screened at Villa Torlonia but we have no evidence that the screening took place—which, via his son, might have allowed the *Cinema* and *Bianco e nero* groups *carte blanche* towards a film that, indeed, showed debatable value from both a formal and a political viewpoint.[92]

Bizarrely, the very last weeks of the regime saw the production of a jazz musical. Riccardo Freda's *Tutta la città canta* was shot in the Tuscan studios of Pisorno (a minor studio created in 1934), with music by Gorni Kramer and singing performances by Natalino Otto. The ruse to avoid censorship was the usual 'Italianness' of the entire production, starting with the setting of the film. However, one only has to watch some of the choreographed pieces that pepper the narrative to see the extent to which Freda was trying to reproduce the feel and look of the great American musicals of the 1930s. It is the story of a provincial schoolteacher living with his two sanctimonious aunts. Bizarrely, he inherits a vaudeville company, which he brings to his home town, with all the comic situations one can easily imagine. Freda was fresh from his debut as director with the adventure film *Don Cesare di Bazan* (1942), which had received much praise for his capacity to give pace and a spectacular look to the narrative. Some critics saw this as modelled on American swashbucklers. He continued in this vein during the post-war years, with popular films such as *Aquila nera* (1946, based on a storyline already made famous by Rodolfo Valentino) and *Beatrice Cenci* (1956), which marked the beginning of a darker style that was to turn him into a cult director of Gothic horror films.[93]

While *Tutta la città canta* was in production, *Cinema* devoted one of its issues to dance in cinema. After articles on waltz and classical music, it was the turn of jazz: this time Giuseppe De Santis managed to deliver a balancing act, first

---

[91] A recent monograph devoted entirely to this film is Luca Martera, *Harlem: Il film più censurato di sempre* (Milan and Rome: La Nave di Teseo–Centro Sperimentale di Cinematografia, 2021).

[92] Martera's book, despite its 345 pages of accurate historical evidence on this single film, cannot give a clear answer. A post-war coda to the distribution of *Harlem* should be mentioned. After a process of self-censorship to free it from the most compromising racist and anti-American traits, the film surprisingly returned to Italian cinemas in 1947 under the title *Knock-Out*. On this see Martera, *Harlem*, 199–262.

[93] On Freda, see Roberto Curti, *Riccardo Freda: The Life and Works of a Born Filmmaker* (Jefferson, NC: McFarland & Company, 2017).

Fig. 10.16. A cameo appearance of Gorni Kramer in Riccardo Freda's *Tutta la città canta* (1946). (courtesy of Cineteca di Milano)

criticizing Hollywood musicals for their superficial and escapist use of jazz music—with Fred Astaire as the ultimate example of jazz dance turned into a virtuoso exercise—but then praising King Vidor's representation of the deep roots of jazz within the American black community. Vidor's *Halleluiah* was also praised by Francesco Pasinetti in his article on dance in cinema within the same issue. Again, it is difficult not to see all this as the clear sign of the survival of a strong 'pro-American' party right at the end of the regime.[94]

A concluding comment concerns the greatest American filmmaker of the interwar years, Charlie Chaplin. As we saw in Chapter 9, the odd reference to the presumed Jewishness of Chaplin was already present in pre-1938 articles, although not necessarily with an anti-Semitic slant. After the legislation, though, the field was open to all sorts of innuendos and vilification. *The Dictator* (1940) was unsurprisingly ignored, but that did not stop journalists and film critics from writing about Chaplin. In a potted history of the Jewish presence in world cinema, published by *Bianco e nero* in May 1939, and perfectly in line with the regime's new racist policies, Chaplin was presented once again as an example of Jewish culture, in this case of the Jewish drive for commercial success, which, according to the author, had turned an art, cinema, into a money-making machine.[95]

---

[94] Giuseppe De Santis, 'Il jazz e le sue danze nel cinema'; Francesco Pasinetti, 'La danza e il ritmo cinematografico', *Cinema*, 8/164 (25 April 1943), 236–8, 232–3. The production of *Tutta la città canta* was interrupted by the collapse of the regime. Indeed, the film was finished and released only after the end of the war with the new title *6x8/48* (1946).

[95] Domenico Paolella, 'Gli ebrei nel cinema', *Bianco e nero*, 3/5 (1939), 45. Paolella was then an aspiring director and scriptwriter, who, soon after the war, became artistic director of Settimana

The peak of anti-Semitism was achieved by a journalist, Marco Ramperti, who had already expressed his racism when writing about Chaplin in a 1933 article for *La Stampa* mentioned in Chapter 9. This time Ramperti was given space in one of the very last issues of *Film* before the regime's implosion, on 10 July 1943. 'Charlot ebreo due volte' once again delved into Chaplin's private life in order to prove the existence of a mean-spirited Jew whose hypocrisy was supposed to throw a revealing light on the filmmaker. Ramperti continued his journalistic militancy during the years of the Repubblica Sociale Italiana, for which he was arrested at the end of the war and released from prison only thanks to the government's amnesty of 1946. He then returned to his work as a fiction writer. In 1950 he published a phantasy novel, *Benito I Imperatore*, in which he imagined Mussolini during the months after the victory of the Axis, achieved thanks to its own use of the atomic bomb in 1945. The USA, according to Ramperti's imagination, was by then falling into the hands of women, and the next American ambassador in Rome was going to be Rita Hayworth.[96]

However, it is perhaps more fitting to end this chapter on a different note. On the same day that the *Film* issue of 10 July 1943 came out, *Cinema* distributed its last issue directed by Vittorio Mussolini before the fall of the regime. It contained an essay by Osvaldo Campassi that was part of a feature dedicated to great masterpieces of the past. The film chosen was King Vidor's *The Crowd*. Once again, a film by Vidor was singled out as an example of a director who had managed to bring the spirit of his times to the screen. *Cinema* was not giving up on America.[97]

## Conclusion

Alfieri's draconian anti-American policies on books, films, music, and comic magazines were part and parcel of the nationalistic clampdown of 1938. If the Nazis had inspired the centralization of culture in the mid-1930s, it was now a question of catching up in time for the final showdown. America was by then a clear enemy-to-be, whose influence had to be eradicated. This forms a final phase of our so-called nationalistic denial of the obvious. Anti-American protectionism hit publishing houses, film distribution, music broadcasts, and peaked—in

---

Incom (the postwar competitor of LUCE's newsreels, co-founded by Luigi Freddi) and, later a prolific director of B-movies in all sorts of different genres. On Paolella and his anti-Semitic writings, see Andrea Minuz, 'I "valori spirituali" del cinema italiano: Antisemitismo e politiche della razza nelle riviste cinematografiche degli anni trenta', *Trauma and Memory*, 5/3 (2017), 96–102.

[96] Marco Ramperti, 'Chaplin ebreo due volte', *Film*, 6/28 (10 July 1943), 5. Ramperti had also singled out Chaplin in a vitriolic anti-Semitic piece entitled 'Più che dalla stella gialla gli ebrei si riconoscono dalla ferocia dello sguardo', published in *Il Popolo di Roma* on 31 December 1941. His 1950 phantasy novel is still in print, thanks to the historic publisher of Italy's neo-Fascist movement, Edizioni di Ar.

[97] Osvaldo Campassi, '"La folla" di King Vidor', *Cinema*, 8/169 (10 July 1943), 21–2.

absurdity—with the 1941 rule that comics should return to the *Belle époque* tradition of rhyming couplets at the bottom of the text.

One could even argue that Nazism was partly responsible for the final failure of Fascism's claim to being a model of European civilization. Hitler's megalomania tragically dictated the pace of the upcoming world war. By June 1940, Fascist Italy was still far from being ready. Mussolini's pride and joy, his super-Fascist air forces, entered the war with outdated aeroplanes. A whole nation was to suffer the tragic cynicism of a decision taken in the wake of Hitler's armies and in the hope that the war would soon be over. From a cultural viewpoint, the Second World War was similarly disastrous for the Fascists. It scuppered Mussolini's dream of showing to the world what Fascism had become by inviting all nations to visit Rome's EUR42 exhibition. The grandiose peak of Italy's regime-controlled architecture, whose iconic giant arch should have competed for time immemorial with Paris's Tour Eiffel and New York's skyscrapers, was left as an unfinished project, a spectacular waste land.[98]

American technology and American mass production did the rest, massively helping to turn the course of the war. By the time the first GIs set foot on Sicilian beaches—some of them proud Italian Americans—the obvious was there for all to see. The superior popularity of US troops over Montgomery's 8th Army had nothing to do with the British character. People could not wait to see 'the Americans'. Their arrival, they knew, was going to mark the return of so many things Italians had learnt to dream of, desire, and cherish. Despite, by then, five years of attempted 'de-Americanization', the appeal of American culture was still present. In the minds of many, the expression 'America' still carried connotations of modernity, fun, and a better lifestyle.

---

[98] On 4 February 1939, when chairing the Grand Council of Fascism, Mussolini was still convinced that the war would break out after the climax of the 1942 Exhibition. As he confessed to industrialist Alberto Pirelli, his idea was that the exhibition would attract millions of foreign visitors, whose precious foreign currency would be invested in strengthening Italy's army. On this see Nicoloso, *Mussolini architetto*, 203–6.

# Conclusion

During the decades preceding the Second World War, rather than eliciting a smooth range of varying opinions, America raised extreme reactions. It provoked wide-eyed gazes and, at the same time, condescending smirks; silent attraction and explicit loathing. It evoked different sounds: the swinging rhythms of a jazz band and the weltering thuds of an assembly line. It concocted different images: a glamorous film star and a lynched African American.

When Italy was unified, in 1861, its politicians and intellectuals had more pressing matters to think about than questions of foreign cultural influence. The ruling elite was in charge of a vast peninsula, populated by more than twenty million people speaking countless different dialects. A sense of national identity was forged from Italy's glorious literary past, but the present proved more difficult to shape. The disastrous war against Austria of 1866, in which the first national army of Italy met with defeat on both land and sea, was followed a month later by a popular uprising in Palermo that saw the young Italian state lose control of Sicily's main city for an entire week. 'Making the Italians' was proving hard work.

Amid the tensions and the suffering of these troubled years, there is one technical detail: the flagship man-of-war of the Italian Royal Navy, which, in September 1867, opened fire on Palermo and quickly deployed the troops that reconquered the city, was the product of American technology. Confusingly named *Re di Portogallo* (to celebrate the Savoy family's Portuguese connection), the ironclad battleship had been launched from its New York shipyard in August 1863. The *Re di Portogallo* had been involved in the disastrous battle of Lissa in July 1866 (when its sibling, the *Re d'Italia*, was sunk) and subsequently redeployed in the Sicilian waters to lead the suppression of the Palermitan uprising. At the other end of the Atlantic, still embroiled in its civil war, the United States of America was emerging as an industrialized country able to compete with and supply its European rivals. The shipyard from which the two battleships had originated was owned by William H. Webb, one of the fathers of America's naval design. His most famous clipper, built in 1853 and considered a paradigm in its class, was symbolically named *Young America*.

The five decades between Italy's unification and the First World War saw the slow appearance of the USA, not just as a distant, exotic country of vast spaces and zany citizens, but as a political, economic, and cultural power to be reckoned with. The two decades of Fascist rule saw the arrival of what today we would call 'mass culture', and in many cases it came with a 'Made in USA' label attached to it.

America was a leading power in the field of middlebrow culture, years ahead of Italy in terms of industrial infrastructure and decades ahead in terms of spending power among its working classes. Italy was slowly becoming a wealthier, better-educated society, and this meant more time and money for free-time activities. Paolo D'Attorre is right to remind us that, in many cases, Italians could only dream of the privileges that their American peers could afford, such as a radio set or a car; but it was nonetheless an aspiration that was real, powerful, and infectious. Italy's 'two nations' of previous decades were much closer than they had ever been. The elite could travel first class to America on the *Rex*, of course, but many did travel in third class; and, in Italy, they all watched the same movies, danced to the same tunes, and, if interested, could read the same books.[1]

In these final pages, brief attention will be paid to what, in the research devoted to this book, emerged as a surprising discovery, somehow fooling expectations. I will then conclude with some considerations on how the whole study falls within the wider discussion on the influence of American culture.

## The Belle Époque

In his *The Americanization of the World* (1901), when writing about the fields in which he thought the USA would 'Americanize' the rest of the planet, W. T. Stead dwelled first on religion. Prophetic in so many other ways, when it came to religion, Stead—the son of a Protestant minister—was blinded by his own anti-Catholicism. To him, the history of the two Americas was the perfect parable of the superiority of Protestantism. The sinful gluttony of Catholic culture had produced corruption and misery in Latin America, while the stern but entrepreneurial faith of Puritanism had produced, up north, the greatest nation of the twentieth century. Now it was the turn of this religion-powered superiority to be exported all over the world. However, when that happened, the religious dimension was gone. Where did Stead get it wrong? His error of judgement, beyond the simplifications of his vision of the Americas' macro-history, was due to the fact that the USA, when it came to exporting its social and economic lifestyle, was more pragmatic and secular than Stead would have hoped. By the first decades of the twentieth century, with the rise on the social ladder of the Irish community, followed by those of both Italian and the Jewish descent, being a good American did not require adherence to any Protestant church. If WASP Americans had founded a promising democratic nation, its economic success was partly due to its capacity to absorb wave after wave of entrepreneurial non-Protestants.

---

[1] D'Attorre, 'Il sogno americano', 24–5.

What was a surprise, when reading articles and travel pieces on the USA written by Italian journalists, scholars, and travellers, was to see short-sightedness equal to Stead's, only of an opposite pole. If Stead had been fooled by his own Protestant fervour, Italian commentators found it difficult to step out of a vision that could be generically defined as nationalistic and anti-Protestant. Difference and diversity were immediately compared to the familiar norm, and judged to fall short of it. Italy's educated elite—Latin and Catholic—looked down on Protestant America. Once again, from his prison cell, Gramsci spotted this trend. He noted the glee with which Italian readers would discuss Sinclair Lewis's *Babbitt* as a denunciation of the empty materialism of American society while they were oblivious to their own close-mindedness.[2]

As a result, the emancipation of women was recurrently criticized and derided as a weakness of the Protestant man. Divorce was the yardstick with which many Italian travellers measured the moral degeneration of American society. Divorce was no rightful progress on women's rights; rather, it was a weapon invented by women to sponge lifelong benefits from their wealthy ex-husbands. Moral hypocrisy was also a sin that was found to define WASP America. In this case, the sin was to proclaim strict moral rulings—such as the ban on alcohol—and then tolerate and partake in their open evasion. If the Italian American community was ever mentioned, it was either to show how it was immune from those sins, or as a denunciation of how this moral weakness was beginning to intoxicate the flesh and mind of the Latin people.

Where the WASP and the WICC met (let us return to the acroynym proposed in chapter 6: White Italian Catholic Commentator) was in their ambivalent attitude towards African Americans. This was an uncomfortable discovery. Despite the immense popularity in Italy of Harriet Beecher Stowe's *Uncle Tom's Cabin* (1852) throughout the second half of the nineteenth century, when it came to face-to-face meetings, in the metropolises of the north-east or, more rarely, in the rural plains of the Deep South, the racist view prevailed. Was the social and political emancipation of African Americans a mistake? The odd word of tolerance for the practice of lynching as the white man's last resort to maintaining law and order marked the lowest ebb of this attitude, made possible by the removal of any memory of the biggest lynching in American history, one that targeted eleven Italian Americans in 1891. Only a handful of Italian journalists and authors escaped this racist attitude. Worst, it often served an instrumental use: trolleyed-out when needed as a further sample of America's dark side, or to justify Italy's own state-racism in the last years of Fascism.

The Italian American community too was subjected to a similar, targeted attention. It was at the centre of the Italian traveller's interest mainly through a

---

[2] Gramsci, Quaderno 6 (1930–1932), §49.

nationalistic narrative of self-defence. Only sporadically was it explored in depth. It felt as though the America imagined from Italy was not supposed to include former Italians. It was the exotic that people sought, not the familiar.

Beyond the perception of America, a surprising feature was the nature of the influence of American culture. For those early decades, one can speak in terms of 'techniques'. Americans mainly taught Italians 'how to do things', through their capacity to produce in vast quantities while containing costs and labour, through their love for the machine, and through their dynamic marketing departments. It is almost a fateful sign of the times that the American philosophical school that gained notoriety at the start of the twentieth century should be called pragmatism. Hence, it is only consequential to find, among the 'early importers' of American culture, the fathers of the Italian industry: from Camillo Olivetti, to Giovanni Agnelli, together with Alberto and Piero Pirelli, who made repeated visits to the USA in order to observe America's cutting-edge hardware and to forge commercial alliances. Even in the world of journalism, on his return to Italy, what Dario Papa brought with him was the technique, the drive, and the pragmatic approach of American journalism. Similarly, the fact-based, bone-dry narrative of Adolfo Rossi was the technique that he had brought with him from New York, and that he so successfully applied as a correspondent for *Corriere della Sera* and *La Tribuna*.

If until the early years of the twentieth century, it was mainly techniques that America exported to Italy, this was soon replaced by the first waves of artefacts. Literary works became more and more popular, but it was American cinema that was to emerge as the stronger influence. By the time young Europeans came out of the trenches and life returned to normality, there was a new beacon illuminating the world with its flickering light. It had been built in the space of a decade, out of the desolated outskirts of a Californian city, so unknown that its inhabitants had to build a giant advertising sign on its hills, spelling 'Hollywood'.

The end of the First World War also brought President Wilson's imposition, at Versailles, of the English language as the language of diplomacy, on equal terms with French. Throughout the nineteenth century, despite its global power, the British Empire had allowed French to continue in its role as the international language *par excellence*. It was no great concession, since the British educated elite, as much as that of any other European country, was fully at ease in that language. In 1919, Wilson broke the spell, in typical uncouth American fashion. Italy's educated elite responded with indifference. After the fiasco of Luigi Credaro's Liceo Moderno—wiped out by Giovanni Gentile's reform of 1923—the Italian education system stabilized itself on the traditional notion of Latin and ancient Greek as the main foreign languages to be learnt. French was the only concession to the modern world. All this while, from below, millions of Italians continued their long journey to America, which implied learning English for those ending up in the USA, however imperfectly spoken. Unsurprisingly, linguists show us how return migration had a bigger 'Americanizing' impact on dialects rather than on the Italian language. Dialect was the mother tongue of those migrants.

## The Jazz Age

In Italy, the jazz age corresponded with the beginning of the Fascist age—hence the importance given in this book to Benito Mussolini's views of America. What emerged was a clear sense of *Il Duce*'s instrumental use of culture. He was neither pro- nor anti-American; rather he was pro- or anti-American according to circumstances and to his political aims at a particular time. Hollywood's grip on Italian cinemas did not bother him, and, when his son Vittorio thought of himself as a film producer, he was happy to let him do business with the Americans until as late as the autumn of 1937. A year later he was equally prepared to let Alfieri declare war on Hollywood when the alliance with Nazi Germany made this desirable. Jazz music too was initially allowed to spread, since it brought an aura of modernity and dynamism that was in tune with Fascism's cult of its own revolutionary ethos. When the racial question made it progressively more 'incorrect', the solution was to allow jazz to continue in its Italian form, composed by Italians and sung in Italian.

Fascism's anti-Americanism was a late policy, dictated by geopolitical rather than cultural circumstances. It became official in 1938 and was later intensified by open warfare between the two countries. In many respects, *Time*'s cover photograph of Mussolini with his two eldest sons, Bruno and Vittorio, published in October 1935, is iconic of the pre-1938 years. It took the invasion of Ethiopia to start to ruin the long honeymoon between Fascism and the American media. In the preceding thirteen years of dictatorship, Italian Fascism and American culture were far from being at loggerheads. Mussolini was praised as a political figure, and he reciprocated by praising America as a young nation that had moved to the centre of the international stage in a way that, he hoped, Fascist Italy would one day follow. In their black shirts, Bruno, the aviator, and Vittorio, the budding film producer, embodied two realms that American and Fascist culture celebrated equally. Bruno and Vittorio represented the new, fearless Fascist Italy, ready to take on the world. America had lessons to teach when it came to technology, regardless of whether it implied producing, with maximum cost-effectiveness, aircrafts or films or any other artefact. Had Mussolini's eldest daughter, Edda, been part of the photograph, with her 'flapper's' shortcut hair, sporty clothing, and love for jazz music, it would have completed the picture of a Italian family whose younger generation was perfectly at ease with American culture.

The anti-American propaganda of the late 1930s, if nothing else, disconnected many Italians from the regime, since it attacked notions and values that Italians had already absorbed or aspired to. The image of a lifestyle based on an individual

Fig. 11.1. The Mussolini family: left, the cover of *Time*, 26/18 (8 October 1935), featuring Mussolini with his sons Bruno (left) and Vittorio (right) (courtesy of BNC, Rome); right, detail from a photograph showing Edda Mussolini with a group of blackshirts during a cruise to India of the Naval League, on 21 February 1929. (courtesy of Archivio Luce, Rome)

search for pleasure and wealth was more attractive to the Italian ethos than the cult of the state and of autarkic frugality churned out by the regime. By 1938, every day, Italians listened to American-style music, watched American films, read American fiction; teenagers read American comics and children played at *indiani e cow-boy*. If pre-First World War Italy imported the 'techniques' of American culture, the interwar years welcomed the transfer and replica of the artefacts themselves. Linking this process to the image of American culture as closely related to modernity, Miriam Bratu Hansen coined the notion of 'vernacular modernism'. It is a notion that manages to encapsulate the concentration of innovation and popular appeal that characterized American culture in different fields such as literature, cinema, and journalism. And, as she adds:

If classical Hollywood cinema succeeded as an international modernist idiom on a mass basis, it did so not because of its presumably universal narrative form but because it meant different things to different people and publics, both at home and abroad. [...] To write the international history of classical American cinema, therefore, is a matter of tracing not just its mechanisms of standardization and hegemony but also the diversity of ways in which this cinema was translated and reconfigured in both local and translocal contexts of reception.[3]

The preceding chapters have, I hope, given an idea of how American culture was transferred and reconfigured in Italy's interwar years.

If there was a surprising discovery for this period, it is related not so much to the well-cultivated fields of music, film, and literature but, rather, to that of architecture. Although the Fascists did not explicitly rival America in the construction of high-rise buildings, it was fascinating to see how this ambition was nonetheless part of the regime's idea of its own modernity. Marcello Piacentini was at the same time Fascism's main architect and the father of Italy's skyscrapers during years in which most European cities spurned the American contribution to world architecture. Piacentini was also the supervisor of the EUR42 project, which was supposed to offer itself as the ultimate showcase of Fascist Italy.

The EUR42 project produced two unexpected offshoots in the post-war years, despite the taboo to which this Roman district was subjected. The first, as we saw in Chapter 10, was the intriguing similarity between Libera's never-built, giant arch at the entrance of EUR42 and Saarinen's one in St Louis's Remembrance Park. The second one is more incidental but nonetheless symbolic. Since 2014, the most iconic building at EUR, the Palazzo della Civiltà Italiana, has become the headquarters of one of Italy's most prestigious fashion houses, Fendi. The peak of Fascism's architectural aesthetics is now part of the image of a leading company in Italy's best export market, designer clothing. What does this tell us about today's Italy? Although this falls outside the remit of this book, one can at least suggest that it is an implicit recognition of the value of Italy's contribution to the early history of high-rise buildings. The writing on the four facades of the *palazzo* is still embarrassing today, but the architectural achievement allows for the toleration of Italy's past political arrogance. It is also the sign of a reconciliation of sorts with Italy's Fascist years. But whether this is a positive symptom of maturity or a sinister return to the past (or perhaps a mixture of the two) is too delicate a question to be tackled here.

Talking of arrogance, the racial attitude with which Italians referred to African Americans remained the same during the interwar years, and if nothing else became harsher. The USA was considered a paradigm of the challenges of

---

[3] Miriam Bratu Hansen, 'The Mass Production of the Senses: Classical Cinema as Vernacular Modernism', *Modernism/Modernity*, 6 (1999), 59–77 (68).

cohabiting with a black community. When open war—from December 1941—required anti-American propaganda to step up a gear and produce shocking illustrations of the American threat, the monstrous, wide-eyed, black GI soldier became the recurrent image.

The Italian American community, too, continued to play an odd part in the representation of America. The prevailing nationalism of the Fascist years should have engendered an explicit praise of the achievements of Italian Americans. Instead, it was a game that was played only at the political level—when praising Italy's 'American colony'—but not culturally. Italian commentators were still reluctant to dwell on the Italian American community. It somehow interfered with the image of the United States of America that readers wanted to hear about. A similar case concerns jazz musicians. The role of Sicilian Americans such as Nick La Rocca was almost entirely ignored, even when the anti-American opposition to jazz would have allowed it as a good excuse for jazz enthusiasts to keep welcoming what was coming from the USA. The 'Other' that America represented had somehow to remain a distant, detached reality, untouched by the traumatic echoes of Italy's mass migration, a migration that, however successful in many cases, had originated from poverty, and disillusionment in one's motherland.

## An Inevitable 'Americanization'?

At the end of one of her by now vintage essays, going back to 1984, Victoria De Grazia suggested that studies on Americanization should ask themselves whether the process was 'natural and inevitable'.[4] 'Americanization' is a loaded expression, and the fact that this study has avoided its use is part of a move towards a more articulated understanding of cultural change. However, if the question is rephrased as referring to the attraction and influence of American culture, then, from this end, it looks as if its tenacity during the nationalistic, autarkic years of Fascism would suggest that there was a degree of inevitability, particularly because of its identification with the notion of 'modernity', as Emilio Gentile had argued.[5]

By 1938, the presence of American culture had reached a point of no return. The case of jazz music is exemplary: to eradicate it would have meant imposing a massive act of cultural censorship, which nobody within the Fascist regime ever thought advisable. This does not mean that the process was entirely uncontrollable. At the other end of the spectrum we have the example of the car industry. Here, thanks to Giovanni Agnelli's influence on Mussolini, the regime imposed such strict protectionist policies against American cars that the result was the best of both worlds, for FIAT: American 'techniques' were transferred but at the same

[4] De Grazia, 'Americanism for Export', 81.
[5] Gentile, 'Impending Modernity: Fascism and the Ambivalent Image of the United States'.

time the doors remained shut to American imports, so that the first low-cost car sold in Italy was a FIAT and not a Ford model. Irony dictated that the protruding lights of the Fiat 500 eventually gave birth to the nickname 'Topolino'. In other words, Agnelli managed to import American industrial practices and, at the same time, avoid America's competition in the car market—all this while the American-influenced film and comics industries indirectly provided a bit of modern, American flavour to his FIAT 500. And, when even the iconic Mickey Mouse—despite Mondadori's strenuous resistance—was taken off the pages of Italian comics, as late as 1942, the regime eventually tolerated the creation of an Italian-made equivalent called Tuffolino. If a straight replica could be banned, an Italian re-elaboration seemed by then necessary.

American cinema, literature, comics, music—all flooded Italy's entertainment markets with their products. If it is debatable whether the image of America as imported through those products actually conveyed an idea of democracy that was implicitly anti-Fascist, there is no doubt that it projected a lifestyle and a culture that were at loggerheads with Fascism's regimented cult of the state. So, when Mussolini decided, in 1938, that Italians had to be taught to be a master race, in the wake of their German neighbours, the regime's proclamations fell on the deaf ears of many Italians—probably most Italians.

When asked for his view of American culture under Fascism, Federico Fellini produced an insightful intuition:

> American literature and cinema were one and the same thing. [...]: it was real life that gloriously opposed the sinister vitalism of party officials dressed in black jumping through circles of fire: it was the individual who prevailed over the collective.[6]

If nothing else, the anti-American policies of the last years of Fascism made many Italians realize how detached they were from a strict understanding of Totalitarianism. Mussolini's anthropological revolution had failed. The individualism that characterizes the Italian ethos was better fed by the narratives coming from America than by the calls for collective sacrifice and subjection to the state that came from Mussolini's ministries.

The year 1938 was also the one in which Italians were told to be racist, not just against their African subjects, but also against their internal enemy, the Jewish community that for years Mussolini had boasted as entirely integrated. After ridiculing Hitler's anti-Semitism, the same credo was now part of Fascism's new, suprematist ethos. Hollywood became the paradigm of America's role as an economy in the hands of Judeo-plutocrats. Italians were asked to give up something they had become familiar with—and had enjoyed—because it denied the principles

---

[6] Federico Fellini, *Intervista sul cinema* (Rome and Bari: Laterza, 1983), 46.

on which Nazi-Fascism's New Order was based. Mussolini, the ultimate sorcerer of Italian politics, this time went too far, asked for too much, and led a nation into years of sufferings, death, and civil war.

From July 1943 until April 1945, the Allied army—mainly understood as 'the Americans'—was welcome in its slow march up the Italian peninsula, not just because it brought an end to the war. It also brought back visions of a lifestyle that was so much more attractive than the late face of Fascism. The fact that some of those GIs were Italian Americans added a further, healthy reconnection with Italy's recent, humble past.

## The End of the Beginning

A few months after the liberation of Rome, writing for a newly founded journal, Emilio Cecchi wrote a review of Chaplin's *The Great Dictator* (1940). It was a lukewarm review, consistent with Cecchi's preference for the early Chaplin. More importantly, when it came to the character of Mussolini, Cecchi condemned the film for having produced a poor caricature, 'entirely missing the point'. It is interesting to note how Cecchi managed to write an entire paragraph on Chaplin's caricature of Mussolini without ever mentioning the dictator's name. *Il Duce* was still alive, then, only four hundred miles further north, an ill man presiding over a Nazi puppet state. Perhaps the journal, or the Allies, did not allow explicit mention of Mussolini, or perhaps it was an act of self-restraint by Cecchi himself. Similarly, Chaplin's attack against Hitler's anti-Semitism was not mentioned in the article. Some topics were perhaps still too heated to be touched upon. But Cecchi was right: the caricature of Mussolini was not particularly good. It presented Mussolini as a buffoon, cheekily bossing around Hitler, a happy-go-lucky charlatan whose main preoccupation was to have a plate of steaming pasta always next to him. What Cecchi could not predict was the fact that Chaplin's caricature was to become a model in the post-war years.

Fifty years later, Gian Piero Brunetta concluded that Chaplin's deformation of Mussolini's character had become mainstream in Italian culture. It was a sort of exorcism through which this gigantic presence in Italy's history of the previous twenty years could be instantly framed and ridiculed. Not that Mussolini did not contribute to it with his theatrical poses and mad looks during his public speeches. But it was as if this single aspect of Mussolini had been turned into the whole of his persona and as such could easily be relegated to the hall of ridiculous fame: detached, removed from any connection he might have had with the life and mind (and heart) of many Italians.[7]

---

[7] Emilio Cecchi, 'Il dittatore', *Mercurio*, 3 (1944); then in Cecchi, *Fra Buster Keaton e Visconti*, 231–2 (232). Brunetta, 'Il sogno a stelle e strisce di Mussolini', 175–6.

From Turin, another 'Americanista', Cesare Pavese, began a new phase in his life, in his case as a pro-Communist intellectual living in a democratic Italy quickly put under the roof of the Atlantic Pact. The USA, in the early post-war years, became a target of Communist propaganda, and Pavese had to deal with this new reality. On 3 August 1946, from the pages of the PCI's daily, *L'Unità*, Pavese suggested that the fertile influence of American culture had run its course: 'it seems to us that American culture has lost is primacy, its naïve and shrewd fervour that put it at the avant-garde of our intellectual world.' The use of the first person plural is indicative of Pavese's attempt to find a formula that could justify a development that was political first and foremost.[8]

In many ways, the cold war had already started. America had ceased to be a mainly imagined place, and, instead, it had become a political presence directly involved in the shaping of post-Fascist Italy. Paradoxically, many of those who had been hailing America as a source of inspiration—and Pavese was one of them—found themselves pushed towards a critical stance as a result of the PCI's unrelenting anti-Americanism. And those who had followed the Fascist regime in their late demonization of American culture found themselves hailing it as a shield against Soviet Union-led Communism. Thanks to these confused times, a film as profoundly racist and anti-American as *Harlem* (1943) could still find its way back into Italy's cinema theatres after a quick editing-out of its more outrageous lines and shots. After all, and absurdly so, it could now be enjoyed by both factions: former Fascists enjoying its nationalistic narrative, and Communist militants appreciating its critique of American society.

The post-war years could not have started in a more complicated manner. Perhaps this contradictory and still ambivalent perception of American culture is also a cause for the scarcity of critical discussion of the links between King Vidor's early films and Italian neorealist cinema, embodied by Rossellini's and De Sica's own humanist, anti-rhetorical take on contemporary society. A similar case was that of neorealist literature, but there the American influence had been more openly recognized. In later years, even the most autochthonous of all narrative genres, the western, was to be appropriated and elaborated: from the popular comic strips of Tex Willer (created in 1948 by Gian Luigi Bonelli and Aurelio Galleppini) to the '"Spaghettification' of the genre, peaking with Bruno Bozzetto's animation *West and Soda* (1965), and Sergio Leone's *Once upon a Time in the West* (1968).

The advance of the American/English language too was a phenomenon that mainly took place in the post-Second World War years. Thanks to lack of change in Italy's education system, secondary schools continued to teach French as the main modern language well into the 1980s—this, despite the fact that linguists could already point to the fact that, since 1945, the English language was by far

---

[8] Cesare Pavese, 'Ieri e oggi', *L'Unità* (Turinese edition), 3 August 1947, p. 3; then in *Letteratura americana e altri saggi*, 193–6.

Fig. 11.2. Film still from Fellini's *La dolce vita* (1960), with Adriano Celentano, in the middle, singing 'Ready Teddy' in his makeshift English. (courtesy of Legenda, Cambridge)

more influential and had—to borrow Giulio Lepschy's words—'replaced French as the most dangerous language'.[9]

Once again, Federico Fellini had a stroke of genius when, in 1959, he asked an unknown rock'n'roll singer who was debuting in Milan's nightclubs, pretending to be able to sing in English, to come and act in his next film. Adriano Celentano's performance, singing his gobbledegook version of Little Richard's 'Ready Teddy' during an Ancient Roman fancy-dress party in *La dolce vita* (1960), became such an iconic scene that Celentano was to continue his successful career composing and singing some of his songs in imaginary English. In the end, it was only as late as 1988 that English overtook French as the most-taught modern language in Italy's secondary schools. In other words, Italy's linguistic turn took place about half a century after American culture had become most influential outside the classroom.

## America and Italy's 'Modern Times'

The inevitability of the penetration by American culture during the interwar period was dependent on the fact that Italy, like other European countries, in those same years experienced the epoch-making expansion of mass culture. Italy's working classes were eventually able to share some of the free-time activities that for centuries had been the privileged domain of the educated elite. It was coincidental that this should have happened during the years in which the American

---

[9] Giulio Lepschy, 'Anglismi e italianismi' (1995), in Lepschy, *L'amanuense analfabeta e altri saggi* (Florence: Olschky, 1992), 169–92 (171).

cultural industries had a leading edge thanks to the strength of the US economy and to the traumas and ruptures brought by the First World War on European soil. Had this happened a generation or two earlier, sociologists today would be writing about the 'Frenchization' of popular culture in the Western world and beyond.

Moving the chronological boundary of this study all the way back to Italy's unification has allowed an in-depth perception of the importance of French culture as a model of modernity. At the same time, what emerged was the stark differentiation between a model that was mainly absorbed and elaborated by a tiny elite as against the mass presence of American culture, reverberating through the walls of thousands of cinema theatres and dance halls all over the country. As Kuisel suggested, in the progressively more globalized world of the early twentieth century, American culture was projecting itself as a transnational force helped by its unrivalled capacity for mass production and for the attractiveness of its artefacts. By the middle of the Twentieth century, this had turned American culture into—as Ellwood condensed it—'a form of global hegemony that none could even dream of matching'. Europeans could selectively appropriate and re-elaborate what came from across the Atlantic, but the cultural trade balance was by then heavily in favour of America.[10]

The chapters of this book stopped the clock in July 1943, so it is only right that this conclusion too should return within those boundaries. A quotation from one of the many enthusiastic letters that Pavese sent to Anthony Chiuminatto after the latter's return to America provides a fitting end. Pavese by then had no doubts about the role that the USA was about to take on the world stage. Here is what he wrote on 5 April 1930 in his slightly awkward English:

> You've got to predominate in this century all over the civilized world as before did Greece, and Italy and France. I'm sure of it. What in their little sphere have American Movies done in old Europe [...] will do the whole of your art and thought. [...] Now you can really go and conquer the earth.[11]

When Pavese wrote these lines, the American century was already in full swing. It was a 'long century', since by the end of the nineteenth century it was already clear that the manufacturing might of US industry could easily outstrip that of any European country. By 1930, American culture was everywhere to be seen, heard, and appropriated. Technology helped. Jazz music flew over the ocean, thanks to long-, medium-, and short-wave transmissions. New York's skyline—built on the prodigies of steel-reinforced concrete—arrived through the images of countless illustrated magazines and Hollywood films. Fascism's late anti-Americanism was destined to fail. By then, the United States of America had become a familiar, attractive place in the mind of too many Italians.

[10] Kuisel, 'The End of Americanization?', 630–4. Ellwood, *The Shock of America*, 524.
[11] Cesare Pavese, *Lettere. 1924–1944* (Turin: Einaudi, 1966), 187.

# Bibliography

Abel, Richard, *The Ciné Goes to Town: French Cinema, 1896-1914* (Berkeley and Los Angeles: University of California Press, 1994).

Abel, Richard, 'The Perils of Pathé, or the Americanization of American Cinema', in Leo Charney and Vanessa Schwartz (eds), *Cinema and the Invention of Modern Life* (Berkeley and Los Angeles: University of California Press, 1995), 183-223.

Adams, David K., and Vaudagna, Maurizio (eds), *Transatlantic Encounters: Essays on the Use and Misuse of History in Europe and America* (Amsterdam: VU University Press, 2000).

Adamson, Walter L., *Avant-Garde Florence: From Modernism to Fascism* (Cambridge, MA: Harvard University Press, 1993).

Adamson, Walter L., 'Modernism in Florence: The Politics of Avant-Garde Culture in the Early Twentieth Century', in Luca Somigli and Mario Moroni (eds), *Italian Modernism: Italian Culture between Decadentism and Avant-Garde* (Toronto: University of Toronto Press, 2004), 221-42.

Adamson, Walter L., 'The Culture of Italian Fascism and the Fascist Crisis of Modernity: The Case of *Il Selvaggio*', *Journal of Contemporary History*, 30/4 (October 1995), 555-75.

Agnoletti, Braccio, 'Contrattaccare l'America', *Lo Schermo*, 1 (August 1935), 57-8.

Agri, Amedeo, 'Filosofia del "Gag"', *Cinema*, 4/69 (10 May 1939), 300-1.

Albano, Lucilla, 'Hollywood: Cinelandia', in Riccardo Redi (ed.), *Cinema italiano sotto il fascismo* (Venice: Marsilio, 1979), 219-32.

Alexander, Jeffrey C., 'Toward a Theory of Cultural Trauma', in Jeffery C. Alexander, Ron Eyerman, Bernhard Giese, Neil J. Smelser, and Piotr Sztompka (eds), *Cultural Trauma and Collective Identity* (Berkeley and Los Angeles: University of California Press, 2004), 1-30.

Alicata, Mario, and De Santis, Giuseppe, 'Verità e poesia', *Cinema*, 6/127 (10 October 1941), 216-17.

Alicata, Mario, and De Santis, Giuseppe, 'Ancora di Verga e del cinema italiano', 6/130 (25 November 1941), 314-15.

Allen, Gay Wilson (ed.), *Walt Whitman Abroad* (Syracuse, NY: Syracuse University Press, 1955).

Allotti, Pierluigi, *Giornalisti di regime: La stampa italiana tra fascismo e antifascism (1922-1948)* (Rome: Carocci, 2012).

Alovisio, Silvio, '"The Pastrone System": Itala Film from its Origins to World War I', *Film History*, 12/3 (2000), 250-61.

Alovisio, Silvio, 'Le riviste del cinema muto: Una fonte per la ricerca tecnologica?', *Bianco e nero*, 549 (2004), 31-44.

Alovisio, Silvio, 'Immaginare un nuovo mondo: Sulle tracce del western nel cinema muto italiano', in Pollone (ed.), *Il western in Italia*, 49-66. This article is an expanded version of Alovisio's 'Quando il western italiano era muto', *Mondo niovo*, 5/2 (2006), 18-24.

Alvaro, Corrado, 'Pirandello della Germania del cinema sonoro e di altre cose', interview in *La Fiera letteraria*, 14 April 1929, pp. 17-19.

Amadelli, Antonio, 'La Fiat in USA: Le origini', *La Manovella*, 1983 (printout held at Archivio Storico Fiat, Turin).

Ambrosoli, Luigi, 'Luigi Credaro e la scuola italiana nell'età giolittiana', *Scuola e città*, 5 (1980), 199–206.

Amerighi, Guglielmo, 'Il "tempo irreale" di Chaplin', *Il Frontespizio*, 7/5 (May 1940), 311.

Andreazza, Fabio, *Identificazione di un'arte: Scrittori e cinema nel primo novecento italiano* (Rome: Bulzoni, 2008).

Angelini, Franca, et al., *Il secondo Ottocento: Lo stato unitario e l'età del positivismo*, 2 vols (Rome and Bari: Laterza, 1975).

Angioletti, Giovanni Battista, 'La decadenza della letteratura francese', *La Stampa*, 28 February 1929, p. 3.

Anon., 'Stati Uniti d'America', *Il Mondo illustrato*, 5 (30 January 1847), 68.

Anon., 'Il padiglione della donne', *L'Esposizione universale di Filadelfia del 1876*, instalment no. 10 [no date specified; presumably May or June 1876], 73–4.

Anon., 'Le nostre incisioni', *L'Illustrazione popolare*, 36 (9 July 1876), 562.

Anon., 'Angelo Mosso in America', *La Stampa*, 10 June 1899, 2.

Anon., 'La statua della Libertà a New York', *Corriere della Sera*, 29–30 October 1886, 1.

Anon., 'Cowboys in Old Verona', *New York Times*, 18 May 1890, p. 17.

Anon., 'Data mondiale', *Corriere della Sera*, 4 July 1918, p. 1.

Anon., 'L'on Mussolini a Centocelle passa in rivista gli aviatori', *Corriere della Sera*, 25 May 1927, p. 5.

Anon., 'Siete voi fotogenico?', *Cinema illustrazione*, 5/52 (24 December 1930), 15.

Anon., 'Indiscrezioni', *Cinema illustrazione*, 5/52 (24 December 1930), 15.

Anon., 'Grattacieli', *Architettura* (April 1932), 189–93.

Anon., 'Nasce una nuova Europa', *Rivista illustrata del Popolo d'Italia*, 17/11 (November 1938), 63–5.

Anon., 'Rassegna della stampa', *Bianco e nero*, 3/5 (1939), 85–96.

Anon., 'Girls', *Cinema*, 4/69 (10 May 1939), 297.

Antonioni, Michelangelo, 'La scuola delle mogli', *Cinema*, 5/88 (25 February 1940), 117–19.

Apollonio, Umbro (ed.), *Documents of 20th Century Art: Futurist Manifestos* (New York: Viking Press, 1973).

Archivio Storico FIAT, *L'industria italiana nel mercato mondiale: Dalla fine dell'800 alla metà del 900* (Turin: Fiat, 1993).

Archivio Storico FIAT, *FIAT: Le fasi della crescita: Le cifre dello sviluppo aziendale* (Turin: Scriptorium, 1996).

Argentieri, Mino (ed.), *Schermi di guerra: Cinema italiano 1939–1943* (Rome: Bulzoni, 1995).

Argentieri, Mino, *L'asse cinematografico Roma–Berlino* (Naples: Sapere, 1986).

Argentieri, Mino, 'Autarchia e internazionalità', in Caldiron (ed.), *Storia del cinema italiano*, 148–65.

Armani, Armando, 'Febbre di gloria', *Gerarchia*, 7/1 (January 1927), 418–21.

Armstrong, Louis, *Swing that Music* (New York: Longman, 1936).

Armus, Seth, *French Anti-Americanism (1930–1948)* (Lanham, MD: Lexington Books, 2008).

Asor Rosa, Alberto, *Scrittori e popolo: Il populismo nella letteratura contemporanea* (Rome: Samonà e Savelli, 1965; Turin: Einaudi, 1988).

Audenino, Patrizia, *Un mestiere per partire: Tradizione migratoria, lavoro e comunità in una vallata alpina* (Milan: Franco Angeli, 1990).

Audenino, Patrizia, 'The Paths of the Trade: Italian Stonemasons in the United States', in George E. Pozzetta (ed.), *Emigration & Immigration: The Old World Confronts the New* (New York: Garland Publishing, 1991), 31–47.

Ajello, Nello, 'I maestri del colore (appunti per una storia del giornalismo letterario in Italia)', *Problemi dell'informazione*, 1/4 (1976), 556-7.

Bakewell, Charles M., *The Story of the American Red Cross in Italy* (New York: Macmillan, 1920).

Bakker, Gerben, 'The Decline and Fall of the European Film Industry: Sunk Costs, Market Size, and Market Structure, 1890-1927', *Economic History Review*, 58/2 (2005), 310-51.

Bakker, Gerben, *Entertainment Industrialised: The Emergence of the International Film Industry, 1890-1940* (Cambridge: Cambridge University Press, 2009).

Balboni, Paolo, *Storia dell'educazione linguistica in Italia: Dalla Legge Casati alla Riforma Gelmini* (Turin: UTET, 2009).

Balboni, Silvano, 'Note 5', *Bianco e nero*, 1/4 (April 1937), 71-3.

Barbata Jackson, Jessica, *Dixie's Italians: Sicilians, Race and Citizens in the Jim Crow Gulf South* (Baton Rouge, LA: Louisiana State University Press, 2020).

Bartolini, Simonetta, *Ardengo Soffici: Il romanzo di una vita* (Florence: Le lettere, 2009).

Barzini, Luigi, 'I "cavalieri della notte" alla caccia degli italiani', *Corriere della Sera*, 5 April 1908, p. 5.

Barzini, Luigi, 'La fantasia dei giornalisti americani', *Corriere della Sera*, 22 April 1908, p. 3.

Barzini, Luigi, Bianchi e neri', *Corriere della Sera*, 5 September 1908, p. 3.

Barzini, Luigi, 'Petrosino e la mano nera', *Corriere della Sera*, 14 March 1909, p. 3.

Barzini, Luigi, Jr, *Nuova York* (Milan: Giacomo Agnelli, 1931).

Barzini, Luigi, Jr, 'La sbalorditiva confusione americana', *Corriere della Sera*, 15 February 1934., p. 3.

Barzini, Luigi, Jr, 'Questa è l'America', *Corriere della Sera*, 1 June 1934, p. 3.

Barzini, Luigi, Jr, 'Un nuovo ciclo sociale negli Stati Uniti', *Corriere della Sera*, 10 November 1936, p. 3.

Barzini, Luigi, Jr, 'Il successo, scopo della vita: La colpa è dell'America', *Corriere della Sera*, 6 April 1939, p. 5.

Barzini, Luigi, Jr,' L'Americano e sua moglie al padiglione italiano', *Corriere della Sera*, 3 June 1939, p. 3.

Barzini, Luigi, Jr, 'Il destino del Mida americano', *Corriere della Sera*, 8 July 1939, p. 3.

Barzini, Luigi, Jr, 'Rivista mattutina', *Corriere della Sera*, 20 September 1939, p. 3.

Barzini, Luigi, Jr, 'Nascita e morte di uno sport', *Corriere della Sera*, 1 October 1939, p. 3.

Bassignana, Pier Luigi, 'Tayloristi loro malgrado', in Bassignana (ed), *Taylorismo e fordismo alla Fiat nelle relazioni di viaggio di tecnici e ingegneri (1919-1955)* (Turin: AMMA, 1998), 7-36.

Bayly, C. A., Beckert, Sven, Connelly, Matthew, Hofmeyr, Isobel, Kozol, Wendy, and Seed, Patricia, 'AHR Conversation: On Transnational History', *American Historical Review*, 111/5 (2006), 1441-64.

Baxter, Devon, '"The Goddess of Spring" (1934)', in the online platform *Cartoon Research*, https://cartoonresearch.com/index.php/walt-disneys-the-goddess-of-spring-1934/, posted 21 September 2016 (accessed 1 July 2021).

Beard, Charles A., and Beard, Mary R. *The Rise of American Civilization* (New York: Macmillan, 1927).

Becciu, Leonardo, *Il fumetto in Italia* (Florence: Sansoni, 1971).

Bedarida, Raffaele, '"Bombs against Skyscrapers": Depero's Strange Love Affair with New York City: 1928-1949', *Italian Modern Art*, 1 (2019), 1-33.

Bellu, Serge, *Histoire mondiale de l'automobile* (Paris: Flammarion, 1998).

Benadusi, Lorenzo, *Il Corriere della sera di Luigi Albertini: Nascita e sviluppo della prima industria culturale di massa* (Rome: Aracne, 2012).

Benjamin, Walter, 'Paris, Capital of the 19th Century' [originally entititled 'Paris, Hauptstadt des XIX. Jahrhunderts', 1935], *Perspecta*, 12 (1969), 163–72.
Benjamin, Walter, *The Arcades Project* (1982; Cambridge, MA: Belknap Press).
Ben-Ghiat, Ruth, *Fascist Modernities: Italy, 1922–1945* (Berkeley and Los Angeles: University of California Press, 2001).
Ben-Ghiat, Ruth, *Italian Fascism's Empire Cinema* (Bloomington, IN: Indiana University Press, 2015).
Bennetta, Jules-Rosette, *Second Skin: Josephine Baker in Art and Life: The Icon and the Image* (Urbana and Chicago: University of Illinois Press, 2007).
Benvenuti, Sergio, *Il fascismo nella Venezia Tridentina (1919–1924)* (Trento: Società di studi trentini di scienze storiche, 1976).
Bergman, Andrew, *We're in the Money: Depression America and its Films* (New York: Harper Colophon Books, 1971).
Bergmeier, Horst J. P., and Lotz, Rainer E., *Hitler's Airwaves: The Inside Story of Nazi Radio Broadcasting and Propaganda Swing* (New Haven: Yale University Press, 1997).
Bergoglio, Franco, 'Pavese, Mila, Gramsci. Letteratura, jazz e antifascismo nella Torino degli anni trenta', *L'impegno*, 20.2 (2000), 40–51.
Bergstrom, Janet, 'Murnau, Movietone and Mussolini', *Film History*, 17 (2005), 187–92.
Beria, Chiara, 'La "Rassegna Settimanale" e la cultura europea', in Romano Luperini (ed.), *Il verismo italiano fra naturalismo francese e cultura europea* (Lecce: Manni, 2007), 119–49.
Bernardini, Aldo, *Cinema muto italiano*, i. *Ambiente, spettacoli e spettatori 1896–1904* (Rome and Bari: Laterza, 1980).
Bernardini, Aldo, *Cinema muto italiano*, iii. *Arte, divismo e mercato 1910–1914* (Bari and Rome: Laterza, 1982).
Bernardy, Amy Allemande, *Italia randagia attraverso gli Stati Uniti* (Turin: Bocca, 1913).
Bertellini, Giorgio, 'Epica spettacolare e splendore del vero: L'influenza del cinema storico italiano in America (1908–1915)', in Gian Piero Brunetta (ed.), *Storia del cinema mondiale*, 5 vols (Turin: Einaudi, 1999–2010), ii (1999), 227–65.
Bertellini, Giorgio, 'DUCE/DIVO: Masculinity, Racial Identity and Politics among Italian Americans in 1920s New York City', *Journal of Urban History*, 31/5 (2005), 685–726.
Bertellini, Giorgio, *The Divo and the Duce: Promoting Film Stardom and Political Leadership in 1920s America* (Oakland, CA: University of California Press, 2019).
Bertellini, Giorgio, 'Strabismi culturali: Zavattini e gli Stati Uniti', in Alberto Ferraboschi (ed.), *Zavattini oltre i confini: Reti, pratiche, ricezione* (Reggio Emilia: Biblioteca Panizzi, 2020), 97–113.
Bertieri, Claudio, 'Fumetto & moschetto: I comics italiani di guerra', in Argentieri (ed.), *Schermi di guerra*, 201–38.
Bertolucci, Attilio, 'Paura di Wright', *Giovedì*, 24 May 1953; then in Bertolucci, *Riflessi da un paradiso perduto*, 443–5.
Bertolucci, Attilio, 'Che emozione quando Fay Wray lanciava violette nello stivale di Von Stroheim', *La Repubblica*, 20 August 1976; repr. as 'Il cinema che ho amato', in Bertolucci, *Riflessi da un paradiso perduto*, 49–51.
Bertolucci, Attilio, *Riflessi da un paradiso perduto: Scritti sul cinema* (Bergamo: Moretti & Vitali, 2009).
Bevilacqua, Piero, De Clementi, Andreina, and Franzina, Emilio (eds), *Storia dell' emigrazione italiana. Partenze*, i (Rome: Donzelli, 2001).
Beynet, Michel, *L'Image de L'Amérique dans la culture italiennes de l'entre-deux guerres*, 3 vols (Aix-Marseille: Publications de l'Université de Provence, 1990).
Biagi, Enzo, *Dinastie: Gli Agnelli, i Rizzoli, i Ferruzzi-Gardini, i Lauro* (Milan: Mondadori, 1988).

Bianco, Carla, *The Two Rosetos: The Folklore of an Italian-American Community in Northeastern Pennsylvania* (Bloomington, IN: Indiana University Press, 1974).
Billiani, Francesca, *Culture nazionali e narrazioni straniere* (Florence: Le Lettere, 2007).
Bishop, Charles, *La France et l'automobile* (Paris: Génin, 1971).
Bizzarri, Libero, and Solaroli, Libero, *L'industria cinematografica italiana* (Florence: Parenti, 1958).
Blasetti, Alessandro, 'Il nostro oro', *Lo Schermo*, 2 (August 1926), 3.
Blasetti, Alessandro, 'I dispiaceri del regista', *Cinema*, 17 (10 March 1937), 174.
Bobbio, Norberto, 'La cultura italiana tra ottocento e novecento', in anon. (ed.), *La cultura italiana tra '800 e '900 e le origini del nazionalismo* (Florence: Olschki, 1981), 1–19.
Boccioni, Umberto, 'Perché non siamo impressionisti', in Boccioni, *Pittura scultura futuriste (dinamismo plastico)* (Milan: Edizioni futuriste di 'Poesia', 1914), 81–99.
Boccioni, Umberto, 'Simultaneità', in Boccioni, *Pittura scultura futuriste (dinamismo plastico)* (Milan: Edizioni futuriste di 'Poesia', 1914), 81–99; then in *Gli scritti editi e inediti* (Milan: Feltrinelli, 1971), 170–81.
Bolzoni, Francesco, 'Vidor visto dall'osservatorio italiano', in Sergio Toffetti and Andrea Morini (eds), *La grande parata: Il cinema di King Vidor* (Turin: Lindau, 1994), 174–88.
Bonalumi, Giovanni, 'Le correzioni del "Garofano rosso" di Vittorini', *Lettere italiane*, 1 (1979), 79–95.
Bond, Emma, Bonsaver, Guido, and Faloppa, Federico (eds), *Destination Italy: Representing Migration in Contemporary Media and Narrative* (Oxford: Peter Lang, 2015).
Bondanella, Peter, *The Italian Cinema Book* (London: Palgrave Macmillan, 2013).
Bonetta, Gaetano, and Fioravanti, Gigliola (eds). *L'istruzione classica (1860–1910)* (Rome: Ministero per i beni culturali e ambientali, 1995).
Bono, Gianni, *Guida al fumetto italiano*, 2 vols (Milan: Epierre, 2003).
Bonsaver, Guido, 'Vittorini's American Translations: Parallels, Borrowings and Betrayals', *Italian Studies*, 53 (1998), 68–97.
Bonsaver, Guido, *Elio Vittorini: The Writer and the Written* (Leeds: Northern Universities Press, 2000; London: Routledge, 2017).
Bonsaver, Guido, 'Fascist Censorship on Literature and the Case of Elio Vittorini', *Modern Italy*, 8/2 (2003), 165–86.
Bonsaver, Guido, *Censorship and Literature in Fascist Italy* (Toronto: Toronto University Press, 2007).
Bonsaver, Guido, *Vita e omicidio di Gaetano Pilati: 1881–1925* (Florence: Cesati, 2010).
Bonsaver, Guido, *Mussolini censore: Storie di letteratura, dissenso e ipocrisia* (Rome and Bari: Laterza, 2013).
Bonsaver, Guido, '"Senti'n po', a Gregori Pècche...": Shavelson's *It Started in Naples* and Fellini's *La dolce vita* between Italian and US Culture', in Bonsaver, Richardson, and Stellardi (eds), *Cultural Reception, Translation and Transformation from Medieval to Modern Italy*, 331–51.
Bonsaver, Guido, 'Turin between French and US Culture: The Car and Film Industries, 1904–14', in Bonsaver, Carlucci, and Reza (eds), *Italy and the USA*, 156–83.
Bonsaver, Guido, 'The Royal Italian Academy', in Patricia Gaborik (ed.), *Pirandello in Context* (Cambridge: Cambridge University Press, 2023), 56–70.
Bonsaver, Guido, and Gordon, Robert (eds), *Culture, Censorship and the State in 20th Century Italy* (Cambridge: Legenda: 2005).
Bonsaver, Guido, and Gussoni, Alice, 'From Sicily to Louisiana: Early Migration and Historiographical Issues', in Lauren Braun-Strumfels, Daniele Fiorentino, and Maddalena Marinari (eds), *Managing Migration in Italy and the United States* (Berlin: De Gruyter, forthcoming 2023).

Bonsaver, Guido, Carlucci, Alessandro, and Reza, Matthew (eds), *Italy and the USA: Understanding Cultural Change in Language and Narrative* (Cambridge: Legenda, 2019).

Bonsaver, Guido, Carlucci, Alessandro, and Reza, Matthew, 'The Dynamics of Cultural Change: A Theoretical Frame with Reference to Italy–USA Relations', *900 Transnazionale/ Transnational 900*, 3/1 (2019), 107–30.

Bonsaver, Guido, Richardson, Brian, and Stellardi, Giuseppe (eds), *Cultural Reception, Translation and Transformation from Medieval to Modern Italy: Essays in Honour of Martin McLaughlin* (Cambridge: Legenda, 2017).

Bontempelli, Massimo, *Stato di grazia* (Florence: Sansoni, 1924).

Bontempelli, Massimo, 'Perché "900" sarà scritto in francese', *Il Tevere*, 18 May 1926, p. 3.

Bontempelli, Massimo, 'Chronique et faits-divers au sujet de la foundation de "900"', in *900: Cahiers d'Italie e d'Europe*, 1 (Autumn 1926), 172–6.

Bontempelli, Massimo, 'La mare aux grenouilles', in *900: Cahiers d'Italie e d'Europe*, 1 (Autumn 1926), 176–8.

Bontempelli, Massimo, 'Morale du Jazz', *900: Cahiers d'Italie e d'Europe*, 2 (Winter 1926-7), 173–5.

Bontempelli, Massimo, 'Analogies', *900: Cahiers d'Italie e d'Europe*, 4 (Summer 1927), 8–13.

Bontempelli, Massimo, *L'avventura novecentista* (Florence: Vallecchi, 1938).

Borgese, Giuseppe Antonio, *La nuova Germania* (Milan: Fratelli Bocca, 1909).

Borgese, Giuseppe Antonio, 'Grecismi dell'America', *Corriere della Sera*, 24 June 1932, p. 3.

Borgese, Giuseppe Antonio, 'In cerca del mare', *Corriere della Sera*, 24 October 1933, p. 3.

Borgese, Giuseppe Antonio, 'Un tema di romanzo', *Corriere della Sera*, 23 July 1933, p. 3.

Borghese, Lucia, 'Storia della ricezione delle fiabe grimmiane in Toscana e della loro prima traduzione italiana', in Pietro Clemente and Mariano Fresta (eds), *Interni e dintorni del Pinocchio: Folkoristi italiani del tempo del Collodi* (Pescia: Editori del Grifo, 1986), 49–58.

Boschi, Luca, Gori, Leonardo, and Lama, Sergio, *I Disney italiani* (Bologna: Granata Press, 1990).

Bosio, Gastone, 'Disegni animati italiani', *La Stampa*, 29 January 1935, p. 6.

Bosio, Gastone, 'Pinocchio sullo schermo', *La Stampa*, 12 February 1935, p. 6.

Bosetti, Gilbert, 'Les Lettres françaises sous le fascism: Le Culte de la "N.R.F" dans l'entre-deux-guerres face à la francophobie fasciste', *Mélanges de l'École Française de Rome*, 98/1 (1986), 383–432.

Bosworth, Richard, *Mussolini* (London: Arnold, 2002).

Botta, Enrico, 'Da una guerra civile all'altra: Lo zio Tom, la secessione e l'unità d'Italia', *Ácoma*, 21 (2021), 22–42.

Bottai, Giuseppe, 'Dichiarazioni a favore della legge', *Lo Spettacolo italiano*, 7 (July 1931).

Bottai, Giuseppe, *Carta della scuola* (Milan: Mondadori, 1939).

Bottai, Giuseppe, *L'Italia dall'emigrazione all'impero* (Rome: Società Nazionale Dante Alighieri, 1940).

Bottai, Giuseppe, *Diario 1935-1944* (Milan: Rizzoli, 1982).

Bottazzi, Luigi, 'Le impressioni d'America di Luigi Pirandello', *Corriere della Sera*, 8 March 1924, in Pupo (ed.), *Interviste a Pirandello*, 235–8.

Bottiglieri, Bruno, 'Strategie di sviluppo, assetti organizzativi e scelte finanziarie nel primo trentennio di vita della Fiat', in Progetto ASF, *FIAT 1899-1930. Storia e documenti* (Milan: Fabbri, 1991), 13–40.

Bourdieu, Pierre, *The Field of Cultural Production* (Cambridge: Polity Press, 1993).

Bourdieu, Pierre, *The Rules of Art* (Cambridge: Polity Press, 1996).

Boyd Caroli, Betty, *Italian Repatriation from the United States, 1900-1914* (New York: Center for Migration Studies, 1973).

Bragaglia, Anton Giulio, 'Lo stile è l'epoca', *Critica fascista*, 22 (15 November 1926), 417–18.
Bragaglia, Anton Giulio, *Jazz Band* (Milan: Corbaccio, 1929).
Brancaleone, David, *Cesare Zavattini's Neo-Realism and the Afterlife of an Idea: An Intellectual Biography* (New York: Bloomsbury Academic, 2021).
Bratu Hansen, Miriam, 'America, Paris, the Alps: Kracauer (and Benjamin) on Cinema and Modernity', in Leo Charney and Vanessa Schwartz (eds), *Cinema and the Invention of Modern Life* (Berkeley and Los Angeles: University of California Press, 1995), 362–402.
Bratu Hansen, Miriam, 'The Mass Production of the Senses: Classical Cinema as Vernacular Modernism', *Modernism/modernity*, 6 (1999), 59–77.
Brazzale, Francesco, Caliaro, Luigino, and Vollman, Andrea, *Grande Guerra, americani in Italia, nascita di una superpotenza* (Valdagno: Rossato, 2017).
Breyer, W, 'Influenza di Hollywood', *Cinema*, 4/69 (10 May 1939), 298–9.
Briosi, Sandro, *Il problema della letteratura in 'Solaria'* (Milan: Mursia, 1976), 15–16.
Brogi, Daniela, 'Tra letteratura e cinema: Pavese, Visconti e la funzione Cain', *Allegoria*, 64/2 (2011), 176–95.
Brown, Sharon A., *Administrative History: Jefferson National Expansion Memorial* (Washington: National Park Service, 1984).
Brownlow, Kevin, *The Parade's Gone By...* (New York: Alfred Kopf, 1968).
Brunello, Piero, 'Agenti di emigrazione, contadini e immagini dell'America nella provincia di Venezia', *Rivista di storia contemporanea*, 11/1 (1982), 95–122; then in Emilio Franzina (ed.), *Un altro Veneto: Saggi e studi di storia dell'emigrazione nei secoli XIX e XX* (Abano Terme: Francisci, 1983), 138–67.
Brunetta, Gian Piero, *Storia del cinema italiano (1895–1945)* (Rome: Editori Riuniti, 1979).
Brunetta, Gian Piero, 'Il sogno a stelle e strisce di Mussolini', in Maurizio Vaudagna (ed.), *L'estetica della politica: Europa e America negli anni trenta* (Rome and Bari: Laterza, 1989), 173–86.
Brunetta, Gian Piero *Storia del cinema italiano,* i. *Il cinema muto (1895–1929)* (Rome: Editori Riuniti, 1993).
Brunetta, Gian Piero, *Storia del cinema italiano,* ii. *Il cinema del regime (1929–1943)* (Rome: Editori Riuniti, 2001).
Brunetta, Gian Piero (ed.), *Storia del cinema mondiale*, 5 vols (Turin: Einaudi, 1999–2010).
Brunetta, Gian Piero, *Il ruggito del leone: Hollywood alla conquista dell'impero dei sogni nell'Italia di Mussolini* (Venice: Marsilio, 2013).
Bruni, Mario, 'La grande parata', *Cinematografo*, 1 (6 March 1927), 11.
Buccini, Stefania, *The Americas in Italian Literature and Culture, 1700–1825* (University Park, PA: Pennsylvania State University Press, 1996).
Buffa, Cristiano, and Ortoleva, Peppino, 'Lingotto, luogo, simbolo', in Carlo Olmo (ed.), *Il Lingotto: 1915–1939: L'architettura, l'immagine, il lavoro* (Turin: Allemandi, 1994), 151–c92.
Busino, Giovanni, 'Il nazionalismo italiano e il nazionalismo europeo', in anon. (ed.), *La cultura italiana tra '800 e '900 e le origini del nazionalismo* (Florence: Olschki, 1981).
Busoni, Mario, *Buffalo Bill in Italia: L'epopea del Wild West Show* (Fidenza: Mattioli 1885, 2011).
C. (sic), 'Come abbiamo fatto "Due milioni per un sorriso"', *Film*, 2/38 (23 September 1939), 9.
Caizzi, Bruno, *Camillo e Adriano Olivetti* (Turin: Unione Tipografico–editrice Torinese, 1962).
Calcagno, Diego, 'Sette giorni a Roma', *Film*, 5/11 (14 March 1942), 6.

Caldiron, Orio, 'Le ambiguità della modernizzazione negli anni del consenso', in Caldiron (ed.) *Storia del cinema italiano*, 3–34.

Caldiron, Orio (ed.). *Storia del cinema italiano*, v (Venice and Rome: Marsilio–Bianco e nero edizioni– Centro Sperimentale di Cinematografia, 2006).

Càllari, Francesco, 'Cose dell'altro mondo', *Film*, 2/50 (16 December 1939), 2.

Calvesi, Maurizio, Guidoni, Enrico, and Lux Simonetta (eds), *E 42: Utopia e scenario del regime* (Venice: Marsilio, 1987).

Calvino, Italo, 'Autobiografia di uno spettatore', preface to Federico Fellini, *Quattro film* (Turin: Einaudi, 1974); repr. in Italo Calvino, *Romanzi e racconti* (Milan: Mondadori, 1994), iii. 27–49.

Camboni, Maria, 'Giovanni Papini e Walt Whitman tra Pragmatismo, Nietzsche e Futurismo', *900 Transnazionale/Transnational 900*, 2/1 (2018), 26–41.

Campassi, Osvaldo, 'Le coppie', *Cinema*, 3/52 (25 August 1938), 119–22.

Campassi, Osvaldo, 'Coppie', *Cinema illustrazione*, 13/38 (21 September 1938), 5.

Campassi, Osvaldo, 'Vera essenza dei film della prateria', *Cinema*, 7/152 (25 October 1942), 614–16.

Campassi, Osvaldo, '"La folla" di King Vidor', *Cinema*, 8/169 (10 July 1943), 21–2.

Campman [pseudonym], 'Commenti alla vita: Dallo "jazz"', *La Tribuna illustrata*, 27/40 (5–12 October 1919), 7.

Canali, Mauro, *La scoperta dell'Italia: Il fascismo raccontato agli americani (1920–1945)* (Venice: Marsilio, 2017).

Cannistraro, Philip V., *La fabbrica del consenso: Fascismo e mass-media* (Rome and Bari: Laterza, 1975).

Cannistraro, Philip V., *Blackshirts in Little Italy: Italian Americans and Fascism, 1921–1929* (West Lafayette: Bordighera, 1999).

Cannistraro, Philip, and Sullivan, Brian R., *Il Duce's Other Woman* (New York: Morrow, 1993).

Cannistraro, Philip V., and Rosoli, Gianfausto, 'Fascist Emigration Policy in the 1920s: An Interpretive Framework', *International Migration Review*, 13/4 (1979), 673–92.

Cannonieri, Giorgio, *La mia avventura tra gli Arussi* (Milan: Mondadori, 1937).

Capellini, Giovanni, *Ricordi di un viaggio scientifico nell'America settentrionale nel 1863* (Bologna: Tipografia Vitali, 1867).

Capirone, Giuseppe, 'Fiat "compra" in America, storia di cent'anni', *Il Registro*, 28/4 (October–December 2014), 12–17.

Capuana, Giuseppe, *Gli americani di Ràbbato* (Milan: Sandron, 1912).

Carabba, Claudio, *Il fascismo a fumetti* (Rimini: Guaraldi, 1973).

Caraceni, Augusto, *Il jazz: Dalle origini ad oggi* (Milan: Suvini Zerboni, 1937).

Carbonelli, Pietro, 'L'America e la questione abissina', *Corriere della Sera*, 5 June 1935, p. 1.

Carducci, Nicola, *Gli intellettuali e l'ideologia americana nell'Italia letteraria negli anni trenta* (Manduria: Lacaita, 1973).

Carega di Muricce, Francesco, *In America (1871–1872)*, 2 vols (Florence and Rome: Banco Annunzi, 1875).

Carey, Gary, *Anita Loos: A Biography* (London: Bloomsbury, 1988).

Caruso, M. Girolama, and Heim, Frank, 'Il livello di istruzione in Italia negli ultimi 150 anni: I dati', in Sveva Avveduto (ed.), *Italia 150 anni: Popolazione, welfare, scienza e società* (Rome: Gangemi, 2015), 121–34.

Casanova, Pascale, 'Paris, méridien de Greenwich de la littérature', in Christophe Charle and Daniel Roche (eds), *Capitales culturelles, capitals symboliques* (Paris: Éditions de la Sorbonne, 2002), 289–96.

Casanova, Pascale, *La République mondiale des lettres* (Paris: Éditions du Seuil, 1999); trans. into English as *The World Republic of Letters* (Cambridge, MA: Harvard Unversity Press, 2004).

Casarini, Athos, 'The Futurist Hears the Call of War: "And I am going" Says Casarini', *World Magazine*, 15 August 1915, p. 11.

Casella, Alfredo, *21 + 26* (Rome: Augustea, 1931).

Casetti, Francesco, Alovisio, Silvio, and Mazzei, Luca (eds), *Early Film Theories in Italy: 1896-1920* (Amsterdam: Amsterdam University Press, 2017).

Castronovo, Valerio, *Giovanni Agnelli: La FIAT dal 1899 al 1945* (Turin: Einaudi, 1977).

Castronovo, Valerio, *FIAT 1899-1999: Un secolo di storia italiana* (Milan: Rizzoli, 1999).

Castronovo, Valerio, Giacheri Fossati, Luciana, and Tranfaglia, Nicola, *La stampa italiana nell'età liberale* (Rome and Bari: Laterza, 1979).

Catalfamo, Antonio, 'La tesi di laurea di Cesare Pavese sul Walt Whitman e i suoi studi successivi sulla letteratura americana', *Forum Italicum*, 47/1 (2013), 80-95.

Catani, Patrizia, and Zuccolini, Roberto (eds), *I fondi archivistici dei consolati in Chicago, Cleveland, Denver, New Orleans e S. Francisco conservati presso l'Archivio Storico Diplomatico* (Rome: Ministero degli Affari Esteri–Archivio Storico Diplomatico, 1990).

Cauli, Alberto, 'Francesco De Pinedo and Ernesto Campanelli's Record-breaking Flight to Australia – Perception, Recognition and Legacy: An Account in the Australian Press', *The Journal of Navigation*, 74.2 (2021), 328-42.

Cavallo, Luigi, 'Una tesi sulla letteratura americana', *L'Unità* (Roman edn), 3 August 1947, p. 3.

Cecchi, Emilio, 'I capolavori di Edgardo Poe', *Cronache letterarie*, 8 (12 June 1910) [available at Fondo Emilio Cecchi, file 6.6.10; Gabinetto Vieusseux, Florence].

Cecchi, Emilio, 'Del tradurre', *Pegaso*, 1 (January 1929), 93-5.

Cecchi, Emilio, '"Guerriero" di Buster Keaton', *L'Italia letteraria*, 44 (November 1931), 5; then in Cecchi, *Fra Buster Keaton e Visconti*, 187-90.

Cecchi, Emilio, 'Cinema 1931', *Scenario*, 1/2 (1932), 5-10; repr. in Cecchi, *Fra Buster Keaton e Visconti*, 135-40.

Cecchi, Emilio, 'E le ragazze?', *Corriere della Sera*, 13 February 1935, p. 3; then in Cecchi, *America amara*, 258.

Cecchi, Emilio, 'Grattacieli', *Corriere della Sera*, 1 March 1935, p. 3; then in Cecchi, *America amara*; then in Cecchi, *Saggi e viaggi* (Milan: Mondadori, 1997), 1121-7.

Cecchi, Emilio, 'Frank Capra', *Cinema*, 2/20 (25 April 1937), 312-19; then in Cecchi, *Fra Buster Keaton e Visconti*, 165-70.

Cecchi, Emilio, 'Gente nera che vuol essere bianca', *Corriere della Sera*, 1 September 1938, p. 3.

Cecchi, Emilio, 'Arrivano le donne', *Corriere della Sera*, 1 January 1938, p. 3.

Cecchi, Emilio, 'L'agape nera', *Corriere della Sera*, 23 August 1938, p. 3.

Cecchi, Emilio, 'Il film a colori', *Bianco e nero*, 3/2 (1939), 29-30.

Cecchi, Emilio, 'Stanchezza del cinema americano', *Bianco e nero*, 3/3 (1939), 13-19.

Cecchi, Emilio, 'Letteratura americana e cinematografo', *Cinema*, 4/84 (25 December 1939), 374-5; then in Cecchi, *Fra Buster Keaton e Visconti*, 117-19. A long extract of the article was published in *Bianco e nero*, 4/2 (1940), 83-4.

Cecchi, Emilio, *America amara* (Florence: Sansoni, 1939).

Cecchi, Emilio, 'Il dittatore', *Mercurio*, 3 (1944); then in Cecchi, *Fra Buster Keaton e Visconti*, 231-2.

Cecchi, Emilio, *Nuovo continente* (Florence: Sansoni, 1958).

Cecchi, Emilio, *Fra Buster Keaton e Visconti*, ed. Francesco Bolzoni (Rome: Centro Sperimentale per la Cinematografia, 1995).

Cecchi, Maria, 'Quando il trucco ha torto', *Cinema*, 1/6 (1936), 216.

Cecchi, 'Introduzione', in Elio Vittorini (ed.), *Americana: Raccolta di narratori* (Milan: Bompiani, 1984), 1037–52.

Cecchi, Maria, and Reanda, Sandro, *Cinecittà* (Rome: Italia Industriale Edizioni, 1939).

Celenza, Anna Harwell, *Jazz Italian Style: From its Origins in New Orleans to Fascist Italy and Sinatra* (Cambridge: Cambridge University Press, 2017).

Cerase, Francesco P., 'Migration and Social Change: Expectations and Reality: A Case of Return Migration from the United States to Italy', *International Migration Review*, 8/2 (1974), 245–61.

Cerase, Francesco P., 'L'onda di ritorno: I rimpatri', in Bevilacqua, De Clementi, and Franzina (eds), *Storia dell'emigrazione italiana*, i. 113–25.

Cerchiari, Luca, *Jazz e fascismo* (Palermo: L'Epos, 2003; Milan: Mimesis, 2019).

Cerchiari, Luca, 'How to Make a Career by Writing against Jazz: Anton Giulio Bragaglia's *Jazz Band* (1929)', *Forum Italicum*, 49/2 (2015), 462–73.

Ceretti, Emilio, 'Rimorso dei comunisti di Hollywood', *Cinema*, 5/86 (25 February 1940), 114–15.

Ceretti, Emilio, 'Il cinema americano contro l'intelligenza europea', *Cinema*, 8/160 (25 February 1943), 116–17.

Chang, Natasha V., 'Forgetting Fascism: Memory, History, and the Literary Text in Umberto Eco's *La misteriosa fiamma della regina Loana*', *Italian Culture*, 26/1 (2008), 105–32.

Chapman, David, *Jazz italiano: A History of Italian Syncopated Music 1904–1946* (Newcastle upon Tyne: Cambridge Scholars Publishing, 2018).

Chard, Chloe, *Pleasure and Guilt on the Grand Tour: Travel Writing and Imaginative Geography 1680–1830* (Manchester: Manchester University Press, 1999).

Charnitzky, Jürgen, *Fascismo e scuola: La politica scolastica del regime (1922–1943)* (Florence: La Nuova Italia, 1996).

Charters, Samuel B., *A Trumpet around the Corner: The Story of New Orleans Jazz* (Jackson, MS: University Press of Mississippi, 2009).

Cherchi Usai, Paolo (ed.), *Giovanni Pastrone: Gli anni d'oro del cinema a Torino* (Turin: UTET, 1985).

Cherchi Usai, Paolo, 'Un americain à Turin à la conquete de l'Italie: George Kleine à Grugliasco 1913–1914', *Archives*, 22–3 (1989), 1–20.

Cherchi Usai, Paolo, 'On the Concept of "Influence" in Early Cinema', in Roland Cosandey and François Albera (eds), *Cinéma sans frontières 1896–1918: Images across Borders* (Payot, Québec: Nuit Blanche Editeur, 1995), 275–86.

Cherchi Usai, Paolo, 'Maciste all'Hell's Kitchen: Il cinema muto torinese negli Stati Uniti', in Paolo Bertetto and Gianni Rondolino (eds), *Cabiria e il suo tempo* (Milan: Il Castoro, 1998).

Chiarini, Luigi, 'Prefazione', *Bianco e nero*, 3/2 (1939), 5–7.

Chiaromonte, Nicola, 'Parigi come modello', *Solaria*, 8 (1933), 59–62.

Choate, Mark, *Emigrant Nation: The Making of Italy Abroad* (Cambridge, MA: Harvard University Press, 2008).

Churchwell, Sarah, *Behold, America: The Entangled History of America First and the American Dream* (London: Bloomsbury, 2018).

Ciampelli, G. M., 'Il "jazz" e la sua storia', *Radiocorriere*, 9/7 (12–19 February 1933), 13.

Ciano, Galeazzo, *Diario: 1937–1943* (Bologna: Cappelli, 1948).

Ciano, Galeazzo, *Diario 1937–1943* (Milan: Rizzoli, 1980).

Ciarlantini, Franco, *Incontro con il nord America* (Milan: Alpes, 1929).

Ciarlantini, Franco, 'Il compito di Roosevelt', *Augustea*, 9/5 (1933), 131–2.

Ciarlantini, Franco, *Roma-New York e ritorno: Tragedie dell'americanismo* (Milan: Giacomo Agnelli, 1934).
Cinel, Dino, *The National Integration of Italian Return Migration, 1870-1929* (Cambridge: Cambridge University Press, 1991).
Cipolla, Arnaldo, 'Grattacieli', *La Stampa*, 19 February 1925, p. 3.
Cipriani, Geppi, 'Fox-trott, ballo sovrano!', *La Tribuna illustrata*, 28/8 (22-9 February 1920), 6.
Cirino, Mark, and Ott, Mark P. (eds), *Hemingway in Italy: Twenty-First Century Perspectives* (Gainesville, FL: University Press of Florida, 2017).
Clair, René 'Ritmo—Il cinema e lo stato', *Bianco e nero*, 3/2 (1939), 153-8.
Clair, René, 'Senso primitivo nel cinema', *Cinema*, 173-4 (25 September-25 October 1943), 110-11.
Cognetti de Martiis, Salvatore, *Gli Stati Uniti d'America nel 1876* (Milan: Stab. Tip. della Perseveranza, 1877).
Colarizi, Simona, *Luigi Barzini: Una storia italiana* (Venice: Marsilio, 2017).
Colasacco, Brett, 'From Men into Gods: American Pragmatism, Italian Proto-Fascism, and Secular Religion', *Politics, Religion & Ideology*, 15/4 (2014), 541-64.
Commissariato generale dell'emigrazione, *Annuario statistico della emigrazione italiana* (Rome: Ed. Commissariato generale dell'emigrazione, 1926).
Confessore, Ornella, *L'americanismo cattolico in Italia* (Rome: Edizioni Studium, 1984).
Contorbia, Franco (ed.), *Lucia Rodocanachi: Le carte, la vita* (Florence: Società editrice fiorentina, 2006).
Consiglio, Alberto, 'I registi: King Vidor', *Cine-Convegno*, 1 (25 April 1933), 37-50.
Consiglio, Alberto, and Debenedetti, Aldo, 'Chaplin Charlot', *Cinema*, 6 (25 September 1936), 224-7.
Consiglio, Alberto, and Debenedetti, Aldo, 'Il senso dell'avventura', *Cinema*, 7 (10 October 1936), 263-6.
Corni, Gustavo, 'Il modello tedesco visto dall'Italia', in Agostino Giovagnoli and Giorgio Del Zanna (eds), *Il mondo visto dall'Italia* (Milan: Guerini, 2004), 34-54.
Cortese, Antonio, and Miccoli, Maria Carmela, 'Il ruolo degli agenti di emigrazione e delle compagnie di navigazione nei flussi in uscita dall'Italia sino alla Prima Guerra Mondiale', *Polis*, V/I (2017), 261-73.
Cotillo, Salvatore A., *Italy in the Great War* (Boston: Christopher House, 1922).
Cottini, Luca, *The Art of Objects: The Birth of Italian Industrial Culture, 1878-1928* (Toronto: University of Toronto Press, 2018).
Cottini, Luca, 'Buffalo Bill and the Italian Myth of the American West', in Bonsaver, Carlucci, and Reza (eds), *Italy and the USA*, 97-102.
Creel, George, Complete Report of the Chairman of the Committee on Public Information, 1917: 1918: 1919 (Washington: Government Printing Office, 1920).
Crespi, Barbara, 'Cinecittà: Utopia fascista e sogno americano', in Caldiron (ed.). *Storia del cinema italiano*, 89-140.
Crisp, Colin, *The Classic French Cinema, 1930-1960* (Bloomington, IN: Indiana University Press, 1997).
Croce, Benedetto, *Filosofia della pratica: Economia ed etica* (Bari: Laterza, 1909).
Cugny, Laurent, *Une histoire du jazz en France*, i. *Du milieu du XIXe siècle à 1929, Jazz en France* (Paris: Outre Mesure, 2014).
Curnutt, Kirk, 'Of Mussolini and Macaroni: Hemingway, Fitzgerald, and Expatriate "Italianicity"', in Rena Sanderson (ed.), *Hemingway's Italy: New Perspectives* (Baton Rouge, LA: Louisiana State University Press, 2005).

Curti, Roberto, *Riccardo Freda: The Life and Works of a Born Filmmaker* (Jefferson, NC: McFarland & Company, 2017).
D'Arcangeli, Marco Antonio, 'Giovanni Gentile–Luigi Credaro: Due protagonisti a confronto fra "pubblico e privato"', in Giuseppe Spadafora (ed.), *Giovanni Gentile: La pedagogia; La scuola* (Rome: Armando Editore, 1997), 461–78.
D'Attorre, Pier Paolo (ed.), *Sogno americano e mito sovietico nell'Italia contemporanea* (Milan: Franco Angeli, 1991).
D'hoker, Elke, and Bonciarelli, Sarah, 'Extending the Middlebrow: Italian Fiction in the Early Twentieth Century', *Belphégor*, 15/2 (2017), 1–16.
Dainotto, Roberto, 'The Saxophone and the Pastoral: Italian Jazz in the Age of Fascist Modernity', *Italica*, 85/2–3 (2008), 273–94.
Dall'Osso, Angela, *Voglia d'America: Il mito americano in Italia tra otto e novecento* (Rome: Donzelli, 2007).
Davies, Judith, *The Realism of Luigi Capuana: A Study in the Evolution of Late Nineteenth-Century Narrative in Italy* (London: Modern Humanities Research Association, 1979).
De Amicis, Edmondo, *In America* (Rome: Voghera, 1897).
De Begnac, Yvon, *Taccuini mussoliniani* (Bologna: Il Mulino, 1990).
De Berti, Raffaele, 'Figure e miti ricorrenti', in Caldiron (ed.), *Storia del cinema italiano*, 294–311.
De Berti, Raffaele, 'Rotocalchi cinematografici e modelli di vita hollywoodiani nell'Italia fra le due guerre', in Raffaele De Berti (ed.), *Immaginario hollywoodiano e cinema italiano degli anni trenta* (Milan: CUEM, 2004), 75–104.
De Berti, Raffaele, 'Rotocalchi tra fotogiornalismo, cronaca e costume', in Raffaele De Berti and Irene Piazzoni (eds), *Forme e modelli del rotocalco italiano tra fascismo e dopoguerra* (Milan: Cisalpino, 2009), 3–64.
De Berti, Raffaele, 'Princess Tam Tam: Josephine Baker una venere in Italia (1928–1936)', *Àgalma 22: Rivista di studi culturale ed estetica*, 22 (2011), 38–47.
De Berti, Raffaele, *Il volo del cinema: Miti moderni nell'Italia fascista* (Milan and Udine: Mimesis, 2012).
De Biasio, Anna, 'Appunti sui primi studi americanistici in Italia: Gustavo Strafforello e il suo *Manuale di letteratura italiana* (1884)', *Annali di Ca' Foscari*, 39/1–2 (2000), 113–33.
De Carlis, Stefania (ed.), *'La Vraie Italie' di G. Papini* (Rome: Bulzoni, 1988).
De Feo, Luciano, 'Editoriale', *Cinema*, 2/20 (25 April 1937), 299–301.
De Grazia, Victoria, 'Mass Culture and Sovereignty: The American Challenge to European Cinemas, 1920–1960', *Journal of Modern History*, 61/1 (1989), 53–87.
De Grazia, Victoria, *How Fascism Ruled Women: Italy, 1922–1945* (Berkeley and Los Angeles: University of California Press, 1993).
De Grazia, Victoria, *Irresistible Empire: America's Advance through 20th-Century Europe* (Cambridge, MA: Harvard University Press, 2005).
D'Elia, Nicola, *Giuseppe Bottai e la Germania nazista: I rapporti italo-tedeschi e la politica culturale fascista* (Rome: Carocci, 2009).
De Marchi, Emilio, *Giacomo l'idealista* (Milan: Hoepli, 1897).
De Noël, Octave, *Le Péril américaine* (Paris: De Soye et Fils, 1899).
De Ritis, Beniamino, 'Il Rubicone americano', *Nuova antologia*, 368 (July 1933), 227.
De Ritis, Beniamino, *Mente puritana in corpo pagano* (Florence: Vallecchi, 1934).
De Ritis, Beniamino, *La terza America* (Florence: Sansoni, 1937).
De Ritis, Beniamino, *Stati Uniti: Dalla guerra civile al 'nuovo trattamento'* (Varese: Tip. A. Nicola, 1938).
De Rivarol, Antoine, *De l'universalité de la langue française* (Paris: Bailly-Dessenne, 1784).

De Romero, Federico, 'Americanization and National Identity: The Case of Postwar Italy', in Luciano Tosi (ed.), *Europe, its Borders and the Others* (Naples: Edizioni Scientifiche Italiane, 2000), 263–79.

De Sanctis, Francesco, *Storia della letteratura Italiana* (1873; Turin: Einaudi, 1965); English trans. by Joan Redfern, from Francesco de Sanctis, *History of Italian Literature*, 2 vols (Oxford: Oxford University Press, 1930).

De Santis, Giuseppe, 'Quattro passi fra le nuvole', *Cinema*, 8/157 (10 January 1943), 27.

De Santis, Giuseppe, 'Harlem', *Cinema*, 165 (10 May 1943), 280.

De Santis, Giuseppe, 'Il jazz e le sue danze nel cinema', *Cinema*, 8/164 (25 April 1943), 236–8.

De Santis, Giuseppe, 'Quando Visconti girava Ossessione tra Ferrara e Pontelagoscuro e io...', *Bologna incontri*, 14/4 (April 1983), 23–32.

De Santis, Giuseppe, 'Visconti's Interpretation of Cain's Setting in *Ossessione*' [trans. Luciana Bohne], *Film Criticism*, 3 (1985), 22–32.

De Santis, Giuseppe, and Puccini, Gianni, 'A proposito dell'ultimo film di Renoir', *Cinema*, 7/133 (10 January 1942), 8–9.

Decleva, Enrico, *Arnoldo Mondadori* (Turin: UTET, 2007).

Del Negro, Piero, *Il mito americano nella Venezia del Settecento* (Rome: Atti della Accademia Nazionale dei Lincei [18], 1975), 445–657.

Del Valle de Paz, Giacomo, 'Critica del jazz', *Il Pensiero musicale*, 8/9–11 (September–November 1928), 132–4.

Della Casa, Stefano, *Mario Mattoli* [Il Castoro Cinema] (Florence: Nuova Italia, 1990).

Della Valle, Giacomo, 'Tempo di jazz', *Radiocorriere*, 8/2 (9–16 January 1932), 9–10.

DeMara, Nicholas A., 'Pathway to Calvino: Fantasy and Reality in "Il Sentiero dei nidi di ragno"', *Italian Quarterly*, 14/55 (1971), 14–33.

Depero, Fortunato, 'Vertigini di Nuova York: Il mulo e la metropoli', *L'Illustrazione italiana*, 25 (June 1935), 1051–2.

Depero, Fortunato, *Fortunato Depero nelle opere e nella vita* (Trento: Mutilati e Invalidi, 1940), revisited and translated in English as *So I think, So I Paint: Ideologies of an Italian Self-Made Painter* (Trento: Tip. Temi, 1947).

Depero, Fortunato, *Un futurista a New York* (Montepulciano: Editori del Grifo, 1990).

Di Capua, Giovanni, *Faccetta nera: Canti dell'ebbrezza fascista: Saggi critici, testi, spartiti, commenti* (Valentano: Scipioni Editore, 2000).

Di Chio, Federico, *Il cinema americano in Italia: Industria, società, immaginari: Dalle origini alla seconda guerra mondiale* (Milan: Vita e Pensiero, 2021).

Di Franco, Manuela, 'US Culture and Fascist Italy: The Case of *Omnibus* (1937–39)', in Bonsaver, Carlucci, and Reza (eds), *Italy and the USA*, 123–39.

Di Gregorio, Luca, 'Per un pugno di romanzi: L'immaginario del West di Emilio Salgari, tra "selvaggismo nero" e western americano (1896–1910)', in Pollone (ed.). *Il western in Italia*, 23–36.

Diggins, John P., *Mussolini and Fascism: The View from America* (Princeton: Princeton University Press, 1972).

Di Spalatro, Antonella, *Censura e politca editoriale: Enrico Piceni alla Mondadori negli anni trenta* (Rome: Lithos, 2021).

Di Stefano, Giulio, 'Appunto sul Vidor minore', *Cinema*, 173–4 (25 September–25 October 1943), 112–13.

Doherty, Thomas Patrick, *Hollywood and Hitler, 1933-1939* (New York: Columbia University Press, 2013).

Doletti, Mino, 'Si gira "Luciano Serra" in Etiopia', *Film*, 1/1 (29 January 1938), 3.

Donaldson, Scott, 'Hemingway of "The Star"', *College Literature*, 7/3 (1980), 263–81.

Dossin, Catherine, *The Rise and Fall of American Art, 1940s–1980s: A Geopolitics of the Western Art World* (Farnham: Ashgate, 2015).

Dos Passos, John, *The Fourteenth Chronicle: Letters and Diaries of John Dos Passos* (Boston: Gambit, 1973).

Dumont, Hervé, *Frank Borzage: The Life and Films of a Hollywood Romantic* (Jefferson NC: McFarland, 2006).

Dunnett, Jane, *The 'Mito Americano' and Italian Literary Culture under Fascism* (Rome: Aracne, 2015).

Eco, Umberto, *A Theory of Semiotics* (London: Macmillan, 1977; 1975 in Italian edn).

Eco, Umberto. 'Il modello americano', in Umberto Eco, Remo Ceserani, and Beniamino Pladico (eds), *La riscoperta dell'America* (Rome and Bari: Laterza, 1984), 3–32.

Eco, Umberto, *La misteriosa fiamma della regina Loana* (Milan: Bompiani, 2004); trans. in English as *The Mysterious Flame of Queen Loana* (London: Secker & Warburg, 2005).

Edmiston, Fred W., *The Coon-Sanders Nighthawks: 'The Band that Made Radio Famous'* (Jefferson, NC: McFarland & Co., 2003).

Einaudi, Luigi, *Un principe mercante: Studi sulla espansione coloniale italiana* (Turin: Bocca, 1900).

Ellwood, David W., *Italy 1943–1945* (Leicester: Leicester University Press, 1985).

Ellwood, David W., *The Shock of America: Europe and the Challenge of the Century* (Oxford: Oxford University Press, 2012).

Erbaggio, Pierluigi, 'Mussolini in American Newsreels: *Il Duce* as Modern Celebrity', in Mark Epstein, Fulvio Orsitto, and Andrea Righi (eds), *Totalitarian Arts: The Visual Arts, Fascism(s) and Mass-Society* (Newcastle upon Tyne: Cambridge Scholars Publishing, 2017), 62–81.

Ercole, Pierluigi, '"The Greatest Film of the Fascist Era": The Distribution of *Camicia nera* in Britain', *Alphaville: Journal of Film and Screen Media*, 6 (Winter 2013), 1–14.

Eschenazi, Gabriele, *Le regine dello Swing: Il Trio Lescano: Una storia fra cronaca e costume* (Turin: Einaudi, 2010).

Esposito, Edoardo, *Con altra voce: La traduzione letteraria fra le due guerre* (Rome: Donzelli, 2018).

Evola, Julius, 'Americanismo e bolscevismo', *Nuova antologia*, 7/165 (May 1929), 110–28.

Ezra, Elizabeth, and Salzberg, Ana, 'The Screen Test 1915–1930: How Stars Were Born', *Celebrity Studies*, 8/3 (2017), 477–88.

Fabbri, Bruno, *Buffalo Bill di Romagna: Storia di Domenico Tambini e della sua misteriosa eredità* (Poggio Rusco: MnM, 2020).

Fabre, Giorgio, *L'elenco: Cnsura fascista, editoria e autori ebrei* (Turin: Zamorani, 1998).

Fabre, Giorgio, *Hitler's Contract: How Mussolini Became Hitler's Publisher* (London: Enigma, 2006).

Faeti, Antonio, 'Starace nel pallone', in Maurizio Vaudagna (ed.), *L'estetica della politica* (Rome: Laterza, 1989), 187–202.

Faina, Eugenio, *Inchiesta parlamentare sulle condizioni dei contadini nelle province meridionali e nella Sicilia*, viii. *Relazione finale* (Rome: Tipografia Nazionale, 1911).

Falasca-Zamponi, Simonetta, *Fascist Spectacle: The Aesthetics of Power in Mussolini's Italy* (Berkeley and Los Angeles: University of California Press, 1997).

Falconi, Dino, 'Joe il rosso raccontato dal suo soggettista', *Cinema illlustrazione*, 11/43 (21 October 1936), 4–5.

Fanfani, Massimo, 'La prima stagione di *Lingua nostra*', in Matteo Santipolo and Matteo Viale (eds), *Bruno Migliorini, l'uomo e il linguista* (Rovigo: Accademia dei Concordi, 2009), 25–96.

Fanfani, Massimo, 'A Century of Americanisms', in Bonsaver, Carlucci, and Reza (eds), *Italy and the USA*, 232–45.
Fauri, Francesca, *Storia economica delle migrazioni italiane* (Bologna: Il Mulino, 2015).
Favaro, A., 'A proposito della prossima Esposizione universale di Filadelfia', *L'Illustrazione italiana*, 23 (2 April 1876), 359–62.
Fellini, Federico, *Intervista sul cinema*, ed. Giovanni Grazzini (Rome and Bari: Laterza, 1983).
Ferme, Valerio, *Tradurre è tradire: La traduzione come sovversione culturale sotto il fascismo* (Ravenna: Longo, 2003).
Fernandez, Dominique, *Il mito dell'America negli intellettuali italiani dal 1930 al 1950* (Caltanissetta and Rome: Sciascia, 1969).
Ferrando, Anna, *Cacciatori di libri: Gli agenti letterari durante il fascismo* (Milan: Franco Angeli, 2019).
Ferrando, Anna (ed.), *Stranieri all'ombra del Duce: Le traduzioni durante il fascismo* (Milan: Franco Angeli, 2019).
Ferrari, Fabio, *Myths and Counter-Myths of America: New World Allegories in 20th-Century Italian Literature and Film* (Ravenna: Longo, 2008).
Ferrero, Felice, 'Gli accampamenti cittadini', *Corriere della Sera*, 11 and 23 August 1910, p. 3.
Ferrero, Felice, 'Battaglia di donne', *Corriere della Sera*, 28 January 1910, p. 3.
Ferrero, Felice, 'Geppì', 3 February 1910, p. 3.
Ferrero, Felice, 'La mano nera', *Corriere della Sera*, 3 February 1911, p. 3.
Ferrero, Felice, 'Bianchi e neri', *Corriere della Sera*, 9 September 1924, p. 3.
Ferrero, Felice, 'L'impero dei negri', *Corriere della Sera*, 21 October 1920, p. 3.
Ferrero, Leo, 'Dialogo sull'ombra', *Solaria*, 2/3 (March 1927), 2c3–30.
Ferrero, Leo, *Paris: Dernier modéle de l'Occident* (Paris: Les Éditions Rieder, 1932).
Ferrero, Leo, *Amérique, miroir grossissant de l'Europe* (Paris: Éditions Rieder, 1939).
Fiamingo, Giuseppe Maria, *Il protezionismo sociale contemporaneo* (Turin: Roux Frassati & Co., 1896).
Fiamingo, Giuseppe Maria, 'L'invasione economica dell'America', *Nuova antologia di lettere, scienze e arti*, 98 (March–April 1902), 484–92.
Finzi, Roberto, 'La cultura italiana e le leggi antiebraiche del 1938', *Studi storici*, 49/4 (2008), 895–929.
Fiorentino, Daniele, '"Those Red-Brick Faces": European Press Reactions to the Indians of Buffalo Bill's Wild West Show', in Christian Feest (ed.), *Indians and Europe: An Interdisciplinary Collection of Essays* (Aachen: Rader, 1987), 403–14.
Fiorentino, Daniele, *Gli Stati Uniti e il Risorgimento d'Italia, 1848–1901* (Rome: Gangemi, 2013).
Flink, James, *The Automobile Age* (Cambridge, MA: MIT Press, 1988).
Foerster, Robert F., *The Italian Emigration of our Time* (Cambridge, MA: Harvard University Press, 1919).
Fontana, Ferdinando, and Papa, Dario, *New York* (Milan: Galli Editore, 1884).
Forgacs, David, 'Americanisation: The Italian Case, 1938–1956', *Borderlines. Studies in American Culture*, 1/2 (1993), 157–69.
Forgacs, David, and Gundle, Stephen, *Mass Culture and Italian Society: From Fascism to the Cold War* (Bloomington, IN: Indiana University Press, 2007).
Forno, Mauro, *Informazione e potere: Storia del giornalismo italiano* (Rome and Bari: Laterza, 2012).
Fortuna, James F., '"Un'arte ancora in embrione": International Expositions, Empire, and the Evolution of Fascist Architectural Design', *Modern Italy*, 25/4 (2020), 455–76.

Fourniol, Étienne, 'L'America nella letteratura francese del 1927', *Nuova antologia*, 7/158 (April 1928), 370–81.
Fraccaroli, Arnaldo, 'Prefazione all'America', *Corriere della Sera*, 27 January 1927, pp. 1–2.
Fraccaroli, Arnaldo, 'S'è udito uno scricchiolìo', *Corriere della Sera*, 5 February 1927, p. 3.
Fraccaroli, Arnaldo, 'Elogio della donna', *Corriere della Sera*, 25 May 1927, p. 3.
Fraccaroli, Arnaldo, 'Una città di fanciulle', *Corriere della Sera*, 27 May 1927, p. 3.
Fraccaroli, Arnaldo, 'Good bye, America!', *Corriere della Sera*, 3 November 1927, p. 3.
Fraccaroli, Arnaldo, *Hollywood, paese d'avventura* (Milan: Treves, 1928).
Fraccaroli, Arnaldo, *New York ciclone di genti* (Milan: Treves, 1928).
Fraccaroli, Arnaldo, *Vita d'America* (Milan: Treves 1928).
Fraccaroli, Arnaldo, *Donne d'America* (Milan: Omenoni, 1930).
Fraccaroli, Arnaldo, *Il paradiso delle fanciulle, ovvero* American Girls (Milan: Treves, 1931).
Fracchia, Umberto, 'Esistere nel tempo', *La fiera letteraria*, 1 (13 December 1925), 1.
Franchi, Adolfo, 'Elogio di Biancaneve e i sette nani', *L'Illustrazione italiana*, 41/1 (1 January 1939), 16.
Franzina, Emilio, *La grande emigrazione: L'esodo dei rurali dal Veneto durante il secolo XIX* (Venice: Marsilio, 1976).
Franzina, Emilio, *L'immaginario degli emigranti: Miti e raffigurazioni dell'esperienza italiana all'estero fra i due secoli* (Treviso: Pagus, 1992).
Franzina, Emilio, *Merica! Merica! Emigrazione e colonizzazione nelle lettere dei contadini veneti e friulani in America Latina; 1876–1902* (Verona: Cierre, 1994).
Franzina, Emilio, *Gli Italiani al nuovo mondo* (Milan: Mondadori, 1995).
Franzina, Emilio, *Dall'Arcadia in America: Attività letteraria ed emigrazione transoceanica in Italia (1850–1940)* (Turin: Edizioni della Fondazione Giovanni Agnelli, 1996).
Franzina, Emilio, *La storia è altrove: Casi nazionali e casi regionali nelle moderne migrazioni di massa* (Verona: Cierre, 1998).
Franzina, Emilio, *Al caleidoscopio della Gran Guerra: Vetrini di donne, di canti e di emigranti, 1914–1918* (Isernia: Cosmo Iannone, 2017).
Freddi, Luigi, *Altre terre* (Florence: Corbaccio, 1933).
Freddi, Luigi, 'Il cinema', *Rivista illustrata del Popolo d'Italia*, 14/4 (April 1936), 67–73.
Freddi, Luigi, 'Arte per il popolo', *Bianco e nero*, 3/2 (1939), 11–12.
Freddi, Luigi, 'Rivista mattutina', *Corriere della Sera*, 20 September 1939, p. 3.
Freddi, Luigi, *Il cinema*, 2 vols (Rome: L'Arnia, 1949); repr. in single vol. as *Il governo dell'immagine* (Rome: Gremese, 1994).
Friedman, Max Paul, 'Beyond "Voting with their Feet": Toward a Conceptual History of "America" in European Migrant Sending Communities, 1860s to 1914', *Journal of Social History*, 40/3 (2007), 557–75.
Frykholm, Joel, *George Kleine and American Cinema: The Movie Business and Film Culture in the Silent Era* (London: Palgrave Macmillan, 2015).
Fulvi, Daniele, '"Compagni di pragmatismo": Giuseppe Papini e William James', *Nóema*, 6/2 (2015), 18–36.
Fumasoni Biondi, Leone, 'Scambi culturali e turismo: Italia e Stati Uniti', *Corriere della Sera*, 18 April 1930, p. 1.
Fumasoni Biondi, Leone, 'L'azione e le idee di Henry Ford', *Corriere della Sera*, 30 December 1930, p. 3.
Gabaccia, Donna, *Militants and Migrants: Rural Sicilians Become American Workers* (New Brunswick, NJ: Rutgers University Press, 1988).
Gabaccia, Donna, *Italy's Many Diasporas* (London: UCL Press, 2000).

Gaborik, Patricia, *Mussolini's Theatre: Fascist Experiments in Art and Politics* (Cambridge: Cambridge University Press, 2021).
Gaborik, Patricia, 'Fascism', in Patricia Gaborik (ed.), *Pirandello in Context* (Cambridge: Cambridge University Press, 2022), 12–24.
Gadda Conti, Giuseppe, 'L'America nel *Corriere della Sera* e nella *Stampa*: Mark Twain', *Studi americani*, 19–20 (1973), 133–54.
Gadducci, Fabio, Gori, Leonardo, and Lama, Sergio, *Eccetto Topolino: Lo scontro culturale tra Fascismo e Fumetti* (Rome: Nicola Pesce Editore, 2011).
Gallagher, Tad, *The Adventures of Roberto Rossellini: His Life and Films* (New York: Da Capo Press, 1998).
Gallo, Claudio, 'Carteggio inedito tra Lorenzo Montano e Arnoldo Mondadori: Alle origini del "Giallo" e di alcune collane Mondadori', *Atti Accademia Roveretana degli Agiati*, VIII.II.A (2002), 181–226.
Garzarelli, Benedetta, 'Cinema e propaganda all'estero nel regime fascista: Le proiezioni di *Camicia nera* a Parigi, Berlino e Londra', *Dimensioni e problemi della ricerca storica*, 2 (2003), 147–65; repr. in Garzarelli, *Parleremo al mondo intero: La propaganda del fascismo all'estero* (Alessandria: Edizioni dell'Orso, 2004).
Gathreaux, Alan, *Italians of Louisiana: History, Heritage, Tradition* (Charleston, SC: History Press, 2014).
Gatti, Alessandro (ed.), *I cineoperatori: La storia della cinematografia italiana dal 1895 al 1940 raccontata dagli autori della fotografia*, i (Rome: Edizioni AIC, 1999).
Geist, Johann Friedrich, *Arcades: The History of a Building Type* (Cambridge, MA: MIT Press, 1985).
Gennaro, Rosario, 'Una guerra italiana combattuta a Parigi: Bontempelli, *900* e i suoi avversari', *Incontri*, 34/2 (2019), 86–99.
Gentile, Emilio, Il mito dello stato nuovo dall'antigiolittismo al fascismo (Rome and Bari: Laterza, 1982).
Gentile, Emilio, 'Impending Modernity: Fascism and the Ambivalent Image of the United States', *Journal of Contemporary History*, 28/1 (1993), 7–29; later repr. as part of his volume *The Struggle for Modernity: Nationalism, Futurism, and Fascism* (Westport, CT: Praeger, 2003), 161–80.
Gentile, Emilio, *Fascismo di pietra* (Rome and Bari: Laterza, 2007).
Gentile, Emilio, 'A Revolution for the Third Italy', in Spencer M. Di Scala and Emilio Gentile (eds), *Mussolini 1883–1915: Triumph and Transformation of a Revolutionary Socialist* (New York: Palgrave Macmillan, 2016).
Gentile, Giovanni, 'Religione e prammatismo nel James' (1904), in Gentile, *Il modernismo e i rapporti tra religione e filosofia: Discorsi di religione* (Bari: Laterza, 1909; Florence: Sansoni, 1965), 171–90.
Gentile, Giovanni, 'Esiste una scuola in Italia? Lettera aperta a S. E. Berenini', *Il Resto del Carlino*, 4 May 1918, pp. 1–2.
Gentile, Giovanni, *Il problema scolastico del dopoguerra* (Naples: Ricciardi, 1919).
Gentile, Giovanni, 'Prammatismo razionale' (1907), in Gentile, *Saggi critici* (Naples: Ricciardi, 1921), 203–14.
Gentile, Giovanni, 'Prefazione a "Cinematografo"', *Bianco e nero*, 3/2 (1939), 13–14.
Gentile, Giovanni (ed.), *Enciclopedia italiana* (Rome: Istituto dell'Enciclopedia Italiana, 1934), https://www.treccani.it/enciclopedia/liceo-ginnasio_%28Enciclopedia-Italiana%29/ (accessed 1 December 2021).
Gerbi, Antonello, 'Teorie sul cinema (A proposito di un "Cahiers du mois")', *Il Convegno*, 7/10 (October 1926), 766–81.

Gerbi, Antonello, *The Dispute of the New World: The History of a Polemic, 1750-1900* (Pittsburgh, PA: University of Pittsburgh Press, 1973).
Getto, Giovanni, 'Pascoli e l'America', in Giovanni Getto, *Carducci e Pascoli* (Bologna: Zanichelli, 1957), 154–84.
Ghez, Didier, *Disney's Grand Tour: Walt and Roy's European Vacation—Summer 1935* (New York: Theme Park Press, 2013).
Ghilardi, Margherita, 'Cronologia', in Emilio Cecchi, *Saggi e viaggi* (Milan: Mondadori, 1997), pp. xxix–lv.
Giacosa, Giuseppe, *Impressioni d'America* (Milan: Cogliati, 1898).
Gigli Marchetti, Ada, and Finocchi, Luisa (eds), *Stampa e piccola editoria tra le due guerre* (Milan: Franco Angeli, 1997).
Giladi, Amotz, 'Les Écrivains florentins d'avant-garde et la France: Échanges, rivalités et conflits, 1900–1920', *Australian Journal of French Studies*, 54/2–3 (2017), 218–34.
Gili, Jean A., *Stato fascista e cinematografia: Repressione e promozione* (Rome: Bulzoni, 1981).
Gili, Jean A., *André Deed: Boireau, cretinetti, gribouille* (Bologna: Cineteca Bologna, 2005).
Ginex, Giovanna, 'L'arte dell'illustrazione nelle pagine de "La Domenica del Corriere" (1899–1989)', in Giovanna Ginex (ed.), *La Domenica del Corriere: Il novecento illustrato* (Milan: Skira, 2007), 17–27.
Ginex, Giovanna, 'Not Just Campari! Depero and Advertizing', *Italian Modern Art*, 1 (January 2019), 1–28, https://www.italianmodernart.org/journal/articles/not-just-campari-depero-and-advertising/#easy-footnote-3-4647 (accessed 15 January 2012).
Giordano, Michele, *La stampa illustrata in Italia: Dalle origini alla Grande Guerra 1834–1915* (Milan: Guanda, 1983).
Girardi, Michele, *Puccini: His International Art* (Chicago: Chicago University Press, 2000) (Italian original publication, 1995).
Girimonti Greco, Giuseppe, '"Adoratori" romanzeschi della Garbo: (De-)figurazioni narrative di un volto divino (1933–2007)', in Matteo Colombi and Stefania Esposito (eds), *L'immagine ripresa in parola: Letteratura, cinema e altre visioni* (Rome: Meltemi, 2008), 147–71.
Girosi, Marcello, 'Marineland o la terra del mare', *L'Illustrazione italiana*, 45/6 (5 February 1939), 255–7.
Gobetti, Piero [signed as: ***], 'La scuola delle padrone, la scuola dei servi, la scuola dei cortigiani', *La Rivoluzione liberale*, 2/13 (8 May 1923), 53.
Goebbels, Joseph, 'Discorso alla Reichsfilmkammer', *Bianco e nero*, 3/2 (1939), 85–105.
Goebbels, Joseph, *The Goebbels' Diaries, 1939–1945* (London: Hamilton, 1982).
Goeschel, Christian, *Mussolini and Hitler: The Forging of the Fascist Alliance* (New Haven: Yale University Press, 2018).
Goetz, Helmut, *Il giuramento rifiutato: I docenti universitari e il regime fascista* (Florence: La Nuova Italia, 2000).
Golino, Carlo L., 'Giovanni Papini and American Pragmatism', *Italica*, 32/1 (1955), 38–48.
Gori, Gigliola, *Italian Fascism and the Female Body: Sport, Submissive Women, and Strong Mothers* (New York: Routledge, 2004).
Gorlier, Claudio, 'L'alternativa americana', in Elio Vittorini, *Americana: Raccolta di narratori* (Milan: Bompiani, 1984), pp. vii–xv.
Graf, Arturo, *L'anglomania e l'influsso inglese in Italia nel secolo XVIII* (Turin: Loescher, 1911).
Gramsci, Antonio, *Quaderni dal carcere*, ed. V. Gerratana, 4 vols (Turin: Einaudi, 1975).
Gramsci, Antonio, *Americanismo e Fordismo: Quaderno 22* (Turin: Einaudi, 1978).
Grandi, Aldo, *Fuori dal coro: Ruggero Zangrandi, una biografia* (Milan: Baldini & Castoldi, 1993).

Grandi, Aldo, *Letteratura e vita nazionale* (Rome: Editori Riuniti, 1971).
Grassi, Tiziana, et al. (eds), *Dizionario Enciclopedico delle migrazioni italiane nel mondo* (Rome: SER, 2014).
Gray, Christopher, 'Mystery of 104 Bronze Statues of Mercury', *New York Times*, 2 February 1997, p. 5.
Grazia, Patrizia, *Editori a Milano (1900–1945)* (Milan: Franco Angeli, 2013).
Graziani, Carlo, 'Luigi Credaro e la politica scolastica nell'età giolittiana', *Problemi della pedagogia*, 1–2 (1961), 76–106, 276–90.
Gromo, Mario, 'Il film del decennale: "Camicia nera"', *La Stampa*, 24 March 1933, p. 3.
Gromo, Mario [m.g.], 'Dietro lo schermo', *La Stampa*, 23 July 1935, p. 3.
Gromo, Mario, 'I quattro moschettieri', *La Stampa*, 30 March 1937, p. 5.
Guglielman, Eleonora, 'Dalla "scuola per signorine" alla "scuola delle padrone": Il Liceo femminile della riforma Gentile e i suoi precedent storici', in Marco Guspini (ed.), *Da un secolo all'altro: Contributi per una 'storia dell'insegnamento della storia'* (Rome: Amicia, 2004), 155–95.
Guidali, Fabio, 'Developing Middlebrow Culture in Fascist Italy: The Case of Rizzoli's Illustrated Magazines', *Journal of European Periodical Studies*, 4/2 (2019), 106–21.
Guidali, Fabio, 'Tradurre in "roto": Periodici popolari e letteratura straniera (1933–1936)', in Anna Ferrando (ed.), *Stranieri all'ombra del duce: Le traduzioni durante il fascismo* (Milan: Franco Angeli, 2019), 87–103.
Gundle, Stephen, *Between Hollywood and Moscow: The Italian Communists and the Challenge of Mass Culture, 1943–1991* (Durham, NC: Duke University Press, 2000).
Gundle, Stephen, *Mussolini's Dream Factory: Film Stardom in Fascist Italy* (New York and Oxford: Berghahn, 2013).
Hansen, Arlen J., *Gentlemen Volunteers: The Story of the American Ambulance Drivers in the Great War: August 1914–September 1918* (New York: Arcade Publishing, 1996).
Hara, Kunio, '"Per noi emigrati": Nostalgia in the Reception of Puccini's *La fanciulla del West* in New York City's Italian-Language Newspapers', *Journal of the Society for American Music*, 13/2 (2019), 177–94.
Hay, James, *Popular Film Culture in Fascist Italy: The Passing of the Rex* (Bloomington, IN: Indiana University Press, 1987).
Hays, Will H., 'Dare e avere', *Cinema*, 4/69 (10 May 1939), 289.
Hays, Will H., *The Memoirs of Will H. Hays* (New York: Doubleday & Company, 1955).
Hertner, Peter, *Il capitale tedesco in Italia dall'Unità alla prima guerra mondiale* (Bologna: Il Mulino, 1984).
Hemingway, Ernest, 'Mussolini, Europe's Prize Bluffer', *Toronto Daily Star*, 27 January 1923.
Hemingway, Ernest, 'Il ritorno del soldato', *Il Convegno*, 6–7 (1925), 339–47.
Hermeter, Anne-Rachel, 'La *NRF* de Paulhan et l'Italie: Regards croisés (1925–1940)', in Jean-Yves Guérin (ed.), *La Nouvelle Revue française de Jean Paulhan (1925–1940 et 1953–1968)* (Paris: Éditions Le Manuscrit, 2006), 45–64.
Higham, Charles, *Merchant of Dreams: Louis B. Mayer, MGM, and the Secret Hollywood* (New York: Sidgwick & Jackson, 1993).
Hughes, H. Stuart, *The United States and Italy* (Cambridge, MA: Harvard University Press, 1979; enlarged edn, 2013).
Iaccio, Pasquale, *Vincere! Vincere! Vincere!: Fascismo e società italiana nelle canzoni e nelle riviste di varietà, 1935–1943* (Rome: Ianua, 1981).
Ingold, Tim, *Being Alive: Essays on Movement, Knowledge and Description* (London: Routledge, 2011).
Interlandi, Telesio, 'Contro il cinema italiano', *Il Tevere*, 20–1 October 1937, p. 1.
Introvigne, Massimo, 'Nick Carter in Italy', *Dime Novel Round-Up*, 75/1 (2006), 12–15.

Isani, Giuseppe, 'Cose dell'altro mondo', *Cinema*, 4/84 (25 December 1939), 393.

Jackson, Frederick, 'An Italian Uncle Tom's Cabin', *Italica*, 35/1 (1958), 38–42.

Jacini, Stefano, *Relazione finale sui risultati dell'Inchiesta agraria*, vol. 15 of *Atti della Giunta per la Inchiesta agraria e sulle condizioni della classe agricola* (Rome: Forzani, 1874).

James, William, *The Will to Believe and Other Essays in Popular Philosophy* (New York: Longmans, Green & Co., 1897).

James, William, 'Giovanni Papini and the Pragmatist Movement in Italy', *Journal of Philosophy, Psychology and Scientific Method*, 3/13 (1906), 337–41 (340).

James, William, *Pragmatism: A New Name for Some Old Ways of Thinking* (Cambridge, MA: Harvard University Press, 1907).

Janni, Mauro, 'Verso la realizzazione delle nostre proposte', *Il Popolo d'Italia*, 7 February 1939, p. 3.

Janni, Mauro, 'La Radio—Musica leggera moderna', *Il Popolo d'Italia*, 19 February 1939, p. 3.

Jeffers, H. Paul, *The Napoleon of New York: Mayor Fiorello La Guardia* (New York: John Wiley & Sons, 2002).

Joyce, James, 'Prime versioni italiane dall'*Ulysses*, con un ritratto e una lettera autografa', *Il Convegno*, 7/11 (1926), 813–28.

Kallis, Aristotle, '"In miglior tempo...": What Fascism did not Build in Rome', *Journal of Modern Italian Studies*, 16 (2011), 59–83.

Kallis, Aristotle, *The Third Rome, 1922–1943: The Making of the Fascist Capital* (Basingstoke: Palgrave Macmillan, 2014).

Kallis, Aristotle, 'Futures Made Present: Architecture, Monument, and the Battle for the "Third Way" in Fascist Italy', *Fascism*, 7 (2018), 45–79.

Kallmann, Alfred, *Die Konzernierung in der Filmindustrie, erläutert an den Filmindustrien Deutschlands und Amerikas*, doctoral thesis (Würzburg, 1932).

Kessner, Thomas, *Fiorello H. La Guardia and the Making of New York* (New York: McGraw-Hill, 1989).

King, Russell, *Il ritorno in patria: Return Migration to Italy in Historical Perspective* (Durham: Department of Geography, University of Durham, 1988).

Kirk, Terry, *The Architecture of Modern Italy*, 2 vols (New York: Princeton Architectural Press, 2005).

Klein, Gabriella, *La politica linguistica del fascismo* (Bologna: Il Mulino, 1986).

Kokubo, Marie, 'L'influenza della letteratura e del cinema americano nei personaggi di *Lavorare stanca* di Cesare Pavese', in Hideyuki Doi, Katsuo Hashimoto, and Takeo Sumi (eds), *Per i sessant'anni del professor Tadahiko Wada* (Tokyo: Sobunsha, 2012), 5–23.

Körner, Axel, *Politics and Culture in Liberal Italy: From Unification to Fascism* (London: Routledge, 1999).

Körner, Axel, 'Uncle Tom on the Ballet Stage: Italy's Barbarous America, 1850–1900', *Journal of Modern History*, 83/4 (2011), 721–52.

Körner, Axel, 'Masked Faces: Verdi, Uncle Tom and the Unification of Italy', *Journal of Modern Italian Studies*, 18/2 (2013), 176–89.

Körner, Axel, *America in Italy: The United States in the Political Thought and Imagination of the Italian Risorgimento, 1763–1865* (Princeton and Oxford: Princeton University Press, 2017).

Körner, Axel, Miller, Nicola, and Smith, Adam I. P. (eds), *America Imagined: Explaining the United States in Nineteenth-Century Europe and Latin America* (New York: Palgrave Macmillan, 2012).

Kornhaber, Donna, '*Charlot* as Cinema: Louis Delluc and Charlie Chaplin at the Dawn of Film Criticism', *Film History*, 27/2 (2015), 140–59.

Kreimeier, Klaus, *The UFA Story: A History of Germany's Greatest Film Company, 1918-1945* (Berkeley and Los Angeles: University of California Press, 1999).
Kroes, Bob, 'America and the European Sense of History', *Journal of American History*, 86/3 (1999), 1135-55.
Kuisel, Richard F., 'The End of Americanization? or Reinventing a Research Field for Historians of Europe', *Journal of Modern History*, 92 (September 2020), 602-34.
La Guardia, Fiorello H., *The Making of an Insurgent: An Autobiography: 1881-1919* (Philadelphia, PA: Lippincott, 1948).
Ladd, Brian, *Autophobia: Love and Hate in the Automotive Age* (Chicago: University of Chicago Press, 2008).
Lanaro, Silvio, 'Mercantilismo agrario e formazione del capitale nel pensiero di Alessandro Rossi', *Quaderni storici*, 6/16 (1971), 48-156.
La Torre, Antonella, 'Arco monumentale', in Calvesi, Guidoni, and Lux (eds), *E 42: Utopia e scenario del regime*, 467-70.
Lauer, Bernhard, 'Les contes des Grimm dans les langues du monde : aller et retour', in Peyrache-Leborgne, Dominique (ed.), *Vies et métamorphoses des contes de Grimm. Traductions, réceptions, adaptations* (Rennes: Presses universitaires de Rennes, 2017), 17-23.
Laughlin, Clara, *So You're Going to Rome!* (Cambridge, MA: Riverside Press, 1925; repr. 1928).
Laux, James, *In First Gear: The French Automobile Industry to 1914* (Liverpool: Liverpool University Press, 1976).
Lazzaro, Claudia, and Crum, Roger J. (eds), *Donatello among the Blackshirts: History and Modernity in the Visual Culture of Fascist Italy* (Ithaca, NY: Cornell University Press, 2005).
Le Corbusier, *Vers une architeture* (Paris: Editions G. Crès et Cie., 1923); English trans. *Towards a New Architecture* (London: Architectural Press, 1987).
Leoncini, Paolo, *Emilio Cecchi: L'etica del visivo e lo stato liberale* (Lecce: Milella, 2017).
Lepschy, Giulio, 'Anglismi e italianismi', in Silvana Monti (ed.), *Scritti di linguistica e dialettologia in onore di Giuseppe Francescato* (Trieste: Edizioni Ricerche, 1995); then in Lepschy, *L'amanuense analfabeta e altri saggi* (Florence: Olschky, 1992), 169-92.
Legge, Doriana, 'Il café chantant: Quella sarabanda attorno al magro albero della cuccagna, 1900-1928', *Teatro e storia*, 38 (2017), 179-208.
Lepri, Sergio, Arbitrio, Francesco, and Cultrera, Giuseppe, *L'agenzia Stefani da Cavour a Mussolini: Informazione e potere in un secolo di storia italiana* (Florence: Le Monnier, 2001).
Leavitt, Charles L., IV, *Italian Neorealism: A Cultural History* (Toronto: Toronto University Press, 2020).
Levi, Carlo, *Cristo si è fermato a Eboli* (Turin: Einaudi, 1945; trans. Frances Frenave, 1947).
Levi, Ezio, and Testoni, Gian Carlo, *Introduzione alla vera musica di jazz* (Milan: Magazzino Musicale, 1938).
Linati, Carlo, 'Tra cannibali e balene', *Corriere della Sera*, 15 April 1927, p. 3.
Linati, Carlo, 'Un cronista del Mid West', *Corriere della Sera*, 5 July 1927, p. 3.
Liuzzi, Fernando, 'Jazz e anti-jazz', *Nuova antologia*, 251 (January 1927), 70-6.
Livi, François, 'Le "Saut vital": Le Monde littéraire italien à Paris (1900-1914)', in André Kaspi and Antoine Marès (eds), *Le Paris des étrangers: Depuis un siècle* (Paris: Imprimerie nationale, 1989), 313-27.
Livingston, Alexander, *Damn Great Empires! William James and the Politics of Pragmatism* (Oxford: Oxford University Press, 2016).
Lettau, Joseph, *In Italy with the 332d Infantry* (Youngstown, OH: Lettau, 1921).
Lief, Shane, 'Anarchist Blues', *Jazz Archivist*, 25 (2012), 34-42.

Lizzani, Carlo, 'Vie del cinema italiano', *Cinema*, 8/60 (25 February 1943), 103.
Longanesi, Leo, 'L'occhio di vetro', *L'Italiano*, 17–18 (January–February 1933), 74–81; repr. in *Bianco e nero*, 3/2 (1939), 74–81.
Lotman, Juri, *Universe of the Mind: A Semiotic Theory of Culture* (London: Tauris, 1990).
Lottini, Irene, 'When Buffalo Bill Crossed the Ocean: Native American Scenes in Early Twentieth Century European Culture', *European Journal of American Culture*, 31/3 (2012), 187–203.
Lotz, Rainer, 'The United States Army Ambulance Service Jazz Band', *Vintage Jazz Mart*, 145 (2007), 2–7.
LP, 'Il cinema straniero alla Mostra di Venezia', *Rivista illustrata del Popolo d'Italia*, 14/9 (September 1936), 48–9.
Luconi, Stefano, *La 'diplomazia parallela': Il regime fascista la mobilitazione degli italo-americani* (Milan: Franco Angeli, 2000).
Luconi, Stefano, 'La città della Grande Depressione: Manlio Morgagni a New York, 1932', *Storia urbana*, 109 (2005), 35–50.
Luconi, Stefano, 'Le comunità italoamericane degli Stati Uniti e la prima guerra mondiale', *Dimensioni e problemi della ricerca storica*, 1 (2015), 91–110.
Ludwig, Emil, *Colloqui con Mussolini* (1932; Milan: Mondadori, 2000).
Luperini, Romano (ed.), *Il verismo italiano fra naturalismo francese e cultura europea* (Lecce: Manni, 2007).
Lussana, Fiamma, 'Luciano De Feo direttore dell'Istituto LUCE', *Studi storici*, 56/4 (2015), 935–61.
Maccari, Mino [as Bisorco, Orco], 'Gazzettino ufficiale di Strapaese', *Il Selvaggio*, 4/13 (15 June 1927), 1.
Maccari, Mino [as Bisorco, Orco].,'Gazzettino ufficiale di Strapaese', *Il Selvaggio*, 5/6 (30 March 1928), 21.
McFarlane, Bruce, 'The Second Battalion', in William Wallace et al., *Ohio Doughboys in Italy: Reminiscences of the 332d Infantry* (Pleasantville, NJ: Penhallow Press, 1921), 59–63.
McGrath Morris, James, *The Ambulance Drivers: Hemingway, Dos Passos and a Friendship Made and Lost in War* (Boston: Da Capo Press, 2017).
Maggi, Raffaello, *Filmindustria-Riflessi economici* (Busto Arsizio: Pianezza, 1934).
Magrin, Alessandra, 'Rough Riders in the Cradle of Civilization: Buffalo Bill's Wild West Show in Italy and the Challenge of American Cultural Scarcity at the fin-de-siècle', *European Journal of American Culture*, 36/1 (2017), 23–38.
Mancini, Elaine, *Struggles of the Italian Film Industry during Fascism, 1930–1935* (Ann Arbor, MI: UMI Research Press, 1985).
Manetti, Daniela, *'Un'arma poderosissima': Industria cinematografica e stato durante il fascismo, 1922–1943* (Milan: Franco Angeli, 2012).
Mangoni, Luisa, *Una crisi fine secolo: La cultura italiana e la Francia tra otto e novecento* (Turin: Einaudi, 1985).
Mangoni, Luisa, *Pensare i libri: La casa editrice Einaudi dagli anni trenta agli anni sessanta* (Turin: Bollati e Boringhieri, 1999).
Mangoni, Luisa, *Civiltà della crisi: Cultura e politica in Italia tra otto e novecento* (Rome: Viella, 2013).
Mantegazza, Vico, *Agli Stati Uniti: Il pericolo americano* (Milan: Treves, 1910).
Manzotti, Fernando, *La polemica sull'emigrazione nell'Italia Unita* (Milan: Dante Alighieri Editrice, 1962; rev. edn, 1969).

Marazzi, Elisa, 'Dalle carte di un mediatore: Gian Dàuli e l'editoria milanese', in Anna Ferrando (ed.), *Stranieri all'ombra del Duce: Le traduzioni durante il fascismo* (Milan: Franco Angeli, 2019), 123–37.

Marazzi, Martino, 'Introduzione: La cultura dell'emigrazione italiana e il ruolo della tradizione', in Marazzi, *A occhi aperti: Letteratura dell'emigrazione e mito americano* (Milan: Franco Angeli, 2011), 11–22.

Margadonna, Ettore, 'King Vidor, poeta della sua terra', *Comoedia*, 12/8 (8 August 1930), 17–21; repr. in Margadonna, *Il cinema degli anni Trenta*, 60–8.

Margadonna, Ettore, 'Chapliniana', *Comoedia*, 13/2 (February–March 1931), 21–4; repr. in Margadonna, *Il cinema degli anni trecnta*, 96–103.

Margadonna, Ettore, *Cinema ieri e oggi* (Milan: Editoriale Domus, 1932).

Margadonna, Ettore, *Il cinema degli anni trenta*, ed. Fabio Andreazza (Florence: Le Lettere, 2013).

Margravio, Anthony V., and Salomone, Jerome J., *Bread and Respect: The Italians of Louisiana* (Gretna, LA: Pelican, 2002).

Marinelli, Dario, 'Da Yeah a Ueee senza passare dal MinCulPop: Strategie di coesistenza e resistenza del jazz italiano durante il fascismo', *California Italian Studies*, 4/1 (2013), 1–15.

Marinetti, Filippo Tommaso, *Fondazione e Manifesto del futurismo*, first pub. in French in *Le Figaro*, 20 February 1909; then in Marinetti, *I manifesti del futurismo* (Florence: Edizioni di 'Lacerba', 1914).

Marinetti, Filippo Tommaso, *Vulcano: Otto sintesi incatenate* (1926); then in Marinetti, *Teatro*, iii (Rome: Bianco, 1960), 137–206.

Marinetti, Filippo Tommaso, 'Contro l'esterofilia: Manifesto futurista alle signore e agli intellettuali', *Gazzetta del Popolo*, 24 September 1931, p. 3; later inserted in *La cucina futurista* (Milan: Sonzogno, 1932).

Marinetti, Filippo Tommaso, *Gli aeropoeti futuristi dedicano al Duce Il Poema di Torre Viscosa* (Milan: Officine Grafiche Esperia, 1938).

Marinetti, Filippo Tommaso, and Corra, Bruno, 'Contro il teatro morto. Contro il romanzone analitico. Contro il negrismo musicale. Manifesto futurista', *La Gazzetta del Popolo*, 22 October 1937, p. 3.

Marinetti, Filippo Tommaso, and Giuntini, Aldo, 'Manifesto futurista dell'aeromusica: Sintetica geometrica e curativa', *Stile futurista*, 1/2 (August 1934), 1–4.

Martelli, Sebastiano, 'America, emigrazione e "follia" nell'opera di Pirandello', in Mario Mignone (ed.), *Pirandello in America: Atti del simposio internazionale 30.10–1.11 1986* (Rome: Bulzoni, 1988), 211–35.

Martelli, Sebastiano (ed.), *Il sogno italo-americano: Realtà e immaginario dell'emigrazione negli Stati Uniti* (Naples: CUEN, 1998).

Martelli, Sebastiano, 'Dal vecchio mondo al sogno americano: Realtà e immaginario dell'emigrazione nella letteratura italiana', in Bevilacqua, De Clementi, and Franzina (eds), *Storia dell'emigrazione italiana*, i. 433–55.

Martellini, Amoreno, *Abasso di un firmamento sconosciuto: Un secolo di emigrazione italiana nelle fonti autonarrative* (Bologna: Il Mulino, 2018).

Martin, Benjamin G., *The Nazi–Fascist New Order for European Culture* (Cambridge, MA: Harvard University Press, 2016).

Martinelli, Vittorio, *Il cinema muto italiano, 1924–1931* (Turin: Nuova ERI, 1996).

Martinelli, Vittorio, 'Laggiù nell'Arizona', *Bianco e nero*, 58/3 (July–September 1997), 107–13.

Maselli, Joseph, *The Italians of New Orleans* (Charleston, SC: Arcadia Publishing, 2004).

Massara, Giuseppe, *Viaggiatori italiani in America (1860-1970)* (Rome: Edizioni di storia e letteratura, 1976).

Martera, Luca, *Harlem: Il film più censurato di sempre* (Milan and Rome: La Nave di Teseo–Centro Sperimentale di Cinematografia, 2021).

Mattioli, Guido, *Mussolini aviatore e la sua opera per l'aviazione* (Rome: Pinciana, 1935).

May, Renato, 'Allelujah!', *Bianco e nero*, 1/10 (31 October 1937), 82–100.

Mayor des Planches, Edmondo, *Attraverso gli Stati Uniti: Per l'emigrazione italiana* (Turin: Unione Tipografica Torinese, 1913).

Mazzarini, Francesca, 'Storia "non breve né facile": La "bonifica della stampa per i ragazzi" nell'Italia fascista', *Storia e problemi contemporanei*, 28/2 (2001), 33–50.

Mazzoletti, Adriano, *Il jazz in Italia*, i (Turin: EDT, 2004).

Mazzucchelli, Chiara, '*La Merica* for Children: Emigration in Luigi Capuana's *Gli "americani" di Ràbbato*', *AltraItalia*, 1 (2019), 60–76.

Meda, Ambra, 'Babilonie stellate: Immagini delle metropoli americane nella letteratura di viaggio degli anni trenta', *Forum Italicum*, 45/1 (2011), 100–23).

Meda, Juri, *Stelle e strips: La stampa italiana a fumetti tra americanismo e antiamericanismo, 1935-1955* (Macerata: EUM, 2007).

Mehrhoff, W. Arthur, *The Gateway Arch: Fact and Symbol* (Bowling Green, OH: Bowling Green State University Popular Press, 1992).

Melani, Costanza, *Effetto Poe: Influssi dello scrittore americano sulla letteratura italiana* (Florence: Florence University Press, 2006).

Mereu Keating, Carla, *The Politics of Dubbing: Film Censorship and State Intervention in the Translation of Foreign Cinema in Fascist Italy* (Oxford and Bern: Peter Lang, 2016).

Micciché, Lino, *Visconti e il neorealismo: Ossessione, La terra trema, Bellissima* (Venice: Marsilio, 1990).

Michaud, Régis, *Littérature américaine* (Paris: Éditions Kra, 1930).

Mida, Massimo, 'Quadrato americano', *Cinema*, 7/136 (25 February 1942), 102–4.

Mida, Massimo, and Quaglietti, Lorenzo (eds), *Dai telefoni bianchi al neorealismo* (Bari and Rome: Laterza, 1980).

Migone, Gian Giacomo, *Problemi di storia dei rapporti tra Italia e Stati Uniti* (Turin: Rosenberg & Sellier, 1971).

Migone, Gian Giacomo, *Gli Stati Uniti e il Fascismo: Alle origini dell'egemonia americana* (Milan: Feltrinelli, 1980); also pub. in English as *The United States and Fascist Italy: The Rise of American Finance in Europe* (Cambridge: Cambridge University Press, 2015).

Miller, Nicola, 'Liberty, Lipstick, and Lobsters', in Körner, Miller, and Smith (eds), *America Imagined*, 81–117.

Miller, Webb, '"Ho fatto del mio organismo un motore costantemente sorvegliato e controllato che marcia con assoluta regolarità"', *Il Popolo d'Italia*, 6 March 1937; then collected in Mussolini, *Opera omnia*, xxviii. 136–9.

Ministero di agricoltura, industria e commercio, *Risultati parziali del censimento della popolazione al 31 dicembre 1881 riguardo al numero degli analfabeti e confronti internazionali* [Bollettino n. 3] (Roma: Tipografia Elzeviriana, 1882).

Minuz, Andrea, 'I "valori spirituali" del cinema italiano: Antisemitismo e politiche della razza nelle riviste cinematografiche degli anni trenta', *Trauma and Memory*, 5/3 (2017), 96–102.

Mirabile, Andrea, *Multimedia Archeologies: Gabriele D'Annunzio, Belle Époque Paris, and the Total Artwork* (Amsterdam: Rodopi, 2014).

Mon, Gijs, *Atlantic Automobilism: The Emergence and Persistence of the Car: 1890-1940* (New York: Berghahn, 2014).

Monelli, Paolo, *Barbaro dominio* (Milan: Hoepli, 1933).

Monga, Luigi, 'Handbooks for Italian Emigrants to the United States: A Bibliographical Survey', *Resources for American Literary Study*, 6/2 (1976), 209-21.
Montemaggiori, Amerigo, *Dizionario della dottrina fascista* (Turin: Paravia, 1934).
Montesano, Maria, 'Gli uomini che mascalzoni!', *Cinema illustrazione*, 7/33 (17 August 1932), 8-9.
Montevecchi, Luisa, and Raicich, Marino (eds), *L'inchiesta Scialoja sulla istruzione secondaria maschile e femminile (1872-1875)* (Rome: Ministero per i beni culturali e ambientali, 1995).
Monticone, Alberto, *Il fascismo al microfono* (Rome: Studium, 1978).
Moore, R. Lawrence, and Vaudagna, Maurizio (eds), *The American Century in Europe* (Ithaca, NY: Cornell University Press, 2003).
Morgan, Thomas P., *The Listening Post: Eighteen Years on Vatican Hill* (New York: G. P. Putnam's Sons, 1944).
Morellini, Amoreno, 'Il commercio dell'emigrazione: Intermediari e agenti', in Bevilacqua, De Clementi, and Franzina (eds), *Storia dell'emigrazione italiana*, i. 293-308.
Moretti, Franco, *Atlas of the European Novel, 1800-1900* (London: Verso, 1998).
Moricola, Giuseppe, *L'albero della cuccagna: L'affare emigrazione nel grande esodo tra '800 e '900* (Rome: Aracne, 2016).
Morosi, Antonio, *Il teatro di varietà in Italia* (Florence: Calvetti, 1901).
Morosi, Antonio, 'La cena di Natale', in *Il café chantant: Guida del varieté italiano*, 1 (1910), 11-12.
Morovich, Enrico, 'Due soggetti per Macario', *Cinema*, 7/152 (25 October 1942), 610.
Moscatelli, Sara, 'Il veicolo della modernità: L'automobile', in Paride Rugafiori (ed.), *La capitale dell'automobile: Imprenditori, cultura e società a Torino* (Venice: Marsilio, 1999), 65-138.
Moscati, Ruggero (ed.), *I documenti diplomatici italiani*, 7th ser., ii (27 April 1923-22 February 1924) (Rome: Istituto Poligrafico dello Stato, 1955), 68-9, n. 102, http://www.farnesina.ipzs.it/series/SETTIMA%20SERIE/volumi/VOLUME%20II (accessed 17 February 2022).
Mosso, Angelo, *La democrazia nella religione e nella scienza: Studi sull'America* (Milan: Treves, 1901).
Mosso, Angelo, 'L'educazione della donna agli Stati Uniti d'America', *Nuova antologia di lettere, scienze ed arti*, 98 (March-April 1902), pub. in two instalments, 193-207, 408-417.
Mosso, Angelo, *Vita moderna degli italiani* (Milan: Treves, 1906).
Mozzoni, Anna Maria, *Un passo avanti nella cultura femminile: Tesi e progetto* (Milan: Tipografia internazionale, 1866).
Muntoni, Alessandra, and Farci, Maria Silvia, 'Palazzo della Civiltà Italiana', in Calvesi, Guidoni, and (eds), *E 42: Utopia e scenario del regime*, 353-70.
Mura [pen name of Maria Volpi], 'Jazz Band', *Il Jazz Band*, 1 (January 1927), 8-9.
Murphy, Libby, 'Charlot Francais: Charlie Chaplin, the First World War, and the Construction of a National Hero', *Contemporary French and Francophone Studies*, 14/1 (2010), 421-9.
Muscio, Giuliana, *Napoli/New York/Hollywood: Film between Italy and the United States* (New York: Fordham University Press, 2019).
Mussolini, Benito, 'La Voce', *Vita trentina*, 13 (3 April 1909), 7.
Mussolini, Benito, 'Al popolo americano', *Il Popolo d'Italia*, 19 January 1924, p. 1.
Mussolini, Benito, 'Roosevelt e il sistema', *Il Popolo d'Italia*, 7 July 1933, p. 1.
Mussolini, Beni, *Opera omnia*, ed. Edoardo and Duilio Susmel, 44 vols (Florence: La Fenice, 1951-80).

Mussolini, Vittorio, 'Emancipazione del cinema italiano', *Cinema*, 1/6 (25 September 1936), 213–15.
Mussolini, Vittorio, 'Si gira', *Il Popolo d'Italia*, 23 April 1937, p. 3.
Mussolini, Vittorio, 'Primi piani', *Il Popolo d'Italia*, 29 April 1937, p. 3.
Mussolini, Vittorio, 'Funzioni della Cinecittà', *Il Popolo d'Italia*, 6 May 1937, p. 2.
Mussolini, Vittorio, *Voli sulle ambe* (Florence: Sansoni, 1937).
Mussolini, Vittorio, 'Anno nuovo, vita nuova?', *Film*, 1/1 (29 January 1938), 1.
Mussolini, Vittorio, 'Un momento critico', *Cinema*, 58 (25 November 1938), 307.
Mussolini, Vittorio, 'Importazione ed esportazione cinematografica', *Cinema*, 4/82 (25 November 1939), 307.
Mussolini, Vittorio [as TSM], 'Constatazioni', *Cinema*, 6/117 (10 May 1941), 297.
Mussolini, Vittorio, 'Nuova situazione', *Cinema*, 6/132 (25 December 1941), 381.
Mussolini, Vittorio, *Vita con mio padre* (Milan: Mondadori, 1957).
MV, 'Una gita di corsa all'Esposizione', *La Stampa*, 18 July 1876, p. 2.
Nardi, Isabella, *Il primo passo: Note sulla formazione di un giornalista-letterato: Ugo Ojetti* (Naples: Edizioni Scientifiche Italiane, 1990).
Navarra, Quinto, *Memorie del cameriere di Mussolini* (1946; repr. Milan: Longanesi, 1972).
Neumann, Dietrich, 'A Skyscraper for Mussolini', *AA Files*, 68 (2014), 141–53.
Newton, Francis, *The Jazz Scene* (Goring by Sea: McGibbon & Key, 1959).
Nicoli, Marina, 'Entrepreneurs and the State in the Italian Film Industry, 1919–1935', *Business History Review*, 85 (Winter 2011), 775–98.
Nicoloso, Paolo, *Mussolini architetto: Propaganda e paesaggio urbano nell'Italia fascista* (Turin: Einaudi, 2008).
Nievo, Ippolito, *Confessioni di un italiano* [pub. posthumously in 1867], 2 vols (Milan: Garzanti, 1973).
Nizza, Angelo, 'Che cosa è il jazz', *La Stampa*, 9 December 1933, p. 6.
Nizza, Angelo, 'Due cantanti d'eccezione nel mondo del jazz', *La Stampa*, 19 May 1934, p. 6.
Nolan, Mary, *The Transatlantic Century: Europe and America, 1890–2010* (Cambridge: Cambridge University Press, 2012).
Notari, Umberto, *Quelle signore: Scene di una grande città moderna* (1904; Milan: Società editrice di giornali illustrati e moderni, 1906).
Notari, Umberto, *La donna tipo tre* (Milan: Società Anonima Notari, 1928; repr. Milan: La Vita Felice, 1998).
Nowell-Smith, Geoffrey, 'Silent Cinema, 1895–1930: Introduction', in Geoffrey Nowell-Smith (ed.). *The Oxford History of World Cinema* (Oxford: Oxford University Press, 1996), 2–5.
O'Hare-McCormick, Anne, 'Behind Fascism Stands a Philosopher', *New York Times Magazine*, 26 September 1926, pp. 3, 18.
Olivetti, Camillo, *Lettere americane* (Milan: Edizioni di Comunità, 1968).
Ojetti, Paola, 'Per uomini soli', *Film*, 2/13 (1 April 1939), 2.
Ojetti, Ugo, *Alla scoperta dei letterati* (Milan: Fratelli Dumolard, 1895).
Ojetti, Ugo, *America vittoriosa* (Milan: Treves, 1899).
Ojetti, Ugo, *L'America e l'avvenire* (Milan: Treves, 1905).
Ojetti, Ugo, 'Per un'architettura italiana', *Corriere della Sera*, 8 August 1911, p. 3.
Ojetti, Ugo, *L'Italia e la civiltà tedesca* (Milan: Rava, 1915).
Ojetti, Ugo, 'Lettera a S. E. Benito Mussolini', *Pegaso*, 1 (January 1929), 89–92.
Pabst, Georg Wilhelm, 'Servitù e grandezza di Hollywood', *Bianco e nero*, 3/2 (1939), 118–21.
Palanti, Mario, *L'Eternale—Mole Littoria* (Milan: Rizzoli, 1926).
Paliotti, Vittorio, *Il salone Margherita e la belle époque* (Rome: Benincasa, 1975).
Paolella, Domenico, 'La razza e il cinema italiano', *Film*, 1/30 (20 August 1938), 1.

Paolella, Domenico, 'Gli ebrei nel cinema', *Bianco e nero*, 3/5 (1939), 45.
Paoletti, Gianni, *Vite ritrovate: Emigrazione e letteratura italiana di otto e novecento* (Foligno: Editoriale Umbra, 2011).
Papini, Giovanni, and Soffici, Ardengo, 'Ciò che dobbiamo alla Francia', *Lacerba*, 2/17 (September 1914), 1–2.
Papini, Giovanni, *Un uomo finito* (Florence: La Voce, 1913).
Papini, Giovanni, 'Su questa letteratura', *Pegaso*, 1 (January 1929), 29–43.
Pardini, Samuele, 'The Automobile', in Sascha Bru, Luca Somigli, and Bart Van den Bossche (eds), *Futurism: A Microhistory* (Oxford: Legenda, 2017), 48–58.
Pareto, Vilfredo, 'Il mito virtuista e la letteratura immorale', first pub. as *Le Mythe vertuiste et la literature immorale* (Paris: Rivière, 1911); rev. and trans. into Italian in 1914. Now in Vilfredo Pareto, *Scritti sociologici* (Turin: UTET, 1966), 481–652.
Parini, Giuseppe, *Il giorno* [1763–5], ed. Dante Isella (Parma: Guanda, 1996).
Parisi, Luciano, *Borgese* (Turin: Tirrenia, 2000).
Pasetti, Aldo, 'Torre di Zuino, capitale della cellulosa', *Rivista illustrata del Popolo d'Italia*, 17/11 (November 1938), 125–8.
Pasinetti, Francesco ['FP'], 'I libri', *Bianco e nero*, 3/3 (1939), 62–4.
Pasinetti, Francesco, 'La danza e il ritmo cinematografico', *Cinema*, 8/164 (25 April 1943), 232–3.
Passerini, Luisa, *Mussolini immaginario* (Rome and Bari: Laterza, 1991).
Pasolini, Pier Paolo, 'Alcuni poeti', *Tempo illustrato*, 5 April 1974; then in Pasolini, *Descrizioni di descrizioni* (Turin: Einaudi, 1979), 190–1.
Patuelli, Raffaello, 'Walt Disney', *Lo Schermo*, 1 (August 1935), 24–6.
Paulicelli, Eugenia, *Fashion under Fascism: Beyond the Black Shirt* (Oxford: Berg, 2004).
Pavese, Cesare, 'Romanzieri americani', *La Cultura*, 11/2 (April–June 1932), 408–9.
Pavese, Cesare, 'John Dos Passos e il romanzo americano', *La Cultura*, 12/1 (January–March 1933); repr. in Pavese, *Saggi letterari*, 105.
Pavese, Cesare, 'Ieri e oggi', *L'Unità*, 3 August 1947; repr. in Pavese, *Saggi letterari*, 173–5.
Pavese, Cesare, 'Ieri e oggi', *L'Unità* (Turinese edn), 3 August 1947, p. 3; repr. in Pavese, *La letteratura americana e altri saggi*, 193–6.
Pavese, Cesare, *La letteratura americana e altri saggi* (Turin: Einaudi, 1951).
Pavese, Cesare, *Saggi letterari* (Turin: Einaudi, 1951).
Pavese, Cesare, *Lettere. 1924–1944*, ed. Lorenzo Mondo (Turin: Einaudi, 1966).
Pavese, Cesare, *Selected Letters 1924–1950* (London: Peter Owen, 1969).
Pavese, Cesare, *Il mestiere di vivere*, 2nd edn (Turin: Einaudi, 1990).
Pavolini, Alessandro, 'Politica della cultura', *Corriere della Sera*, 24 November 1938, p. 1.
Pavone, Claudio, *Una guerra civile: Saggio storico sulla moralità della Resistenza* (Turin: Bollati Boringhieri, 1991); pub. in English as *A Civil War: A History of the Resistance* (London: Verso, 2013).
Pearse, Holly A., 'Charlie Chaplin: Jewish or Goyish?', *Jewish Quarterly*, 57 (2010), 38–41.
Pecorini, Alberto, *Gli americani nella vita moderna osservati da un italiano* (Milan: Treves, 1909).
Peden, Charles, *Newsreel Man* (Garden City, NY: Doubleday, Doran & Co., 1932).
Pemberton, Jo-Anne, *Global Metaphors: Modernity and the Quest for One World* (London: Pluto Press, 2001).
Peressutti, Gino, 'Cinecittà', *Cinema*, 2/20 (25 April 1937), 302–6.
Petacco, Arrigo, *Il superfascista: Vita e morte di Alessandro Pavolini* (Milan: Mondadori, 1999).
Piacentini, Marcello, 'In tema di grattacieli', *Architettura e arti decorative*, 2/8 (1923), 311–17.

Piazzoni, Irene, *Valentino Bompiani: Un editore italiano tra fascismo e dopoguerra* (Milan: LED, 2007).
Pietralunga, Mark (ed.), *Cesare Pavese and Antonio Chiuminatto: Their Correspondence* (Toronto: Toronto University Press, 2007).
Pietrangeli, Antonio, 'Analisi spettrale del film realistico', *Cinema*, 7/146 (25 July 1942), 393.
Pietrangeli, Antonio, 'Harlem', *Bianco e nero*, 7/6 (June 1943), 32–5.
Pini, Giorgio, *Filo diretto con Palazzo Venezia* (Bologna: Cappelli, 1950).
Pischedda, Bruno, *L'idioma molesto: Cecchi e la letteratura novecentesca a sfondo razziale* (Turin: Aragno, 2015).
Pitigrilli [Segre, Dino], *Cocaina* (Milan: Sonzogno, 1921).
Pizzi, Katia, *Italian Futurism and the Machine* (Manchester: Manchester University Press, 2019).
Poesio, Camilla, *Tutto è ritmo, tutto è swing: Il Jazz, il fascismo e la società italiana* (Florence: Le Monnier Università, 2018).
Poggioli-Kaftan, Giordana, 'The "Third Space" in Luigi Capuana's Gli americani di Ràbbato', *Studi d'Italianistica nell'Africa Australe/Italian Studies in Southern Africa*, 31.2 (2018), 29–51.
Polan, Dana, *Scenes of Instruction: The Beginnings of the US Study of Film* (Berkeley and Los Angeles: University of California Press, 2007).
Pollone, Matteo, 'L'anonimo fondale dell'avventura: Lo spazio astratto del fumetto western italiano delle origini (1935–1965)', *Between*, 8/15 (2018), 10–11.
Pollone, Matteo (ed.), *Il western in Italia: Cinema, musica, letteratura e fumetto* (Turin: Graphot, 2020).
Pollone, Matteo, 'Non solo Spaghetti: Il western italiano prima e dopo Leone', in Pollone (ed.), *Il western in Italia*, 3–22.
Possenti, Eligio, 'Colloquio con Luigi Pirandello', *Corriere della Sera*, 28 October 1930, p. 3; in Pupo (ed.), *Interviste a Pirandello*, 292–4.
Praz, Mario, ' "Gentlemen Prefer Blondes": L'ultimo successo inglese', *La Fiera letteraria*, 34 (August 1926), 5.
Praz, Mario, 'Un giovane narratore americano', *La Stampa*, 13 June 1929, p. 3.
Praz, Mario, 'America nera', *La Stampa*, 6 June 1930, p. 3.
Praz, Mario, 'Hemingway in Italy', *Partisan Review*, 15/10 1948), 1086–1100.
Praz, Mario, 'Impressioni italiane di americani nell'ottocento', *Studi americani*, 4 (1958), 85–107.
Praz, Mario, *Il patto col serpente* (Milan: Mondadori, 1972).
Prendergast, Christopher, *Paris and the Nineteenth Century* (Oxford: Blackwell, 1992).
Pretelli, Matteo, *La via Fascista alla democrazia americana: Cultura e propaganda nelle comunità italo-americane* (Viterbo: ASEI-Sette Città, 2012).
Pretelli, Matteo, *L'emigrazione italiana negli Stati Uniti* (Bologna: Il Mulino, 2011).
Pretelli, Matteo, 'Mussolini's Mobilities: Transnational Movements between Fascist Italy and Italian Communities Abroad', *Journal of Migration History*, 1 (2015), 100–20.
Preziosi, Ernesto, *Il Vittorioso: Storia di un settimanale per ragazzi 1937–1966* (Bologna: Il Mulino, 2012).
Prezzolini, Giuseppe, *La coltura italiana* (Florence: Lumachi, 1906; then, in a new edn enriched with more chapters, Florence: La Voce, 1923).
Prezzolini, Giuseppe, *Diario 1900–1941* (Milan: Rusconi, 1978).
Prezzolini, Giuseppe, *Diario per Dolores*, ed. Giuliano Prezzolini and Maria Cristina Chiesa (Milan: Rusconi, 1993).
Progetto Archivio Storico FIAT, *I primi quindici anni della FIAT: Verbali dei Consigli di amministrazione 1899–1915* (Milan: Franco Angeli, 1987).

Progetto Archivio Storico FIAT, *FIAT 1899–1930: Storia e documenti* (Milan: Fabbri, 1991).
Prolo, Maria Adriana, 'Francesi nel cinema italiano muto', *Bianco e nero*, 14/8–9 (1953), 69–74.
Puck, 'Galleria: LIXI James Stewart', *Cinema*, 4/69 (10 May 1939), 306–7.
Pulcini, Virginia, 'The English Language and Anglo-American Culture in Twentieth Century Italy', in Bonsaver, Carlucci, and Reza (eds), *Italy and the USA*, 31–46.
Pupo, Ivan (ed.), *Interviste a Pirandello: 'Parole da dire, uomo, agli altri uomini'* (Soveria Manelli: Rubbettino, 2002).
Purificato, Domenico, 'Timore per Pinocchio', *Cinema*, 4/69 (10 May 1939), 290–1.
Quaglietti, Lorenzo, 'Cinema americano, vecchio amore', in Argentieri (ed.), *Schermi di guerra*, 307–27.
Rabagliati, Alberto, *Quattro anni fra le 'stelle': Aneddoti e impressioni* (Milan: Giovanni Bolla, 1932).
Radice, Mark A., '"Futurismo": Its Origins, Context, Repertory, and Influence', *Musical Quarterly*, 73/1 (1989), 1–17.
Raeburn, Bruce Boyd, 'Stars of David and Sons of Sicily: Constellations beyond the Canon in Early New Orleans Jazz', *Jazz Perspectives*, 3/2 (2009), 123–52.
Rafanelli, Leda, *Una donna e Mussolini* (Milan: Rusconi, 1946).
Ramades Ferrarin, A., 'Joséphine Baker, "Self Made Woman"', *Comoedia*, 9/9 (September 1927), 31, 48.
Ramperti, Marco, 'Chaplin contro Charlot', *La Stampa*, 19 January 1933, p. 3.
Ramperti, Marco, 'Più che dalla stella gialla gli ebrei si riconoscono dalla ferocia dello sguardo', *Il Popolo di Roma*, 31 December 1941.
Ramperti, Marco, 'Chaplin ebreo due volte', *Film*, 6/28 (10 July 1943), 5.
Randall, Annie J., and Gray Davis, Rosalind, *Puccini and the Girl: History and Reception of 'The Girl of the Golden West'* (Chicago: University of Chicago Press, 2005).
Rapisarda, Stefano, 'A proposito dello studio delle lingue straniere in epoca fascista', *Le Forme e la storia*, 8/1–2 (2015), 705–14.
Ravasio, Carlo, 'Fascismo e tradizione', *Il Popolo d'Italia*, 30 March 1928, p. 3.
Redaelli, Cesare, *Iniziando Mussolini alle vie del cielo* (Milan: Ufficio Storico del Partito Nazionale Fascista, 1933).
Redi, Riccardo, *La Cines: Storia di una casa di produzione italiana* (Bologna: Persiani, 2011).
Reeder, Linda, *Widows in White: Migration and the Transformation of Rural Women, Sicily 1880–1928* (Toronto: University of Toronto Press, 2003).
Reich, Jacqueline, *The Maciste Films of Italian Silent Cinema* (Bloomington, IN: Indiana University Press, 2015).
Révész, Andrés, 'Special Interview with Mussolini. "Why I Broke with Socialism"', *Sunday Times*, 11 April 1926, pp. 15–16.
Ricciardi, Caterina, 'Scott Fitzgerald in Rome', *RSA Journal*, 10 (1999), 29–46.
Richter, Dieter, *Il paese di Cuccagna: Storia di un'utopia popolare* (Florence: Nuova Italia, 1998).
Rimondi, Giorgio, *La scrittura sincopata: Jazz e letteratura nel novecento italiano* (Milan: Bruno Mondadori, 1999).
Robbe, Federico, 'Da "civiltà mercantile" a "grande popolo": Il mito americano nel nazionalismo italiano durante la Grande Guerra', *Eunomia*, 4/4 (2015), 333–70.
Robey, David, '*Romantic, romantico, romanzesco*: An Aspect of Walter Scott's Reception in Italy', in Bonsaver, Richardson and Stellardi (eds), *Cultural Reception, Translation and Transformation from Medieval to Modern Italy*, 199–214.
Rochat, Giorgio, *Italo Balbo* (Turin: UTET, 1986).
Roger, Philippe, *The American Enemy: The History of French Anti-Americanism* (Chicago: Chicago University Press, 2005; French original, 2002).

Rodondi, Raffaella, *Il presente vince sempre: Tre studi su Vittorini* (Palermo: Sellerio, 1985).
Rondolino, Gianni, *Torino Come Hollywood* (Bologna: Capelli, 1980).
Rondolino, Gianni, *Roberto Rossellini* (Turin: UTET, 1989).
Roger, Philippe, *The American Enemy: The History of French Anti-Americanism* (Chicago: Chicago University Press, 2005; 2002 in the French original).
Roma, Enrico, 'I nuovi film: Gli uomini che mascalzoni', *L'Illustrazione italiana*, 7/42 (19 October1932), 12.
Romanelli, Raffaele, *L'Italia liberale* (Bologna: Il Mulino, 1979).
Romano, Sergio, 'Prefazione', in Teodori, *Maledetti americani*, pp. vii–xi.
Romussi, Carlo, *Storia degli Stati Uniti d'America* (Milan: Sonzogno, 1877).
Rosa, Enrico, 'Americanismo', Treccani online, http://www.treccani.it/enciclopedia/americanismo_res-545223ec-8bab-11dc-8e9d-0016357eee51_%28Enciclopedia-Italiana%29/ (accessed 30 March 2023).
Rosher, Chas (Charles), ASC, 'An Analysis of the Film Industry in Italy', *American Cinematographer*, 2/9 (15 September 1922), 7–9.
Rosoli, Gianfausto (ed.), *Un secolo di emigrazione italiana 1876–1976* (Rome: Centro Studi Emigrazione, 1978), 343–83.
Ross, Corey, 'Mass Culture and Divided Audiences: Cinema and Social Change in Inter-War Germany', *Past & Present*, 193 (2006), 157–95.
Rossi, Adolfo, *Nacociù, la Venere americana: Avventure degli emigranti al Nuovo Mondo* (Rome: Edoardo Perino, 1889); this book saw two further editions with different titles: *Vita d'America* (Rome: Edoardo Perino, 1891) and *Un italiano in America* (Milan: Treves, 1892).
Rossi, Adolfo, *Il paese dei dollari* (Milan: Tipografia degli Operai, 1892); later edn: *Nel paese dei dollari (Tre anni a New York)* (Milan: Max Kantorowicz Editore, 1893).
Rossi, Adolfo, 'Viaggiando in Sardegna', *Corriere della Sera*, 22–3 November 1934, p. 1.
Rossi, Adolfo, *L'Italia della vergogna nelle cronache di Adolfo Rossi (1875–1921)* (Ravenna: Longo, 2010).
Rossi, Egisto, *Gli Stati Uniti e la concorrenza americana: Studi di agricultura, industria e commercio da un recente viaggio* (Florence: Tipografia Barbera, 1884).
Rossi, Sergio, 'E. A. Poe e la scapigliatura lombarda', *Studi americani*, 5 (1959) 119–39.
Rossini, Daniela, 'La propaganda americana in Italia durante la Grande Guerra: Guglielmina Ronconi', *Contemporanea*, 8/2 (2005), 299–310.
Rossini, Daniela, *Il mito americano nell'Italia della Grande Guerra* (Rome and Bari: Laterza, 2000); pub. in English as *Woodrow Wilson and the American Myth in Italy* (Cambridge, MA: Harvard University Press, 2008).
Rossini, Daniela, 'La donna nuova Americana nell'illustrazione: Reazioni italiane tra Belle Époque e fascismo', in Rossini (ed.), *Le americane: Donne e immagini di donne fra belle époque e fascismo* (Rome: Biblink, 2008), 95–114.
Roth, Paul, 'Introduzione al cinema', *Bianco e nero*, 3/2 (1939), 124–50.
Ruggiero, Amerigo, 'L'influenza femminile nella vita americana', *La Stampa*, 24 January 1930, pp. 1–2.
Ruggiero, Amerigo, 'La donna americana nella bufera', *La Stampa*, 10 June 1933, p. 3.
Ruggiero, Amerigo, 'La donna emancipata', *La Stampa*, 28 May 1933, p. 1.
Ruggiero, Amerigo, 'Ondata di linciaggi', *La Stampa*, 2 January 1934, p. 1.
Ruggiero, Amerigo, *L'America al bivio* (Turin: Einaudi, 1934).
Ruggiero, Amerigo, *Gli italiani d'America* (Milan: Treves, 1937).
Rundle, Christopher, *Publishing Translations in Fascist Italy* (Oxford: Peter Lang, 2010).
Russo, Valentina, *Le lingue estere: Storia, linguistica e ideologia nell'Italia fascista* (Rome: Aracne, 2013).

Rydell, Robert W., and Kroes, Rob, *Buffalo Bill in Bologna: The Americanization of the World, 1869-1922* (Chicago: Chicago University Press, 2005).
Sabatello, Dario, 'I sette nani e Biancaneve', *Cinema illustrazione*, 13/23 (8 June 193c8), 4-5.
Sacchi, Filippo, 'La serata italiana al Festival del Lido', *Corriere della Sera*, 12 August 1932, p. 5.
Sacchi, Filippo [f.p.], 'Joe il rosso', *Corriere della Sera*, 19 November 1935, p. 5.
Sacchi, Filippo, 'Per uomini soli', *Corriere della Sera*, 10 April 1939, p. 4.
Saibene, Alberto, 'Il secolo americano di Adriano Olivetti', in Adriano Olivetti, *Dall'America: Lettere ai familiari (1925-26)* (Rome and Ivrea: Edizioni di Comunità, 2016), 118-39.
Salgari, Emilio, *Arriva Buffalo Bill!* (Verona: Perosini, 1993).
Salvetti, Patrizia, *Corda e sapone: Storie di linciaggi di italiani negli Stati Uniti* (Milan: Donzelli, 2003).
Saiu, Liliana, *Stati Uniti e Italia nella Grande Guerra 1914-1918* (Florence: Olschki, 2003).
Salvemini, Gaetano, *Mussolini diplomatico* (Paris: Éditions Contemporaines, 1932); also pub. in French as *Mussolini diplomate* (Paris: Grasset, 1932).
Sanfilippo, Matteo, 'La grande emigrazione nelle pagine dei viaggiatori', in Martelli (ed.), *Il sogno italo-americano*, 351-76.
Sanfilippo, Matteo, 'L'emigrazione siciliana', *Archivio storico dell'emigrazione Italiana*, 3/1 (2007), 79-95.
Santipolo, Matteo, and Viale, Matteo (eds). *Bruno Migliorini, l'uomo e il linguista* (Rovigo: Accademia dei Concordi, 2009).
Sarfatti, Margherita, *The Life of Benito Mussolini* (London: Butterworth, 1925).
Sarfatti, Margherita, *America, ricerca della felicità* (Milan: Mondadori, 1937).
Sassone, Irmo, 'La conquista delle 8 ore nel 1906', *L'Impegno*, 2/1 (1982), https://impegno.istorbive.it/wp-content/uploads/2020/04/Sassone-n.-1-1982.pdf (accessed 2 June 2022).
Sassoon, Donald, *The Culture of the Europeans: From 1800 to the Present* (London: Harper Press, 2006).
Saunders, Thomas J., *Hollywood in Berlin: American Cinema and Weimar Germany* (Berkeley and Los Angeles: California University Press, 1994).
Savio, Francesco, *Ma l'amore no: Realismo, formalismo, propaganda e telefoni bianchi nel cinema italiano di genere (1930-1943)* (Milan: Sonzogno, 1975).
Savio, Francesco, *Cinecittà anni trenta: Parlano 116 protagonisti del secondo cinema italiano, 1930-1943* (Rome: Bulzoni, 1979).
Scarpa, Domenico, 'Il diavolo in bottiglia', in Mario Soldati (ed.), *Cinematografo* (Palermo: Sellerio, 2006), 9-28.
Scarpaci, Jean Ann, *Italian Immigrants in Louisiana's Sugar Parishes: Recuitment, Labor Conditions, and Community Relations, 1880-1910* (New York: Arno Press, 1980).
Scarrocchia, Sandro, *Albert Speer e Marcello Piacentini: L'architettura del totalitarismo negli anni trenta* (Milan: Skira, 1999; 2nd edn, 2013).
Schaffer, Ronald, *America in the Great War: The Rise of the War Welfare State* (Oxford: Oxford University Press, 1991).
Schivelbusch, Wolfgang, *Three New Deals: Reflections on Roosevelt's America, Mussolini's Italy and Hitler's Germany, 1933-1939* (New York: Picador, 2006).
Schnapp, Jeffrey, 'Why Speed is a Religion-Morality', in Schnapp, *Modernitalia* (Bern: Peter Lang, 2012), 1-21.
Sciascia, Leonardo, 'Introduzione', in Stefano Vilardo (ed.), *Tutti dicono Germania Germania* (Milan: Garzanti, 1975), 5-7.
Scurati, Antonio M., *L'uomo della provvidenza* (Milan: Bompiani, 2020).
Sedita, Giovanni, 'Vittorio Mussolini, Hollywood and Neorealism', *Journal of Modern Italian Studies*, 15/3 (2010), 431-57.

Seelinger, Matthew J., '"Viva l'America!"': The 332nd Infantry on the Italian Front', *On Point*, 4/3 (1998), available on the National Museum of the United States Army website.
Segrè, Claudio G., *Italo Balbo: A Fascist Life* (Berkeley and Los Angeles: University of California Press, 1987).
Serri, Mirella, *Il breve viaggio* (Venice: Marsilio, 2002).
Settis, Bruno, 'Rethinking Fordism', in Francesca Antonini, Aaron Bernstein, Lorenzo Fusaro, and Robert Jackson (eds), *Revisting Gramsci's Notebooks* (Leiden: Brill, 2020), 376–87.
Severino, Agostino, 'I nuovi programmi per l'insegnamento delle lingue straniere', *Le Lingue estere*, 9/4 (1942), 84–5.
Shepherd, David J., *The Bible on Silent Film: Spectacle, Story and Scripture in the Early Cinema* (Cambridge: Cambridge University Press, 2013).
Shipton, Alyn, *A New History of Jazz* (London: Continuum 2001).
Shores, Christopher, Massimello, Giovanni, and Guest, Russell, *A History of the Mediterranean Air War 1940–45*, i. North Africa (London: Grub Street, 2012).
SIAE, *La vita nello spettacolo in Italia nel decennio 1924–1942* (Rome: SIAE, 1935).
Silk, Gerald, '"Il Primo Pilota": Mussolini, Fascist Aeronautical Symbolism, and Imperial Rome', in Lazzaro and Crum (eds.), *Donatello among the Blackshirts*, 67–81.
Sinibaldi, Caterina, 'Dangerous Children and Children in Danger: Reading American Comics under the Italian Fascist Regime', in Christopher Kelen and Björn Sundmark (eds), *The National in Children's Literature: Nations of Childhood* (New York and London: Routledge, 2012), 53–67.
Sinibaldi, Caterina, 'Between Censorship and Innovation: The Translation of American Comics during Italian Fascism', *New Readings*, 16 (2016), 1–21.
Smith, Lawrence G., *Cesare Pavese and America: Life, Love, and Literature* (Amherst, MA: University of Massachusetts Press, 2008).
Smolderen, Thierry, *The Origins of Comics: From William Hogarth to Winsor McCay* (Jackson, MS: University Press of Mississippi, 2014).
Smucker, John R., *The History of the United States Army Ambulance Service—1917, 1918, 1919* (Allentown, PA: USAAS Association, 1967).
Soldati, Mario, 'Il segreto di Hollywood', *Pan*, 2/4 (December 1934), 551–65.
Soldati, Mario, *America primo amore* (Florence: Bemporad, 1935); then in Soldati, *America e altri amori*, 40–9.
Soldati Mario (pub. under the pseudonym Franco Pallavera), *24 ore in uno studio cinematografico* (Milan: Corticelli, 1935).
Soldati, Mario, 'Viaggio alla ricerca del cinema genuino', *L'Europeo*, 15 December 1963; then in Soldati, *America e altri amori*, 1143–7.
Soldati, Mario, *America e altri amori: Diari e scritti di viaggio* (Milan: Mondadori, 2011).
Solmi, Franco, *Athos Casarini pittore. 1883–1917* (Bologna: Alfa, 1963).
Solmi, Sergio, *Scrittori negli anni: Saggi e note sulla letteratura italiana del 900* (Milan: Il Saggiatore, 1963).
Sommaiolo, Paolo, *Il café-chantant: Artisti e ribalte nella Napoli Belle Époque* (Naples: Tempo Lungo, 1998).
Sorani, Aldo, 'L'offensiva letteraria americana', *La Stampa*, 21 September 1928, p. 3.
Sorano, Aldo, 'Régis Michaud, *Panorama de la Littérature américaine*, Kra, Paris, 1928', *Pegaso*, 1 (January 1929), 125–9.
Soria, Massimo, 'Chiaroscuro del jazz', *Radiocorriere*, 10/31 (29 July–4 August 1933), 17.
Sormani, Giuseppe, *Eco d'America* (Milan: Tipografia degli Operai, 1888).
Spagnol, Tito A., 'Una serata al cinema', *Cinema*, 7/146 (25 July 1942), 378–9.

Spagnol, Tito A., 'Idee e metodi americani', in Spagnol, *Hollywood Boulevard* (Turin: Aragno, 2006).
Speer, Alfred, *Spandau: The Secret Diaries* (London: Collins, 1976; originally pub. in German, 1975).
Spina, Luigi, 'Gramsci e il jazz', *Belfagor*, 44.4 (1989), 450-4.
Spini, Giorgio, 'Prefazione', in Giorgio Spini, Gian Giacomo Migone, and Massimo Teodori (eds), *Italia e America dalla Grande Guerra a oggi* (Venice: Marsilio, 1976), 9-22.
Spini, Giorgio, 'Prefazione', in Giorgio and Massimo Spini, Gian Giacomo Migone, Teodori (eds), *Italia e America dal settecento all'età dell'imperialismo* (Venice: Marsilio, 1976), 9-24.
Spini, Giorgio, 'I Puritani della Nuova Inghilterra e la cultura italiana', in Raimondo Luraghi (ed.), *Atti del I Congresso Internazionale di Storia Americana: Italia e Stati Uniti dall'indipendenza americana ad oggi (1776-1976)* (Genoa: Tilgher, 1978), 23-31.
Spini, Giorgio, Migone, Gian Giacomo, and Teodori, Massimo (eds), *Italia e America dal settecento all'età dell'imperialismo* (Venice: Marsilio, 1976).
Spinosa, Antonio, *I figli del duce* (Milan: Rizzoli, 1983).
Stead, W. T., *The Americanization of the World or The Trend of the Twentieth Century* (New York and London: H. Markey, 1901).
Sterba, Christopher M., *Good Americans: Italian and Jewish Immigrants during the First World War* (Oxford: Oxford University Press, 2003).
Steward, William Kilborne, 'The Mentors of Mussolini', *American Political Science Review*, 22/4 (November 1928), 843-69.
St Johns, Ivan, 'Fifty-Fifty: June Mathis Meets the Perfect Collaborator—and Marries him', *Photoplay*, 30/5 (October 1926), 46, 123-4.
Stone, Marla, *The Patron State: Culture and Politics in Fascist Italy* (Princeton: Princeton University Press, 1998).
Storchi, Simona, 'Ardengo Soffici's *Rete mediterranea*: The Aesthetics and Politics of Post-War Modernism', *Annali d'italianistica*, 33 (2015), 321-40.
Studlar, Gaylyn, 'The Perils of Pleasure? Fan Magazine Discourse as Women's Commodified Culture in the 1920s', in Richard Abel (ed.), *Silent Film* (New Brunswick: Rutgers University Press, 1999), 263-97.
Studdert, Will, *The Jazz War: Radio, Nazism and the Struggle for the Airwaves in World War II* (London: I. B. Tauris, 2017).
Sullam, Sara, '(Middle)browsing Mondadori's Archive: British Novels in the *Medusa* Series, 1933-1945', *Textus: English Studies in Italy*, 28/3 (2015), 179-201.
Swanson, Carl A., 'D'Annunzio's "Ode all'America in armi" (IV LUGLIO MCMXVIII)', *Italica*, 30/3 (1953), 135-43.
Tanfani, Roberto, *I figli del deserto: Romanzo d'avventure fra le Pelli-Rosse* (Rome: Perino, 1891).
Tedeschi, Rubens, 'Mal di melodramma', in Luca Ronconi (ed.), *D'Annunzio: La scena del vate* (Milan: Electa, 1988), 19-26.
Teodori, Massimo, *Maledetti americani: Destra, sinistra e cattolici: Storia del pregiudizio antiamericano* (Milan: Mondadori, 2002).
Teodori, Massimo, *Benedetti americani: Dall'alleanza atlantica alla guerra al terrorismo* (Milan: Mondadori, 2003).
The Florence Pragmatist Club, 'Il pragmatismo messo in ordine', *Leonardo*, 3/2 (April 1905), 45-7.
Thomason, Sarah Grey, 'Contact as a Source of Language Change', in Brian D. Joseph and Richard D. Janda (eds), *The Handbook of Historical Linguistics* (Oxford: Blackwell, 2004), 687-712.

Thompson, Jonathan, *Italian Civil and Military Aircraft, 1930–1945* (Fallbrook, CA: Aero Publishers, 1963).

Thompson, Kristin, *Exporting Entertainment: America in the World Film Market 1907–34* (London: BFI Publishing, 1985).

Tirabassi, Maddalena, *Ripensare la patria grande: Gli scritti di Amy Allemande Bernardy sulle migrazioni italiane (1900–1930)* (Isernia: Cosmo Iannone, 2005).

Tirabassi, Maddalena, 'Why Italians Left Italy: The Physics and Politics of Migration', in William J. Connell and Stanislao Pugliese (eds), *The Routledge History of Italian Americans* (New York: Routledge, 2018), 117–51.

Todd, David, *A Velvet Empire: French Informal Imperialism in the Nineteenth Century* (Princeton: Princeton University Press, 2021).

Toninelli, Pier Angelo, 'Between Agnelli and Mussolini: Ford's Unsuccessful Attempt and the Italian Automobile Market in the Interwar Period', *Enterprise & Society*, 10/2 (2009), 335–75.

Tomadjoglou, Kimberly, 'Rome's Premiere Film Studio: Società Italiana Cines', *Film History*, 12/3 (2000), 262–75.

Tomasi, Silvano (ed.), *For the Love of Immigrants: Migration Writings and Letters of Bishop John Baptist Scalabrini* (New York: Center for Migration Studies, 2000).

Tomasi di Lampedusa, Giuseppe, *Il gattopardo* (1958; Milan: Feltrinelli, 1967); English trans. by Archibald Colquhoun, *The Leopard* (New York: Pantheon, 1960).

Tommaseo, Nicolò, and Bellini, Bernardo, *Dizionario della lingua italiana* (Turin: Società L'Unione Tipografico-editrice, 1861–79).

Tonelli, Anna, 'La "sana musica italiana": Divieti e censure fasciste contro jazz e fox-trot', *Storia e problemi contemporanei*, 28 (2001), 17–31.

Torrielli, Andrew J., *Italian Opinion on America: As Revealed by Italian Travellers, 1850–1900* (Cambridge, MA: Harvard University Press, 1941).

Tranfaglia, Nicola, *La stampa del regime: 1932–1943 Le veline del Minculpop per orientare l'informazione* (Milan: Bompiani, 1995).

Turco, Maria Grazia (ed.), *Dal teatro all'italiana alle sale cinematografiche: Questioni di storia e prospettive di valorizzazione* (Rome: Quasar, 2017).

Turco, Vincenzo, 'Un liberatore: Walt Disney: "Biancaneve e i sette nani"', *Lo Schermo*, 7/16 (July 1938), 23–5.

Turconi, Davide, 'I film storici italiani e la critica americana dal 1910 alla fine del muto', *Bianco e nero*, 1/2 (1963), 40–54.

Turi, Gabriele, *Casa Einaudi: Libri uomini idee oltre il fascismo* (Bologna: Il Mulino, 1990).

Ulbach, Louis (ed.), *Paris Guide par le principaux ècrivains et artistes de la France*, 2 vols (Paris: Librairie Internationale, 1867).

Urso, Simona, *Margherita Sarfatti: Dal mito del Dux al mito americano* (Venice: Marsilio, 2003).

Van Watson, William, 'Luchino Visconti's (Homosexual) Ossessione', in Jacqueline J. Reich and Piero Garofalo (eds), *Re-Viewing Fascism: Italian Cinema 1922–1943* (Bloomington, IN: Indiana University Press, 2002), 172–93.

Vaudagna, Maurizio, 'New Deal e corporativismo nelle riviste politiche ed economiche italiane', in Giorgio Spini, Gian Giacomo Migone, and Maurizio Teodori (eds), *Italia e America dalla Grande Guerra a oggi* (Venice: Marsilio, 1976), 101–40.

Vaudagna, Maurizio, '"Drammatizzare l'America!": I simboli politici del New Deal', in Vaudagna (ed.), *L'estetica della politica* (Rome: Laterza, 1989), 77–102.

Vaudagna, Maurizio, 'Mussolini and Franklin D. Roosevelt', in Cornelis A. van Minnen and John S. Fears (eds), *FDR and his Contemporaries: Foreign Perceptions of an American President* (London: Macmillan, 1992), 157–70.

Varvaro Pojero, Francesco, *Una corsa nel nuovo mondo*, 2 vols (Milan: Treves, 1878).

Vecchi, Giovanni, *Measuring Wellbeing: A History of Italian Living Standards* (Oxford: Oxford University Press, 2017).
Ventresca, Robert A., 'Mussolini's Ghost: Italy's Duce in History and Memory', *History and Memory*, 18/1 (2006), 86–119.
Vergher, Mario, 'Il Pinocchio incompiuto', *Animazione*, 3 (2001), 34–5.
Veritas [pseudonym], 'Il cavaliere Ambrosio di ritorno dall'America', *La Vita cinematografica*, 7/15 (February 1916), 74.
Vezzani, Roberto, 'Fascist Indirect Propaganda in 1930s America: The Distribution and Exhibition of Italian Fiction Films', *Italianist*, 38/2 (2018), 156–73.
Viallet, Jean-Pierre, 'Statistiques et histoire des relations culturelles franco-italiannes: L'Example des traductions (1932–1938)', in Jean-Baptist Duroselle and Enrico Serra (eds), *Il vincolo culturale tra Italia e Francia negli anni trenta e quaranta* (Milan: Franco Angeli, 1986), 246–94.
Vigolo, Giorgio, 'Roma e Hollywood', *Cinema*, 10 (24 November 1936), 373–4.
Villari, Pasquale, *L'Italia, la civiltà latina e la civiltà germanica* (Florence: Le Monnier, 1861).
Villaroel, Giuseppe, 'Colloqui con Pirandello', *Il Giornale d'Italia*, 8 May 1924, in Pupo (ed.), *Interviste a Pirandello*, 248–51.
Vinall, Shirley, 'In the Footsteps of D'Annunzio: Anthologie-Revue de France et d'Italie and the Promotion of Italian Culture in France', *The Italianist*, 26 (2006), 274–310.
Vincendeau, Ginette, 'Hollywood Babel: The Coming of Sound and the Multiple-Language Version', in Andrew Higson and Richard Maltby (eds), *'Film Europe' and 'Film America': Cinema, Commerce, and Cultural Exchange 1920–1939* (Exeter: University of Exeter Press, 1999), 207–24.
Visconti, Luchino, 'Cinema antropomorfico', *Cinema*, 173–4 (25 September–25 October 1943), 108–9.
Visconti, Luchino, 'Vita difficile del film "Ossessione"', *Il Contemporaneo* (24 April 1965), 7–8.
Visentini, Gino, 'Fuochi d'artificio', *Cinema*, 3/59 (10 December 1938), 360–1.
Vittorini, Elio, 'American Influences on Contemporary Italian Literature', *American Quarterly*, 1 (1949), 5–6.
Vittorini, Elio, *Conversation in Sicily* (New York: New Directions, 1951).
Vittorini, Elio, *Conversazione in Sicilia* (Milan: Bompiani, 1941).
Vittorini, Elio, *Si diverte tanto a tradurre? Lettere a Lucia Rodocanachi, 1933–1943*, ed. Anna Chiara Cavallari and Edoardo Esposito (Milan: Archinto, 2016).
Volpato, Giuseppe, 'L'internazionalizzazione dell'industria automobilistica italiana', in Archivio Storico Fiat, *L'industria italiana nel mercato mondiale: Dalla fine dell'800 alla metà del 900* (Turin: Fiat, 1993), 157–216.
VS, 'Le divise militari americane e il mercato degli schiavi nella Carolina del Sud', *Il Mondo illustrato*, 4/11 (16 March 1861), 172–3.
Wagnleitner, Reinhold, *Coca-Colonization and the Cold War: The Cultural Mission of the United States in Austria after the Second World War* (Chapel Hill, NC: University of North Carolina Press, 1994).
Wagstaff, Christopher, *Italian Neorealist Cinema: An Aesthetic Approach* (Toronto: University of Toronto Press, 2008).
Wakeman, Rosemary, *A Modern History of European Cities: 1815 to the Present* (London: Bloomsbury Academic, 2020).
Wallace, William, 'A Summary', in Wallace et al., *Ohio Doughboys in Italy: Reminiscences of the 332d Infantry* (Pleasantville, NJ: Penhallow Press, 1921), 64–72.
Walton, Benjamin, 'Rossini and France', in Emanuele Senici (ed.), *The Cambridge Companion to Rossini* (Cambridge: Cambridge University Press, 2004), 25–36.

Ward, Richard Lewis, *A History of the Hal Roach Studios* (Carbondale, IL: Southern Illinois University Press, 2005).

Welge, Jobst, 'Fascism *Triumphans*: On the Architectural Translation of Rome', in Lazzaro and Crum (eds), *Donatello among the Blackshirts*, 83–94.

Wells, H. G., *The Future in America* (New York and London: Harper and Brothers Publishers, 1906).

Werner, M. R., *Fiorello H. La Guardia and the Making of New York* (New York: McGraw-Hill, 1989).

Wilcox, Vanda, *Morale and the Italian Army during the First World War* (Cambridge: Cambridge University Press, 2016).

Winderling, Gustavo, *Ricordi d'America* (Milan: Treves, 1878).

Woodhouse, John, *Gabriele D'Annunzio: Defiant Archangel* (Oxford: Oxford University Press, 1998).

Woodress, James, 'The Fortunes of Cooper in Italy', *Studi americani*, 10/2 (1965), 53–76.

Wyke, Maria, *Projecting the Past: Ancient Rome, Cinema and History* (London: Routledge, 1997).

Zagarrio, Vito, *Cinema e fascismo: Film, modelli, immaginari* (Venice: Marsilio, 2004).

Zane, Marcello, 'Strisce senza stelle: Per uno studio sull'iconografia italiana dell'emigrazione negli Stati Uniti', in Martelli (ed.), *Il sogno italo-americano*, 322–49.

Zangrandi, Ruggero, *Il lungo viaggio: Contributo alla storia di una generazione* (Turin: Einaudi, 1948); repr., in an enlarged version: *Il lungo viaggio attraverso il fascismo* (Milan: Feltrinelli, 1961).

Zanini, Rita, 'I quattro moschettieri: Un film di marionette', *Cinema*, 8 (25 October 1936), 314.

Zavattini, Cesare [alias Giulio Tani], 'La beneficiata dei direttori: Da Fitzmaurice a King Vidor', *Cinema illustrazione*, 8/22 (31 May 1933), 14.

Zavattini, Cesare, *Neorealismo ecc.* (Milan: Bompiani, 1979).

Zavattini, Cesare, *Cronache da Hollywood* (Rome: Editori Riuniti, 1996).

Zavattini, Cesare, *Io: Un'autobiografia* (posthumously edited by Paolo Nuzzi) (Turin: Einaudi, 2002).

Zavattini, Cesare, *Selected Writings*, ed. David Brancaleone, 2 vols (New York: Bloomsbury Academic, 2021).

Zucchi, John E., *The Little Slaves of the Harp: Italian Child Street Musicians in Nineteenth Century Paris, London and New York* (Montreal and Kingston: McGill–Queen's University Press, 1992).

Zucconi, Benedetta, 'Esordi della riflessione discografica in Italia: *Il Disco. Bollettino discografico mensile (1933–37)*', *Forum Italicum*, 49/2 (2015), 474–90.

Zuculin, Bruno, 'Musiche e danze americane', *La Lettura*, 19.8 (August 1919), 599–600.

Zvereva, Irina, 'Per una storia della riflessione teorica sulla traduzione in Italia: La sfortuna di Shakespeare', *Entymema*, 11 (2013), 257–68.

# Index

For the benefit of digital users, indexed terms that span two pages (e.g., 52–53) may, on occasion, appear on only one of those pages.

Abel, Richard  113n.12
Abraham, Paul  410
Adamson, Walter L.  xi, 37, 222n.76
Addison, Joseph  26
Agenzia Stefani  42–3, 62–3, 81, 196, 201
Agnelli, Giovanni  2, 109, 125–30, 223, 229–30, 410–11, 493, 497–8
Agri, Amedeo  474
Aimard, Gustave  138
Ajello, Nello  63
Alain-Fournier  272–3
Albertarelli, Rino  292
Albertini, Luigi  81–2, 195–6, 198–9, 269, 286
Alcock, John  224
Alcott, Louisa May  134, 150, 260
Alessandrini, Goffredo  350, 359–60, 383, 387–8, 406–7, 409, 454, 464–5
Alexander, Jeffrey  145
Alfieri, Dino  293–5, 319–20, 325, 354, 356n.43, 357–8, 373–6, 383–4, 422–3, 442–3, 446, 448, 452–3, 455, 464–5, 470–1, 488–9
Alfieri, Vittorio  48
Alicata, Mario  395, 477
Alighieri, Dante  54–5, 109, 115–16, 299
Allen, Gay Wilson  137n.7
Allotti, Pierluigi  424n.10
Alvaro, Corrado  20n.31
Alovisio, Silvio  xi, 93n.90, 101n.101, 114n.14, 115, 116n.19
Amadelli, Antonio  126n.41
Ambrosio, Film  113–15, 117–18, 130
Ambrosio, Rinaldo Arturo  111, 113–15, 118–21, 124
Ambrosoli, Luigi  45n.47
*Americanata*  2, 68–70, 72–3, 155, 201–2, 234, 246, 315–16, 423–7, 449–50
Americanism  1–2, 42n.43, 51–2, 80–1, 182n.15, 191, 218–19, 221–3, 233, 255–6, 285n.50, 302, 320–1, 360n.51, 422–3
Americanization  viii, 1–2, 7, 13, 123n.33, 231–2, 244, 247, 491, 497
American Red Cross in Italy  156–9
Amidei, Sergio  480

Anderson, Sherwood  262–3, 278, 280n.45, 485
Andreazza, Fabio  337n.10
Antonioni, Michelangelo  475
Apollinaire, Guillaume  253
Arbitrio, Francesco  43n.44
Architecture  14, 39–41, 70–3, 82–3, 107–9, 124, 184–91, 194, 202–4, 222, 354, 410–11, 425, 430–40, 484, 489, 496
Argentieri, Mino  373n.66, 415n.128
Armani, Armando  226n.81
Armstrong, Louis  168–9, 296, 307–8, 329n.51
Armus, Seth  2n.2, 181n.11
Asor Rosa, Alberto  267n.33
Astaire, Fred  385
*Audace L'*  288, 454
Audenino, Patrizia  100n.98
Aviation  14, 82–3, 163, 165–6, 219, 223–9, 350–1, 359–60, 427–30, 489, 494
*Avventuroso L'*  288–91

Bacchini, Romolo  404–6
Badoglio, Pietro  451–2
Baker, Joséphine  180–1, 180n.10, 184–5
Bakewell Charles M.  158n.15, 159
Bakker, Gerben  113n.13, 338n.12, 347–8, 348n.29
Balbo, Italo  226–9, 241, 246, 321–3, 425–30
Balboni, Paolo  44n.45
Balboni, Silvano  344, 358
Baldini, Giovanni  36–7
Balistreri, Gioacchino  xi, 301n.9
Balla, Giacomo  299
Bampton, Claude  325–6
Barbara, Mameli  404–6
Barbarani, Berto  146
Barbaro, Umberto  357–8, 390n.90, 467, 471
Barnum, Phineas Taylor  60
Bartolini, Francesco  115–16
Bartolini, Simonetta  253n.12, 254n.13
Barzini, Luigi  78–9, 82–5, 189, 198–9, 219
Barzini, Luigi jr  198–9, 423–4, 428n.15
Barzizza, Giuseppe 'Pippo'  325–8, 460, 462–3
Bassani, Giorgio  236, 477–8

## 540 INDEX

Bassignana, Pier Luigi 127n.44
Battaglia, Salvatore 69n.43
Battisti, Cesare 30–1
Baudelaire, Charles 26–7, 136–7, 252
Baxter, Devon 408n.120
Beard, Charles 109, 111–12
Beard, Mary 109, 111–12
Becciu, Leonardo 283, 290n.54, 455n.53
Beckert, Sven 12n.22
Bedarida, Raffaele xi, 183n.16
Beethoven, Ludwig van 29–30
Belasco, David 140–2, 150
Bellini, Vincenzo 34
Bellu, Serge 125n.36
Benadusi, Lorenzo 82n.75
Benda, Julien 389
Ben-Ghiat, Ruth 10–11, 190–1, 353n.37, 386, 422n.5
Benjamin, Walter vii, 32, 39–40
Bennetta, Jules-Rosette 181n.12
Benvenuti, Sergio 248n.1
Benzi, Carlo 15, 312–13
Berenson, Bernard 189
Bergman, Andrew 398n.105
Bergmayer, Horst J. P. 460n.59
Bergoglio, Franco 281n.47
Bergson, Henri 147–8, 211
Bergstrom, Janet 214n.64
Beria, Chiara 35n.28
Bernardini, Aldo 114n.14, 115n.17
Bernardy, Amy Allemande 102–4
Bertellini, Giorgio xi, 115n.17, 207n.48, 215nn.65, 379n.73, 383n.77
Bertieri, Claudio 455n.53
Bertini, Francesca 377–8
Bertolucci, Attilio 335
Beynet, Michel 6, 186, 191–2, 200–1, 219–20, 222nn.74, 76, 229n.84, 233, 235, 236n.98, 245, 257n.18, 264n.28, 336n.7, 337n.10, 379n.71
Biagi, Enzo 379n.72
Bianco, Carla 244
*Bianco e nero* 336, 357–8, 390n.90, 395, 412–13, 467–74, 484–7
Bilenchi, Romano 274
Billiani, Francesca 260n.24, 263n.26
Bingham, Jocelyn Frisco 306
Bishop, Charles 125n.37
Bismark, Otto von 28
Bixio, Cesare A. 480–1
Bizzarri, Libero 344n.20, 358n.47
Blackburn, Howard 69–70
Blasetti, Alessandro 238–9, 336n.8, 345, 356–8, 390, 392, 482

Bobbio, Norberto 149n.23
Boccaccio, Giovanni 274–5
Bocchini, Arturo 365
Boccioni, Umberto 37, 182, 298
Boese, Carl 398
Boito, Arrigo 119
Bolzoni, Francesco 392n.94
Bompiani, publishing house 247, 260, 273, 277–9, 447–52
Bompiani, Valentino 277–8, 444–5, 447–52
Bonelli, Gian Luigi 500
Bonetta, Gaetano 44n.45
Bonciarelli, Sarah 18n.28
Bono, Gianni 288n.53
Bonnard, Mario 402n.112
Bonsanti, Alessandro 273
Bonsaver, Gianni 19
Bonsaver, Guido 11n.20, 12n.21, 13n.23, 16n.26, 18n.29, 178n.4, 210n.54, 251n.8, 264n.28, 267n.33, 273n.38, 274n.40, 280n.45, 355n.41, 419n.3, 446n.41
Bontempelli, Massimo 254–6
Borgese, Giuseppe Antonio 32, 192–3, 196–8, 234–5, 245
Borghese Bruschi, Lucia xi, 27n.12
Borghesio, Carlo 416–17
Borgnetto, Luigi Romano 115–16
Borrelli, Aldo 424
Borrelli, Lyda 377–8
Borzage, Frank 175–6, 238–9, 245, 384
Boschi, Luca 292n.58
Bosetti, Gilbert 258n.20
Bosio, Gastone 405–6
Boswell, Sisters The 327
Bosworth, Richard xi, 224n.78, 263n.27
Botta, Carlo 48
Botta, Enrico 133n.2
Bottai, Giuseppe 226, 245, 315, 353, 357–8, 422–3, 440–2, 444
Bottazzi, Luigi 178n.4
Bottiglieri, Bruno 128n.45
Bourdieu, Pierre 9–10, 12, 376
Boyd Caroli, Betty 102n.102
Bozza, Umberto 312
Bozzetto, Bruno 500
Brabin, Charles 343
Bragaglia, Anton Giulio 300–4, 330–1, 337, 342n.16, 357–8
Bragaglia, Carlo Ludovico 301, 460–1
Brahms, Johannes 29–30
Bragato, Stefano xi
Brancaleone, David 396n.101
Bratu Hansen, Miriam 32, 494–6
Brazzale, Francesco 162n.19

## INDEX

Brenon, Herbert 339–40
Brignone, Guido 409, 413, 477
Briosi, Sergio 258n.20
British culture 25–7, 34–5, 44–6, 81–2, 107–8, 132, 134, 138, 259, 264–5, 279, 282–5, 311–12, 325–6, 471, 474
Brogi, Daniela 280n.45
Brown, Arthur 224
Brown, Clarence 337
Brown, Sharon A. 439n.28
Browning, Robert 134
Browning, Elizabeth 134
Brownlow, Kevin 122n.29, 343, 344n.19, 392n.93
Brunello, Pietro 99n.96
Brunetta Gian Piero 213n.62, 335n.5, 337n.10, 342n.16, 351n.34, 354n.39, 357n.44, 358n.47, 375n.68, 464–5, 465n.64, 499
Bruni, Mario 392n.94
Bruno, C. 311
Bryer, Winifred 474
Buccini, Stefania 24n.3
Buck, Pearl S. 272–3
Buffa, Cristiano 411n.123
Buffalo Bill, *see* Cody, William
Bulwer-Lytton, Edward 339–40
Busch, Wilhelm 283
Busino, Giovanni 27n.9
Busoni, Mauro 86n.80
Butler, Frank 115
Butler, Nicholas Murray 220

Cabanne, Christy 338–9
Caetani, Gelasio 213–14
*Café chantant: Guida del varieté italiano* 39–40
Caffarelli, Enzo 97
Cagney, James 367
Cain, James M. 274–5, 280, 477–8
CAIR (Cartoni Animati Italiani Roma), studios 404–9
Caizzi, Bruno 108n.2
Calamai, Clara 478
Caldiron, Orio 349n.30, 362n.53
Caldwell, Erskine 273–5, 280, 485
Calcagno, Diego 482
Càllari, Francesco 480n.85
Caliaro, Luigino 162n.19
Calvesi, Maurizio 436n.25
Calvino, Italo 281–2, 335
Camerini, Mario 190–1, 231–2, 347, 350–2, 369–70, 379–80, 386n.84, 397–8, 412–13, 465, 481–2
Campassi, Osvaldo 465n.65, 466, 482–3, 488
Canali, Mauro 286n.52

Cannistraro, Philip 213n.60, 217n.69, 221n.73, 241n.107, 263n.27, 320n.39, 355n.41, 357n.45, 422n.7
Cannonieri, Giorgio 454
Canudo, Riccio 36, 355n.40
Capellini, Giovanni 50
Capone, Alphonse Gabriel 'Al' 175–6, 414–15
Cappiello, Leonetto 36–7
Capirone, Giuseppe 126n.41
Capra, Frank 175–6, 238–9, 245–6, 337, 349, 349n.30, 351, 359, 384, 388, 398–400, 474–6
Capuana, Luigi 35–6, 142–3, 145, 150
Carabba, Claudio 455n.53
Caraceni, Augusto 330–3
Carbonelli, Pietro 199–200, 423–4
Carducci, Giosuè 134–5, 137
Carega di Muricce, Francesco 51, 59–60
Carlucci, Alessandro xi, 11–12, 69n.43
Carné, Marcel 478–9
Carnegie, Dale 277–8
Carnera, Primo 15, 16, 325, 381–3, 454–5, 484, 485–6
Carpenter, Edith 262–3
Caruso, M. Girolama 47n.2
Caruso, Pino 140–2
Casanova, Pascale 12, 257
Casavola, Franco 300–1, 307–8
Casarini, Athos 182
Casella, Alfredo 316, 321
Caselotti, Adele 407–8
Casetti, Francesco 116n.19
Casini, Gherardo 444–7
Castronovo, Valerio 56n.21, 126n.38, 230n.86, 411n.122
Casucci, Leonello 307–8
Catalfamo, Antonio 252n.9
Cauli, Alberto 226n.81
Cavalieri, Lina 140–1
Cavour, Camillo Benso di 42
Cecchi, Emilio 136–7, 149, 178–9, 189–93, 199–201, 234, 246, 265–6, 269–71, 274, 350, 352, 383, 392n.94, 424, 447–52, 472–4, 484–6, 499
Cecchi, Maria 343n.18
Celentano, Adriano 501
Cendrars, Blaise 389
Centro Sperimentale di Cinematografia 357–8, 383–4, 395
Cerase, Francesco Paolo 104n.107, 245n.113
Cerchiari, Luca 297n.2, 303, 317n.36, 327n.45, 331n.53
Ceretti, Emilio 475n.75
Cerio, Ferruccio 354n.39
Cermak, Anton 209n.52

Cervi, Gino  482
Chang, Natasha C.  457–8
Chaplin, Charlie  6–7, 15, 16, 282, 296, 335, 336, 352–3, 364–5, 384, 389–91, 389n.88, 394, 482–3, 487–8, 499
Chapman, David  305n.18, 312n.27, 317n.36, 327n.45
Chard, Chloe  193n.28
Charlot  6–7
Charnitzky, Jürgen  250n.5
Charters, Samuel B.  169n.33
Chenal, Pierre  477–9
Cherchi Usai, Paolo  112, 115n.17, 117n.21
Chiarelli, Luigi  412–13
Chiarini, Luigi  336n.8, 357–8, 390n.90, 467–74, 484–5
Chiaromonte, Nicola  179n.7
Chicago  viii
Child, Richard Washburn  206–7, 214–15
Chiodelli, Raoul  325
Chiuminatto, Anthony  251–2, 502
Choate, Mark I.  80n.71, 96n.94, 245n.113
Churchwell, Sarah  210n.55
Ciampelli, G.M.  330n.52
Ciano, Costanzo  315, 318–19
Ciano, Edda, see Mussolini, Edda
Ciano, Galeazzo  210, 226, 290, 318–20, 355–6, 373n.66, 374–6, 404, 418–19, 422–3, 442–3
Ciarlantini, Franco  221–2, 257
Cinecittà, studios  344, 352, 359, 365, 371, 373, 376–84, 417
*Cinema*  336, 343n.18, 359–63, 370, 388, 395, 402–6, 412–13, 417, 465, 473–80, 482, 486–7
*Cinema illustrazione*  349, 379–83, 390n.90, 395, 407–8, 415–16, 465–8, 484–5
Cines, Film  115, 118, 118n.24, 122–3, 178–9, 301, 345, 347–52, 358n.47, 381, 383, 397–8, 410, 484–6
Cipolla, Arnaldo  186, 189
Cipriani, Geppi  308n.23
Cirino, Mark  157n.13
Clair, René  395, 471, 478–9
Clarke, Gilmore D.  439–40
Cleveland, Stephen Grover  81
Cody, William (Buffalo Bill)  5, 7–8, 48, 85–93, 108, 115, 138, 150–1, 181, 184–5, 457
Cognetti de Martiis, Salvatore  50–1, 59, 136
Colarizi, Simona  198n.37
Colasacco, Bret  148n.22
Colizzi, Gioachino  404–5
Colla, brothers  402
Collodi, Carlo  404–7, 474
Comics  4–5, 247

*Commercio Il*  52
Comte de Rivarol (Rivaroli, Antoine)  23
Confessore, Ornella  81n.72
Consiglio, Alberto  388, 389n.89, 394–5
Contorbia, Franco  251n.8
*Convegno Il*  258, 336
Coolidge, Calvin  194, 208, 338–9
Cooper, Gary  347, 383–5, 454–5
Cooper, Jackie  391–2
Cooper, James Fenimore  133, 136, 138–9, 150
Cornetta, Angelo  66
Corni, Gustavo  30n.16
Corona, Pietro 'Pete'  312–13
Corradini, Enrico  143, 150
*Corriere d'America*  198–9, 219–20
*Corriere dei Piccoli*  4–5, 282–5, 287–8, 292–4
*Corriere della Sera*  43, 56n.21, 60–1, 63–9, 78–9, 81–5, 94–5, 154, 159–60, 178–9, 186, 189, 192–200, 225–6, 245–6, 264–5, 269, 286, 310, 321, 423–4, 429n.17, 493
Corsi, Mario  395n.99
Corsi, Pietro  xi
Cortese, Antonio  99n.96
Cortese, Valentina  482
Coryell, John R.  138
Cotillo, Salvatore A.  164–5, 167
Cottini, Luca  xi, 86n.80, 91, 108n.3
Crawford, Joan  466–7
Credaro, Luigi  29, 44–5, 247–8, 493–4
Creel, George  164n.23
Cremonesi, Filippo  187–9
Crespi, Barbara  358n.47
Crialese, Emanuele  93–4
Crisp, Colin  347n.26
Crispi, Francesco  42
Croce, Benedetto  31, 149, 176–7, 196–7, 279, 353–4, 394–5, 419n.3, 448, 452
Crosby, Bing  307–8
Crossio, Carlo  454–5
Crossland, Alan  345
Cugny, Laurent  181n.12, 298
Cultrera, Giuseppe  43n.44
Curiel, Eugenio  451–2
Curnutt, Kirk  306n.20
Curti, Roberto  486n.93
Custer, George Armstrong  88–9, 91

Dall'Oglio, Enrico  263
Dall'Osso, Angela  69n.43, 182n.14
Dainotto, Roberto  181n.12
Damrosch, Walter  320–1
D'Annunzio, Gabriele  35–6, 45–6, 117, 134–7, 144–5, 147–9, 163, 165–6, 172, 216, 223, 241, 269, 314, 337, 392, 458–61

## INDEX

Dàuli, Gian 261–3, 265
Dante, *see* Alighieri, Dante
Da Ponte, Lorenzo 139
D'Arcangeli, Marco Antonio 248n.1
D'Attorre, Paolo 7–9, 490–1
Davies, Judith 36n.31
De Amicis, Edmondo 143, 145, 150
De Begnac, Yvon 316–17, 319n.38, 363
Debenedetti, Giacomo 388, 389n.89, 480
De Benedetti, Aldo 397–8
De Berti, Raffaele 181n.12, 381n.75, 396–7, 400n.108
Debussy, Claude 35–6, 298, 316
De Carlis, Stefania 253n.11
De Chirico, Giorgio 15
De Chomòn, Segundo 119
Decleva, Enrico 272n.37, 423n.8
Deed, André 113–14
De Feo, Luciano 352–3, 359, 362–4, 370–6, 405–6, 409
De Flaviis, Carlo 68–9
Defoe, Daniel 279
De Franciscis 476
De Grazia, Victoria xi, 8, 17, 32, 107, 224n.79, 230, 233, 236, 334, 344, 352n.35, 376–7, 497
Deiro, Guido 331–2
Delavigne, Casimir 139
Del Duca, Cino 289–90
Deledda, Grazia 250
Deleuze, Gilles 193n.28
D'Elia, Nicola 445n.39
Della Casa, Stefano 400n.109
Delluc, Louis 336–7, 389, 389n.89
Del Negro, Pietro 24n.3
Del Valle de Paz, Giacomo 328–9
De Marchi, Emilio 45
De Musset, Alfred 139
De Noël, Octave 76n.60
Depero, Fortunato 183–4, 299
De Pinedo, Francesco 225–6
De Renzi, Mario 354n.38
De Ritis, Beniamino 219
De Roberto, Federico 46
De Sanctis, Francesco 24–5, 30
De Santis, Giuseppe 363, 395, 477–9, 482, 483n.89, 484–7
De Sica, Vittorio 231–2, 237, 350–1, 366n.60, 369–70, 391–2, 397–9, 401, 465, 481–2, 500
De Staël, Germaine 26–7, 34, 147
Devoto, Giacomo 443
De Waals, Edmund 19
D'hoker, Elke 18n.28
Diaz, Armando 163, 165
Di Capua, Giovanni 328n.48, 459n.58

Di Chio, Federico 114n.15, 464n.62
Dickens, Charles 279, 335
Dickie, John xi
Dietrich, Marlene 466–7
Diggins, John 215n.65
Di Franco, Manuela 379n.73
Di Gregorio, Luca 91n.87, 138n.10
Di Maggio, Joe 245–6
Dinale, Ottavio 186–7
Di Savoia, Luigi Amedeo (Duca degli Abruzzi) 82–3
Disney, Walt 286, 291, 371, 384, 404–9
Disney, Walt (Company) 4, 290–1, 296, 401–9, 425–7, 472, 474
Di Spalatro, Antonella 273n.38
Disraeli, Benjamin 47
Distefano, Giulio 395n.99
Doherty, Thomas Patrick 364n.57
Doletti, Mino 465n.63
*Domenica del Corriere (La)* 2, 68–70, 94–5, 160–1, 201–2, 381, 425–7
D'Omerville, Carlo 55–6
Donizetti, Gaetano 34
Dos Passos, John Roderigo 157–8, 278, 394
Dossin, Catherine 15n.25
Dowd, Nancy 392n.93
Drieu La Rochelle, Pierre 392–3
Duane Gillespie, Elizabeth 56–7
Du Bose Heyward, Edwin 392–3
Ducis, Jean-François 26–7
Duhamel, Georges 180–1
Dumas, Alexandre 212, 292, 402
Duncan, Isadora 180, 180n.10
Dunnett, Jane 10–11, 256n.16, 267–8
Duranti, Doris 381–3
Duse, Eleonora 377–8

Earhart, Amelia 231–2
*Eco d'Italia L'* 60–1
Eco, Umberto 4–5, 9, 12–13, 335, 449–50, 457–8
Edison, Thomas 3, 72, 107–8, 112–14
Edmiston, Fred W. 331n.54
Edwards, James Gordon 340
EIAR (Ente Italiano Audizioni Radiofoniche) 296, 314–28, 460, 462–3
Eiffel Tower viii–ix, 33
Einaudi, Giulio 278–9
Einaudi, Luigi 278–9
Einaudi, publishing house 247, 260, 278–9
Elkins, Katherine 82–3
Eliot, T. S. 266
Ellington, Duke 326–7
Ellwood, David W. xi, 8, 11, 222n.76, 224n.79, 376, 502

Emanuel, Guglielmo  286–8, 452–3
Emerson, Ralph Waldo  72, 147
Empire State Building  viii–ix
English language learning, see Foreign language learning in Italy
ENIC (Ente Nazionale Industrie Cinematografiche)  383, 460–1, 464, 465n.64
ERA Film  366, 369–70, 379n.72, 475
Erbaggio, Pierluigi  215, 215n.65
Ercole, Pierluigi  355n.40
Eschenazi, Gabriele  327n.45, 464n.61
Escobar, Mario  306, 314
Esposito, Edoardo  276n.42
*Esposizione universale di Filadelfia L'*  55–6, 58
EUR42 (Esposizione Universale Roma 1942)  431–40, 489, 496
Evola, Julius  257
Ezra, Elizabeth  381n.76

Fabre, Giorgio  277n.43, 419n.3, 445n.39, 446n.42
Fabre, Marcel  113–14
Factor, Max  237
Faina, Eugenio  103
Fairbanks, Douglas  346–7, 384–5
Falasca-Zamponi, Simonetta  215n.66
Falconi, Armando  415
Falconi, Dino  415–16
Fanfani, Massimo  xi, 443n.35
Farabegoli, Giorgio  xi
Farci, Maria Silvia  438n.26
Fassini, Alberto  122
Faulkner, William  273–6, 280, 450–1, 485
Fauriel, Claude  34
Favaro, A.  57n.24
Febeo, Augusto  310
Fellini, Federico  16, 192, 335, 498, 501
Ferme, Valerio  xi, 136, 260, 264n.28, 445n.40
Fernandez, Dominique  267
Ferrando, Anna  257n.17, 263n.26
Ferrando, Lidio  xi
Ferrari, Fabio  280n.45
Ferrarin, A. Ramades  180n.10
Ferraris, Galileo  107–8
Ferrero, Felice  83–5, 192–3
Ferrero, Leo  179–80, 336n.7
Ferretti, Lando  406–7
Ferroni, Giorgio  483n.89
Ferry, Gabriel  138
FIAT (Fabbrica Italiana Automobili Torino), car and aircraft company  82–3, 125–31, 208, 223, 229–30, 410–12, 428–9, 497–8
Fiamingo, Giuseppe Maria  109
Filippini, Gino  320–1, 324

Filippini, Ugo  299, 306–7, 312
Finocchi, Luisa  263n.26
Finzi, Roberto  441n.30
Fioravanti, Gigliola  44n.45
Fiorentino, Daniele  10–11, 90n.85
Fitzgerald, Francis Scott  180, 299, 305–8, 331–2, 339–40
Fitzgeral, Zelda  305–6
Fitzmaurice, George  395
Flynn, Errol  384–6
Foà, Augusto  257n.17
Foerster, Robert F.  240n.105
Fontana, Ferdinando  54–5, 59–61, 75–6
Ford, Henry  127–30, 229–30, 410–11
Ford, John  482–3
Forde, Walter  485
Foreign language learning in Italy  6–7, 14, 43–6, 103–4, 119, 148n.22, 247–55, 261–2, 265–6, 277, 349–50, 350n.33, 440–4, 493–4, 500–1
Forgacs, David  xi, 10–11, 313, 352n.35, 455n.54
Formiggini, Angelo Fortunato  419n.3
Forno, Mauro  63n.36
Fortuna, James J.  433n.21
Forzano, Giovacchino  354, 361n.52, 409, 413–14
Foscolo, Ugo  25, 26n.8
Fourniol, Étienne  257
Fox Film Corporation  213, 215, 338, 340–3, 359, 368–9, 372–3, 378–9, 400, 464
Fox, William  338, 340, 342–3
Fraccaroli, Arnaldo  156n.12, 192–6, 225n.80, 233–4, 337n.10
Fracchia, Umberto  268
Franchetti, Leopoldo  34–5, 94
Franchi, Aldo  427n.14
Francis, Kay  359
Franco, Francisco  211, 364–5
Frank, Joseph Maria  231–2
Frank, Waldo  189, 392–3
Franklin, Benjamin  48–9, 56–7
Franzina, Emilio  xi, 94, 99n.96, 101n.100, 105n.109, 143nn.14, 15, 145n.17, 151n.1, 240n.105
Frassinelli, Carlos  278
Freda, Riccardo  486–7
Freddi, Luigi  336n.8, 337–8, 352–4, 356–60, 362, 364, 370–6, 381, 383–4, 404, 406, 417, 424–5, 464–5, 465n.64, 469–73, 484–6, 487n.95
French culture  vii–viii, 9–10, 23, 33–46, 55n.18, 111, 167–8
  and architecture  38–42
  and art  36–7, 41–2, 182
  and the car industry  124–7

and cinema 110–15, 119, 121, 123, 238–9, 336, 337n.10, 338, 347, 360, 389, 392–3, 477–9
and classical music 34, 38, 54, 316
and jazz 180–2, 298–9, 302, 307–8, 310, 312, 328–9, 331
and foreign language learning 29, 43–6, 247–53, 442–4
and literature 23–5, 28, 34–8, 132–4, 136–9, 179–80, 247, 251–9, 261, 263–5, 267n.31, 269–71, 449–50
and the press 24, 42–3, 52–3, 53n.15, 63n.36, 69, 81n.74, 201–2
Friedman, Max Paul 101n.101
Fritsch, Willy 466–7
Frykholm, Joel 118n.22
Fuller, Loïe 180n.10
Fuller, Margaret 147
Fulvi, Daniele 148n.21
Fumasoni Biondi, Leone 195–7, 199, 229
Futurism 1, 16, 29–30, 37, 168–9, 182–3, 211, 219, 255–6, 296–305, 317, 328, 330n.52, 421

Gabaccia, Donna xi, 5, 47, 105
Gable, Clark 237, 351, 383, 466–7
Gable, Ria 466–7
Gaboriau, Émile 212
Gaborik, Patricia xi, 178n.4, 303nn.13, 14
Gadda Conti, Giuseppe 68n.42
Gadducci, Fabio 285n.50, 290n.55, 291n.56, 292n.58, 454n.52
Gallagher, Tad 386n.83
Galleppini, Aurelio 500
Gallo, Claudio 257n.17
Gallone, Carmine 333, 356–7, 451–2, 482, 484–6
Galtier-Boissière, Jean 389
Galzigna, Bruno 442
Gamberale, Luigi 137
Gandolfi, Alfredo 118–21
Garbo, Greta 231–2, 237, 337, 343–4, 413, 466–7
Garella, Luisa 415
Garibaldi, Giuseppe 61, 75, 207n.48
Garnett, Tay 478–9
Garzanti, Aldo 419n.3
Garzarelli, Benedetta 355n.40
Gaskill, Nicholas xi
Gatti, Alessandro 344n.20
Gatti Casazza, Giulio 139–40
*Gazzetta d'Italia* 51
Geist, Johann Friedrich 41n.42
Gennaro, Rosario 256n.15
Genovese, Vito 364–5
Gentile, Emilio 10, 28n.13, 31n.19, 177, 187n.20, 191–2, 211, 222n.74, 436n.25, 497

Gentile, Federico 443
Gentile, Giovanni 31, 44–5, 149, 176–7, 212–13, 218–19, 220n.72, 247–50, 249n.2, 253–4, 269, 291, 353–4, 357, 441, 443–4, 470
Gerbi, Antonello 49n.4, 336
Gerswhin, George 175, 308–10, 322–3, 392–3
German culture 25, 27–32, 34, 45–6, 73–4, 123, 123n.33, 138, 152, 248, 259, 338, 360
 in Nazi Germany 209–10, 221, 335, 353–5, 357, 372–3, 398, 406–7, 410, 418, 421–7, 429–30, 434–6, 442–4, 460n.59, 462, 465–8, 489, 498–9
Getto, Giovanni 137n.8
Ghez, Didier 290n.55, 404nn.114, 115
Ghilardi, Margherita xi, 179n.6
Giacheri Fossati, Luciana 56n.21
Giachetti, Fosco 383n.78
Giacosa, Giuseppe 69–71, 74–6
Giannini, Amadeo 175–6, 245
Giannini, Guglielmo 483
Gibbons, James 80–1
Gide André 269–71, 392–3
Gigli Marchetti, Ada 263n.26
Giladi, Amotz 36, 253n.11
Gilbert, Claudette 351
Gili, Jean A. 114n.14, 347n.27, 473n.71
Ginex, Giovanna 69n.45, 183n.16
Ginzburg, Carlo 13–14
Ginzburg, Leone 278–9
Giolitti, Giovanni 29
Giordano, Michele 53n.15
*Giornale della letteratura straniera* 34–5
*Giornale di Sicilia Il* 94–5
Girardi, Michele 142n.13
Girimonti Greco, Giuseppe 231n.89
Girosi, Marcello 427n.14
Girotti, Massimo 478–9, 484
Giuntini, Aldo 303–4
Gobetti, Piero 179, 251, 278–9
Goebbels, Joseph 210, 355–6, 373–4, 421–3, 468, 471, 473
Goeschel, Christian 418n.1
Goethe, Johann Wolfgang 25
Goetz, Helmut 197n.34
Goldsoll, Frank Joseph 121
Golino, Carlo L. 148n.21
Gompers, Samuel 169
Goncourt brothers 35–6
Gordon, Robert xi, 11
Gori, Gigliola 230n.87
Gori, Leonardo 285n.50, 290n.55, 291n.56, 292n.58, 454n.52
Gorlier, Claudio 449
Graf, Arturo 27

Gramsci, Antonio 9–10, 10n.15, 12, 20, 41–2, 42n.43, 107, 138, 145–6, 315n.33, 492
Grandi, Aldo 362n.53
Grandi, Dino 209
Grant, Cary 383
Grasset, Bernard 179
Gravina, Cesare 85n.78
Gray, Christopher 204n.46
Gray Davis, Rosalind 142n.13
Grazia, Patrizia 447n.43
Graziani, Carlo 45n.47
Green, Jamie 248n.1
Grey Thomason, Sarah 13n.23
Griffith, D. W. 88–9, 121–2, 151, 335, 389, 394, 484–5
Grimm brothers 27, 407–8
Gromo, Mario 337, 354, 402n.113, 404n.115
Guarente, Frank 331–2
Guattari, Félix 193n.28
Guazzoni, Enrico 116–17, 122–3
Guerrini, Giovanni 437
Guest, Russell 429n.16
Guglielman, Eleonora 249n.2, 250n.5
Guidali, Fabio 18n.28, 259n.22
Guidoni, Enrico 436n.25
Gundle, Stephen xi, 7, 10–11, 313, 335n.6, 352n.35, 381n.76, 383n.78, 455n.54
Gussoni, Alice xi, 69n.44, 100n.97, 201n.43

Hainsworth, Peter xi
Haley, Bill 310n.25
Hall Caine, Henry 213–14
Halliburton, Richard 277
Hammett, Dashiell 288
Hamp, Charles W. 170
Hansen, Arlen J. 156n.11, 158n.15
Hara, Kunio 142n.13
Harding, Warren G. 352
Hardy, Oliver 389, 402, 480n.85
Harmsworth, Alfred 283–5
Harwell Celenza, Anna 169n.33, 181n.12, 297–8, 298nn.4, 5, 308n.22, 317n.36, 319n.38, 327n.45, 328–9, 328n.47, 329n.50, 330n.52
Havas 42–3, 81n.74
Hawks, Howard 414–15
Hawthorn, Nathaniel 132–3
Hay, James 335n.4, 338n.11, 397–8, 412n.124, 413n.125
Hayes, Will H. 213–14, 237, 373–6, 474
Hayworth, Rita 488
Heim, Frank 47n.2
Hemingway, Ernest 156–8, 180, 266–7, 273–5, 279–81, 485

Henabery, Joseph 121–2
Hennessy, David 74–5
Hermeter, Anne-Rachel 258n.20
Higham, Charles 344n.19, 364n.57
Hillyer, Lambert 485
Hitler, Adolf 209–11, 277, 353–4, 364n.57, 418–20, 425, 430, 434–6, 489, 498–9
Hobsbawn, Eric 3–4
Holland, Katrin 231–2
*Hollywood Reporter* 366n.60, 367–9, 371–2
Hoover, Herbert 160
Hopkins, J. Ernest 298n.4
Hopper, Edward 15
Hugenberg, Alfred 355–6
Hughes Howard 476
Hughes, Lachlan xi
Hugo, Victor 25, 139
Huysman, Joris-Karl 35–6

Iaccio, Pasquale 318n.37
*Illustrazione italiana L'* 57, 69, 201, 425–7
*Illustrazione popolare L'* 55–7, 69, 86–7, 201
Ingold, Tim 19
Ingrao, Pietro 395n.100
Interlandi, Telesio 371–2
Introvigne, Massimo 138n.10
Isani, Giuseppe 480n.85
Itala, Film 113–17
*Italia: Giornale del popolo L'* 62–5
Italian Americans 5, 19
  during 1861–1914 49–50, 54–5, 61–2, 66, 74–9, 83–5, 93–106, 121–2, 132, 150, 168–9
  during World War One 151, 156, 160, 162, 164–7, 182
  during the interwar years 5–6, 175–6, 183, 194–201, 196n.33, 208–10, 213–14, 223, 227, 239–46, 252, 276, 296–7, 312–13, 316n.34, 327–33, 345–6, 356n.43, 407–17, 454–5, 484–6, 492–3, 497
*Italiano L'* 219, 421, 470

Jackson, Frederick 133n.2
Jacini, Stefano 94
James, Henry 132–3, 189
James, William 1, 72, 147–9, 176–7, 211–12, 261–2
Jannaccone, Pasquale 136
Janni, Mauro 459n.58, 460n.59
Janssen, Werner 320–1
Jazz music 1, 3–4, 13–15, 18, 32, 105, 142, 153, 168–72, 175, 201–2, 255–6, 281, 296–333, 399–400, 412, 421–2, 458–64, 480–2, 494, 497–8
Jeffers, H. Paul 166n.28

*Jeune Fille La* 46
Joel, Otto 29
*Journal des savants* 46
Joyce, James 255

Kahn, Otto 139–40
Kallis, Aristotle 187n.20, 433n.21
Kallmann, Alfred 123n.33
Keaton, Buster 296, 335, 389
Kelly, Joseph xi
Kessner, Thomas 166n.28
King Features Syndicate 4–5, 286, 452–3
King, Russell 104n.107, 240n.104, 245n.113
Kirk, Terry 354n.38, 411n.121, 431–3
Klein, Gabriella 442n.34, 443n.35
Kleine, George 115–22, 339–40, 342
Kokubo, Marie xi, 280n.45
Körner, Axel xi, 11, 30n.16, 49n.4, 133n.2, 139
Kornhaber, Donna 389n.88
Kracauer, Sigfried 32
Kramer, Gorni 326–8, 464, 486–7
Kreimer, Klaus 356n.42
Kroes, Rob 7–8, 55n.19, 89–90
Kuisel, Richard viii, 502

*Lacerba* 37–8
Ladd, Brian 131n.48
Lafitte, Paul 112–13
La Guardia, Fiorello H. 165–7, 170, 204n.46
Lama, Sergio 285n.50, 290n.55, 291n.56, 292n.58, 454n.52
Lanaro, Silvio 52n.13
Lanfranchi-Guilloux, Stéphanie xi
Lang, Eddie 329
Lang, Fritz 392
Langdon, Rose 389
La Padula, Ernesto 436–8
La Piana, Angelina 279
Lardner, Ring 274–5
La Rocca, Dominic James "Nick" 15, 168–9, 175–6, 296–7, 328, 331–3, 497
Laterza, Giovanni 419n.3, 448
La Torre, Antonella 439n.28
Lauer, Bernhard 27–8
Laughlin, Clara 306–7
Laurel, Stan 389, 402, 480n.85
Laux, James 125n.36
Laval, Pierre 228–9
Lawrence, D. H. 272–3
Leander, Zarah 466–7
Leavitt, Charles xi, 366n.60, 479n.83
Le Bon, Gustave 263–4
Le Corbusier 410–11
Lederman, D. Ross 485

Lenin, Vladimir 216
Leo XIII, Pope 80–1
Leoncini, Paolo xi
Leone, Sergio 13, 115n.18, 500
Leopardi, Giacomo 26, 424
Lepri, Sergio 43n.44
Lepschy, Giulio 500–1
Leslie, Thomas xi
Le Tourneur, Pierre 34
Lettau, Joseph 162n.19, 168n.32, 169n.35, 171–2
Levi, Carlo 190–1, 242–4
Levi, Ezio 330–1
Lewis, Richard 364n.57, 388
Lewis, Sinclair 257, 262–3, 265–6, 278–9, 392–3, 450–1, 492
Libera, Adalberto 354n.38, 438–40
Liceo Femminile 7
Lief, Shane 169n.33
Linati, Carlo 264–5
Lincoln, Abraham 48–51
Lindberg, Charles 224–6, 371–2
Liuzzi, Fernando 329n.50
Livi, François 36n.32
Livingston, Alexander 148n.22, 212
Lizzani, Carlo 363, 479
Lombardo, Agostino 7
London, Jack 17–18, 136, 261–4
Longanesi, Leo 393–4, 424, 449–50, 470–2
Loos, Anita 266, 268–71, 299
Lotman, Yuri 12–13
Lottini, Irene 91n.86
Lotz, Rainer 170n.36, 460n.59
Louis, Joe 15, 325, 484
Louÿs, Pierre 140–1
Loy, Myrna 475
LUCE, Istituto 350–1, 353–4, 356, 359, 364, 371–2, 406–9, 487n.95
Lubitsch, Emil 388, 399
Luconi, Stefano 151n.1, 196n.33, 240n.105, 241n.107
Ludwig, Emil 208–9
Lumière brothers 39, 112–13, 123
Luperini, Romano 36n.31
Lussana, Fiamma 353n.36
Lux, Simonetta 436n.25

Macario, Erminio 482–3
Maccari, Mino 222, 253–4
MacDonald, James Ramsey 228–9
Maciste, *see* Pagano, Bartolomeo
Maggi, Luigi 115–16
Maggi, Raffaello 348
Maggio, Antonio 168–9
Maggio, Antonino "Anthony" 296–7

Magnani, Anna 461n.60
Magrin, Alessandra 86n.80
Maiori, Antonio 85n.78
Malaparte, Curzio 254–5
Malasomma, Nunzio 410, 480–1
Malipiero, Gian Francesco 321
Mallarmé, Stéphane 137
Malthe-Brun, Conrad 26
Mamoulian, Rouben 395, 404
Mancini, Elaine 346n.25, 348n.29, 351n.34
Mandrake 4–5
Manetti, Daniela 334n.1, 355n.41, 358n.46, 473n.71
Mangoni, Luisa 28n.13, 31n.21, 35, 279n.44
Mantegazza, Vico 76–80
Manzi, Armando 312–13
Manzoni, Alessandro 34
Marazzi, Elisa 263n.26
Marazzi, Martino xi, 145n.17
March, Fredric 367
Marconi, Guglielmo 220n.72, 314
Margadonna, Ettore 336–7, 336n.7, 379, 387–9, 392–3, 402n.112
Margravio, Anthony V. 100n.97
Mari, Febo 144, 150
Marinelli, Dario 461n.60
Marinetti, Filippo Tommaso 36–7, 36n.32, 111, 222, 233, 249, 297–301, 303–5, 315n.32, 317, 446
Martellini, Amoreno xi, 94n.91, 101n.100
Martelli, Sebastiano 3n.3, 144n.16
Martin, Benjamin G. 422n.5
Martinelli, Vittorio 115n.18, 414n.127
Mascagni, Pietro 300–1, 315–16
Maspero, Mauro xi
Massara, Giuseppe 54n.16
Massinello, Giovanni 429n.16
Mastrocinque, Camillo 366n.60
Matarazzo, Raffaele 397, 413–16, 482
Martera, Luca 486n.91
Mathis, June 343–4
Matté Trucco, Giacomo 127–8, 411
Matteotti, Giacomo 178, 187–9, 306
Mattioli, Guido 224n.78
Mattioli, Mauro 232n.90
Mattoli, Mario 398–400, 481–2
Mauri, Francesca 96n.94
Maurois, André 257
Mayer, Louis B. 343–4, 364, 367–9
Mayer, Teodoro 43n.44
Mayo, Archie 347–8
Mayor des Planches, Edmondo 77
Mazzarini, Francesca 295n.59
Mazzei, Luca 116n.19

Mazzini, Giuseppe 23, 48–9
Mazzoletti, Adriano xi, 169nn.33, 35, 298n.6, 299, 303n.12, 306n.20, 308n.22, 310n.25, 312nn.26, 27, 315nn.32, 33, 317n.36, 325nn.42, 49, 328n.49, 330n.52
Mazzotti, Fernando 96
Mazzucchelli, Chiara 143n.14
May, Renato 395
McBride, John 358
McFarlane, Bruce 162n.19
McGrath Morris, James 158n.15
McLaughlin, Martin xi
Meda, Juri 285n.50
Mehrhoff, W. Arthur 440n.29
Melani, Costanza 137n.6
Méliès, Georges 113–14, 119, 298
Melis de Villa, Armando 431
Meloney, Marie Mattingly "Missy" 220
Melville, Herman 264–5, 278
Mendelssohn, Felix 29–30
*Mercure de France* 36
Mereu Keating, Claudia 347n.27
Merriam, Charles E. 163, 167
Metro Goldwyn Mayer (MGM) 338–9, 343–4, 350, 350n.32, 358, 366–70, 378–9, 417, 464
Meucci, Antonio 61, 75
Mezzasoma, Fernando 448–9
MGM, *see* Metro Goldwyn Mayer
Micciché, Lino 478n.79
Miccoli, Maria Carmela 99n.96
Michaud, Régis 256, 269–71
Mida, Massimo 394n.96, 395n.99, 477n.78
Mickey Mouse (Topolino) 4, 286, 287, 291, 292, 294, 400, 401, 410–11, 452–3, 455, 456, 497–8
Migliorini, Bruno 443
Migone, Gian Giacomo 208nn.49–51, 240n.104
Mix, Tom 384–5
Mila, Massimo 278–9, 281n.47
Miller, Nicola 59n.25
Miller, Webb 316–17
Minuz, Andrea 487n.95
Mirabile, Andrea 36n.31
Mirador (Agazzi, Arturo) 311–12
Miranda, Isa 381–3
Mistinguett, Florentine Bourgeois 308
*Mito americano* 17–18, 135, 247, 260, 267–82
Modernissima, publishing house 261–5
Modigliani, Amedeo 36–7, 182, 478
Moleschott, Jacob 29
Molino, Walter 292, 454
Mon, Gijs 125n.36
Monaco, Eitel 473n.71
Monanni, Giuseppe 263–4

Mondadori, Alberto  423
Mondadori, Arnoldo  256, 271–3, 277, 289–92, 295, 379, 423, 444–7, 452–5
Mondadori, publishing house  180, 216n.67, 217, 220–1, 231–2, 256–8, 260, 265, 271–2, 274n.40, 277–9, 293, 338–9, 379, 401, 423n.8, 475n.75
*Mondo illustrato Il*  52–3, 55–6
Monga, Luigi  101n.99
Montemaggiorni, Amerigo  241
Monelli, Paolo  329, 443
Montevecchi, Luisa  44n.45
Montale, Eugenio  421–3
Montano, Lorenzo  256–7, 265
Montesano, Maria  398n.106
Monti, August  278–9
Monti, Vincenzo  26n.8
Monticone, Alberto  314n.30
Moravia, Alberto  274–5
Morbelli, Riccardo  402
Morellini, Moreno  99n.96
Moretti, Franco  12, 26
Morgagni, Manlio  43n.44, 196, 201, 204
Morgan, J. P.  85, 208
Morgan, Thomas P.  217n.69
Moricola, Giuseppe  94n.91
Moroni, Guido Celsi  292
Morosi, Antonio  39
Morovich, Enrico  483n.89
Moscatelli, Sara  130n.47
Mosco, Antonio  481n.86
Mosso, Angelo  29, 104
Mozzoni, Anna Maria  57–9
Muntoni, Alessandra  438n.26
Mura (Volpi, Maria)  310
Murphy, Libby  389n.88
Muscio, Giuliana  85n.78, 115n.17, 214n.63, 327n.46, 341n.15
Musolino, Nick  331
Mussolini, Arnaldo  201, 315n.32, 362–3
Mussolini, Benito  14, 18, 19–20, 30–1, 176–7, 196, 196–7, 213, 238–9, 258, 290, 318–19, 324–5, 410–11, 418–20, 422–3, 424n.9, 425, 427–8, 429–30, 441, 443, 451–2, 489, 495, 497–8, 498–9, 499
  and American politics  205–11, 220–1, 268, 494
  and art  212–13, 421
  and architecture  186–9, 430–40
  and cinema  18, 213–14, 335, 337–8, 352–76, 404, 406, 417, 464, 470–1, 479, 485–6, 494, 499
  and Italian Americans  213–14, 240–1, 409
  and jazz music  18, 315–19, 330n.52, 331, 494
  and literature  213–14, 263–4, 269–71, 295, 446, 448–9
  and pragmatism  14, 132, 148–9, 176–7
Mussolini, Bruno  226, 362, 494–5
Mussolini, Edda  237, 318–19, 319n.38, 404, 494–5
Mussolini, Rachele  404
Mussolini, Romano  290n.55, 315–16, 318–19
Mussolini, Vito  362–3
Mussolini, Vittorio  18, 132, 147–8, 219, 226, 318–19, 330–1, 336n.8, 337–8, 359–74, 379–80, 397, 417, 454, 464–5, 475–9, 488, 494–5

Napoleon III  25, 28
Naumburg, Nancy  473
Navarra, Quinto  353n.36
Nazzari, Amedeo  383, 386, 412–13, 480–2
Negroni, Baldassarre  410
Nelson, Graham  xi
Nencioni, Enrico  134–7, 149
Nerbini, Giuseppe  286
Nerbini, Mario  286–95, 401, 446–7, 457
Neri, Ferdinando  251–2
Nervetti, Milietto  313
Neumann, Dietrich  187n.20
Newton, Francis  4n.4
New York  viii, 1, 5
Nicoli, Marina  345n.23, 347n.27
Nicoloso, Paolo  187n.20, 433n.21, 436n.25
Nietzsche, Friedrich  147–8, 211–12, 263n.27
Nievo, Ippolito  24–5
Nizza, Angelo  329, 329n.51, 402
Nolan, Mary  8, 206, 209n.52
Noris, Assia  232, 351, 381–3, 462–3, 465, 481–2
Norris, Frank  450–1
Notari, Umberto  233–4
*Nouvelle Revue Française La* (*NRF*)  36, 256, 258, 269–71
Novarro, Ramon  339–40, 343
Nowell-Smith, Geoffrey  334
*Nuova antologia di lettere, scienze ed arti*  35, 109, 134, 136, 219–21, 257, 328–9
Nuzzi, Paolo  381n.76

Oakley, Annie  89–91, 115, 140–1
O'Hare-McCormick, Anne  177
Ojetti, Paola  413n.126
Ojetti, Ugo  31, 69–74, 76, 79–80, 135, 269–71, 413n.126
Olcott, Sidney  85n.78
Olivetti, Camillo  2, 59, 107–9, 130, 493
Omegna, Roberto  111
*Omnibus*  273, 424, 449–50, 470–1
O'Neil, Eugene  303n.13

550  INDEX

Orazi, Vezio 473
Orlando, Vittorio Emanuele 163
Orteig, Raymond 224
Ortoleva, Peppino 411n.123
Ortuso, Michele 'Mike' 312–13
O'Sullivan, Maureen 475
Ott, Mark P. 157n.13
Otto, Natalino 327–8

Pabst, Georg Wilhelm 471
Padoan, Adolfo 115–16
Pagano, Bartolomeo 381–3, 413–14
Pagano, Giuseppe 222, 433–6
Page, Thomas Nelson 151–2
Palanti, Mario 186–9, 430
Palermi, Amleto 398, 412–13
Paliotti, Vittorio 38n.38
Palma di Cesnola, Luigi 75
Paolella, Domenico 487n.95
Paoletti, Gianni 143n.14
Papa, Dario 49–50, 59–63, 59n.27, 493
Papini, Giovanni 14, 30–1, 36, 136, 147–9, 176–7, 211, 252–5, 261–2, 269–71
Pardini, Samuele 111n.8
Parenti, Tony 331–2
Pareto, Vilfredo 74
Parini, Giuseppe 23–4
Parisi, Luciano 197n.34
Parrott, Ursula 271–2
Pascoli, Giovanni 134–5, 137, 144–5, 149–50
Pasetti, Aldo 425n.12
Pasinetti, Francesco 473n.70, 486–7
Pasolini, Pier Paolo 146, 305
Passerini, Luisa 215n.66
Pastrone, Giovanni 113–16, 117n.21, 120–2, 338, 381–3
Pathé-Frères 112–14
Patuelli, Raffaello 404n.115
Paulicelli, Eugenia 238–9
Pavese, Cesare 136, 247, 251–2, 256, 260, 262–5, 267, 267n.32, 274–82, 394, 449–52, 500, 502
Pavese, Luigi 415
Pavolini, Alessandro 226, 272–3, 291, 336n.8, 373n.66, 421–3, 442–3, 446–9, 451–2, 455, 476–7, 479, 485–6
Pavolini, Corrado 336n.8
Pearse, Holly A. 390n.90
Pecorini, Alberto 73–4, 78
Peden, Charles 215
Peirce, Charles Sanders 147–8
Pemberton, Jo-Anne 148n.22
Peressutti, Gino 358, 359n.48
Perino, Edoardo 92

Perseveranza La 50–1
Petacci, Emilio 415
Petacco, Arrigo 479n.83
Petrolini, Ettore 390
Petrosino, Giuseppe 83–5
Pezzetti Tonion, Fabio xi
Phillipoteaux, Paul Dominique 92n.89
Photo Drama Producing Co. 118–21
Piacentini, Marcello 187–9, 222, 354, 430–40, 463
Piacentini, Pio 430–1
Piceni, Enrico 272–3
Pickford, Mary 85n.78, 346–7
Pietralunga, Mark 252n.9
Pietrangeli, Antonio 477, 481–2, 484–6
Pignatelli, Valerio 286n.52
Pilati, Gaetano 18
Pillepich, Narciso 428–9
Pilotto, Camillo 401
Pini, Giorgio 320n.39, 362–3, 422
Pintor, Giaime 421–3
Pirandello, Luigi 20, 29, 143–4, 177–8, 180–1, 250–1, 268, 297–8, 337, 345–6, 350
Pirelli, Alberto 48–9, 493
Pirelli, Piero 493
Pischedda, Bruno 451n.47
Pitigrilli (Segre Dino) 238–9, 279n.44
Pittaluga, Stefano 344–8, 350, 378–9, 413–14
Pizzetti, Ildebrando 117, 321, 329
Pizzi, Katia 183
Poe, Edgar Allan 26–7, 72, 134–9, 150, 260, 273
Poesio, Camilla 201n.44, 230–1, 317n.36
Poggiolo-Kaftan, Giordana 143n.14
Polan, Dana 131n.48
Pollone, Matteo 138n.10, 292n.57
Polo, Marco 240–1, 347–8
Polverelli, Gaetano 355, 448–9, 485–6
Ponti, Gio 433
Pope, Generoso 198–9
Popolo Il 30–1
Popolo d'Italia Il 283, 315n.32, 321, 356, 361, 364–5, 422, 458–60
Porter, Edwin, S. 388
Possenti, Eligio 178n.5
Potious, Costantino 481n.86
Poulaille, Henri 389
Pound, Ezra 354n.39
Power, Tyrone 368–9
Pragmatism 1n.1, 14, 136n.5, 147–9, 176–7, 211–12
Pratella, Francesco Balilla 299n.8, 300–1
Prato, Paolo xi
Praz, Mario 6–7, 137n.8, 200, 264–71

Prendergast, Christopher 37n.34
Pretelli, Matteo 104n.107, 241n.107, 245n.114
Preziosi, Ernesto 288n.53
Prezzolini, Giuseppe 30–1, 147–9, 211, 220, 249, 260–2
*Progresso Italo-americano Il* 60–1, 66, 81, 198–200
Prolo, Maria Adriana 114n.14
Proust, Marcel 36n.31
Puccini, Giacomo 54, 93, 139–42, 150, 304, 482–3
Puccini, Gianni 477
Pulcini, Virginia 443n.35

Quaglietti, Lorenzo 394n.96, 395n.99, 464n.62, 474n.74

Rabagliati, Alberto 327–8, 460–2, 464, 480–1
Radice, Mark A. 299n.8
Radio 4, 109–12
*Radiocorriere* 314, 316–28, 461
Raeburn, Bruce Boyd 169n.33
Rafanelli, Leda 263–4
Ragusa Moleti, Girolamo 137
Raicich, Marino 44n.45
RAM (Roach and Mussolini) Pictures 366–7, 370–2, 376, 417, 475, 475n.75
Ramperti, Marco 390, 488
Randall, Annie J. 142n.13
Rapisarda, Stefano 442n.33
*Rassegna settimanale di politica, scienze, lettere e arti* 34–5
Ravasio, Carlo 315
Ravel, Maurice 316
Rayal, Guillaume Thomas 24
RCA (Radio Corporation of America) 345, 358n.47
Redaelli, Cesare 224n.78
Redi, Riccardo 118n.24, 122n.30, 123n.32
Reeder, Linda 103n.105, 105n.108
Reich, Jacqueline 383n.77, 413–14
Renoir, Jean 395, 475, 478–9
Respighi, Ottorino 321
Reuters 42–3
Révész, Andrés 211
Reynaud, Paul 420
Reza, Matthew 11–12
Ricciardi, Caterina 305n.19
Richter, Dieter 101n.101
Richter, Hans 471
Ridolfi, Eleuterio 413–14
Riefenstahl, Leni 406–7
Righelli, Gennaro 345, 350–1, 412–13
Rimondi, Giorgio 281n.47, 297n.2

*Rivista illustrata del Popolo d'Italia La* 201–4, 424–5
Rizzoli, Angelo 379–81, 424
Roach, Hal 364–70, 417, 470–1
Robbe, Federico 153n.6, 155n.8
Roberto, Roberti 115n.18
Robey, David xi, 26n.8
Rocca, Gino 336–7
Rocco, Alfredo 28, 268, 404–6
Rocco, Ferdinando 404–5
Rochat, Giorgio 228n.82
Rodocanachi, Lucia 251, 272–3
Rodondi, Raffaela 274n.40
Roger, Philippe 2n.2, 81n.74, 181n.11
Roma, Enrico 398n.106
Roman Catholic Church 1, 28, 49, 67n.39, 73, 80–1, 96–7, 213n.62, 218, 222, 234–6, 246, 288, 291–2, 374–5, 479, 491–2
Romanelli, Raffaele 52n.13
Romano, Mario 437
Romano, Sergio 47–8
Romussi, Carlo 55n.20
Ronconi, Guglielmina 156n.10
Rondolino, Gianni 110–11, 359n.49
Roosevelt, Eleanor 220
Roosevelt, Franklin Delano 175, 198–9, 206, 208–11, 219–21, 243, 268, 369–70, 420, 422
Roosevelt, Theodore 82–3, 89
Roppolo, Leon 331–2
Rosa, Enrico 217n.69
Rosher, Charles 'Chas' 340–2
Rosny, Aîné J.-H. 257
Rosoli, Gianfausto 102n.102
Ross, Corey 338n.11
Rossellini, Roberto 359–60, 391–2, 475, 480n.85, 500
Rossi, Adolfo 33–4, 49–50, 60–8, 74, 81, 493
Rossi, Alessandro 51–2
Rossi, Egisto 51–2
Rossini, Daniela 10–11, 46n.49, 151, 152n.3, 153n.5, 156nn.10,12, 164n.24, 167n.29
Rossini, Gioachino 34, 139, 317
Rosso, Medardo 36–7
Rosson, Richard 414–15
Rota, Giuseppe 133
Rotha, Paul 471
Ruggiero, Amerigo 85, 200–1, 229, 235–6, 245
Rulli, Dino 181n.12, 311
Rundle, Christopher 259n.22, 446n.41, 447n.43, 449n.44
Russell, Jack 306
Russo, Valentina 442n.34
Russolo, Luigi 299–301
Rydell, Robert W. 7–8, 55n.19, 89–90

Saarinen, Eero 439–40, 496
Sabatello, Dario 407–8
Sacchi, Filippo 337n.9, 398n.106, 413n.126, 416n.129
Saibene, Alberto 109
Saiu, Liliana 153n.5
Salandra, Antonio 31–2
Salgari, Emilio 91, 117, 292, 343n.18, 454
Salierno Mason, Alane 276n.42
Salomone, Jerome J. 100n.97
Salvatorelli, Luigi 278–9
Salvemini, Gaetano 258
Salvetti, Patrizia 75n.56
Salzberg, Ana 381n.76
Sanfilippo, Matteo xi, 77n.64, 94n.91
Sarfatti, Margherita 212–13, 215–23, 236, 246, 353–4, 421–3, 433n.19
Saroyan, William 273–6, 476
Sassoon, Donald xi, 9–10, 35, 38, 176
Saunders, Thomas J. 123n.33
Savio, Francesco 350n.33, 359n.49, 390, 392n.94, 412n.124
Sbardellotto, Angelo 209n.52
Scalabrini, Giovanni Battista 80, 96–7
Scapigliatura 134–5, 137, 149
Scarfiotti, Lodovico 126
Scarpaci, Jean Ann 100n.97
Scarpino, Cinzia xi
Scarrocchia, Sandro 436n.25
Schaffer, Ronald 163n.21
*Schermo Lo* 336n.8
Schirru, Michele 209n.52
Schivelbush, Wolfgang 209n.52
Schlegel, A. W. 27
Schnapp, Jeffrey 111n.8
Sciascia, Leonardo 145–6, 335
Scotto, Walter 26–7
Scribe, Eugène 139
Scurati, Antonio 209n.52
Sebald, W. G. 19
*Secolo Il* 56n.21, 63n.36, 81–2
Sedita, Giovanni 364n.57, 477n.77, 478–9
Seelinger, Matthew xi, 161n.18
Segrè, Claudio 228n.82
*Selvaggio Il* 219, 222–3, 253–4, 421
Senise, Carmine 365
Senise, Renato 365, 367
Senise, Vincenzo 365n.59
Serri, Mirella 422n.5
Settis, Bruno 42n.43
Severino, Agostino 444n.38
Shakespeare, William 25–7, 346–7, 443–4
Shapiro, Nat Meyer 189

Shearer, Norma 271
Shipton, Alyn 169n.33
Shores, Christopher 429n.16
Siegfried, André 257
Siemens, Carl Friedric von 359
Sienkiewicz, Henryk 116–17
Silk, Donald 229n.83
Silone, Ignazio 101n.101
Silvi, Lilia 480–1
Simonin, Louis 60
Sinclair, Upton 185–6
Sinibaldi, Caterina 285n.50
Smith, Luther Ely 439n.28
Smith, Lawrence G. 252n.9
Smith, Mary 311–12
Smith, Mons 306, 311–12
Smolderen, Thierry 283n.48
Smucker, John R. 170n.36, 171
Soffici, Ardengo 37–8, 252–4
*Solaria* 6–7, 179, 258, 272–3, 336, 389
Solaroli, Libero 344n.20, 358n.47, 478
Soldati, Mario 5–6, 190–1, 223, 252, 350–1, 397–8, 410, 416–17
Solloway, Eddie 311–12
Solmi, Franco 182n.14
Solmi, Sergio 258
Sommaiolo, Paolo 38n.38
Sonnino, Sidney 34–5, 94
Sorani, Aldo 257, 257n.18, 271n.36
Sorel, Georges 147–8, 211–12
Soria, Massimo 330n.52
Sormani, Giuseppe 52, 81
Souvestre, Émile 55–6
Spagnol, Tito Antonio 349–50, 384, 417, 477, 481–2
Spencer, Herbert 26–7
Speer, Aldred 434–6
*Spettatore italiano Lo* 26, 43
Spina, Luigi 315n.33
Spina, Vittorio 170–1
Spini, Giorgio 49
Spinosa, Antonio 364n.57
Staiola, Enzo 391–2
*Stampa La* 57, 68n.42, 85, 200, 235–6, 266, 321, 329n.51, 337, 354–5, 390, 405–6, 473
Stead, W.T. 1, 491–2
Steele, Richard 26
Stefani, *see* Agenzia Stefani
Stein, Gertrude 279
Steinbeck, John 273–5, 277–8, 280, 449
Stella, Antonio Fortunato 26
Stemmle, Robert 466–7
Sterba, Christopher M. 160n.16
Stevani, Mario Alberto 118–22

Steward, James 474
Steward, William Kilborne 212n.58
Stiller, Maurice 343–4
St Johns, Ivan 344n.20
Stone, Marla 15, 356n.43, 421–2
Storchi, Simona xi, 254n.13
Storero, Luigi 125–6
Stowe, Harriet Beecher 133, 136, 150, 260, 492
Strafforello, Gustavo 135–6
Stuart, Stuart Henry 152n.4
Studdert, Will 460n.59
Studlar, Gaylyn 381n.75
Sullam, Sara xi, 18n.28, 257n.17
Sullivan, Brian R. 213n.60, 217n.69, 221n.73, 263n.27, 422n.7
Sutter, Johan 'John' 416n.130
Swanson, Carl A. 163n.22

Taft, William Howard 83, 85
Tambini, Domenico 457
Tamburri, Anthony Julian xi
Tanfani, Edoardo 92
Tasso, Torquato 115–16, 122–3
Taviani, brothers 122n.29, 151
Taylor, Sam 346–7
Taylorism 14, 127, 155, 186n.18, 229–30
Tedeschi, Rubens 36n.31
Temple, Shirley 369, 400
Teodori, Massimo 8
Terragni, Giuseppe 433n.19
Testoni, Gian Carlo 330–1
Thompson, Christine 113n.13
Thompson, Jonathan 429n.16
Thoreau, David 147
Thornton, Niven Wilder 257
Tirabassi, Maddalena 103n.106, 240n.104
Tittoni, Tommaso 220n.72
Tobagi, Benedetta 19
Todd, David 10, 25n.5, 44n.46
Toeplitz, Ludovico 350, 352, 383
Tolomei, Ettore 248
Tolstoy, Leo 45, 335
Tomadjoglou, Kimberly 123n.31
Tomasi di Lampedusa, Giuseppe 46
Tomasi, Silvano 80n.71
Tommaseo, Niccolò 25–6
Tonelli, Anna 444n.37
Toninelli, Pier Angelo 129n.46, 230n.86
Topolino, *see* Mickey Mouse
Torelli Viollier, Eugenio 81–2
Torrielli, Andrew J. 49n.6
Toscanini, Arturo 85, 139–42, 315
Totò (Antonio De Curtis) 318, 390

Tranfaglia, Nicola 56n.21, 210n.55, 236n.100, 320n.39
Trenker, Luis 416n.130
Tresca, Carlo 365
Treves, Fratelli (publishing house) 55–7, 60, 73, 76, 250n.6, 419n.3
Trio Lescano 327–8, 462–4
Turco, Vincenzo 407n.119
Turconi, Davide 115n.16, 117n.20
Turi, Gabriele 279n.44
Turpin, Ben 389
Twain, Mark 134, 136, 260

UFA (Universum-Film Aktiengeselleschaft GmBH) 123, 355–6, 358, 466–7
Umberto, di Savoia 457–8
Ungaretti, Giuseppe 268
URI (Unione Radiofonica Italiana), *see* EIAR
Urso, Simona 213n.60, 221n.73

Valentino, Rodolfo/Rudolph 175–6, 327, 383n.77, 486–7
Valéry, Paul 179
Valle, Cesare 433–4, 436
Van Loon, Hendrik Willem 277
Van Watson, William 479n.82
Varvaro Pojero, Francesco 54, 60
Vatican, *see under* Roman Catholic Church
Vaudagna, Maurizio 8, 209n.52, 210n.55, 354n.39
Vecchi, Giovanni 47n.1
Vecchi, Lotario 285–6, 289–90, 454
Venice Film Festival 232, 336–7, 373–4, 406–7, 416, 416n.130, 424–5, 427
Veniero, Ugo 241
Ventresca, Robert A. 452n.48
Venuti, Joe 327–9, 331–2
Verdi, Giuseppe 133, 139, 317
Verdini, Raoul 404–5
Verga, Giovanni 35–6, 46, 392–3
Vergher, Mario 405n.116
Vezzani, Roberto xi, 346n.24
Viallet, Jean-Pierre 258–9
Vidor, King 337, 346–7, 362, 384, 387–8, 391–7, 399–400, 470, 482–3, 486–8, 500
Vigolo, Giorgio 360n.51
Villaroel, Giuseppe 178n.4, 250n.6
Vincendeau, Ginette 347n.26
Vittorio Emanuele III 160, 163, 165–6, 208, 239, 260, 463
Vilardo, Stefano 146n.19
Villari, Luigi 241
Villari, Pasquale 30, 102–3
Vinall, Shirley 36n.32

Visconti, Luchino  363, 394–5, 475, 477–9, 482, 484
Visentini, Gino  413n.125
Vitetti, Leonardo  155
Vittorini, Elio  211, 247, 251, 265, 267, 267n.33, 272–8, 421–3, 447–52
*Voce La*  30–1, 279, 281
Vollman, Andrea  162n.19
Volpato, Giuseppe  126n.41
Von Kurowski, Agnes  156–7
Von Mackensen, Georg  442–3
Von Nagy Käthe  466–7
*Vraie Italie La*  252–5

Wagner, Richard  29–30, 317
Wagnleitner, Reinhold  13
Wagstaff, Christopher  391–2
Wakeman, Rosemary  38n.37, 182n.15
Wallace, Edgar  446–7
Wallace, Lewis  339–40
Wallace, William  160
Walsch, George  343
Wanger, Walter  365n.59
Warren, Harry  331–2
Washington, Booker T.  76–7
Washington, George  48
Wayne, John  384–5
Webb, William H.  490
Welge, Jobst  440n.29
Wells, H. G.  1
Western films  13, 91, 93, 101, 115
White, Alice  201–2
Whiteman, Paul  308–10, 325–8
Whitman, Walt  72, 134–6, 138–9, 147–8

Wilcock, Vanda  156n.10
Wilder, Thornton  303n.14
Wilson, Thomas Woodrow  152–4, 162–4, 168, 206–7, 252–3, 352, 493–4
Winderling, Gustavo  54
Wolff  42–3
Women in America  2, 17, 56–9, 66–7, 74, 85, 89–90, 102–3, 115, 133–4, 150, 176, 178–81, 230–9, 244, 351–2, 381–2, 386–7, 399, 425–7, 466–7, 475, 488, 492
Woodhouse, John  36n.31
Wooding, Sam  296
Woodress, James  133n.1
Wright, Frank Lloyd  189
Wurster, William  439–40
Wyke, Maria  126n.39

YMCA (Young Men's Christian Association)  167–8, 170–1

Zagarrio, Vito  335n.5, 395n.100, 397–8, 415n.128
Zamdomeneghi, Federico  36–7
Zandonai, Riccardo  140–1, 321
Zanelli, Dario  386n.83
Zangara, Giuseppe  209n.52
Zangrandi, Ruggero  361–2
Zanini, Rita  402n.113
Zavattini, Cesare  238–9, 277, 292, 335, 351–2, 379, 381, 390–1, 395–6, 423, 460–1
Zola, Émile  35–8
Zucchi, John E.  97n.95
Zucconi, Benedetta  319n.38
Zuculin, Bruno  328–9, 330n.52, 332–3
Zvereva, Irina  26n.8